JCPenny
Johnson & Johnson

KinderCare Learning Centers
Kmart Corporation
Kohlberg, Kravis, Roberts, & Company
Kraft Foods, Inc.

Lanier Worldwide, Inc.
Levi Strauss & Co.
Lincoln Electric Company

Mariott International Corporation
Mars
Mary Kay, Inc.
MasterCard International Corp
Mazda Motor Corp
McDonald's Corporation
McDonnell Douglas Corporation
McKinsey & Company
McNeil Consumer Products
Media Metrix
Mercedes-Benz
Mercer Management Consulting
Merrill Lynch & Co
Microsoft Corporation
Minolta Co, Ltd
Mitsubishi
Monsanto Chemical Co.
Moody's Investor Service
Morgan Stanley Dean Witter
Motorola, Inc.

National Assn. Of Purchasing
Management
Netscape
Nike, Inc.
Nikon, Inc.
Nissan Motor Corporation
Nordstrom, Inc.
Novell, Inc.
Nucor Corporation
NYNEX

Old Navy
Otis Elevator Co
Oxford Health Plans, Inc.

PepsiCo, Inc.
Philip Morris, Inc.
Philips Electronics
Pioneer Hi-bred International, Inc.
Pratt & Whitney
PricewaterhouseCoopers
Proctor & Gamble
Prudential Insurance Company of
America

Quaker Oats Company
Qwest Communications

Ramada (Cendant Corp)
RCIPA, Inc.
Reebok International, Ltd
Revco
Rice Aircraft Company
RJR Nabisco
RKO Warner Video
Robert Plan Corporation
Ryder System, Inc.

Sabre Interactive
Salomon Smith Barney, Inc.
Scott, O.M., & Sons, Co.
Sears Auto Centers
Sears, Roebuck & Co
Searle, G.D., & Co.
Sharp Electronic Corporation
Sony Corporation
Southeast Airlines (Delta Air Lines)
Sun Microsystems, Inc.

Taiwan Semiconductor Manufacturing Co.
Tandy Corporation
Target Corporation
Tenneco Automotive, Inc.
Texaco, Inc.
Texas Instruments, Inc.
Time Warner, Inc.
Towers Perrin
Toyota Motor Corporation

Union Pacific Corp.
United Airlines, Inc.
United Technologies
UPS of America, Inc.

Volvo

Wachovia Corporation
Wallace Company
Wal-Mart Stores, Inc.
Wal-Mart.com
Walt Disney Company
Westinghouse Electric Company
Winston and Strawn
Wm Wrigley, Jr. Company

Xerox

Yahoo! Inc.

Managerial Economics and Organizational Architecture

Managerial Economics and Organizational Architecture

Second Edition

JAMES A. BRICKLEY
CLIFFORD W. SMITH, Jr.
JEROLD L. ZIMMERMAN

*William E. Simon Graduate School
of Business Administration*

University of Rochester

Boston   Burr Ridge, IL   Dubuque, IA   Madison, WI   New York   San Francisco   St. Louis
Bangkok   Bogotá   Caracas   Lisbon   London   Madrid
Mexico City   Milan   New Delhi   Seoul   Singapore   Sydney   Taipei   Toronto

McGraw-Hill Higher Education

A Division of The McGraw-Hill Companies

MANAGERIAL ECONOMICS AND ORGANIZATIONAL ARCHITECTURE
Published by McGraw-Hill/Irwin, an imprint of The McGraw-Hill Companies, Inc. 1221 Avenue of the Americas, New York, NY, 10020. Copyright © 2001, 1997, by The McGraw-Hill Companies, Inc. All rights reserved. No part of this publication may be reproduced or distributed in any form or by any means, or stored in a data base or retrieval system, without the prior written consent of The McGraw-Hill Companies, Inc., including, but not limited to, in any network or other electronic storage or transmission, or broadcast for distance learning.
Some ancillaries, including electronic and print components, may not be available to customers outside the United States.

This book is printed on acid-free paper.

1 2 3 4 5 6 7 8 9 0 DOW/DOW 0 9 8 7 6 5 4 3 2 1 0

ISBN   0-07-231447-8

Senior sponsoring editor: *Paul Shensa/Marilea Fried*
Marketing manager: *Nelson Black/Martin Quinn*
Senior project manager: *Gladys True*
Production supervisor: *Rose Hepburn*
Supplement coordinator: *Betty Hadala*
Media technology producer: *Ann Rogula*
Art director: *Francis Owens*
Cover and interior design: *Brad Thomas*
Compositor: *Interactive Composition Corporation*
Typeface: *10.75/12 Adobe Garamond*
Printer: *R. R. Donnelley & Sons Company*

Library of Congress Cataloging-in-Publication Data

Brickley, James A.
    Managerial economics and organizational architecture / James A. Brickley, Clifford W. Smith, Jr., Jerold L. Zimmerman.—2nd ed.
      p.   cm.
    Includes index.
    ISBN 0-07-231447-8 (alk. paper)
    1. Managerial economics. 2. Organizational effectiveness. I. Smith, Clifford W. II. Zimmerman, Jerold L., 1947-III. Title.

HD 30.22 .B75 2001
658–dc21   00-036959

www.mhhe.com

Dedicated to Ronald Bittner, Henry Epstein, and James Gleason— steadfast supporters and cherished friends.

PREFACE

A quiet revolution is occurring within business schools. Bright, young economists are conducting path-breaking research in organizational economics, and then using this research to revitalize the curriculum. Armed with powerful theories and access to unprecedented data, we now have a rich set of managerial insights to teach about the workings of organizations and markets.

Thirty years ago, teaching managerial economics to business students was truly a "dismal science." Many students dismissed the standard economic tools of marginal analysis, production theory, and market structure as too esoteric to have real relevance to the business problems they believed they would encounter. Most of these students knew they would not be responsible for the pricing decisions of their future employers. They sought positions in large firms, eventually hoping to manage operations, marketing, finance, or information systems staffs. But a new generation of economists began applying traditional microeconomic tools—initially to problems involving corporate governance, executive compensation, mergers, and acquisitions. More recently, economists have turned their attention to the internal structure of the firm. Consequently, the managerial economics course now presents a rich menu of topics that can be used to demonstrate the power of traditional microeconomics tools.

We have been extremely gratified by the reception afforded the first edition of *Managerial Economics and Organizational Architecture*. Adopters report that the first edition helped them transform their managerial economics course into one of the most popular required courses within their core curriculum. The first edition had as its foundation recent economics research that applies powerful economic tools of analysis, such as optimization and equilibrium, to examine how managers can design organizations that motivate individuals to make choices that increase a firm's value. Our second edition continues to focus on the fundamental importance of markets and organizational design. In other books, there has been little coverage of such managerially important topics as developing effective performance-evaluation systems and compensation plans, assigning decision-making authority among employees, or managing transfer-pricing disputes among divisions. Given the increased pressures on managers to structure more effective organizations, this omission has been both significant and problematic. Our first objective in writing this book has been to provide current and aspiring managers enrolled in business programs with a systematic, comprehensive framework for addressing such organizational problems.

Before our first edition, faculty who wished to teach courses based on this emerging literature had to rely primarily on academic articles, which frequently were accessible only to the most determined students. This lack of accessible teaching materials severely limited the breadth of topics that could be covered in such a course. To that end, we have strived to write the underlying theoretical concepts in simple, intuitive terms and to illustrate them with numerous examples, most drawn from actual company practice.

Changing Nature of the Curriculum

Increasing global competition and rapid technological change are prompting firms to undertake major organizational restructurings as well as producing fundamental industry realignments. Firms now attack problems with focused, cross-functional teams. Many firms are shifting from functional organizational structures (manufacturing, marketing, and distribution) to flatter, more process-oriented organizations. Moreover, this pace of change shows no sign of slowing. Business and economics students recognize these issues; they want skills that will make them effective managers and prepare them to manage organizational change.

Business school programs are evolving in response to these changes. Narrow technical expertise in a single functional area (whether operations, accounting, finance, information systems, or marketing) is not sufficient. To be effective managers within this environment, students must develop cross-functional skills. To meet these challenges, business schools are becoming more integrated. Courses build on one another. Problems faced by managers are not just finance problems or operations problems or marketing problems. Rather, most business problems involve elements that cut across traditional functional areas. And for that reason, the curriculum must encourage students to apply concepts they have mastered across a variety of courses.

A second reason for writing the book has been to provide a multidisciplinary, cross-functional approach to organizational economics. We believe that this is critically important. Our interests span economics, finance, accounting, information systems, and financial institutions; this has allowed us to draw examples across a number of functional areas to demonstrate how this underlying economic framework can be used to analyze a variety of problems managers face regularly.

The Conceptual Framework

Although the popular press and existing literature on organizations are replete with jargon—TQM, reengineering, outsourcing, teaming, venturing, empowerment, and corporate culture—they fail to provide managers with a systematic, comprehensive framework for examining organizational problems. This book uses economic analysis to develop such a framework. We present this important material in an organized, integrated, accessible manner.

Through this text, readers will gain an understanding of the basic tools of economics and how to apply them to solve important business problems. Although the book covers the standard managerial economics problems of pricing and production, it pays special attention to organizational issues. In particular, the book will help readers understand

- How the elements of business environment (technology, competition in input and output markets, and regulation) drive the firm's choice of strategy.
- How strategy and the business environment affect the firm's choice of organizational design—what we call *organizational architecture*.
- How the three key features of organizational architecture—the assignment of decision-making authority, the reward system, and the performance-evaluation system—can be structured to allow managers to achieve their desired results.
- How corporate policies such as strategy, financing, accounting, marketing, information systems, operations, compensation, and human resources are interrelated and thus why it is critically important that they be coordinated.

Moreover, organizational architecture provides a more integrated and comprehensive view of material presented elsewhere in the business curriculum.

Our View of Content and Pedagogy

A variety of topics could be covered in an economics textbook. This book focuses on topics that we believe are most relevant to managers. For instance, the book provides an in-depth treatment of compensation policy, outsourcing, transfer pricing, and management innovations. But we spend little time on public policy aspects of topics, such as minimum-wage legislation, antitrust policy, and income redistribution through the welfare system or the tax code. A number of other important features differentiate this book from others currently available:

- Our book provides a comprehensive, cross-functional framework for analyzing organizational problems. We do this by first describing and integrating important research findings published across several functional areas. We then demonstrate how to apply the framework to specific organizational problems.
- We have tried to write a readable book. Reviewers, instructors, and students found the first edition accessible and interesting. The analysis in the text uses intuitive descriptions and simple examples; more technical material is provided in chapter appendices for those who wish to pursue it.
- Numerous examples drawn from the business press and our experiences illustrate the theoretical concepts. These examples, many highlighted in boxes, reinforce the underlying principles and help the reader better visualize the application of abstract ideas. Each chapter begins with a specific case history that is used throughout the chapter. This provides an important pedagogical device that unifies the chapter and aids the reader in recalling and applying the key constructs.
- Nontraditional economics topics dealing with strategy, outsourcing, leadership, ethics, and implementing management innovations are examined. Business school curricula often are criticized for being slow in covering topics of current interest to business, such as ethics. The last five chapters examine recent management trends and demonstrate how the book's framework can be used to analyze and understand topical issues.
- Cases and end-of-chapter problems are drawn from real organizational experience, from the business press as well as our contact with executive MBA students and consulting engagements. We have structured exercises that provide readers with a broad array of opportunities to apply the framework to problems like those they might encounter as managers.

Alternative Uses for the Text

Our book is an effective tool for a variety of classes at the MBA, executive MBA, or undergraduate level. The literature on the economics of organizations provides the foundation for this book. The basic material on managerial economics is presented in Parts 1 and 2—the first 10 chapters. The tools necessary for understanding and applying the organizational framework we develop within this text have been selected for their managerial relevance. In our experience, these economics tools are invaluable for those students who have been out working (and hence not in a classroom) for some time and for those who did not major in economics as an undergraduate. Those with an economics background may choose to forgo components of this material. We have structured our discussions of demand, production/cost, market structure, pricing, and strategy to be optional. Thus, readers who do not want to review these tools can skip Chapters 4 through 9 without loss of continuity. The inclusion of this material allows this book to be used in an introductory managerial economics course as well as in a course that specifically focuses on organizations, where students would have had a prior economics course.

We strongly recommend that all readers cover Chapters 1 to 3 and 10; these chapters introduce the underlying tools and framework for the text. Chapters 4 to 9, as we noted above, cover the basic managerial economics topics of demand, costs, production, market structure, pricing, and strategy. Part 3 (Chapters 10 to 17) develops the organizational architecture framework; we recommend that these be covered in sequence. Finally, Part 4 (Chapters 18 to 22) covers special managerial topics: outsourcing, leadership, regulation, ethics, the process of management innovations, and managing organizational change. They are capstone chapters—chapters that apply and illustrate the framework. Chapter 22 offers a particularly useful summary of the implications of our analysis. Instructors can assign these chapters based on their specific interests and available time.

Second Edition

This edition differs from the first in several ways:

- The core microeconomics material in Chapters 4 to 7 has been enriched. For example, we expanded our analysis of pricing with market power and made it a separate chapter (Chapter 7).
- Two chapters on the economics of strategy (Chapters 8 and 9) have been added—the second providing a broad array of game theory applications.
- A chapter on the economics of regulation (Chapter 20) has been added. We focus on how regulation constrains a firm's decisions and how firms participate in the political markets for regulation.
- We end the book with a general discussion of the economics of changing organizational architecture and the role played by management innovations (like TQM or reengineering) in this process.
- Many of the examples used throughout the text have been updated, with new ones added that focus especially on international and e-commerce.
- More end-of-chapter cases and problems are included.
- Each chapter has been revised to enhance the book's readability.

Acknowledgments

No textbook springs from virgin soil. This book has its intellectual roots firmly planted in the work of dozens who have toiled to develop, test, and apply organization theory. As we detailed in the preface to the first edition, the genesis of this book was a course William Meckling and Michael Jensen taught on the economics of organizations at the University of Rochester in the 1970s. Bill's and Mike's research and teaching stimulated our interest in the economics of organizations, prompted much of our research focused on organizational issues, and had a profound effect on this text. No amount of citation or acknowledgments can adequately reflect the encouragement and stimulation that Bill and Mike provided, both personally and through their writings.

Bill and Mike emphasized three critical features of organizational design: (1) the assignment of decision rights within the organization, (2) the reward system, and (3) the performance-evaluation system. These three elements, which we call *organizational architecture,* serve as an important organizing device for this book. As readers will discover, this structure makes a rich body of knowledge more useful for managerial decision making.

Important contributions to the literature on the economics of organizations have been made by a host of scholars. Through the work of these individuals, we have learned a tremendous amount. A number of our colleagues at Rochester also contributed to the development of the book. Ray Ball, Rajiv Dewan, Scott Keating, Stacey Kole, Larry Matteson, Glenn MacDonald, Kevin Murphy, Mike Ryall, Greg Schaffer, Ronald

Schmidt, Karen Van Nuys, Ross Watts, Michael Weisbach, and Ron Yeaple offered thoughtful comments and suggestions that helped clarify our thinking on key issues. Don Chew, editor of the *Journal of Applied Corporate Finance,* provided invaluable assistance in publishing a series of articles based on the book; his assistance in writing these articles improved the exposition of this book enormously.

This project also has benefited from an extensive development effort. In addition to generations of Simon School students, dozens of colleagues both in the United States and overseas formally reviewed the manuscript and gave us detailed feedback, for which we are very grateful.[1] New material for this addition was reviewed by Gordon H. Dash, Gary Ferrier, Luke Froeb, Charles M. Gray, Philip Grossman, James Henderson, Harvey James, Jr., Alejandro Manelli, Robert Michaels, Edward G. Weiss, Robert Windle, Daryl Winn, and Pan G. Yatrakis. We owe special thanks to Henry Butler, Luke Froeb, Mel Gray, and Chris James, each of whom provided insightful comments on the material. In addition, we are grateful for feedback from over 500 individuals who completed various surveys. Their thoughts served to guide our refinement of this work. We appreciate the efforts of Lena Cardone and Kathy Jones who provided secretarial support. Finally, we wish to thank our colleagues at Irwin/McGraw-Hill: Michael Junior, Paul Shensa, Gary Nelson, Ellen Cleary, and Marilea Fried. They encouraged us to pursue this project. Through their vision and publishing expertise, they provided us with insights and feedback to help expand our audience while adhering to our mission.

This book represents the current state of the art. Nonetheless, development is ongoing as research continues to evolve and as we continue to learn. *Managerial Economics and Organizational Architecture* covers an exciting, dynamic area. We hope that a small portion of that excitement is communicated through this text. Reviewers, instructors, and students frequently mention the relevance of material to the business community, the accessibility of the text, and the logical flow within the framework we have developed. However, in the final analysis, it is the instructors and their students who will determine the true value of our efforts.

We welcome—in fact, urge—feedback. We appreciate the extensive feedback we have received from many readers; their generous comments have improved this edition substantially. Although we had a definite objective in mind as we began writing this book, it is important to be open to suggestions and willing to learn from others who are traveling a similar yet distinct path. Although we are unlikely to please everyone, we will continue to evaluate suggestions critically and to be responsive where consistent with our mission. If readers would like to share their thoughts on this work or their classroom experiences, please feel free to contact any of us at the University of Rochester. Many thanks in advance for the assistance.

Brickley @simon.rochester.edu
Smith@simon.rochester.edu
Zimmerman@simon.rochester.edu

---

[1]The first edition benefited from reviews by: John H. Brown, Luke Froeb, Michael Gibbs, Charles M. Gray, Daniel R. LeClair, Robert Maness, Stephen E. Margolis, J. Peter Mattila, Daniel L. McConaughy, Seth W. Norton, Richard R. Pace, David Parker, Tim Sorenson, Martin Stahl, Michael Sykuta, Steven Tomlinson, Roger Tutterow, Walter Verdon, Mike Williams, and Huizhong Zhou.

Contents in Brief

Contents

Part 1 Basic Concepts

Part 2   Managerial Economics

Part 3   Designing Organizational Architecture

Part 4   Applications of Organizational Architecture

Part 1
Basic Concepts

Chapter 1
Introduction*

Francis Baring with his brother John established Barings Bank in London in 1762. Their bank prospered by facilitating international trade. Barings helped finance the British effort in the American Revolutionary War; thereafter, Barings credit reopened trade with the United States. In 1803, Barings helped the United States finance the Louisiana Purchase and helped Britain finance its campaigns against Napoleon. The bank's influence was such that in 1818 Duc de Richelieu observed, "There are six great powers in Europe: England, France, Prussia, Austria, Russia, and Barings Brothers."

The bank almost failed in 1890 when loans that it had made in Argentina defaulted. But it survived with the help of a bailout engineered by the Bank of England. The family rebuilt the bank over the following decades. Although it never regained its former preeminence, Barings retained its reputation as a gilt-edged institution run largely by members of the family and owned primarily by a charitable foundation. In the first half of the 1990s, its influence expanded substantially, in part due to its substantial Far East securities business.

In late February 1995, Barings' board of directors met to review the 1994 results. The bank had a small rise in profits—a quite reasonable result in what had been simply a dreadful year for most of its competitors. One big contributor to those results had been

---

*Portions of this chapter were published in J. Brickley, C. Smith, and J. Zimmerman (1995), "The Economics of Organizational Architecture," *Journal of Applied Corporate Finance* 8:2, 19–31.

an extremely profitable securities operation in Singapore. But that afternoon, things changed dramatically. The Singapore office trading star, Nick Leeson, unexpectedly walked out of the office and disappeared. As senior management examined the bank's records, it became clear that something was seriously amiss.

In principle, Leeson engaged in a simple operation: arbitraging security prices between the Osaka Stock Exchange and the Singapore International Monetary Exchange (SIMEX).[1] Leeson should have been able to lock in a virtually riskless profit by selling the security on the exchange with the higher price while simultaneously buying an equivalent instrument on the exchange with the lower price. And although price differences are typically small, such arbitrage can produce a substantial profit if done in enough volume. In this arbitrage business, although Barings might accumulate large positions on both exchanges, those securities it bought and those it sold should balance. The bank was supposed to face no net exposure to price changes.

Yet what management found as they reviewed the bank's records was that Leeson had bought securities in both markets. In effect, he had made an enormous bet that the security price would rise. But it had fallen, and now the very solvency of the bank was threatened.

How could this have happened? It appears that Leeson circumvented the bank's internal controls. The Singapore branch was small, and Leeson had effective authority over both trading as well as the branch's back office systems (bookkeeping, clearing, and settlement). He used that power to conceal losses and disguise the true nature of his activities—and thus he was able to "cook the books." For example, he apparently told senior management that a number of his trades were on behalf not of the bank but clients. And the bank's internal control systems failed to uncover the deceit.

By early March, the bank's aggregate losses totaled $1.4 billion. Leeson was arrested by German police at the Frankfurt Airport. Eventually Leeson was returned to Singapore where he was tried and sentenced to three years in prison. And Barings, Britain's oldest merchant bank, had been sold to ING (the large Dutch financial institution) for £1. Thus, Barings' owners had lost their entire investment.

The Barings collapse was caused ultimately by a poorly designed organization. For instance, *The Wall Street Journal* noted:

> *What is emerging from the documents and from interviews with current and former Barings executives is a fatally flawed organization: one that ignored at least several warning signs going back not just weeks and months, but years; one that so wanted to ensure the continuation of profits from Singapore—which boosted bonuses—that it was reluctant to impose tight controls; one that had a deeply split staff, which ultimately may have contributed to its downfall.*[2]

Three general aspects of the bank's organization contributed to the failure: the broad range of authority and responsibilities granted to Leeson, aspects of the firm's compensation system, and gaps in the bank's systems for evaluating, monitoring, and controlling its employees. Let's examine each in more detail.

First, Leeson had responsibility for both proprietary and customer trading as well as effective control of the settlement of trades within his unit. Granting him such a broad

---

[1]The specific securities Leeson traded were futures contracts on the Nikkei 225, the main Japanese stock market index.

[2]M. Branchli, N. Bray, and M. Sesit (1995), "Barings PLC Officials May Have Been Aware of Trading Position," *The Wall Street Journal* (March 6), A1.

Changing Architecture Exposes Fraud

While Leeson's actions are unusual in that they resulted in the insolvency of his employer, others have engaged in similar deception. Toshihide Iguchi of Daiwa Bank's New York office, allegedly hid $1.1 billion of trading losses from more than 30,000 unauthorized trades in US treasury securities over 11 years. Like Leeson, Iguchi had responsibility for both trading and back-office operations for the bank. Daiwa's decisions in 1993 to separate these operations and to bolster internal audits led to the uncovering of the fraud. In July 1995, Iguchi, then in charge only of settlements, wrote a letter to the bank's president confessing his misrepresentation. He noted it had become increasingly difficult to maintain the deceit. Thus, although Iguchi's unauthorized trading resulted in the loss of 10 percent of the total regulatory capital of one of Japan's largest banks, these problems were uncovered and stopped before the bank was ruined.

Source: J. Sapsford, M. Sesit, and T. O'Brien (1995), "Daiwa Bank Executive
Is Charged in New York in $1.1 Billion Debacle," *The Wall Street Journal*
(September 22), A2.

scope of decision-making authority created the opportunity to circumvent the bank's internal controls. As the *Financial Times* observed:

> *In Singapore, Mr. Leeson was in the process of settling transactions as well as initiating them. A watertight line between dealing and operational responsibility, crucial to internal control, was missing.*[3]

In reaction to the Barings collapse, the SIMEX changed its rules. It required that member firms use different traders for proprietary trading and customer business. It also prohibited the head of trading from taking charge of the settlement process.

Second, the bank's compensation system encouraged Leeson to speculate while providing senior managers with limited incentives to exercise tighter control over their star trader. Barings traditionally had paid out approximately 50 percent of gross earnings as annual bonuses. Yet a system where managers participate in annual profits—but not in losses—can encourage excessive risk taking. This perverse incentive can be most pronounced when a small bet loses and the employee tries to make it up by doubling the bet. If this second bet also loses, there can be a strong incentive to double up again and "go for broke."

Third, Leeson compromised the firm's performance-evaluation system. He misrepresented his trades as customer trades and hid losses. A better designed and executed monitoring system would have identified these problems long before the solvency of the institution was threatened.

Managerial Economics and Organizational Architecture

Standard managerial economics books address a number of questions that are important for organizational success:

- Which markets will the firm enter?
- How differentiated will the firm's products be?
- What mix of inputs should the firm use in its production?
- How should the firm price its products?
- Who are the firm's competitors, and how are they likely to respond to the firm's product offerings?

[3]"The Box That Can Never Be Shut," *Financial Times* (February 28, 1995), 17.

Addressing these questions is certainly important—and in this book, we do—yet this tale of Barings' untimely end suggests that this list is woefully incomplete. It is also important to address questions about the internal organization of the firm. A poorly designed organization can result in lost profits and even in the failure of the institution.

With the benefit of hindsight, it seems easy to identify elements of the Barings organization that if changed might have prevented this debacle. But the critical managerial question is whether before the fact one reasonably could be expected to identify the potential problems and to structure a more productive organization. Barings' management did not. We believe the answer to this fundamental managerial question is a resounding *yes.* To examine these issues, a rich framework that can be applied consistently is required.

We are not, of course, the first to recognize the importance of corporate organization or to offer advice on how to improve it. The business section of any good bookstore displays a virtually endless array of prescriptions: *benchmarking, empowerment, total quality management, reengineering, outsourcing, teaming, corporate culture, venturing, matrix organizations, just-in-time production, downsizing.* The authors of all these books would strongly agree that the firm's organization and the associated policies adopted by management can have profound effects on performance and firm value. And all buttress their recommendations with selected stories of firms that followed their advice and realized fabulous successes.

The problem with such approaches, however, is that each tends to focus on a particular facet of the organization—whether it be quality control, or worker empowerment, or the compensation system—to the virtual exclusion of all others. As a consequence, the suggestions offered by the business press are often myopic. These publications tend to offer little guidance as to which tools are most appropriate in which circumstances. The implicit assumption of most is that their technique can be successfully adopted by all companies. This presumption, however, is invariably wrong. Ultimately, this literature fails to provide managers with a productive framework for identifying and resolving organizational problems.

Organizational Architecture

In contrast to the approach of most business best-sellers, we seek to provide a systematic framework for analyzing such issues, one that can be applied consistently in addressing organizational problems and structuring more effective organizations. In this book, we offer a framework that identifies three critical aspects of corporate organization:

- The assignment of decision rights within the company
- The methods of rewarding individuals
- The structure of systems to evaluate the performance of both individuals and business units

Not coincidentally, these are the same three aspects of the organization we identified in the Barings case.

We introduce the term *organizational architecture* to refer specifically to these three key aspects of the firm. We hesitate to simply use "organization" to refer to these three corporate features because common usage of that term refers only to the hierarchical structure—that is, decision-right assignments and reporting relationships—while it generally ignores the performance-evaluation and reward systems. We thus use organizational architecture to help focus attention on all three of these critical aspects of the organization.

R&D and Executive Turnover

Suppose a firm links the CEO's bonus to earnings and the CEO will be retiring in two years. The CEO might reduce the firm's research and development budget to boost earnings this year and next. Five years down the road, earnings will suffer with no new products coming on stream. By then, however, this CEO will be long gone. In fact, research suggests that this can be a problem for some R&D-intensive firms.

Source: P. Dechow and R. Sloan (1991), "Executive Incentives and the Horizon Problem," *Journal of Accounting and Economics* 14, 51–89.

Stated as briefly as possible, our argument is that successful firms assign decision rights in ways that effectively link decision-making authority with the relevant information for making good decisions. When assigning decision rights, however, senior management must also ensure that the company's reward and performance-evaluation systems provide decision makers with appropriate incentives to make value-increasing decisions.

Depending on its specific circumstances, the firm will assign decision-making authority differently (some will decentralize particular decisions but centralize others) and will tailor its reward and performance-evaluation systems. Even though no two firms might adopt precisely the same architecture, successful firms ensure that the three critical aspects of organizational architecture are coordinated.

Our approach is integrative in the sense that it draws on a number of disciplines: accounting, finance, information systems, marketing, management, operations, political science, and strategy. But what also distinguishes this approach most clearly from that of the best-sellers is its central reliance on the basic principles of economics.

Economic Analysis

Economics long has been applied to questions of pricing policy—for example, "How would raising the price of the firm's products affect sales and firm value?" This book addresses standard managerial-economics questions involving pricing, advertising, scale, and the choice of inputs to employ in production. In addition, we apply these same tools to examine questions of organizational architecture. For example, "How would changing a division from a cost center to a profit center change incentives, alter employee decisions, and impact firm value?"

In essence, economics provides a theory to explain the way individuals make choices. For example, in designing organizations, it is important to keep in mind that individuals respond to incentives. Managers and employees can be incredibly resourceful in devising methods to exploit the opportunities they face. This also means, however, that when their incentives are structured inappropriately, they can act in ways that reduce the firm's value. In choosing corporate policies, it is critical that managers anticipate potential responses by customers, suppliers, or employees that might produce undesirable outcomes. Not doing so invites individuals to "game" the system and can result in utter failure of well-intentioned policies.

We use economics to examine how managers can design organizations that motivate individuals to make choices that will increase a firm's value. For example, the evidence suggests that the problem highlighted in the accompanying box on chief executive

---

Creative Responses to a Poorly Designed Incentive System

A manager at a software company wanted to find and fix software bugs more quickly. He devised an incentive plan that paid $20 for each bug the Quality Assurance people found and $20 for each bug the programmers fixed. Since the programmers that created the bugs were also in charge of fixing them, they responded to the plan by creating bugs in software programs. This action increased their payoffs under the plan—there were more bugs to detect and fix. The plan was canceled within a single week after one employee netted $1,700 under the new program.

Source: S. Adams (1995), "Manager's Journal: The Dilbert Principle," *The Wall Street Journal* (May 22), A12.

---

officers slashing R&D budgets prior to their retirement is not widespread.[4] The research suggests that these perverse incentives can be controlled by basing the CEO's incentive compensation on stock prices and by managing CEO succession so that decision rights are gradually transferred to the successor over the years prior to the final departure. Moreover, CEOs' postretirement opportunities for election to board seats appear linked to performance over the final years of their tenure.[5]

Traditional economic analysis generally characterized the firm simply as a "black box" that transforms inputs (labor, capital, and raw materials) into outputs. Little consideration was given to the internal architecture of the firm.[6] In recent years, economists have focused more on questions of organizational architecture.[7] But little effort has been devoted to synthesizing the material in an accessible form that emphasizes the managerial implications of the analysis. We apply the basic tools of economics to examine the likely effect on a firm's value of decisions such as centralization versus decentralization, the bundling of tasks into specific jobs and jobs into business units within the firm, the use of objective versus subjective performance measures, compensating employees through fixed versus variable (or "incentive") compensation, and retaining activities within the firm versus outsourcing. In sum, we examine how managers can structure organizational architecture to motivate individuals to make choices that increase the firm's value.

In this analysis, ideas of equilibrium—the interplay of supply and demand in product, labor, and capital markets—represent important constraints on managerial

---

[4]K. Murphy and J. Zimmerman (1993), "Financial Performance Surrounding CEO Turnover," *Journal of Accounting and Economics* 16, 273–315.

[5]J. Brickley, J. Linck, and J. Coles (1999), "What Happens to CEOs After They Retire? New Evidence on Career Concerns, Horizon Problems, and CEO Incentives," *Journal of Financial Economics* 52, 341–378.

[6]Of course, there are several notable exceptions: F. Knight (1921), *Risk, Uncertainty, and Profit* (London School of Economics: London); R. Coase (1937), "The Nature of the Firm," *Economica* 4, 386–405; and F. Hayek (1945), "The Use of Knowledge in Society," *American Economic Review* 35, 519–530.

[7]For example, R. Coase (1960), "The Problem of Social Cost," *Journal of Law and Economics* 3, 1–44; S. Cheung (1969), "Transaction Costs, Risk Aversion, and the Choice of Contractual Arrangements," *Journal of Law and Economics* 12, 23–42; A. Alchian and H. Demsetz (1972), "Production, Information Costs, and Economic Organization," *American Economic Review* 62, 777–795; K. Arrow (1974), *The Limits of Organization* (W.W. Norton: New York); M. Jensen and W. Meckling (1976), "Theory of the Firm: Managerial Behavior, Agency Costs and Ownership Structure," *Journal of Financial Economics* 3, 305–360; Y. Barzel (1982), "Measurement Costs and the Organization of Markets," *Journal of Law and Economics* 25, 27–48; O. Williamson (1985), *The Economic Institutions of Capitalism: Firms, Markets, Rational Contracting* (Free Press: New York); and B. Holmstrom and J. Tirole (1989), "The Theory of the Firm," in R. Schmalensee and R. Willig (Eds.), *Handbook of Industrial Economics* (North-Holland: New York).

decisions. Understanding how prices and quantities change in response to changes in costs, product characteristics, or the terms of sale is a critical managerial skill. For example, the doubling of crude oil prices in 2000 prompted oil companies to increase production, encouraged petrochemical companies to alter their input mix to economize on a now-more-expensive input, made salespeople reevaluate their decisions about contacting potential customers by phone rather than in person, and encouraged auto producers to focus more on gas economy in the design of new models. Yet these incentives to change depend on the structure of the organization. For instance, a salesperson is less likely to switch to greater reliance on telephone and mail when the firm reimburses all selling expenses than when salespeople are responsible for the costs of contacting potential customers.

Economic Darwinism

Survival of the Fittest[8]

The collapse of Barings, Charles Darwin might have noted, is an example of how competition tends to weed out the less fit. As described in *The Origin of the Species,* natural history illustrates the principle of "survival of the fittest." In industry, we see *economic Darwinism* in operation as competition weeds out ill-designed organizations that fail to adapt. Competition in the marketplace provides strong pressures for efficient decisions—including organizational decisions. Competition among firms dictates that only those firms with low costs survive. If firms adopt inefficient, high-cost policies—including their organizational architecture—competition will place strong pressures on these firms to either adapt or close.

Fama and Jensen suggest that "the form of organization that survives in an activity is the one that delivers the product demanded by customers at the lowest price while covering costs." This survival criterion helps highlight that while a well-crafted organizational architecture can contribute to a firm's success, it is not sufficient for success. The firm must have a business strategy that includes products for which the prices customers are willing to pay exceed costs. The potential for value creation by a company that manufactures only buggy whips is quite limited no matter how well structured the firm's organizational architecture.

Nonetheless, given a firm's business strategy (including its product mix), its choice of organizational architecture can have an important impact on profitability and value. An appropriate architecture can lower costs by promoting efficient production; it also can boost the prices customers are willing to pay by helping to ensure high-quality production, reliable delivery, and responsive service.

Economic Darwinism and Benchmarking

In the biological systems that Darwin analyzed, the major forces at work were random mutations in organisms and shocks from the external environment (for instance, from changes in weather). But in the economic systems on which we focus, purposeful voluntary changes occur. For instance, in order to compete better with Coke, Pepsi copied

[8]This section draws on A. Alchian (1950), "Uncertainty, Evolution, and Economic Theory," *Journal of Political Economy* 58, 211–221; G. Stigler (1951), "The Economics of Scale," *Journal of Law and Economics* 1, 54–71; and E. Fama and M. Jensen (1983), "Separation of Ownership and Control," *Journal of Law and Economics* 26, 301–325.

Economic Darwinism: General Motors and Chrysler

In the US auto industry at the beginning of 1994, two different organizational architectures competed in new model development. General Motors placed strong emphasis on functional specialties. GM has established small teams that consist of experts from the same functional field. Each team is charged with a particular assignment that relates to its area of specialization. For example, one team might have the primary responsibility for the design of the body of the vehicle while another team might be charged with developing the drive train. These teams work simultaneously on their specific tasks. Some of the individuals on these teams also serve on additional cross-functional teams that are charged with coordinating the development process across the functional areas.

In contrast to GM, Chrysler Corporation places nearly all decisions about the development of a new vehicle in the hands of a single cross-functional product team. Chrysler's platform teams include engineers, designers, financial analysts, marketing experts, and manufacturing people who all report to a single project leader. This leader has authority over each of the team members and their work.

General Motors' CEO, Jack Smith, attributed important differences in the operation of Chrysler and GM to these differences in organization. Chrysler took three years to bring the Viper to market; GM regularly takes more than five. And at the bottom line—Chrysler earned about $7 for every $100 in sales for 1994; GM earned $.70.

GM and Chrysler offer but two illustrations of how firms differ when they make fundamental decisions about the organization of their activities. Fortunately, for firms like GM, this decision-making process is ongoing. In 1995, GM reorganized its product development process along lines that more closely resemble the Chrysler model. Thus, economic Darwinism is a major force at work in industries around the globe.

Source: A. Stertz (1992), "Detroit's New Strategy to Beat Back Japanese Is to Copy Their Ideas," *The Wall Street Journal* (October 1), A1.

many of Coke's practices. Pepsi spun off its fast-food chains (Taco Bell, KFC, and Pizza Hut) to focus on its core business—just as Coca Cola had done. Also, Pepsi is changing its network of bottlers. One analyst remarked, "Pepsi is starting to look a lot more like Coke."[9] In fact, this practice has been formalized in the process of *benchmarking*.

Benchmarking generally means looking at those companies that are doing something best and learning how they do it in order to emulate them. But this process also occurs in less formal ways. As Armen Alchian argued, "Whenever successful enterprises are observed, the elements common to those observed successes will be associated with success and copied by others in their pursuit of profits or success."[10] For example, if the cover article in the next *Fortune* reports an innovative inventory control system at Toyota, managers across the country—indeed, around the globe—will read it and ask, *Would that work in my company, too?* Undoubtedly, the managers with the strongest interest in trying it will be those within firms currently suffering through inventory problems.[11] Some will achieve success, but others may experience disastrous results caused by unintended though largely predictable organizational "side effects" (like Leeson's unchecked incentive for risk taking).

Although competition tends to produce efficiently organized firms over the longer run, uncritical experimentation with the organizational innovation *du jour* can expose the firm to an uncomfortably high risk of failure. Successful organizations are not just a collection of "good ideas." The elements of a successful organization must be carefully

[9]N. Harris (1997), "If You Can't Beat 'Em, Copy 'Em," *Business Week* (November), 50.

[10]Alchian (1950), 218.

[11]This raises the question of why any firm with an innovative idea would voluntarily disclose it. Perhaps the free publicity outweighs the lost competitive advantage.

Random Mutations (Experimentation) in Firms

Within organizations some changes approximate Darwin's random mutations. Firms sometimes adopt changes without detailed understanding of their implications. If the change appears productive, it is likely to be exported to other locations. The more successful the company and its strategy, the more likely the innovation will be copied by competitors. For example, Just for Feet CEO, Harold Ruttenberg, admits he works by trial and error. Plenty of ideas have vanished like out-of-style sneakers. Gone are the in-store nursery, "Too busy for it," says Ruttenberg and a $100,000 drive-through window. "Things weren't well planned in the beginning," he says, "When I look back on it, it was just pure luck and a miracle that it worked."

Source: N. Harris (1998), "Just for Feet," *Business Week* (July 20), 70–71.

coordinated: The different elements of the firm's architecture must be structured to work together to achieve the firm's goals. For this reason, it is important to be able to analyze the likely consequences of a contemplated organizational change and forecast its impact on the entire firm.

This concept of economic Darwinism thus has important managerial implications. First, existing architectures are not random; there are sound economic explanations for the dominant organization of firms in most industries. Second, surviving architectures at any point in time are optimal in a *relative* rather than an *absolute* sense; that is, they are the best among the competition—not necessarily the best possible. Third, if the environment in which the firm operates changes—if technology, competition, or regulation change—then the appropriate organizational architecture normally changes as well. These three observations together suggest that although improvements in architecture

Transfers of Organizational Architecture Across the Global Economy

In 1996, Tianjin Optical & Electrical Communication Group was typical of a Chinese state-owned company. Although the electronics manufacturer boasted skilled technicians, mismanagement left the company at the brink of bankruptcy. Motorola, Inc., changed that. It offered to take Tianjin Optical as a supplier, but only if Tianjin adopted the US telecommunications company's quality-control and management practices. By 1999, Tianjin Optical was selling a third of its production to Motorola and reported a small profit. "Now, we think we can survive," says Zhang Bingjun, Tianjin Optical's chairman.

Each Tianjin employee receives an average of two weeks a year in classroom instruction stressing modern management practices. That effort has paid off: The Tianjin assembly lines produce a slim cellular phone every $2\frac{1}{2}$ seconds with virtually the same defect rate as in Motorola's US plants. Motorola also provides training for more than 100 outside suppliers to boost the quality of their output. Motorola budgets about $2 million annually to "show [potential suppliers] Western management practices and create a mindset where they understand what we're doing and why," says a training director, Ying Shea.

This assistance in establishing a more effective organizational architecture and internal operating policies provided by a US multinational corporation to its Chinese partners is but one example of the vital role that foreign businesses play within the Chinese business sector. Since Communist China opened itself to foreign investment two decades ago, foreign companies have become an important conduit for economic reform. They have introduced not just modern production technology but also more efficient organizational architecture to the Chinese business community. Some estimates suggest that including these collateral benefits, foreign firms and their joint ventures account for as much as a fifth of China's trillion-dollar economy.

Source: E. Guyot (1999), "Foreign Companies Bring China More Than
Jobs," *The Wall Street Journal* (September 15), A26.

are certainly always possible, a manager should resist condemning prevailing structures without careful analysis. Before undertaking major changes, executives should therefore have a good understanding of how the firm arrived at its existing architecture and, more generally, develop a broader perspective of why specific types of organizations work well in particular settings. Finally, an executive generally should be more skeptical of claimed benefits of proposed organizational changes if the environment has been relatively stable.

Purpose of the Book

The primary thrust of this book is to provide a solid conceptual framework for analyzing organizational problems and structuring a more effective organizational architecture. The book also provides basic material on managerial economics and discusses how it can be used for making operational decisions—for example, input, output, and pricing decisions. This material additionally supplies a set of tools and an understanding of markets that is important for making good organizational decisions.

Our Approach to Organizations

We begin with two basic notions: People act in their own self-interest, and information often is asymmetric—individuals do not all share the same information. As we have indicated, this framework suggests that the three critical elements of organizational architecture are the assignment of decision rights, the reward system, and the performance-evaluation system. Successful organizations assign decision rights in a manner that effectively links decision-making authority with the relevant information to make good decisions. Correspondingly, successful organizations develop reward and performance-evaluation systems that provide self-interested decision makers with appropriate incentives to make decisions that increase the values of their organizations.

It is also important to note that modern organizations are extremely complex and that developing an understanding of how people within them behave is difficult. As in any book that addresses this set of topics, we face difficult trade-offs between adding more institutional richness to embrace more texture of the actual environment versus omitting details to keep the analysis more focused and manageable. At certain points (especially where little prior formal analysis of the problem exists), we take quite complex problems and discuss them in terms of simplified examples. Nonetheless, we believe that in these cases, we can provide important managerial insights to these topics through our admittedly simple examples.

Finally, we believe that a powerful feature of this economic framework is that it can be extended readily to incorporate a broad array of other managerial policies such as finance, accounting, information systems, human relations, operations, and marketing. In this sense, this book can play an important integrating role across the entire business curriculum. This type of integration is becoming increasingly important with the expanded use of cross-functional teams within the business community.

Overview of the Book

- **Part 1: Basic Concepts** lays the groundwork for the book. Chapter 2 summarizes the economic view of behavior, stressing management implications. Chapter 3 presents an overview of markets, provides a rationale for the existence of organizations, and stresses the critical role of the distribution of knowledge within the organization.

- **Part 2: Managerial Economics** applies the basic tools of economic theory to the firm. Chapters 4 through 7 cover the traditional managerial-economics topics of demand, production and cost, market structure, and pricing. These four chapters provide the reader with a fundamental set of microeconomic tools and use these tools to analyze basic operational policies such as input, output, and product pricing decisions. Chapters 8 and 9 focus on corporate strategy—the former on creating and capturing values and the latter on using game theory to examine the interaction between the firm and its competitors, suppliers, and other parties. These chapters also provide important background material for the subsequent chapters on organizations: A good understanding of the market environment is important for making sound organizational decisions.[12] Chapter 10 examines conflicts of interest that exist within firms and how contracts can be structured to reduce or control these conflicts.

- **Part 3: Designing Organizational Architecture** develops the core framework of the book. Chapter 11 provides a basic overview of the organizational-design problem. Chapters 12 and 13 focus on two aspects of the assignment of decision rights within the firm—the level of decentralization chosen for various decisions and the bundling of various tasks into jobs and then jobs into subunits. Chapters 14 and 15 examine compensation policy. First we focus on the level of compensation necessary to attract and retain an appropriate group of employees. Then we discuss the composition of the compensation package, focusing on how the mix of salary, fringe benefits, and incentive compensation affects the value of the firm. In Chapters 16 and 17, we analyze individual and divisional performance evaluation.

- **Part 4: Applications of Organizational Architecture** uses the framework that we have developed to provide insights into contemporary management issues. Chapters 18 through 22 discuss outsourcing, leadership, regulation, ethics, and management innovations.

Suggested Readings	

A. Alchian (1950), "Uncertainty, Evolution, and Economic Theory," *Journal of Political Economy* 58, 211–221.

M. Jensen (1983), "Organization Theory and Methodology," *The Accounting Review* 58, 319–339.

M. Jensen and W. Meckling (1992), "Specific and General Knowledge, and Organizational Structure," *Journal of Applied Corporate Finance* 8:2, 4–18.

Review Questions

1–1. What are the three aspects of *organizational architecture*?

1–2. Xerox has developed an expert system to assist employees who answer the company service center's 800 number to help callers who have problems with their photocopy machines. The system is designed to lead the employee through a set of questions to diagnose and fix the problem. If the machine operator cannot fix the problem with the assistance of the input from the service center employee, a service representative is dispatched to make a service call. This expert system is designed to evolve more effective prompts as experience accumulates. This will be accomplished by having service representatives call the service center after a service call. The

[12]Chapters 2 and 3 should be read by all. A reader familiar with managerial economics and corporate strategy can proceed directly to Chapter 10 to focus on organizational issues. (Such a reader, however, should find the material in Chapters 4 to 9 a helpful review.) Others should read Part 2 before proceeding to the material on organizations.

nature of the problem and the actions taken are to be entered into the system. Xerox bases pay for the individuals who answer the 800 number on the number of service calls they handle; it bases compensation for service representatives on the number of service calls they make. What incentives does this create?

1–3. Briefly describe *economic Darwinism.*

1–4. *The Wall Street Journal*[13] reports that

> *Franchisees, who pay fees and royalties in exchange for using franchisers' business formats, have become much more militant in recent years about what they see as mistreatment by franchisers. In general, Ms. Kezios is seeking federal and state laws to give franchisees more power in franchise arrangements. Among her goals: creating legally protected exclusive territories for franchisees.*

> How would you expect existing franchisees to react to this proposed regulation? How would you expect a potential new franchisee to react to this proposed regulation?

1–5. In the process of benchmarking, a colleague of yours notes that Lincoln Electric, a producer of electric arc welders, has much higher productivity than does your company. Unlike your firm, Lincoln has an extensive piece-rate compensation system; much of its employees' total compensation is simply the number of units produced times the piece rate for that type unit. Your colleague recommends that our company adopt a piece-rate compensation system to boost productivity. What do you advise?

1–6. In the life insurance industry, we see two major ownership structures—common stock insurers and mutual insurers. In a common stock company, the owners—its stockholders—are a separate group from its customers—the policyholders. In a mutual, the policyholders are also the owners of the company. It has been argued that mutual insurance companies are dinosaurs—they are large, slow, bureaucratic, and inefficient. How would you respond to such an argument?

---

[13]J.A. Tannenbaum (1995), "Focus on Franchising: Franchisee Gains," *The Wall Street Journal* (June 19), B2.

Chapter 2
Economists' View of Behavior

CHAPTER OUTLINE

In June 1992, the state of California filed charges alleging that Sears Auto Centers were overcharging customers an average of $230 for unneeded or unperformed repairs. These charges were followed by similar allegations by the state of New Jersey. Ultimately, Sears admitted that "some mistakes did occur" and agreed to a settlement for an amount up to $20 million. Sears maintained that its senior management had been unaware of the problem and neither condoned nor encouraged defrauding customers. This auto repair scandal imposed significant costs on Sears. As the complaints became public, the price of Sears' stock fell by about 6 percent, and sales at its auto centers declined substantially.

To limit these costs, Sears' management had to act quickly to address the problem. As a first step, management had to understand what could have motivated employees to recommend unneeded repairs. Only then could management choose a policy to redress the situation. If management thought the problem was caused by a few dishonest employees, the appropriate response would have been to try to identify and fire those employees. If, instead, management thought the problem was caused by disgruntled employees taking out their frustrations on customers, a potential response would have been to adopt a job enrichment program to increase employee satisfaction and, it would be hoped, customer service. Many alternate assumptions and responses are possible.

This example involving Sears illustrates a general point. Managers' responses to problems are likely to depend on their understanding of people's motives and their forecast of people's reactions—their responses depend on their underlying model of behavior. Most managerial actions involve trying to affect the behavior of individuals such as employees, customers, union officials, or subcontractors. Managers with different understandings (or models) of what motivates behavior are likely to make different decisions and take different actions.

We begin this chapter by briefly summarizing the general framework economists use to examine individual behavior. Some graphical tools are introduced to aid our analysis. Next, we use this economic framework to analyze the problem at Sears Auto Centers. The managerial implications of this analysis are discussed. We contrast this economic view of behavior with alternative views and explore why the economic framework is particularly useful in managerial decision making. Finally, we analyze decision making under uncertainty.

Economic Behavior: An Overview

Individuals have unlimited wants. People generally want greater wealth, more attentive service, larger houses, more luxurious cars, and additional personal material items. They want more time for leisure activities. Many people also want to improve the plight of others—starving children, the homeless, and disaster victims. People are concerned about vitality, religion, integrity, and gaining the respect and affection of others.

In contrast to wants, resources are limited. Households face limited incomes that preclude all the purchases and expenditures that members of the households might like to make. The available amount of land, trees, and other natural resources is finite. There are only 24 hours in the day. People become ill; death is inevitable.

Economic Choice

Economic analysis is based on the notion that individuals assign priorities to their wants and choose their most preferred options from among the available alternatives. If Kathy Measer is confronted with a choice between a laptop or a desktop computer, she can tell you whether she prefers one over the other or whether she is indifferent between the two. She correspondingly purchases her preferred alternative. If Kathy has a weekly budget of $400, she considers the many ways she might spend the money and then chooses the package of goods and services that will maximize her personal happiness. She cannot make all desired purchases on her limited budget. However, this choice is optimal for Kathy, given her limited resources.

Economists do not assert that people are selfish in the sense that they care only about their own personal wealth. Within the economic paradigm, people also care about such things as charity, family, religion, and society. For instance, Kathy will donate $100 to her church, as long as the donation provides greater satisfaction than alternative uses of the money.

Neither do economists contend that individuals are supercomputers that make infallible decisions. Individuals are not endowed with perfect knowledge and foresight, nor is additional information costless to acquire and process.[1] For example, Kathy might order an item from a restaurant menu only to find that she does not like what she is served. Within this economic paradigm, she simply does the best she can in the face of her imperfect knowledge. But she learns from her experience and does not repeat the same mistakes in judgment time after time.[2]

Marginal Analysis

Marginal costs and benefits are the incremental costs and benefits that are associated with making a decision.[3] It is the marginal costs and benefits that are important in economic decision making. An action should be taken whenever the marginal benefits of that action exceed its marginal costs. Mary O'Dwyer has a contract to help sell products for an office supply company. She is paid $50 for every sales call that she makes to customers. Thus, Mary's marginal benefit for making each additional sales call is $50. Mary enjoys playing tennis more than selling. If she places a marginal value of more than $50 on the tennis that she would forgo by making an extra call, she should not make any more sales calls that day—the marginal costs would have exceeded the marginal benefits. She continues to make additional sales calls as long as the reduction in tennis playing is valued at less than $50.[4]

Marginal analysis is a cornerstone of modern economic analysis. In economic decision making, "bygones are forever bygones." Costs and benefits that have already been incurred are *sunk* (assuming they are nonrecoverable) and hence are irrelevant to the current economic decision. Mary paid $5,000 to join a tennis club last month. This fee does not affect her current decision of whether to play tennis or make an extra sales call. That expenditure is ancient history and does not affect Mary's current trade-offs.

---

[1] Economists sometimes use the idea of *bounded rationality.* Under this concept, individuals act in a purposeful and *intendedly rational* manner. However, they have cognitive limitations in storing, processing, and communicating information. It is these limitations which make the question of how to organize economic activity particularly interesting. H. Simon (1957), *Models of Man* (John Wiley & Sons: New York).

[2] At least this learning appears to occur outside the comics. For decades, Charlie Brown from *Peanuts* has continued to try to kick the football held by Lucy van Pelt. Yet Lucy always pulled the ball at the last second. Few individuals are as incurably optimistic as Charlie Brown—they learn.

[3] Technical note: *Marginal* costs and benefits are typically defined as changes in costs and benefits associated with very *small changes* in a decision variable. For instance, the marginal costs of production are the additional costs from producing a small additional amount of the product (for instance, one more unit). Often decisions involve discrete choices, such as whether or not to build a new plant. In these cases, it is not possible to define a small change in the decision variable. *Incremental* costs and benefits are those costs and benefits which vary with such a decision. For our present discussion, the technical distinction between marginal and incremental is not important.

[4] To keep this example simple, we abstract from several issues. We ignore any pleasure Mary receives from the process of selling. Also, selling effort today is likely to have some effect on her future professional progress. Finally, if Mary values a tennis game at 9 AM and one at 7 PM equally, she will sell during the business day and postpone tennis to the evening.

Opportunity Costs

Because resources are constrained, individuals are faced with *trade-offs*. Using limited resources for one purpose precludes their use for something else. For example, if Larry Matteson takes four hours to play golf, he cannot use that same four hours to paint his house. The *opportunity cost* of using a resource for a given purpose is its value in its best alternative use. The opportunity cost of using four hours to play golf is the value of using the four hours in its next best alternative use.

Marginal analysis frequently involves a careful consideration of the relevant opportunity costs. If Larry starts a new pizza parlor and hires a manager at $30,000 per year, the $30,000 is an *explicit* cost (a direct dollar expenditure). Is he better off managing the restaurant himself, since he can avoid the explicit cost of $30,000 by not paying himself a salary? The answer to this question depends (at least in part) on the opportunity cost of his time. If he can earn exactly $30,000 in his best alternative job, the *implicit* cost of self-management is the same as the explicit cost of hiring an outside manager: He forgoes $30,000 worth of income if he manages the parlor himself. Both explicit and implicit costs are opportunity costs that should be considered in the analysis. Suppose that Larry's gross profit from the pizza parlor, before paying the manager a salary, is

Opportunity Costs and V-8

The Campbell Soup Company used the idea of an opportunity cost to create a successful ad campaign for its V-8 vegetable juice. Upon finishing a soft drink, the fellow in the ad would look into the camera, slap his forehead, and exclaim: "Wow—I coulda had a V-8." Since one is unlikely to drink both a soft drink and a V-8, the opportunity cost of the soft drink is the forgone V-8—a cost that these commercials sought to convince the viewing audience is quite high.

$35,000 and that he can earn $40,000 in an outside job. Hiring a manager for $30,000 yields a net profit of $5,000 from the pizza parlor. He also earns $40,000 from the outside job, for total earnings of $45,000. If he manages the pizza parlor himself, he earns only $35,000. In this example, it is better for him to work at the outside job and hire a manager to run the restaurant.[5]

Creativity of Individuals[6]

Within this economic framework, individuals maximize their personal happiness given resource constraints. Indeed, people are quite creative and resourceful in minimizing the effects of constraints. For instance, when the government adopts new taxes, almost immediately accountants and financial planners begin developing clever ways to reduce their impact. Some self-employed individuals were able to reduce the impact of recent tax increases by changing the status of their incorporation.

As another example, a 33-year-old Brazilian farm hand recently retired with full social security benefits after he satisfied social security auditors that he had been working since he was three years old. Because Brazil doesn't specify a minimum retirement age, the average Brazilian retires at age 49.[7]

Similarly, when hackers and corporate spies continue to develop more sophisticated schemes to steal information from Web sites or networks, software tools that detect break-ins also have grown in popularity and sophistication. This intrusion-detection software was about a $100 million industry in 1999 and is expected to grow to a billion dollar industry within a few years.[8]

Understanding this creative nature of individuals has important managerial implications which we discuss later in this chapter, as well as throughout the book.

Graphical Tools

Economists often employ a set of graphical tools to illustrate how individuals make choices. We use these tools throughout this book. They also are used in other courses within the typical business school curriculum, such as in finance, human relations, and marketing courses. Our intent is to introduce these tools so that the reader is comfortable

---

[5]Again, to keep the example simple, we assume there is no difference in personal satisfaction between Larry's outside job and managing the pizza parlor. We also postpone the discussion of consequences for the success of the pizza parlor from hiring a manager versus self-management until Chapter 10.

[6]This section draws on W. Meckling (1976), "Values and the Choice of the Model of the Individual in the Social Sciences," *Schweizerische Zeitschrift für Volkswirtschaft und Statistik*, 112, 545–560.

[7]P. Fritsch (1999), "In Brazil Retirement Has Become a Benefit Nearly All Can Enjoy," *The Wall Street Journal* (September 9), A1.

[8]J. D'Allegro (1999), "Intrusion Detection Matures," *National Underwriter* (March 8), 9.

Creative Gaming of the System

An MIS manager bought computers for his company one at a time, charging them on his personal credit card. He then filed for reimbursement on his expense account. Although this process imposed delay costs on the firm—it required almost a year for the company to acquire twenty computers—the manager received frequent flyer miles given by his credit card company.

Source: S. Adams (1996), *The Dilbert Principle* (Harper Business: New York), 326.

---

using them in simple applications. (We avoid discussion of the more technical considerations that underlie their development.) We then apply the tools to analyze the problems at Sears Auto Centers.

Individual Objectives

Goods are things that people value. Goods include standard products like food and clothing, services like haircuts and education, as well as less tangible emotions such as love of family and charity. The economic model of behavior posits that people acquire goods that maximize their personal happiness, given their resource constraints (such as a limited income). Economists frequently use the term *utility* in referring to personal happiness.

To provide a more detailed analysis of how people make choices, economists represent an individual's preferences by a *utility function.* This function expresses the relation between total utility and the level of goods consumed. The individual's objective is to maximize this function, given the resource constraints.[9] The concept can be illustrated most conveniently through a simple example where an individual cares about only two goods. The insights from this two-good analysis can be extended readily to the case of additional goods such as food, housing, clothing, respect, and charity.

Suppose that Dominique Lalisse values only food and clothing. In general form, his utility function can be written as follows:

$$\text{Utility} = F(\overset{+}{\text{Food}}, \overset{+}{\text{Clothing}}) \tag{2.1}$$

Dom prefers more of each good—thus, his utility rises with both food and clothing. In Dom's case, his specific utility function is

$$\text{Utility} = \text{Food}^{1/2} \times \text{Clothing}^{1/2} \tag{2.2}$$

For instance, if Dom has 16 units of food and 25 units of clothing, his total utility is 20 (that is, utility $= 16^{1/2} \times 25^{1/2} = 4 \times 5 = 20$). Dom is better off with 25 units of both food and clothing. Here, his utility is 25 (utility $= 25^{1/2} \times 25^{1/2} = 5 \times 5 = 25$).

Utility functions rank alternative bundles of food and clothing in the *order* of most preferred to least preferred, but they do not indicate how much one bundle is preferred

---

[9]Clearly, most individuals do not actually consider maximizing a mathematical function when they make these choices. However, this formulation can provide useful insights into actual behavior to the extent that it *approximates* how individuals make choices. Mathematicians have shown that if an individual's behavior is consistent with some basic "axioms of choice" (comparability, transitivity, nonsatiation, and willingness to substitute), the individual will make choices *as if* he or she were trying to maximize some utility function.

to another. If the utility index is 100 for one combination of food and clothing and 200 for another, Dom will prefer the second combination. The second bundle does not necessarily make him twice as well off as the first bundle.[10] This formulation does not allow one person's utility of a bundle to be compared to another person's utility.

Indifference Curves

Preferences implied by the utility function can be illustrated graphically through *indifference curves*. An indifference curve pictures all combinations of goods that yield the same utility. Given his utility function in Equation (2.2), Dom is indifferent between either 16 units of food and 25 units of clothing or 25 units of food and 16 units of clothing. Both combinations yield 20 units of utility, and hence are on the same indifference curve. Figure 2.1 shows two of Dom's indifference curves. For example, if given a choice between any two points on curve 1, Dom would say that he does not care which one is selected—in either case, he obtains 8 units of utility.

The slope at any point along one of Dom's indifference curves indicates how much food he would be *willing to give up* for a small increase in clothing (his utility remains unchanged by this exchange).[11] Standard indifference curves that illustrate trade-offs between two goods have negative slopes. If Dom obtains a smaller amount of one good such as food, the only way he can be equally as well off is to obtain more of another good like clothing. If the slope at a point along an indifference curve is -2, Dom is willing to give up 2 units of food to obtain 1 unit of clothing. Alternatively he is willing to give up $1/2$ unit of clothing to obtain 1 unit of food. This *willingness to substitute* has important implications, which we discuss below.

North and east movements in graphs like Figure 2.1 are utility-increasing. Holding the amount of food constant, utility increases by increasing clothing (an eastward movement). Holding the amount of clothing constant, utility increases by increasing the

---

[10]This is like rankings on a test—an individual who scores in the 80th percentile is not twice as smart as one from the 40th.

[11]Recall that the slope of a line is a measure of steepness, defined as the increase or decrease in height per unit of distance along the horizontal axis. Slopes of curves are found geometrically by drawing a line tangent to the curve at the point of interest and determining the slope of this tangent line. The slope at a point along one of Dom's indifference curves indicates how the quantity of food changes for small changes in the amount of clothing in order to hold utility constant. Since by definition Dom is indifferent to this exchange (he remains on the same indifference curve), he is *willing* to make the exchange.

Figure 2.1 Indifference Curves

These indifference curves picture all combinations of food and clothing that yield the same amount of utility. The specific utility function in this example is $U = F^{1/2} \times C^{1/2}$, where F is food and C is clothing. Northeast movements are utility-increasing. Indifference curve 2 represents all combinations of food and clothing that yield 20 units of utility, whereas curve 1 pictures all combinations that yield 8 units of utility. Other indifference curves could be drawn for different levels of utility.

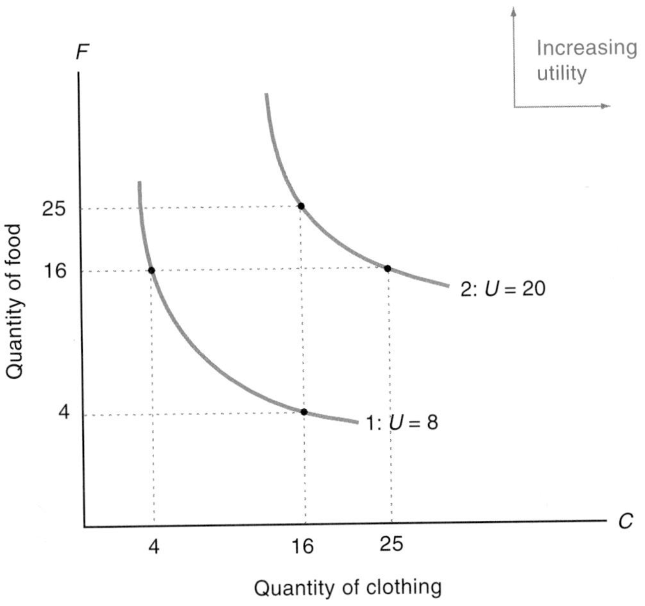

amount of food (a northward movement). Thus, in Figure 2.1, Dom would rather be on indifference curve 2 than on 1. He obtains 20 units of utility rather than 8.

Economists typically picture indifference curves as convex to the origin (they bow in, as in Figure 2.1). Convexity implies that if Dom has a relatively large amount of food, he would exchange a relatively large quantity of food for a small amount of additional clothing. Thus, the indifference curves in Figure 2.1 are steep when the level of food is high relative to the level of clothing. In contrast, if he has a relatively large amount of clothing, he would be willing to substitute only a small amount of food for additional clothing. Correspondingly, the indifference curves in Figure 2.1 flatten as Dom has less food and more clothing. The behavior implied by the convexity of indifference curves is consistent with the observed behavior of many individuals—most people purchase balanced combinations of food and clothing.

Constraints

Dom would like more of both food and clothing. Unfortunately, he faces a budget constraint that limits his purchases. Suppose that he has an income of I and the prices per unit of food and clothing are P_f and P_c, respectively. Since he cannot spend more than I, he faces the following constraint:

$$I \geq P_f F + P_c C \tag{2.3}$$

where F and C represent the units of food and clothing purchased. The constraint indicates that only combinations of food and clothing that cost no more than I are feasible. Rearranging terms, this constraint can be written as

$$F \leq I/P_f - (P_c/P_f)C \tag{2.4}$$

Figure 2.2   Constraint

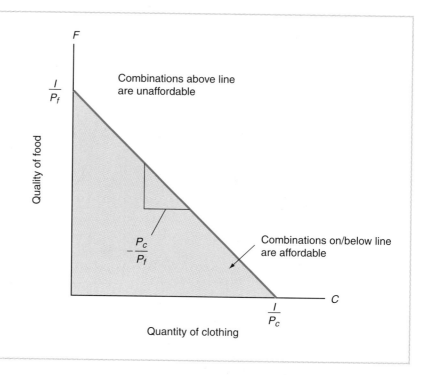

The constraint reflects the feasible combinations of food and clothing that are attainable given the person's income (*I*). The vertical and horizontal intercepts, respectively, show the amounts of food and clothing that can be purchased if no income is spent on the other good. The slope of the constraint is equal to −1 times the ratio of the prices of the two goods. For instance, if the price of clothing is $8 and the price of food is $2, the slope will be −4. This slope implies that 4 units of food must be given up for 1 unit of clothing. If both goods have the same price, the slope will be −1.

Figure 2.2 pictures this constraint—sometimes called a *budget line.* All combinations of food and clothing on or below the line are attainable. Combinations above the line are not feasible given an income of *I.* The *F* intercept (on the vertical axis) of the line I/P_f indicates how much food Dom can purchase if his entire income is spent on food and no clothing is purchased. The *C* intercept is correspondingly I/P_c. The slope of the line $-P_c/P_f$ is −1 times the ratio of the two prices. The ratio P_c/P_f is the *relative price* of clothing in terms of food. It represents how many units of food must be given up to acquire a unit of clothing: It is the opportunity cost of clothing. For example, if the price of clothing is $8 and the price of food is $2, the relative price of clothing is 4. To keep total expenditures constant, 4 units of food must be given up for every unit of clothing purchased. The relative price of food is P_f/P_c (in this example, 0.25); 1/4 unit of clothing must be given up for each unit of food purchased.

The constraint changes with changes in Dom's income and the relative prices of the two goods. As shown in Figure 2.3, changes in income result in parallel shifts of the constraint: Its slope is unaffected. An increase in income shifts the constraint outward (up and to the right), while a decrease in income shifts the constraint inward. The slope of the constraint changes with the relative prices of the two goods. As shown in Figure 2.4, if the price of clothing increases relative to the price of food, the constraint becomes steeper. If the price of clothing falls relative to the price of food, the constraint becomes flatter.

Individual Choice

Within this economic framework, Dom's goal is to maximize utility given the constraint. Utility is maximized at the point of tangency between the constraint and an indifference

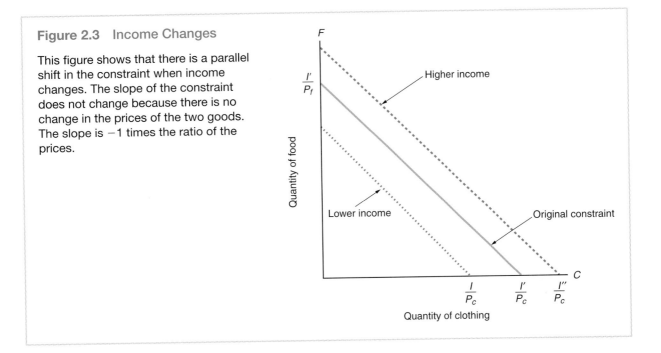

Figure 2.3 Income Changes

This figure shows that there is a parallel shift in the constraint when income changes. The slope of the constraint does not change because there is no change in the prices of the two goods. The slope is −1 times the ratio of the prices.

curve.[12] Figure 2.5 portrays the optimal choice. Dom could choose points like *b* and *c* on indifference curve 1. However, point *a* on curve 2 is preferred. Dom would prefer to be at any point on curve 3. Yet, these points are not attainable given his income.

This graphical solution to Dom's choice problem has a simple intuitive interpretation. At the point of tangency, the indifference curve and the constraint have equal slopes. Recall that the slope of the indifference curve represents Dom's willingness to trade food for clothing, whereas the slope of the constraint represents the terms of trade available in the marketplace. At the optimal choice, the *willingness and ability to trade are equal.* At other feasible combinations of food and clothing, Dom's utility could be increased by making substitutions. For instance, if Dom were at a point where he was willing to trade 5 units of food for 1 unit of clothing and if the relative price of clothing were 4 (the slope of the indifference curve is steeper than the constraint), Dom would be better off purchasing less food and more clothing. (He is willing to trade 5 units of food for one unit of clothing, but only has to give up 4 units of food to obtain 1 unit of clothing in the marketplace.) Alternatively, if Dom were at a point where he was only willing to give up 1 unit of food for 1 unit of clothing (the slope of the indifference curve is flatter than the constraint), he would be better off purchasing more food and less clothing—since he receives 5 units of food for each unit of clothing given up.

Changes in Choice

Dom's constraint will change whenever prices or income change. Correspondingly, he will make different choices. Recall that changes in relative prices alter the slope of the

---

[12]For simplicity, we ignore the possibility of corner solutions—the points where the budget constraint intersects the axes. With corner solutions, the individual spends all income on only one good.

Figure 2.4 Price Changes

This figure shows how the slope of the constraint changes with changes in the price of clothing. The slope of the line is $-(P_f/P_c)$. Thus, an increase in the price of clothing (from P_c' to P_c'') produces a steeper line, while a decrease (from P_c' to P_c) produces a flatter line. Changes in the price of food also affect the slope of the line.

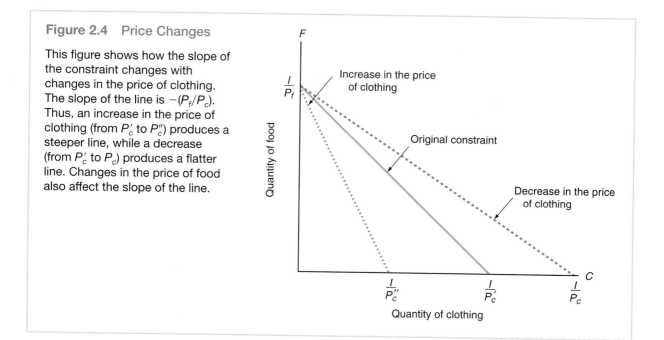

constraint. When the relative price of a good increases, individuals typically choose less of that good.[13] Figure 2.6 shows how Dom will purchase less food as its relative price increases—food is more expensive and so less attractive than it was at a lower price. Generally the amount of clothing purchased can either go up or down; it depends on the location of the new tangency point. (Given the particular utility function used in this example, the amount of clothing purchased remains unchanged.) Even though the price of clothing is relatively more attractive, the increase in food prices can limit available income so as to reduce the amount purchased of both goods. Changes in Dom's income cause parallel shifts in the constraint and will change his optimal choice. In Chapter 4, we examine in more detail how changes in income and prices affect consumption choices.

Choices also change if preferences change. Now changes in preferences undoubtedly occur. (Do you really believe that Toys 'R' Us will have any difficulty satisfying the demands for Teenage Mutant Ninja Turtle action figures, Tomaguchi virtual pets, Tickle-Me-Elmo dolls, or Pokemon Cards next Christmas?) Yet, economists rarely focus on such explanations. Economics has little theory to explain what might cause preferences to change. And since a large premium is placed on operationalism in managerial economics, preference-based explanations generally are appealed to only after other potential explanations are exhausted. In a sense, these preference-based explanations are too easy—they work too well. Virtually any observed behavior can be explained by appealing to preferences: Why did the consumption of frozen yogurt increase relative to that of ice cream? People's preferences changed so that more frozen yogurt and less ice cream was demanded. But a reduction in consumption could be "explained" just as readily. Without a deeper understanding of why preferences change, one is left "explaining" everything but with an analysis that allows you to predict nothing.

[13]In principle, some individuals might purchase more of a good if the price increases, but this outcome is rarely observed.

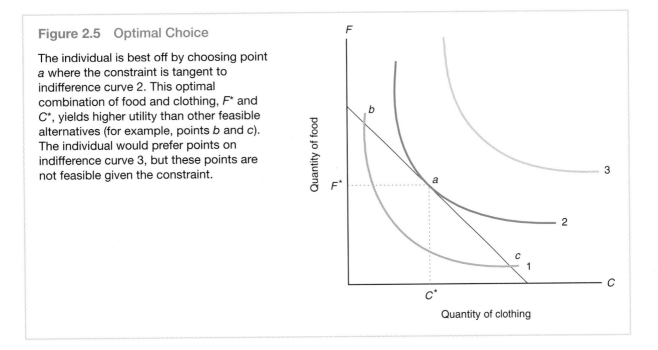

Figure 2.5 Optimal Choice

The individual is best off by choosing point *a* where the constraint is tangent to indifference curve 2. This optimal combination of food and clothing, *F** and *C**, yields higher utility than other feasible alternatives (for example, points *b* and *c*). The individual would prefer points on indifference curve 3, but these points are not feasible given the constraint.

Ultimately, the managerial usefulness of this analysis comes from its power to identify policy instruments that have a predictable impact on the problems at hand. Across a broad array of problems, assuming that underlying preferences are reasonably stable and analyzing the impact of changes in constraints regularly will yield important managerial insights and identify productive managerial tools.

Motivating Honesty at Sears

Often, economists focus on consumption goods such as food and clothing. This focus is natural given the interests economists have in understanding consumer behavior. Yet this analysis can easily be extended to consider other goods that people care about, such as love and respect.[14] Such an extension can be used to analyze the problem at Sears Auto Centers.

Suppose that Susan Chen, like other employees at Sears, values two goods—money and integrity. Her utility function is

$$
\overset{+}{} \quad \overset{+}{}
$$
$$
\text{Utility} = F(\text{Money, Integrity}) \tag{2.5}
$$

Money is meant to symbolize general purchasing power; it allows the purchase of goods such as food, clothing, and housing. Integrity is something Sue values for its own sake—being honest in her dealings with other people makes Sue feel good and she values it for that reason.

Suppose that integrity can be measured on a numerical scale with Sue preferring higher values. For example, 5 units of integrity provide more utility than 4 units of integrity. (In actuality, measuring a good like integrity on a numerical scale may be quite

[14]G. Becker (1993), "Nobel Lecture: The Economic Way of Looking at Behavior," *Journal of Political Economy* 101, 385–409.

Figure 2.6   Optimal Choice and Price Changes

This figure shows how the optimal choice changes with an increase in the price of food. In this example, the individual chooses less food (F_1^* rather than F_0^*). This is the typical case—usually, an individual will purchase less of a good when its price increases. Due to the particular utility function used in this example, the amount of clothing purchased remains unchanged (C^*). More generally, the amount of clothing purchased can either go up or down. It depends on the location of the new tangency point.

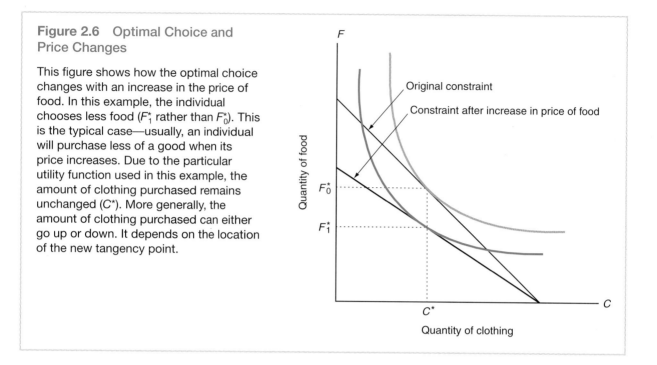

difficult. Yet this complication does not limit the qualitative insights that we can derive from the analysis.)

Salespeople at Sears Auto Centers were paid a commission based on total sales. In addition, they had sales quotas for particular products and services. Missing these quotas could result in job loss as well as lower pay. Individual sales apparently could be increased and sales quotas met by being dishonest—for example, telling customers that they needed new shock absorbers when in fact they did not.

Given the customer volume at the store and the commission rate, there is some maximum amount that Sue can earn even if she recommends repairs to every customer. If she recommends fewer repairs, income will decline. If she is completely honest and recommends no unnecessary repairs, sales quotas would be difficult to meet. Although this might result in a potential layoff and less future income, our analysis in this chapter is framed in a simple one-period context and does not consider future monetary returns from developing a good reputation. (In Chapters 10 and 21 we extend the analysis and consider such multiperiod effects.)

Figure 2.7 pictures Sue's implied constraint. This constraint depicts the maximum amounts of income and integrity that are possible given the compensation plan and conditions at the store.[15] If Sue sacrifices all integrity, she earns $\$_{max}$ a month. If she is scrupulously honest, she earns much less (there is some floor on income that depends on the traffic from customers with legitimate problems). Intermediate options along the

---

[15]For simplicity, we draw the constraint as linear. Linearity is not necessary for our analysis. Also, we want to emphasize that we put dollars on the vertical axis only because it is a convenient general indication of value, not because money is more important than other things. We could illustrate Sue's willingness to trade integrity against anything else Sue values, such as big Macs, pianos, or pairs of jeans.

Figure 2.7   Nature of the Constraint Facing a Worker at Sears Auto Center

The constraint pictures the maximum amounts of money and integrity that are possible for the employee given the compensation scheme and conditions at the store. If the employee sacrifices all integrity and recommends many unnecessary repairs, the employee earns a maximum of $\$_{max}$ a month. Fewer sales are made if the employee recommends fewer unnecessary repairs (selects a higher level of integrity), and income is lower since the worker is paid a commission on sales. I_c represents complete honesty.

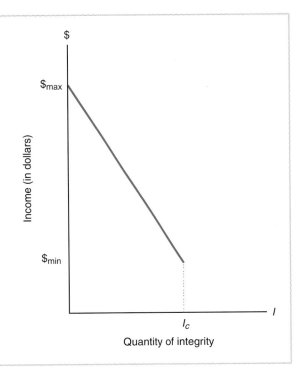

constraint are possible. While Sue would like to earn more than $\$_{max}$, higher income is not feasible in this job.

She chooses the combination of integrity and income that places Sue on her highest attainable indifference curve. This choice occurs at the point of tangency between her indifference curve and the constraint. Sue ends up selecting relatively low amounts of integrity because the commission plan adopted by Sears management has made integrity expensive: If Sue chooses more integrity, she must forfeit a relatively large amount of income.

Management can alter the constraint facing Sue and her colleagues by changing the compensation scheme. In the Sears case, lowering the sales commission (and raising the fixed hourly wage) reduces the monetary gains from selling additional products through

Money and Job Satisfaction

In surveys of 400 executives by the Young President's Organization, they admitted that the "pursuit of money consumed them," yet played down the importance of money in career choices. Some equated wealth with self-worth and others said, "There's never enough." However in attitude surveys, career-development programs consistently top employees' list of wants. Managers often insist they would never make career decisions primarily based on money. One manager ranks his family's well-being and happiness as most important, but still appreciates the monetary value of the job. One manager who received a large bonus said he will use the money for his children's education, "It's given me a sense of relief. Now I can redirect some money to things we haven't done or divert it into a retirement fund." Thus, these executives clearly value things other than money and regularly make choices that trade off money for other things that they value.

Source: H. Lancaster (1998), "Needy or Greedy?" *The Wall Street Journal* (June 30), B1.

dishonest behavior and thus flattens the constraint. Changes in the slope of the constraint result in a different tangency point and thus a different choice. Figure 2.8 shows how Sue's optimal choice changes when the sales commission is decreased.[16] The result is more honest behavior. In essence, Sue "purchases" more integrity because it is less expensive. Consistent with this analysis, Sears actually responded to the problem by changing the compensation scheme from commission to straight salary. It also eliminated sales quotas and introduced a program to reward personnel for high levels of customer satisfaction.

Managerial Implications

This analysis illustrates how the economic framework can be used to analyze and address management problems. Managers are interested in affecting the behavior of individuals such as employees, customers, union leaders, or subcontractors. Understanding what motivates individuals is critical. The economic approach views individual actions as the outcomes of maximizing personal utility. People are willing to make substitutions (for example, less leisure time for more income) if the terms of trade are advantageous. Managers can affect behavior by appropriately designing the constraints faced by individuals. The design of the constraints affects the trade-offs that individuals face and hence their choices. For example, management can motivate employees through the structure of compensation plans or customers through pricing decisions.

The outcome of individuals making economic choices is a function of both constraints and preferences. Individuals try to achieve their highest level of satisfaction given the constraints they face. Our discussion of management implications, however, intentionally focuses on constraints, not preferences. As a management tool, the usefulness of focusing on personal preferences often is limited. Preferences rarely are observable, and (as we noted earlier) virtually any observed change in choice can be "explained" as simply a matter of a change in personal tastes. But, it is difficult to change what a person likes or does not like. A preference-based explanation as to why employees were dishonest at Sears is that these employees gained personal utility from being dishonest (or compared to employees at other firms, Sears employees were willing to trade large amounts of personal integrity for small financial rewards). This explanation is not very helpful in giving management guidance on how to address the problem. It suggests that Sears might try to fire dishonest employees and replace them with employees who care more about personal integrity. But the difficulty of observing personal preferences limits the viability of this approach. How would Sears know if, as a group, the new hires would be any less dishonest than the old employees? You cannot just ask applicants if they are honest—if they are not, they will have no qualms about claiming that they are.

The fact that individuals are clever and creative in minimizing the effects of constraints greatly complicates management problems. Changing incentives will affect employee behavior, though sometimes in a perverse and unintended manner. Consider two of the Soviet Union's early attempts to adopt incentive compensation to motivate employees. To discourage taxi drivers from simply parking their cabs, they were rewarded

---

[16]We have altered the compensation scheme in a manner that places Sue on the same indifference curve. The rationale for doing this is as follows. Sears must provide Sue with sufficient utility to retain her at the firm. Below this level of utility, Sue will quit and work elsewhere. Sears is unlikely to want to pay Sue more than this minimum utility because it reduces firm profits. Thus, Sears has an incentive to adjust compensation in a manner that keeps her on the same indifference curve. Sue's indifference curve in Figure 2.8 can be viewed as this "reservation" utility. These issues are covered in more detail in Chapter 14.

Figure 2.8 Optimal Choices of a Worker at Sears Auto Center under Two Different Compensation Plans

Case 1 reflects the original compensation plan. In this case, compensation consists of a high sales commission and the constraint is relatively steep. In Case 2, the firm pays a higher portion of the wage as a fixed salary and a lower commission rate. The slope of the constraint is flatter. The result is that the individual chooses a higher level of integrity in Case 2 than in Case 1.

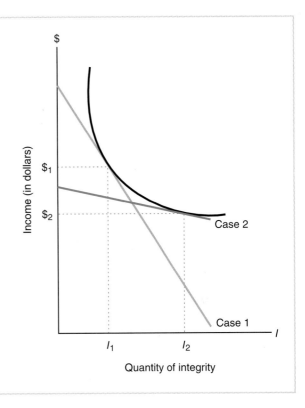

for total miles traveled; to encourage additional production, chandelier manufacturers were rewarded on total volume of production—measured in kilograms. In response to these incentive plans, taxi drivers began driving empty cabs at high speeds on highways outside Moscow, and chandelier manufacturers started producing such massive fixtures that they literally would collapse ceilings. (It is less costly to make one 100-kilo chandelier than five 20-kilo chandeliers; manufacturers also substituted lead for lighter-weight inputs.) Sears initially adopted a commission plan to motivate salespeople to work harder. The dishonest behavior was a side effect that undoubtedly was not anticipated when the plan was adopted.

In summary, the economic approach to behavior has important managerial implications. The framework suggests that a manager can motivate desired actions by establishing

Perverse Incentives at Lincoln Electric

Lincoln Electric is a successful company that manufactures arc welding equipment. It is famous for a strong emphasis on incentive compensation. Their incentive program appears to be an important source of the high productivity of Lincoln's production workers. At one point, Lincoln Electric decided to extend its incentive compensation program to clerical workers. Counters were installed on typewriters and secretaries were paid on the number of characters typed. This policy resulted in an increase in the amount of typing. The program, however, was discontinued when it was discovered that a secretary spent her lunch hour typing worthless pages by depressing a repeating key in order to increase her compensation.

Source: N. Fast and N. Berg (1975), "The Lincoln Electric Company," Harvard Business School Case #376–028.

appropriate incentives. However, managers must be careful because setting improper incentives can motivate perverse behavior.

It is worth noting that economic analysis is limited in its ability to forecast the precise choices of a given individual because individual preferences are largely unobservable. The focus is on aggregate behavior or on what the typical person tends to do. For example, an economist might not be very good at predicting the individual responses of a group of employees to a new incentive plan. An economist will be successful in predicting that the typical employee will work harder—and thus output for the group will rise when compensation is tied to output—than when a fixed salary independent of performance is paid. Managers typically are interested in structuring an organizational architecture that will work well and does not depend on specific people filling particular jobs. Individuals come and go, and the manager wants an organization that will work well as these changes occur. In this context, the economic framework is likely to be very useful. To solve management problems where the characteristics of a specific individual are more important, other frameworks may be more valuable. For example, if the board is interviewing a potential new CEO, insights into that individual's behavior derived from psychology might be extremely useful.

Alternative Models of Behavior[17]

We have shown how the economic view of behavior can be used in managerial decision making. We now discuss four other models that are commonly used by managers (either explicitly or implicitly) to explain behavior. Our discussion of each of these models is simplified. The intent, however, is to capture the essence of a few of the more prominent views that managers have about behavior and to illustrate how managerial decision making is affected by the particular view. We contrast these alternative views with the economic view and argue why the economic framework is a particularly useful tool for managers.

Only-Money-Matters Model

Some people believe that the only important component of the job is the level of monetary compensation. But as we have already suggested, people have an incredibly broad range of interests, extending far beyond money. And these interests are reflected in a diverse array of activities. As examples, much of the work through the Red Cross is undertaken by unpaid volunteers; people frequently choose early retirement, walking away from a regular paycheck to enjoy additional leisure time; riskier occupations command higher pay in order to attract people into those jobs.

Some of this confusion can result from a misinterpretation of standard economic analysis. Central to economics is the study of trade-offs (recall our discussion of indifference curves illustrating trade-offs between food and clothing). Economists frequently use money as one of the goods being considered. But in these cases, money is merely a convenient unit of value: It represents general purchasing power. Its use does not suggest that only money matters.

Happy-Is-Productive Model

Managers sometimes assert that happy employees are more productive than unhappy employees. Managers following this happy-is-productive model see as their goal the

---

[17]This section draws on W. Meckling (1976).

Happy-Is-Productive versus Economic Explanations of the Hawthorne Experiments

Seven productivity studies were conducted at Western Electric's Hawthorne plant over the period 1924–1932. All seven studies focused on the response of assembly workers' productivity when different aspects of the work environment were manipulated (for example, length of break times and workday). Surprisingly, productivity rose virtually regardless of the particular manipulation. For example, it is claimed that productivity increased whenever illumination of the work area was changed, regardless of the direction of the change. When the lights were turned up, productivity increased, and when they were turned down, productivity increased, as well. This result is known as the Hawthorne Effect and is among the most discussed findings in psychology; it often is taken as support for the happy-is-productive model. The workers in the experiment were given special attention and nonauthoritarian supervision relative to other workers at the plant. Also, the affected workers' views on the experiments were solicited by management, and the workers were given more responsibility. These actions, it has been argued, increased job satisfaction and performance.

Parsons (1974) presents evidence that the findings of the Hawthorne experiments also can be explained by accompanying changes in the compensation system. Prior to the experiment, all workers were paid based on the output of a group of about 100 workers. During the experiment, the compensation plan was changed to base pay on the output of only five workers. In this case, a given worker's output more directly affects her own pay, and economic theory predicts increased output. Interestingly, the last of the original Hawthorne experiments observed workers where the compensation system was not changed. In that seventh experiment, there was no change in output.

Source: H. Parsons (1974), "What Happened at Hawthorne?" *Science* 183, 922–932.

designing of work environments that satisfy employees. Psychological theories, such as Maslow's and Herzberg's, are frequently used as guides in efforts to increase job satisfaction.[18]

A manager adhering to the happy-is-productive model might suggest that the problem at Sears was motivated by disgruntled employees who took out their frustrations on customers. This view implies that Sears could reduce the problem by promoting employee satisfaction through such actions as designing more interesting jobs, increasing the rates of pay, and improving the work environment. Happier employees would be expected to provide customers with better service.

The economic and happy-is-productive models do not differ based on what people care about. The economic model allows individuals to value love, esteem, interesting work, and pleasant work environments, as well as more standard economic goods such as food, clothing, and shelter. The primary difference in the models is what motivates individual actions. In the happy-is-productive model, employees exert high effort when they are happy. In the economic model, employees exert effort because of the rewards.

To contrast the two models, consider offering an employee guaranteed lifetime employment plus a large salary, which will be paid independent of performance. The happy-is-productive model suggests that the employee will be more productive, because the additional job security and high salary are likely to increase job satisfaction. The economic model suggests that the employee would exert less effort—since the employee receives no additional rewards for working harder and will not be fired for exerting low effort.

[18]F. Herzberg, B. Mausner and B. Snyderman (1959), *The Motivation to Work* (John Wiley & Sons: New York); and A. Maslow (1970), *Motivation and Personality* (Harper & Row: New York).

Good-Citizen Model

Some managers subscribe to the good-citizen model. The basic assumption is that employees have a strong personal desire to do a good job; they take pride in their work and want to excel. Under this view, managers have three primary roles. First, they need to communicate the goals and objectives of the organization to employees. Second, they must help employees discover how to achieve these goals and objectives. Finally, managers should provide feedback on performance so that employees can continue to improve their efforts. There is no reason to have incentive pay, since individuals are interested intrinsically in doing a good job.

This view suggests that the problems at Sears occurred because employees misunderstood what was good for the company. Employees might have thought that increasing sales was in the company's best interests, even if it required a certain amount of dishonesty. Under the good-citizen view, the management of Sears could motivate employee honesty by clearly communicating to its salespeople that Sears would be better off in the long run if they did not deceive their customers. Managers of each automotive center might be instructed to hold a series of employee meetings to stress the value of honesty and customer service.

In the good-citizen model, employees place the interests of the company first. There is never a conflict between an employee's personal interest and the interest of the company. In contrast, the economic model posits that employees maximize their own utility. Potential conflicts of interest often arise. The economic view predicts that pleas from Sears management that employees be more honest would have little affect on behavior unless they also changed the reward system to make it in the interests of employees to be more honest.

Product-of-the-Environment Model

The product-of-the-environment model argues that the behaviors of individuals are largely determined by their upbringings. Some cultures and households encourage positive values in individuals, such as industry and integrity, whereas others promote negative traits, such as laziness and dishonesty. This model suggests that Sears had dishonest individuals in its automotive centers. A response would have been to fire these employees and replace them with honest salespeople from better backgrounds.

Economics and Attracting Russian Workers

Near the Arctic Circle, Siberia offers two main seasons: frostbite and mosquito swarms. It also boasts large mineral deposits. Attracting workers to Siberia has been difficult until companies raised salaries. Now, despite its inhospitable climate, private companies draw people to work the giant oil, gold, and diamond deposits with salaries as much as ten times those offered in the rest of the country. With the rest of the economy in shambles where people are sometimes paid in tires and brassieres, Siberia is more enticing with monthly wages of $720 in cash deposits—about seven times the median Russian salary.

Source: M. Brzezinski (1998), "A Paradise on Ice? Hardly, but to Many, Siberia Is a Hot Spot," *The Wall Street Journal* (July 1), A1.

The Economic Framework and Criminal Behavior

Criminals often are viewed as psychologically disturbed. Evidence, however, suggests that criminal behavior can be explained, at least in part, by the economic framework. This framework predicts that a criminal will consider the marginal costs and benefits of a crime and will commit the crime only when the benefits exceed the costs. Under this view, increasing the likelihood of detection and/or the severity of punishment will reduce crimes. In a pioneering study, Issac Ehrlich examined whether the incidence of major felonies varied across states with the expected punishment. He found that the incidence of robberies decreased about 1.3 percent in response to each 1 percent increase in the proportionate likelihood of punishment. The incidence of crime also decreased with the severity of the punishment. Since Ehrlich's study, scholars have conducted extensive research on this topic. In general, the results support the conclusion that the economic model plays a useful role in predicting criminal activity.

Source: I. Ehrlich (1973), "Participation in Illegitimate Activities: A Theoretical and Empirical Investigation," *Journal of Political Economy* 81, 521–565.

Which Model Should Managers Use?

Behavior is a complex topic. No behavioral model is likely to be useful in all contexts. For example, the economic model is unlikely to be helpful in predicting whether a given individual will prefer a red shirt to a blue shirt (selling at the same price). But our focus is on managerial decision making. In this context, there are reasons to believe that the economic model is particularly useful.

Managers are frequently interested in fostering *changes* in behavior. For example, managers want consumers to buy more of their products, employees to exert more effort, and labor unions to accept smaller wage increases. In contrast to other models, the economic framework provides managers with concrete guidance on how to alter behavior. Desired behavior can be encouraged by changing the relevant costs and benefits facing the decision maker. For example, incentive compensation can be used to motivate employees, and price changes can be used to affect consumer behavior.

There is ample evidence to support the hypothesis that this economic framework is useful in explaining changes in behavior. The most common example is that consumers tend to buy fewer products at higher prices. The evidence suggests that the model is also useful in explaining aspects of behavior in many other contexts, including voting; the formation, dissolution, and structure of families; drug addiction; and the incidence of crime.[19]

The good-citizen model appears less successful in predicting behavior in business settings. Management would be an easy task if employees would work harder and produce higher-quality products simply on request. The happy-is-productive model also has material limitations. Most importantly, the existing evidence suggests that there is little relation between job satisfaction and performance (see Scott's "Criticisms of the Happy-Is-Productive Model" in the accompanying box). Happy employees are not necessarily more productive. Sometimes, managers might want to follow the implications of the product-of-the-environment model and fire employees with undesirable traits. Yet, this approach is unlikely to be useful in solving most managerial problems. Also, given laws

[19]G. Becker (1993).

Criticisms of the Happy-Is-Productive Model

W. Richard Scott summarizes some of the major concerns about the happy-is-productive model (sometimes referred to as the human-relations movement):

> Virtually all of these applications of the human-relations movement have come under severe criticism on both ideological and empirical grounds. Paradoxically, the human-relations movement, ostensibly developed to humanize the cold and calculating rationality of the factory and shop, rapidly came under attack on the grounds that it represented simply a more subtle and refined form of exploitation. Critics charged that workers' legitimate economic interests were being inappropriately deemphasized; actual conflicts of interest were denied and "therapeutically" managed; and the roles attributed to managers represented a new brand of elitism. The entire movement was branded as "cow sociology" just as contented cows were alleged to produce more milk, satisfied workers were expected to produce more output.
>
> The ideological criticisms were the first to erupt, but reservations raised by researchers on the basis of empirical evidence may in the long run prove to be more devastating. Several decades of research have demonstrated no clear relation between worker satisfaction and productivity.

Source: W. Scott (1981), *Organizations: Rational, Natural and Open Systems* (Prentice Hall: Englewood Cliffs, NJ), 89–90.

---

that limit discrimination, this approach can subject the firm to potentially serious legal sanctions.

Decision Making under Uncertainty

Throughout this chapter, we have considered cases where the decision maker has complete certainty about the items of choice. For instance, Dom Lalisse knew the exact prices of food and clothing, and Sue Chen knew the precise trade-off between integrity and compensation at Sears. Decision makers, however, often face uncertainty. For instance, in choosing among risky investment alternatives (such as stocks and bonds), an individual must forecast the likely payoffs. Even so, there can be significant uncertainty about the eventual outcomes. The analysis presented in this chapter can be extended readily to incorporate decision making under uncertainty.[20] A detailed analysis of decision making under uncertainty is beyond the scope of this book. This section introduces a few key concepts that we will use later in this book.

Expected Value   Taylor McClure sells real estate for RealCo. He receives a sales commission from his employer. For simplicity, suppose that Taylor has three possible incomes for the year. In a good year, he sells many houses and earns $200,000, whereas in a bad year he earns nothing. In other years, he receives $100,000. Probability refers to the likelihood that an outcome will occur. In this example, each outcome is equally likely, and thus has a probability of 1/3 of occurring. The *expected value* of an uncertain payoff is defined as the weighted average of all possible outcomes, where the probability of each outcome is used as the weights. The expected value is a measure of central tendency—the payoff that will occur on average. In our example, the expected value is[21]:

$$\text{Expected value} = (1/3 \times 0)\ (1/3 \times 100{,}000)\ (1/3 \times 200{,}000) = \$100{,}000 \quad (2.6)$$

---

[20]For example, E. Fama and M. Miller (1972), *The Theory of Finance* (Dryden Press: New York), Chapter 5.

[21]Note that the expected value need not equal one of the possible outcomes. As a weighted average, it can be a value between outcomes. In this example, it happens to correspond to one of the possible outcomes, $100,000.

Variability   Although Taylor can expect average earnings of $100,000, his income is not certain. The *variance* is a measure of the variability of the payoff. It is defined as the expected value of the squared difference between each possible payoff and the expected value. In this example, the variance is

$$\text{Variance} = 1/3(0 - 100{,}000)^2 + 1/3(100{,}000 - 100{,}000)^2$$
$$+ \ 1/3(200{,}000 - 100{,}000)^2$$
$$= 6.7 \text{ billion} \qquad\qquad (2.7)$$

The *standard deviation* is the square root of the variance:

$$\text{Standard deviation} = (6.7 \text{ billion})^{1/2} = \$81{,}650 \qquad\qquad (2.8)$$

Variances and standard deviations are used as measures of risk. It does not really matter which we use, since one is a simple transformation of the other (higher standard deviations correspond to higher variances). In this example, we focus on the standard deviation. Higher standard deviations reflect more risk. An event with a definite outcome has a standard deviation of zero.

Risk Aversion

Like most people, Taylor is *risk-averse:* Holding the expected payoff fixed, he prefers a lower standard deviation. He therefore gains utility from an increase in expected value, but he experiences a reduction in utility from increases in standard deviation. Figure 2.9 shows three of Taylor's indifference curves. Each curve shows all combinations of expected value and standard deviation that give Taylor equal utility. In contrast to our previous analysis, here one of the objects of choice is a "bad"—Taylor does not like risk. Thus, in this figure, the indifference curves have positive slopes, and northwest movements are utility-increasing (recall in the standard analysis that the curves have negative slopes, and northeast movements are utility-increasing). The slopes of the indifference curves indicate Taylor's degree of risk aversion. Steeper slopes translate into higher risk aversion. (If the slopes of the indifference curves are steep, Taylor must receive a relatively large increase in expected value for each additional unit of risk to maintain a constant level of utility.) If his indifference curves were totally flat, he would be *risk-neutral.* A risk-neutral person cares only about expected value and is indifferent to the amount of risk. Indifference curve 3 is associated with the highest level of utility, whereas curve 1 is associated with the lowest utility. Taylor is currently on curve 2. Given a choice among compensation plans with different expected payoffs and risk, Taylor will choose the combination that places him on the highest attainable indifference curve.

Certainty Equivalent and Risk Premium

Figure 2.9 indicates that Taylor is indifferent between the risky commission scheme, which has an expected payoff of $100,000 and a certain income of $80,000. The $80,000 is Taylor's *certainty equivalent* for the risky income stream—he is willing to trade the uncertain income of $100,000 for a certain income of $80,000. The difference between the expected value of the risky income stream and the certainty equivalent is called the *risk premium.* This $20,000 premium, which comes in the form of a higher

Figure 2.9 Indifference Curves for Expected Value and Standard Deviation

This figure displays three indifference curves for a *risk-averse* individual. The individual prefers higher expected value but lower standard deviation. Standard deviation is a measure of risk. Since risk is a "bad," the indifference curves are positively sloped. Northwest moves are utility-increasing. Currently, the individual has a compensation package that has an expected value of $100,000 and a standard deviation of $81,650. The *certainty equivalent* of this package is $80,000. The *risk premium* is $20,000.

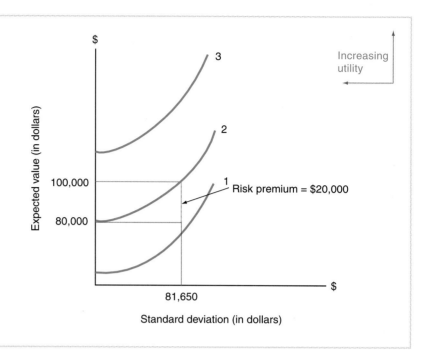

expected payoff, must be paid to keep Taylor indifferent between the risky income stream and his certainty equivalent.

Suppose that Taylor receives a job offer from a competing real estate company that would pay him a fixed salary of $90,000 per year. Taylor considers the new job to be the same as his current job in all dimensions other than the compensation plan. Taylor's current compensation plan will not be sufficient to motivate him to continue to work for RealCo. Even though his current plan has a higher expected payoff, he would prefer the certain $90,000 to RealCo's risky commission plan. If RealCo wants to retain Taylor, it must offer him a compensation package that provides the same level of utility as the $90,000 for certain. We expand on this issue in more detail later in the book.

Risk Aversion versus Risk Taking

Lauren Arbittier decides to bet $2,000 on number 35 of the roulette wheel in a Las Vegas casino. Almost immediately she starts to question her decision. Lauren normally is a risk avoider who hardly ever gambles. But she works at Trilogy Software where the CEO understands that taking risks and suffering the consequences are critical to the firm's success. The CEO wants to develop people who take chances. "You don't win points . . . for trying." Lauren is participating in Trilogy's three-month training program for all new recruits. It educates employees about, among other things, how to evaluate risky projects, not just to immediately accept or reject the project because it is risky. The program also suggests to employees that they will not be rewarded at Trilogy unless they take risks. Thus, although Lauren does not like taking risks, working for Trilogy, she has economic incentives to do so.

Source: E. Ramstad (1998), "High Rollers, How Trilogy Software Trains Its Raw Recruits to Be Risk Takers," *The Wall Street Journal* (September 21), A1.

CASE STUDY: *Interwest Healthcare Corp*

Interwest Healthcare is a nonprofit organization that owns ten hospitals located in three western states. Cynthia Manzoni is Interwest's chief executive officer. Vijay Singh, Interwest's Chief Financial Officer, and the administrators of the ten hospitals report to Manzoni.

Singh is deeply concerned because the hospital staffs are not being careful when entering data into the firm's management information system. This data involves information on patient intake, treatment, and release. The information system is used to compile management reports such as those relating to the costs of various treatments. Also, the system is used to compile reports that are required by the federal government under various grant programs. Singh reasons that without good information, the management and government reports are less useful and potentially misleading. Singh is worried about the managerial implications and the potential loss of federal funds. The federal government periodically audits Interwest and might discontinue aid if the reports are deemed inaccurate.

Singh has convinced Manzoni that a problem exists. She also realizes the importance of an accurate system both for management planning and maintaining federal aid. Six months ago, she invited the hospital administrators and staff members from the corporate financial office to a retreat at a resort. The purpose was to communicate to the hospital administrators the problems with the data entry and to stress the importance of doing a better job. The meeting was acrimonious. The hospital people accused Singh of being a bureaucrat who did not care about patient services. Singh accused the hospital staffs of not understanding the importance of accurate reporting. By the end of the meeting, Manzoni thought that she had a commitment by the hospital administrators to increase the accuracy of data entry at their hospitals. However, six months later, Singh claims that the problem is as bad as ever.

Manzoni has hired you as a consultant to analyze the problem and to make recommendations that might improve the situation.

Discussion Questions

1. What are the potential sources of the problem?
2. What information would you want to analyze?
3. What actions might you recommend to increase the accuracy of the data entry?
4. How does your view of behavior affect how you might address this consulting assignment?

Summary

In this chapter we summarize the way economists view behavior. In the economic model, individuals are seen as having unlimited wants but limited resources. They rank alternative uses of limited resources in terms of preference, and choose the most preferred alternative. Individuals are clever in figuring out ways of maximizing their utility (happiness) in the face of resource constraints. Individuals are not necessarily selfish in the sense that they care only about their personal wealth: They also care about charity, family, religion, and society. They are not infallible supercomputers.

The *opportunity cost* of using a resource is the value of the resource in its best alternative use. For example, the cost of having a manager use five hours to work on a project is the value of the manager's time in working on the next best alternative project. Economic decision making requires careful consideration of the relevant opportunity costs.

Marginal costs and benefits are the incremental costs and benefits that are associated with a decision. In calculating marginal costs, it is important to use the opportunity costs of the incremental resources. For example, in deciding whether to purchase a new laptop computer, the marginal cost is its price and the marginal benefit is the value that the person places on the new computer. It is the marginal costs and benefits that are important in economic decision making. Action should be taken when the marginal benefits are greater than the marginal costs. *Sunk costs* that are not affected by the decision (for example, unrecoverable funds previously spent on computers) are not relevant.

A *utility function* is a mathematical function that relates total utility to the amounts that an individual has of whatever items the individual cares about *(goods)*. Preferences implied by a utility function are pictured graphically by *indifference curves.* Indifference curves picture all combinations of goods that yield the same level of utility. Individual choice involves maximizing utility given resource *constraints.* Graphically, the constraint shows all combinations of goods that are feasible to acquire. The optimal choice is where the indifference curve is tangent to the constraint. At this point, the individual is at the highest level of utility possible given the constraint.

Changes in the constraint result in changes in the optimal choice. An important implication is that managers can affect behavior by affecting constraints. Managers, however, have to be careful. Individuals are clever at maximizing their utility, and setting the wrong incentives can have perverse consequences.

We contrast the economic model with other models of human behavior that managers often use. We argue that the economic model is often more useful than alternative models in managerial decision making.

The analysis in this chapter can be extended to the case where the decision maker faces uncertainty about the items of choice. An example of decision making under uncertainty is choosing among risky investment alternatives. One concept that we will rely on later in this book is *risk aversion.* When confronted with both a risky and a certain alternative having the same expected (or average) payoffs, a risk-averse person always will choose the certain outcome. A *risk premium* must be offered to entice the person to choose the risky alternative.

Throughout this chapter, we focus primarily on how managers might use the economic view to analyze and influence the behavior of employees. As we will see, the economic view is quite powerful and is useful in explaining behavior in a variety of different contexts.

<table>
<tr><td>Suggested
Readings</td><td>G. Becker (1993), "Nobel Lecture: The Economic Way of Looking at Behavior," Journal of Political Economy 101, 385–409.

M. Jensen and W. Meckling (1994), "The Nature of Man," Journal of Applied Corporate Finance 7, 4–19.</td></tr>
</table>

<table>
<tr><td>Review
Questions</td><td>

2–1. Which costs are pertinent to economic decision making? Which costs are *not* relevant?

2–2. **a.** Briefly describe the five models of behavior presented in this chapter.
    b. What are the implications of these models for managers attempting to influence their employees' behavior?

2–3. Employees in a plant in Minnesota are observed to be industrious and very productive. Employees in a similar plant in Southern California are observed to be lazy and unproductive. Discuss how alternative views of human behavior and motivation might suggest different explanations for this observed behavior.

2–4. Employees at a department store are observed engaging in the following behavior: (a) they hide items that are on sale from the customers, and (b) they exert little effort in designing merchandise

</td></tr>
</table>

displays. They are also uncooperative with one another. What do you think might be causing this behavior, and what might you do to improve the situation?

2–5. One of the main tenets of economic analysis is that people act in their own narrow self-interest. Why then do people leave tips in restaurants? If a study were to compare the size of tips earned by servers in restaurants on interstate highways with those in restaurants near residential neighborhoods, what would you expect to find? Why?

2–6. Several school districts have attempted to increase teacher productivity by paying teachers based on the scores their students achieve on standardized tests (administered by outside testing agencies). The goal is to produce higher-quality classroom instruction. Do you think that this type of compensation scheme will produce the desired outcome? Explain.

2–7. A company recently raised the pay of employees by 20 percent. Employee productivity remained the same. The CEO of the company was quoted as saying, "it just goes to show that money does not motivate people." Provide a critical evaluation of this statement.

2–8. One physician who worked for a large health maintenance organization was quoted as saying:

One day I was listening to a patient's heart and realized there was an abnormal rhythm. My first thought was that I hoped that I did not have to refer the patient to a specialist.

Indeed, HMO physicians have been criticized for not making referrals when they are warranted. How do you think the physician was compensated by the HMO? Explain.

2–9. Insurance companies have to generate enough revenue to cover their costs and make a normal profit—otherwise, they will go out of business. This implies that the premiums charged for insurance policies must be greater than the expected payouts to the policyholders. Why would a person ever buy insurance, knowing that the price is greater than the expected payout?

2–10. Critically evaluate the following statement: "Risk-averse people never take gambles."

2–11. Suppose that an investment can yield three possible cash flows: $5,000; $1,000; or $0. The probability of each outcome is 1/3.
   a. What is the expected value and standard deviation of the investment?
   b. How much would a risk-neutral person be willing to pay for the investment?
   c. How much would a risk-averse person be willing to pay for the investment?

2–12. In order to spur consumer spending in 1998, the Japanese government considered an $85 billion voucher system whereby every Japanese consumer would receive a shopping voucher that could be used to purchase Japanese products. For simplicity, assume the following: each consumer has wealth of 1 million yen, consumers must allocate this wealth between consumption now (c_1) and consumption later (c_2), the interest rate is zero, the voucher is worth 100,000 yen, and it can be spent only in the current period. If it is not spent, it is lost.
   a. Plot a budget line for a representative consumer both before and after the voucher program (c_1 and c_2 are on the axes).
   b. Do you expect that current consumption of a typical consumer will increase by the full 100,000 yen of the voucher? Explain.
   c. How does the impact of this 100,000-yen voucher differ from simply giving the individual 100,000 yen?

2–13. Refer to the box titled, "Risk Aversion versus Risk Taking." There are at least three ways in which the Trilogy training program might be effective: (1) It changes employees' preferences regarding risk bearing. (2) It more effectively identifies individuals with the risk to tolerances that Trilogy desires. (3) It better communicates the consequences to Trilogy employees of undertaking risky ventures. Discuss the likely importance of these three mechanisms.

2–14. People give to charity.
   a. Is this action consistent with the "economic view of behavior"? Explain.
   b. Suppose there is a big drop in charitable giving. At the same time there has been no decline in per capita income or total employment. Using the economic model, what potential factors might have led to this decline in giving?
   c. How might the decline in giving be explained by the product-of-the environment model?

2–15. Some states in the United States allow citizens to carry handguns. Citizens can protect themselves in the case of robberies by using these guns. Other states do not allow citizens to carry handguns. Criminals, however, tend to have handguns in all states. *Use economic analysis* to predict the effects of handgun laws on the behavior of the typical criminal. In particular: (1) Do you think criminals will commit more or fewer robberies in the states with the laws? (2) How do you think the laws will affect the *types of robberies* criminals commit? Be sure to explain your *economic reasoning*.

2–16. Discuss the following statement: "Sunk costs matter. People who pay $20,000 to join a golf club play golf more frequently than people who play on public golf courses."

Chapter 3
Markets, Organizations, and the Role of Knowledge

During much of the twentieth century, the Soviet Union and the United States were involved in an acrimonious debate over the merits of free-market versus centrally planned economies. The Soviet belief in the superiority of central planning was summarized eloquently in Premier Nikita Khruschev's ominous prophecy, "We will bury you." The 1990s, however, witnessed the rapid collapse of many of the centrally planned economies around the world. The Soviet Union broke apart. The Berlin Wall was dismantled, and West and East Germany were reunified. Communist governments across Eastern Europe were replaced, while market economies in countries like Singapore and the United States thrived.

These events appear to support the contention that central economic planning does not work as well as free markets. Yet on closer inspection, it is evident that a substantial amount of central economic planning occurs within market economies. Indeed, most of the production in modern economies takes place within firms, where resource allocation decisions are made by managers in ways that often are closely akin to central planning.

Management, through administrative actions, dictates the output mix of the firm as well as methods of production. These decisions can involve thousands of employees and billions of dollars in resources. Indeed, the monetary size of the world's largest firms exceeds that of many national economies. For instance, the 1997 gross national products of Peru, Kenya, and Portugal were $110 billion, $45 billion, and $150 billion, respectively; the 1997 net sales at General Motors were $178 billion. If central planning is so bad, why do firms within market economies rely on it so extensively?

In this chapter, we examine three questions: How do market systems work? What are the relative advantages of market systems compared to central planning in large economies? Why do we observe so much economic activity conducted within firms in market economies?

Answers to these questions are particularly important to managers for two reasons. First, an understanding of how markets work helps managers make appropriate input, output, and pricing decisions. Second, national economies are like firms in that both are human creations to organize economic activity. Understanding the relative advantages and disadvantages of markets, central planning, and firms is directly relevant to understanding firm-level issues such as whether to decentralize decision rights to employees and whether to make or buy each of the firm's inputs.

Goals of Economic Systems

Every economic entity—be it a national economy, firm, or household—is confronted with three basic issues:

- What to produce
- How to produce it
- How to allocate the final output

Economic entities can be organized in alternative ways to address these issues. For instance, national economies can rely on either central planning or free markets. Similarly, firms and households can use centralized decision making, where the CEO or head of household makes all major decisions. Alternatively, other people in the firm or household can be granted substantial decision-making authority.

Given the alternatives, what is the best way to organize economic activities? To answer this question, we need some criterion for comparing alternative systems. Unfortunately, disagreement over such a criterion is likely. For instance, you might argue that an ideal system would produce your preferred mix of products and give them all to you, whereas your neighbor is certain to disagree. Given these differences in opinion, economists focus on a relatively uncontroversial but narrow criterion for comparing the effectiveness of economic systems: *Pareto efficiency*.[1] A distribution of resources is said to be Pareto-efficient if there is no alternative allocation that keeps all individuals at least as well off but makes even one person better off. If an economic system is not producing an efficient allocation of resources, it is possible to make its members better off by adopting Pareto-improving changes (thus benefiting some members without hurting others).

As an example, assume that the economy produces 1,000 personal computers and no VCRs. This distribution of resources is not Pareto-efficient if there is a subset of individuals who prefer to substitute a VCR for a computer and could make this substitution without reducing the utility of other individuals in the society. Based on the concept of

---

[1]The term is named after Vilfredo Pareto, 1848–1923, an Italian economist and sociologist.

Pareto efficiency, its citizens would be better off if the economy produced more VCRs and fewer computers. If this action adversely affects even one person, the move would not be Pareto-improving and an economist would have little formal basis to conclude whether the move would be good or bad from a societal viewpoint.[2] Pareto efficiency also requires that goods be produced in an efficient manner. The resource allocation would not be Pareto-efficient if production could be rearranged so that more VCRs were produced without lowering computer production (and vice versa).

Within centrally planned economies, government officials decide what to produce, how to produce it, and who obtains the final output. In free markets, these decisions are decentralized to individuals within the economy. At least in concept, a central planner could order any feasible production and distribution of goods. Thus, any allocation of resources that could be achieved by a market economy also could be achieved by a centrally planned economy—at least in principle. We begin by discussing how market systems work and how they can produce a Pareto-efficient allocation of resources. We then discuss why in large economies a market is more likely to produce an efficient resource allocation than central planning.

Property Rights and Exchange in a Market Economy

A *property right* is a legally enforced right to select the uses of an economic good. A property right is *private* when it is assigned to a specific person. Private property rights are *alienable* in that they can be transferred (sold or given) to another individual. For example, if Valerie Fong owns an automobile, she can use the automobile as she sees fit (within limits set by traffic laws). Valerie can restrict others from using her vehicle. She also can sell the automobile (transfer to another person whatever property rights she has in the vehicle). The government maintains police and a court system to help enforce these property rights.

An important feature of a market economy is the use of private property rights. Owners of land and other resources have the legal rights to decide how to use these resources and frequently trade these rights to other individuals. They are free to start new businesses and to close existing businesses. In contrast, in centrally planned economies, property tends to be owned by the state; government officials decide how to use these resources.

Dimensions of Property Rights

Ownership involves two general dimensions: *use rights* and *alienability rights*. These aspects of ownership are not always bundled together. You own your body in the sense that you can decide what activities to pursue. Yet, there are significant legal restrictions on alienability. For instance, you cannot enter a legally enforceable contract to sell one of your kidneys, despite the fact that you have two, can live comfortably with one, and might value your second kidney much less than a wealthy individual dying from kidney failure. This restriction eliminates the possibility of a free market in kidneys. In some transactions, it is possible to sell use rights while retaining alienability rights. For instance, in a rental contract, the renter obtains the rights to use an apartment, but does

---

[2]Therefore, economics does not address the question of which of the many possible efficient resource allocations is best for a society. Producing your preferred set of products and giving them all to you is efficient (the allocation cannot be changed without making you worse off). However, others will argue that the allocation is not fair or equitable. Economists have no special training in resolving these issues and thus rarely attempt to settle these types of debates.

Patent for Priceline.com

Government-enforced patents better-define property rights in new inventions. Patents in the United States are awarded for processes, machines, manufacturers, or compositions of matter that are considered useful, novel, and unobvious. Patents protect the intellectual property rights of the inventor and thus protect the common good by providing incentives to innovate novel and unobvious inventions.

Priceline.com received a patent for the world's first buyer-driven e-commerce system where users can go to the Internet to name their price for goods and services. Some question whether Priceline.com's process is really novel and unobvious. If the patent is upheld, future Internet businesses where consumers can name their own price will have to pay Priceline.com a royalty. This royalty is a tax on all Internet consumers, which will lead to unnecessary litigation and impede development of online commerce. Awarding a patent for something that is obvious lowers incentives for future innovations that use this process.

Source: J. Gurley (1999), "The Trouble with Internet Patents," *Fortune* (July 19), 118.

not have the right to sell the unit. Conversely, the landlord has the right to sell the apartment, but does not have the right to use it while the lease is in force. (Rental, lease, and franchise agreements separate alienability and use rights; we examine these contracts in Chapter 18.)

Gains from Trade

To understand how a market economy works, we must understand the motives for trading property rights. Why do people buy and sell? The basic answer is to make themselves better off.

Within the economic framework, people order their preferences and take actions that maximize their level of satisfaction (utility). Trade takes place because the buyer places a higher value on the item than the seller. The corresponding *gains from trade* make both parties better off—voluntary trade is *mutually advantageous*. For example, if José Coronas is willing to pay up to $16,000 for a particular automobile and Rochester Motors is willing to sell the automobile for as little as $10,000, the potential gains from trade are $6,000 ($16,000 − $10,000). If the automobile trades at $13,000, both parties are $3,000 better off. José gives up $13,000 to buy something that he values at $16,000, while Rochester Motors obtains $13,000 for something it values at only $10,000. At other prices between $10,000 and $16,000, the total gains are still $6,000

Lack of Well-Defined Property Rights Inhibits Repairs

Two years after the massive 1994 earthquake that leveled Kobe, Japan, 51,000 people were still living in shelters and seven of every ten buildings remained damaged. The problem was ill-defined property rights. Everybody had rights: tenants, subtenants, landowners, landlords. In one city block, there were 303 renters, lessees, subletters, and so forth, often with overlapping claims. All had to agree to the rebuilding plan before construction could begin—thereby snarling the process. Kobe hired 1,000 arbitrators and set up a property-rights hot line. But despite $30 billion of rebuilding money available, only 4 of 100 "construction teams" actually had begun rebuilding.

Source: J. Sapsford (1996), "Building Blocked," *The Wall Street Journal* (December 12), A1.

Tom Sawyer, Huckleberry Finn, and Gains from Trade

An example of gains from trade is provided by Mark Twain in a dialogue between Tom Sawyer and Huck Finn:

"Say—what's that?"

"Nothing but a tick."

"Where'd you get him?"

"Out in the woods."

"What'll you take for him?"

"I don't know. I don't want to sell him."

"All right. It's a mighty small tick, anyway."

"Oh, anybody can run a tick down that don't belong to them. I'm satisfied with it. It's good enough for me."

"Sho, there's ticks a-plenty. I could have a thousand of 'em if I wanted to."

"Well, why don't you? Becuz you know mighty well you can't. This is a pretty early tick, I reckon. It's the first one I've seen this year."

"Say, Huck—I'll give you my tooth for him."

"Le's see it."

Tom got out a bit of paper and carefully unrolled it. Huckleberry viewed it wistfully. The temptation was very strong. At last he said:

"Is it genuwyne?"

Tom lifted his lip and showed the vacancy.

"Well, all right," said Huckleberry, "it's a trade."

Tom enclosed the tick in the percussion-cap box that had lately been the pinch bug's prison, and the boys separated, each feeling wealthier than before.

Source: M. Twain (1944), *The Adventures of Tom Sawyer* (Whitman: Racine, WI), 54–55.

but they are not split evenly. For example, at a price of $15,000, José gains $1,000 in value, while Rochester Motors gains $5,000.[3]

From where do these gains from trade come? One source is differences in preferences. The buyer and seller simply may place different values on the traded item. For example, some people value new automobiles more than other people do. Another important source of gains is that the seller may be able to produce the item more cheaply than the buyer and thus has a *comparative advantage* in its production. In advanced economies, individuals specialize in producing goods where they have a comparative advantage; they then trade to acquire other goods. Specialization greatly enhances the standard of living of a society. Imagine that you had to be completely self-sufficient, making your own clothing, growing your own food, building your own house, and producing your own vehicles for transportation. Your overall standard of living would be much lower than it is now, living in a modern, specialized economy.

[3]Sometimes, individuals regret a trade after the fact. For instance, José might be unhappy that he purchased a particular automobile from Rochester Motors. On average, he must find it advantageous to purchase automobiles or else he would quit purchasing them (at least from Rochester Motors). José's ability to say no limits the extent to which he can be exploited in any voluntary trade.

Strategic Business Planning: Ignoring Economics of Trade

During the 1970s, many firms adopted a particular form of strategic business planning. All projects of the firm were ranked based on growth potential and market share. Projects with high growth potential and high market share were called stars, while projects with low growth potential and market share were referred to as dogs. Dogs were sold, while stars were kept. Funding for the stars came from cash cows, projects with high market share and low growth potential.

The idea behind this process is to treat the projects of a firm like stocks in a portfolio. Through systematic analysis, winners are to be kept and losers sold. Money is invested in the winners to enhance the firm's competitive advantage. While the idea might sound intriguing, its underpinnings are inconsistent with the basic economics of trade—sell if, and only if, you can get a price that exceeds the value of keeping the item yourself. This principle implies that, contrary to the process, dogs should be kept unless they can be sold at sufficiently high prices. Moreover, stars should be sold if the price is sufficiently high.

By the 1980s, many firms found that violating the basic economics of trade had led them to accumulate suboptimal collections of projects. Large increases in stock prices were observed as these firms reshuffled plants, divisions, and subsidiaries through sell-offs, spin-offs, and divestitures.

Source: "The New Breed of Strategic Planner" (1984), *Business Week* (September 17), 62–68.

A common misconception is that trade takes place because people have too much of some goods—people sell to others what they cannot use themselves. This view, however, does not explain why individuals sell houses, cars, jewelry, land, and other resources (such as Tom's tooth and Huck's tick) that they value highly and have in short supply. The economic explanation for trade argues that trade takes place not because people have too little or too much of a good. Rather, trade takes place because a person is willing to pay a higher price for a good than it is worth to its current owner. While you might love your new sports car, you would still sell it if someone offered you a high-enough price. And winning bidders of collectibles auctioned on eBay are frequently individuals with collections of related items.

It is important to recognize that trade is an important form of value creation. Trading produces value that makes individuals better off. Gains from trade also provide important incentives to move resources to more productive uses. If George Nichols can make the most productive use of a piece of land, he will be willing to pay a higher price for the land than other potential users. The current owner, Jody Crowe, has the incentive to sell the land to George, because she gets to keep the proceeds from the sale. It is

Gains from Trade: The Story of McDonald's

McDonald's Corporation, with over 24,000 restaurants in 114 countries, is the largest fast-food company in the world. Its worldwide sales in 1998 were over $36 billion. Although Ray Kroc often is given credit for founding this company, the history of the restaurant goes back to 1937 when two brothers, Dick and Mac McDonald, opened a drive-in restaurant. These brothers conceived of the idea of a clean, efficient, quick-service restaurant with a limited menu featuring hamburgers and french fries. However, Kroc had the vision and the ability to take this idea and expand it nationwide. Taking advantage of potential gains from trade, the McDonald brothers sold Kroc the exclusive rights to franchise copies of their operation. This transaction resulted in one of the most successful business operations of all time.

Source: C. Shook and R. Shook (1993), *Franchising: The Business Strategy That Changed the World* (Prentice Hall: Englewood Cliffs, NJ).

these incentives that help to promote a Pareto-efficient allocation of resources in a market economy. After all mutually advantageous trades are completed, it is impossible to change this allocation without making someone worse off.

Basics of Supply and Demand

Gains from trade explain why individuals buy and sell. But what coordinates the separate decisions of millions of individuals in a market economy to prevent chaos? Why are there not massive surpluses of some goods and huge shortages of other goods? What restricts the amounts demanded by the public to the amounts supplied? Answers to these questions come from an understanding of the market price system.

The Price Mechanism

The basic economics of a price system can be illustrated through standard supply-and-demand diagrams. Figure 3.1 displays a supply-and-demand diagram for a particular model of personal computer—for example, a Pentium III machine with standard quality and features. The vertical axis on the graph shows the price for a PC, and the horizontal axis shows the total quantity of PCs demanded and supplied in the market for the period (for example, a month).

The market includes all potential buyers and sellers of this type of PC. Suppose that in this market there are many buyers and sellers and that individual transactions are so small in relation to the overall market that the price is unaffected by any single sale or purchase. In this case, no buyer or seller has market power: All trades are made at the going market price. We label this type of market as *competitive.* (In Chapter 6, we extend our analysis of competitive markets; we also examine *noncompetitive* market structures.)

The *demand curve* depicts how many total PCs consumers are willing to buy at each price. The demand curve slopes downward because consumers typically buy more if the price is lower. For example, consumers are likely to buy more PCs if the price is P' (say, $500) than if the price is P'' (say, $1,500).

The *supply curve* depicts how many PCs producers are willing to sell at each price. The curve slopes upward: At higher prices, producers are able and willing to produce and sell more units. For example, at a price of $500, many potential producers cannot cover their costs, and thus they refrain from entering production. At a price of $1,500, more units are manufactured and brought to market.

Shifts in Demand, Quantity, and Price at the Ryder Cup

The Ryder Cup features competition between top American and European golfers. It has become one of the more prominent golfing events in the world. In 1995, the Ryder Cup was held at Oak Hill Country Club in Rochester, New York. The event attracted over 30,000 spectators a day. Many of these spectators (for example, Prince Andrew of Great Britain) were from outside the Rochester area.

A significant number of these visitors were avid golfers who wanted to play while they were in Rochester. Rochester has several courses that are open to the public. However, many courses in the area are private (only members and their guests can play). Facing this dramatic temporary increase in the demand for public golf courses, several of the private courses decided to become public during the week of the Ryder Cup. These courses charged high fees ranging from $100 to $250 per round (their normal guest fees were approximately $50). This example highlights that shifts in demand motivate increases in the quantity supplied and the price of a product (in this case, golf times).

Figure 3.1 Supply and Demand in the PC Industry

The demand curve shows the number of PCs that consumers want to purchase at each price. The supply curve shows the number of PCs that producers want to sell at each price. Equilibrium occurs where the two curves intersect. Here, the quantity supplied equals the quantity demanded. If the price is above the market-clearing price of P^*, there is a surplus of PCs. Producers supply more PCs than consumers want to purchase, and inventories shrink. If the price is below the market-clearing price, there is a shortage. Producers supply fewer PCs than consumers want to purchase and inventories build. Surpluses and shortages put pressure on prices and quantities to move to equilibrium levels of P^*.

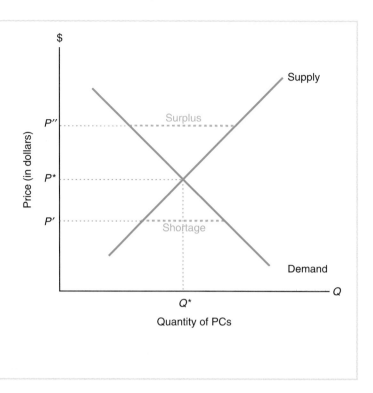

The two curves cross at the *market-clearing price P^** and *quantity Q^**. At the market-clearing price, the quantity of PCs demanded exactly equals the quantity supplied. Here, the market is said to be in *equilibrium.*

There are strong pressures within markets that push prices and quantities toward their equilibrium levels. To see why, suppose that the market price is above the equilibrium price, such as P'' in Figure 3.1. At this higher price, there is a *surplus* of PCs—suppliers produce more PCs than consumers are willing to purchase. As inventories of unsold PCs build, this surplus places downward pressure on prices as suppliers compete to try to sell their products. As prices fall, fewer PCs will be produced and more will be demanded, thus reducing the surplus. In contrast, if the price is below the market-clearing price, such as P' in Figure 3.1, inventories dwindle and back orders accumulate—there is a *shortage* of computers. Here, consumers will bid up the price of PCs as they compete for the limited supply. As prices rise, producers increase their output and consumers demand fewer PCs, thus reducing the shortage. When the market is in equilibrium, there is no pressure on prices and quantities—the quantity demanded exactly equals the quantity supplied. Inventories are stable at their desired levels, and the market price is stable at this point.

Supply-and-demand diagrams like that in Figure 3.1 are snapshots at a point in time. As time passes, both the supply and the demand curves are likely to change. Figure 3.2 shows the effects of a shift in the demand curve in the PC market. The left panel pictures an increase in demand. Here, there is a shift in the demand curve to the right, since at each price, consumers demand more PCs. Demand for PCs might increase for a variety of reasons, including an increase in the purchasing power of consumers or a decline in the prices of supporting software. These types of changes motivate consumers to purchase more PCs at any given price. After the demand shift at the old

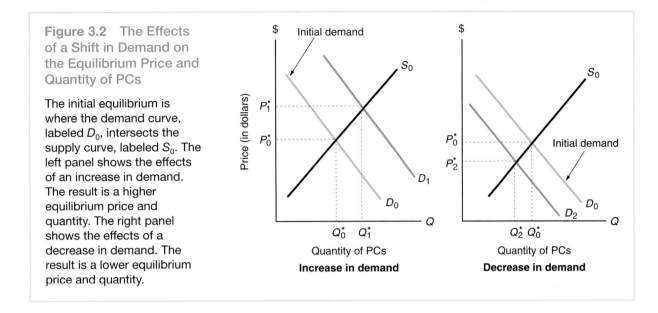

Figure 3.2 The Effects of a Shift in Demand on the Equilibrium Price and Quantity of PCs

The initial equilibrium is where the demand curve, labeled D_0, intersects the supply curve, labeled S_0. The left panel shows the effects of an increase in demand. The result is a higher equilibrium price and quantity. The right panel shows the effects of a decrease in demand. The result is a lower equilibrium price and quantity.

equilibrium price, inventories shrink and there is a shortage of PCs. This shortage places upward pressure on prices; higher prices in turn stimulate more production. The end result is a higher equilibrium price and quantity. The right panel shows that the opposite effect occurs with a reduction in demand. This shift to the left in the demand curve also can be caused by a variety of factors (for example, a recession that causes businesses to reduce their purchases of PCs or an increase in personal tax rates that reduces consumers' purchasing power).

Figure 3.3 shows the effects of a shift in supply in the PC market. The left panel displays a shift in the supply curve to the right. A rightward shift implies an increase in supply, because at each price producers make and offer more PCs. Many factors might cause an increase in supply. For example, a decline in the prices of labor and other inputs used for manufacturing PCs will make PC production more profitable and increase supply. Supply also might increase because of changes in technology that allow for less expensive, more efficient production. After the supply shift at the old equilibrium price, inventories accumulate and there is a surplus of PCs. This surplus places downward

High Prices and Criminal Activity: Computer Chips Become a Big Black-Market Item

The strong incentives that high prices provide to suppliers to bring products to market unfortunately can be seen in the activities of criminals. Intel 486 chips sold for about $450 to $500 in 1993. These prices motivated increased theft of computer chips. For example, in September 1993, six masked men overwhelmed employees at one of Intel's eight distributors, making off with $739,000 of microprocessors. Many similar robberies have been reported. According to *The Wall Street Journal,* "Forget drugs. Forget arms. If you want to make a black-market killing these days, steal computer chips. Chips are the dope of the 90's." Fortunately, the high prices of computer chips also have motivated legal activity to increase chip supply—other computer companies have developed products to compete with Intel.

Source: E. Gonzales (1993), "Chips Become Big Black-Market Item," *The Wall Street Journal* (September 16), B1.

Figure 3.3 The Effects of a Shift in Supply on the Equilibrium Price and Quantity of PCs

The initial equilibrium is where the demand curve, labeled D_0, intersects the supply curve, labeled S_0. The left panel shows the effects of an increase in supply. The result is a lower equilibrium price and an increase in equilibrium quantity. The right panel shows the effects of a decrease in supply. The result is a higher equilibrium price and a lower equilibrium quantity.

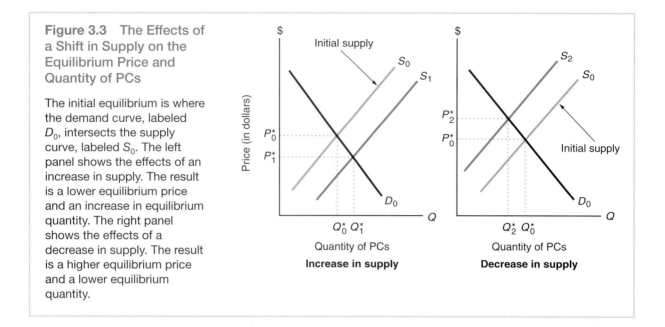

pressure on prices, which in turn stimulates more demand. The end result is a lower equilibrium price and higher equilibrium quantity. The right panel shows that the opposite effect occurs when supply shifts to the left.

Prices as Social Coordinators

The equilibrium of supply and demand highlights the crucial role that prices play in coordinating the consumption and production decisions of individuals. For example, if too few PCs are being produced, inventories will shrink and dealers will raise prices. High prices signal would-be producers to shift from producing lower-valued products to producing computers. Because property rights are private, individuals reap the reward from redirecting their efforts and therefore have strong incentives to shift production. Higher prices also motivate consumers to reduce the quantity of PCs demanded. The end result is that the quantity demanded equals the quantity supplied. This is what Adam Smith referred to as "the invisible hand."

If everyone trades in the marketplace and all mutually advantageous trades are completed, the price system results in a Pareto-efficient resource allocation.[4] No government intervention or central planning is required. Rather, consumers and producers, acting in their own self-interest, react to price signals in a manner that produces an efficient resource allocation. Prices act to control and coordinate the many individual decisions made in the economy. After trading is completed, the output mix and final distribution of products cannot be changed without making someone worse off. Also, suppliers engage in efficient production.

The basic logic for efficiency in a competitive economy is straightforward. At equilibrium prices, the quantity supplied equals the quantity demanded for all goods and

---

[4]These conditions will be met in a competitive market when trading costs are sufficiently low. Later, we will discuss factors that can motivate inefficiency in a market economy.

Supply of Online Résumés Bogs Down Employers

The Internet has reduced significantly the cost of submitting résumés to would-be employers. Job seekers no longer must print their résumés on high-quality paper, address, stamp, and mail an envelope. A click of the mouse and the résumé is gone. Some companies have thousands of résumés dumped into their e-mail boxes each day. During 1999 there were almost 5 million résumés on the Internet—200 times more than in 1994. When the cost of a good (like submitting a résumé) falls, the quantity supplied increases.

Source: S. Armour (1999), "Online Resumes Bogging Down Employers," *Democrat and Chronicle* (July 19), 1F.

there are no shortages or surpluses. Everyone who wants to make trades has done so, and all gains from trade have been exhausted. In making supply decisions, firms have strong private incentives to adopt the most efficient production methods and the value-maximizing output mix (these production choices maximize their profits). No changes in either production or distribution can be made without making someone worse off.

Externalities and the Coase Theorem[5]

Externalities exist when the actions of one party affect the well-being or production possibilities of another party outside an exchange relationship. Externalities can prevent a free market from being efficient. If a firm emits pollution into the air, it can adversely affect the welfare of the firm's neighbors. If the firm does not bear these costs, it is likely to select an inefficient level of pollution (that is, to overpollute). In choosing how much to invest in pollution control equipment, the firm's managers will consider only its own costs and benefits. Efficient investment would require them also to consider costs and benefits imposed on neighbors (the efficient level of investment is where the total marginal costs of additional investment equal the total marginal benefits—not just those incurred privately by the firm).

Economists used to think that externalities surely would prevent a market system from producing an efficient allocation of resources. Government intervention seemed to be required to enhance efficiency. For example, the traditional recommendation was to tax firms based on their levels of pollution. This tax would give firms incentives to reduce pollution.

In 1960, Nobel Prize–winner Ronald Coase presented a convincing argument that exchange in a free market is more powerful in producing efficient results than had been thought previously. As long as property rights can be traded, there is an incentive to rearrange these rights to enhance economic efficiency. The often-recommended government intervention might be unnecessary and in many cases undesirable. Suppose that a firm has the legal right to pollute as much as it wants. The neighbors always can offer to pay the firm to reduce its pollution level. Thus, the firm faces a cost for polluting (if the firm pollutes, there is an opportunity cost of not receiving compensation from its neighbors). The firm will pollute only if the pollution is more valuable to the firm than the costs it imposes on its neighbors. This efficient solution is obtained without a pollution tax. The same level of pollution can occur even if the neighbors have the legal right to

---

[5]This section draws on R. Coase (1960), "The Problem of Social Cost," *Journal of Law and Economics* 3, 1–44.

Property Rights in Russia

An exchange transaction is an agreement among individuals on property rights to goods. Exchange is limited dramatically if property rights are not enforceable. Within well-functioning economies, the legal system is an important institution for enforcing property rights and increases trade in the economy. Former communist countries, such as Russia, have had difficulty converting to a market system because they do not have established legal systems for enforcing property rights. Although there are court systems, the inefficiencies of these systems significantly limited their usefulness to private companies and individuals (the courts are quite slow, expensive, and sometimes corrupt).

The lack of a good legal system offers profit opportunities for firms to create their own mechanisms for enforcing property rights and facilitating trade. Large firms in Russia have established their own security forces. If another party does not honor a contract, the security force uses coercive power to force compliance (much like the Mafia). In turn, these large companies have incentives to honor contracts, because it is important for them to maintain good reputations to encourage other parties to deal with them in the future (see Chapters 10 and 21). Allegedly, the ability of large firms to enforce contracts in Russia serves as a source of competitive advantage (profits). Small firms have difficulty competing with large firms because they do not have these security forces or the reputations to ensure contract compliance.

Utilizing legal systems can be expensive, even in developed economies. Managers, throughout the world, have the potential to create value if they can devise more efficient methods for contract enforcement. Many firms invest substantial resources to develop reputations as honest trading partners.

Source: A. Grief and E. Kandel (1995), "Contract Enforcement Institutions: Historical Perspective and Current Status in Russia," in *Economic Transition in Eastern Europe and Russia* (Hoover Institution: Palo Alto, CA), 291–321.

stop the firm from emitting any pollution as opposed to the firm's having the legal right to pollute as much as it wants. In this case, the firm can pay its neighbors for the right to pollute. Regardless of whether the firm or the neighbors have the legal right, the gains from trade are exhausted when the marginal benefit to the firm of polluting is equal to the sum of the marginal costs imposed on its neighbors plus those which the firm bears.

Coase's argument convinced most economists that externalities were less of a problem than previously thought. It also implied that the distribution of property (legal) rights might have less of an effect on the ultimate use of resources than it has on the distribution of income—as long as these rights can be exchanged. In our example, the firm might emit the same amount of pollution regardless of who initially is assigned the property right. However, the party with the property right obtains more wealth (since it is the one receiving payments).

Nonetheless, as Coase points out, market exchange will not always solve the problem of externalities. The transactions that are necessary to overcome this problem are not free: There are *contracting costs*. These costs include search and information costs, bargaining and decision costs, and drafting, policing, and enforcement costs.[6] These costs can prevent a preferred outcome from occurring. In our example, the firm might limit its pollution for a payment that is far lower than the collective damage imposed on its neighbors. Nonetheless, the costs of bargaining with the firm and the costs of reaching agreement on how the neighbors should split the payment can prevent this mutually beneficial agreement from being reached. Generally, the costs of reaching an agreement increase with the number of bargainers. In our example, the likelihood of reaching an

---

[6]C. Dahlman (1979), "The Problem of Externality," *The Journal of Law and Economics* 22, 148–162.

The Coase Theorem and the "Fable of the Bees"

A prominently discussed case of externalities is the so-called "Fable of the Bees." Beekeepers provide pollination services for the surrounding fruit growers, and the growers, in turn, provide nectar for the bees. Many economists would consider this to be a classic case of externalities. If beekeepers and growers do not receive compensation for the benefits they bestow on other parties, they will underinvest in their activities (from a social standpoint).

The Coase Theorem suggests that beekeepers and growers can privately negotiate to overcome this externality problem. This is exactly what is done. Beekeepers and growers often enter into contracts. Fruit growers hire beekeepers to supply hives of bees for pollination of those trees that give little suitable nectar, while the beekeepers pay growers for the privilege of "grazing" their bees on high nectar-producing trees. Given these payments, beekeepers and growers have incentives to consider the effects on the other party when they make their investment decisions. Through this process, beekeepers and growers can reach efficient levels of investment without help from the government.

Source: S. Cheung (1973), "The Fable of the Bees: An Economic Investigation," *Journal of Law and Economics* 16, 11–34.

efficient agreement is highest if the firm has to bargain only with a single neighbor who owns all the surrounding property.

It also is important that property rights be clearly assigned, enforced, and exchangeable. Suppose there were no legal system to enforce property rights. Neighbors would be reluctant to pay a firm not to pollute—they do not obtain an enforceable property right to prevent the firm from polluting. After collecting the payment, the firm could renege on its promise to reduce pollution and the neighbors would have no recourse.

> **The Coase Theorem**
> The ultimate resource allocation will be efficient, regardless of the initial assignment of property rights, as long as contracting costs are sufficiently low and the property rights are assigned clearly, are well enforced, and can be exchanged readily.

This discussion suggests that market economies will tend to produce an efficient resource allocation whenever property rights are clearly assigned and contracting costs of exchanging them are sufficiently low. When these conditions are met, efficiency will occur regardless of the initial distribution of property rights. This general principle is often referred to as the *Coase Theorem*.

The driving force behind the Coase Theorem is gains from trade: Individuals have incentives to search out and undertake mutually advantageous trades. This principle has important managerial implications. Even if a manager does not have all the property rights necessary to undertake a particular project, it does not mean that the project cannot be undertaken. If the proposed project creates enough value, the manager often can acquire the necessary property rights from their current owners. Suppose the Watts Construction Company can create substantial value by developing a shopping center on a site that currently is zoned for residential housing. Surrounding property owners might support a change in the zoning requirement, as long as they share in the value creation. Watts might be able to increase this support by offering to develop a new neighborhood park near the shopping mall.

The Coase Theorem also suggests that contracting costs are central to the study of organizations. In the absence of contracting costs, efficient outcomes will occur independent of the way decision rights are assigned. From an efficiency standpoint, it does not matter whether decision rights are centralized or decentralized. It is contracting costs that make these organizational considerations important. We elaborate on this issue in the section that follows.

Public versus Private Arctic Exploration

From 1818 to 1909, 35 government and 56 privately funded expeditions sought to locate and navigate a Northwest Passage, discover the North Pole, and make other significant discoveries in arctic regions. Most major arctic discoveries were made by private expeditions. Most tragedies were publicly funded. By other measures as well, publicly funded expeditions performed poorly. On average, 5.9 (8.0 percent) of their crew members died compared to 0.9 (6.2 percent) for private expeditions. Publicly funded expeditions based on ships used an average of 1.63 ships and lost 0.53 of them. In contrast, private ship–based expeditions used 1.15 ships and lost 0.24 of them. Of public expeditions that lasted longer than one year, 46.7 percent were debilitated by scurvy, compared to 13.2 percent for private expeditions.

The evidence indicates that these differences are not attributable to differences in the exploratory objectives sought, country of origin, the number of previous expeditions on which the leader served, or the decade in which the expedition occurred. Rather, they are due to systematic differences in the ways public and private expeditions were organized. Historical accounts indicate that, compared to private expeditions, public expeditions employed leaders that were relatively unmotivated and unprepared for arctic exploration, separated the initiation and implementation functions of executive leadership, and adapted slowly to new information about clothing, diet, shelter, modes of arctic travel, organizational structure, and optimal party size.

Source: J. Karpoff (1999), "Public Versus Private Initiative in Arctic
Exploration: The Effects of Incentives and Organizational Structure,"
Working Paper, University of Washington.

Markets versus Central Planning

History suggests that the price system is more efficient at controlling and coordinating production and consumption decisions in large economies than is central planning. Without the aid of government planners, market economies have produced products that are highly valued by consumers while avoiding large shortages or surpluses. In planned economies such as the former Soviet Union, shortages, surpluses, and other production mistakes are common.

There are at least two reasons why markets have been more successful than central planning in large economies. First, the price system motivates better use of knowledge and information in economic decisions. Second, it provides stronger incentives for individuals to make productive decisions.

General versus Specific Knowledge[7]

Figure 3.4 shows how the costs of transferring knowledge can be displayed on a continuum. At one end of this continuum is *general knowledge*. General knowledge essentially is free to transfer. Examples of general knowledge are prices and quantities—a store-keeper easily can tell you that the price of sugar is $1 per pound. As the costs of information transfer increase, the information is said to become more *specific*. We use the term *specific knowledge* to denote knowledge that is relatively high on this scale: It is expensive to transfer.

At least three factors influence the costs of transferring information. First are the characteristics of the sender and receiver. Generally, it is less expensive for people of similar training, language, and culture to communicate than for people from different

---

[7]This section draws on M. Jensen and W. Meckling (1995), "Specific and General Knowledge, and Organizational Structure," *Journal of Applied Corporate Finance* 8:2, 4–18.

Figure 3.4 The Cost of Transferring Knowledge

The costs of transferring knowledge can be displayed on a continuum. At one end is *general knowledge,* which essentially is free to transfer. As the costs of information transfer increase, the information is said to become more *specific*. We use the term *specific knowledge* to denote knowledge that is relatively expensive to transfer.

General knowledge   Specific knowledge

Information transfer costs

backgrounds. Second is the technology available for communication. For example, the development of electronic mail (e-mail) has lowered the costs of transferring information. Third is the nature of the knowledge itself. Some knowledge is difficult to summarize, comprehend, or transfer in a timely fashion. Depending on the exact setting, the following types of knowledge often are specific in nature:

- **Idiosyncratic knowledge of particular circumstances.** The employee on the spot is most likely to know if a particular truck has room for additional cargo or if a certain customer wants to purchase a specific product. If this information is not used immediately, it may become useless. For example, by the time the information about the truck is transferred to another person (such as a central planner), the opportunity to load the truck with additional cargo can be lost (for instance, if the truck has left).

- **Scientific knowledge.** Knowledge of how recombinant DNA works is not easily transferred to nonscientists.

- **Assembled knowledge.** An accountant who has completed a client's tax returns for several years is likely to have assembled important knowledge about the relevant parts of the tax code and the idiosyncrasies of the individual's income and deductions. Another example is learning to operate a complex machine. In neither case is this information easily transferred to others.

Failure to Use Specific Knowledge at GE

In the late 1970s, aggregate data indicated that houses and families were shrinking. Based on this data, strategic planners at General Electric concluded that smaller appliances were the wave of the future. Correspondingly, General Electric invested heavily in developing smaller refrigerators and other appliances.

But GE's planners had little contact with homebuilders and retailers. They failed to realize that bathrooms and kitchens were not shrinking. Indeed, working couples actually wanted larger refrigerators to reduce the number of trips to the supermarket. Moreover, top management, which also lacked contact with the market, failed to catch the planners' mistakes. As a result, General Electric wasted a lot of time and money designing smaller appliances. This loss occurred because the relevant specific knowledge about trends in homebuilding was not incorporated in the decision-making process.

Source: "The New Breed of Strategic Planner," *Business Week* (September 17, 1984), 62.

The Dynamic Nature of Specific Knowledge

Historically, economies of scale have motivated firms in retailing to concentrate on standardized production and distribution. Knowledge about the idiosyncratic demands of people in particular neighborhoods tended to be ignored in stocking individual stores within a large retail chain: The information simply was too expensive to collect and process. This limited their ability to compete with small local stores that catered to the specific demands of local customers

But the development of computers and electronic scanners has made information about idiosyncratic demands of individuals less specific. As a result, retail companies have begun to engage in more micromarketing. For instance, the Sears outlet in the North Hollywood section of Los Angeles is tailor-made to suit the neighborhood's Hispanic population. Signs are in Spanish. The store is stocked with ethnic items, such as a broad selection of compact discs and tapes by Latin American artists. A few hundred miles to the north, the Sears store in San Jose offers a large number of clothing items in extra-small sizes to attract the area's Asian population. On the other hand, Sears stores in Florida carry large, roomy clothes that appeal to the large population of elderly residents.

Source: "Customers on Target," *Financial Times* (August 18, 1995).

Specific knowledge is critical in properly allocating resources. Many economic opportunities are short-lived and must be acted on quickly by the person on the spot (who has the specific information of the opportunity) or lost. Not incorporating the proper scientific or assembled knowledge into economic decisions can have costly implications. For an economic system to be successful, it must promote the use of relevant specific knowledge in economic decisions.

Figure 3.4 displays knowledge on a continuum at a *point in time.* It is important to realize that knowledge is dynamic. There are at least two factors that can motivate changes in the costs of transferring knowledge. The first is technology: Improved communications and computer technology have greatly lowered the costs of transferring certain types of information, making it more general. Second, individuals can take actions to convert specific knowledge to more general knowledge, for example, by drafting an operating manual.

Use of Specific Knowledge at Apple Computer

Apple's first portable Mac had so many bells and whistles that it weighed 17 pounds. It did poorly in the market. In 1990, Apple began completely reworking the design of the computer from the customer's viewpoint. The entire product-development team of software designers, industrial engineers, marketing people, and industrial designers were sent into the field to observe potential customers using other products. The team discovered that people used laptops on airplanes, in cars, and at home in bed. People did not want just small computers but mobile computers. In response, Apple designed two distinctive features for its PowerBook computer—the TrackBall pointer and the palm rest in the front of the keyboard. The new product was easy to use and distinctive. Sales improved.

The knowledge of what customers really wanted in a laptop computer was acquired by a team of employees who interacted closely with customers. The team members also had important scientific and assembled knowledge that allowed them to take this new information and use it to design a marketable product. Finally, they had the authority to modify the product based on their findings. It is less likely that such specific knowledge would be incorporated in product design within a large centrally planned economy—where a central office is in charge of making decisions on literally millions of products.

Source: "Hot Products, Smart Design Is the Common Thread," *Business Week* (June 7, 1993), 54–57.

Markets versus Central Planning in Russia

Since 1994 the Republic of Georgia moved toward a market economy by privatizing many businesses and creating labor and product markets where prices are unregulated. The Republic of Uzbekistan privatized only a small part of its economy, and government monopolies and central planners still control various economic activities tightly. From 1995–1998 gross domestic product has been growing between 7 and 11 percent in Georgia, whereas the Uzbekistan economy is stagnant. Nonetheless, most ex-Soviet republics are reluctant to adopt a decentralized economy. Free markets benefit the young and energetic and often hurt politically influential groups who benefit from the old system: pensioners, employees at inefficient state enterprises, and government officials.

Source: G. Becker (1998), "A Free-Market Winner vs. a Soviet Style Loser," *Business Week* (August 3), 22.

Nonaka and Takeuchi argue that converting hunches, perceptions, mental models, beliefs, experiences, and other types of specific knowledge into a form that can be communicated and transmitted in formal and systematic language is a key aspect of successful new product innovation.[8] As one example, consider Matsushita's development of an automated fresh bread maker in the 1980s. Specific knowledge of how to knead dough to produce tasty bread was held by master bakers. This knowledge was not easily transferred to others, and past attempts to produce fully automated bread makers had failed because they produced poor-quality bread. Yet specific knowledge about how to manufacture automated bread machines was held by engineers. To produce a successful bread machine, relevant specific knowledge had to be transferred between bakers and engineers. To accomplish this transfer, managers from Matsushita took bread-making lessons from a master baker at an Osaka hotel. Eventually, the managers discovered that the key to good bread making is to twist and stretch the dough during the kneading process. This concept was general knowledge that could be passed along to design engineers. Matsushita's "Home Baker" was the first fully automatic bread-making machine for home use and has become a quite successful product.

Specific Knowledge and the Economic System[9]

Nobel Prize–winner Friedrich Hayek offered a convincing argument that market economies are more likely than centrally planned economies to incorporate relevant specific knowledge in economic decision making. He argued that the relevant specific knowledge for economic decision making is not given to any one individual; instead, it is distributed among many people in the economy. This knowledge, by definition, does not lend itself to statistical aggregation; it is costly to transfer. A central planner generally lacks the mental or computing ability to process large volumes of this sort of information. Hayek concluded that central planners often will ignore important specific knowledge in economic decisions.

In contrast, economic decisions in a market system are decentralized to individuals who are likely to have the relevant specific knowledge. Technical and marketing geniuses, like William Gates at Microsoft and Michael Dell at Dell Computer, are free to

---

[8]I. Nonaka and H. Takeuchi (1995), *The Knowledge-Creating Company* (Oxford University Press: New York).

[9]This section draws on F. Hayek (1945), "The Use of Knowledge in Society," *American Economic Review* 35, 519–530.

Fiat—Using Specific Knowledge about Developing Markets

Traditionally, leading car manufacturers simply have adapted their existing models for sales in developing countries, in spite of the fact that unique conditions prevail in these markets. Fiat, however, has invested about $2 billion in developing a new car, the A178, to meet the particular demands of people in developing countries. The car is attractively styled and inexpensive but built tough to withstand poor road conditions. Specific knowledge about the appropriate design features was obtained from a task force of engineers from Brazil, Italy, Turkey, Poland, Argentina, India, South Africa, and Morocco. Fiat forecasts that it will sell up to 900,000 A178s a year once production goes into full swing. Fiat has the decision rights to produce this product and does not have to convince some central planner of its merits.

Source: "Fiat Steers New Model Towards Developing Markets," *Financial Times* (August, 24, 1995).

---

start new businesses and to market products of their choosing. The information that motivates these decisions does not have to be transferred to some central office in Washington where centralized production decisions are made. Thus, the information is more likely to be used effectively.

The activities of decentralized decision makers are coordinated by prices. For instance, an increase in market-determined wage rates (the price of labor) signals to producers that labor is in short supply and should be conserved. Higher wages, in turn, motivate producers to use less labor. An important advantage of the price system that is stressed by Hayek is that prices economize on the costs of transferring information to coordinate decisions. Companies normally do not have to know all the details of why labor costs have increased. The simple fact that wages have increased tells them most of the things they need to know to make value-maximizing decisions.[10]

Incentives in Markets

Private property rights are critical for making a market economy work because they provide strong incentives for decentralized decision makers to act on their specific information—the wealth effects of economic decisions are borne directly by the resource owners. If Alice Chan owns a piece of property, she has incentives to use the land productively because she gets to keep the profits. If Jamal Hammoud can make more productive use of the land, Alice will sell the land to Jamal (there are gains from trade). Property rights are rearranged so that decision rights over resources are linked with the relevant specific knowledge.

In contrast, decision makers in centrally planned economies have limited incentives to make productive use of information (even if they have it) since they do not own the resources under their control. Further, lower-level bureaucrats have limited incentives to carry out decisions made by the central authority. The best use of a particular automobile might be to transport tourists from a local airport. A central planner, however, might give the car to his brother because he is more concerned about making his brother happy than in making the economy more productive. After all, he does not keep the profits from transporting tourists—they go to the state.

---

[10]Producers also might want to know the expected future prices of labor. For instance, if the price increase is expected to be transitory, the company might want to avoid making layoffs.

Nobel Prize–Winner F. A. Hayek on the "Miracle" of the Price System

It is worth contemplating for a moment a very simple and commonplace instance of the action of the price system to see what precisely it accomplishes. Assume that somewhere in the world a new opportunity for the use of some raw material, say, tin, has arisen, or that one of the sources of supply of tin has been eliminated. It does not matter for our purpose—and it is significant that it does not matter—which of these two causes has made tin more scarce. All that the users of tin need to know is that some of the tin they used to consume is now more profitably employed elsewhere and that, in consequence they must economize tin. There is no need for the great majority of them even to know where the more urgent need has arisen, or in favor of what other needs they ought to husband the supply. If only some of them know directly of the new demand and switch resources over to it, and if the people who are aware of the new gap thus created in turn fill it from still other sources, the effect will rapidly spread throughout the entire economic system. This influences not only all the uses of tin but also those of its substitutes and the substitutes of these substitutes, the supply of all things made of tin, and their substitutes, and so on. All this takes place without the great majority of those instrumental in bringing about these substitutions knowing anything at all about the original cause of these changes. The whole acts as one market, not because any of its members surveys the whole field, but because their limited individual fields of vision sufficiently overlap so that through many intermediaries the relevant information is communicated to all. The mere fact that there is one price for any commodity—or rather that local prices are connected in a manner determined by the cost of transport, etc.—brings about the solution which (if conceptually possible) might have been arrived at by one single mind possessing all the information which is in fact dispersed among all the people involved in the process.

Source: F. Hayek (1945), "The Use of Knowledge in Society," *American Economic Review* 35, 1–18.

Contracting Costs and Existence of Firms

Hayek's argument suggests that markets are better than central planning. Why, then, is so much activity conducted within firms, where resource allocation decisions are made by managers in a manner that often is akin to central planning?[11] Conceptually, firms do not have to exist. All production and exchange could be carried out by market transactions. In the case of the PC, each consumer could buy all the parts that make up the PC in separate market transactions and then pay someone to assemble them. In reality, of course, most computers are made by firms and only the final products are sold to the consumer.

Ronald Coase provides an answer to the question as to why resources are allocated both by markets and firms.[12] His basic argument is that economic transactions involve contracting costs, including search and information costs, bargaining and decision costs, and policing and enforcement costs. There is also an opportunity cost if the transaction results in an inefficient resource allocation (we discuss this in detail in Chapter 10). The optimal method of organizing a given economic transaction is the one that minimizes contracting costs.[13] In some cases, the method will be market exchange. In other cases, the method will involve firms.

---

[11]Within a firm, resources often are transferred from one division to another by an administrative order from management. For example, managers often are transferred among divisions by administrative decisions. Prices are not used to make these decisions—the divisions typically do not bid for the managers.

[12]R. Coase (1937), *Economica,* "The Nature of the Firm," New Series, IV, 386–405.

[13]It is not always possible to separate contracting costs from the basic costs of production. The optimal method of production can depend on the way the transaction is organized. Therefore, it is more precise to say that the optimal method of organization is the one that minimizes total costs (production and contracting costs). The basic arguments are easier to explain if we focus on contracting costs.

Japan, Computers, and Industrial Policy

In the early 1990s, a group of prominent policy advocates argued that Japan's output of computers and computer-related products would pass that of the United States during the decade due to the alleged power and success of Japanese government planners. It was argued that the United States was at a competitive disadvantage because it did not rely on central economic planning. By 1995, "it is not Fujitsu or an NEC or a Hitachi that you stare at every day at the office, but a Compaq or IBM or Apple—all American designed and manufactured." Japanese companies have also been "crushed" in software. In 1994, US computer companies "invaded" the Japanese market for personal computers in a serious manner. In 1994, US companies doubled their share of the Japanese computer market to more than 30 percent.

Source: "Japan, Computers, and Industrial Policy," *The American Enterprise*
(July/August, 1995), 86.

Contracting Costs in Markets

A primary set of costs of using markets for exchange involves the discovery and negotiation of prices.[14] For example, firms have the following two potential advantages:

- **Fewer transactions.** If there are N customers and M factors of production, a firm can hire the M factors and sell to the N customers. The total transactions are $N + M$. In contrast, if each customer contracts separately with each factor of production, there are $N \times M$ transactions. For example, 10 workers might be required to assemble a computer. If there are 1,000 customers and each customer negotiates with each worker, there are a total of 10,000 transactions. If a firm hires the 10 workers and sells computers to the 1,000 customers, there are 1,010 transactions.

- **Informational specialization.** Think of buying a PC. How much do you know about buying each separate part? PC producers, on the other hand, specialize in this knowledge. The consumer buying from a firm only has to be concerned with the quality of the end product.

In Chapter 18, we shall elaborate on one particularly important set of contracting costs that motivates the existence of firms, those associated with *specific assets*. Assets are specific when they are worth more in their current use than in alternative uses. An example is a machine that is used to produce parts that can be used only by one particular producer. The machine is valuable in producing parts for the particular buyer but is essentially worthless in alternative uses. In this case, independent suppliers are reluctant to purchase the machine since they do not want to be at the mercy of a single buyer. For instance, suppliers might worry that the buyer will try to force a reduction in future prices, make unreasonable quality or quantity demands, or curtail purchases. It is these concerns that make simple market transactions between buyers and sellers unlikely when the relevant assets are highly specific. A potential response to this problem is for the producer to own the machine and make the input parts within a single larger firm.

Another potential advantage of firms is that in some cases they can reduce contracting costs through established reputations. Individuals are likely to have confidence in trading with parties who are expected to continue to participate in the marketplace over a long

---

[14]Economists generally agree that contracting costs motivate the existence of firms. There is disagreement concerning which contracting costs are most important. Our intent in this chapter is to give the reader a general sampling of the kinds of costs that can be important.

Herbert Simon on Organizations and Markets

The United States often is referred to as a market economy. In reality, much of the economic activity in the United States, as well as in other market economies, is conducted within firms. To quote Herbert Simon, a former Nobel Prize winner,

> Suppose a visitor from Mars approaches the earth from space, equipped with a telescope that reveals social structures. The firms reveal themselves, say, as solid green areas with faint interior contours marking out divisions and departments. Market contracting costs show as red lines connecting firms, forming a network in the spaces between them. Within the firms the approaching visitor also sees pale blue lines, the lines of authority connecting bosses with various levels of workers. . . . No matter whether the visitor approached the United States or the Soviet Union, urban China or the European Community, the greater part of the space below would be within the green areas, for almost all the inhabitants would be employees, within firm boundaries. Organizations would be the dominant feature on the landscape. A message sent back home, describing the scene, would speak of "large green areas interconnected by red lines." It would not likely speak of a "network of red lines connecting green spots."

Source: H. Simon (1991), "Organizations and Markets," *Journal of Economic Perspectives* 5, 25–44.

time. They understand that these parties have incentives to be honorable in order to enhance their reputation and future business opportunities. Organizations tend to have longer lives than individuals and thus might be expected to be more likely to honor agreements than unknown individuals (some major corporations date back to the nineteenth century). This increased trust can motivate lower expenditures on negotiating and policing agreements. We discuss this issue in greater detail in Chapters 10 and 21.

Government regulation also helps explain the existence of some firms. Sometimes firms can produce more cheaply because they avoid taxes at various stages of production compared to market transactions.

Contracting Costs within Firms

We have discussed several contracting costs that can motivate the existence of firms. Given these costs, why isn't the economy just one big firm? The answer is that resource allocation by firms also involves contracting costs. For example, as firms become larger, it becomes increasingly difficult for managers to make efficient and timely decisions. They are more likely to make errors and to be less responsive to changing circumstances. As a firm grows important decisions must be delegated to employees who are not owners of the firm, thereby generating costs to motivate these nonowners to work in the

General Motors and Fisher Body

In the 1920s, General Motors and Fisher Body were separate companies. General Motors produced cars with auto bodies supplied by Fisher. To improve efficiency, General Motors asked Fisher to construct a new auto body plant next to a new General Motors assembly plant. Fisher refused, probably in part because it feared investing in such a specific asset (the proposed plant was tailored closely to the General Motors production process). By making this investment, Fisher would have made itself vulnerable to subsequent unreasonable demands from General Motors (for example, to reduce prices). Ultimately, this problem was resolved by General Motors' purchase of Fisher Body to form a single large firm.

Corporate Focus and Stock Returns

Ronald Coase argues that the use of markets involves contracting costs and that sometimes these costs can be reduced by including transactions within firms. However, firms also involve contracting costs. In the 1990s, many companies concluded that they had become too large and diversified. These companies, in turn, decided to refocus on their core businesses and to shed unrelated activities (for example, through asset sales). Evidence suggests that on average, these firms increased their stock market values by increasing their focus on core activities.

Source: R. Comment and G. Jarrell (1995), "Corporate Focus and Stock
Returns," *Journal of Financial Economics* 37, 67–87.

---

interests of the owners. Chapters 10 and 18 contain more detailed discussions of these contracting costs within firms.

Efficient Organization   Individuals involved in trade and production have incentives to implement cost-reducing methods of organization because there are greater gains to be shared. For example, at a given price, more profits can be generated if costs are reduced.[15] In competitive markets, individuals will constantly search for new and better ways to reduce costs to improve their competitive advantage and profits. The bottom line is that firms will be used to organize economic activities whenever their cost is lower than that of using markets, and vice versa. Also, as we will see, this same process has important implications for the internal design of organizations.

Managerial Objectives   Our discussion to this point has treated decision makers within firms as owners. Owners have a strong interest in increasing the profits of the firm, since they get to keep the proceeds. In public corporations managers are rarely major owners of the firm. Nonetheless, in Part 2 of the book, we assume that managers strive to maximize firm profits: They make input, output, and pricing decisions with profit maximization as their sole objective. This perspective is a reasonable starting point because if firms fail to make profits over time, they cease to exist. Most managers are under constant pressure to create value. There also are other mechanisms, such as incentive compensation, that work to align the interests of managers and owners. These mechanisms help make profit maximization a reasonable first approximation of the

---

CEO Turnover and Firm Profits

A standard assumption in microeconomics is that managers strive to maximize profits. One reason that managers are likely to be concerned about profits is that poor profits and stock price performance increase the likelihood that they will be fired. For instance, research suggests that the worst performing firms are about 1.5 times as likely to have a management change as the best performers.

Source: J. Warner, R. Watts, and K. Wruck (1988), "Stock Prices and Top
Management Changes," *Journal of Financial Economics* 20, 461–492; and
M. Weisbach (1988), "Outside Directors and CEO Turnover," *Journal of
Financial Economics* 20, 431–460.

---

[15]A firm's profit (Π) is the difference between its total revenues (TR) and total costs (TC): $\Pi = TR - TC$. If a company has sales of $1 million and costs of $750,000 it earns a profit of $250,000.

Firms versus Markets: When Markets Ruled

Economic theory argues that activities are organized within firms when the cost is lower than using markets, and vice versa. Today, much of the economic activity in the world is conducted within firms. It is hard to envision a world where large firms do not play an important role in the production and distribution of products. The importance of firms, however, is a relatively recent phenomenon. Prior to the middle of the nineteenth century, there were virtually no large firms. Most production was conducted by small, owner-managed operations. The activities of these operations were coordinated almost entirely through market transactions and prices. To quote Alfred Chandler in describing business organization before 1850,

> The traditional American business was a single-unit business enterprise. In such an enterprise an individual or a small number of owners operated a shop, factory, bank, or transportation line out of a single office. Normally this type of firm handled only a single economic function, dealt in a single product line, and operated in one geographic area. Before the rise of the modern firm, the activities of one of these small, personally owned and managed enterprises were coordinated and monitored by market and price mechanisms.

The large firm became feasible only with the development of improved energy sources, transportation, and communications. Coal-fired steam power generators provided a source of energy that made it possible for the factory to replace artisans and small mill owners, and railroads enabled firms to ship production in large quantities to newly emerging urban centers. The telegraph allowed firms to coordinate activities of workers over larger geographic areas. These developments tended to make it less expensive to coordinate production and distribution using administrative controls, rather than to rely on numerous market transactions among all the intermediaries in the system.

Source: A. Chandler (1977), *The Visible Hand: The Managerial Revolution in American Business* (Harvard University Press: Cambridge, MA).

managers' objective function. Profit maximization is the basic premise used in most economics textbooks. Starting in Chapter 10, however, we shall present a richer characterization of the firm and analyze management/owner conflicts in greater detail.

Managerial Implications

We began this chapter with an overview of how market economies operate. An understanding of this topic is critical if managers are to make productive economic decisions. It is important to understand how a shift in either supply or demand affects product prices. (In Part 2, we shall extend this analysis and examine in more detail how managers might make optimal input, output, and pricing decisions.)

Hewlett-Packard and Corporate Focus

Many companies often split themselves into several companies when their operations have grown too large and unwieldy. In 1996 AT&T spun off its equipment arm as Lucent Technologies and sold its computer-manufacturing division to NCR. In 1999, Hewlett-Packard announced it would spin off as a separate company its $7.6 billion a year test and measurement operations, leaving the remaining $39.5 billion a year computers and printers business. This was intended to allow H-P to become more focused on making these products. H-P faced slowing revenue growth in 1998–1999, partly because it moved slower than its rivals to capitalize on new developments like the Internet. One analyst commented, "H-P needs to be more agile and faster-moving, if it's going to keep pace with the Dells and Sun Microsystems."

Source: D. Hamilton and S. Thurm (1999), "H-P to Spin Off Its Measurement Operations," *The Wall Street Journal* (March 3), A3.

CASE STUDY: *Property Right Security in Russian Deprivatization*

Since 1992, approximately 70,000 state-owned enterprises in Russia were privatized. Many of the private buyers were foreign companies and investors, for example from the United States and Western Europe. The idea was to move from a centrally planned economy to a market system.

Yet in the late 1990s a weak economy caused great concern among Russian voters. Politicians, such as Moscow's Mayor Yuri M. Luzhkov, began promoting "deprivatization" or as the locals put it, *deprivatizatsia.* Under this policy certain past privatizations would be declared illegal and the transactions would be reversed. The company then either would be run as a state-owned enterprise or sold to another party. For example, in October 1999, a court stripped Wall Street's Kohlberg Kravis Roberts and the US-Russia Investment Fund of their majority interest in the Lomonosov Porcelain Factory in St. Petersburg. These companies had purchased the factory in 1998, but the courts ruled that the company's initial privatization five years earlier was illegal. Sources suggested that the company was likely to be resold to Soviet-era managers who were set to lose their jobs when the new investors entered the picture.

Politicians, such as Luzhkov, vow that not all privatizations will be reversed—only the illegal ones. But one current problem is that privatization legislation is nebulous about what could be termed a violation. Anything from a missing piece of paper in the original tender offer to investment requirements not being met might be ruled a violation. And virtually anyone could file a complaint to trigger an inquiry into a past deal.

Discussion Questions

1. What impact will the prospect of deprivatization have on investment by managers of privatized firms?
2. What effect will deprivatization have on foreign investment in Russia?
3. Do you think that mass deprivatization is in the long-run best interests of Russia?
4. Who gains from deprivatization? Who loses?
5. Assuming more people are hurt by deprivatization than helped, why would a local politician support such a policy?

SOURCE: M. Coker (1999). "That Russian Company You Bought? Maybe You Didn't," *Business Week* (December 13), 70.

We also discussed the role of knowledge and incentives in determining the effectiveness of alternative economic systems and the importance of contracting costs in determining whether or not economic transactions are conducted within markets or organizations. Although we have focused our discussion at the economic-system level, these issues are directly relevant to understanding firm-level decisions on organizational architecture. If firms are to be productive, they must be structured in ways that promote the use of the relevant specific knowledge and economize on the costs of organization. They also must establish appropriate incentives, so that their employees act in a productive manner. Starting in Chapter 10, we shall extend the concepts introduced in this chapter to questions of organizational architecture.

Summary

There are many different ways of organizing economic activities. Economists focus on *Pareto efficiency* in evaluating the effectiveness of alternative economic systems. An allocation is Pareto-efficient if there is no alternative that keeps all individuals at least as well off but makes at least one person better off. Pareto-improving changes in a resource allocation are viewed as welfare-increasing.

An important feature of a market economy is the use of *private property rights*. A property right is a legally enforced right to select the uses of an economic good. A property right is private when it is assigned to a specific person. Private property rights are *alienable* in that they can be transferred (sold or gifted) to other individuals.

In free markets, property rights frequently are exchanged. Trade occurs because it is mutually advantageous. The buyer values the good more than the seller, and there are *gains from trade*. Trade is an important form of value creation. Trading produces value that makes individuals better off. Gains from trade also motivate the movement of resources to more productive users.

Prices coordinate the individual actions in a market economy. If too little of a good is being produced, inventories will shrink, prices will rise, and producers will have incentives to increase output to exploit the profit opportunity. If too much of a good is being produced, prices will fall, inventories will build, and producers will have incentives to cut production. The market is in *equilibrium* when the quantity supplied of a product equals the quantity demanded. There are strong pressures in competitive economies that move the market toward equilibrium. In equilibrium, there are no *shortages* or *surpluses* and inventories are stable at their desired levels. Equilibrium prices and quantities change with changes in the supply and demand for products.

Externalities exist when the actions of one party affect the consumption or production possibilities of another party outside an exchange relationship. Externalities can cause markets to fail to produce an efficient resource allocation. Competitive markets will produce a Pareto-efficient allocation of resources if the costs of making mutually advantageous trades are sufficiently low. The *Coase Theorem* indicates that the ultimate resource allocation will be efficient, regardless of the initial assignment of property rights, as long as *contracting costs* are sufficiently low and property rights are clearly assigned, well enforced, and readily exchangeable.

General knowledge is inexpensive to transfer, whereas *specific knowledge* is expensive to transfer. Specific knowledge is quite important in economic decisions. Central planning often fails because important specific knowledge is not incorporated in the planning process. Within market systems, economic decisions are decentralized to individuals with the relevant specific knowledge. Prices convey general knowledge that coordinates the decisions of individuals. Private property rights provide important incentives to individuals to act productively, since they bear the wealth effects of their decisions.

In principle, all economic activity could be conducted through market transactions. However, even in market economies, much economic activity occurs within firms, where administrative decisions rather than market prices are used to allocate resources. Firms exist because of the contracting costs of using markets. However, organizing transactions within firms also involves costs. Individuals have incentives to organize transactions in the most efficient manner—to increase the gains from trade. Economic activities tend to be organized within firms when the cost is lower than that of using markets, and vice versa.

This chapter provides important background information on both markets and organizations. In Part 2, we shall extend the analysis of markets and study important managerial decisions such as output, inputs, pricing, and strategy. In these next six chapters, we assume that managers strive to maximize firm profits. In the remainder of the book, we shall extend the analysis of organizations and cover a variety of important topics about organizational design. A reader interested primarily in organizational design can move directly to Chapter 10 without loss of continuity.

Suggested Readings

R. Coase (1988), *The Firm, the Market, and the Law* (The University of Chicago Press: Chicago).

J. Eatwell, M. Milgate, and P. Newman (1989a), *Allocation, Information, and Markets* (W.W. Norton: New York).

———— (1989b), *The Invisible Hand* (W.W. Norton: New York).

F. Hayek (1945), "The Use of Knowledge in Society," *American Economic Review* 35, 519–530.

M. Jensen and W. Meckling (1995), "Specific and General Knowledge, and Organizational Structure," *Journal of Applied Corporate Finance* 8:2, 4–18.

O. Williamson (1985), *The Economic Institutions of Capitalism* (Free Press: New York).

Review Questions

3–1. What is Pareto efficiency? Why do economists use this criterion for comparing alternative economic systems?

3–2. What is a property right? What role do property rights play in a market economy?

3-3. Twin brothers, Tom and Bill, constantly fight over toys. For instance, Tom will argue it is his turn to play with a toy, while Bill argues it is his turn. Their parents frequently have to intervene in these disputes. Their mom has conceived an idea that might reduce these conflicts. In particular, every toy in the house would be "owned" by one of the boys. The owner would have complete authority over the use of the toy. The mom reasons that ownership would cut down on disputes. Any time there is an argument over a toy, the owner gets the final and immediate say. The boys' dad is concerned that this idea will prevent the boys from learning to "share." He envisions that under the new system, Tom will not allow Bill to play with his toys and Bill will not allow Tom to play with his toys. The current system forces them to figure out a way to share the toys. Do you think that their dad's concerns are valid? Explain.

3-4. What do you think will happen to the price and quantity of DVD players if
   a. The availability of good movies to play on DVD players increases?
   b. Personal income increases?
   c. The price of inputs used to produce DVD players decreases?
   d. Ticket prices at local movie theaters decline substantially?

3–5. **a.** What is an externality?
   b. Why might externalities lead a firm to discharge too much pollution into a river?
   c. Congress has passed a law that limits the level of cotton dust within textile factories. Why might a textile firm allow too much cotton dust within its workplace?

3–6. What is the difference between general and specific knowledge? How can specific knowledge motivate the use of decentralized decision making?

3–7. Evaluate the following statement:

Using free markets and the price system always results in a more efficient resource allocation than central planning. Just look at what happened in Eastern Europe.

3–8. **a.** What are contracting costs?
   b. Give a few examples of contracting costs.
   c. What effect does the existence of contracting costs have on market economies?

3–9. If markets are so wonderful, why do firms exist?

3–10. Some people (for example, Hayek) argue that decentralization of economic decisions in the economy leads to an efficient resource allocation. What differences exist within the firm that make the link between decentralization and efficiency less clear?

3–11. In certain professional sports, team owners "own" the players. Owners can sell or trade players to another team. However, players are not free to negotiate with other team owners on their own behalf. The team owners initially obtain the rights to players through an annual draft that is used to allocate new players among the teams in the league. They also can obtain the rights to players by purchasing them from another team. Players do not like this process and often argue that they should be free to negotiate with all teams in the sporting league. In this case, they would be free to play for the team that offers the most desirable contract. Owners argue that this change in rights would have a negative effect on the distribution of talent across teams. In particular, they argue that all the good players would end up on rich, media-center teams such as New York or Los Angeles (because these teams could afford to pay higher salaries). The inequity of players across teams would make the sport less interesting to fans and thus destroy the league. Do you think the owners' argument is correct? Explain.

3–12. The guide at the Washington Monument tells your 10-year-old nephew, "Enjoy the monument. As a citizen, you are one of its owners." Your nephew asks you if that is true. What do you say?

3–13. Locust Hill Golf Club is a private country club. It charges an initiation fee of $23,000. When members quit the club, they receive no refund on their initiation fees. They simply lose their membership. Salt Lake Country Club is also a private golf course. At this club, members join by buying a membership certificate from a member who is leaving the club. The price of the membership is determined by supply and demand. Suppose that both clubs are considering installing a watering system. In each case, the watering system is expected to enhance the quality of the golf course significantly. To finance these systems, members would pay a special assessment of $2,000 per year for the next 3 years. The proposals will be voted on by the memberships. Do you think that the membership is more likely to vote in favor of the proposal at Locust Hill or for the one at Salt Lake Country Club? Explain.

3–14. Critically evaluate the advice of the Providence Consulting Group, which recommended to your company,

That you analyze all the business divisions in your company. Rank them on growth potential. Sell all the low-growth units and invest the money in the high-growth units. Make sure not to sell the high-growth units.

3–15. Suppose that the US government begins charging a $1 sales tax to all consumers for each dress shirt they buy.
  a. What is likely to happen to the price (not including the tax) and quantity demanded of dress shirts? Show using supply and demand graphs.
  b. What is likely to happen to the demand for sport shirts (not taxed) and undershirts (which are worn primarily with dress shirts)? Explain.

3–16. Title-loan firms offer high-interest loans (the interest rate can exceed 200 percent per year) to high-risk customers. The title of a car often is used as collateral. If the borrower defaults on the loan, the company can repossess the car. Recently, the financial press has reported stories of poor people who have had their cars repossessed by title lending companies. Legislation is being proposed in some states to make this lending practice illegal. A proponent of the law made the following argument. "The market for loans is very competitive given all of the banks, savings and loans, and finance companies. Outlawing title lending will make poor people better off. It will motivate the lending companies to provide loans with less onerous terms. Thus low income people and people with bad credit histories will be able to obtain credit on more favorable terms." Do you agree with this argument? Explain.

Part 2
Managerial Economics

Chapter 4
Demand

The Players Theater Company is a regional repertory theater in the Midwest. Each year, it produces six plays, ranging from Shakespeare to contemporary musicals. PTC has priced its tickets at $30. On a typical night, about 200 of the theater's 500 seats are filled. The PTC board met recently to discuss a possible price decrease to $25 for next season. Advocates of the proposal argued that the decrease in ticket prices would increase the theater's customer base, the number of tickets sold, and revenues for the company.

At the meeting, the PTC board engaged in a heated debate over the proposal. It soon became evident that the board had insufficient information to make a sound decision. For instance, nearby restaurants, which serve PTC customers, have indicated that they are planning to implement substantial price increases before the beginning of the next season. Would this increase affect the demand faced by PTC and thus the appropriate ticket price? Although customers might buy more tickets at lower prices, would total revenue or profits necessarily increase? Would it be better to attract additional customers by lowering price or by improving the quality of PTC plays? After a lively discussion, the proposed decrease in price was tabled for further study.

This discussion at the PTC board meeting highlights the fact that managers require a detailed understanding of product demand to make sound pricing decisions. Understanding product demand also is important for decisions on advertising, production levels, new product development, and capital investment projects.

Chapter 3 offered a brief introduction to supply and demand analysis. In that chapter, we introduced the notion of a demand curve and briefly discussed some of the factors that might cause a demand curve to shift. In this chapter we provide a more extensive analysis of demand. Important topics include: demand functions, demand curves, factors affecting demand, industry versus firm-level demand, network effects, demand for product attributes, product life cycles, and demand estimation. In the technical appendix to this chapter, we derive point elasticities, analyze marginal revenue for a linear demand curve, and examine a special (log-linear) demand function.

Demand Functions

Managers require a fundamental knowledge of the factors that affect the demand for their product. Only by understanding these factors can they make sound decisions on pricing, output, capital expenditures, and other strategic issues. A *demand function* is a mathematical representation of the relation between the quantity demanded of a product and all factors that influence this demand. In its most general form, a demand function can be written as

$$Q = f(X_1, X_2, \ldots X_n) \tag{4.1}$$

where the X_is are those factors that affect the demand for this product.

The quantity demanded Q is the dependent variable in the demand function, since its value depends on the variables on the right-hand side of the equation. The X_is are the independent variables. In this chapter, we focus on three particularly important independent variables: the price of the product, the prices of related products, and the incomes of potential customers. This analysis can be extended to include other variables, such as advertising expenditures, tastes and preferences, and consumer expectations (for example, about future prices).

For concreteness, we continue to focus on PTC as an example. We assume that PTC faces a demand function for tickets on any given night that can be expressed by the following function[1]:

$$Q = 117 - 6.6P + 1.66P_s - 3.3P_r + 0.0066I \tag{4.2}$$

where P is the price of PTC tickets, P_s is the ticket price at a nearby symphony hall, P_r is the average meal price at nearby restaurants, and I is the average household income of area residents.

---

[1]Note that this function assumes that PTC can sell fractional tickets. This assumption does not have a material effect on our analysis. However, it allows us to draw continuous demand curves. One way to think of quantity in this example is as the *average* number of tickets sold for a performance. In this case, fractional tickets are possible. Note also that we assume that demand is constant for each performance by PTC. PTC performances are all scheduled for Friday and Saturday nights. If they expand their schedule to include weeknights or matinees, it is likely that demand conditions for these performances will differ and hence so should prices. These issues are discussed in Chapter 7.

Figure 4.1 Demand Curves

The left panel shows the demand curve for the Players Theater Company tickets. By convention, price is placed on the vertical axis, while quantity is placed on the horizontal axis. The equation for PTC's demand curve is: $P = 60 - 0.15Q$. The curve indicates that, for example, 200 tickets are purchased at $30 and 133 tickets are purchased at $40. The right panel indicates that the demand curve shifts to the right as income increases from $50,000 to $51,000—at each price, consumers buy more tickets. Movements along a demand curve are motivated by changes in price and are called *changes in the quantity demanded.* Movements of the entire demand curve are motivated by other factors, such as changes in income, and are referred to as *changes in demand.*

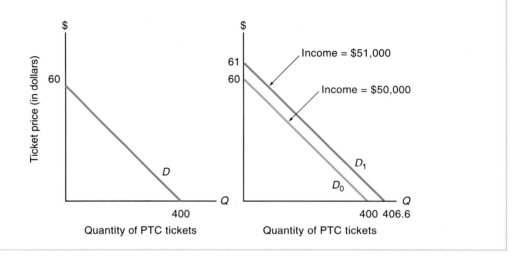

As our starting point, we assume PTC tickets are currently priced at $30; symphony tickets and meals are priced at $50 and $40, respectively; income is $50,000. Given these values, the demand function implies that PTC sells 200 tickets per night. We now examine each of the independent variables in the demand function in more detail.

Demand Curves

The price of the product is particularly important in demand analysis for two reasons: First, prices are among the most important variables that customers consider in making purchasing decisions. Second, managers choose the price of their products, while variables such as the prices of other products and income levels largely are beyond their control. Given its special importance, economic analysis traditionally singles out the effects of price from other independent variables in the demand function.

A *demand curve* for a product displays for a particular period of time how many units will be purchased at each possible price, holding all other factors fixed.[2] The left panel of Figure 4.1 depicts the demand curve for PTC tickets. By convention, price is placed

[2]Technical note: It is possible to derive an individual's demand curve from the indifference curve/budget line analysis presented in Chapter 2. The price of one good—say, food—is varied, holding the price of other goods and income fixed. The person's optimal choices are recorded. The individual's demand curve simply plots the optimal choices of the good (in this case, food) against the associated prices. The firm-level demand curve, in turn, is the sum of the demands of all individuals at each price.

Learning the Law of Demand the Hard Way

Mercury One-2-One is a British mobile-phone company. In a promotion to attract new customers, the company offered *free* telephone calls on Christmas to customers who signed on between November 8th and Christmas Eve.

The company "never dreamed its customers would be so generous in spreading the holiday cheer." The promotion generated more than 33,000 hours of calls, jamming the network and prompting hundreds of complaints from people who couldn't get through to place their calls. The volume on Christmas was about 10 times the daily average. Many people placed overseas calls and simply left the phone line open, logging free international calls of up to 12 hours. The average call was about $1\frac{1}{2}$ hours long; the typical caller rang up about $60 worth of calls—equal to the average *monthly bill* of a cellular company in the United States. The promotion ended up costing the firm millions of dollars. One member of Parliament vowed to file a complaint with Britain's Board of Trade. To quote one executive of the company, "There's certainly been insatiable demand."

Source: K. Pope (1994), "Phone Company's Gift of Gab Jams Its Lines,"
The Wall Street Journal (December 28), B1.

---

on the vertical axis, while quantity is placed on the horizontal axis.[3] The equation for PTC's demand curve is:

$$P = 60 - 0.15Q \qquad (4.3)$$

This expression is obtained by substituting the current values of the other variables into Equation (4.2) and solving for P. The equation indicates that, for example, 200 tickets are purchased at $30 and 133 tickets are purchased at $40.[4]

Demand curves hold other factors fixed. Changes in income or the prices of symphony tickets or restaurant meals will cause shifts in the position of the demand curve (the intercept changes). For instance, the right panel of Figure 4.1 indicates that the demand curve shifts to the right as income increases from $50,000 to $51,000—at each price, patrons purchase 6.6 more tickets. Movements along a demand curve reflect changes in price and are called *changes in the quantity demanded*. Movements of the entire demand curve are caused by other factors (such as this change in income) and are referred to as *changes in demand*.

Law of Demand

As we discussed in Chapter 3, demand curves generally slope downward—individuals purchase less (or certainly no more) of a product as the price increases. PTC's demand curve has a slope of -0.15. Although it is conceptually possible that individuals might purchase more of a product as the price rises, as a practical consideration, managers are quite safe in assuming that the quantity demanded for their products varies inversely with price. It would be foolish for PTC board members to think that they would sell more tickets if they raised the price. The negative slope of demand curves has become known as the *law of demand*.

Elasticity of Demand

Demand curves vary in their sensitivity of quantity demanded to price. In some cases, a small change in price leads to a big change in quantity demanded, whereas in other cases

---

[3]In subsequent chapters, we consider costs which are a function of quantity produced. Placing P on the vertical axis allows us to display both demand (revenue) and costs on the same graph in a convenient fashion.

[4]Rounded to the nearest dollar.

Increased Foreign Competition and Demand Elasticities

Price elasticities for products usually increase with available substitutes. In recent years, there has been a dramatic increase in the amount of foreign competition facing many American companies. One result has been an increase in the demand elasticities for many American products. A specific example is film produced by Eastman Kodak. For years, Kodak had a virtual worldwide monopoly in the production of film. Correspondingly, consumers were relatively insensitive to the price of Kodak film—they had no alternative sources. Kodak now faces intense pressure from Japan's Fuji Corporation. Competition also comes from producers of store-brand film, such as the 3-M Corporation in the United States (store-brand film is sold under the store name at large discount drug, retail, and grocery stores). As a result, the demand for Kodak film is much more price-elastic. This change in price elasticities has motivated Kodak to change its pricing and product development strategies: It can no longer focus exclusively on selling high-quality film at high prices.

a big price change leads to only a small change in quantity demanded. Information on this sensitivity is critically important for managerial decision making. For instance, the board would not want to lower ticket prices to $25 if it could fill the theater by reducing prices only to $28.

One measure of the responsiveness of quantity demanded to price is simply the slope of the demand curve. But this measure is of limited usefulness, in part because it depends on the particular dimensions in which quantities are quoted. For instance, if the slope of a demand curve is -2 when the quantity is expressed in tons, it is only -0.001 when the quantity is stated in pounds. Using the magnitude of the slope coefficient to derive insights into the sensitivity of quantity demanded to price requires additional computation. Economists more frequently use a dimensionless measure of this sensitivity known as the *price elasticity of demand,* η. (Frequently, this elasticity is simply referred to as the *elasticity of demand.*)

Price elasticity measures the *percentage change in quantity demanded given a percentage change in its price.* The law of demand indicates that price elasticities are negative; convention, however, dictates that we state this elasticity as a positive number. Higher price elasticities mean greater price sensitivity. The elasticity of demand, η, thus is given by

$$\eta = -(\% \text{ change in } Q)/(\% \text{ change in } P) \tag{4.4}$$

Calculating Price Elasticities   This elasticity can be approximated between any two points using the concept of *arc elasticity.*[5] The formula for an arc elasticity is

$$\eta = -[\Delta Q/(Q_1 + Q_2)/2] \div [\Delta P/(P_1 + P_2)/2] \tag{4.5}$$

where Δ represents the change between the two points.[6] Figure 4.2 displays two points on PTC's demand curve for theater tickets. As shown in the figure, the arc elasticity between these two points is 1.4. Hence, over this region, for every 1 percent increase in price, patrons reduce the quantity of tickets purchased by approximately 1.4 percent.

[5]Price elasticity can be measured at a point on the demand curve. The concept of *point elasticity* requires elementary knowledge of calculus and, more importantly, a smooth mathematical demand curve. While our example assumes such a curve, data on demand often is available for only a few price-quantity combinations. We show how to calculate point elasticities in the appendix to this chapter.

[6]Equation (4.4) can be expressed as $\eta = -\Delta Q/Q \div \Delta P/P$. When calculating the elasticity between two points, the question arises as to which Q and P to use in this expression, the starting or ending values. Equation (4.5) uses the average of these two values—the initial plus the ending values divided by 2.

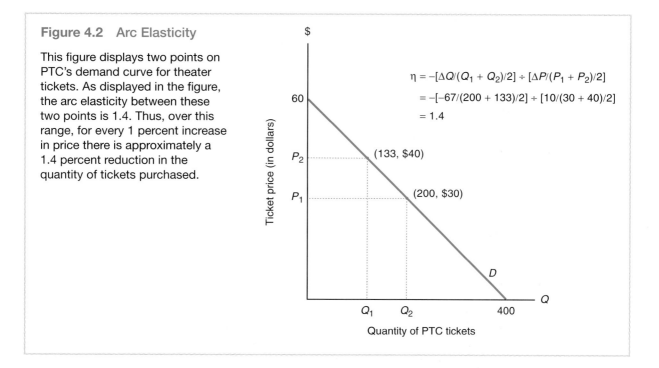

Figure 4.2 Arc Elasticity

This figure displays two points on PTC's demand curve for theater tickets. As displayed in the figure, the arc elasticity between these two points is 1.4. Thus, over this range, for every 1 percent increase in price there is approximately a 1.4 percent reduction in the quantity of tickets purchased.

$$\eta = -[\Delta Q/(Q_1 + Q_2)/2] \div [\Delta P/(P_1 + P_2)/2]$$
$$= -[-67/(200 + 133)/2] \div [10/(30 + 40)/2]$$
$$= 1.4$$

Price elasticities lie between zero and infinity. If the price elasticity is zero, quantity demanded is unaffected by price. In this case, as depicted in the left panel of Figure 4.3, the demand curve is vertical. If the price elasticity is infinite, a small increase in price will

Figure 4.3 Range of Price Elasticities

Price elasticities lie between zero and infinity. If the price elasticity is zero, quantity demanded is unaffected by price. In this case, as depicted in the left panel of the figure, the demand curve is vertical. If the price elasticity is infinite, as in the right panel, a small increase in price will cause people to purchase none of the product, and the demand curve is a horizontal line.

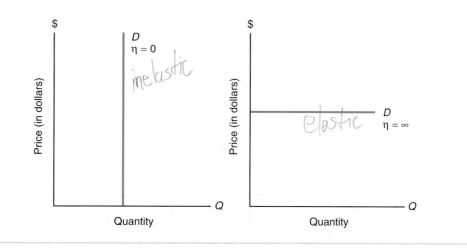

Figure 4.4   Price Elasticities, Price Changes, and Total Revenue

How total expenditures on a product change with price depends directly on the price elasticity. This figure displays the relation between small price changes, total revenue, and price elasticities.

Inelastic demand ($\eta < 1$)
$\Uparrow P \Rightarrow \Uparrow$ Total revenue
$\Downarrow P \Rightarrow \Downarrow$ Total revenue

Unitary elasticity ($\eta = 1$)
$\Delta P =$ No change in total revenue

Elastic demand ($\eta > 1$)
$\Uparrow P \Rightarrow \Downarrow$ Total revenue
$\Downarrow P \Rightarrow \Uparrow$ Total revenue

lead customers to purchase none of the product. In this case, as displayed in the right panel of Figure 4.3, the demand curve is a horizontal line. For instance, a small farmer might not be able to sell any soybeans if they were priced above the prevailing market price. Demand is elastic if the price elasticity is greater than one, unitary if equal to one, and inelastic if less than one.

Elasticity varies along most demand curves. For instance, with a linear demand curve, elasticity will be high when quantities are low and approach zero as the quantities become large. (Try calculating some arc elasticities along PTC's demand curve.) We discuss this topic in greater detail below. (In the appendix to this chapter, we present a special demand curve that has constant elasticity—it does not vary along the curve).

Price Changes and Total Revenue   One of the board's concerns is how total revenue changes if it lowers ticket prices. We now demonstrate that the relation between revenue and price depends on the demand elasticity. Total revenue is calculated by multiplying the quantity purchased times the price (that is, $P \times Q$). If price elasticity is *inelastic* (less than one), a 1 percent increase in price results in less than a 1 percent decrease in quantity, and thus total revenue increases. Conversely, a price decrease results in a decrease in revenue. In contrast, if demand elasticity is *unitary* (equal to one), a 1 percent change in price results in an offsetting 1 percent change in quantity and hence total revenue is unchanged. Finally, if demand is *elastic* (value greater than one), a small increase in price results in a decline in revenue, whereas a small decrease in price results in an increase in revenue. These relations are summarized in Figure 4.4. We discuss these relations in greater detail below.

Determinants of Price Elasticities   The elasticity of demand tends to be high when there are good substitutes for the product. For instance, the elasticity of demand for PTC tickets is likely to increase with the number of competing events in the city. With many entertainment options, a small increase in the price of PTC tickets might be sufficient to induce a substantial number of potential consumers to attend other events. When alternatives are more limited, additional customers will decide to pay the higher price for PTC tickets rather than just stay at home.

Demand elasticities also can depend on the importance of the goods within consumers' budgets. Goods such as salt and pepper, which consume a relatively small proportion of a person's income tend to be relatively price-insensitive, or inelastic. On the other hand, goods such as major appliances and automobiles represent more substantial purchases. Customers are more likely to comparison-shop to collect product information and thus are more likely to be price-sensitive.

A third determinant of price elasticity is the length of the period to which the demand curve pertains. Demand tends to be more elastic or responsive to price changes

Short-Run versus Long-Run Effects of Increases in Gasoline Prices

In the 1960s, gasoline sold for about 25 cents per gallon in the United States. At this price, Americans tended to purchase large, powerful automobiles with poor gas mileage. In the early 1970s, Americans experienced an extraordinarily disruptive gasoline crisis. Not only did the price rise but for a time there were shortages of gasoline; people had to wait in line sometimes for hours to fill their tanks. The increase in gasoline prices and waiting times resulted in a near-term decline in the quantity demanded of gasoline (people carpooled, drove less frequently, etc.). The longer-term effect was much greater; in response to changes in consumer demand, car companies began designing smaller, more fuel-efficient automobiles. Currently, many cars travel at least 20 miles per gallon (and often much more). In the 1960s, many cars traveled fewer than 10 miles per gallon.

over a longer period than within a shorter period. An increase in PTC ticket prices is likely to result in an immediate decline in tickets sold. Long-run effects will be even larger as consumers identify other entertainment options or fail to renew season tickets (these effects will cause the demand curve to shift to the left). Similarly, a large increase in the price of heating oil will result in a near-term decline in the quantity of oil demanded. Over time, the effect will be larger as consumers insulate their homes better and shift to alternative energy sources.

Linear Demand Curves

The PTC board's decision on whether or not to lower prices depends on the relation between price and total revenue and thus its demand elasticity: It would make little sense for the board to lower prices if a price reduction would lower total revenue. We now provide a more in-depth analysis of the relation between price and revenue and discuss the PTC board's optimal pricing policy. Through this analysis, we illustrate the properties of

Price Elasticities

Economists have estimated the price elasticities of various products, such as

Sugar	=	0.31
Potatoes	=	0.31
Tires	=	1.20
Electricity	=	1.20
Haddock	=	2.20
Movies	=	3.70

These estimates indicate that sugar and potatoes have relatively low price elasticities. This might be expected given that these products represent a small portion of most people's budgets. Also, sugar has few close substitutes. Haddock and movies have high elasticities. Haddock is a narrowly defined product (as opposed to fish) and has many close substitutes. Movies are a luxury item for many people; higher prices cause individuals to consume other forms of entertainment.

Source: E. Mansfield (1988), *Microeconomics* (W.W. Norton: New York), 142.

Demand Elasticities and Airline Pricing

Round-trip airfares are substantially lower if the traveler stays over a Saturday night. Airline companies offer this discount to increase revenues (and profits). The typical traveler who stays over a Saturday night is a tourist. Tourists have relatively high price elasticities for air travel. Lowering the price from the standard fare correspondingly increases revenue: The price decrease is more than offset by the increase in tickets sold. Airline companies do not offer comparable discounts to travelers who complete the round-trip midweek. These customers are primarily business travelers who have relatively inelastic demands. Lowering price would decrease revenue because the decrease in price would not be offset by an increase in tickets sold. Airline companies also offer fewer discounts during peak periods, such as the period around the Thanksgiving holiday. During these periods, demand is relatively inelastic and they can fill the planes without offering substantial discounts. (Chapter 7 presents a detailed discussion of product pricing.)

linear demand curves. Knowing these properties is useful for understanding the subsequent analysis in this book.[7]

Total Revenue   PTC's total revenue (TR) for any given performance is equal to the quantity of tickets sold times the price. Price is given by the demand curve in Equation (4.3). Thus, total revenue can be expressed as

$$\text{TR} = P \times Q$$
$$= (60 - 0.15Q)Q$$
$$= 60Q - 0.15Q^2 \qquad (4.6)$$

Figure 4.5 displays PTC's demand and total revenue curves. Total revenue increases as price decreases up to the midpoint of the demand curve. Over this range, demand is elastic: The percentage decline in price is smaller than the percentage increase in quantity demanded. The elasticity is unitary at the midpoint. Past the midpoint, price declines result in reduced total revenue; thus, demand is inelastic over this range. These are general properties of linear demand curves.

Marginal Revenue   An important concept in economics is *marginal revenue,* which is defined as the *change in total revenue given a one-unit change in quantity.* Intuitively, marginal revenue for the first unit is just its price. Thus, the intercepts of the demand and marginal revenue curves are the same. As quantity increases, marginal revenue is below price—to sell an extra unit, the price charged for all units must decrease. Marginal revenue is positive up to the midpoint of the demand curve (total revenue is increasing over this interval). At the midpoint, demand elasticity is unitary and marginal revenue is zero. Beyond the midpoint, marginal revenue is negative—the increase in revenue from selling another unit is less than the decline in revenue from lowering price (see the appendix). Hence, marginal revenue (MR) for a linear demand curve is a line with the

---

[7]There is no reason to believe that most demand curves are linear. We focus on linear demand curves for two reasons. First, even though a demand curve is not linear, it might be reasonably approximated by a linear demand curve over the range of potential prices being considered by management. Second, linear demand curves are used throughout the economics literature because they simplify the calculations in examples and at the same time illustrate more general principles. Given the widespread use of linear demand curves, it is important to understand their basic properties.

Figure 4.5   Demand, Total Revenue, and Marginal Revenue for Linear Demand Curves

This figure displays PTC's demand and total revenue curves in the upper and lower panels. Total revenue increases as price decreases up to the midpoint of the demand curve. Thus, over this range, demand is elastic: The percentage decline in price is smaller than the percentage increase in quantity demanded. The elasticity is unitary at the midpoint. Past the midpoint, price declines result in reduced total revenue; and thus, demand is inelastic over this range. An important concept in economics is *marginal revenue,* which is defined as the *change in total revenue given a unitary change in quantity.* In the appendix, we show that marginal revenue (MR) for a linear demand curve is a line with the same intercept as the demand curve but with twice the negative slope. The marginal revenue curve for PTC is pictured in the figure.

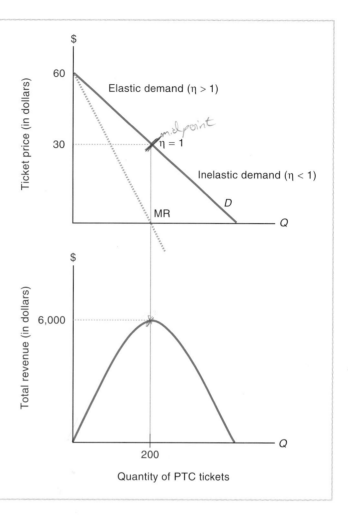

same intercept as the demand curve but with twice the negative slope (see Figure 4.5). The equation for PTC's marginal revenue is

$$MR = 60 - 0.3Q \tag{4.7}$$

Profit Maximization   All of PTC's costs are fixed and do not depend on the quantity of tickets sold on a given evening—actors and utilities have to be paid regardless of how many people attend the performance. Thus, the PTC board's objective is to maximize total revenue (for PTC, with costs fixed, maximizing total revenue is equivalent to maximizing total profit). Figure 4.5 indicates that revenues are maximized at a price of $30. Hence under current conditions, the PTC board should not lower the ticket price to $25. Currently, the company is collecting $30 × 200 = $6,000 in revenue per night. If the price is decreased to $25, total revenue would be $25 × 233 = $5,825 per night.[8] (The upcoming increase in restaurant prices will change the optimal pricing policy. A practice problem at the end of this chapter explores this policy change.)

---

[8]From the demand curve: $25 = 60 − 0.15Q. Therefore, Q = 233.

Complementarity between Computer Hardware and Software

Over the past decade, there has been a dramatic decrease in the price of personal computers. Not only has the price of PCs decreased, but their quality and computing power have improved significantly as well. This decrease in the price of personal computers has increased the quantity of PCs demanded enormously. In addition, it also has increased the demand for software products. Today, some of the largest companies in the world (for example, the Microsoft Corporation) specialize in the production of software for PCs. Computer hardware and software are complements and thus have negative cross elasticities.

Note that, in contrast to this example, most firms do not want to maximize total revenue. PTC, with only fixed costs, is a special case. In most firms, both costs and revenues vary with output. A profit-maximizing firm must consider both effects. We discuss these considerations in greater detail in Chapters 5 through 7.

Other Factors That Influence Demand

In addition to a product's own price, the prices of related products and incomes of potential customers are among the more important factors that influence product demand.

Prices of Related Products

Complements versus Substitutes   The demand for a product can be affected by the prices of related products. For instance, if the local symphony raises its ticket prices, arts patrons will be less likely to attend the symphony and more likely to attend the PTC. Thus, there is a positive relation in Equation (4.3) between the demand for PTC tickets and the price of symphony tickets. Goods that compete with each other in this manner are referred to as *substitutes*. In contrast, if local restaurants raise their prices, the demand for PTC tickets falls (note the negative sign in the demand function). For instance, some potential PTC customers will choose to stay home because the total cost of an evening on the town has increased. Products like theater tickets and meals at restaurants, which tend to be consumed together, are *complements*. Another example of complements is digital video disk players and DVD movies. Between 1997 and 1999, the price of DVD players fell from $600 to $299. Sales of DVD players rose from under 50,000 to 600,000 over these two years. And as consumers experience the better sound quality and video, they also are buying bigger TVs and better sound systems. Big-screen TVs were up 12 percent and audio sales 11 percent. "The biggest market driver is DVD," said

Derived Demand

Some products are demanded, not because individuals receive pleasure from consuming them, but rather because they are useful in the consumption of other products. Demands for these products are derived from the demands from other products. Take motor oil, for example. Few people derive satisfaction from purchasing oil for their automobiles. Rather, this oil is a derived demand from consuming transportation services provided by your car. Procter & Gamble (P&G) discovered that spraying a bit of their Clean Shower bathroom cleaning product on a razor each day can extend the razor's life three or four times. They are formulating a product targeted to this use. Thus, this new product's demand is derived from the demand for razor blades.

Estimates of Cross Elasticities

Economists have estimated the cross elasticities for various commodities. Below are a few of these estimates:

Electricity and natural gas	=	0.20
Beef and pork	=	0.20
Natural gas and fuel oil	=	0.44
Margarine and butter	=	0.81

All the pairs of commodities listed above are substitutes. Complements such as DVD players and DVD movies have negative cross elasticities. Natural gas apparently is not a very strong substitute for electricity. Although people can use either gas or electricity for heating, natural gas is not generally used for lighting. On the other hand, natural gas and fuel oil are closer substitutes (both tend to be used for heating). Margarine and butter are strong substitutes.

Source: E. Mansfield (1988), *Microeconomics* (W.W. Norton: New York), 143.

Terry Shimek, owner of Shimek's Audio Video in Anchorage, Alaska. Moreover, the demand for DVD movies increased as well. Initially caught flat-footed, Hollywood started making more movies available on DVD. The number jumped from 1,800 in 1988 to 5,000 in 1999. (That is compared to 18,000 on VHS tape.)[9]

Cross Elasticities   One frequently used measure of substitution between two products is the *cross elasticity of demand*. Cross elasticity is defined as the *percentage change in the quantity demanded of a good, given a percentage change in the price of some other good.* Cross elasticities between any two goods, *X* and *Y*, can be calculated using a formula that is analogous to Equation (4.5):

$$\eta_{xy} = [\Delta Q_x / (Q_{x1} + Q_{x2})/2] \div [\Delta P_y / (P_{y1} + P_{y2})/2] \qquad (4.8)$$

Unlike price elasticities, which are invariably positive (at least when you multiply them by -1), cross elasticities can be either positive or negative—substitutes have positive cross elasticities whereas complements have negative cross elasticities. Whether a commodity has strong substitutes or complements depends, in part, on how finely the commodity is defined. Pepsi and Coke might have relatively large cross elasticities. The cross elasticities between colas, more broadly defined, and other soft drinks are likely to be smaller.[10]

Cross elasticities are useful because managers frequently want to forecast what will happen to their own sales as other companies change their prices. The PTC board is concerned about the effects that a forthcoming increase in restaurant prices would have on its ticket demand. If meals in local restaurants and theater tickets are strong complements, a substantial increase in restaurant prices would cause a serious decline in the demand for PTC tickets. In this case, the PTC board might want to offset this shift in demand by lowering ticket prices or advertising more heavily. In contrast, if meals and tickets are weak complements, the increase in meal prices would have little effect on ticket demand. In our example, a $10 increase in meal prices will result in

[9]E. Ramsted (1999), "As Prices Tumble, Sales of DVD Players Explode for the Holidays," *The Wall Street Journal* (December 9), 31.

[10]Below, we extend this discussion to show how cross elasticities can be used by managers to define a firm's industry.

33 fewer ticket sales per night. Using the formula in Equation (4.8), the corresponding cross elasticity between these two points [(200, $40); (167, $50)] is −0.81: For every 1 percent increase in meal prices over this range there is, on average, a 0.81 percent decline in ticket sales. This elasticity suggests that PTC tickets and restaurant meals are rather strong complements.

Income

Normal versus Inferior Goods   Another factor that frequently affects the demand for a product is the income of potential buyers. As a person's income increases, more products are purchased, and the combined expenditures across all products rise. The demand for specific products, however, can either rise or fall as income increases. The demand for goods such as gourmet foods or jewelry would be expected to increase with income, whereas the demand for other goods like canned processed meat or cabbage might decline. Goods for which demand increases with income are called *normal goods*. PTC tickets are normal goods. Goods for which demand declines with income are called *inferior goods*.

Income Elasticities   The sensitivity of demand to income is measured by their *income elasticity*. The income elasticity is defined as the *percentage change in the demand for a good, given a percentage change in income (I)*. Income elasticities can be calculated using the following formula.

$$\eta_I = [\Delta Q/(Q_1 + Q_2)/2] \div [\Delta I/(I_1 + I_2)/2] \tag{4.9}$$

The income elasticity is positive for normal goods and negative for inferior goods.

The income elasticity of a firm's product has important implications. Firms producing products with high income elasticities are more affected by cyclical fluctuations; they tend to grow more rapidly in expanding economies but contract more sharply in depressed economies. Managers must anticipate these fluctuations in managing cash flows and hiring decisions. Demands for products with small income elasticities are more stable over economic cycles. Studies indicate that goods like domestic servants, medical care, education for children, and restaurant meals tend to have relatively large income elasticities, whereas goods such as most food products, gasoline, oil, and liquor have relatively small (in absolute value) income elasticities.

Russian Cola Wars

In 1999, Crazy Cola had a 48 percent market share in Krasnoyarsk, Russia. Crazy Cola, produced locally by OAO Pikra, is headed by a 60-year-old former communist factory worker named Yevgeniya Kuznetsova. Ms. Kuznetsova formerly bottled Pepsi at a state-run plant.

A 1.5-liter bottle of Crazy Cola sold for about 39 cents, compared to 77 cents for a two-liter bottle of Coke or Pepsi. Krasnoyarsk is a poor community, and many residents are unwilling to pay a premium for brand-name colas. To quote one 25-year-old graduate student, Viktoria Pimenova, "Crazy Cola is fun, and it's our local product. But it is a drink for people who don't have money. Coke and Pepsi taste better." This statement suggests that Crazy Cola is an *inferior good*, while Coke and Pepsi are *normal goods*. This implies that if the incomes of local residents increase, demand for Coke and Pepsi will increase, while the demand for Crazy Cola will decrease.

Source: B. McKay (1999), "Siberian Soft-Drink Queen Outmarkets Coke and Pepsi," *The Wall Street Journal* (August 23), B1.

Estimates of Income Elasticities

Economists have estimated the income elasticities for various products. Below are a few of these estimates:

Flour	=	−0.36
Natural gas and fuel oil	=	0.44
Margarine	=	−0.20
Milk and cream	=	0.07
Dentist services	=	1.41
Restaurant consumption	=	1.48

According to these estimates, flour and margarine are inferior goods. People spend less on these goods as their incomes rise. The other goods are normal goods (expenditures on the products rise with income). Dentist services and restaurant consumption are particularly sensitive to income changes.

Source: E. Mansfield (1988), *Microeconomics* (W. W. Norton: New York), 143.

Income elasticities also can influence location decisions. For instance, PTC has a relatively high income elasticity (above 1.6). This elasticity was one of the factors that motivated the founders to locate their theater in a community with a high per capita income. They anticipated that they would have fewer customers if they located in a less affluent area.

Other Variables

We have concentrated on three of the more important independent variables in most demand functions—the product's own price, prices of related products, and income. Other variables, such as advertising expenditures, also can be important. In all cases, the analysis is similar. Demand responds to a change in some other variable. Sensitivity can be measured by the appropriate elasticity—for instance, an advertising elasticity. Obviously, managers do not have the time to consider all the conceivable variables that might have small impacts on the demand for their products. Good decision making requires that managers understand the effects of the more important factors, which usually include the product's own price, the prices of close substitutes and important complements, and incomes.

Store Layout Affects Demand

Paco Underhill calls himself a "retail anthropologist." His consulting firm videotapes consumers as they shop at his clients' stores such as Sears, The Gap, and McDonald's. He then offers recommendations for store layout. For example, most North Americans turn right after entering a store while most British and Australian customers turn left. Consumers tend to avoid narrow aisles; they apparently dislike being jostled from behind (what he calls the "butt-brush factor"). Junk food should be placed on low or middle shelves so kids can reach them. After finding that women spend only half the time in the store when accompanied by a man, he recommends placing numerous chairs around stores so men can sit comfortably while the women shop.

Source: K. Labich (1999), "Attention Shoppers: This Man Is Watching You,"
Fortune (July 19), 131–133.

Industry versus Firm Demand

Industry Demand Curves   Although we have concentrated our analysis on firm-level demand, demand functions and demand curves can be defined for entire industries. For instance, a demand function could be specified for the entertainment industry in PTC's market area. Such a function would relate the total ticket sales for all entertainment events to factors that affect this demand. Managers often are interested in total industry demand because it provides important information on the size of their potential markets and trends that affect them. For instance, a company's executives might judge the performance of a store manager that reports flat sales quite differently if market demand is shrinking and the store is increasing market share versus a case where market demand is increasing but the store is losing market share. Moreover, estimates of industry demand sometimes can be obtained at modest cost from outside analysts or business publications.

Firms within an industry compete directly and their products are likely to be relatively strong substitutes. The overall industry, on the other hand, is less likely to have strong substitutes. A person wanting to go to an entertainment event might choose among several options based on price. Entertainment events more broadly defined have fewer alternatives. Thus, demands facing individual firms within an industry tend to be more price-elastic than those for the entire industry.

Defining Industry and Market Area   We have indicated that managers can gain important insights by analyzing industry-level demand. One problem that managers face in conducting this type of analysis is defining the relevant industry and market area. Is PTC competing in the live theater industry or in a more broadly defined entertainment industry? Cross elasticities provide important information to answer these types of questions. The cross elasticity between PTC tickets and symphony tickets is 0.4. This relatively high value (see the box titled Estimates of Cross Elasticities presented earlier in this chapter) suggests that PTC competes against companies in a broader entertainment industry than just live theater.[11] The managers at PTC also must define the relevant geographic area of their marketplace. If PTC raises its prices, will its customers shift to theaters in other nearby cities? If so, these cities should be included in the definition of PTC's market area.

Network Effects

For some products, demand increases with the number of users. For example, fax machines and telephones are not particularly useful unless there is a *network* of users. This consideration is quite important for many of today's communication and information products. For instance, consumers were reluctant to buy new products, such as high-definition television sets, DVD players, and new word processing programs, until they became convinced that the products had the potential for widespread use. Consumers understand that if a product does not garner sufficient demand, important complementary products, such as DVD movies, will not be produced in high volumes or at attractive

---

[11]Cross elasticities also are used as evidence in antitrust cases. Antitrust cases generally focus on whether or not a company has significant market power within an industry. Thus, the definition of the industry is quite important. A company might have a significant market share (and thus apparent power) in a narrowly defined industry, but a small market share in a more broadly defined market. For instance, the government suggested that the ReaLemon Company had monopolized the reconstituted concentrated lemon juice market—supplying over 90 percent of that market. The company responded that the appropriate market definition was broader: They faced vigorous competition from reconstituted natural-strength lemon juice, fresh lemons, frozen lemonade, lime juice, and so on.

prices. Also they worry that it will be difficult to acquire reliable, inexpensive service for the new product. They may learn to use a new technology only to find that it is discontinued because of insufficient demand. For example, despite vigorous efforts by Sony to promote its Betamax technology for video recording, the technology was displaced completely by the VHS format.

Products where these network concerns are important often have relatively elastic demands. When price is lowered, there are two effects. One is the standard price effect: Consumers purchase more of the product because it is being sold at a more attractive price. The second is the *network effect:* Demand for the product increases even more because more people are using the product. When a new consumer purchases the product, there is an externality for other users; because there is an additional user of the product, the product becomes more attractive for other current and potential users.

Network effects not only have important implications on product pricing (we discuss this issue more in Chapter 7), but on product design as well. For instance, when software manufacturers are designing software upgrades, they have to decide whether to make the new product compatible with prior versions of the software and with competing products on the market. Making a new product compatible with competing products can reduce the uniqueness of the product. However, the net effect can be to increase overall demand for the product because of network effects. For example, a consumer might be more willing to buy Microsoft Word if it is compatible with WordPerfect because of the enhanced ability to interact with WordPerfect users.

Product Attributes

Thus far, we have taken the *attributes* of the product as given. Our analysis of the demand for PTC tickets is based on the existing quality and selection of plays, their starting times, the quality of seating, and so on. Given these characteristics, we examined how price and other factors affect the demand for PTC tickets.

Understanding consumer demand also plays an important role in the design of the product. For instance, do local patrons prefer Shakespeare or more contemporary plays? Do they prefer mysteries or musicals? Do they value comfortable seating with additional leg room or seating that is closer to the stage? Can the anticipated decrease in demand from increased restaurant prices be offset by changing the starting time of the plays? (Delaying the starting time by thirty minutes might give people more time to eat at home before going to the play.)

Answers to these types of questions are important in managerial decision making and establishing corporate strategy. Indeed, when managers speak of the importance of understanding consumer demand, they often are referring to understanding the specific product attributes that are important to customers. (We discuss corporate strategy formulation in Chapter 8.) Marketing managers are responsible for understanding the broad range of product attributes that affect demand. These include price, product design, packaging, promotion and advertising, and distribution channels.[12] This broad focus on demand has played an especially important role in management innovations like total quality management programs (see Chapter 22).

An important problem facing most firms is how to incorporate information that may be held by many people throughout a firm—for example, about such matters as consumer demand—into the decision-making process for product design. We defer discussions of this problem until Parts 3 and 4 of this book. These sections provide insights into how to design the firm's organizational architecture to help ensure that relevant information is incorporated in the decision-making process.

Product Life Cycles

Our discussion of product attributes suggests that managers constantly seek to develop new and better ways to identify and respond to consumer demands. This activity leads to the introduction of new products. Managers generally recognize that market demand for a new product is unlikely to remain stable over time. Often, the industry demand curve for a new product shifts outward as the product becomes more widely known. Eventually, however, the demand is likely to shift inward as consumers shift toward other new and improved products. This pattern in the demand for new products is known as the *product life cycle*.

As depicted in Figure 4.6, the product-life-cycle hypothesis suggests that the demand for a product can be categorized into four main phases: introduction, growth, maturity, and decline. In the growth phase, the industry-level demand increases rapidly. In the maturity phase, the demand continues to increase and then begins to decrease. In the decline phase, the demand continues to fall. Eventually, the product is withdrawn from the market. Managers should recognize these trends in new-product planning, as well as in entry, exit, and pricing decisions for given products.

The increase in demand during the growth phase encourages new firms to enter the industry. For instance, the growth in the demand for personal computers (PCs) during the 1990s prompted many firms to begin production. Given the entry of new firms, original firms typically lose market share. If industry demand grows at a faster rate than the number of firms, existing firms realize sales growth, even though their market share falls. If the number of new firms grows faster than industry demand, existing firms will experience a reduction in demand, depressing prices and firm profits.

---

[12]For a more formal economic analysis of the demand for product attributes, see K. Lancaster (1966), "A New Approach to Consumer Theory," *Journal of Political Economy* 74, 132–157.

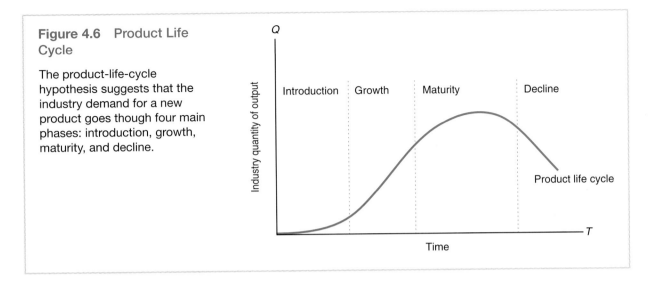

Figure 4.6   Product Life Cycle

The product-life-cycle hypothesis suggests that the industry demand for a new product goes though four main phases: introduction, growth, maturity, and decline.

This discussion suggests that the first firms to introduce a successful product sometimes can have "first-mover advantages." In this case, they enjoy high profits until competitive entry occurs. They also can develop a customer base and have a longer time period to learn how to produce the product efficiently. These advantages explain why firms frequently strive to be the first to develop and launch new products. However, in attempting to exploit an innovative product, managers must anticipate the impact that their policies are likely to have on entry decisions by potential rivals (see Chapters 8 and 9).

First-Mover Advantages and Financial Innovation

US investment banks have introduced an impressive list of innovative financial products. Bankers estimate that developing a new financial product requires an investment of $50,000 to $5 million. Yet the securities they create cannot be patented and SEC regulations compel innovators to disclose quite detailed information about product design. Thus rivals can copy the product at low cost and exploit the innovating bank's investment in educating investors, issuers, and regulators. Bankers estimate that imitators incur costs that are only 25 to 50 percent of the costs incurred by innovators. If financial innovation is profitable, these cost disadvantages of innovation must be offset by other benefits—first-mover advantages. These advantages might include higher prices, lower costs, or larger volume.

In a study of 58 financial innovations that raised almost $280 billion over the period 1974–1987, there is no evidence that innovative banks charged higher prices during the brief "monopoly" period prior to the introduction of imitative products. In the longer run, they actually charged prices that were lower than those of their imitative rivals. This result should not be extraordinarily surprising. Investment banks typically choose one of their best customers as the issuer of an innovative product. These issuers will have special burdens placed on them in explaining the innovative product to investors, regulators, and rating agencies. If immediately following the offering, a rival firm were to issue an imitative product at a lower cost using a competing investment bank, the firm's managers might be understandably annoyed. Thus, investment banks profit from product innovation in ways other than charging higher prices. They underwrite more offers of the products they innovate than do imitating rivals. Innovation also appears to lower costs by allowing banks to exploit economics of scope and learning effects. (In Chapter 5, we discuss such cost considerations.)

Source: P. Tufano (1989), "Financial Innovation and First-Mover Advantages," *Journal of Financial Economics* 25, 213–240.

The analysis also suggests that managers should be careful in evaluating whether to enter an industry during its growth phase. Competition during this phase can be intense; moreover, the demand they face is expected to decline at some point in the future. To prosper in such an environment, a new firm must have some type of *competitive advantage* over its rivals (for example, being a low-cost producer). We discuss this issue in more detail in Chapter 8.

Demand Estimation[13]

In our PTC example, we knew the demand function. Most managers are not so lucky: They must estimate their demand functions. Sometimes it is easy to estimate demand, at least for the very near term. Other times it is quite difficult. Some companies employ statistical techniques to provide numerical estimates of demand functions. Other companies use more qualitative approaches.

Demand estimation is a complex topic that is largely beyond the scope of this book. Here, we simply provide a brief discussion of three general techniques used in estimating demand: *interviews, price experimentation, and statistical analysis.* Our intent is to provide insights into the basic costs and benefits of each approach. These insights make managers more informed consumers of demand estimates and offer guidance as to the type of demand analysis to employ in a given situation. Although each approach has its limitations, the approaches are not mutually exclusive. Because the limitations differ, many managers employ several methods and aggregate the estimates to increase their understanding of demand.

Interviews

Interview approaches attempt to estimate demand through customer surveys, questionnaires, and focus groups. Perhaps the most naive version of this approach is simply to ask consumers what they would purchase if faced with different prices. The answers to these questions can be remarkably unreliable. First, people have incentives to be less than completely truthful since customers would like the firm to offer lower prices. Second, even if they try to be truthful, they might have difficulty forecasting what they would actually purchase given the array of alternatives available in the marketplace.

More sophisticated approaches to customer interviews are possible. For example, an individual might be asked about the difference in price between two competing products. Now if you found that individuals had purchased one of the products but did not know the price of the other, you might conclude that customers were relatively insensitive to price.

Sometimes companies use a *simulated market* where people are given play money and asked to simulate purchase decisions. These experiments can yield useful insights. Again, however, the decisions people make with play money need not mirror the decisions they would make with their own money.

Consumer surveys play a particularly important role in providing information about the attributes that are valued by customers. Many businesses request that buyers fill out customer-service and complaint forms. Businesses often follow up sales or service with telephone calls to customers to ask about product and service quality and customer

---

[13]This section draws on W. Baumol (1977), *Economic Theory and Operations Analysis* (Prentice Hall: Englewood Cliffs, NJ), 234–236.

Using Technology to Assess Demand

The ACNielsen Corporation has been using handheld computers known as *la maquinita*—the little machine—to collect information on the buying habits of Hispanics. As part of a pilot program in Los Angeles, 500 Latino households are taking all their household purchases and scanning their bar codes into the device. This is the first time that comprehensive information has been collected on the buying habits of the Latino community, which now represents 12 percent of the US population. Eventually ACNielsen will sell the database to consumer product firms. The likely upshot will be more spending on ads targeting the Latino community. In 1998, an estimated $1.71 billion was spent on advertising to Latinos, representing about 2 percent of total advertising dollars in the United States. This example highlights how new technologies are being employed to assess product demand.

Source: R. Wartzman (1999), "A Push to Probe Buying Habits in Latino
Homes," *The Wall Street Journal* (August 5), B1.

---

satisfaction. Among the most important sources of information about customer preferences are the direct contacts that salespeople and other company representatives have with their customers.

All the interview approaches, however, can produce remarkably inaccurate information if the sample is not representative of the population of the firm's customers. For instance, if you are interested in estimating demand for a good with a negative income elasticity, distributing surveys at an up-scale mall might be a poor way to proceed. More subtle problems with eliciting interview information also can arise. One team of researchers cautions, "The curious, the exhibitionistic, and the succorant are likely to overpopulate any sample of volunteers. How secure a base can volunteers be with such groups over-represented and the shy, suspicious, and inhibited under-represented?"[14]

Price Experimentation

A second approach is to undertake price experiments. For instance, the board might decrease PTC's ticket price to $25 and carefully track changes in ticket sales. However as part of the company's marketing strategy, PTC prints brochures that detail the season's plays, costs, dates, and ticket prices. Thus, experimenting with their ticket prices would require reprinting their brochures. This raises the cost to PTC of this type of price experimentation. Some other types of firms incur few costs in changing prices; for instance, it is particularly easy for companies that market through the Internet to experiment with their prices.

Many firms are unlike PTC in that they operate at multiple locations. If a firm has the flexibility to vary prices across different geographic markets, it has the potential to gain more information than if it is limited to experimenting at a single location. But care must be exercised. Ideally, the local markets are separated geographically and have their own media outlets. Thus advertising lower prices in one market will not shift demand from the firm's other locations.

There are at least three limitations in the use of price experimentation. First, demand can differ, depending on whether customers anticipate that a price change will be permanent or temporary. And it can be difficult to identify customers' expectations about future prices. Second, direct-market tests are not controlled experiments; several

---

[14]E. Webb, D. Campbell, R. Schwartz, and L. Schrest (1966), *Unobtrusive Measures* (Rand McNally College Publishing Company: Chicago).

changes might be occurring simultaneously. For instance, the board might lower PTC's ticket prices at the same time that the symphony changes its prices. The observed change in demand would reflect both effects. Third, some managers worry that price experimentation is risky. They are concerned that customers lost as a result of a price increase might be difficult to regain even if subsequently the price were lowered. Alternatively, it might be difficult to raise the price once a firm had lowered it (customers might be annoyed and purchase from rivals).

Statistical Analysis

Often, companies use statistical techniques such as regression analysis to estimate demand functions. Computers and large databases on sales, prices, and other relevant factors have increased the usefulness of this approach materially. By using statistical techniques, the effects of specific factors often can be isolated. It is possible to analyze large samples of actual market data to obtain more reliable results.

Even though statistical approaches can provide managers with important information on demand, they must recognize that there are potential problems. Just because a researcher can produce reams of computer output formatted into tables and multicolored graphs implies neither that the analysis is well done nor that the results are reliable. Below, we briefly discuss three types of problems that managers encounter regularly in statistical approaches to estimating demand.

On Estimating Demand Curves for Common Stocks

There has been a long-running debate over the demand elasticities of common stocks of individual firms. Many economists argue that these demand curves are perfectly elastic, since there are numerous stocks with similar risk-return characteristics available in the market. In this case, the demand curves for individual stocks are horizontal. Others argue that each stock is unique and has very few substitutes. Here, the individual demand curves would be downward-sloping.

Managers care about the slopes of the demand curves for their common stock since these slopes affect the price at which they can sell new securities. If demand curves slope downward, price must be decreased below the current market price to sell new securities. If demand curves are horizontal, new securities can be issued at the current market price. Managers, of course, want to sell new stock at the highest possible price.

The existing empirical evidence suggests that stock prices decline by about 3 percent when firms announce new issues of common stock. This finding seems to suggest that the demand curves for common stocks are downward-sloping. This finding, however, is subject to alternative interpretations. If the stock market thinks that firms tend to issue new stock when they are overvalued, an announcement of a new issue will cause the entire demand curve to shift down and price will decline (since the market infers from the new information that the firm is overvalued). The observation that prices decline when new stock is issued is not sufficient to allow us to identify the price elasticity of a firm's common stock—the price decrease might be due to either a shift in demand or a shift in quantity demanded.

This example illustrates that it is not always easy to estimate demand curves, even when data on prices and quantities are readily available. Indeed, the data on prices and volumes for publicly traded securities are among the best available in the world.

Source: C. Smith (1986), "Investment Banking and the Capital Acquisition Process," *Journal of Financial Economics* 15, 3–29.

	1998	*1999*	*2000*
Income (*I*)	$3,000	$4,000	$3,500
Advertising (*A*)	2	3	2.5
Price (*P*)	10	10	10
Sales (*S*)	236	284	260
True demand	$S = 120 - 2P + 8A + 0.04I$		
Estimated demand	$S = 140 + 48A$		

Table 4.1 An Example of the Omitted-Variables Problem

The true demand curve of the company in this example is: Sales = $120 - 2P + 8A + 0.04I$. The data for 1998 to 2000 are presented in the table. If the analyst omits income and uses statistical techniques to estimate a relation between advertising and sales, the analyst will obtain the following equation: Sales = $140 + 48A$. The model predicts sales perfectly (based on the data in the table). The estimated equation, however, significantly overstates the influence of advertising. The omitted-variables problem is present whenever important variables are left out of the analysis that are correlated with the explanatory variables that are included in the analysis.

Omission of Important Variables The problem of *omitted variables* can be illustrated by an example. Assume that the actual demand function for a company is

$$\text{Sales} = 120 - 2P + 8A + 0.04I \tag{4.10}$$

where *P* is the price of the product
 A is advertising expenditures
 I is income

Table 4.1 presents the data for 1998, 1999, and 2000. While this data is potentially available to the marketing manager, Brendis Isaccsdottir, who wants to estimate demand, she does not necessarily know that both advertising and income are important determinants of demand. Suppose that Brendis ignores income and uses statistical techniques to estimate a relation between sales and advertising.[15] Standard regression techniques would yield the following equation:

$$\text{Sales} = 140 + 48A \tag{4.11}$$

The model appears to predict sales perfectly (based on the data in the table). The equation, however, materially overstates the true influence of advertising and can lead to spectacular mistakes in decision making. Based on this analysis, Brendis might budget far too much for advertising. This omitted-variables problem is present whenever important excluded variables are correlated with explanatory variables that are included in the statistical analysis.[16] Including unimportant variables does not bias estimated coefficients for the other variables (however, including irrelevant variables reduces the precision of the various estimates).

[15]The manager does not have to worry about controlling for price, since it was constant over the period ($10).

[16]The problem does not always result in overstated coefficients on the explanatory variables. Depending on the nature of the correlation among the explanatory variables, the coefficients can either be overstated or understated. The estimated coefficient in this example is overstated because advertising and income are positively correlated.

Figure 4.7   An Example of the Identification Problem

An analyst has collected data on past prices and sales for her firm's industry. The demand and supply curves have shifted over the three years. Connecting the three price-quantity points provides a poor estimate of the current industry demand curve (labeled D_3 in the graph). The three points are *equilibrium* points, given all conditions that affect the demand and supply of the product at each point in time. They are not three points along the same demand (or supply) curve.

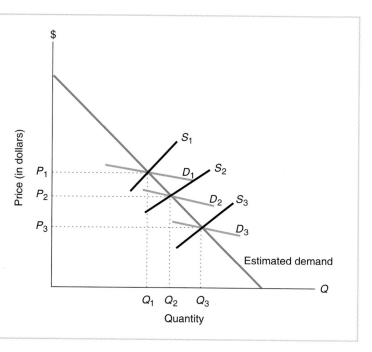

Multicollinearity   If the factors that affect demand are highly correlated (tend to move together), it might be impossible to estimate their individual effects with much precision. For instance, two important variables in the demand function might be income and education. If in the data set to be analyzed high income is always associated with high education, it might be impossible to separate the two effects.

Identification Problem   Another potentially important problem that can confront Brendis is the *identification problem*. This problem also can be illustrated by example. Suppose the marketing manager has collected data on past prices and sales for a given industry with the aim of estimating an industry demand curve. In the past three years, the following sales and price combinations have been observed: (10, $10), (12, $8), and (14, $6). Is it valid for Brendis to connect these three points as an estimate of the demand curve? Because of the identification problem, the answer is generally no.

Each data combination reflects the intersection of the demand curve and supply curve for the industry for each year. If the demand curve has shifted over the three years due to changes in factors such as personal income, the points come from three different demand curves. Connecting the points does not provide an estimate of the current demand curve. In fact, if supply considerations have been stable while demand has shifted, it will trace out the industry's supply curve. Suppose in our example that both the demand and supply curves have shifted in each year. As shown in Figure 4.7, the resulting combinations of price and quantity are observed *equilibrium* points, given the conditions during the relevant time periods. Connecting these points provides a poor estimate of the current demand curve D_3.

Sometimes, Brendis will not have enough information to solve the identification problem and is better off using consumer interviews or market experiments to estimate demand. Other times, she has enough information to identify the demand function (she needs to be able to specify factors that influence demand, but not supply, and vice versa).

One special case in which Brendis does not have to worry about the identification problem is when the *demand curve is stable.* Suppose the demand curve did not shift over the three years and all the different sales-price combinations were caused by changes in supply. In this case, she can obtain a reasonable estimate of the demand curve simply by connecting the observed sales-price combinations.

Implications

We have discussed some of the difficulties that managers face in trying to estimate the demand for their product. These problems can be difficult to solve. Nonetheless, estimates of demand play a critical role in decision making—especially the pricing decision. Successful managers address these problems the best they can, given imperfect knowledge and limited resources.

Summary

Understanding product demand is critical for many managerial decisions such as pricing, setting production levels, undertaking capital investment, and establishing an advertising budget. This chapter provides a basic analysis of demand.

A *demand function* is a mathematical representation of the relations among the quantity demanded of a product over a specified time period and the various factors that influence this quantity. We focus on three independent variables in the demand function: the price of the product, the prices of related products, and customers' incomes.

A *demand curve* for a product displays how many units will be purchased over a given period at each price holding all other factors fixed. Movements along a demand curve reflect changes in price and are called *changes in the quantity demanded.* Movements of the entire demand curve are caused by other factors, such as changes in income, and are referred to as *changes in demand.*

Demand curves generally slope downward to the right: Quantity demanded varies inversely with price. This relation often is referred to as the *law of demand.* Demand curves vary in their sensitivities of the quantity demanded to price. *Price elasticity* is defined as the percentage change in quantity demanded from a percentage change in price (expressed as a positive number). The price elasticity tends to be high when there are close substitutes for the product and when the good represents a significant expenditure for the consumer. Demand tends to be more elastic over the long run than over the short run. How total revenue from a product changes with price depends on the price elasticity. A small price increase results in an increase in expenditures when demand is *inelastic* and a decrease in expenditures when demand is *elastic.* Total expenditures remain unchanged when the demand elasticity is *unitary.*

An important concept in economics is *marginal revenue,* which is defined as the *change in total revenue given a one-unit change in quantity.* Marginal revenue for a linear demand curve is given by the line with the same intercept as the demand curve but with twice the negative slope. Total revenue increases with quantity when marginal revenue is positive and decreases with quantity when marginal revenue is negative.

The price of related products can affect the demand for a product. Goods that compete with each other are referred to as *substitutes.* Products that tend to be consumed together are *complements.* One frequently used measure of substitution between two products is the *cross elasticity of demand.* The cross elasticity is positive for substitutes and negative for complements.

Another factor that can affect the demand for a product is the income of potential buyers. The sensitivity of demand to income is measured by the *income elasticity.* The income elasticity is positive for *normal goods,* and negative for *inferior goods.*

Demand curves can be defined for individual firms or entire industries. The price elasticities for individual firms within an industry are generally higher than for the industry as a whole. Cross elasticities can be helpful in defining the appropriate industry.

For some products, demand increases with the number of users. For example, fax machines and telephones are not very useful unless there is a *network* of users. Products where these network concerns are important often have relatively elastic demands. When price is lowered, there is both a *standard price effect* and a *network effect.*

The standard economic analysis of demand takes the *attributes* of the product as given. Information about consumer demand, however, is also important in the initial design of products. Parts 3 and 4 of this book provide important insights into how to design the firm's organizational architecture to help ensure that this type of information is incorporated in the decision-making process.

Managers use three basic approaches to estimate demand: *interviews, price experimentation,* and *statistical analysis.* All three approaches can suffer from potentially serious problems. Managers have to do the best they can given imperfect information and limited resources. Knowledge of the potential pitfalls can make managers more intelligent producers and users of demand estimates.

Appendix

Demand[17]

In the chapter, we presented formulas for arc elasticities that estimate elasticities between two points on the demand curve. This appendix shows how to calculate elasticities at single points on the demand curve. It also derives the equation for marginal revenue for a linear demand curve and discusses a special (log-linear) demand function.

Point Elasticities   Elasticities measure the percentage change in quantity demanded for a percentage change in some other variable. There are several ways to express the formula for an elasticity. One way, using price elasticity as an example, follows:

$$\eta = -(\Delta Q/Q)/(\Delta P/P)$$
$$= -(\Delta Q/\Delta P) \times (P/Q) \tag{4.12}$$

By definition, as the change in P goes to zero, the limit of the first term $(\Delta Q/\Delta P)$ is the partial derivative of Q with respect to P. At a particular point on the demand curve, the elasticity of demand for small changes in P is given by

$$\eta = -(\partial Q/\partial P) \times (P/Q) \tag{4.13}$$

As an example, consider the demand function for PTC theater tickets:

$$Q = 117 - 6.6P + 1.66P_S - 3.3P_R + 0.0066I \tag{4.14}$$

The point elasticity at the current price-quantity combination of \$30 and 200 tickets is

$$\eta = -(-6.6) \times (30/200) = 1 \tag{4.15}$$

Recall that this is the value that we derived graphically in the text (see Figure 4.5).

---

[17]This appendix requires elementary knowledge of calculus.

Other point elasticities—for example, point cross elasticities—can be calculated in a similar fashion. Simply substitute the appropriate variable (for example, the price of another product) for P in Equation (4.13).

Marginal Revenue for Linear Demand Curves Marginal revenue (MR) is the change in total revenue for an additional unit of quantity. As the change in quantity becomes very small, the limit of this definition is the partial derivative of total revenue with respect to Q.

Linear demand curves take the following form:

$$P = a - bQ \tag{4.16}$$

Thus, total revenue, $P \times Q$ can be written:

$$\begin{aligned} TR &= (a - bQ) \times Q \\ &= aQ - bQ^2 \end{aligned} \tag{4.17}$$

Marginal revenue is

$$MR = \partial TR / \partial Q = a - 2bQ \tag{4.18}$$

This formula is a line that has the same intercept as the demand curve, but with twice the negative slope.

Log-Linear Demand Functions The following demand function is frequently used in empirical demand estimation:

$$Q = \lambda P^\alpha I^\gamma \tag{4.19}$$

where Q is the quantity demanded
   P is price
   I is income
(Other variables such as advertising and the price of other goods are commonly included as other explanatory variables.) An important property of this demand function is that the *price and income elasticities are constant* (they do not vary along the demand function) and are equal to $-\alpha$ and γ, respectively. In particular:

$$\begin{aligned} \eta &= -(\partial Q / \partial P) \times (P/Q) \\ &= -(\lambda \alpha P^{\alpha-1} I^\gamma) \times (P/\lambda P^\alpha I^\gamma) \\ &= -\alpha \end{aligned} \tag{4.20}$$

Similarly, γ is the income elasticity

Taking the natural logarithm of the demand function in Equation (4.19) yields

$$\ln Q = \ln \lambda + \alpha \ln P + \gamma \ln I \tag{4.21}$$

This equation is linear in the logarithms; it thus can be estimated by standard regression analysis using data on Q, P, and I. The estimated coefficients α and γ are estimates of the price and income elasticities. Other types of elasticities—for example, cross elasticities—can be estimated by including other variables in the demand equation.

Appendix Problem The BJC Company has the following demand function:

$$Q = 300 - 30 \text{ (price)} + 0.01 \text{ (income)}$$

Currently, price is $5 and income is $20,000.

1. Calculate the point elasticities for price and income.
2. Is the product a normal or an inferior good?

3.   Is demand elastic or inelastic?

4.   What will happen to revenue if the company raises its price?

Suggested Readings

G. Stigler (1987), *The Theory of Price* (Macmillan: New York), Chapter 3.

Review Questions

4–1.   What is the difference between a demand function and a demand curve?

4–2.   How will each of the following affect the position of the demand curve for videocassette recorders (VCRs)?
   a.   An increase in the price of VCR tapes.
   b.   A decrease in the price of VCRs.
   c.   An increase in per capita income.
   d.   A decrease in the price of movie tickets.

4–3.   If the demand for a product is inelastic, what will happen to total revenue if price is increased? Explain.

4–4.   What signs are the cross elasticities for substitute products? Explain.

4–5.   Distinguish between normal and inferior goods.

4–6.   How can cross elasticities be used to help define the relevant firms in an industry?

4–7.   Suppose the price of heating oil increases significantly. Discuss the likely short-run and long-run effects.

4–8.   The Alexander Machine Tool Company faces a linear demand curve. Currently, it is selling at a price and quantity where its demand elasticity is 1.5. Consultants have suggested that the company expand output because it is facing an elastic demand curve. Do you agree with this recommendation?

4–9.   For three years in a row, income among consumers has increased. Alexander Machine Tool has had sales increases in each of these three years. Does Alexander Machine Tool produce inferior or normal goods? Forecasts predict that income will continue to rise in the future. Should Alexander Machine Tool anticipate that demand for its products will continue to rise? Explain.

4–10.   The cross elasticity between product A and product B is 10. Do you think that product A is likely to face an elastic or inelastic demand curve? Explain.

4–11.   Vijay Bhattacharya is interested in estimating the industry demand curve for a particular product. He has gathered data on historical prices and quantities sold in the industry. He knows that the industry supply curve has been stable over the entire period. He is considering estimating a regression between price and quantity and using the result as an estimate of the demand curve. Do you think this technique will result in a good estimate of the demand curve? Explain.

4–12.   Maria Tejada, a civil engineer, uses data on population trends to forecast the use of a particular highway. Her forecasts indicate severe road congestion by the year 2010. She suggests building a new road. Comment on this approach.

4–13.   Alexander Machine Tool faces the demand curve: $P = \$70 - 0.001Q$. What price and quantity maximize total revenue? What is the price elasticity at this point?

4–14.   Studies indicate that the income elasticity of demand for servants in the United States exceeds 1. Nevertheless, the number of servants has been decreasing during the last 75 years, while incomes have risen significantly. How can these facts be reconciled?

4–15.   Prior to a price increase, the price and quantity demanded for a product were $10 and 100, respectively. After the price increase, they were $12 and 90.
   a.   Calculate the arc elasticity of demand.
   b.   Is the demand elastic or inelastic over this region?
   c.   What happened to total revenue?

4–16. Define marginal revenue. Explain why marginal revenue is less than price when demand curves slope downward.

4–17. In 1991, Rochester, New York, had a serious ice storm. Electric power was out in houses for days. The demand for power generators increased dramatically. Yet the local merchants did not increase their prices, even though they could have sold the units for substantially higher prices. Why do you think the merchants adopted this policy?

4–18. Seven teenagers, four boys and three girls, were given $200 each to go on a shopping spree. An advertising agency, which specializes in youth markets, gave the teens the money. An account executive accompanied the teens while they were shopping. Not only did the agency want to learn what they bought, but also what they talked about to see what was on their minds. "It's not so much to stay in tune with trends, because trends are elusive. It's more what's really happening with teens and what's important to them."[18]

    a. Discuss the trade-offs between sample size (7 teens), cost, and reliability of what is learned from this experiment.

    b. An agent accompanied the teens while they were shopping. Why didn't the ad agency avoid this expense and just look at what the teens bought?

4–19. Southwest Airlines estimates the short-run price elasticity of business air travel to be 2 and the long-run elasticity to be 5. Is ticket demand more elastic in the short-run or long-run? Does this seem reasonable? Explain.

---

[18]"Teens Track Retail Trends for Ad Agency," *Democrat and Chronicle* (September 5, 1999), 1E.

Chapter 5
Production and Cost

Metals prices were quite volatile in the 1990s. For instance, in 1994, domestic steel prices increased as the US economy recovered from a recession.[1] Indeed, the steel market was the strongest it had been in 20 years: Specifically, steel prices had risen from below $90 to over $135 per ton between 1992 and 1994. After significant price increases earlier in the year, domestic steel companies were planning to increase sheet-steel prices by another 10 percent at year's end. In the tight electrogalvanized markets, price increases as high as 20 percent were

---

[1]Details of this example are from "General Motors Eyes Imports to Counter Price Increases," *Metal Bulletin* (July 11, 1994), 21.

expected. (In fact, in 1995, prices exceeded $142 per ton.) US automobile manufacturers were among the companies most affected by these price increases, since they are major users of domestic steel.

To counter the effects of the increase in domestic steel prices, US auto companies actively pursued new overseas suppliers. For instance, in July 1994, General Motors invited bids for sheet steel from foreign companies such as Sidmar, Solldac, Thyssen, and Klockner. The increases in steel prices affected both companies' pricing and output decisions. The increases in steel prices also placed pressure on US automakers to use other raw materials in the production process. For example, auto companies increased their use of aluminum in engines, transmissions, body components, heating and cooling systems, and suspension systems in 1995.[2] (Aluminum prices had been relatively stable; they were $.534 per pound at the beginning of 1992 and $.533 in January 1994.) Potential applications focused on replacing cast iron or steel with aluminum. In addition, auto companies increased research on new ways to use plastics, magnesium, and recyclable materials in their production process.

By 1999, some of this pressure to substitute aluminum for steel had moderated. Steel fell to under $70 per ton, and aluminum, after reaching over $.90 in 1995, fell below $.69 per pound in 1999.

These events raise a number of questions that are of interest to managers. First, how do firms choose among substitutable inputs in the production process? How does the optimal input mix change with changes in the input prices? How do changes in input prices affect the ultimate cost of production and the output choices of firms? In this chapter we address these and related questions. Major topics include production functions, choice of inputs, costs, profit maximization, cost estimation, and factor demand curves. In the appendix, we derive the factor-balance equation.

Production Functions

A *production function* is a descriptive relation that connects inputs with output. It specifies the *maximum* feasible output that can be produced for given amounts of inputs. Production functions are determined by the available technology. Production functions can be expressed mathematically. For instance, given current technology, an automobile supplier is able to transform inputs like steel, aluminum, plastics, and labor into finished auto parts. In its most general form, the production function is expressed as

$$Q = f(x_1, x_2, \ldots x_n) \tag{5.1}$$

where Q is the quantity produced and $x_1, x_2, \ldots x_n$ are the various inputs used in the production process.

To simplify the exposition, suppose that the auto part in this example is produced from just two inputs—steel and aluminum. An example of a specific production function[3] in this context is

$$Q = S^{1/2}A^{1/2} \tag{5.2}$$

---

[2]A. Wrigley (1994), "Automotive Aluminum Use Climbing in 1995's Models: Automotive Applications Will Use Some 120 Million Lbs. in 1995," *American Metal Market* (August 9), 1.

[3]This production function is an example of a Cobb-Douglas production function, which takes the general form: $Q = \lambda S^{\alpha} A^{\gamma}$. Cobb-Douglas production functions are used frequently in empirical estimation. Not all firms, however, have production processes that are well described by this particular type of production function.

Increasing Returns to Scale at Volkswagen

In order to compete globally, VW and Volvo have long had a cooperative relationship whereby VW modifies or installs VW engines in certain Volvo cars. This allows VW to produce proportionally more engines with a proportionally smaller increase in inputs, thereby increasing VW's productivity. Some of these productivity gains can be passed through to Volvo in terms of lower engine costs. This is an example of increasing returns to scale. (Note, in 1999 Ford purchased Volvo's car division.)

Source: B. Mitchener, A. Latour, and S. Moore (1998), "VW-Volvo Talks Suggest Success Isn't Enough to Ensure Independence in Automotive Industry," *The Wall Street Journal* (July 2), A17.

---

where S is pounds of steel, A is pounds of aluminum, and Q is the number of auto parts produced.

With this production function, 100 pounds of steel and 100 pounds of aluminum will produce 100 auto parts over the relevant time period, 400 pounds of steel and 100 pounds of aluminum will produce 200 auto parts, and so on.[4]

Returns to Scale

The term *returns to scale* refers to the relation between output and the *proportional variation of all inputs* taken together. With *constant returns to scale,* a 1 percent change in all inputs results in a 1 percent change in output. For example, Equation (5.2) presents a production function with constant returns to scale. If the firm uses 100 pounds of each input, it produces 100 auto parts. If the firm increases both inputs by 1 percent to 101 pounds, it produces 101 auto parts.[5]

With *increasing returns to scale,* a 1 percent change in all inputs results in a greater than 1 percent change in output. An example of such a production function is

$$Q = SA \tag{5.3}$$

Here, 100 pounds of steel and 100 pounds of aluminum produce 10,000 auto parts, while 101 pounds of steel and aluminum produce 10,201 auto parts (a 2 percent increase in output). Firms often experience increasing returns to scale over at least some region of output. One major reason is that a firm operating on a larger scale can engage in more extensive specialization. For instance, if an automobile company has only three employees and three machines, each employee and each machine has to perform a myriad of tasks for the company to produce automobiles. Given the broad array of tasks that each worker and machine has to perform, efficiency is likely to be low. In contrast, a large firm employing thousands of workers and machines can engage in much greater specialization. (As noted in Chapter 3, specialization often produces efficiency gains.)

With *decreasing returns to scale,* a 1 percent change in all inputs results in a less than 1 percent change in output. An example is

$$Q = S^{1/3}A^{1/3} \tag{5.4}$$

---

[4]$100^{1/2} \times 100^{1/2} = 10 \times 10 = 100$, and $400^{1/2} \times 100^{1/2} = 20 \times 10 = 200$.

[5]$[(100 \times 1.01)^{1/2}] \times [(100 \times 1.01)^{1/2}] = 101$.

The likelihood that a firm will choose to operate where it experiences decreasing returns to scale is open to debate. Some economists argue that firms should seldom display decreasing returns to scale. If a facility of a given size can produce a given output, why can't the firm simply replicate that facility and produce twice the output with twice the inputs? Indeed, most empirical studies on the subject suggest that the typical firm initially experiences increasing returns to scale, followed by constant returns to scale over a quite broad range of output. On the other hand, several empirical studies indicate that some firms probably do experience decreasing returns to scale.[6] Also, casual observation suggests that some larger firms suffer from inefficiencies to a greater extent than do smaller firms—for example, coordination and control problems become more severe as a firm becomes larger. (We focus on these organizational issues in Part 3.)

In our examples, the returns to scale are the same over all ranges of output. For instance, Equation (5.2) always displays constant returns to scale, while Equation (5.4) always displays decreasing returns. Most production functions vary in returns to scale over the range of output. Most frequently, production functions have increasing returns to scale when output is relatively low, followed by constant returns to scale as output continues to increase, and possibly decreasing returns to scale when output is high. Other combinations are possible.

Returns to a Factor

Returns to a factor refers to the relation between output and the variation in a single input, *holding other inputs fixed.* Returns to a factor can be expressed as total, marginal, or average quantities. The *total product* of an input is the schedule of output obtained as that input increases, holding other inputs fixed. The *marginal product* of an input is the change in total output associated with a one-unit change in the input, holding other inputs fixed. Finally, the *average product* is the total product divided by the number of units of the input employed.

To illustrate these concepts, consider the production function in Equation (5.2): $Q = S^{1/2}A^{1/2}$. Table 5.1 presents the total, marginal, and average product of S, holding A fixed at 9.[7] For this production function, total product increases as S increases; marginal product, however, declines. This means that although total product increases with S, it does so at a decreasing rate. Average product also decreases over the entire range.

More generally, marginal and average products do not have to decline over the entire range of output. Indeed, many production functions display increasing marginal and average products over some ranges. However, most production functions reach a point after which the marginal product of an input declines. This observation is often called the *law of diminishing returns* (or law of diminishing marginal product), which states that the marginal product of a variable factor eventually will decline as the use of an input is increased. To illustrate this principle, consider the classic example of farming a plot of land. Land is fixed at 1 acre, and no output can be harvested without any

---

[6]For example, E. Berndt, A. Friedlaender, and J. Chiang (1990), "Interdependent Pricing and Markup Behavior: An Empirical Analysis of GM, Ford, and Chrysler," working paper, National Bureau of Economic Research, Cambridge, MA.

[7]The production function assumes that production does not have to take place in discrete units. For instance, output might be expressed in tons; clearly production in fractions of tons is possible.

Units of S	Units of A	Total Product of S	Marginal Product of S	Average Product of S
1	9	3.00	3.00	3.00
2	9	4.24	1.24	2.12
3	9	5.20	0.96	1.73
4	9	6.00	0.80	1.50
5	9	6.70	0.70	1.34

Table 5.1   Returns to a Factor

This table shows the total, marginal, and average products of steel for the production function $Q = S^{1/2}A^{1/2}$. Aluminum is held fixed at 9 units. The total product of S is the total output for each level of S; the marginal product of S is the incremental output from one additional unit of S; and the average product of S is output devided by the total units of S.

workers. If 10 bushels of grain can be produced by one worker, the marginal product of the first unit of labor is 10 bushels. The change in output might be even greater as the firm moves from one to two workers. For instance, two workers might be able to produce 25 bushels of grain by working together and specializing in various tasks. The marginal product of labor is 15 bushels and thus, over this range, marginal product is increasing. Eventually, as the firm continues to add more workers, while holding land fixed, output will grow at a slower rate. At some point, total output might actually decline with additional workers because of coordination or congestion problems. In this case, the marginal product is negative.

Figure 5.1 illustrates returns to a factor in this common case. The upper panel displays total product, and the lower panel displays marginal and average products. As the use of input S goes from zero to S_1, marginal product rises. Over this range total product is convex—total product increases at an increasing rate.[8] At S_1, diminishing

Food Intake and Productivity: An Example of Diminishing Returns

Economist John Strauss analyzed data from a survey of farmers from Sierra Leone in West Africa. Through this analysis, he was able to estimate the relation between an individual's agricultural output and daily caloric intake. Between 0 and 5,200 calories per day, he found a positive association between output and caloric intake. The relation, however, was subject to diminishing marginal returns. For instance, for workers consuming about 1,500 calories per day, a 1 percent increase in caloric consumption increased agricultural output by about 0.5 percent. This impact of caloric consumption on output declined steadily with increases in caloric consumption. For workers consuming 4,500 calories per day, a 1 percent increase in calories increased output by only 0.12 percent. Beyond 5,200 calories per day, the estimated relation was negative—additional caloric intake *reduced output.* Apparently, beyond that point the marginal product of food intake was negative.

Source: J. Strauss (1986), "Does Better Nutrition Raise Productivity?"
Journal of Political Economy 94, 297–320.

[8]Technical note: The marginal product at a point is equal to the slope of the total product curve at that point ($MP = \partial TP/\partial S$). Thus, marginal product is decreasing when the total cost curve is concave and increasing when it is convex.

Figure 5.1 Returns to a Factor: A Common Case

This figure illustrates a common pattern for total product, marginal product, and returns to a factor. In the lower panel, marginal product rises, then falls, and eventually becomes negative. When marginal product is rising (between zero and S_1), total product increases at an increasing rate (the curve is convex) in the lower panel. When marginal product is falling but positive (between S_1 and S_2), total product continues to increase but does so at a decreasing rate. Beyond S_2, marginal product is negative and total product falls with additional output. Average product is rising where it is below marginal product and is falling where it is above marginal product. Average and marginal products are equal where average product is at a maximum.

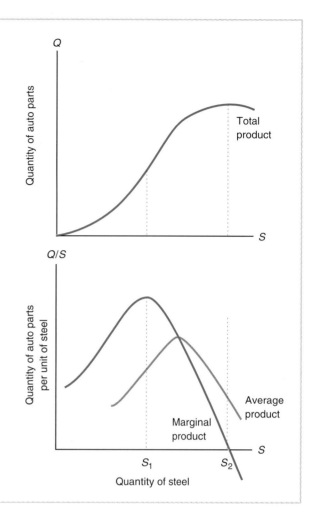

returns set in and the marginal product begins to fall. Between S_1 and S_2, marginal product is positive and so total product continues to increase. However, it does so at a decreasing rate (the curve is concave). Beyond S_2, marginal product is negative, hence total output falls with increases in S. Average product is rising where marginal product is above average product and is falling where marginal product is below average product. Marginal product and average product are equal where average product

Baseball Averages

Marginal product is above average product when average product is rising and below average product when average product is falling. This relation is a general property of marginals and averages. A useful illustration is a baseball player's batting average. The batting average is defined as the number of hits divided by the number of times at bat. Suppose a player starts a game with an average of .300. If the player gets two hits out of four at bats, the marginal batting average for the day is .500 and the player's batting average must rise. If the player gets one hit out of four at bats, the marginal is .250 and the overall average must drop.

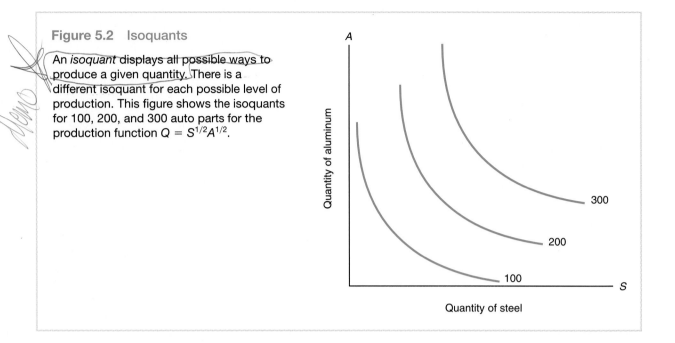

Figure 5.2 Isoquants

An *isoquant* displays all possible ways to produce a given quantity. There is a different isoquant for each possible level of production. This figure shows the isoquants for 100, 200, and 300 auto parts for the production function $Q = S^{1/2}A^{1/2}$.

is at its maximum.[9] This relation is a general rule.[10] The accompanying box on baseball averages illustrates the intuition behind this relation.

Choice of Inputs

Production Isoquants

Most production functions allow some substitution among inputs. For example, suppose that Alexi Dyachenko is chief operating officer, managing a firm with the production function $Q = S^{1/2}A^{1/2}$, and he wants to produce 100 auto parts. In this case, there are many different combinations of steel and aluminum that will yield 100 auto parts. For instance, 100 auto parts can be produced using 100 pounds of steel and 100 pounds of aluminum, 25 pounds of steel and 400 pounds of aluminum, or 400 pounds of steel and 25 pounds of aluminum. Figure 5.2 displays all the possible combinations of inputs that can be used to produce exactly 100 auto parts. Obviously, 100 auto parts also could be produced with more inputs—points above or to the right of a point on this isoquant—but those points represent inefficient production methods. This curve is called an *isoquant* (*iso,* meaning the same, and *quant* from quantity). An isoquant shows all input combinations that produce the same quantity assuming efficient production. There is a different isoquant for each possible level of production. Figure 5.2 shows the isoquants for 100, 200, and 300 auto parts.

Production functions vary in terms of how easily inputs can be substituted one for another. In some cases, no substitution is possible. Suppose that in order to produce

[9]Graphically, marginal product is the slope of a line drawn tangent to the total product curve of that level of output; average product is the slope of the line connecting a point on the total product curve with the origin.

[10]Averages and marginals also are equal when the average is at a minimum.

Figure 5.3 Isoquants for Fixed Proportion Production Functions, Perfect Substitutes, and the Normal Case

Production functions vary in terms of how easily inputs can be substituted for one another. In some cases, inputs must be used in *fixed proportions* and no substitution is possible. Here, isoquants take the shape of right angles. At the other extreme are *perfect substitutes,* where the inputs can be freely substituted for one another. Here, isoquants are straight lines. Most production functions have isoquants that are between the two extremes. The isoquants in the normal case have curvature but are not right angles.

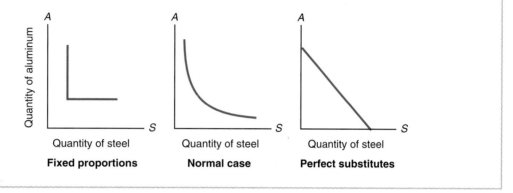

100 auto parts you must have 100 pounds of aluminum and 100 pounds of steel, to produce 200 auto parts you must have 200 pounds of aluminum and 200 pounds of steel, and so on. Having extra steel or aluminum without the other metal yields no additional output—they must be used in *fixed proportions.* As shown in Figure 5.3, isoquants from fixed-proportion production functions are shaped as right angles. At the other extreme are *perfect* substitutes: The inputs can be substituted freely one for another. Suppose that one auto part always can be produced using either 2 pounds of steel or 2 pounds of aluminum. In this case, the firm can produce 100 auto parts by using either 200 pounds of aluminum or 200 pounds of steel, or any combination in between. As shown in Figure 5.3, the corresponding isoquant is a straight line. Most production technologies imply isoquants that are between these two extremes. As depicted in Figure 5.3, typical isoquants have curvature, but are not right angles. The degree of substitutability of the inputs is reflected in the curvature: The closer the isoquant is to a right angle (the more convex), the lower the degree of substitutability.

Substitution of Inputs in Home Building

Builders in the Pacific Northwest use large quantities of wood in the construction of residential houses. For instance, wood is used for framing, siding, floors, roofs, and so on. Homebuilders in the Southwest (for example, Arizona) use much more stucco and tile in home construction. An important reason for this difference is that, in contrast to the Pacific Northwest, the Southwest does not have large nearby forests. This example suggests that homebuilders are able to substitute among inputs in building a home. Homebuilders in the Southwest, however, still use wood to frame the house: The substitution of other inputs for wood is not complete.

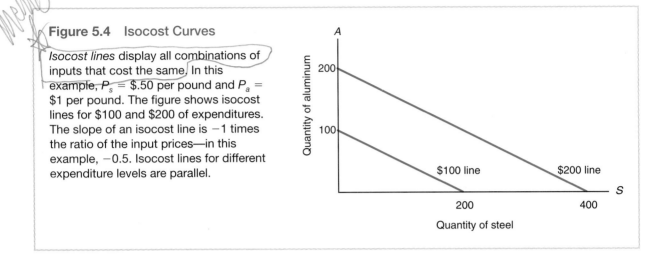

Figure 5.4   Isocost Curves

Isocost lines display all combinations of inputs that cost the same. In this example, P_s = $.50 per pound and P_a = $1 per pound. The figure shows isocost lines for $100 and $200 of expenditures. The slope of an isocost line is −1 times the ratio of the input prices—in this example, −0.5. Isocost lines for different expenditure levels are parallel.

Generally, isoquants are convex to the origin (as pictured in the center panel in Figure 5.3—the typical case). Convexity implies that the substitutability of one input for another declines as less of the first input is used. In our example, if the firm is using a large quantity of steel and little aluminum, it can eliminate a relatively large quantity of steel with the addition of only a small quantity of aluminum while keeping output the same (see Figure 5.2). In this case, aluminum would be much better suited than steel to construct some components of the auto part. But as the firm uses higher proportions of aluminum, its ability to substitute aluminum for steel declines: Steel is better suited for other components. Most production processes display this property.

Isocost Lines

Given that there are many ways to produce a given level of output, how does Alexi choose the most efficient input mix? The answer depends on the costs of the inputs. Suppose that the firm faces competitive input markets and can buy as much of each input as it wants at prevailing market prices. The price of steel is denoted P_s, whereas the price of aluminum is denoted P_a. Total cost (TC) is equal to the sum of the quantities of each input used in the production process times their respective prices. Thus,

$$\text{TC} = P_s S + P_a A \qquad (5.5)$$

Isocost lines display all combinations of S and A with the same cost. Suppose P_s = $.50 per pound and P_a = $1 per pound, and the given cost level is $100. In this case,

$$\$100 = \$.50S + \$A \qquad (5.6)$$

or equivalently,

$$A = 100 - 0.5S \qquad (5.7)$$

Figure 5.4 graphs this isocost line. Note that the intercept, 100, indicates how many pounds of aluminum could be purchased if the entire $100 were spent on aluminum. The slope of −0.5 is −1 times the ratio of the two prices (P_s/P_a): Since aluminum is twice as expensive as steel, 0.5 pounds of aluminum can be given up for 1 pound of steel and costs remain the same.

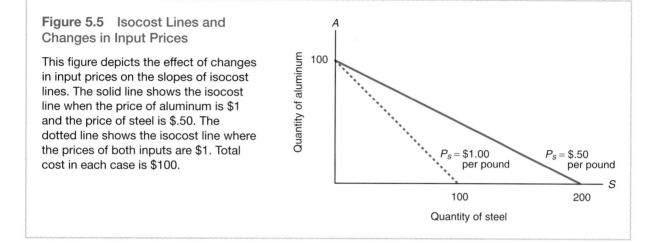

Figure 5.5 Isocost Lines and Changes in Input Prices

This figure depicts the effect of changes in input prices on the slopes of isocost lines. The solid line shows the isocost line when the price of aluminum is $1 and the price of steel is $.50. The dotted line shows the isocost line where the prices of both inputs are $1. Total cost in each case is $100.

Holding the prices of the inputs constant, isocost lines for different cost levels are parallel. Figure 5.4 illustrates this property using the isocost lines for $100 and $200. Note that the further away the line is from the origin, the higher the total cost. Thus, holding output constant, the firm would like to be on the lowest possible isocost line.

The slope of an isocost line changes with changes in the ratio of the input prices. As depicted in Figure 5.5, if the price of steel increases to $1, the line becomes steeper (slope of -1). Here, the firm must give up 1 pound of aluminum to obtain 1 pound of steel. Alternatively, if the price of steel falls to $.25 (not pictured in the figure), the line becomes flatter (slope of -0.25). In this case, the firm has to give up only 0.25 pound of aluminum for every pound of steel. Similarly, the slope of the line also changes with changes in the price of aluminum. What determines the slope of the line are the *relative prices* (recall the slope is $-P_s/P_a$).

Cost Minimization

For any given level of output, Q^*, Alexi will want to choose the input mix that minimizes total costs. As shown in Figure 5.6, the cost-minimizing mix (S^*, A^*) occurs at the

General Motors Is Shanghaied

In the late 1990s, General Motors participated in a $1.5 billion joint venture with a state-owned enterprise in China. The Buicks produced at the resulting state-of-the-art Shanghai plant were considered to be the highest-quality cars of that model being produced anywhere in the world. Production costs, however, were extremely high. One important reason for the high costs was government regulation. The Chinese government dictated what products could be built, as well as how many, and at what price. The government also restricted the input mix. For instance, in 1999 GM was required to use locally made components equaling 40 percent in terms of value and 60 percent in 2000. Thus although GM has shared important technology with its Chinese partner, government constraints have precluded efficient production. High costs have limited the joint venture's ability to export cars to other countries.

Source: L Kraar (1999), "China's Car Guy," *Fortune* (October 11), 238–246.

Figure 5.6 Cost Minimization

The input mix that minimizes the cost of producing any given output, Q*, occurs where an isocost line is tangent to the relevant isoquant. In this example, the tangency occurs at (S*, A*). The firm would prefer to be on an isocost line closer to the origin. However, the firm would not have sufficient resources to produce Q*. The firm could produce Q* using other input mixes, such as (S', A'). However, the cost of production would increase.

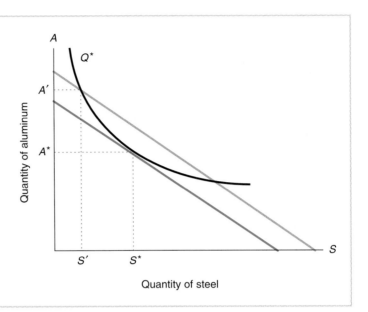

point of tangency between the isoquant for Q^* with the isocost line. Alexi would like to produce the output less expensively (using an isocost line closer to the origin). However, lower-cost production is not feasible. Alexi could select other input mixes to produce Q^*.[11] But any other input mix would place the firm on a higher isocost line. Consider the combination (S', A') in Figure 5.6. This combination of inputs also produces Q^* units of output. Yet this output can be produced at a lower cost by using less aluminum and more steel.

In the appendix to this chapter, we show that at the optimal input mix, the following condition holds:

$$MP_s/P_s = MP_a/P_a \qquad (5.8)$$

where MP_i is the marginal product of input i. (Recall that the marginal product of an input is described in Table 5.1.) Condition (5.8) has a straightforward interpretation. The ratio of the marginal product to price indicates how much additional output can be obtained by spending an extra dollar on the input. At the optimal output mix this quantity must be the same across all inputs. Otherwise, it would be possible to increase output without increasing costs by reducing the use of inputs with low ratios and increasing the use of inputs with high ratios. For instance, if the ratio is 10 units per dollar for aluminum and 20 units per dollar for steel, the firm could hold costs constant but increase output by 10 units by spending one less dollar on aluminum and one more dollar on steel. Alexi has not chosen an optimal input mix when such substitution is possible.

---

[11]Note the similarity between this cost minimization problem and the consumer's utility maximization problem introduced in Chapter 2. The mathematics are the same—both are constrained optimization problems. The consumer maximizes utility for a given budget. Cost minimization is equivalent to maximizing output for a given budget (where the budget is that associated with the lowest-cost method of producing the output).

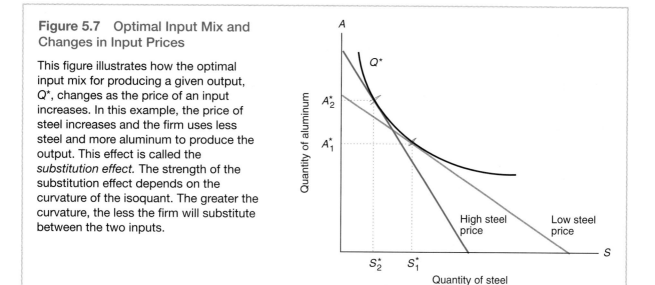

Figure 5.7 Optimal Input Mix and Changes in Input Prices

This figure illustrates how the optimal input mix for producing a given output, Q^*, changes as the price of an input increases. In this example, the price of steel increases and the firm uses less steel and more aluminum to produce the output. This effect is called the *substitution effect.* The strength of the substitution effect depends on the curvature of the isoquant. The greater the curvature, the less the firm will substitute between the two inputs.

Changes in Input Prices

An increase in the relative price of an input will motivate Alexi to use less of that input and more of other inputs. Figure 5.7 illustrates how the optimal input mix for producing Q^* changes as the price of steel increases: Alexi chooses less steel and more aluminum to produce the output. This effect is called the *substitution effect.* The strength of the substitution effect depends on the curvature of the isoquant. The greater the curvature, the less Alexi will substitute between the two inputs for any given change in prices. The substitution effect helps explain the reactions of automobile companies to the 1994 increases in domestic steel prices. These companies increased their use of foreign steel. They also searched for additional ways to replace steel with other inputs such as aluminum.

Minimum Wage Laws

The minimum wage in the United States was increased to $5.15 on September 1, 1997. President Clinton and other proponents of this action argued that the poor would be substantially better off as a result of this increase. The analysis in this chapter indicates why many economists and politicians are skeptical about this claim. Although it is true that the increase in minimum wage makes some workers better off by increasing their wages, other individuals would be made worse off. In particular, the increase in the wage rate is likely to motivate firms to substitute away from low-skilled workers toward more automation and additional high-skilled workers. Thus, the number of employees hired at the minimum wage is likely to decline with an increase in the wage. Estimates suggest that when the minimum wage was increased from $3.35 to $4.25, employment among teenage men fell by 7.29 percent, and employment among teenage women fell by 11.34 percent; employment among teenage blacks fell by 10 percent. Minimum wage workers who retain their jobs are better off; but individuals who want a job, yet cannot find one, are worse off.

Source: D. Deere, K. Murphy, and F. Welch (1995), "Employment and the 1990–1991 Minimum-Wage Hike," *American Economic Review* 85:2, 232–237.

Costs

We have analyzed how firms should choose their input mix to minimize costs of production. We now extend this analysis to focus more specifically on costs of producing different levels of output. Analysis of these costs plays an important role in output and pricing decisions.

Cost Curves

The *total cost curve* depicts the relation between total costs and output. Conceptually, the total cost curve can be derived from the isoquant/isocost analysis discussed above. For each feasible level of output, there is a least-cost method of production—as depicted by the tangency between the isoquant and the isocost line. The total cost curve simply displays the cost of production associated with the isocost line and the corresponding output. For instance, if the least-cost method of producing 100 auto parts is $1,000, one point on the total cost curve is (100, $1000). If the least-cost method of producing 200 parts is $1,500, another point is (200, $1,500). *Marginal cost* is the change in total costs associated with a one-unit change in output. *Average cost* is total cost divided by total output. Managers sometimes refer to marginal cost as incremental cost, whereas they use the term *unit cost* to refer to average cost.

Figure 5.8 displays the total, marginal, and average cost curves for a hypothetical firm. (This figure illustrates a common pattern for cost curves, although not all firms have cost curves with this same shape.) The upper panel indicates that total cost increases with output. Between zero and Q_1, total cost increases but at a decreasing rate (the curve is concave). As shown in the lower panel, over this range, marginal cost decreases.[12] Past Q_1, total cost increases at an increasing rate (the total cost curve is convex) and marginal cost increases. Average cost is declining where marginal cost is below average cost and is rising where marginal cost is above average cost. Average cost equals marginal cost where average

[12]Technical note: The marginal cost at a point is the derivative of total cost ($MC = \partial TC/\partial Q$). Graphically, it is equal to the slope of the total cost curve at that point. Thus, marginal cost decreases when the total cost curve is concave and increases when it is convex. The average cost curve is the slope of the line connecting a point on the total cost curve with the origin.

Figure 5.8 Cost Curves

This figure displays the total, marginal, and average cost curves of a hypothetical firm. The upper panel pictures total cost. Total cost increases with output. Between zero and Q_1, total cost increases but at a decreasing rate (the curve is concave). As shown in the lower panel, over this range, marginal cost decreases. Past Q_1, total cost increases at an increasing rate (the curve is convex) and marginal cost increases. Average cost declines where marginal cost is below average cost and rises where marginal cost is above average cost. This relation is a general rule.

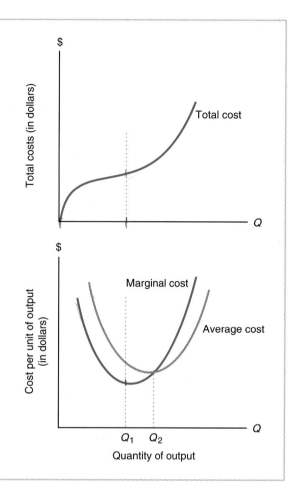

cost is at its minimum point. As previously discussed, these relations are general rules: They apply to average costs and average products, as well as batting averages and GPAs.

Production Functions and Cost Curves With constant input prices, the shapes of cost curves are determined by the underlying production function. For instance, if the production function displays increasing returns to scale over some range of output, long-run average cost must decline over that range. With increasing returns to scale, a 1 percent increase in input expenditures results in a greater than 1 percent increase in output and average cost must fall. In contrast, with decreasing returns to scale, a 1 percent increase in input expenditures results in a less than 1 percent increase in output and average cost must rise. Finally, constant returns to scale imply constant average cost. U-shaped curves (as pictured in Figure 5.8) normally are used to illustrate average costs. This slope suggests an initial region of increasing returns to scale, followed by decreasing returns to scale.[13]

[13]Some economists argue that the typical long-run average cost curve is flat to the right of its minimum efficient scale. Once that output is reached, additional output can be produced at a constant average cost by simply replicating the process (the production function does not experience decreasing returns to scale). But this argument presumes that organizational costs do not increase disproportionally with firm size. See P. McAfee and J. McMillan (1995), "Organizational Diseconomies of Scale," *Journal of Economics and Management Strategy* 4:3, 399–426.

There is also a direct link between the marginal cost curve and the underlying production function. Recall from Equation (5.8) that cost minimization requires the ratio of the marginal product to price to be equal across all inputs. For illustration, suppose at the optimal input mix to produce 100 auto parts, the ratio of the marginal product to price for both steel and aluminum is 2. By expending $1 more on either input, output increases by 2 units. The reciprocal of this ratio (1/2) is their marginal cost of producing one additional unit of output—if 2 units are produced with $1 of additional expenditure on inputs, the marginal cost of producing one extra unit is $.50. This example indicates that, holding input prices constant, marginal cost is determined by the marginal productivity of the inputs: The higher their marginal productivity, the lower the marginal cost. If the marginal productivities in our example were doubled, the ratio of the marginal product to price would be 4 and the marginal cost would be $.25. The inverse relation between marginal productivity and marginal cost makes intuitive sense. If with a given increase in inputs more output can be produced, the marginal cost of producing that output is lower.

Input prices also can affect the shapes of the cost curves. For instance, a declining average cost can be motivated by discounts on large volume purchases. Similarly, a machine that produces 20,000 units might not be twice as expensive as a machine that produces only 10,000 units. Alternatively, if the firm bids up the price of inputs with large purchases, average cost can rise with increased output. Thus, the long-run average cost curve can slope upward even if the firm does not experience decreasing returns to scale.

Opportunity Costs   Managers must be careful to use the correct set of input prices in constructing cost curves. In Chapter 2, we defined *opportunity cost* as the value of a resource in its next best alternative use. Current market prices for inputs more accurately reflect opportunity costs than *historical costs*. For instance, if an auto supplier purchases 1,000 pounds of aluminum for $600 and subsequently the market price increases to $900, the opportunity cost of using the aluminum is $900. If the company uses the aluminum, its replacement cost is $900. Alternatively, the current inventory could be sold to another firm for $900. In either case, the firm forgoes $900 if it uses the aluminum in its production process.

The *relevant costs* for managerial decision making are opportunity costs. It is important to include the opportunity costs of all inputs whether or not they have actually been purchased in the marketplace. For instance, if an owner spends time working in the firm, the opportunity cost is the value of the owner's time in its next best alternative use.

Short Run versus Long Run

Cost curves can be depicted for both the *short run* and the *long run*. The short run is the operating period during which at least one input (typically capital) is fixed in supply. For instance, in the short run it might be infeasible to change plant size or change the number of machines. In the long run, the firm has complete flexibility—no inputs are fixed.

The definitions of short run and long run are not based on calendar time. The length of each period depends on how long it takes the firm to vary all inputs. For a cleaning-services firm operating out of rented office space, the short run is a relatively brief period—perhaps only a few days. For a large manufacturing firm with heavy investments in long-lived specialized plant and equipment, the short run might be a relatively long time period—it might be a matter of years.

Figure 5.9 Short-Run Cost Curves

This figure displays the short-run cost curves of a hypothetical firm. The upper panel depicts total cost (TC) and total variable cost (TVC). Fixed costs simply shift the position of the variable cost curve. The lower panel depicts marginal and average costs. Average fixed cost declines with output since the fixed cost is being spread over more units. Marginal cost (MC) declines to Q_1 and then increases beyond that point due to diminishing returns. Marginal cost depends only on the variable input factors and is *completely independent of the fixed cost.* Average total cost (ATC) and AVC decline as long as marginal cost is lower than the average cost and increase beyond that point. Marginal cost is equal to both ATC and AVC at their respective minimum points. Average total cost is always larger than AVC, since ATC = AFC + AVC. However, this difference becomes smaller as output increases and AFC declines.

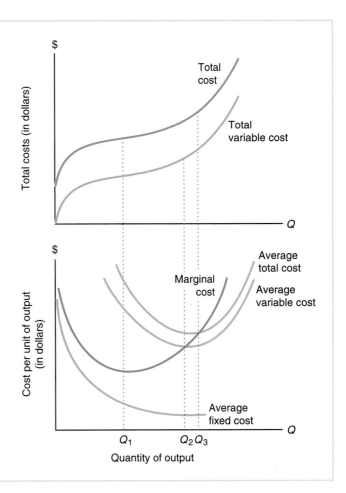

Short-run cost curves sometimes are called *operating curves* because they are used in making near-term production and pricing decisions. For these decisions, it often is appropriate to take the plant size and certain other factors as given (since these factors are beyond the control of the managers in the short term). Long-run cost curves frequently are referred to as *planning curves,* since they play a key role in longer-run planning decisions relating to plant size and equipment acquisitions.

Fixed and Variable Costs   In the short run, some costs are fixed and do not vary with output. These *fixed costs* are incurred even if the firm produces no output. For instance, the firm has to pay managers' salaries, interest on borrowed capital, lease payments, insurance premiums, and property taxes whether or not it produces any output. *Variable costs* change with the level of output. These costs include items like raw material, fuel, and certain labor costs. In the long run, all costs are variable.

Short-Run Cost Curves   Figure 5.9 displays the short-run cost curves for the TAM Corporation. For this firm, suppose that the basic plant size is fixed and that all other inputs are variable. The upper panel depicts total cost. Total cost is the sum of the fixed cost (FC) and total variable cost (TVC). The shape of the total cost curve is completely determined by the shape of the total variable cost curve. Fixed costs simply shift up the location of the curve. Between 0 and Q_1, the total cost curve is concave. Over this range, the marginal productivity of variable factors increases (assuming fixed input prices). Past Q_1, the total cost curve is convex and the marginal productivity of variable factors decreases. This type of pattern is expected given the law of diminishing returns. At low output levels, fixed inputs are not efficiently utilized. Increasing the variable inputs increases output materially. Over this range, total cost increases—but does so at a decreasing rate. Eventually, the marginal productivity of the variable inputs declines and it becomes increasingly expensive to produce extra units of output.

The lower panel depicts marginal and average costs. Average fixed cost (AFC) is total fixed cost divided by output. Average fixed cost declines with output since the fixed cost is spread over more units. Marginal cost (MC) declines up to Q_1 and then increases beyond that point due to diminishing returns. Note that marginal cost depends only on the variable input factors and is *completely independent of the fixed cost*. Average variable costs (AVC) are total variable costs divided by output. Both average total cost (ATC) and average variable cost decline as long as marginal cost is lower than average cost; they increase beyond that point. Marginal cost is equal to both average total cost and average variable cost at their respective minimum points. Average total cost is always larger than average variable cost, since ATC = AFC + AVC. However, this difference becomes smaller as average fixed cost declines with higher output.

Long-Run Cost Curves   In the short run, firms are unable to adjust their plant sizes. In the long run, however, if a firm wants to produce more output, it can build a larger, more efficient plant. In the long run, the average cost (LRAC) of production is less than or equal to the short-run average cost of production. Indeed, the LRAC curve can be thought of as an *envelope* of the short-run average cost curves. Figure 5.10 illustrates this concept. The figure shows four potential plant sizes. Each of the four plants provides the low-cost method of production over some range of output, assuming that only these four plant sizes are feasible. For instance, the smallest plant provides the lowest-cost method of producing any output from zero to Q_1, while the next largest plant provides the low-cost method of producing outputs from Q_1 to Q_2, and so on. The heavy portion of each curve indicates the minimum long-run average cost for producing each level of output.

DeLorean Automobiles

The difficulties of competing with plant sizes significantly below the minimum efficient scale are highlighted by the experience of the DeLorean Motor Company. John Z. DeLorean had been a high-ranking executive at General Motors. He left GM in 1979 to form his own automobile company, the DeLorean Motor Company. The strategy of the new company was to specialize in high-priced luxury sports cars. The company's first (and only) car was the stainless-steel DMC12 with a list price of $29,000—quite a high car price in the early 1980s. Although the minimum efficient scale is relatively large in auto production, DeLorean felt he could compete by designing higher-quality sports cars than the large auto companies. Planned production for 1980 was 3,000 cars. The company soon ran into financial difficulties. In 1982, DeLorean was accused of conspiring to buy and distribute 220 pounds of cocaine valued at $24 million. Federal officials asserted that DeLorean was entering the drug business to help save his ailing automobile company. Although DeLorean was later acquitted on these charges, the company still faced insurmountable financial difficulties and soon went out of business.

Figure 5.10 Long-Run Average Costs as an Envelope of Short-Run Average Cost Curves

In the long run, the average cost (LRAC) of production is less than or equal to the short-run average cost (SRAC) of production. The LRAC curve can be thought of as an *envelope* of the short-run average cost curves. The figure shows four potential plant sizes. Each of the four plants provides the low-cost method of production over some range of output. For instance, the smallest plant provides the lowest-cost method of producing any output from zero to Q_1, while the next largest plant provides the low-cost method of producing output from Q_1 to Q_2, and so on. The heavy portion of each curve indicates the minimum long-run average cost for producing each level of output, assuming that there are only these four possible plant sizes.

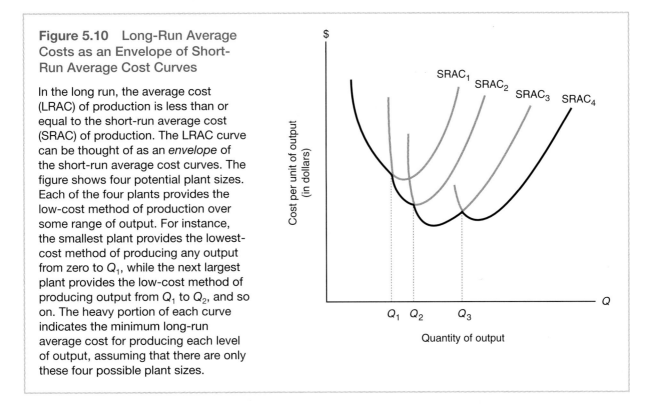

If we extend this analysis by assuming there are many different feasible plant sizes that vary only slightly in size, the resulting LRAC curve will be relatively smooth, as pictured in Figure 5.11. This figure also pictures the long-run marginal cost curve (LRMC). As we have discussed, the marginal cost is below average cost where average cost is falling and above average cost where it is rising. The two are equal at the minimum average cost.

Minimum Efficient Scale

Minimum efficient scale is defined as that plant size at which long-run average cost first reaches its minimum point. In Figure 5.11, this minimum occurs at Q^*. The minimum efficient scale affects both the optimal plant size and the level of potential competition.

Public Utilities

The production of electric power typically is associated with large economies of scale: The average cost of producing electricity decreases with the quantity produced. This production characteristic implies that it is generally more efficient to have one large plant that produces power for an area than several smaller plants. A problem with having one producer of electric power in an area, however, is that the firm has the potential to overcharge consumers for electricity since there are limited alternative sources of supply. Concerns about this problem provide one motivation for the formation of public utility commissions that regulate the prices that utility companies can charge consumers.

Figure 5.11   Long-Run Average and Marginal Cost Curves

If there are many different plant sizes that vary only slightly in size, the resulting long-run average cost (LRAC) curve is relatively smooth, as pictured in this figure. The long-run marginal cost (LRMC) is below average cost where average cost is falling and above average cost where it is rising. The two are equal at the minimum average cost. The minimum efficient scale is defined as the plant size at which LRACs are first minimized (Q* in this example).

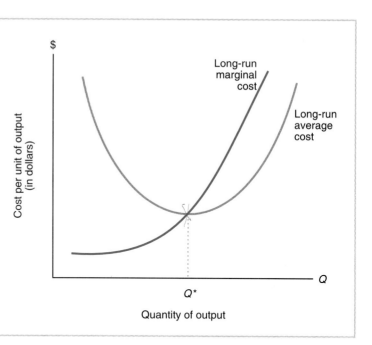

Average production cost is minimized at the minimum efficient scale. As we discuss in the next chapter, competition provides incentives for firms to adopt this plant size. If firms build plants that depart materially from minimum efficient scale, they will be at a competitive disadvantage and could be forced out of business. One complicating factor is transportation costs. If transportation costs are high, cost disadvantages of smaller regional plants can be more than offset by cost savings in transporting the product to customers. In this case, when total production and distribution costs are considered, firms with plants that are smaller than the minimum efficient scale can survive in a competitive marketplace.

Generally, the number of competitors will be large and competition more vigorous when the minimum efficient scale is small relative to total industry demand. For instance, suppose that Kate Polk is evaluating the possibility of entering an industry where she sees established firms reporting substantial profits. If her firm would have to produce 10 percent of the market's output to be cost-efficient, Kate should be concerned that her entry is likely to drive the price down and thus would be less likely to enter the market than if she needed to produce only 1 percent of the market's output for efficient production.

Industries where average cost declines over a broad range of output are characterized as having *economies of scale*. Significant economies of scale limit the number of firms in the industry. For instance, if the minimum efficient scale is 25 percent of total industry sales, there is room for only four firms to produce at that volume. The level of competition among existing firms can vary significantly, even if there are only a few firms in the industry. However, threat of entry is less pressing than in industries where scale economies are low. The threat of potential new competitors is often an important consideration in a firm's strategic planning. In subsequent chapters, we examine how a firm's market structure affects managerial decision making.

Figure 5.12 Learning Curve

A learning curve displays the relation between average cost for a given output period, Q^*, and cumulative past production. In this example, there are significant learning effects in the early stages of production. These effects become minimal as the firm continues to produce the product.

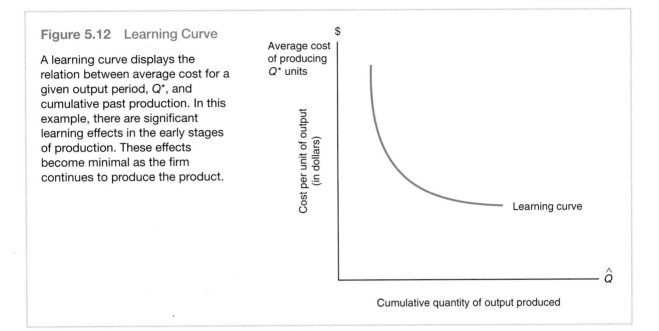

Cumulative quantity of output produced

Learning Curves

For some firms, the long-run average cost of producing a given level of output declines as the firm gains production experience. For example, with more output, employees might gain important information on how to improve production processes. They also become more proficient as they gain experience on the job.[14] A *learning curve* displays the relation between average cost and cumulative production volume. Cumulative production is the total amount of the product produced by the firm across all previous production periods. Figure 5.12 presents an example where there are significant learning effects in the early stages of production. Eventually, however, these effects frequently become minimal as the firm continues to produce the product.

Economies of Scale and Learning Effects in the Chemical Processing Industry

Marvin Lieberman studied economies of scale and learning effects in the chemical processing industry. He found that for each doubling in plant size, average production costs fell by about 11 percent. For each doubling of cumulative volume, the average cost of production fell by about 27 percent. Thus, there is evidence of both economies of scale and learning effects in the chemical processing industry. The size of the estimates suggests that learning effects are more important than economies of scale in explaining the observed decline in costs within the industry from the 1950s to the 1970s.

Source: M. Lieberman (1984), "The Learning Curve and Pricing in the Chemical Processing Industries," *Rand Journal* 15, 213–288.

[14]A. Alchian (1959), "Costs and Outputs," in *The Allocation of Economic Resources,* by M. Abramovitz and others (Stanford University Press: Palo Alto, CA), 23–40.

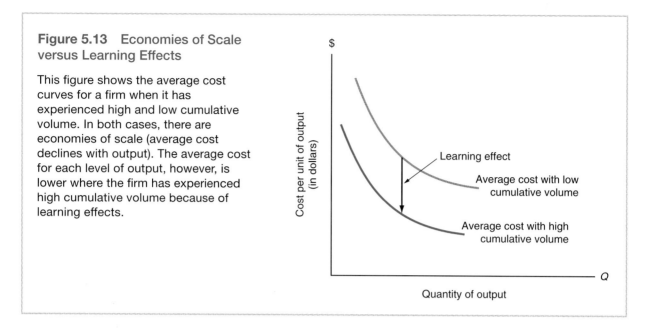

Figure 5.13 Economies of Scale versus Learning Effects

This figure shows the average cost curves for a firm when it has experienced high and low cumulative volume. In both cases, there are economies of scale (average cost declines with output). The average cost for each level of output, however, is lower where the firm has experienced high cumulative volume because of learning effects.

Figure 5.13 illustrates the difference between economies of scale and learning effects. Economies of scale imply reductions in average cost as the quantity being produced within the production period increases. Learning effects imply a shift in the entire average cost curve: The average cost for producing a given quantity in a production period decreases with cumulative volume. Learning effects sometimes can provide existing firms in an industry a competitive advantage over potential entrants; it depends on the nature of the information (Chapter 3) and the distribution of that information across employees. We discuss this issue in more detail in Chapter 8.

Economies of Scope

Thus far, we have focused on the production of a single product. Most firms, however, produce multiple products. *Economies of scope* exist when the cost of jointly producing a set of products within one firm is less than the cost of producing the products separately

Economies of Scale and Scope in Apartment Management

Home Properties of New York is a real estate investment trust specializing in apartment communities in select Northeast, Midwest, and Mid-Atlantic markets. Board Chairman Norman Leenhouts noted: "Since the beginning of last year, we have more than doubled the size of our owned portfolio. By concentrating our growth in our core markets, we are realizing material scale economies—especially in advertising and personnel costs. Moreover, we exploit scope economies by identifying best practices in our different markets and exporting those practices to properties throughout our portfolio."

Source: "Home Properties Reports Record Second Quarter 1999 Results"
(August 5, 1999), *PR Newswire*.

across independent firms. Joint production can produce cost savings for a variety of reasons. Efficiencies can result from common use of production facilities, coordinated marketing programs, and sharing management systems. Also, the production of some products provides unavoidable by-products that are valuable to the firm. For instance, a sheep rancher jointly produces both mutton and wool.

Economies of scope help explain why firms produce multiple products. For instance, PepsiCo is a major producer of soft drinks; yet it also produces a wide range of snack foods (for example, corn chips and cookies). These multiple products allow PepsiCo to leverage its product development, distribution, and marketing systems. These issues are discussed in greater detail in Chapter 8.

Economies of scope and economies of scale are different concepts. Economies of scope involve cost savings that result from joint production, whereas economies of scale involve efficiencies from producing higher volumes of a given product. It is possible to have economies of scope without having economies of scale and vice versa.

Profit Maximization

Thus far, we have focused on the costs of producing different levels of output. However, what output level should a manager choose to maximize firm profits? To answer this question, we return to the concept of *marginal analysis* that we initially introduced in Chapter 2.

Marginal costs and benefits are the incremental costs and benefits that are associated with a particular decision. It is these incremental costs and benefits that are important in economic decision making. An action should be taken whenever the incremental benefits of that action exceed its incremental costs. In deciding whether or not to produce one more unit of a product, the incremental benefit is marginal revenue (see Chapter 4), while the incremental cost is equal to marginal production cost (including any distribution costs)—fixed costs do not affect the decision. Therefore the firm should

Economies of Scale and Scope in DSP Production

In 1999, Texas Instruments was the leading producer of DSPs (digital signal processors). Its DSPs powered roughly two of every three digital phones, most high-performance disk drives, and a third of all modems. They also are used in a myriad of other products including digital cameras, Internet audio, digital speakers, hand-held information appliances, printers, electric-motor controls, and wireless networking equipment. DSPs are programmable. They are especially good at performing superfast real-time calculations, which come in handy when you want to compress, decompress, encrypt, or filter signals and images. Programmability helps keep DSPs inexpensive to produce. The major difference between a DSP in a cell phone and a DSP in a digital camera is the software that tells it what to do. Thus TI gains substantial *economies of scale* in DSP production even though the chips are used in a variety of products. It also enjoys *economies of scope*. For instance, it is able to leverage technological developments across its various products. While TI was notably slow in technology development a few years ago, it is now a world leader. For example , it makes a cell-phone chip whose circuits are just 0.18 micron (millionth of a meter) apart. This distance is similar to Intel's and IBM's most advanced chips.

Source: E. Schonefeld (1999), "Hotter than Intel" *Fortune* (October 11), 179–184.

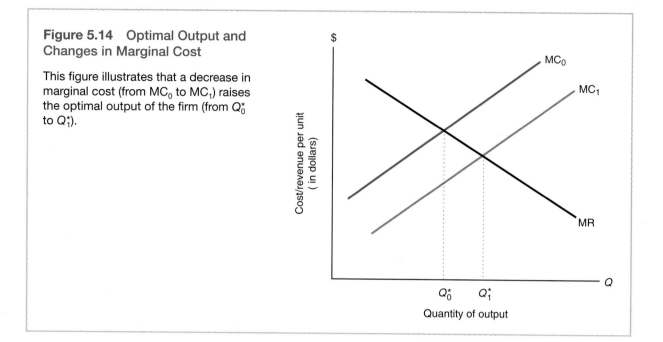

Figure 5.14 Optimal Output and Changes in Marginal Cost

This figure illustrates that a decrease in marginal cost (from MC_0 to MC_1) raises the optimal output of the firm (from Q_0^* to Q_1^*).

produce extra units so long as marginal revenue exceeds marginal cost; the firm should not produce extra units if marginal revenue is less than marginal cost. At the *profit-maximizing level of production,* the following condition holds[15]:

$$MR = MC \tag{5.9}$$

As we saw in Chapter 4, marginal revenue depends on the demand curve for the product. The effective demand curve that the firm faces will be affected by the degree of competition in the product market. In Chapter 6, we examine how the output decisions of firms vary across different market settings.

The changes in metal prices throughout the 1990s changed the total cost of automobile manufacturing. Typically, such changes are accompanied by changes in the *marginal cost* of production. For example, a reduction in steel prices would mean not only a substitution toward steel from other inputs but also an increase in output. Figure 5.14 illustrates this effect. Note that this analysis holds other factors constant. If the demand for automobiles is falling at the same time (thus shifting marginal revenue downward), the net effect could be an increase in output. However, the increase in output would be less than if steel prices were constant.

Factor Demand Curves

In discussing the optimal input mix, we noted that the following condition must hold for efficient production:

$$MP_i/P_i = MP_j/P_j \tag{5.10}$$

[15]Technical note: Since profits equal total revenues minus total costs, Equation (5.9) is the first-order condition for profit maximization. This condition holds at both minimum and maximum profits. At the maximum, the marginal cost curve cuts the marginal revenue curve from below—the second-order condition.

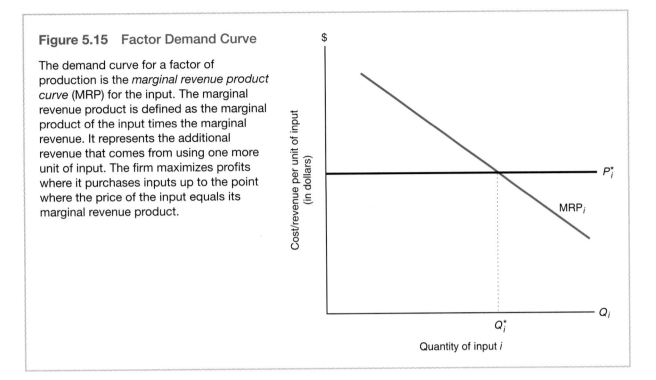

Figure 5.15   Factor Demand Curve

The demand curve for a factor of production is the *marginal revenue product curve* (MRP) for the input. The marginal revenue product is defined as the marginal product of the input times the marginal revenue. It represents the additional revenue that comes from using one more unit of input. The firm maximizes profits where it purchases inputs up to the point where the price of the input equals its marginal revenue product.

for all inputs i and j. The ratios of marginal product to price reflect the incremental output from an input associated with an additional dollar expenditure on that input. The reciprocals of these ratios reflect the dollar cost for incremental output or the marginal cost:

$$P_i/\text{MP}_i = P_j/\text{MP}_j = \text{MC} \tag{5.11}$$

At the profit-maximizing output level, $\text{MR} = \text{MC}$. Therefore, at the optimal output level the following condition must hold:

$$P_i/\text{MP}_i = \text{MR} \tag{5.12}$$

or equivalently,

$$P_i = \text{MR} \times \text{MP}_i \tag{5.13}$$

Equation (5.13) is the firm's demand curve for input i.[16] It has a straightforward interpretation. The right-hand side of the equation represents the incremental revenue that the firm obtains from employing one more unit of the input (the incremental output times the incremental revenue). We call this incremental revenue the *marginal revenue product* (MRP$_i$) of input i. Figure 5.15 illustrates the demand curve for an input.[17] At the current input price of P_i^*, the firm optimally uses Q_i^* units of the input. The firm optimally employs additional units of the input up to the point where the marginal cost of

---

[16]Technical note: The marginal product of input i can depend on the levels of other inputs used in the production process. Thus, the demand curve for an input must allow other inputs to adjust to their optimal levels as the price of input i changes. This adjustment is not important if the marginal product of input i is not affected by the levels of the other inputs.

[17]Technical note: The second-order condition for maximum profits ensures that the demand curve for the input is the *downward-sloping* portion of the marginal revenue product curve. Thus, Figure 5.15 displays only the downward-sloping portion of the curve.

the input (its price with constant input prices) is equal to the marginal revenue product of the input. Intuitively, if the marginal revenue product is greater than the input price, the firm increases its profitability by using more of the input. If the marginal revenue product is less than the price of the input, the firm increases profitability by reducing the use of the input. Profits are maximized when the two are equal.

Our discussion of the profit-maximizing output level and the optimal use of an input might appear to suggest that these decisions are two distinct choices. The two decisions, however, are linked directly. Once the firm chooses the quantities of inputs, output is determined by the production function. Thus, profit-maximizing firms choose the output where marginal revenue equals marginal cost and produce that output so that the price of each input is equal to its marginal revenue product. In our auto example, an increase in steel prices would be expected to motivate *simultaneous* adjustments in both the number of automobiles produced and the methods used to produce them.

Cost Estimation

Our discussion indicates that a detailed knowledge of costs is important for managerial decision making. Short-run costs play an extremely important role in operating decisions. For instance, when the marginal revenue from increased output is above the short-run marginal cost of production, profits increase by expanding production. Alternatively, if marginal revenue is below short-run marginal cost, reducing output increases profits. Long-run costs, in turn, provide important information for decisions on optimal plant size and location. For instance, if economies of scale are important, one large plant is more likely optimal with the product transported to regional markets. Alternatively, if scale economies are small, smaller regional plants, which reduce transportation costs, are more likely optimal.

If managers are to incorporate costs in their analyses in this manner, they must have accurate estimates of how short-run and long-run costs are related to various factors both within and beyond the control of the firm.[18] Among the most commonly used statistical techniques for estimating cost curves is regression analysis. A regression estimates the relation between costs and output (possibly controlling for other factors, such as the product mix or the weather, which affect costs). The data for this analysis can be either time-series data on costs, output, and other variables, or cross-sectional data, which includes observations on variables across firms or plants at a point in time. For instance, in many applications, it is assumed that short-run total costs are approximately linear[19]:

$$VC = a + bQ \tag{5.14}$$

where VC is total variable costs for the period and Q is the quantity of output produced.

A detailed discussion of cost estimation is beyond the scope of this book. Suffice it to say that similar problems arise in cost estimation as arise in the case of demand estimation (for example, omitted-variables problems). Among the most common problems in cost estimation are difficulties in obtaining data on relevant costs. Cost estimates often are based on accounting reports, which record historical costs. As we have indicated, these

---

[18]In addition, some firms estimate cost curves to obtain insights into their underlying production functions. Recall that the shapes of cost curves depend on the underlying production functions. Thus, it often is possible to infer the characteristics of a production function from the shape of the corresponding cost curves. Typically, the data for estimating cost curves is more readily available than the necessary data for estimating production functions.

[19]Variable costs are normally estimated with an intercept. Although variable costs undoubtedly are zero when output is zero, most cost curves are nonlinear. Forcing the intercept to be zero yields a less precise estimate of this slope—the change in costs associated with a change in output.

CASE STUDY: *Rich Manufacturing*

Gina Picaretto is production manager at the Rich Manufacturing Company. Each year her unit buys up to 100,000 machine parts from Bhagat Incorporated. The contract specifies that Rich will pay Bhagat its production costs plus a $5 markup (*cost-plus pricing*). Currently, Bhagat's costs per part are $10 for labor and $10 for other costs. Thus the current price is $25 per part. The contract provides an option to Rich to buy up to 100,000 parts at this price. It must purchase a minimum volume of 50,000 parts.

Bhagat's workforce is heavily unionized. During recent contract negotiations, Bhagat agreed to a 30 percent raise for workers. In this labor contract, wages and benefits are specified. However, Bhagat is free to choose the quantity of labor it employs.

Bhagat has announced a $3 price increase for its machine parts. This figure represents the projected $3 increase in labor costs due to its new union contract. It is Gina's responsibility to evaluate this announcement.

Discussion Questions

1. Why do many firms use cost-plus pricing for supply contracts?
2. What potential problems do you envision with cost-plus pricing?
3. Should Gina contest the price increase? Explain.
4. Is the increase more likely to be justified in the short run or the long run? Explain.
5. How will a $3 increase in the price of machine parts affect Gina's own production decisions?

historical costs do not necessarily reflect the opportunity costs of using resources. Moreover, there is the issue of choosing the appropriate functional form. Equation (5.14) presumes a linear model. However, cost curves need not be linear. For instance, it might be appropriate to use a quadratic model, which would include an additional Q^2 term.

One of the more serious problems complicating cost estimation is the fact that most plants produce multiple products. Multiple products are produced in the same plant because there are economies of scope. Rather than produce two different types of cereals in two separate plants, it typically is cheaper to produce them in one plant; fixed resources can be used more efficiently. If a plant produces multiple products, total and average costs for each product can be calculated only by allocating fixed costs across the products. This allocation often is arbitrary and complicated further by the existence of joint costs. Cost accountants use accounting records to track costs of individual products. Fixed and variable resources used by each product are recorded. These product costs, calculated by the cost accountants, typically are used to estimate short-run and long-run average and marginal costs.

Despite these estimation problems, cost curves play an important role in managerial decision making. Nonetheless, it is important that managers maintain a healthy skepticism when using these estimates. For instance, in making major decisions, it generally is instructive for managers to examine whether a proposed decision is still attractive with reasonable variation in the estimated parameters of the cost function—that is, to conduct *sensitivity analysis*.

Summary

A *production function* is a descriptive relation that connects inputs with outputs. It specifies the *maximum* possible output that can be produced for given amounts of inputs. *Returns to scale* refers to the relation between output and a proportional variation in *all inputs* taken together. A production function displays *constant returns to scale* when a 1 percent change in all inputs results in a 1 percent change in output. With *increasing returns to scale,* a 1 percent change in all inputs results in a greater than 1 percent change in output. Finally, with *decreasing returns to scale,* a 1 percent change in all inputs results in a less than 1 percent change in output. *Returns to a factor* refers to the relation between output and the variation in only one input, *holding other inputs fixed.* Returns to a factor can be expressed as total, marginal, or average quantities. The *law of diminishing returns* states that the marginal product of a variable factor will eventually decline as the use of the input is increased.

Most production functions allow some substitution of inputs. An *isoquant* displays all combinations of inputs that produce the same quantity of output. The optimal input mix to produce any given output depends on the costs of the inputs. An *isocost line* displays all combinations of inputs that cost the same. *Cost minimization* for a given output occurs where the isoquant is tangent to the isocost line. Changes in input prices change the slope of the isocost line and the point of tangency. When the price of an input increases, the firm will reduce its use of this input and increase its use of other inputs (*substitution effect*).

Cost curves can be derived from the isoquant/isocost analysis. The *total cost curve* depicts the relation between total costs and output. *Marginal cost* is the change in total cost associated with a one-unit change in output. *Average cost* is total cost divided by total output. Average cost falls when marginal cost is below average cost; average cost rises when marginal cost is above average cost. Average and marginal costs are equal when average cost is at a minimum. There is a direct link between the production function and cost curves. Holding input prices constant, the slopes of cost curves are determined by the underlying production technology.

Opportunity cost is the value of a resource in its next best alternative use. Current market prices more closely reflect the opportunity costs of inputs than *historical costs.* The *relevant costs* for managerial decision making are the opportunity costs.

Cost curves can be depicted for both the *short run* and the *long run.* The short run is the operating period during which at least one input (typically capital) is fixed in supply. During this period, *fixed costs* can be incurred even if the firm produces no output. In the long run, there are no fixed costs—all inputs and costs are *variable.* Short-run cost curves are sometimes called *operating curves* because they are used in making near-term production and pricing decisions. Fixed costs are irrelevant for these decisions. Long-run cost curves are referred to as *planning curves,* since they play a key role in longer-run planning decisions relating to plant size and equipment acquisitions.

The *minimum efficient scale* is defined as that plant size at which long-run average cost is first minimized. The minimum efficient scale affects both the optimal plant size and the level of potential competition. Industries where the average cost declines over a broad range of output are characterized as having *economies of scale.*

A *learning curve* displays the relation between average cost and the cumulative volume of production. For some firms, the long-run average cost for producing a given level of output declines as the firm gains experience from producing the output (that is, there are significant learning effects).

Economies of scope exist when the cost of producing a joint set of products in one firm is less than the cost of producing the products separately across independent firms. Economies of scope help explain why firms often produce multiple products.

The profit-maximizing output level occurs at the point where *marginal revenue equals marginal cost.* At this point, the marginal benefits of increasing output are offset exactly by the marginal costs.

The *marginal revenue product* of input *i* (MRP$_i$) equals the marginal product of the input times marginal revenue. Profit-maximizing firms use an input up to the point where the MRP of the input equals the input price. At this point, the marginal benefit of employing more of the input is offset exactly by its marginal cost.

Managers often use estimates of cost curves in decision making. A common statistical tool for estimating these curves is regression analysis. One common problem in statistical estimation is the difficulty of obtaining good information on the opportunity costs of resources. Another problem with estimating cost curves involves allocating fixed costs in a multiproduct plant. Cost accountants track the costs and estimate product costs.

| Appendix | **The Factor-Balance Equation**[20] |

This appendix derives the factor-balance equation—Equation (5.9) in the text:

$$MP_i/P_i = MP_j/P_j \qquad (5.15)$$

This condition must hold if the firm is producing output in a manner that minimizes costs (assuming an interior solution).

Recall that at the cost-minimizing method of production, the isoquant curve and isocost line are tangent. Thus, they must have equal slopes. The factor-balance equation is found by setting the slope of the isoquant equal to the slope of the isocost line and rearranging the expression. In the text, we showed that the slope of the isocost line is $-P_j/P_i$. We now derive the slope of an isoquant.

Slope of an Isoquant The production function in the two-input case takes the following general form:

$$Q = f(x_i, x_j) \qquad (5.16)$$

To find the slope of an isoquant, we totally differentiate Equation (5.16). We set this differential equal to zero, since quantity does not change along an isoquant:

$$dQ = [\partial Q/\partial x_i \, dx_i] + [\partial Q/\partial x_j \, dx_j] = 0 \qquad (5.17)$$

The slope of the isoquant is defined by dx_i/dx_j. Thus,

$$\text{Slope of an isoquant} = -(\partial Q/\partial x_j)/(\partial Q/\partial x_i) \qquad (5.18)$$

$$= -MP_j/MP_i \qquad (5.19)$$

This expression has a straightforward interpretation. For illustration, assume that at some fixed combination of x_i and x_j, the marginal product of i is 1 and the marginal product of j is 2. At this point, the slope of the isoquant is -2. This means that 2 units of i can be given up for 1 unit of j and output will stay the same. This is true by definition since j has twice the marginal product of i.

Factor-Balance Equation When employing the cost-minimizing production method, the slope of the isoquant is the same as the slope of the isocost line:

$$-MP_j/MP_i = -P_j/P_i \qquad (5.20)$$

Rearranging this expression gives us the factor-balance equation:

$$MP_i/P_i = MP_j/P_j \qquad (5.21)$$

[20]This appendix requires a basic knowledge of calculus.

This expression immediately generalizes to production functions with more than two inputs.

| Suggested Readings | G. Stigler (1987), *The Theory of Price* (Macmillan: New York), Chapters 6–10. |

Review Questions

5–1. Distinguish between returns to scale and returns to a factor.

5–2. Your company currently uses steel and aluminum in a production process. Steel costs $.50 per pound, and aluminum costs $1.00 per pound. Suppose the government imposes a tax of $.25 per pound on all metals. What affect will this have on your optimal input mix? Show using isoquants and isocost lines.

5–3. Your company currently uses steel and aluminum in a production process. Steel costs $.50 per pound, and aluminum costs $1.00 per pound. Suppose that inflation doubles the price of both inputs. What affect will this have on your optimal input mix? Show using isoquants and isocost lines.

5–4. Is the "long run" the same calendar time for all firms? Explain.

5–5. You want to estimate the cost of materials used to produce a particular product. According to accounting reports, you initially paid $50 for the materials that are necessary to produce each unit. Is $50 a good estimate of your current production costs? Explain.

5–6. Suppose that average cost is minimized at 50 units and equals $1. What is marginal cost at this output level?

5–7. What is the difference between economies of scale and economies of scope?

5–8. What is the difference between economies of scale and learning effects?

5–9. Suppose that you can sell as much of a product as you want at $100 per unit. Your marginal cost is: $MC = 2Q$. Your fixed cost is $50. What is the optimal output level? What is the optimal output, if your fixed cost is $60?

5–10. Discuss two problems that arise in estimating cost curves.

5–11. Suppose that the marginal product of labor is: $MP = 100 - L$, where L is the number of workers hired. You can sell the product in the marketplace for $50 per unit, and the wage rate for labor is $100. How many workers should you hire?

5–12. Textbook writers typically receive a simple percentage of total revenue generated from book sales. The publisher bears all the production costs and chooses the output level. Suppose the retail price of a book is fixed at $50. The author receives $10 per copy, and the firm receives $40 per copy. The firm is interested in maximizing its own profits. Will the author be happy with the book company's output choice? Does the selected output maximize the joint profits (for both the author and company) from the book?

5–13. Suppose your company produces one product and that you are currently at an output level where your price elasticity is 0.5. Are you at the optimal output level for profit maximization? How can you tell?

5–14. Semiconductor chips are used to store information in electronic products, such as personal computers. One of the early leaders in the production of these chips was Texas Instruments (TI). During the early period in the development of this industry, TI made the decision to price its semiconductors substantially below its production costs. This decision increased sales, but resulted in near-term reductions in profits. Explain why TI might have made this decision.

5–15. The AFL-CIO has been a steadfast proponent of increasing the minimum wage. Offer at least two reasons why they might lobby for such increases.

5–16. The Zimmerman Company digs ditches. It faces the production function, $Q = L^{1/2}K$, where Q is the number of ditches dug, L is hours of labor, and K is the number of digging tools.

a. Complete the following table:

	K = 0	K = 1	K = 2	K = 3
L = 0				
L = 1				
L = 2				
L = 3				

b. Does the production function display increasing, decreasing, or constant returns to scale? Explain.

c. Are the marginal products of K and L increasing, decreasing, or constant? Explain.

d. Assume constant input prices. Draw the *general shapes* of the following: (1) long-run average cost, (2) short-run marginal cost, assuming L is fixed, (3) short-run marginal cost, assuming K is fixed.

5–17. Mountain Springs Water Company produces bottled water. Internal consultants estimate the company's production function to be $Q = 300L^2K$, where Q is the number of bottles of water produced each week, L is the hours of labor per week, and K is the number of machine hours per week. Each machine can operate 100 hours a week. Labor costs $20 per hour, and each machine costs $1,000 per week.

a. Suppose the firm has 20 machines and is producing its current output using an optimal K/L ratio. How many people does Mountain Springs employ? Assume each person works 40 hours a week.

b. Recent technological advancements have caused machine prices to drop. Mountain Springs can now lease each machine for $800 a week. How will this affect the optimal K/L ratio (i.e., will the optimal K/L ratio be smaller or larger)? Show why.

5–18. The Workerbee Company employs 100 high school graduates and 50 college graduates at respective wages of $10 and $20. The total product for high school graduates is $1,000 + 100Q_H$, whereas the total product for college graduates is $5,000 + 50Q_C$. $Q_H =$ the number of high school graduates, while $Q_L =$ the number of college graduates. Is the company hiring the optimal amount of each type of worker? If not, has it hired too many high school or too many college graduates? Explain.

Chapter 6
Market Structure

Sealed Air Corporation manufactures a wide variety of protective packaging materials and systems.[1] Among its most famous products are the packing bubbles that "everyone loves to pop." Other products include padded mailing envelopes, pads for absorbing moisture in supermarket meat packages, and equipment and supplies for creating customized foam for packaging fragile or unusually shaped items.

Founded in 1960, Sealed Air initially enjoyed strong patent protection for its major products. This protection shielded the company from competition and allowed it to post 45 to 50 percent profit margins. This market environment faced the company with little competitive pressure to contain costs or invest carefully. Rather, Sealed Air simply concentrated on developing its sales force and selling its products. The company grew and prospered. Yet by the late 1980s, Sealed Air was confronting a quite different set of market circumstances. Most of its major patents were about to expire, and corporate

---

[1]Details of this example are from K. Wruck (1991), "Sealed Air Corporation's Leveraged Recapitalization," Harvard Business School, Case #9-391-067.

executives anticipated a substantial increase in competition. Management knew that it would have to lower its product prices as new competitors entered their markets. It also expected the firm to suffer a competitive disadvantage, given its inefficient operations and high costs. Historically, Sealed Air had encountered more competition in Europe, where it lacked strong patent protection; in those markets it had fared poorly.

In response to increased competition, management at Sealed Air initiated several major policy changes to increase the company's efficiency. It launched a manufacturing improvement program to boost its production quality and reduce costs. It instituted stringent capital budgeting procedures to limit unproductive investment. It increased the firm's leverage substantially to place pressure on employees to generate sufficient cash flow to service its debt (and avoid bankruptcy). It also structured financial incentives throughout the firm to focus more on efficiency and cash flow. For the most part, these changes appear to have had the desired effect: Earnings and stock price performance showed substantial improvement following these policy changes.

This example of Sealed Air illustrates how appropriate policy choices by a firm—such as pricing, leverage, and production techniques—are influenced critically by its market environment. Policies that work within a protected market environment often have to be amended radically when facing a more competitive environment. It is important that managers understand the firm's market environment and how this set of market circumstances affects decision making. The purpose of this chapter is to enhance that understanding by exploring the implications of alternative market structures. Our primary focus is on output and pricing decisions within different market structures. Subsequent chapters examine in more detail how other policies, such as aspects of the firm's strategy and organizational architecture, depend on the market environment.

We begin by discussing markets and market structure in greater detail. We then provide an analysis of competitive industries. Perfect competition is at one end of a continuum based on the environment in which prices are determined within the industry. Competitive markets provide important managerial implications for firms operating within a broad class of market settings. Next, we discuss barriers to entry that can limit competition within an industry. This section is followed by an analysis of the market structure at the other end of the continuum: monopoly. In a monopolistic industry, there is but one firm. In contrast to firms in competitive industries, a monopolist has substantial discretion in setting prices. After a brief discussion of a hybrid structure— monopolistic competition—we consider the case of oligopoly, where a small number of rival firms constitute the industry.

Markets

A *market* consists of all firms and individuals who are willing and able to buy or sell a particular product.[2] These parties include those currently engaged in buying and selling the product, as well as potential entrants. *Potential entrants* are all individuals and firms that pose a sufficiently credible threat of market entry to affect the pricing and output decisions of incumbent firms.

Market structure refers to the basic characteristics of the market environment, including: (1) the number and size of buyers, sellers, and potential entrants, (2) the degree of product differentiation, (3) the amount and cost of information about product price

---

[2]The specific characteristics of a product often vary across firms. Knowing which firms and individuals to group together as a market, therefore, is not always straightforward. As discussed in Chapter 4, cross elasticities are helpful in defining markets. Products with high cross elasticities can be considered in the same market because they are "close substitutes."

Figure 6.1   Firm Demand Curve in Perfect Competition

In competitive markets, firms take the market price of the product as given. The demand curve is horizontal. Both marginal revenue and average revenue are equal to the market price.

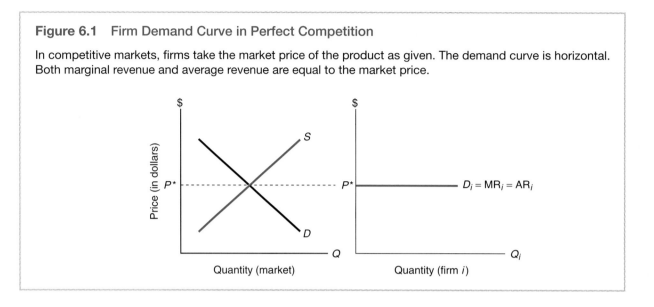

and quality, and (4) the conditions for entry and exit. We begin our analysis of alternative market structures by examining competitive markets.

Competitive Markets

Economists generally characterize competitive markets by four basic conditions:

- A large number of potential buyers and sellers
- Product homogeneity
- Rapid dissemination of accurate information at low cost
- Free entry into and exit from the market

Although few markets are perfectly competitive, many markets closely approximate this description. Moreover, competition establishes a benchmark that yields useful insights into other market settings. An example of a market that comfortably satisfies the conditions for a competitive market is the market for soybeans. In this market, a relatively large number of farmers grow soybeans, and a large number of firms and individuals purchase soybeans. Soybeans are a relatively homogeneous commodity; the product varies little across producers. There are limited informational disparities, and entry as well as exit are reasonably costless.

In competitive markets, individual buyers and sellers take the market price for the product as given—no individual has any real control over price. If a seller charges more than the market price, buyers simply will purchase the product from other suppliers. And firms always can sell their output at the market price; thus they have no reason to offer discounts to attract buyers. In this setting, firms view their demand curves as horizontal—a firm can sell any feasible output at the market price, P^*—but sells no output at a price above P^*. Figure 6.1 illustrates a horizontal demand curve. With a horizontal demand curve, both marginal revenue (MR) and average revenue (AR) equal price.

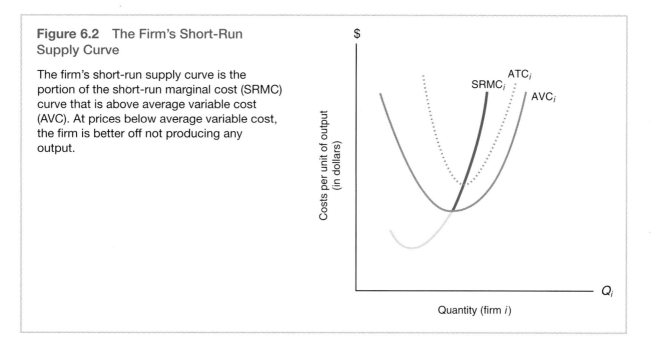

Figure 6.2 The Firm's Short-Run Supply Curve

The firm's short-run supply curve is the portion of the short-run marginal cost (SRMC) curve that is above average variable cost (AVC). At prices below average variable cost, the firm is better off not producing any output.

Firm Supply

Short-Run Supply Decisions In the last chapter, we saw that a firm's profit is maximized at the output where marginal revenue equals marginal cost. The intuition of this result is straightforward—it makes sense to expand output as long as incremental revenue is greater than incremental cost. Past this point, profits decline with additional output since incremental revenue is less than incremental cost. In a competitive market, marginal revenue is equal to price (P). In the short run, the firm takes its plant size (and possibly other inputs) as given. The relevant cost is *short-run marginal cost* (SRMC). The condition for short-run profit maximization in a competitive industry is

$$P^* = \text{SRMC} \tag{6.1}$$

This condition—one of the more important propositions in economics—indicates that at any price, a competitive firm should produce the output where price equals short-run marginal cost. The firm, however, has the additional option of producing no output at all. When the price of the product is insufficient to cover its *average variable cost* (AVC), the firm is better off if it ceases production. With no output, the firm loses money since it generates no revenue to cover its fixed costs. However, this loss is smaller than the one it would incur if the firm produced any other level of output (since revenue from sales would be lower than its variable production costs). Hence the *shutdown condition for the short run* is

$$P^* < \text{AVC} \tag{6.2}$$

A firm's supply curve depicts the quantity that the firm will produce at each price. Therefore the firm's short-run supply curve is that portion of its short-run marginal cost curve above average variable cost. Figure 6.2 displays this supply curve.

Figure 6.3 The Firm's Long-Run Supply Curve

The long-run supply curve for firm i is the portion of the long-run marginal cost (LRMC) curve that is above long-run average cost (LRAC). If price is below LRAC, the firm should go out of business.

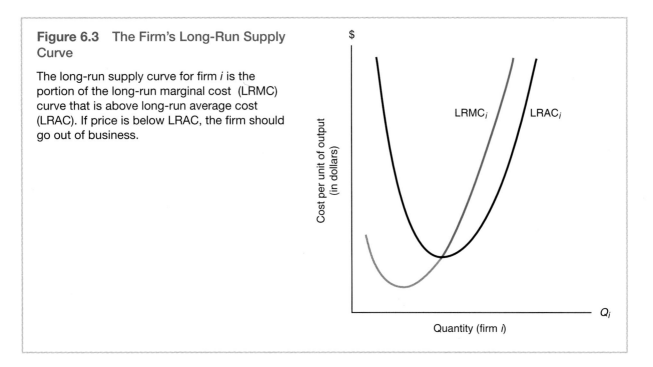

Long-Run Supply Decisions Firms can lose money in the short run yet still find it optimal to stay in business. In the long run, however, a firm must be profitable or it is better to exit this market. Price must equal or exceed *long-run average cost* (LRAC). Thus, the *shutdown condition for the long run* is

$$P^* < \text{LRAC} \tag{6.3}$$

In the long run, a firm can adjust its plant size. The long-run supply decision of a firm is based on *long-run marginal costs* (LRMC). The long-run supply curve of a firm is that portion of its long-run marginal cost curve above long-run average cost. This supply curve is depicted in Figure 6.3.[3]

Competitive Equilibrium

In Chapter 3, we explained that the market price in a competitive market is determined by the intersection of the industry demand and supply curves. The industry demand curve depicts total quantities demanded aggregated across all buyers in the marketplace at each price. Similarly, the industry supply curve is the sum of all individual supply decisions (discussed above).

Consider, as an example, the supply and demand curves, labeled S_0 and D_0 in the right panel of Figure 6.4. Here, the market price is P_0^*. The left panel depicts the long-run supply decision of a typical firm in the industry, firm i. At the price P_0^*, firm i produces the quantity of output Q_{i0}^*. Cost curves are defined to include a normal rate of profit (a normal return on capital is one component of LRAC). Thus, at the price P_0^*,

---

[3]There is no inconsistency between short-run and long-run profit maximization. The LRMC at any given output is equal to the SRMC, given that the firm has the optimal plant size for the output. Hence, the firm simultaneously can choose an output where $P^* = \text{SRMC} = \text{LRMC}$.

Figure 6.4 Competitive Equilibrium

The left panel illustrates the long-run supply decision of firm i, a representative firm in the industry. In the right panel, supply and demand curves (labeled S_0 and D_0) determine the market price, P_0^*. At the price, P_0^*, the firm produces Q_{i0}^*. At the price P_0^*, the firm is earning an *economic profit*. This economic profit is the profit per unit ($P_0^* -$ LRAC$_i$) times the total output Q_{i0}^* and is depicted by the shaded rectangle. Economic profits will motivate other firms to enter the industry. This entry will shift the supply curve to the right and lower the price. Additional entry will occur up to the point where there are no economic profits. This condition occurs at a price of P_1^*. Here, there are no incentives for firms to enter or leave the industry (incumbents are earning a normal rate of profit and inventories are stable at their desired levels), and the market is in *equilibrium*. In a competitive equilibrium, firms produce output at the low point on their average cost curves ($P_1^* =$ LRMC$_i =$ LRAC$_i$). Thus, the equilibrium is associated with efficient production.

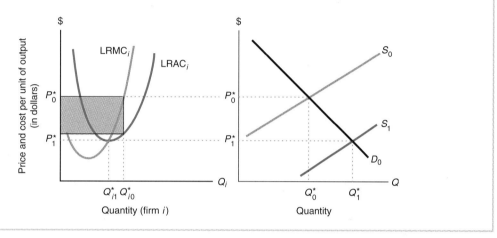

firm i is earning an *economic profit* (above normal profit). This economic profit is the profit per unit ($P_0^* -$ LRAC) times the output Q_{i0}^* and is depicted by the shaded rectangle. The existence of economic profits will motivate other firms to enter the industry.[4] This entry will shift the supply curve to the right; inventories will build above their desired levels because of the increased production; hence firms will lower price. Additional entry will occur up to the point where there are no longer economic profits. This condition is pictured in Figure 6.4 at a price of P_1^*. Here, there are no incentives for firms to enter or leave the industry (incumbents are earning a normal rate of profit); inventories are stable at their desired levels and the market is in *equilibrium*. In a competitive equilibrium, firms produce output at the minimum point on their average cost curves ($P^* =$ LRMC $=$ LRAC). Thus, this equilibrium is associated with efficient production.

Strategic Considerations   Although few markets exactly match economists' idealized conditions for perfect competition, many markets approximate this structure. In most industries, there are strong competitive forces that reduce economic profits over time.

---

[4]Profits reported by firms are based on the accounting definition: sales revenue minus the explicit costs of doing business. The calculation of *accounting profits,* therefore, does not include the opportunity cost of the owner's entrepreneurial effort or equity capital. Economic profits include these costs. Positive economic profits attract entry because the returns are higher than the returns in the alternative activities. Positive accounting profits do not always invite entry—the returns do not always cover the opportunity costs of the owners.

Entry into the Market for Personal Computers

IBM entered the personal computer market in 1981. Its PC quickly became a standard for the industry. IBM, however, had little effective patent protection on its PC, and it had negotiated nonexclusive licenses to key elements like the MS-DOS operating system. Profits quickly attracted rivals (such as Dell, Leading Edge, Packard Bell, and Compaq) to produce IBM clones. Within only a few years, IBM lost substantial market share in the PC market. Margins (the difference between price and average cost) for PC hardware became razor-thin.

These forces imply that many strategic advantages (for example, being the first in a new market) are likely to be short-lived. If the conditions in the market resemble the competitive model, it is important to move quickly to take advantage of transitory opportunities. In addition, potential entrants should realize that observed economic profits in an industry are likely to be bid away as time passes. This consideration can affect both long-range capital spending and entry decisions. For instance, given the threat of increased competition, Sealed Air increased the level of scrutiny it applied to internal investment proposals. In a competitive market, firms must strive for efficiency and cost control; inefficient firms lose money and are forced out of the market. Sealed Air's management understood this when it undertook substantive steps to enhance efficiency.

Superior Firms Even in relatively competitive industries, there are firms that do exceptionally well over long time periods—for example, by being a low-cost producer or having some particular advantage, such as location, relative to competitors. The excess returns, however, often do not go to the owner of the enterprise but rather to the factor input responsible for the particular advantage. For example, land close to a highway interchange (and thus offering customers convenient access) often sells for higher prices than land farther from the interchange. Similarly, the salary of an exceptionally talented manager will be bid up by other firms. In many cases, the firms employing these superior factors of production earn only a normal rate of return ($P^* = $ LRAC). (These issues are discussed in more detail in Chapter 8.)

Phantom Freight

Most plywood in the United States is produced in the Pacific Northwest. Due to this dominance, plywood prices throughout the country are essentially the Northwest price plus shipping. If this condition did not hold, Northwest suppliers would curtail shipping plywood to cities with low prices and increase shipping to cities with high prices. The changes in supply would affect the prices in the cities until, in equilibrium, the prices across cities would differ only by transportation costs.

In a US court case, Southeast timber producers were sued for charging customers Northwest's price plus shipping and then delivering locally produced plywood. It was ruled that these companies were making unjust profits because they did not actually incur the shipping costs. The jury awarded billions of dollars to the customers. Were these companies really making economic profits? The answer is probably not. The local production in the Southeast had a shipping advantage to Southeast customers. The factor that made this advantage possible was scarce timber land in the Southeast. Presumably, the price of this scarce timber land was bid up to the point where plywood producers were making only a normal profit given the prevailing price for plywood in the Southeast (which was the Northwest price plus shipping).

Source: A. Alchian and W. Allen (1983), *Exchange and Production: Competition, Coordination and Control* (Wadsworth Publishing: Belmont, CA), 228–231.

Barriers to Entry[5]

Although the competitive model is a reasonable approximation in many markets, there are other industries where firms have notable market power—output decisions of individual firms have a noticeable impact on prices. A necessary condition for market power to exist is that there are effective *barriers to entry* into the industry.

To understand what constitutes an effective entry barrier, it is useful to consider the decisions of individual firms to enter an industry. Firms consider entering a new market when they observe extant firms reporting large profits. For instance, if Wen Ho observes a firm such as Sealed Air reporting large profits producing packaging materials, his firm (like a number of other firms) is likely to consider entering the industry. Entry decisions depend on three important factors: First, Wen will be concerned about whether his entry will affect product prices. This depends, at least in part, on how existing firms are likely to respond to a new entrant. For example, are they likely to cut prices? Second, Wen will be concerned about incumbent advantages. Do existing firms have advantages that an entering firm will have difficulty duplicating—ones that make it unlikely that the new firm will enjoy similar profits? Third, Wen will be concerned about costs of exit. How much will it cost to leave the industry if this incursion fails? We discuss each of these factors in turn.

Incumbent Reactions

Specific Assets   Specific assets are assets that have more value in their current use than in their next best alternative use. Consider the case of the Alaskan Pipeline. It has a high value in its current use. Yet it is completely specialized for transporting oil from the North Slope to Prudoe Bay—it has virtually no other use. Moreover, it could be moved only at enormous expense. If existing firms in an industry have invested heavily in assets quite specialized to that market, they are likely to fight harder to maintain their positions than if their assets are less specific and can be shifted at low cost to alternative activities.

Scale Economies   Industries with significant economies of scale have minimum efficient scales that occur at high output levels (see Chapter 5). In such industries, a new entrant must produce at high volume to be cost-effective. Large-scale production is more likely to have a material effect on price. For example, if the minimum efficient scale is 30 percent of total market demand, price certainly will decline if a new entrant tries to capture such a large share of the market—its entry undoubtedly would trigger vigorous price competition from incumbents. Note that the absolute size of the minimum efficient scale is not as important as is this scale relative to the size of the total market. Minimum efficient scale varies enormously across industries. In one study, estimates of minimum efficient scale, as a percentage of industry capacity, ranged from 0.5 percent (fruit/vegetable canning) to 33 percent (gypsum products).[6] Globalization of markets increases effective market size, thereby reducing this entry barrier—for example, consider the size of American versus global automobile markets.

Reputation Effects   Potential entrants can be influenced by the reputations of existing firms in the industry for reactions to new entrants. In certain circumstances, it can pay

---

[5]This section provides a brief summary of the literature in economics on barriers to entry; it draws on S. M. Oster (1994), *Modern Competitive Analysis* (Oxford Press: New York).

[6]K. Lancaster and R. Dulaney (1979), *Modern Economics: Principles and Policy* (Rand McNally: New York), 211.

Excess Capacity at Alcoa

In 1940, Alcoa Aluminum lost an important antitrust case involving its production strategy of maintaining excess capacity. The judge ruled that he could think of no better "effective" deterrent to entry.

for an existing firm to react more aggressively than would be implied by considering only its immediate interests. For example, facing a new rival, the firm might engage in extensive price cutting to establish a reputation as a formidable competitor. Note, however, that threats by firms to cut prices if entry occurs sometimes lack credibility. If new firms actually enter, existing firms might not follow through with their threats because they would be harmed by their own price cuts. Thus, it can be reasonable for a potential entrant to ignore threats—if the entrant believes that incumbents are bluffing. We examine these considerations in greater detail in Chapter 9.

Excess Capacity   If firms with excess capacity cut production, they can be confronted with much higher average costs (depending on the slopes of their average cost curves). Also, firms with excess capacity are able to satisfy better the demands of new customers should they lower price and force a rival out of business. Potential competitors, therefore, may be less likely to enter when there is excess capacity in the industry because they anticipate more aggressive reactions on the part of incumbents.[7] Excess capacity frequently exists for completely innocuous reasons. For example, a firm facing cyclical production or anticipating growth has excess capacity over some time spans because it has invested in additional capacity to satisfy better peak demands. In other cases, excess capacity may be chosen specifically to deter entry.

Incumbent Advantages

Precommitment Contracts   Existing firms often have long-term contracts for raw materials, distribution outlets, shelf space, and delivery of the final product. These contracts can serve as a deterrent to entry, since they limit the opportunities for customers and suppliers to switch from incumbent firms to new entrants.

Licenses and Patents   Sometimes, entry is limited through government restrictions such as licensing requirements and patents. For instance, the number of doctors is limited effectively by state medical licensing requirements. This restriction allows doctors to charge higher prices than if entry were unrestricted. Regulators and licensed physicians justify such restrictions with arguments based on consumer protection. Yet, whether or not consumers benefit from stringent licensing is debatable—given that they pay higher prices.

Normal patent life is 17 years. Over this period, other firms are prohibited from copying the innovation; thus a patent provides a firm with potential market power. Patents also provide important incentives to innovate. From a practical standpoint, the effectiveness of a patent in blocking entry varies dramatically (some patents can be circumvented by clever design, for example). Historically, Sealed Air had derived its market

---

[7]Excess capacity can occur because of significant declines in industry demand. In this case, profits are likely to be low and entry will not be attractive. Our current discussion focuses on cases where incumbents are making economic profits and have excess capacity. These economic profits might not induce entry because of the fear of price cutting by incumbents.

Government Restrictions on Exit

Some regulators want to restrict companies from closing plants. These regulators appear motivated by concerns over people who lose their jobs when a company closes a plant. Restrictions on plant closings, however, are likely to reduce the desirability of entry into an industry—firms will be reluctant to enter an industry if they cannot exit easily when they are losing money. Thus, potential effects of government restrictions on exit are less vigorous competition in the affected industries, higher consumer prices, and lower levels of employment.

---

power from strong patent protection. Much of this protection was expiring by the late 1980s, leaving the firm vulnerable to increased competition.

Learning-Curve Effects   In Chapter 5, we discussed how average costs are reduced in some industries through production experience. As production experience accumulates, the firm learns how to lower unit costs. Learning-curve effects can result in new rivals having a cost disadvantage relative to existing firms. Whether these effects are important depends on whether the new entrants simply can copy the techniques learned by existing firms through their experience. In Sealed Air's case, costs had not been driven down by learning effects—indeed, entry was invited by Sealed Air's inefficient production.

Pioneering Brand Advantages   Sometimes, a firm benefits from being first in an industry. In some industries—over-the-counter drugs, for example—a satisfied customer might be reluctant to switch brands even if the price of a competing product is substantially lower. This tendency is likely to be strongest in *experience goods,* which have to be tried by the customer to ascertain quality. For instance, customers might hesitate to try a new pain reliever because they fear that it might not be as effective as their regular brand. Where quality can be judged by inspection prior to purchase, this advantage of incumbents is lower. Sometimes the incumbent's advantage with an experience good can be overcome by a new entrant through free samples, endorsements, or government certification. Each of these methods entails additional costs—these costs of overcoming incumbent advantages deter entry.

Exit Costs

Another important entry consideration centers on the costs of exit. In some industries, it is possible to "hit and run." For instance, forming a new company to seal asphalt driveways requires little investment in specialized equipment or training. A new firm can enter quickly when the profit potential is high and exit at low cost if profits decline. In other industries, especially those with specific assets, exit costs can be high. Here, firms bear significant costs, such as moving employees to new locations and liquidating plants and other assets when they decide to exit. High exit costs deter initial entry.

Monopoly

Effective barriers to entry limit the threat of competition and give incumbent firms market power. Although competitive markets are at one end of the spectrum, at the other end is *monopoly*—where there is but a single firm in the industry. Here, industry and firm demand curves are one and the same.

Figure 6.5 Monopoly

This figure illustrates the price and output decisions of a monopolist. In the example, demand is $P = 200 - Q$. Marginal costs are $10. The profit-maximizing output occurs at 95 units, where MR = MC. To sell this output, the firm charges a price of $105. The firm makes $95 per unit profit ($105 − $10) for a total profit of $9,025 ($95 × 95), as indicated by the shaded rectangle *abcd*. Some consumers are willing to pay more than the marginal cost of production, yet do not receive the product. The associated loss in potential gains from trade is pictured by the shaded triangle *cde*. The firm does not lower the price to sell to these consumers because it does not want to lower the price for other customers.

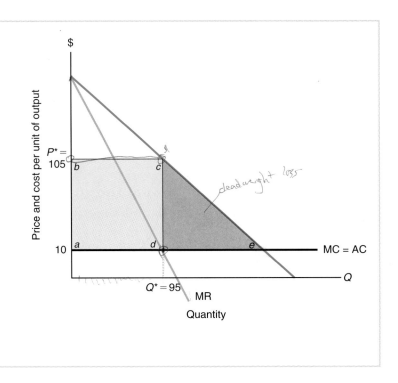

Profit Maximization Suppose that a monopolist charges the same price to all customers. (As discussed shortly, such a pricing policy might be motivated by either government regulation or the inability to prevent resale among customers; in Chapter 7, we relax this restriction.) The firm's objective is to choose the price-quantity combination along the demand curve that maximizes profits. This combination occurs where marginal revenue equals marginal cost.

For purposes of illustration, consider the following linear demand curve:

$$P = 200 - Q \qquad (6.4)$$

(Assume that marginal cost is constant at $10.) Recall from Chapter 4 that the marginal revenue curve for a linear demand curve is a line with the same intercept and twice the negative slope. Figure 6.5 displays the demand curve, marginal revenue curve, and marginal cost curve in this example. Optimal output occurs at 95 units—where MR = MC. To sell this output, the firm charges a price of $105. The firm makes $95 profit per unit ($105 − $10) for a total profit of $9,025 ($95 × 95); this is indicated by the shaded rectangle *abcd*.

As opposed to pure competition, monopolistic suppliers charge customers more than the marginal and average costs of production and distribution; the firm thus earns an economic profit. For instance, up until the time its patents expired, Sealed Air enjoyed a virtual monopoly in some markets and consequently generated substantial profits. Monopolies restrict output compared to competitive industries. In our example, if the industry were competitive, the market price would be $10 (marginal cost) and total quantity sold would be 190 units. (Pricing by firms with market power is discussed in additional detail in Chapter 7.)

Unexploited Gains from Trade   Given the monopolist's output and pricing choices, some consumers are willing to pay more than the marginal cost of production and distribution, yet do not purchase the product. Thus, not all gains from trade are exhausted. The associated loss in potential gains from trade is pictured by the shaded triangle *cde* in Figure 6.5. Consumers along this segment of the demand curve value the product at more than $10 but less than $105. The firm does not lower the price to sell to these consumers because it does not want to lower the price for other customers (recall that in this chapter we presume the firm charges the same price to all customers). From the firm's standpoint, any gain from selling to additional customers would be more than offset by the loss from lowering its price to all its customers.[8]

Monopolistic Competition

As the name implies, *monopolistic competition* is a market structure that is a hybrid between competition and monopoly. In this market structure, there are multiple firms that produce similar products. There is free exit from and entry into the industry. Yet competition does not eliminate market power because the firms sell differentiated products. Examples of such industries include toothpaste, golf balls, skis, tennis rackets, shampoo, and deodorant. For instance, although Colgate and Crest compete directly, many customers do not view these brands of toothpaste as perfect substitutes. These companies thus have some market power. New toothpaste firms are likely to enter the industry if the existing firms report large profits—there are no significant barriers to entry.

Monopolistic competition is similar to monopoly in that firms under both market structures face downward-sloping demand curves: A toothpaste company can raise its price without losing all sales. Given that the firms face downward-sloping demand curves, each strives to select the price-quantity combination that maximizes its profits. The output decision is based on the same analysis as for the pure monopolist—choose that output where MC = MR.

The difference between monopoly and monopolistic competition is that in monopolistic competition, economic profits invite entry. If a toothpaste with a new whitening formula is a hot seller, other companies will imitate the product. This entry will shift the

Monopolistic Competition in Golf Balls

There are many brands of golf balls. Some golfers view the balls as perfect substitutes and simply purchase the lowest-priced brand. Other golfers prefer one brand to another. For instance, they might believe one brand of ball flies farther or provides greater control than competing brands. These golfers are willing to pay a higher price for their favorite ball than for competing balls. However, they often will substitute if the price difference is more than a few dollars a dozen. Also, if a company develops some popular feature, like a larger number of dimples on the ball, the feature is typically copied by other companies within a short time period. Since a golf equipment company has a *monopoly* in producing its own brand, it has some market power. However, this power is limited given the *competition* in the industry.

---

[8]Economists frequently refer to these lost gains from trade as a *dead-weight loss*. This inefficiency (or *social cost*) is one reason why governments might pass regulations like antitrust laws to restrict the formation of monopolies. But these regulations also can be motivated by concerns about the higher prices that consumers pay when they face monopolistic suppliers. Although government regulation has the potential to reduce inefficiencies and wealth transfers from consumers to firms, it is important to keep in mind that government regulation is not costless. There are salaries for regulators and court costs, for instance. From a societal viewpoint, the costs of government regulation should be weighed against the benefits. These issues are discussed in greater detail in Chapter 20.

Figure 6.6   Monopolistic Competition

In monopolistic competition, firms sell differentiated products. This figure shows the demand curve for firm *i* in such an industry. The curve is downward-sloping. Similar to monopoly pricing, the firm selects the output where marginal revenue equals marginal cost. Monopolistic competition differs from monopoly in that abnormal profits will invite entry. Entry shifts the demand curve for the firm to the left (as some of the customers buy from the new firms). The firm makes no economic profits when price is equal to average cost. This condition occurs at price P_i^* and quantity Q_i^*.

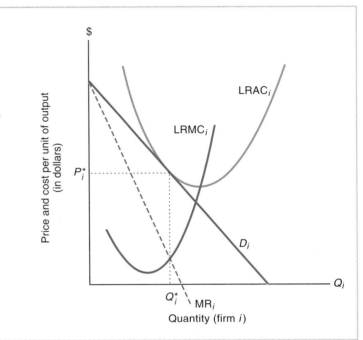

original firm's demand curve to the left and reduce profits. Zero economic profits exist when the demand curve is shifted to the point where average cost equals price. Figure 6.6 shows this condition.

Entry will tend to force profits to zero. Yet some brands continue to be more distinctive than others. Also, costs can vary because of differences in production techniques and inputs. It is possible for some firms to earn economic profits in monopolistic competition.[9]

Oligopoly

Within *oligopolistic markets,* only a few firms produce most of the output. Examples of oligopolistic industries include automobiles and steel during the 1950s. These industries had important scale economies and other substantial entry barriers. In 1995, the top four cereal makers in the United States produced about 90 percent of industry output, while the top eight accounted for virtually all production. Products may or may not be differentiated. Firms can earn substantial profits. These profits are not reduced through new entry because of effective entry barriers. Yet as we shall see, economic profits sometimes can be eliminated in oligopolistic industries through competition among the existing firms.

In our analysis of other market structures, we assume that firms take the prices of their competitors as given. A firm was not expected to respond to announcements of changes in prices by rival firms. This assumption certainly is reasonable in the case of competitive

---

[9]Monopolistic competition does not exhaust all gains from trade for two reasons. First, as in monopoly, the firms do not sell to all consumers who value the product at above marginal cost. Second, firms do not operate at the bottom of their average cost curves (see Figure 6.6). Lower average cost would be obtained with fewer firms, each producing more output. Nonetheless, regulation to address these inefficiencies is unlikely to be effective. Consumers value product differentiation and are arguably better off with more variety at slightly higher average cost than with lower variety produced at lower average cost. Second, with few entry barriers, the market power of firms is unlikely to be great.

markets with many small firms, as well as in the case of monopoly with [...] firm. But this assumption rarely is valid within oligopolistic industrie[...] when American Airlines considers lowering its prices on particular rout[...] must be concerned about whether United Airlines and its other competitors will follow suit. In fact, firms in oligopolistic industries ordinarily will be quite concerned about how their rivals will react to most major policy decisions, be they advertising campaigns or product design decisions. Decision making within these industries requires *strategic thinking*. Decision makers must realize that competitors are rational parties operating in their own self-interest. Thus, it is important for decision makers to place themselves in their rivals' positions and consider how they might react. (This basic principle, which we now examine briefly, is developed more completely in Chapter 9.[10])

Nash Equilibrium

To analyze oligopolies, we need an underlying principle to define an equilibrium when rival firms make decisions that explicitly take each other's behavior into account. Previously, we used the concept that a market is in equilibrium when firms are doing the best they can given their circumstances and have no reason to change price or output. For example, in a competitive equilibrium, there is no reason for entry or exit (existing firms are making "normal" profits). No existing firm has any reason to change its output level (all are producing where $MC = MR = P^*$ and inventories are stable at their desired levels).

We can apply this same basic idea to oligopolistic markets with minor modification. In the following analysis, a firm does the best it can, given what its rivals are doing. In doing so, the firm anticipates that other firms will respond to any action it takes by doing the best they can as well. Actions are *noncooperative* in that each firm makes decisions that maximize its profits, given the actions of the other firms. The firms do not collude to maximize joint profits. An equilibrium exists when each firm is doing the best it can, given the actions of its rivals. Economists call this a *Nash equilibrium* for Nobel laureate John Nash who first developed these general concepts.

To illustrate this approach, assume a simple setting: There are two firms in an industry—a *duopoly*. Each independently chooses a price for an identical product. The firms either choose a high price or a low price. The payoffs are given in Figure 6.7. (The entry on the upper left in each cell is for WonCo, while the entry on the lower right is for TuInc.) For example, if both firms charge a high price, WonCo's profits are $400 and TuInc's profits are $200.[11]

The equilibrium is for WonCo to charge a high price and TuInc to charge a low price. Any other combination is unstable: Given the action of one of the firms, the other firm has the incentive to change its price. For instance, if both firms charge a high price, it is in the interests of TuInc to lower its price—its profits go from $200 to $250. The other combinations of WonCo charging a low price and TuInc a high price and both firms charging a low price are similarly unstable: Each firm has an incentive to alter its price given the other firm's choice. A Nash equilibrium is self-enforcing. If WonCo charges a

---

[10]This chapter presents a basic introduction to game theory. The material provides sufficient background for the game theory applications found in subsequent parts of the book (these are in the appendices of several chapters). Chapter 9 extends this introduction of game theory and discusses in more detail how managers might use this theory as a tool in decision making. Readers interested in a more detailed treatment of game theory should read Chapter 9.

[11]The profits differ due to differences in the underlying production costs.

Figure 6.7 Nash Equilibrium

In this example, there are two firms in an industry—WonCo and TuInc. Each independently chooses a price for an identical product. The firms either choose a high price or a low price. The payoffs are given in the table (the upper-left entry in a cell displays the profits for WonCo, the lower right shows the profits for TuInc). The equilibrium is for WonCo to charge a high price and TuInc to charge a low price—the shaded cell. Any other combination is unstable: That is, given the action of one of the firms, the other firm has the incentive to deviate. This equilibrium is called a *Nash equilibrium*.

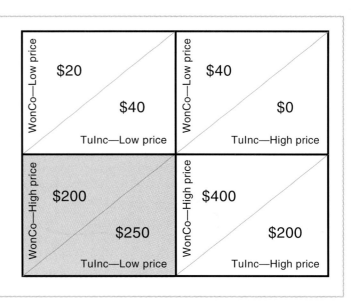

high price, it is optimal for TuInc to charge a low price. Similarly, if TuInc charges a low price, it is optimal for WonCo to charge a high price. Given the choice of one firm, there is no reason for the other to alter its strategy.

In this example, the Nash equilibrium is not the outcome that maximizes the joint profits of the two companies. Combined profits would be higher if both firms charged a high price. Conceptually, the combined profits under this pricing policy could be split in a manner that would make both firms better off than in the Nash equilibrium. For instance, the combined profits of $600 could be split, with each firm receiving $300. As this example illustrates, noncooperative equilibria are not necessarily Pareto-efficient. (Since the potential gains from trade are not exhausted, it is often the case that one or more firms can be made better off, without making other firms worse off, by changing the joint decisions.)

Output Competition

The first major analysis of oligopoly was published by Augustine Cournot in 1838. To illustrate his model, suppose again that there are only two firms in the industry and that they produce identical products. In the *Cournot model,* each firm treats the *output* level of its competitor as fixed and then decides how much to produce. In equilibrium, neither firm has an incentive to change its output level, given the other firm's choice. (Thus, this is a Nash equilibrium.)

Suppose the duopolists face the following total industry demand:

$$P = 100 - Q \tag{6.5}$$

where $Q = Q_A + Q_B$. For simplicity, assume that both firms have marginal costs of zero: $MC_A = MC_B = 0$. Each firm takes the other firm's output as fixed. Thus, the anticipated demand curve for firm i ($i =$ A or B) is

$$P_i = (100 - \overline{Q}_j) - Q_i \tag{6.6}$$

Figure 6.8 Cournot Equilibrium

The duopolists in this example face the total industry demand curve, $P = 100 - Q$, where Q is the sum of the two outputs. Both firms face a marginal cost of zero. The figure shows the reaction curves for each firm. The reaction curve indicates firm i's optimal output given the output choice of firm j (i, j = A or B). The Cournot equilibrium occurs where the two reaction curves cross. Each firm produces 33.33 units. The market price is $33.34. The output for the firms is lower and the profits are greater than in the competitive equilibrium. The output for the firms is greater and the profits are lower than in the collusive (monopoly) equilibrium.

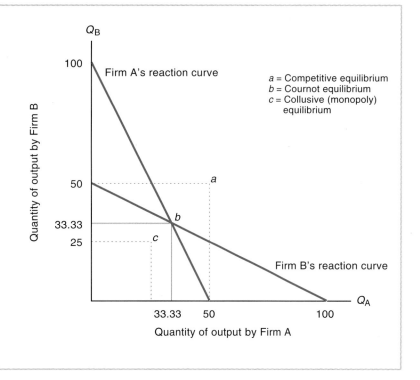

a = Competitive equilibrium
b = Cournot equilibrium
c = Collusive (monopoly) equilibrium

Quantity of output by Firm A

where $\overline{Q}_j$ = expected output of the other firm. The marginal revenue for firm i is[12]

$$\text{MR}_i = (100 - \overline{Q}_j) - 2Q_i \qquad (6.7)$$

Firm i's profits are maximized by setting marginal revenue equal to marginal cost (in this case, zero). Doing so, and rearranging the expression, yields the following *reaction curve:*

$$Q_i = 50 - 0.5Q_j \qquad (6.8)$$

The reaction curve indicates firm i's optimal output given the output choice of firm j. Both firms have the same reaction curve in this example, except that the subscripts are reversed.

Equilibrium occurs where the two curves cross. At these output levels, each firm is maximizing profit given the other firm's output choice. Neither firm has an incentive to alter its output. The equilibrium is pictured in Figure 6.8. In equilibrium, each firm produces 33 units for a total output of 66 units; the price is $33.34. This output level is lower than in a competitive market. With competition, total output would be 100 units and the price would be zero (where $P^* = \text{MC}$). In the Cournot equilibrium, firms make economic profits: price is $33.34, average costs are zero. Each firm thus reports profits of $1,110.89. This profit is lower than the two firms could obtain if they directly colluded and jointly produced the monopolistic output of 50 units (for example, 25 units per firm). With effective collusion, joint profits would be $2,500 rather than

---

[12]Recall that marginal revenue for a linear demand curve is a line with the same intercept, but twice the negative slope.

Figure 6.9 Comparison of Prices and Outputs among Collusive, Cournot, and Competitive Equilibria

In this example, the total industry demand curve is $P = 100 - Q$. Marginal cost is zero. The figure shows the price-quantity outputs for the industry under collusive, Cournot, and competitive equilibria. The output is smallest and the price is highest for the collusive equilibrium. The output is largest and the price is smallest for the competitive equilibrium.

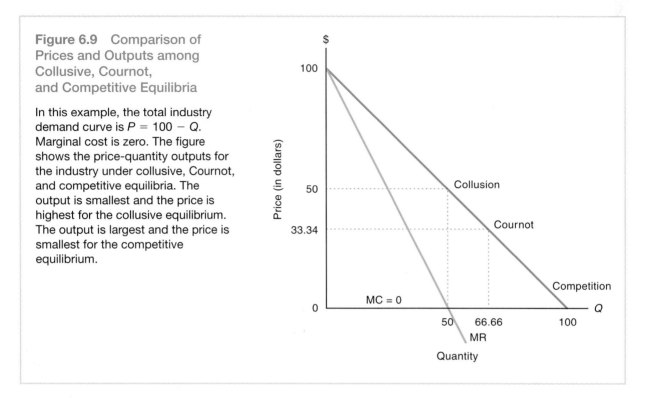

$2,221.78. Figure 6.9 displays the three price-quantity outcomes using the original industry demand curve. (This model can be extended readily to more than two firms. The same general results hold: As the number of firms grows, outcomes approach those of a competitive market.)

Price Competition

In the Cournot model, firms focus on choosing output levels. An alternative possibility is that firms might focus on choosing product price.[13] Here, the Nash equilibrium is for both firms to choose a price equal to marginal cost—the competitive outcome. To see why, suppose one of the firms chooses a price, $P' > $ MC. In this case, it is optimal for the rival firm to charge a price just below P' to capture all industry sales. (Since we assume the firms' products are identical, customers buy the product from the firm that offers the lowest price.) Given that the second firm charges a price just below P', it is now optimal for the first firm to charge a slightly lower price. This process continues; only when price equals marginal cost does neither firm have an incentive to lower price. (Lowering price further would result in selling below cost, thus generating a loss.) Of course, both firms would like to devise a way of avoiding competition and capturing higher profits. Yet as we discuss below, fostering cooperation can be difficult—and in certain cases, illegal.

[13]This situation often is referred to as the Bertrand model. Bertrand was a French economist who wrote a short note almost 50 years after Cournot's work was published arguing that in some markets, producers set prices rather than quantities.

Airline Fare Wars

Firms in oligopolistic industries sometimes engage in intense price competition to their mutual detriment. An example is the US airline industry in the early 1990s. During this period, the major airlines, including American, United, Delta, and Northwest, repeatedly entered fare wars that lowered the price of air travel for consumers and thus lowered the combined profits of the industry. For instance, one company would lower its summer fares in the hope of gaining new passengers. Invariably, the price reduction was matched by other rivals within hours. Outside analysts generally agreed that the firms in the industry lost profits through these price cuts. Indeed, many of these companies reported losses during the period.

Empirical Evidence

There are various economic models of oligopoly. We have presented but two of them to illustrate that economic theory does not make unambiguous predictions about what to expect within such industries. Some models yield outcomes close to pure competition—firms sell at marginal cost and make no economic profits. Other models yield outcomes closer to pure monopoly. What actually occurs in specific oligopolistic markets is an empirical issue. Available evidence suggests that oligopolies result in less output than competitive markets and that firms earn economic profits—at least in some industries.[14] Firms sometimes compete on price, to each other's detriment, and typically earn less in aggregate than a monopolist could.

Cooperation and the Prisoners' Dilemma

As we have discussed, in oligopolistic industries it is in the private interests of firms to find ways to cooperate and capture more profits than through competition. In principle, firms are most profitable if they effectively collude and act as a monopolist in jointly setting price and output for the industry. Collusion maximizes joint profits, which then can be divided among the firms in the industry. Many governments understand these incentives and have passed a variety of antitrust laws to limit firms' ability to engage in fixing prices. These laws are designed to lower the prices consumers pay for products. Some of the more restrictive of these laws have been adopted in the United States. Internationally, firms tend to have more latitude in forming cooperative agreements to increase profits—for example, consider the OPEC cartel.[15]

Prisoners' Dilemma   Even when free to cooperate, firms find that cooperation is not always easy to achieve. Individual firms have incentives to "cheat" and not adhere to output and price agreements. This incentive can be illustrated by the well-known *prisoners' dilemma*. In the original prisoners' dilemma, there are two suspects; hence, suppose Avi Wasserman and Bea Haefner are arrested and charged with a crime. Police have insufficient evidence to convict the suspects unless one of them confesses. The police place Avi

---

[14]D. Carlton and J. Perloff (1990), *Modern Industrial Organization* (HarperCollins: New York), Chapter 10, discusses some of the relevant empirical literature.

[15]In smaller countries, much of the local production of key products is exported. In this case, it can be in the countries' interests to allow the formation of cartels. Ultimately, consumers pay higher prices and there are inefficiencies. However, many of these costs are imposed on people in other countries.

Figure 6.10 Prisoners' Dilemma

In the prisoners' dilemma, there are two suspects: Suppose Avi Wasserman and Bea Haefner are arrested and charged with a crime. The police do not have sufficient evidence to convict the suspects unless one of them confesses. The police place the suspects in separate rooms and ask them to confess. If neither confesses, they are convicted of a minor crime (for example, loitering) and are sentenced to 2 months. If both confess, they spend 12 months in jail. However, if one confesses and the other does not, the confessor is released immediately but the other is sentenced to 18 months in jail—12 for the crime and 6 for obstructing justice. The payoffs in terms of jail time faced by each individual are displayed. Each entry in the table lists the jail sentences for Avi and Bea, respectively. The Nash equilibrium is for both suspects to confess—the shaded cell. Given the payoffs, it is always in the *individual interests* of each suspect to confess (taking the action of the other party as given).

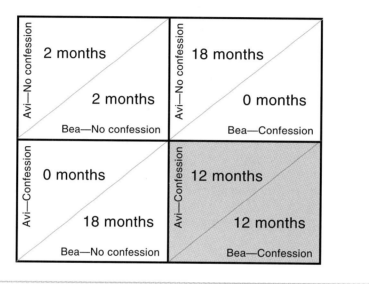

and Bea in separate rooms and try to get them to confess. If neither confesses, they are convicted of less serious crimes and are sentenced to only 2 months in jail. If both confess, they spend 12 months in jail. However, if one confesses but the other does not, the confessor is released while the other is sentenced to 18 months in jail—12 for the crime and 6 for obstructing justice. The payoffs in terms of jail time faced by each individual are displayed in Figure 6.10.

The Nash equilibrium is for both suspects to confess. Given these payoffs, it is always in the *individual interests* of each suspect to confess, taking the action of the other party as given. If Avi does not confess, Bea is set free by confessing. Alternatively, if Avi confesses, Bea reduces her jail sentence from 18 to 12 months by also confessing. Either way, it is in Bea's interests to confess—confessing is a *dominant strategy*. Since the payoffs are symmetrical, it also is optimal for Avi to confess. Although it is in the individual interests of each party to confess, it is clearly in their *joint interests* not to confess. By not confessing, each only serves 2 months in jail, compared to 12 months if both confess. The prisoners' dilemma suggests that any agreement for neither to confess is likely to break down when they make their individual choices unless there is some mechanism to

Figure 6.11 Cartel's Dilemma

Two firms, AVInc and BeaCo, attempt to form a cartel. If both firms restrict output, prices are high and each firm's profit is $500. If both cheat on the cartel and increase output, price will be low and each firm's profit is $200. If one firm expands output while the other restricts output, the market price will be at an intermediate level; the firm with the high output will make $600 (because of the increased sales), but the other firm will only make $150 (because of the lower price). These payoffs are displayed. The Nash equilibrium is for both firms to increase output—the shaded cell. Given the payoffs, it is always in the interest of each firm to increase output (taking the output of the other firm as given).

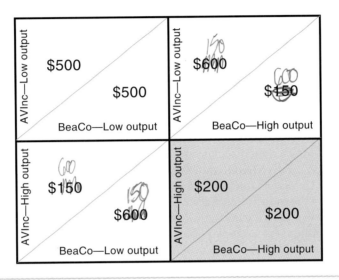

enforce their joint commitment not to confess. (One such mechanism might be the Mob: Both suspects have incentives not to confess if they expect to be executed for providing evidence to the police.)

Cartels   *Cartels* consist of formal agreements to cooperate in setting price and output levels. (These activities are generally illegal in the United States.) Firms trying to maintain cartels can face a problem like the prisoners' dilemma—we might call it the *cartel's dilemma.* Members can agree to restrict output to increase joint profits. However, individual firms have incentives to cheat. If all other firms restrict output, prices will not be affected significantly by the extra output of one firm. However, that firm's profits will increase from selling additional output at the cartel-maintained high price. But if all firms react to these incentives by increasing output, the cartel breaks down. Actual cartels often unravel because of such incentives. This outcome is pictured in Figure 6.11, which displays the payoffs for two firms attempting to form a cartel. It is in their joint interests to restrict output. Yet, as in the prisoners' dilemma, both firms have individual incentives to renege and increase output. The Nash equilibrium is for each to increase output.

A cartel can persist if it can impose sufficient penalties on cheaters—like the Mob in the prisoners' dilemma. But for these penalties to be effective, cartel members must be able to observe (or reliably infer) that a firm has cheated. To the extent that cartel members expect to interact on a *repeated basis,* there are greater incentives to cooperate.

Collusion in the Lysine Industry

Mark Whitacre was a high-ranking executive at Archer Daniels Midland Corporation (ADM). He has accused his former employer of engaging in price fixing. Lysine is an amino acid derived from corn used in swine and poultry feed to promote growth. ADM entered the lysine market in 1991. Prior to that time, the market had been dominated by two Japanese companies. ADM quickly gained market share. However, with the competition, the price of lysine fell from about $1.30 per pound to $.60 per pound. According to Whitacre, ADM executives began discussions in 1992 with their Japanese competitors about how it would be in their mutual self-interest to collude and fix prices. Collectively, the competitors were forgoing millions of dollars of profit per month because of the competition among the three companies. Whitacre indicates that a favorite saying at ADM is:

The competitor is our friend, and the customer is our enemy.

As of 1995, ADM was currently under investigation for price fixing. In addition, it faced numerous lawsuits over the issue.

Source: M. Whitacre, as told to R. Henkoff (1995), "My Life as a Corporate Mole for the FBI," *Fortune Magazine* (September 4), 52–62.

Repeated interaction also increases incentives to invest in developing effective enforcement mechanisms to limit cheating. Potentially, these incentives can be strong enough to resolve the cartel's dilemma. In general, cooperation is easier to enforce if the number of firms in the industry is small: It is easier to identify and punish cheaters.

Even when firms are not permitted to form cartels, there may be ways of cooperating to increase profits. For example, over time, a firm might become known as a price leader. Such a firm changes prices in the face of new demand or cost conditions in a way that approximates what a cartel would do. Other firms follow the price changes, thus acting like members of a cartel. Individually, firms still can have short-run incentives to cheat (for example, reducing price to get more sales). However, firms might resist this short-run temptation to foster cooperation in the long run and hence obtain higher long-run profits.[16]

Another potential mechanism to foster cooperation is the structure of contracts with buyers employed by firms in the industry. *Most-favored-nation clauses* provide buyers with guarantees that the seller will not sell to another buyer at a lower price. These clauses reduce incentives of sellers to lower the price for one buyer because that same price concession would have to be offered to other buyers as well. *Meeting-the-competition clauses* guarantee that a seller will meet the price of a competitor. Such a clause makes it difficult for firms to cheat on an agreement not to lower price since price concessions are more likely to be brought to each other's attention by customers.

Our discussion of these strategic interactions among rivals in output markets is meant only to provide a basic introduction to these issues. A more extensive analysis is provided in Chapter 9.

Summary

A *market* consists of all firms and individuals who are willing and able to buy or sell a particular product. These parties include those currently engaged in buying and selling the product, as well as *potential entrants. Market structure* refers to the basic characteristics of the market environment, including: (1) the number and size of buyers, sellers,

---

[16]Indeed, economists have shown that within any long-term relationship, with no specified ending date, cooperation is a *possible equilibrium*—the parties need not succumb to the cartel's dilemma. We discuss this issue in more detail in Chapter 9 and in the appendix to Chapter 10.

and potential entrants, (2) the degree of product differentiation, (3) the amount and cost of information about product price and quality, and (4) the conditions for entry and exit.

Competitive markets are characterized by four basic conditions: A large number of potential buyers and sellers; product homogeneity; rapid, low-cost dissemination of information; and free entry into and exit from the market. In competitive markets, individual buyers and sellers take the market price of the product as given: They have no control over price. Firms thus view their demand curves as horizontal. The firm's short-run supply curve is that portion of its short-run marginal cost curve above short-run average variable cost. The long-run supply curve is that portion of its long-run marginal cost curve above long-run average cost. In a competitive equilibrium, firms make no economic profits. Production is efficient in that firms produce at their minimum long-run average cost. Firms in competitive industries must move rapidly to take advantage of transitory opportunities. They also must strive for efficient production in order to survive. Some firms in the industry can employ resources that give them a competitive advantage (for example, an extremely talented manager). Yet in such cases, any excess returns often go to the factor of production responsible for the particular advantage, rather than to the firm's owners.

Although the competitive model provides a useful description of the interaction between buyers and sellers for many industries, there are others where firms have substantial market power—prices are affected materially by the output decisions of individual firms. Market power can exist when there are substantial *barriers to entry* into the industry. Expectations about incumbent reactions, incumbent advantages, and exit costs all can serve as entry barriers.

The extreme case of a firm with market power is *monopoly*, where the industry consists of only one firm. Here, industry and firm demand curves are one and the same. In contrast to competitive markets, consumers pay more than marginal cost and the firm earns economic profits. Output is restricted from competitive levels. With a monopoly, not all the potential gains from trade are exhausted.

Monopolistic competition is a hybrid between competition and monopoly. It is like monopoly in that firms under both market structures face downward-sloping demand curves. Market power comes from differentiated products. Examples include the toothpaste, golf ball, tennis racket, and shampoo markets. The analyses of output and pricing policies are similar in the two cases. The difference between monopoly and monopolistic competition is that in monopolistic competition, economic profits invite entry that limits profits.

In *oligopolistic markets,* only a few firms account for most production. Products may or may not be differentiated. Firms can earn substantial profits. However, these profits can be eliminated through competition among existing firms in the industry. To analyze output and pricing decisions in oligopolistic industries, we use the concept of a *Nash equilibrium:* A *Nash equilibrium* exists when each firm is doing the best it can given the actions of its rivals. In the *Cournot model,* each firm treats the *output* level of its competitor as fixed and then decides how much to produce. In equilibrium, firms make economic profits. However, these profits are not as large as would be made if the firms effectively colluded and posted the monopoly price. Other models of oligopoly yield different equilibria. For instance, one model based on *price competition* yields the competitive solution: Price equals marginal cost with no economic profits. Economic theory makes no clear-cut prediction about the behavior of firms in oligopolistic industries. Available evidence suggests that in some oligopolistic industries, firms restrict output from competitive levels and hence capture some economic profits.

It is in the economic interests of firms in oligopolistic industries to find ways to cooperate, thereby capturing higher profits. Even when firms are free to cooperate, effective cooperation is not always easy to achieve. Individual firms have incentives to deviate from agreed-on outputs and prices. This incentive is illustrated by the *prisoners' dilemma*. This model highlights incentives that can cause cartels to be unstable. However, firms sometimes can cooperate successfully when they can impose penalties on noncooperative firms. Cooperation also can be sustained through the incentives provided by long-run, *repeated relationships*.

Suggested Readings	

A. Dixit and B. Nalebuff (1991), *Thinking Strategically* (Norton: New York).

G. Stigler (1987), *The Theory of Price* (Macmillan: New York), Chapter 3.

R. Pindyck and D. Rubinfeld (1992), *Microeconomics* (Macmillan: New York), Chapters 8–13.

Review Questions

6–1. What four basic conditions characterize a competitive market?

6–2. The short-run marginal cost of the Ohio Bag Company is $2Q$. Price is $100. The company operates in a competitive industry. Currently, the company is producing 40 units per period. What is the optimal short-run output? Calculate the profits that Ohio Bag is losing through suboptimal output.

6–3. Should a company ever produce an output if the managers know it will lose money over the period? Explain.

6–4. What are economic profits? Does a firm in a competitive industry earn long-run economic profits? Explain.

6–5. The Johnson Oil Company has just hired the best manager in the industry. Should the owners of the company anticipate economic profits? Explain.

6–6. A Michigan court ruled in the 1990s that General Motors did not have the right to close a particular Michigan plant and lay people off. Do you think this ruling benefited the people of Michigan? Explain.

6–7. The Suji Corporation has a monopoly in a particular chemical market. The industry demand curve is $P = 1,000 - 5Q$. Marginal cost is $3Q$. What is Suji's profit-maximizing output and price? Calculate the corresponding profits.

6–8. Assume the industry demand for a product is: $P = 1,000 - 20Q$. Assume that the marginal cost of product is $10 per unit.
  a. What price and output will occur under pure competition? What price and output will occur under pure monopoly (assume one price is charged to all customers)?
  b. Draw a graph that shows the lost gains from trade that result from having a monopoly.

6–9. In 1981, the United States negotiated an agreement with the Japanese. The agreement called for Japanese auto firms to limit exports to the United States. The Japanese government was charged with helping make sure the agreement was met by Japanese firms. Were the Japanese firms necessarily hurt by this limited ability to export? Explain.

6–10. Compare the industry output and price in a Cournot versus a competitive equilibrium. Do firms earn economic profits in the Cournot model? Does economic theory predict that firms always earn economic profits in oligopolistic industries? Explain. What does the empirical evidence indicate?

6–11. What is a Nash equilibrium? Explain why a joint confession is the Nash equilibrium in the prisoners' dilemma.

Chapter 7
Pricing with Market Power

Beyond.com began selling software over the Internet in 1994. Initially, the company consisted of three employees working above a barbershop in Menlo Park, California. By 1999, it had grown tremendously, becoming a publicly traded company selling commercial, off-the-shelf software to individuals, corporations, and government agencies.

Customers purchase products from Beyond.com through its cyber store. In 1999, approximately 30,000 software stock-keeping units (SKUs) were available for online purchase with more than 3,300 SKUs available for immediate, electronic delivery—including software from such major publishers as Adobe, Lotus, Microsoft, and Sun.

Beyond.com sells popular software at discount prices. A visit to its cyber store in 1999 would have revealed many interesting pricing decisions. Consider the following examples: (1) *Quicken Deluxe,* a leading financial software, is priced at $54.97 for MacIntosh users, and $59.95 for Windows users. Windows' customers, however, could obtain a $30 rebate from the manufacturer, bringing the net price to $29.95; no rebate is offered to Mac users. (2) *Encarta Encyclopedia 99* is priced at $35; but after a $25 rebate from Microsoft and a $10 rebate from Beyond.com, it is free. (3) *Expedia Streets* and *Expedia Trip Planner,* two software products from Microsoft, are offered only as a *bundle* at a price of $35 (before rebate). (4) Additional price discounts are given to large-volume purchasers in the government and corporate sectors.

Pricing is a key managerial decision. These examples illustrate some of the complexities associated with product pricing. For example, how should managers set their basic prices? Why do firms use coupons and rebates? Why are some customers charged higher prices for the same product than others? Why do firms bundle products? Why would a firm ever give its product away for free? Why do some firms offer volume discounts?

This chapter presents a basic analysis of pricing with market power and provides answers to these and related questions. The remainder of the chapter is organized as follows. First, we discuss the underlying objective of pricing decisions. Next, we analyze the benchmark case where the firm charges the same price to all customers. Subsequently, we consider more complex pricing policies. The chapter ends with a brief discussion of several other issues, including multiperiod considerations, strategic interactions, legal and implementation issues.

Pricing Objective

A firm has *market power* when it faces a downward-sloping demand curve. Firms with market power can raise price without losing all customers to competitors. The ultimate objective is to choose a pricing policy that maximizes the firm's value. We continue with the standard economic analysis in which managers seek to maximize profits over a single period. Although managers actually seek to maximize the present value of all future profits, if the business setting is expected to be stationary, these problems are equivalent. Later in this chapter, we discuss how concerns about future profits can affect the current pricing decision. Nonetheless, our single-period analysis provides useful insights into pricing decisions.

Figure 7.1 pictures a firm's demand curve for and its marginal cost of producing the product. The demand curve reflects what consumers are willing to pay for the product. Only in quite special cases is it in the interests of the firm to sell the product at below marginal cost: It can do better by not producing the product. (Later in this chapter, we examine multiperiod considerations that might prompt firms to set current price below marginal cost.) Thus, the maximum potential gains from trade are given by the shaded triangle. If the firm were to sell the product at marginal cost, all the gains would go to consumers in the form of *consumer surplus.* Consumer surplus is defined as the difference between what the consumer is willing to pay for a product and what the consumer actually pays when buying it. Profit-maximizing managers try to devise pricing policies that capture as much of the available gains from trade as possible: The managerial ideal would be to capture all the potential consumer surplus as company profit.

We begin by reviewing the benchmark case where the firm charges all customers the same price. In this case (which was introduced in Chapters 4 and 6), the firm captures some, but not all, of the potential gains from trade. Subsequently, we consider more complex pricing policies.

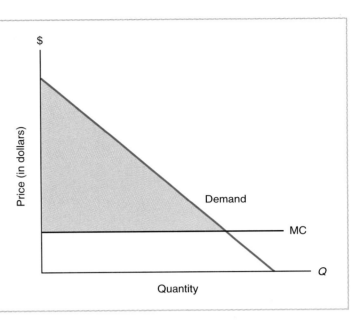

Figure 7.1 Pricing with Market Power

The demand curve reflects what consumers are willing to pay for the product. It typically is not in the firm's interest to sell the product below marginal cost, since it can do better by not producing the product. Thus, the maximum potential gains from trade are given by the shaded triangle. The firm's objective is to select a pricing policy that maximizes its share of the gains from trade and thus firm profit.

Benchmark Case: Single Price per Unit
Profit Maximization

Suppose that Beyond.com sells a software product called *Checkware*. It purchases the product at $10 from the manufacturer and selects a retail price to post on the Internet. All customers buy at this price independently of the quantity purchased. Beyond.com has no other incremental costs and faces the following demand curve:

$$P = 85 - 0.5Q \tag{7.1}$$

where P is price and Q is quantity (in thousands of units).

What price should Beyond.com select to maximize profits?

Chapter 6 shows that profits are maximized by selecting a price-output combination in which marginal revenue equals marginal cost. Marginal revenue is $85 - Q$, and marginal cost is $10 in this example.[1] Thus the optimal quantity and price are 75 and $47.50, respectively. Profits are $2,812,500. Figure 7.2 illustrates the solution graphically.

We focus on this example to provide a number of important insights. It is important to note, however, that this analysis simplifies the pricing problem in at least four important ways. First, all consumers are charged the same unit price, regardless of the quantity purchased. Thus more complicated pricing strategies are not considered. Second, the firm sells only one product; thus interactions among products are not considered. Third, the demand curve is for a single period. The analysis focuses on maximizing single-period profits and abstracts from longer-term considerations (for example, how pricing this period might affect either demand or costs in future periods). Fourth,

---

[1]For expositional simplicity, we assume marginal cost is constant; in the more general case, one also requires information about the marginal cost function.

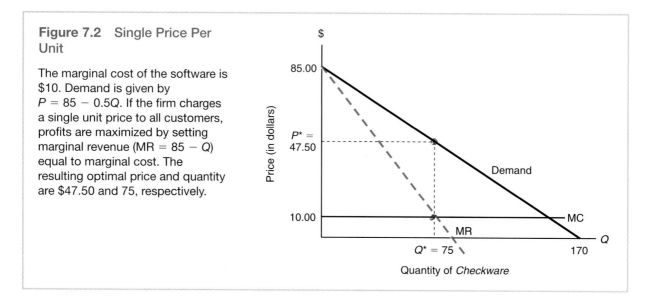

Figure 7.2 Single Price Per Unit

The marginal cost of the software is $10. Demand is given by $P = 85 - 0.5Q$. If the firm charges a single unit price to all customers, profits are maximized by setting marginal revenue (MR = $85 - Q$) equal to marginal cost. The resulting optimal price and quantity are $47.50 and 75, respectively.

the demand curve assumes that the prices of competing products are constant no matter what price Beyond.com charges. In some markets, there is likely to be interaction in the pricing decisions of firms within the industry. Later in this chapter, we consider the implications of relaxing these assumptions.

Relevant Costs   Managers maximize profits by setting marginal cost equal to marginal revenue. As emphasized throughout this book, sunk costs are irrelevant for the pricing-output decision—only *incremental costs* matter. Suppose that Beyond.com previously had spent $100,000 for developing its cyber store and establishing and promoting its web site. While Beyond.com hopes to generate enough profits to offset this initial investment, this expenditure is sunk and hence is irrelevant for its current pricing decisions.

Also as discussed earlier, it is important for managers to focus on *opportunity costs* not accounting costs. For instance, suppose that Beyond.com has some *Checkware* packages in inventory that it had previously purchased from the manufacturer at $18. This historical cost is not relevant for the current pricing decision. Rather what is important is the current cost for replacing the inventory—$10.[2]

Price Sensitivity   Additional insights into a monopolist's pricing decision can be developed using the concept of price elasticity introduced in Chapter 4. Recall that the price elasticity η is a measure of price sensitivity. The higher the price elasticity, the more sensitive is the quantity demanded to price changes. With some algebra, it is easy to show that the monopolist's optimal pricing policy of setting marginal revenue equal to marginal cost can be rewritten as

$$P^* = MC^*/[1 - 1/\eta^*] \tag{7.2}$$

where P^* is the profit-maximizing price, $MC^* =$ marginal cost, and η^* is the elasticity of demand, both at the optimal output level.

[2]Suppose that a package was sold for $16 that originally cost $18. The company reports an accounting loss of $2. However, if the company has to pay $10 to replace the unit in inventory, it actually has an economic profit of $6.

Recall that the elasticity of demand ranges between 0 (totally inelastic) and ∞ (infinitely elastic). Market power decreases as demand becomes more elastic.

No firm should operate on the inelastic portion of its demand curve ($\eta < 1$). With inelastic demand, total revenue increases with an increase in price. As price is increased, fewer units are sold and production costs fall. With an increase in revenue and a reduction in costs, profits must increase with price: Hence the maximum profit cannot lie on the inelastic portion of the demand curve. Thus, we are assured that $\eta^* > 1$, and the optimal price is greater than marginal cost.

If a firm has substantial market power, its demand will be less elastic and the markup over marginal cost will be high. In contrast, if the firm has limited market power (for example, there are many good substitutes), elasticity will be high and the markup low.

In our *Checkware* example, the markup is $37.50 ($47.50 − $10). The elasticity at the optimal price-quantity combination is 1.27 (using the technique from the appendix of Chapter 4). Figure 7.3 compares this case with that of a more elastic demand curve for another software product—*Illustrator*[3]:

$$P = 42.50 - 0.25Q \tag{7.3}$$

With this demand curve, the optimal output and price are 65 and $26.25, respectively. The elasticity at this combination is 1.62 compared to 1.27 in the first example. Correspondingly, the markup is lower ($16.25 versus $37.50).

Estimating the Profit-Maximizing Price

Economic theory suggests that managers should price so that marginal revenue equals marginal cost. One practical problem in applying this principle is that managers often do not have precise information about their demand curves and thus their marginal revenue (Chapter 4 discusses methods of estimating demand). Thus, depending on the circumstances, policies like cost-plus or markup pricing (discussed below) can serve as useful approximations or rules of thumb in the absence of better information.

Linear Approximation   One technique that can be employed with limited information is the *linear approximation method*. This method requires that the pricing manager have estimates of the current price, the current quantity sold, the quantity sold if the price is changed (say by 10 percent), and the marginal cost of production.

 Suppose in our example that Beyond.com's pricing manager, Sally McGraw, currently is pricing the product at $70 and is selling 30 units per period. Sally estimates that if she lowers her price by $5 to $65, she will sell 40 units. This estimate might be based on knowledge about what competitors are charging for the same product, results from past experiences in altering prices, and so on. This information gives her two points on her demand curve. If she assumes the demand curve is linear, she can solve for it. The estimated slope of the line is $(65 - 70)/(40 - 30) = -0.5$. To solve for the intercept, she would substitute the current price and quantity into the equation for a line ($P = a + bQ$) with slope equal to -0.5:

$$\$70 = a - 0.5(30)$$

---

[3]For both demand curves, the quantity sold is 170 when price is zero; however, quantity declines more rapidly with price increases in the second case.

Figure 7.3   Price Sensitivity and Optimal Markup

The optimal price markup above marginal cost depends on the elasticity of demand. The optimal markup decreases with the elasticity of demand. The demand curve for *Checkware* on the left is less elastic than the demand curve for *Illustrator* on the right. Correspondingly, the optimal markup is higher for the demand curve on the left ($37.50 above cost versus $16.25 above cost). At the optimal price and quantities, the elasticity for the demand curve on the left is 1.27 versus 1.62 for the demand curve on the right.

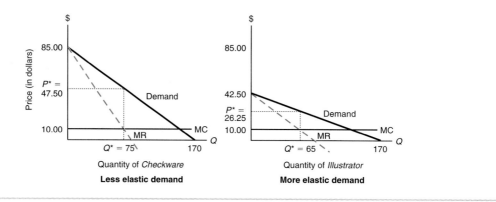

Solving for the intercept yields

$$a = 85$$

Hence, the estimated demand curve is

$$P = 85 - 0.5Q \tag{7.4}$$

Given this estimated demand curve and a marginal cost of $10, Sally has enough information to solve for the "optimal" price. Whether or not this price is close to the true optimal price depends on the accuracy of her cost and sensitivity estimates and on whether the demand curve is close to being linear. Even if the demand curve is not linear, linearity may not be a bad approximation, especially if she begins at a price that is not too far from the optimal price.

In this example, Sally will lower the price from $70 to $47.50. The corresponding change in sales will provide her with additional information, which will be useful for future pricing decisions. For example, was the increase in sales close to what she predicted? If she worries that a $23.50 price reduction is too drastic given a lack of confidence in her estimate of the demand curve, she might start with a smaller price reduction, followed by more reductions if additional experience warrants it. Alternatively, she might offer a $23.50 rebate on the purchase price. If the price cut turns out to be a bad idea, she can simply eliminate the rebate (rebates are discussed in greater detail below).

Cost-Plus Pricing   One of the more common pricing methods used by firms is *cost-plus pricing*. Firms that use this technique calculate average total cost and then mark up the price to yield a target rate of return.

For example, suppose that Sally expects to sell 75 (000) units and targets a 20 percent return on sales. Total costs include the $10 variable cost per unit and the $100,000 of up-front investment. To solve for the implied price, Sally begins by calculating a *unit cost:*

$$\text{Unit cost} = \text{variable cost} + (\text{fixed costs/unit sales}) \tag{7.5}$$

so in this case,

$$\text{Unit cost} = \$10 + (\$100/75) = \$11.33$$

The price that will yield the target rate of return is found using the following formula:

$$\text{Price} = \text{unit cost}/(1 - \text{target rate of return}) \tag{7.6}$$

In our example, this formula implies a price of \$14.16 (\$11.33/0.8); the return on sales is (\$14.16 − \$11.33)/\$14.16 = 0.20.

We have stressed how profit-maximizing pricing considers only incremental costs and depends on the price sensitivity of customers. Cost-plus pricing appears to ignore both of these considerations. The cost-plus price marks up average total cost and seems to ignore the demand for the product—just because Sally targets a 20 percent return on sales does not mean that customers will necessarily buy the product in the required quantities at the implied price.

Firms that consistently use bad pricing policies will find themselves earning lower profits than they could with better pricing techniques and even may go out of business. But if cost-plus pricing is so unsound, why is it so widely used in the marketplace? One explanation is that managers implicitly consider market demand in choosing the target return and the target sales volume. If Sally knows that the product faces little competition, more units can be sold and a higher return will be chosen than when facing greater competition. Conceptually, there is always some target volume and return on total cost that produces the profit-maximizing price.

In our first example, the optimal price and quantity for *Checkware* are \$47.50 and 75,000, respectively. The corresponding unit cost is \$11.33. Using a target return of 76.15 percent in Equation (7.6) will produce the profit-maximizing price of \$47.50. If Sally realizes that she has substantial market power with *Checkware,* she should select a high target return (in this case—76.15 percent). Correspondingly, for products where she has less market power, she should choose lower target returns.

The idea that managers choose target returns and volumes based on market power when they do cost-plus pricing is supported empirically. Consider the price markups by a typical grocery store employing cost-plus pricing. Stable products such as bread, hamburger, milk, and soup are relatively price-sensitive and carry low margins (markups of under 10 percent above cost). Products with high margins tend to be those with relatively inelastic demand, such as spices, seasonal fresh fruit, and nonprescription drugs (markups as high as 50 percent or more). One experienced grocery store manager noted that "price sensitivity is the primary consideration in setting margins."[4] Cost-plus pricing is more useful when the rate of return that yields the profit-maximizing price on the product is relatively stable over the relevant range of cost variation for a given product and varies little across a related set of products.

Markup Pricing Many managerial economics textbooks suggest a pricing rule-of-thumb based on Equation (7.2): $P^* = MC^*/[1 - 1/\eta^*]$. This method—typically referred to as *markup pricing*—consists of substituting an estimate of the current price elasticity and marginal cost into Equation (7.2) and solving for the optimal price.

---

[4] J. Pappas and M. Hirschey (1990), *Managerial Economics,* 6th edition (Chicago: Dryden Press).

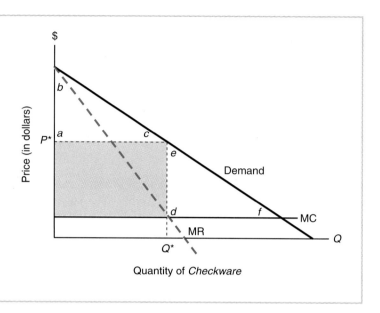

Figure 7.4 Potential for Higher Profits

If the firm charges a single unit price, profits are maximized at a price of *P** and a corresponding quantity of *Q**. The corresponding profits are shown by the shaded rectangle. Consumers receive surplus equal to triangle *abc*, and triangle *def* represents unrealized gains from trade (consumers who value the product at more than cost but who do not buy the product because of the high price). The firm can earn higher profits if it can devise a more complex pricing policy that allows it to capture some of the potential profits represented by these two triangles.

Equation (7.2) is a condition that holds at the optimal price-quantity combination. Price elasticity frequently varies along the demand curve. If Sally currently is at a suboptimal price-quantity combination, the current elasticity will differ from that at the optimal point. Using the current price elasticity in Equation (7.2) will yield a good estimate of the optimal price only when it is close to the elasticity at the optimal price and quantity. Although price elasticity varies along a linear demand curve, it can be constant across a range of values for some nonlinear demand curves. In fact, some demand curves are *isoelastic*—the elasticity is constant along the entire demand curve. (An example is $P = a/Q$.) Assuming the estimate of the current elasticity is close to the actual elasticity, the markup pricing rule will yield a good approximation of the optimal price, regardless of the initial starting point.

On the Importance of Assumptions In our *Checkware* example, the underlying demand curve is linear. Unsurprisingly, the linear approximation works well. In contrast, the markup pricing rule does not. If Sally begins at a price of $70 and a quantity of 30, then the demand curve ($P = 85 - 0.5Q$) implies that the elasticity is 4.66 (this can be derived using the technique from the appendix of Chapter 4). Plugging 4.66 into Equation (7.2) along with the marginal cost of $10 yields an "optimal" price of $12.73. But this is not very close to the optimal price of $47.50. This illustration highlights the importance of considering the underlying assumptions in choosing among alternative rules of thumb. It is easy to imagine other circumstances where the markup pricing rule yields a better estimate than the linear approximation.

Potential for Higher Profits

In the benchmark case of a single unit price, the firm captures some, but not all of the potential gains from trade. Figure 7.4 provides an illustration. Firm profits are displayed by the shaded rectangle, and the associated consumer surplus is the triangle labeled *abc*. The triangle, labeled *def*, shows additional potential gains from trade that would accrue from selling to customers who value the product above its marginal cost, but who do not buy the product at the higher unit price P^*. Below we discuss how a firm might increase profits through more complicated pricing strategies that allow it to capture some of the gains from trade displayed by these two triangles.

Homogeneous Consumer Demands

Potential customers for a product might have quite similar individual demand curves, or they might vary widely in their demands for the product. For instance, in the *Checkware* example, all potential customers might be willing to pay the same maximum price for the product. Alternatively, some customers might be willing to pay a high price for the product, whereas others might be willing to buy the product only at a quite low price. We begin our discussion of more complicated pricing strategies by examining the case of homogeneous demands—in the limit they are identical. These same techniques are appropriate where the firm is dealing with a single given customer and wants to extract maximum profit. Subsequently, we examine the case of heterogeneous demands.

Block Pricing

The overall demand curve for a product is the sum of individual customer demands at each price. For many products, individual customers are likely to consider purchasing multiple units (consider fruit, clothes, and so on). In the benchmark case, individuals pay the same price per unit independent of the number of units purchased. More generally, the company might charge a given customer different prices per unit, depending on the number of units purchased. Profits sometimes can be increased (even if all customers have similar demand curves) by basing the price per unit on the number of units purchased.[5]

Individuals have downward-sloping demand curves for products. This implies that the marginal value that a customer places on each additional unit declines as the quantity purchased increases. Conceptually, the firm could capture all the potential gains from trade with a customer by charging a price equal to the marginal value of each unit. Thus it might charge $100 for the first unit, $99 for the second unit, $98 for the third unit, and so on (where the prices represent the customer's marginal value of each additional unit). Practical considerations often will preclude such a pricing policy. However, the policy might be approximated by charging a high price for the first purchase block (for example, up to 5 units) and declining prices for subsequent blocks. For example, the company might charge the customer $98 per unit up to the first five, $95 per unit for the next five, and so on. As discussed below, block pricing not only is used to extract additional profits from a homogeneous customer base, but also is used in certain circumstances to increase profits when customer demands are more heterogeneous.[6]

Another type of block pricing can occur in the choice of package size. Suppose a typical customer values a first T-shirt at $16 and a second at $10. If vendors sell the shirts individually, they have to charge $10 or less to get a customer to buy two. If they offer

---

[5]Note that in the following discussion we assume that a customer cannot buy a large quantity and then resell it to other customers (undercutting the prices that the company charges to other customers for small quantities). The importance of this assumption is discussed in more detail below.

[6]For expositional simplicity, we have assumed that marginal cost is constant. If production, packaging, or distribution costs decline with volume, price discounts would be offered, even without market power. With market power, the price reductions will exceed the cost reduction as volume increases.

Block Pricing at Hickey-Freeman

Hickey-Freeman is a major producer of high-quality business suits and men's clothing. Each winter and fall it holds a sale at its factory stores in New York, Indiana, and Maine. During a recent spring sale, Hickey-Freeman priced its high-end suits in the following manner. One suit could be purchased at about $700. A second suit could be purchased for around $600. Greater discounts were given if the customer purchased more than two suits. Many customers require at least one good business suit for work. Thus they are likely to be willing to pay a high price for the first suit. While many customers might prefer to own several suits, their willingness to pay is likely to decline significantly with the number of suits purchased. Hickey-Freeman's pricing policy generates more profits than if it sold all suits at 1 unit price. For instance, if it priced all suits at $700 it would fail to sell additional suits to customers who value the extra suits more than the marginal cost of production (but less than $700). Alternatively, if the company priced all suits at $600, it would miss out on the opportunity to charge higher prices for some of the suits.

---

them in packs of two at a price of $26, customers will be willing to purchase the package and pay an effective price of $13 per shirt.

Two-Part Tariffs

With a *two-part tariff*, the customer pays an up-front fee for the right to buy the product and then pays additional fees for each unit of the product consumed. A classic example is an amusement park, where a customer pays a fee to get in and then so much per ride (Disneyland used to price in this manner).[7] Golf and tennis clubs, computer information services, and telephone service providers are examples of companies that frequently use two-part tariffs.

The benchmark case of charging one price to all customers is a special case of a two-part tariff. The entry fee is zero and the additional units can be purchased at the quoted price. Making more general use of two-part pricing (charging a positive entry fee and a subsequent usage price) can sometimes increase profits substantially relative to the benchmark case. As we discuss below, this is most likely to be true when potential consumers have relatively homogeneous demands for the product.

For illustration, consider an example where all consumers have identical demands for the product, $P = 10 - Q$. Figure 7.5 displays a demand curve for a representative consumer. The marginal cost of producing the product is $1. The potential gains from trade that the firm could capture are shown by the shaded triangle and are equal to $40.50 ($0.5 \times 9 \times 9$). Maximum profits can be extracted by charging an up-front fee equal to all the gains from trade (or slightly less) and then charging a price equal to marginal cost, $1. With this pricing strategy, the consumer purchases 9 units. In contrast, if the firm charged a single unit price, the best it could do would be a profit of $20.25 (by setting marginal revenue equal to marginal cost). In this case, the price is $5.50 per unit and the consumer purchases 4.5 units.

Two-part tariffs also can be used profitably when customers' demands are not identical, but this pricing strategy tends to be less effective the more consumers vary in their demands for the product. From a practical or legal standpoint, a company might have to offer the same two-part tariff to all potential customers. Charging a high entry fee

---

[7]W. Oi (1971), "A Disneyland Dilemma: Two-Part Tariffs for a Mickey Mouse Monopoly," *Quarterly Journal of Economics* (February), 77–96.

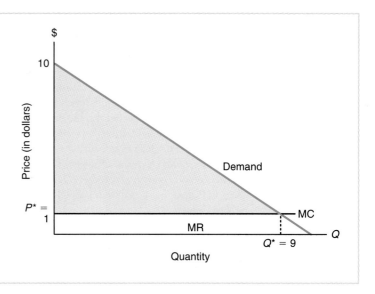

Figure 7.5 Two-Part Tariff

In this example, all potential customers had identical demands. The figure displays a demand curve for a representative consumer, $P = 10 - Q$. The managerial cost of producing the product is $1. The potential consumer surplus that the firm could capture is $40.50, as shown by the shaded triangle. Maximum profits can be extracted by charging an up-front fee equal to all the consumer surplus (or slightly less) and then charging a price equal to marginal cost, $1. Under such a scheme, the consumer purchases 9 units.

allows the firm to extract more surplus from customers who have high demands for the product, but potential customers with lower demands will choose not to purchase. When customers vary widely in demand, it often is best to charge a low entry fee (possibly zero) and then charge a price above marginal cost for use. In this case, given the costs of implementing a two-part tariff (devising the pricing strategy, collecting the fees, and so on), the firm frequently is better off just charging a single price. However, in the next section, we discuss other pricing policies that can increase profits facing more heterogeneous demand.

Price Discrimination—Heterogeneous Consumer Demands

Potential customers often vary materially in their willingness to pay for a product. In our benchmark case, the firm charges the same price to all potential customers. With a heterogeneous customer base, the company can make higher profits if it is able to charge higher prices to those customers who are willing to pay more for the product.

Price discrimination occurs whenever a firm charges differential prices across customers that are not related to differences in production and distribution costs. With price discrimination, the markup or profit margin realized varies across customers. Two conditions are necessary for profitable price discrimination. First, different price elasticities of demand must exist among potential customers for the product (demand must be

Two-Part Pricing for Capital Goods

Frequently a consumer buys a capital good from a firm and then purchases another good to obtain the services of the capital good. For example, Gillette sells razors and razor blades, Hidden Fence installs pet containment systems that require special batteries sold only by Hidden Fence. This situation is like a two-part tariff. With homogeneous consumers, profits are maximized by setting the price of the capital good to extract all consumer surplus and pricing the consumable at marginal cost. With heterogeneous consumers it is typically optimal to charge a lower price for the capital good and a price above marginal cost for the consumable.

As Cigarette Prices Soar, A Gray Market Booms

To price-discriminate successfully, a firm must not only be able to identify submarkets with different price elasticities, but also be able to restrict trade among these submarkets.

Cigarette companies have historically charged much higher prices in the United States than in foreign markets for their premium brands. Due to the fact that United States cigarette prices increased by over 50 percent in the late 1990s, made-for-export cigarettes have appeared for sale in United States stores and on the Internet. These cigarettes were returned for sale in the United States "through a complex and shadowy distribution network."

For example, in 1999, Cigarettes Cheaper, a California-based discounter, sold 45,000 cartons of made-for-export cigarettes produced by R.J. Reynolds. A carton of diverted Winstons sold for $24.89 compared to $30.39 for regular Winstons. In addition, the Internet contains web sites offering cheap export cigarettes. In Brasschaat, Belgium, merchant Tehoe Rooijakkers indicated that hits have increased to 150 a day on his web site advertising low-cost Marlboros, Winstons, and Camels.

These activities reduce the ability of the tobacco companies to charge premium prices for their brand-name cigarettes in the United States.

Source: S. Hwang (1999), "As Cigarette Prices Soar, a Gray Market Booms,"
The Wall Street Journal (January 28), B1.

heterogeneous). Otherwise, there is no point in segmenting the market. When different price elasticities do exist, it is generally more profitable to charge higher prices to those customers who are less sensitive to price. Second, the firm must be able to identify submarkets and restrict transfers among consumers across different submarkets. Otherwise, any attempt to charge differential prices to customers will be undercut by resale across the submarkets. One group of consumers can buy at the low price, then resell to the other groups at a price below the firm's prices to these groups.

Sometimes managers have quite good information about individuals' product demands (which specific customers are willing to pay more for the product). For instance, if Andrew Leone has sold automobiles to the same customers on repeated occasions, he is likely to have relatively good information about each customer's price sensitivity. In other cases, managers have poor information about individual product demands. For example, early in his career Andy had less experience and accumulated information to differentiate among customers who came to the dealership. But he still might be able to engage in certain kinds of price discrimination with information only about the range or distribution of customer demands. We begin our examination of price discrimination by considering the case where the manager has good information about individual demands. We then consider the case where the manager has information only about the distribution of demands.

Exploiting Information about Individual Demands

Personalized Pricing[8] Suppose there are many potential customers. Each customer places a value on the product that signifies the maximum that that individual would pay for the product—their reservation price. For simplicity, suppose each customer

---

[8]Economists often categorize price discrimination as first-, second-, or third-degree. These terms were originated by A.C. Pigou (1950), *The Economics of Welfare* (Macmillan: London). Unfortunately, they are not very descriptive. Following C. Shapiro and H. Varian (1999), *Information Rules: A Strategic Guide to the Network Economy* (Harvard Business School Press: Boston), we use more descriptive terms like personalized pricing, menu pricing, and group pricing.

Tuition Pricing

Firms engaging in personalized pricing strive to extract the maximum willingness to pay from each customer. While colleges and universities do not engage in perfect personalized pricing, they effectively charge different prices to students for tuition through the use of financial aid packages. Stated tuition is the maximum price that any student is charged. Low-income students, who are likely to be relatively price-sensitive, typically are offered more financial aid than high-income students. In addition, top students who are likely to have numerous scholarship offers, and thus more options, are offered significant discounts. An average student from a high-income family typically pays much higher effective tuition than other students.

purchases at most 1 unit. Personalized pricing (*first-degree price discrimination*) extracts the maximum amount each customer is willing to pay for the product. Each consumer is charged a price that makes him or her indifferent between purchasing and not purchasing the product. In this case, the firm extracts all the potential gains from trade. This extreme form of price discrimination is rare and typically is possible only when the number of customers is extremely small and resale is impossible. With personalized pricing, the firm sells to all customers who are willing to pay more than the marginal cost of production. All gains from trade are exhausted, and the outcome is efficient. All the gains from trade, however, go to the firm.

While perfect personalized pricing is rare, new technologies are making it easier for companies to customize quoted prices. For example, companies selling over the Internet can vary quoted prices based on past buying histories, demographic information obtained through electronic registration, clickstreams, and so on. Similarly, companies that sell through catalogs can—and often do—include personalized inserts, where the quoted prices vary depending on the customer's buying history and personal characteristics (for example, zip code). This type of personalized pricing was more difficult under older printing technologies and before the existence of computerized databases that store customer information.[9]

Group Pricing Managers sometimes can gauge an individual's price sensitivity by observing a characteristic of the individual such as age, income, or dress. In these cases, the manager can have a fairly good idea of a specific individual's demand for the product, even if the manager never has interacted with the customer in the past.

Group pricing (*third-degree price discrimination*) results when a firm separates its customers into several groups and sets a different price for each group. For example, utility companies charge different rates to individual versus commercial users, computer companies give educational discounts, and airlines charge different rates based on the amount of notice given for the reservation. Beyond.com charges government agencies and large companies lower prices than other customers. As illustrated in the following example, a firm that can segment its market maximizes profits by setting marginal revenue equal to marginal cost for each market segment.

Firms use a variety of characteristics to divide customers into groups. Three prominent examples are age, time of purchase, and income. For instance, movie theaters frequently give discounts to senior citizens and students, price lower for matinees than for

---

[9]Note, however, that the Internet also lowers information costs and that this makes market segmentation (a necessary aspect of effective price discrimination) more difficult (recall the earlier box on made-for-export cigarettes).

Virtual Vineyards

Virtual Vineyards offers premium wines and specialty foods—such as El Serpis Anchovy Stuffed Olives and Fox's Fine Foods Killer Corn Relish—over the Internet. The company also offers advice, monthly wine programs, and a variety of other services at its web site. Virtual Vineyards tracks the clickstream of each user and instantaneously makes special offers based on the behavior. In a similar vein, Amazon.com tracks the purchases of each consumer and recommends additional related books the next time the user logs on. The Internet has made possible many marketing opportunities not available through other media.

Source: C. Shapiro and H. Varian (1999), *Information Rules: A Strategic Guide to the Network Economy* (Harvard Business School Press: Boston).

evening performances, and vary prices across locations depending on the average income in the area. The objective is to charge a higher price to the groups who are less price-sensitive.

Consider the Snowfish Ski Resort, which can separate its demand into local skiers and out-of-town skiers. The marginal cost of servicing a skier of either type is $10. Suppose the resort faces the following demand curves:

$$\text{Out of town:} \qquad Q_0 = 500 - 10P \qquad (7.7)$$

$$\text{Local:} \qquad Q_1 = 500 - 20P \qquad (7.8)$$

Total demand at any one price is the sum of the demands for the two types of consumers[10]:

$$Q = 1{,}000 - 30P \qquad (7.9)$$

If the company sells all tickets at one price, profit maximization will occur at[11]:

$$P^* = \$21.66; \quad Q^* = 350; \quad Q_0^* = 283; \quad Q_1^* = 67; \quad \text{Profit} = \$4{,}081$$

The company can make higher profits by charging different prices to the two sets of skiers. The optimal prices are found by setting the marginal revenue equal to the marginal cost in each of the two market segments. Under this pricing policy, the following prices, quantities, and profits are observed:

$$P_0^* = \$30; \quad Q_0^* = 200; \quad P_1^* = \$17.50; \quad Q_1^* = 150; \quad \text{Profit} = \$5{,}125$$

where P_0^* and P_1^* = prices charged to out-of-town and local skiers, respectively. The resort charges higher prices to the out-of-town skiers, who are less sensitive to ticket prices than local skiers.

Figure 7.6 displays the optimal pricing policy for each market segment. Snowfish treats the two markets as separate and charges the optimal monopolistic price to each segment. Consistent with Equation (7.2), the optimal markup is lower in the more elastic local market. Using the point-elasticity formula developed in the appendix to

---

[10]This demand curve assumes that price is lower than or equal to $25. At higher prices, the local skiers purchase no tickets and the total demand curve is simply the demand curve for out-of-town skiers ($Q = 500 - 10P$).

[11]The reader should know by now that the solution to this problem is found by setting marginal revenue equal to marginal cost and solving for Q^*. Price can then be found from the equation for the demand curve. For instance, the total demand curve can be obtained by rearranging Equation (7.9): $P = 33.33 - 0.033Q$. When the tickets are sold at one price to all consumers, the marginal revenue is MR $= 33.33 - 0.067Q$. Since marginal cost is $10, the optimal quantity is 350; price is $21.66. The optimal prices and quantities for the individual market segments are found by completing similar calculations using Equations (7.7) and (7.8).

Figure 7.6 Optimal Pricing at Snowfish Ski Resort

Snowfish can segment its customers into two market segments, out-of-town skiers and local skiers. The marginal cost of serving either type of skier is $10. The optimal pricing policy is to set the monopoly price in each market segment. The markup is higher for out-of-town skiers because they have less elastic demands than local skiers. At the optimal prices ($30 and $17.50), the demand elasticities are 1.50 for out-of-town skiers and 2.33 for local skiers.

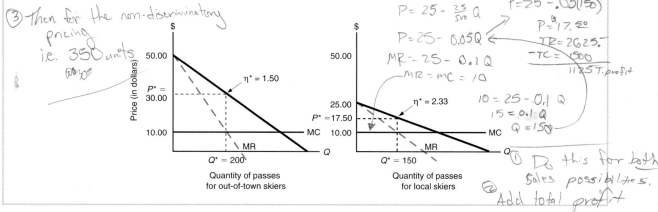

[Handwritten notes: ③ Then for the non-discriminatory pricing i.e. 350 units

P = a - bQ
P = 25 - (25/500)Q
P = 25 - 0.05Q
P = 25 - .05(150)
P = 17.50
TR = 2625.
-TC = 1500
1125 T. profit
MR = 25 - 0.1Q
MR = MC = 10
10 = 25 - 0.1Q
15 = 0.1Q
Q = 150
① Do this for both sales possibilities.
② Add total profit]

Chapter 4, it can be shown that at the optimal prices, the elasticities for the local and out-of-town skier markets are 2.33 and 1.5, respectively. The respective markups above marginal cost are $7.50 and $20 (given the prices of $17.50 and $30).

There are a number of methods that Snowfish might use to charge the two groups different prices. Discount coupons might be sold at supermarkets away from major resort hotels. Presumably, most of the sales at these supermarkets will be to local customers. Alternatively, discount books of tickets (nontransferable) could be sold locally prior to the start of ski season. Ski resorts use both techniques. These policies are more profitable, the more difficult it is for out-of-town skiers to buy the tickets at prices less than $30.

Pricing of Books

Firms divide customers into groups based on various characteristics. Different prices are charged to each group, depending on their elasticity of demand.

One characteristic used by book publishers to segment the market is time. When a new book comes to market, it usually is offered only in a hardback edition for a relatively high price. Subsequently, it is offered in paperback at a substantially reduced price. Individuals who have a high demand for the book (and thus a low price elasticity) do not want to wait for the paperback edition and thus pay a high price for the book. Those with lower demands wait for the cheaper edition. After the paperback edition comes to market, the publisher generally will continue to offer the hardback edition. Hardback books are likely to make better gifts than paperbacks. Also customers are likely to prefer hardbacks for their libraries. Thus there continues to be a market for both types of books. Continuing to offer multiple versions is an example of menu pricing (discussed below).

In 1999 Amazon.com offered four versions of the popular bestseller *Memoirs of a Geisha* by Arthur S. Golden. A hardback version sold for $17.50, whereas the paperback sold for $7.00. In addition, there was a hardback, large-print edition that sold for $28.95 and an audiocassette that sold for $37.56. When the book first entered the market, it was sold only in hardback.

Using Information about the Distribution of Demands

In some settings, the manager does not have enough information to divide customers into meaningful groups. For instance, even if a retailer knows that low-income individuals are more price-sensitive than high-income individuals, the retailer may not be able to gauge the incomes of customers when they come to the store.[12] Nonetheless, the manager might have enough information about the range or distribution of individual demands to engage in profitable price discrimination. In this section we discuss two prominent methods that can be used in this setting. Both rely on the principle of *self-selection*. Consumers are provided with options. They then reveal information about their individual price sensitivities by their choices.

Menu Pricing   With menu pricing (*second-degree price discrimination*), all potential customers are offered the same menu of purchase options. The classic example involves block pricing, where the price per unit depends on the quantity purchased.[13] For instance, cellular phone companies typically give customers a choice among several rate plans, where the price per minute varies with the minimum number of minutes per month specified across each plan. Customers use their private information about likely usage to select the best rate plan for themselves. By carefully constructing the menu of options, the company makes more profits than if it simply offered the product at one price to all potential customers (for example, offering phone service at $.10 per minute, independent of volume). If such quantity discounts are based solely on costs, then there is no price discrimination. However, large-quantity users have incentives to search and thus are likely to be more price-sensitive than low-quantity users, and thus block pricing allows different rates to be charged to the two groups even if per-unit costs are similar. Public utilities frequently price in this manner.

A related pricing strategy is to offer potential customers a menu of price-quality combinations. For instance, *Turbo Tax* markets both a deluxe and standard version of its software. The deluxe version contains additional features that are likely to appeal to sophisticated users. The marginal costs of producing and distributing both versions are virtually equal. However, the company marks up the deluxe version more because the typical customer choosing this version is likely to be less price-sensitive than the typical customer choosing the standard version.

Table 7.1 presents a numerical example of menu pricing. Here the market for *Turbo Tax* software is divided into two types of users, sophisticated and unsophisticated. The reservation prices (maximum willingness to pay) for the deluxe and standard versions are given for both types of users. The marginal cost of producing the software is assumed to be zero.

Ideally, the company would like to identify the two types of users prior to purchase. Assuming it could prevent reselling the software among consumers, the company would maximize profits by charging $100 to the sophisticated users, who would purchase the deluxe version, and $20 to the unsophisticated users, who would purchase the standard version. This pricing strategy is equivalent to personalized pricing.

Since the company cannot identify the type of user prior to purchase, it prices the standard version at $20 and the deluxe version at just below $85 (for example, $84.99).

[12]Also it may be neither practical nor legal to charge customers different prices for the same products even if the retailer knows each customer's income.

[13]Recall that block pricing can be used to increase profit either by extracting more profits from a given homogeneous customer population or by increasing profits through charging different prices to high- versus low-volume customers. In this section, we discuss the second use.

	Sophisticated User	Unsophisticated User
Standard edition	$ 35	$20
Deluxe edition	$100	$20

Table 7.1 Example of Menu Pricing

In this example, there are two versions of *Turbo Tax* and two types of users. The table shows the maximum price that customers in each group are willing to pay for the product (reservation prices). The marginal cost of producing both versions is zero. With menu pricing, the firm will price the standard version at $20 and the deluxe version at $85 (or just below). Consumers acting to maximize consumer surplus will self-select. Sophisticated users will buy the deluxe version (surplus of $15) and the unsophisticated users will buy the standard version (surplus of zero). Unlike personalized pricing, the firm does not obtain all the gains from trade. The firm would like to charge more for the deluxe version. However, if it does, the sophisticated user will purchase the standard version.

The customers, who know their own type, choose the quality-price combination that maximizes their individual consumer surplus. Unsophisticated buyers purchase the standard version (which yields no consumer surplus). Sophisticated users buy the deluxe version and gain a surplus of just over $15 (the surplus they would enjoy if they purchased the standard version). The potential for the sophisticated buyer to purchase the lower-quality product limits the price that can be charged for the deluxe version. If the deluxe version were priced above $85, sophisticated users would obtain greater consumer surplus by buying the standard version at $20, and no deluxe versions would be sold.

The end result is that the sophisticated user gains some consumer surplus and the company makes less profit than it would if it could engage in personalized pricing. Nonetheless, it does better than if it offered only one version at a single price. For instance, the company could offer just the deluxe version at a price of $100 and sell only to sophisticated users or offer the product at $20 and sell to both types of users. But it generally is more profitable to offer both quality-price combinations.[14]

Coupons and Rebates Firms frequently use coupons in product pricing. For instance, most Sunday papers contain numerous coupons offering discounts to customers who use the coupon before its expiration date. Coupons also are distributed through direct mailings, product packages, and magazines.

Firms also frequently offer rebates, where the customer using the rebate is refunded some portion of the purchase price. For instance, automobile manufacturers often offer significant rebates (for example $1,000) to customers who purchase cars during the rebate period. Software manufacturers and retailers (for example, Microsoft and Beyond.com) frequently offer rebates for their products. Rebate offers often are attached to products sold at grocery stores.

Coupons and rebates give price discounts to customers. Price discounts in turn might be given to attract new customers (new first-time users or brand switchers) or to increase sales among current customers. Price discrimination is one primary reason why some

---

[14]If the number of sophisticated users is large relative to the number of unsophisticated users, it might be better to price the deluxe version at $100 and sell only to sophisticated users.

The Little Mermaid: An Example of Price Discrimination

When Disney first distributed *The Little Mermaid* videotapes, the tape retailed for around $20. A customer could obtain a rebate form at the store and mail it in for a $5 rebate. What was going on? Why not simply sell the tapes for $15? Wouldn't costs be avoided? For example, it is expensive to issue and mail checks and print posters and coupons.

To illustrate the potential benefits of the policy, suppose that if the tapes were sold at the same price to all customers, Disney would have priced them at $20. With this policy, Disney would lose the potential profit from selling to consumers who are willing to pay a price above Disney's production cost but less than $20. Disney's apparent objective was to find a way to sell to these consumers at a lower price without having to lower the price to other consumers. One way to accomplish this objective was through rebates. Presumably, those willing to purchase at $20 had higher opportunity costs for their time (on average). This made them less likely to fill out and mail in the coupons. Customers not using the rebates paid a price of $20, whereas the customers using the rebate coupons paid $15.

There are a variety of issues to consider in deciding on such a rebate program. First, there is a trade-off between the costs of administering the program and the benefits of additional sales. Also, there is the loss of $20 sales to customers who would have purchased at $20 but now use the rebate coupons. Disney offered other videotapes without rebates. Deciding whether or not to implement such a program requires careful analysis.

firms use coupons and rebates to make price discounts rather than simply lowering the price.

Coupons have to be clipped and brought to the store, whereas rebates often require customers to complete and mail rebate forms to the manufacturer. Many customers do not use available coupons or rebates to purchase products because the money saved through using the coupon or rebate is less than the value of the time it takes to search for and redeem the offer. The typical coupon/rebate user is likely to have a relatively low opportunity cost of time (for example, the user might not work outside the home or have a low income); such consumers are likely to be more price-sensitive. Thus, issuing coupons and rebates is one way of lowering effective prices to potential customers with more elastic demands.[15]

In 1999 Beyond.com offered a $30 manufacturer's rebate for the Windows version of *Quicken Deluxe*. Customers who applied for the rebate paid a net price of $29.95, whereas a customer failing to use the rebate paid a price of $59.95. Most customers would be expected to use a $30 rebate. Customers failing to redeem a $30 rebate presumably place a high value on their time and are not likely to be very price-sensitive.[16] Consistent with the principles of price discrimination, they pay a higher price for the product than the more price-sensitive rebate user.

Coupon/rebate programs can be expensive. For instance, there are the costs of designing the promotion, printing and circulating the offer, and handling the redemptions. These costs can be significant and should be compared with the benefits in

---

[15]Price discrimination is unlikely to explain the use of large rebates or coupons. For instance, if an automobile company offers customers a $2,000 rebate, it reasonably can forecast that all customers will take advantage of this offer. Thus rebates are essentially equivalent to giving all customers a price reduction, for example, by having a sale. Rebates, however, often are offered by the manufacturer who does not have direct control over the retail price. For a more extensive discussion of coupons, rebates, and other sales promotions see R. Blattberg and S. Neslin (1990), *Sales Promotion: Concepts, Methods, and Strategies* (Prentice Hall: Englewood Cliffs, NJ).

[16]Alternatively, customers might be purchasing the product on the behalf of their companies. In this case, since the company is paying the bill, the customer might be less price-sensitive.

choosing whether to offer the program. We have indicated that one of the potential benefits of these programs is increased profit through price discrimination. Another potential benefit is the increase in future profits from new customers who start using the product due to the sales promotion—if they like the product, they might purchase it in the future even if a coupon is not offered.[17] Coupons (for example, in newspapers and magazines) sometimes can be viewed as a form of advertising that lowers information costs about the product.

Interestingly, Beyond.com offered no rebate for the Mac version of *Quicken Deluxe*. Mac users typically have fewer software products to choose among than Windows users. Also, local software retailers are likely to carry a smaller inventory of Mac products than Windows products. The lack of available substitutes implies that the typical Mac customer is likely to be less price-sensitive than the typical Windows customer. Beyond.com thus offered coupons to Windows users with their higher price sensitivity, and no coupons to the less price-sensitive Mac users. Finally, if Macs are less likely to exist in the future than Windows-based machines, the benefits of attracting new customers for future sales are lower for Macs.

Bundling

To this point, we have considered the case where the firm sells a single product. This section extends the analysis by providing an introduction to the case of multiple products.[18]

Companies frequently bundle products for sale. For example, in 1999 Beyond.com only offered *Expedia Streets* and *Expedia Trip Planner* as a bundle at a price of $35 (before rebate). This bundle combined leading street-mapping and trip-planning technologies into a single package. Other examples include retailers bundling free parking with a purchase at their store, newspapers selling advertising in both morning and afternoon editions at one price, season tickets for sporting events, and restaurants offering fixed-price complete dinners.

One reason for bundling products is to extract additional profits from a customer base with heterogeneous product demands.[19] For example, Table 7.2 presents two types of potential customers: consumers and professional users. The figure displays the maximum prices (reservation prices) that the individual customers within each group are willing to pay for *Expedia Streets* and *Expedia Trip Planner*. The marginal cost of producing either product is assumed to be zero (to simplify the discussion). Potential customers purchase a product only if their surplus is nonnegative.

Why would the company bundle the products, forcing customers to purchase both in order to obtain either? If the firm did not bundle, the most it could charge for *Streets* would be $20 and for *Planner* $10 if it wanted to sell to both groups of customers. Using this policy, it would collect $30 from each customer. The company, however, can bundle

---

[17]Sometimes this benefit can be obtained simply by lowering the purchase price (for example, by having a sale).

[18]The topic of pricing multiple products can be relatively complex. Our intent here is to provide a brief introduction to the idea of product bundling. For a more detailed analysis, see J. Long (1984), "Comments on 'Gaussian Demand and Commodity Bundling'" *Journal of Business* 57, S235–S246.

[19]Products also might be bundled to reduce packaging costs or to reduce the costs to customers who want to buy the products together. For example, to the extent that most users want to utilize features of both street mapping and trip planning, the technologies might be combined to lower the costs to the customer of obtaining and integrating the two products.

	Expedia Streets	Expedia Trip Planner	Bundle
Consumer	$20	$15	$35
Professional	$30	$10	$40

Table 7.2   Product Bundling

In this example, there are two types of customers, professionals and ordinary consumers. The table shows the reservation prices for *Expedia Streets* and *Expedia Trip Planner.* The reservation price for the bundle for any consumer is the sum of the reservation prices for the individual products. If the firm wants to sell both products to both types of customers, it must price the products at $20 and $10, respectively (the minimum reservation prices for each product). It collects $30 from each customer. It can do better by selling the products in a bundle for a price of $35 (the minimum reservation price for the bundle). Bundling increases profits in this example because the two groups have opposite *relative valuations* of the two products. Professionals are willing to pay more for *Streets* than consumers, while the opposite holds for *Trip Planner.* Thus the minimum reservation price for the bundle is greater than the sum of the minimum reservation prices for the separate products.

the products and sell to all customers at a price of $35 (the minimum reservation price for the bundle).

Although both groups in this example value *Streets* higher than *Planner,* the two groups have opposite *relative valuations* of the two products. Professional users are willing to pay more for *Streets* than consumers, whereas consumers are willing to pay more for *Planner* than professional users. This feature implies that the minimum bundle value is greater than the sum of the minimum reservation prices for each product. Thus the firm makes more money selling the bundle than selling the products separately. If one group valued both products higher than the other group, there would be no gains from bundling (the minimum bundle value would be the same as the sum of the minimum individual reservation prices).

Typically, products are not just sold in bundles. Often firms use a tactic of *optional* (*mixed*) bundling, where the products can be purchased separately or in a bundle at a price below the sum of the individual prices. Optional bundling can be more profitable than pure bundling when some customers value one product highly, but value the other product below the marginal cost of production. For these customers, the extra revenue the firm would earn from selling the bundle would be lower than the extra cost of producing it.

Optional Bundling at Burger King

In 1999, Burger King offered a Whopper Value Meal at $3.39. The meal included a hamburger, medium fries, and medium soft drink. Individually, these products could be purchased at $2.09, $.99, and $.99, respectively. When customers purchase a hamburger and soft drink at $3.08, the inference is that they value the fries at less than $.31— otherwise, they would have purchased the Value Meal. Burger King probably could entice these customers to buy the Value Meal by lowering its price (effectively selling the fries at a lower price). However, it is more profitable to sell just the hamburger and drink to these customers and offer the Value Meal at a higher price to other customers who place a higher value on the combination.

Other Concerns

Multiperiod Considerations

Future Demand   In 1999, Beyond.com priced *Encarta Encyclopedia 99* at $35. How-ever, after rebates the net price was zero. If the objective is to maximize single-period profits for a single product (as in the benchmark case), it is never optimal to set a price of zero.[20] Managers, however, are concerned not only with sales in the current period but in future periods as well. Giving the product away can attract new customers; it low-ers the full cost of consuming the good below that of competing products. If they like the product, they will purchase the product in the future at positive prices. This is a major reason why firms provide "free samples" of their products.

Offering a product at a price below marginal cost is a more effective pricing strategy if information costs are higher. If a customer takes the time to learn to use a new soft-ware product (such as *Encarta*), the customer often will want to continue to use the pro-gram in the future, rather than take the time to learn to use a new product. Thus at sim-ilar prices, the customer is more likely to buy upgrades and future editions of the current software rather than switch to a competing product. This *lock-in effect* is a reason why some software firms give away their products (or charge low prices) in the early stages of development.

Firms sometimes charge lower prices than the optimal single-period price because they value maintaining customer goodwill. For example, a severe ice storm in March 1991 produced a major power outage in upstate New York. Electric generators were in high demand and could have been sold to customers at extremely high prices. But local stores did not raise the price of generators substantially. One concern apparently was that they would be seen as taking advantage of customers—that such a tactic would un-dermine the firm's reputation and reduce future demand. Drug companies face similar concerns when they price new drugs. These companies have an incentive to charge the profit-maximizing price for their products (to help reimburse them for their develop-ment and other costs). However, in setting prices these companies have to consider the reactions of "public-interest" groups and government regulators.

Future Costs   As discussed in Chapter 5, for some firms the long-run average cost of producing a given level of output declines as the firm gains experience in producing the product. For instance, employees can gain important information on how to improve the production process as they gain more experience. When these *learning effects* are im-portant, it can be optimal for the firm to produce a high volume of the product initially to gain experience and thus a cost advantage over competing firms in subsequent peri-ods. This high output is correspondingly sold at lower prices than if the firm produced the lower volume associated with optimizing single-period profits.

Many cost advantages, however, are short-lived because competing firms often can copy innovations. Thus managers should consider carefully whether it is appropriate to adopt such a high-volume, low-price strategy. Chapter 8 discusses this issue in more detail.

---

[20]Firms that sell multiple products can have incentives to price selected individual products below marginal cost. For example, McDonald's sometimes has promotions that sell hamburgers at below cost. The intent is to attract customers who buy other products, such as fries, at prices substantially above cost.

Giving Away Internet Products

Giving away services and products has become a common strategy for startup companies on the Internet. For example, in 1998 Egreetings Network sold e-mail birthday cards for $.50 to $2.50 apiece; in 1999, all its online cards were free. Yahoo offered its Internet Directory Service at no charge.

These companies view the no-charge policy as a "cheap way" to attract a customer base (compared to advertising and other marketing promotions). For instance, in less than a year, 1.2 million people signed up for Netzero's free Internet Connection service. The hope is that they can make money in the future by either selling products to these customers or by charging fees to other companies who want to use their customer base for advertising. For instance, FreePC and NetZero are free Internet service providers who make money by charging advertisers for displaying banners on users' monitors when they sign on. Users must supply detailed information to get the free service, and this information is forwarded to advertisers. These Internet service providers don't really provide "free" connections—consumers pay for it via the commercials they receive, just like "free" TV.

Some of these pricing strategies appear to have paid off. For example, in 1994 Netscape gave its browser away. Within two months of initial release, some 1.5 million users had tried it. Some paid after 90 days but most didn't. It encouraged users to complain about software bugs, and Netscape learned how to improve the product. The free browser helped sell other Netscape products. By 1998 some 100 million copies of Netscape Navigator were in use, most at no cost. AOL acquired Netscape for $4.2 billion. Microsoft also bought Hotmail Incorporated (which provided free e-mail) for $400 million. Nonetheless, this pricing strategy is risky and certainly will not pay for all firms.

Source: G. Anders (1999), "Eager to Boost Traffic, More Internet Firms Give
Away Services," *The Wall Street Journal* (July 28), A1, and "No Charge,"
Attaché (September 1999), 14–16.

Storable Products   In a number of our examples, we have discussed products that can be stored. This means that sales of the product and consumption of the product are not the same. When you lower the price of a product, the quantity demanded rises for two reasons: first, as demand curves slope downward and as prices drop, there is more consumption; second, if the price reduction is temporary, the customer will purchase additional units to be consumed at future dates. Thus, for storable goods, the variation over time in sales is greater than the variation in consumption.

Strategic Interaction

The analysis in this chapter starts with a demand curve for the product. Managers choose a pricing strategy that maximizes profits given demand and its cost structure. This approach holds the price of substitute products constant (recall the definition of a demand curve). Thus the reactions of competitors are not considered explicitly in this analysis. Although this approach serves as a useful starting point in many practical applications, it is not as useful in markets with only a few major competitors. In these markets, it often is foolish to ignore rival reactions in setting prices. For example, if United Airlines offers a major price reduction to customers, it is reasonably safe to assume that the other major airlines (for example, American Airlines and Delta) will not hold their prices constant. In these situations, it is important for managers to consider explicitly the reactions of rival firms when they price their products. Chapter 9 provides a set of tools (derived from game theory) that is useful for managers within these interactive settings.

Legal Issues

There are laws that restrict the ability of firms to charge different prices to different customers. For example, the Robinson-Patman Act limits the ability of firms in the United States to charge different prices to customers in wholesale markets. Laws also can limit price levels. For instance, in many countries public utility companies are regulated in terms of the prices that they are allowed to charge customers. Managers contemplating the pricing policies discussed in this chapter should check the legality of a proposed pricing policy given the laws they face within a particular jurisdiction.

Legal constraints can drive the firm's choice of pricing policy in a variety of ways. For example, prompted by complaints from local merchants in a college town, the city council passed a law to restrict street vendors from selling hand-crafted items. But the law exempted flower vendors: There was a long-standing tradition of giving flowers to dates before ball games, and local ladies had long supplied the cut flowers. Undeterred, the craft vendors bought bouquets of flowers, placed a flower on each item, and sold the flower with the craft item bundled in for "free." Some manufacturers in the 1970s began offering rebates rather than cutting product price because when price controls were implemented by the US government, rebates and price cuts were treated differentially.

Xerox originally leased copying machines with a requirement that the lessee buy Xerox paper; it set the paper price above marginal cost. IBM used a similar pricing plan for tabulation machines and IBM cards. The intent was to extract higher profits from higher-volume users. The government successfully charged both companies with employing illegal tying arrangements. These companies could have achieved the same result with less legal exposure. Rather than sell paper and punch cards at prices above cost, they could have offered these items at marginal cost and rented the machines with a two-part price—a fixed amount per month plus so much per copy or card read.

Implementing a Pricing Strategy

In this chapter we have provided an introduction to product pricing. We have discussed the objective of pricing decisions, presented a basic economic analysis of product pricing, and provided a rationale for many observed pricing policies. We also have identified key features in the business environment (such as the nature of the customer base and the type of information that is held by managers) that can affect pricing decisions.

Given our intent, we have kept the analysis relatively simple. The actual implementation of a pricing strategy is complicated by a number of important factors: First, the pricing policies presented in this chapter are not mutually exclusive. Many companies can and do use a combination of pricing policies (consider Beyond.com). Second, our analysis has focused primarily on pricing a single product, but most firms sell a variety of products. In many cases, it is important to consider the interactions of demands and costs of multiple products in developing a pricing strategy. Third, optimal pricing policies can change across time. Fourth, firms have to give more detailed consideration to the legal and strategic issues in formulating pricing strategies. Thus, to manage product pricing effectively, it is important to supplement the basic material presented in this chapter with industry experience and additional training in the economics of pricing.[21]

---

[21]The high salaries paid to successful pricing managers highlight the complexity of pricing decisions in some industries. For instance, top pricing managers are among the highest-paid professionals in major airline companies.

Summary

A firm has *market power* when it faces a downward-sloping demand curve. Firms with market power can raise price without losing all customers to competitors. The ultimate objective is to choose a pricing policy that maximizes the value of the firm.

Consumer surplus is defined as the difference between what the consumer is willing to pay for a product and what the consumer actually pays when buying it. Managers, in maximizing profits, try to devise a pricing policy that captures as much of the gains from trade as possible. Thus, they try to capture potential consumer surplus as company profit.

In the benchmark case, the firm chooses a single per-unit price for all customers. Profits are maximized at the price and output level where *marginal revenue equals marginal cost*. Fixed and sunk costs are irrelevant; only *incremental costs* matter in the pricing decision. The optimal price markup over marginal cost depends on the elasticity of demand. The optimal markup decreases as demand becomes more elastic: It is optimal to charge high prices when customers are not very price-sensitive.

Economic theory suggests that managers should price so that marginal revenue equals marginal cost. One practical problem in applying this principle is that managers often do not have precise information about their demand curves and thus their marginal revenue (Chapter 4 discusses methods of estimating demand). The *linear approximation technique* can be used when the demand curve is roughly linear and the manager has basic information about current price-quantity, price sensitivity, and marginal cost. *Markup pricing* is a technique that managers can use when they have limited information and reason to believe that price elasticity varies little across the demand curve. One of the most common pricing methods used by firms is *cost-plus pricing*. Managers using this technique calculate average total cost and mark up the price to yield a desired rate of return. Cost-plus pricing appears inconsistent with profit maximization since it includes fixed and sunk costs and does not consider consumer demand explicitly. Managers, however, can consider consumer demand implicitly by choosing appropriate target returns (lower target returns are chosen when demand is more elastic). The widespread use of this pricing policy suggests that it can be a useful rule of thumb in some settings.

The benchmark policy charges the same price to all customers independent of the quantity purchased. Sometimes a firm can do better with more complicated pricing policies. With *block pricing* a high price is charged for the first block and declining prices for subsequent blocks. Block pricing can be used either to extract additional profits from a set of customers with similar demands or can be used to price-discriminate. With a *two-part tariff,* the customer pays an up-front fee for the right to buy the product and then pays additional fees for each unit of the product consumed. Two-part tariffs tend to work best when customer demand is relatively homogeneous.

Price discrimination occurs whenever a firm charges differential prices across customers that are not related to differences in production and distribution costs. With price discrimination, the markup or profit margin realized varies across customers. Two conditions are necessary for profitable price discrimination. First, different price elasticities of demand must exist in various submarkets for the product (customers must be heterogeneous). Second, the firm must be able to identify submarkets and restrict transfers among consumers across different submarkets.

Personalized pricing extracts the maximum amount each customer is willing to pay for the product. Each consumer is charged a price that makes him or her indifferent between purchasing and not purchasing the product. *Group pricing* results when a firm separates its customers into several groups and sets a different price for each group.

A firm that can segment its market maximizes profits by setting marginal revenue equal to marginal cost in each market segment (higher prices are charged to the less price-sensitive groups). Both personalized and group pricing require relatively good information about individual customer demands.

Even if the manager does not have detailed information about individual demands, price discrimination still is possible with sufficient information about the distribution of individual demands. With *menu pricing* all potential customers are given the same menu of options. The classic example involves block pricing, where the price per unit depends on the quantity purchased. Customers use their private information to select the best option for them. By carefully constructing the menu of options, the firm makes more profits than if it simply offered the product at one price to all potential customers.

Coupons and rebates offer price discounts to customers. Price discrimination is one reason why firms use coupons and rebates to make price discounts rather than simply lowering the price. Price-sensitive customers are more likely to use coupons and rebates—and thus are charged lower effective prices—than customers who are less price-sensitive. Similar to menu pricing, customers self-select, depending on private information about their personal characteristics. Coupon and rebate programs are expensive to administer. These costs have to be compared to the benefits in deciding whether to adopt such a program.

Firms frequently *bundle* products for sale. One reason for bundling products is to extract additional profits from a customer base with heterogeneous product demands. Bundling can be more profitable than selling the products separately when the *relative values* that the customers place on the individual products vary.

This chapter focuses on a single-period pricing problem, in which managers face a fixed demand curve and cost structure. The prices of competing products are held constant. In some situations, concerns about future demand and costs, as well as the reactions of competitors, can motivate managers to choose pricing policies that would not be appropriate in the simple single-period analysis. Chapter 9 addresses issues of strategic interaction in greater detail.

Suggested Readings	

T. Nagel (1994), *The Strategy and Tactics of Pricing: A Guide to Profitable Decision Making,* 2nd edition (Prentice Hall: Englewood Cliffs, NJ).

C. Shapiro and H. Varian (1999), *Information Rules: A Strategic Guide to the Network Economy* (Harvard Business School Press: Boston).

Review Questions

7–1. Macrosoft is a new producer of word processing software. Recently, it announced that it is giving away its product to the first 100,000 customers. Using the concepts from this chapter, explain why this might be an optimal policy.

7–2. The local space museum has hired you to assist them in setting admission prices. The museum's managers recognize that there are two distinct demand curves for admission. One demand curve applies to people ages 12 to 64, whereas the other is for children and senior citizens. The two demand curves are

$$P_A = 9.6 - 0.08Q_A$$
$$P_{CS} = 4 - 0.05Q_{CS}$$

where P_A is the adult price, P_{CS} is the child/senior citizen price, Q_A is the adult quantity, and Q_{CS} is the child/senior citizen quantity. Crowding is not a problem at the museum, and so managers consider marginal cost to be zero.

    a. What price should they charge to each group to maximize profits?

    b. How many adults will visit the museum? How many children and senior citizens?

    c. What are the museum's profits?

7–3. Textbook publishers have traditionally produced both United States and international editions of most leading textbooks. The United States version typically sells at a higher price than the international edition. (a) Discuss why publishers use this pricing plan. (b) Discuss how the Internet might affect the ability of companies to implement this type of policy.

7–4. Suppose in Table 7.2 (Product Bundling) that the professional user values *Expedia Streets* at $15 rather than $30. Keep all other valuations the same. Discuss how this change affects the optimal pricing strategy.

7–5. Explain why perfect personalized pricing is typically more profitable than menu pricing. Why then do companies use menu pricing?

7–6. In the example in this chapter, the linear approximation method produced the profit-maximizing price, whereas the markup pricing rule did not. Does this imply that the linear rule is always better than the markup rule? Explain.

7–7. Why do companies grant discounts to senior citizens and students?

7–8. You own a theater with 200 seats. The demand for seats is $Q = 300 - 100P$. You are charging $1.25 per ticket and selling tickets to 175 people. Your costs are fixed and do not depend on the number of people attending. Should you cut your price to fill the theater? Explain. What other pricing policies might you use to increase your profits?

7–9. The Snow City Ski Resort caters to both out-of-town skiers and local skiers. The demand for ski tickets for each market segment is independent of the other market segments. The marginal cost of servicing a skier of either type is $10. Suppose the demand curves for the two market segments are:

$$\begin{aligned} \text{Out of town:} \quad & Q_0 = 600 - 10P \\ \text{Local:} \quad & Q_1 = 600 - 20P \end{aligned}$$

    a. If the resort charges one price to all skiers, what is the profit-maximizing price? Calculate how many lift tickets will be sold to each group. What is the total profit?

    b. Which market segment has the highest price elasticity at this outcome?

    c. If the company sells tickets at different prices to the two market segments, what is the optimal price and quantity for each segment? What are the total profits for the resort?

    d. What techniques might the resort use to implement such a pricing policy? What must the resort guard against, if the pricing policy is to work effectively?

7–10. All consumers have identical demand for a product. Each person's demand curve is $P = 30 - 2Q$. The marginal cost of production is $2. Devise a two-part tariff that will exhaust all consumer surplus.

7–11. Xerox sells both copiers and a toner for their copiers. While customers are not required to buy Xerox toner, most do because specified machines use toner only for that machine. The Xerox toner and machines are closely designed and non-Xerox toner in Xerox machines produces inferior copies. Evaluate the statement: "Xerox makes 75 percent of its profits selling toner and 25 percent of its profits selling machines."

7–12. Some tennis clubs charge an up-front fee to join and a per-hour charge for court time. Others do not charge a membership fee but charge a higher per-hour fee for court time. Consider clubs in two different locations. One is located in a suburban area where the residents tend to be of similar age, income, and occupation. The other is in the city with a more diverse population. Which of the locations is more likely to charge a membership fee? Explain.

7–13. Consider three firms: a shoe store at the mall, an automobile dealership, and a house painting firm.

    a. Which firm would you expect to engage in the most price discrimination? Why?

    b. How has the Internet changed the pricing policies of these businesses?

Chapter 8
Economics of Strategy: Creating and Capturing Value

Over the past four decades, Wal-Mart Stores has become the largest, most profitable retailer in the world.[1] Its discount-variety stores, Sam's Clubs, and supercenters (combined discount retail and bulk grocery stores) are located throughout the United States, as well as in many other countries such as Mexico, Canada, Puerto Rico, Germany, Brazil, Argentina, China, Korea, and Indonesia.

---

[1]Details for this example are from S. Foley (1994), "Wal-Mart Stores, Inc.," Harvard Business School Case 9-794-024 and the financial press.

In 1999, it reported $165 billion in sales and net income of over $5.6 billion; its 1,140,000 employees worked at 4,000 stores.

Since Sam Walton opened his first store in 1962, the overall financial performance of the company has been nothing less than phenomenal. To illustrate, suppose you had purchased $1,000 of the stock at the initial offering in 1970 and held it through 1999. This investment would be worth more than $6 million (that is a 36 percent compound annual growth rate); in addition, you would have received cash dividends paid by the company over the period. This performance made Wal-Mart one of the hottest stocks in the market.

While Wal-Mart's performance has been spectacular, it has not been flawless. Following a large price drop in the second quarter of 1993 (over 20 percent during a period when the overall market was essentially flat), Wal-Mart's stock price continued to decline modestly until 1997, even though the overall stock market was rising. In addition, sales growth at Wal-Mart, which for a long period had outpaced the retail industry, fell to unremarkable levels.

In an attempt to increase performance during the 1990s, Wal-Mart took a variety of actions; it opened new stores internationally, opened new supercenters, and logged on to the world of electronic commerce. In 1998, Wal-Mart entered the traditional grocery store business in Arkansas where it opened three "experimental" 40,000 square foot grocery stores (about the same size as traditional supermarkets). During 1997 and 1998, Wal-Mart stock again performed well relative to the general stock market and retail industry.

All managers would like to outperform the general market as well as their specific industry over a sustained period. Examples like that of Wal-Mart suggest that such performance is possible but raise at least five important questions:

- What accounts for the success of these firms?
- Should all properly managed firms expect sustained superior performance?
- What actions can managers take to generate superior performance?
- Can managers enhance financial returns through diversification (as Wal-Mart was attempting to do by opening grocery stores)?
- Do all high-performing firms ultimately "fall back with the rest of the pack" as Wal-Mart did in the mid-1990s?

This chapter applies the basic economic concepts developed in this book to address these and related questions.

Strategy

Strategy refers to the general policies that managers adopt to generate profits. For example, in what industries does the firm operate? What products and services does it offer and to which customers? In what basic ways does it compete or cooperate with other firms within its business environment? Rather than focusing on operational detail, a firm's strategy addresses broad, long-term issues facing the firm.[2] Typically, strategies do not remain constant but evolve through time. For example, Wal-Mart's strategy focuses on discount retailing and the related grocery industry. It owns and operates four basic

---

[2]In the strategy literature, these questions are frequently divided: corporate strategy refers to the choice of industries, whereas business strategy refers to the choice of how to compete within the chosen industries (for example, whether to focus on cost or quality, or on some combination of the two).

types of stores: discount-variety stores, Sam's Clubs, supercenters, and grocery stores. It offers a wide product assortment, "every-day low prices" (supported by a low cost structure), limited advertising, and friendly, well-informed "sales associates." Originally, its strategy focused on placing stores in the rural Southeast. Wal-Mart now operates stores throughout the world. Ultimately, along with the *organizational architecture* of the firm (discussed in Part 3 of this book), strategy is a key determinant of the success or failure of the enterprise.

The ultimate objective of strategic decision making is to realize sustained profits.[3] To achieve this objective, managers must devise ways both to *create and capture value*. Earlier chapters focused on how value might be created and captured through input, output, and pricing policies. Those chapters also analyzed how competition constrains the ability of managers to capture value. But they (like most discussions in the traditional managerial economics literature) focused on a single product, taking the industry and product characteristics as given.

This chapter takes a broader look at how managers create and capture value. The next section presents an analysis of value creation within a given industry. Subsequent sections examine capturing value and the choice of industries. The final section offers a general framework for implementing the concepts in this chapter.

Firms often compete against a few identifiable rivals. For example, Boeing competes largely with Airbus in the production of commercial jet airplanes. It is particularly important for managers in such firms to consider likely responses of rivals when making strategic decisions about pricing, new investment, advertising, and so on. For example, it would be foolish if Boeing failed to consider likely responses by Airbus in setting the prices of its wide-body jets. In this chapter, we concentrate on the broader issues of how firms create and capture value; thus we abstract from how reactions by rivals might be incorporated explicitly in the analysis. In Chapter 9 we use game theory to provide an explicit analysis of reactions by rivals in the strategic decision-making process.

Value Creation

Figure 8.1 displays supply and demand curves for an industry. It differs from our previous supply and demand figures in one important respect: It explicitly displays both consumer-borne and producer-borne transaction costs. Consumer transaction costs include such things as the costs of searching for the product, learning product characteristics and quality, negotiating terms of sale with a supplier, and enforcing agreements. If these costs were lower, demanders would be willing to pay more for the product. For example, automatic teller machines increase the demand for banking services by reducing the amount of time customers spend in line and by providing basic banking services around the clock. The dotted demand curve indicates potential demand—what demand would be if there were no consumer transaction costs. The solid demand curve displays the effective demand given a per-unit consumer transaction cost of *a*. Similarly, producers bear costs in transacting with consumers and suppliers (for example, negotiating terms with customers and paying attorneys

---

[3]If stock market participants anticipate that a company is going to earn sustained abnormal profits, its stock price will be bid up so that in equilibrium investors will earn only a normal rate of return by buying the stock. The fact that Wal-Mart has generated both high profits and high stock returns over a long time period suggests that the company has continually surprised the stock market with its earnings performance. In this book, we concentrate on the underlying profits of the company, not the stock market valuation of these profits. Stock market valuation is covered in finance classes and textbooks.

Figure 8.1 Ways to Create Value

This figure displays the supply and demand curves for an industry. It differs from previous diagrams by including producer and consumer transaction costs. [Per-unit consumer-borne (producer-borne) transaction cost is $a(b)$.] Consumers would demand more and producers would supply more if these costs were lower. Value consists of the sum of consumer and producer surplus. Managers can increase value by reducing transaction or production costs or by increasing the demand for the product—for example, by increasing the perceived quality of the product.

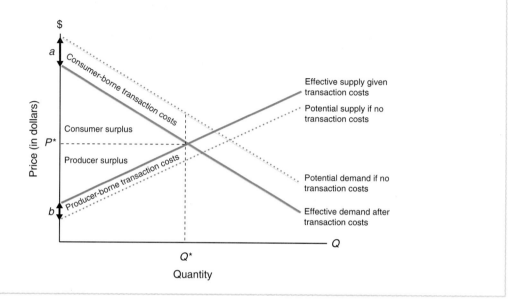

to draft a supply agreement). The dotted supply curve indicates potential supply—the willingness of producers to supply the product in the absence of producer transaction costs. The solid line shows the effective supply curve given a per-unit transaction cost of b.[4]

The area under the dotted demand curve (demand before transaction costs) and above the dotted supply curve (supply before transaction costs) up to Q^* is divided into four areas. First, there are the two parallelograms representing consumer and producer transaction costs. Next, there are the two triangles representing consumer and producer surpluses. *Total value* created by the industry is the sum of producer surplus and consumer surplus.

An important first step in making profits is discovering ways to create value. The second step, discussed below, devises ways to capture this value. Figure 8.1 suggests at least four general ways that managers within the industry might increase value.

- They can take actions to lower production costs or producer transaction costs, thus shifting the effective supply curve to the right.

- Managers can implement policies to reduce consumer transaction costs, thus shifting the effective demand curve to the right.

[4]For expositional convenience, we assume that supply costs are separable into production and transaction costs. Admittedly, there are cases where they are joint or where the allocation is arbitrary.

Dell Computers: Reducing Producer and Consumer Transaction Costs

Dell has developed a system to collect information from customers and assemble a customized product quickly and inexpensively. This allows Dell to bypass a dealer network and their required markups, thereby offering computers at lower prices. (Note, however, that by adopting this strategy of competing with more emphasis on price than service, their product is more likely to appeal to knowledgeable customers than first-time buyers.) Extending this strategy, Dell offers customized services to large accounts. For example, Dell has loaded specialized software along with associated peripherals and network servers at Dell's factory for First Union Capital Markets Group, which uses over 2,500 PCs. The package then is tagged and shipped directly to the specific First Union trader for whom the unit had been designed. This process reportedly has saved First Union over $500,000 annually. These are just a few examples of how companies, like Dell, have reduced transaction costs, both for themselves and their customers.

Source: A. Serwer (1998), "Michael Dell Rocks," *Fortune* (May 11), 58–70.

- They can take actions other than reducing consumer transaction costs to increase demand, shifting both the potential and effective demand curves to the right.
- Managers can devise new products or services—in essence creating a new figure.

We discuss each of these strategies in turn.[5]

Production and Producer Transaction Costs

Chapter 5 discussed how managers should choose inputs to minimize production costs. Over time, managers can discover new technological opportunities to reduce these costs and increase value. They also can devise ways to lower the costs of transacting with customers and suppliers. For example, when personal computers first were developed, they were relatively expensive to produce. Over time, companies learned to reduce these production costs. As a result, the quantity of personal computers sold in the market has increased substantially—as has the total value (consumer plus producer surplus) created within this industry. Computer manufacturers also have devised ways to reduce their costs of transacting with suppliers and customers. For instance, large computer manufacturers have developed electronic connections with major software producers to lower the cost of ordering software programs. They also have developed computer links that reduce their costs of transacting with customers.

Wal-Mart has shifted its effective supply curve to the right by developing new low-cost methods for producing and distributing retail services and products. For example, its extremely efficient hub-and-spoke distribution system has lowered the costs of stocking its stores. Wal-Mart has reduced transaction costs through direct computer links with major suppliers, such as Procter and Gamble. These links have cut the costs of restocking products and essentially have eliminated writing paper checks to these vendors—they are paid through an electronic payment system.

Consumer Transaction Costs

Reducing consumer transaction costs also can increase value. For example, early Wal-Marts were established in small rural towns. One way that these stores added value was

---

[5]We depict demand and supply at the industry level because it facilitates our subsequent discussion on capturing value (which involves competition within the industry). The same four value-creating factors are important if we frame the problem using a firm's demand and costs.

Reducing Consumer Transactions Costs: Kraft Lunchables

Kraft Foods plant in Avon, NY, once had been on the verge of being closed. But during the late 1990s it tripled employment thanks to booming demand for Lunchables, a line of finger food for kids. Kraft prepackages kids' meals to provide a convenience for parents preparing lunch for children to take to school. Included in the package are meat, cheese, crackers, and a drink box. Other Lunchables include pizzas, tacos, hot dogs, and hamburgers. With flashy, colorful packaging and contests to win trips to amusement parks, Lunchables are aimed dead center at the kid consumer. And since the product line was introduced in 1988, they have become huge business for Kraft. The basic idea for Lunchables was to provide convenience for parents while allowing kids to have a hand in selecting their lunches, said Jeff Meyer, brand manager for Lunchables. Grocery Manufacturers of America spokeswoman Lisa McCue added, "People don't have to think about shopping for ingredients, slicing and dicing, cooking, etc. And nowadays, people aren't spending a lot of time in the kitchen. The whole convenience trend just is going to continue."

Source: M. Daneman (1999), "Cashing in on Kids," *Democrat and Chronicle* (July 19), 1F.

through reducing travel time for local residents, who previously had to drive to urban centers to do a larger part of their shopping. Wal-Mart also reduces consumer-borne transactions costs by the layout of their stores. For example, Wal-Mart captures "market-basket data" from customer receipts at all its stores. By analyzing this data, Wal-Mart can tell which products are likely to be purchased together. Wal-Mart uses this knowledge to reduce customers' costs in navigating their stores by placing commonly purchased bundles of products together. Examples of such pairings include bananas with cereal, snack cakes with coffee, bug spray with hunting gear, tissues with cold medicine, measuring spoons with baking supplies, and flashlights with Halloween costumes.[6]

The entire industry that involves marketing over the Internet is another example of reducing consumers' transaction costs. For instance, when prospective customers use search engines to explore the Internet, they often are presented with a list of related books, which can be ordered electronically at a discount through companies such as Amazon.com. This service reduces consumer transaction/search costs by identifying books of potential interest and making it easier to place an order.

Other Ways to Increase Demand

The demand curve holds variables other than the price of the product constant. We already have discussed how managers can increase demand by reducing consumer transaction costs. They also can increase the effective demand for their products—and thus total value created by their transactions—by affecting variables such as expected product quality, prices of complements, or prices of substitutes.

Product Quality   Actions that enhance perceived quality increase demand; total value also is raised unless these actions entail larger increases in production costs. For instance, the innovation of titanium golf clubs increased the demand for golf equipment, while the invention of parabolic skis increased the demand for skis and skiing. The resulting increases in demand have been greater than the associated increases in production costs—thus, total value created within these industries has increased.

[6]E. Nelson (1998), "Why Wal-Mart Sings, 'Yes, We Have Bananas!'" *The Wall Street Journal* (October 6), B1.

Increasing Demand at Serbian McDonald's

During the 78-day air war led by NATO against Yugoslavia in 1999, 15 McDonald's restaurants in Belgrade were closed. Angry mobs—who saw McDonald's as a symbol of America and the West—vandalized the units. To increase the demand for their products, the Yugoslavian McDonald's undertook an anti-NATO, pro-Serbian marketing campaign. For example, as a national flourish to evoke local pride and identity, they produced posters and lapel buttons showing the golden arches topped with a traditional Serbian cap called the *sajkaka*. They also handed out free cheeseburgers at anti-NATO rallies, and allowed the basement of one of their restaurants to be used as a bomb shelter. They also began promoting the McCountry, a domestic pork burger with paprika garnish. After the war was over, the demand for McDonald's products soared in Belgrade. Said 16-year-old Jovan Stojanovic, "I don't associate McDonald's with America. Mac is ours."

Source: R. Block (1999), "How Big Mac Kept from Becoming a Serb Archenemy," *The Wall Street Journal* (September 30), B1.

Price of Complements Managers sometimes can act to reduce the price of complements, thus increasing the demand for their products. To illustrate, consider CompuInc, which produces personal computers, and PrintCo, which produces a complementary printer.[7] For simplicity, suppose that customers purchase either both products or neither product (they are quite strong complements), the price of CompuInc's personal computers is P_c, and the price of PrintCo's printers is P_p, and the demand for each product is

$$Q = 12 - (P_c + P_p) \quad \text{when } P_c + P_p \text{ is 12 or less, 0, otherwise} \quad (8.1)$$

Q is the number of computer-printer combinations sold and the marginal cost of producing both products is 0.

If the two companies do not cooperate in setting prices, each will seek to maximize its individual profits, given its expectation of the other firm's price.[8] In this case, CompuInc will view its demand curve as

$$P_c = (12 - \bar{P}_p) - Q \quad (8.2)$$

while the PrintCo demand curve is

$$P_p = (12 - \bar{P}_c) - Q \quad (8.3)$$

where $\bar{P}_p$ and $\bar{P}_c$ represent the expectations about the other firm's price.[9] Each firm's profit is maximized by setting MR = MC (0 in this example):

$$\text{CompuInc} \quad (12 - \bar{P}_p) - 2Q = 0 \quad (8.4)$$

$$\text{PrintCo} \quad (12 - \bar{P}_c) - 2Q = 0 \quad (8.5)$$

Substituting for Q from Equation (8.1) and rearranging the terms yields the following two reaction curves (see Chapter 6):

$$P_c = 6 - 0.5\bar{P}_p \quad (8.6)$$

$$P_p = 6 - 0.5\bar{P}_c \quad (8.7)$$

---

[7]See A. Brandenburger (1996), "Cheap Complements?" (mimeographed text, Harvard Business School).

[8]We solve for these prices using simple algebra and the fact from Chapter 4 that marginal revenue (MR) for a linear demand curve is a line with the same intercept as the demand curve but with twice the negative slope. (The problem could be solved in fewer steps using calculus.)

[9]There is no reason to place a subscript on Q. By assumption it is the same for both firms.

The equilibrium consists of prices P_p^* and P_c^* that simultaneously solve these two equations.[10] Figure 8.2 displays the solution graphically. In equilibrium, both firms choose a price of 4; thus, a total of 4 units of each product is sold. The profit for each firm is 16; combined profits are 32.

Now consider what happens if the firms were to coordinate the prices, for example, through a joint venture. To maximize the combined profits, the companies jointly set marginal revenue equal to marginal cost[11]:

$$12 - 2Q = 0 \tag{8.8}$$

They sell 6 units at a combined price of 6 (for example, $P_c = P_p = 3$). In this case, they make a combined profit of 36. This combined profit by pricing the products jointly is higher than the profit they would receive if they do not cooperate in setting prices. When the firms price independently, they do not consider the negative effect that their higher prices have on the other's profit. Pricing cooperatively, they take this interaction into account. Note that in this case, consumers also would be better off because the prices of both products are lower.

Prices of Substitutes   Low-priced substitutes reduce the demand for a product. Sometimes managers can affect the price of substitutes. For example, movie theaters frequently prohibit patrons from bringing food into the theater. These restrictions on lower-priced substitutes increase the demand for snacks offered by the theater.

New Products and Services

To this point, our discussion has focused on creating value by increasing demand or reducing the costs of producing existing products. Inventing new products and services also creates value. For example, consider the consumer electronics industry. Many of today's products that create significant value are relatively new developments; for instance, MP3 technology, digital cameras, and digital video displays (DVDs).[12]

---

[10]Recall from Chapter 6 that a Nash equilibrium is where each firm is doing the best it can, given the actions of its rivals.

[11]Note that the combined demand curve is $(P_c + P_p) = 12 - Q$; MR = $12 - 2Q$.

[12]Obviously, the classification of whether a product development constitutes a product improvement or a new product is somewhat arbitrary. For example, are miniature cell phones separate products or improvements over previously existing larger cell phones? This classification problem is not central to our focus. The basic point is that value often is created through the development/enhancement of products.

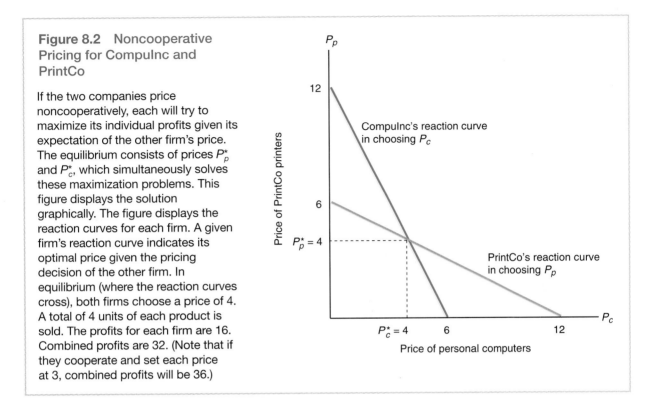

Figure 8.2 Noncooperative Pricing for CompuInc and PrintCo

If the two companies price noncooperatively, each will try to maximize its individual profits given its expectation of the other firm's price. The equilibrium consists of prices P_p^* and P_c^*, which simultaneously solves these maximization problems. This figure displays the solution graphically. The figure displays the reaction curves for each firm. A given firm's reaction curve indicates its optimal price given the pricing decision of the other firm. In equilibrium (where the reaction curves cross), both firms choose a price of 4. A total of 4 units of each product is sold. The profits for each firm are 16. Combined profits are 32. (Note that if they cooperate and set each price at 3, combined profits will be 36.)

Cooperating to Increase Value

Our example of computers and printers shows that firms sometimes can increase value through cooperating with each other, rather than competing. In this case, the companies were producers of complementary products. Opportunities to increase value through cooperation also can arise with customers, suppliers, and even competitors. For instance, cooperating with suppliers and customers in developing computer and information links

Airlines Restrict Cell Phone Use

American Airlines warns passengers that cell phones "may interfere with the aircraft's communication and navigation systems." What American does not tell passengers is that there is no scientific evidence to support these claims. A 1996 study commissioned by the Federal Aviation Administration looked at records from thousands of flights; it failed to find even one instance where equipment was affected by a cell phone. Also plane makers, Boeing and Airbus, have bombarded their aircraft with cell-phone frequencies and found no interference with communication, navigation, or other systems. A likely reason for the lack of impact—cell phones do not operate on any of the frequencies used by airplane systems. Why then are airlines so interested in restricting cell phone use? Airlines have an economic incentive to restrict it—they receive about 15 percent of the revenues from the telephones installed on board. The two major providers of air-phone service, GTE and AT&T, charge about $6 for a 1-minute call (more than 20 times the typical cell-phone rates).

Source: J. Auerbach, (1999), "Connecting Flights: Cell-Phone Use Aloft May Not Be the Danger That Airlines Claim," *The Wall Street Journal* (October 5), A1.

Technology and Value

During the latter part of the twentieth century there has been a massive change in information, communication, and production technologies. This technological change has provided important opportunities for increasing value. For example, the "business process reengineering" movement in the 1990s used computer and information technology to lower costs (for instance, by streamlining systems used to process orders, shipments, payables, and receivables). Flexible production technologies have allowed firms to custom-design certain products to fit specific customer demands better. Computer and information technologies have been used to reduce the costs of transacting with suppliers. Using technology to increase value is likely to remain a significant focus well into the twenty-first century.

can reduce supply costs and lead to the production of more valuable products—ones more tailor-made for the customer (recall the example of Dell Computers). One way competitors cooperate is in development projects to reduce joint costs. For example, major automobile manufacturers have participated jointly in the research and development of batteries for electric cars. Longer-lived batteries are essential for these companies to market electric cars on a wide-scale basis. If each company acts independently, development costs are expected to be higher. As another example, offshore drilling is quite expensive. Prior to soliciting bids for offshore sites, the US government allows the oil firms to conduct a survey of the area jointly; they share the data and divide the costs.

American antitrust laws generally make it illegal for rival firms to cooperate for the purpose of monopoly pricing. Nonetheless, many forms of cooperation are legal and increase the welfare of both producers and consumers (again consider our PC-printer example).

Capturing Value

Creating value is an essential first step in generating profits. But it also is necessary to capture this value. It does the firm little good to reduce transaction/production costs or to increase consumer demand if rivals can copy these changes quickly and enter the market—such competition will eliminate the profits.

Figure 8.3 compares a firm in a competitive market to a firm with market power. In competitive markets, firms face horizontal demand curves and are price takers. With

Advanced Photo System

Firms can increase value by cooperating with other firms. Consider the Advanced Photo System developed in the 1990s. This system has several advantages over traditional photo systems. The film comes in a convenient cartridge that is loaded easily into the bottom of the camera. There are special encoding features that allow enhanced developing. The customer is able to choose from several formats when taking pictures (for example, classic 35 mm or panoramic). The customer receives a print of all photos with index numbers for subsequent reprints.

To maximize consumer appeal for the new system, it was important for the film and camera companies to adopt a set of standard system parameters. Demand for the products would be lower if the market consisted of several incompatible brands of films, cameras, and finishing equipment. The mutual benefits from cooperating on the development of this photo system motivated traditional rivals such as Kodak and Fuji in film and Canon, Minolta, and Nikon in cameras to cooperate in a joint venture to develop the new system. Now that the system is developed and a set of standard parameters adopted, these companies again compete in their respective film and camera markets.

Figure 8.3   Firm with Market Power versus a Firm in a Competitive Industry

The firm on the left has a downward-sloping demand curve and thus has market power. It can choose price-quantity combinations. Chapters 6 and 7 demonstrated that firms with market power often can capture economic profits. The other firm is in a competitive industry and thus faces a horizontal demand curve. Chapter 6 indicated that earning economic profits in this market setting is difficult. Firms along the dotted section on the supply curve (below the market clearing price of *P**) still would produce the product if demand and price fell. The shaded triangle represents producer surplus. This chapter discusses how a firm sometimes (but not always) can capture a portion of this producer surplus as an economic profit.

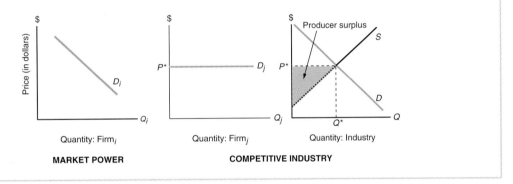

market power, firms choose price-quantity combinations. Chapters 6 and 7 indicated that firms often can capture value if they exploit their market power. Sometimes firms can capture value, even without market power, if they employ superior factors of production that allow them to be more productive than their rivals. In a competitive market, there are typically firms that would be willing to continue to produce the product even if demand and the market price fell. This production corresponds to the dashed section of the supply curve (below the market price *P**) in Figure 8.3. Also shown is the corresponding producer surplus. Sometimes (but not always) a firm can capture a portion of this producer surplus as economic profit. Below, we discuss the conditions under which market power and superior resources lead to economic profits.[13]

Market Power

Entry Barriers   If there are no *barriers to entry,* competition from new firms tends to erode profits within the industry.[14] Entry barriers exist when it is difficult or uneconomic for a would-be entrant to replicate the position of industry incumbents. Chapter 6 discussed a variety of entry barriers. These barriers include factors that make

---

[13]A note on vocabulary: Economists say a firm is earning *rents* when it sells its product for a price higher than average total cost (which includes a "normal" rate of return). A positive rent implies that the firm is earning more than is necessary to motivate it to continue to produce the product over the long run (it is earning an economic profit). It is useful to distinguish between two types of rents: *Monopoly rents,* which correspond to our discussion of market power, and *Ricardian rents,* which correspond to our discussion of superior factors of production.

[14]As discussed in Chapter 6, a firm can have market power when there are limited entry barriers (in the case of differentiated products—monopolistic competition). Entry, however, often will eliminate or at least substantially limit economic profits.

Creating but Not Capturing Value: Eli Whitney

A great problem in southern US agriculture during the eighteenth century in the harvesting of cotton was separating cotton from its seed. This laborious task was done by hand. It was so difficult that it took a worker a whole day to clean 1 pound of staple cotton. Eli Whitney, while visiting Georgia, was intrigued by this problem. Within a few weeks, he produced a machine he called a "cotton gin" (a shortened form of cotton engine). It greatly increased the amount of cotton that could be cleaned in a day and soon led to cotton becoming the chief crop in the South. Clearly, the invention of the cotton gin created significant value. Yet, before Whitney's invention was completed and patented, his first model had been widely copied. Virtually all his profits went into lawsuits to protect and enforce his rights. He did, however, make profits in the financial markets speculating on the price of cotton.

price cuts likely if a new firm enters (such as economies of scale), incumbent advantages (such as patents and brand names), and high costs of exit.

Numerous researchers have tested the theoretical link between entry barriers and profit potential.[15] Consistent with the theory, these studies generally confirm that price-cost margins tend to be lower in competitive industries. Researchers also have found a positive correlation between profit and specific entry barriers (such as economies of scale or advertising) as well as a positive correlation between profit and concentration (combined market share of the top few firms) across geographic markets *within* a given industry.[16]

While theory and evidence suggest that profit potential increases with entry barriers, the existence of such barriers is no guarantee of economic profits. There are at least four additional factors that are important. These include the degree of rivalry within the industry, threat of substitutes, buyer power, and supplier power.[17]

Degree of Rivalry   When the degree of rivalry is high, profits will be low even if there are entry barriers (see Chapter 6). Two factors that help determine the level of rivalry are the number and relative sizes of competitors. The fewer the number of competitors (the more concentrated the industry), the more likely that firms will recognize their mutual dependence and refrain from cutthroat competition. The presence of a large, dominant firm (as opposed to a comparable number of similarly sized firms) also can reduce rivalry because a dominant firm frequently takes the lead in setting prices and takes actions to sanction others that do not follow its lead (within the limits of antitrust constraints). The level of rivalry can change over time as basic conditions within the industry change. For example, if existing firms within an industry have excess capacity, they often will engage in price competition in an attempt to increase their individual outputs. In general, excess capacity, high fixed costs, lack of product differentiation, and slow growth all increase the degree of rivalry within the industry.

[15]For a survey of some of the relevant studies, see R. Schmalensee (1989), "Studies of Structure and Performance," in R. Schmalensee and R. Willig (Eds.), *The Handbook of Industrial Organization* (North Holland: Amsterdam).

[16]In apparent contrast to the theory, researchers have failed to document a strong positive correlation between profits and concentration *across* industries. This is due in part to the difficulty of comparing accounting data across industries. Cross-industry differences in the treatment of depreciation and other accounting choices make interindustry comparisons problematic. Another difficulty is that industries can be concentrated for at least two quite different reasons. First, there can be actual barriers to entry. Second, there can be few firms in an industry because it lacks profit potential. If the sample contains both types of industries, it is not surprising that researchers find mixed results.

[17]M. Porter (1980), *Competitive Strategy* (Free Press: New York), labels these factors, along with the threat of entry, as the "five factors."

Software Pirates Reduce Profits

The Business Software Alliance estimates that 1998 losses to software piracy totaled $3.2 billion in North America, $2.9 billion in Asia, and $3.4 billion in Europe. Most of the stolen sales, perhaps two-thirds, came at Microsoft's expense. Thieves, forgers, and counterfeiters work together to produce shrink-wrapped products, packaged with stolen certificates of authenticity, and forged user manuals. Europe has become a particularly congenial place to sell pirated ware. Its gray markets—from flea markets in Barcelona to trade fairs in Hanover—are ideal venues for the pirates. And with Europe's open borders and variety of different police jurisdictions, it is easy for the pirates to play hide and seek with both product and money.

Source: S. Baker and I. Resch (1999), "Piracy!" *Business Week* (July 26), 90–94.

Threat of Substitutes   Even if entry is limited, firms within an industry are not immune to outside competition. There is the threat of substitutes. For instance, the large scale of investment potentially limits entry into the overnight delivery market (populated by firms such as FedEx and UPS). However, in recent years effective substitutes, such as e-mail and fax machines, have reduced the demand for delivery services (relative to what would have been without these technological developments). Similarly, banks face competition from money market accounts that offer customers the ability to write negotiable orders of withdrawal (usually restricted to amounts in excess of $100).

Buyer and Supplier Power   The final two factors that help determine a firm's market power are buyer and supplier power. If the industry has only a few large customers, profit is likely to be low since these customers will use their buying power to extract lower prices. Similarly, if the key suppliers to an industry are large, concentrated, or well organized (for example, unionized), they will attempt to extract industry profits through high input prices. During the 1990s Intel and Microsoft were essentially sole suppliers of certain key inputs for the production of personal computers; hence they have been quite profitable.

Market Power and Strategy   Firms sometimes can increase economic profit by taking actions that promote entry barriers, reduce intraindustry rivalry, limit the availability of substitutes, or reduce buyer/supplier power. Examples of each type of activity are easy to find. For instance, American manufacturers frequently lobby for taxes or restrictions on imports to reduce entry by foreign firms. Firms in certain industries form

Competition and the Number of Competitors

The degree of rivalry generally increases with the number of competitors. Depending on the nature of the industry, however, competition can be quite fierce even with only a few competitors. Coca-Cola has had about 50 percent of global soft drink sales, while PepsiCo has had about 13 percent. Yet the battle between Coke and Pepsi has been intense for decades, with costly promotional contests and intense competition for distribution. Similarly, competition has been strong in the US tobacco industry, although the three largest companies have had about 90 percent of the market. In detergents, two large companies, Procter and Gamble and Unilever, have conducted a global "soap war." To varying degrees, each of these industries is characterized by excess capacity, high fixed costs, lack of product differentiation, and slow growth—all factors that lead to greater rivalry.

Fear of Supplier Power at Amazon.com

Amazon.com pioneered book retailing through the Internet. Amazon maintains a small inventory of popular titles. Most books, however, are not ordered from the distributor until a customer places an order. Although the company had not reported a profit into 2000, stock market analysts predicted a brisk future for the company. Indeed, in the late 1990s, the stock market value of Amazon.com surpassed that of Barnes and Noble, "king of the brick-and-mortar booksellers." In looking forward, one of Amazon's biggest fears was the power of its suppliers. As *Business Week* notes, "next year it could be Amazon calling the shots, or it could be Yahoo, or America Online, dictating prices and terms." Both search engines and Internet links are important inputs for Amazon's major product—selling books over the Internet. Amazon's chief financial officer acknowledged, "This is the biggest wild card in our business model."

Source: C. Mayer (1998), "Does Amazon = 2 Barnes & Nobles?" *The New York Times* (July 19), 3.4.

---

cartels or other collusive agreements to reduce competition.[18] As we have discussed, organizations like the AMA act to limit the availability of substitute products or services (in their case new physicians, nurses, physician assistants, and midwives). Firms reduce buyer power by opposing buyer-cooperatives. Finally, firms thwart supplier power by opposing labor unions and expanding capacity in nonunionized locations—especially internationally.

Historically, many managers focused on capturing value through anticompetitive activities, such as erecting entry barriers. They have found that often it is difficult to limit competition—especially in a global marketplace. Also, as discussed in Chapter 20, regulators extract much of the producer surplus created through limits on competition, for example, through campaign contributions to encourage the adoption and enforcement of entry restrictions. Due to these considerations, much of the contemporary focus in strategy is on superior resources—the subject of the next section.[19]

Superior Factors of Production

Both human as well as physical assets vary in productivity. For example, Sammy Sosa is a great baseball player, Jack Welch of General Electric is a superb CEO, land in California's Imperial Valley is incredibly fertile, land adjacent to an expressway interchange offers customers quite convenient access, and so on. If an asset allows the firm to make a profit because of its superior productivity, other firms will compete for this resource and bid up its price. Thus, with well-functioning markets, the gains from superior productivity accrue to the responsible asset.

Producer Surplus Captured by Superior Assets   Figure 8.1 divides value into consumer surplus and producer surplus. Consumers receive the consumer surplus. Producer surplus goes to the owners of superior assets. As an example, consider Pete Irving, General Manager of Speedy Modems. Last year, Speedy was just breaking even in producing modems at a price of $100. Demand for the particular type of modem increased, and the price rose to $150; Speedy began making a profit (producer surplus) of $50 per unit.

---

[18]Managers must be careful undertaking these types of actions in the United States since many are illegal under American antitrust law.

[19]An example of the contemporary focus in the strategy literature is D. Collis and C. Montgomery (1995), "Competing on Resources: Strategy in the 1990s," *Harvard Business Review*, 118–128.

Sugar Prices

The 2000 wholesale price for sugar in world markets was about $.06 per pound. In contrast, the price in United States markets was over $.22 per pound. The dramatic difference between the two prices is due largely to American tariffs on sugar imports. Foreign producers would be willing to sell to Americans at lower prices. Yet, they are not permitted to do so. This restriction benefits domestic sugar producers, who are able to sell their sugar at the higher price. Without entry restrictions, the United States price would be driven down to about $.07 per pound. Such a domestic price decline would benefit American consumers but hurt American sugar producers.

This profit motivated other firms to produce the same type of modems. They were less productive than Speedy solely because they lacked a manager with Pete's talents. The rival firms began making job offers to Pete. To dissuade him from going to a rival firm, Speedy had to increase Pete's salary. Through this process, Pete's salary increased to the point where Speedy was making only a normal rate of profit—the same as the competing modem companies. The gains from his special talents went to Pete, not to the firm. This same process works for physical assets. For instance, if a firm rents a prime piece of land or a unique piece of equipment, rental rates will be bid up to reflect the asset's superior productivity. And if the firm owns the asset, its value (and thus the opportunity costs for continuing to use it) will be bid up—in effect, the firm pays the rent to itself for its continued use of the asset.

Figure 8.4 displays a graphical analysis of this general phenomenon. The illustration on the right depicts supply and demand in the marketplace. The initial price is P_0^*. A typical firm in the industry is depicted on the left and is making no economic profits—price equals long-run average cost ($LRAC_0$). The demand for the product increases and the market price goes up to P_1^*. The firm appears to have the potential to make an economic profit, since the price is above its initial long-run average cost. Competitors and new entrants, however, will bid for the special resources (such as a talented manager or a productive piece of land) that would allow the firm to produce the product at an average cost below price. In equilibrium, the firm's costs would increase to the point where its long-run average cost ($LRAC_1$) again equals price.[20] The additional producer surplus created by the increase in price (shaded area) is reflected in the price or opportunity cost of the scarce assets, which made lower-cost production possible at the initial price and output level.

If the firm owns the scarce asset (for example, a piece of land), the wealth of the firm's owners increases as the price of the asset is bid up. It is important, however, to realize that a firm does not have to use a superior asset to realize this value. In fact, the firm might be better off selling the assets to another firm. Managers sometimes overlook this alternative.

As an example, it has been argued that Arco has a competitive advantage in producing retail gasoline because it owns productive oil fields in Alaska that it bought long ago at low prices.[21] Potential competitors are disadvantaged, it is argued, because they have to buy oil on the open market at a higher price than Arco's current cost of extracting its oil. This argument is flawed because it fails to apply the concept of

---

[20]This analysis assumes that the asset is equally valuable to all firms. If this assumption does not hold, the firm's costs will not necessarily be bid up to the point where it makes no economic profits. Price will not be bid above the value to the next highest valued user. We discuss this issue below.

[21]This example is taken from a strategy textbook. Similar examples are easy to find throughout the management literature.

Figure 8.4 Producer Surplus Is Captured by Superior Assets

The illustration on the right depicts supply and demand in the marketplace. The initial price is P_0^*. The typical firm in the industry is depicted on the left and is making no economic profits—price equals long-run average cost (LRAC$_0$). The demand for the product increases and the market price goes up to P_1^*. The firm appears to have the potential to make an economic profit, since the price is above its initial long-run average cost. Competitors and new entrants, however, will bid for the special resources (such as a talented manager or a piece of land) that would allow the firm to produce the product at an average cost below price. In equilibrium, the firm's cost would have increased to the point where its long-run average cost (LRAC$_1$) equals price. The additional producer surplus created by the increase in price (shaded area) goes to the scarce assets, which made lower-cost production possible at the initial price and output level.

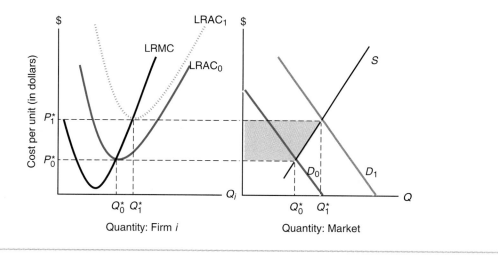

Quantity: Firm *i*

Quantity: Market

opportunity costs appropriately (see Chapter 5). If Arco can sell its oil on the open market, the cost of using it internally is the revenue forgone from not selling it—and that is the current spot market price of oil, not just Arco's production cost. If other companies were more efficient in refining crude oil and producing gasoline for retail customers, Arco would be more profitable if it sold the oil on the open market and did not compete in the production of gasoline. The wealth of Arco shareholders is certainly greater because the company owns valuable oil rights in Alaska. But the critical question is how do managers best exploit this valuable asset. It might be best either to sell the land to another company, sell the oil from the land to another company, or refine the oil internally to produce and sell retail gasoline (or some other petroleum product). Its best course of action depends on the relative efficiency of Arco versus its competitors in the extraction and distribution of oil or the production and distribution of gasoline. Arco should not extract oil or produce retail gasoline simply because it owns its oil reserves.

Table 8.1 presents a numerical example. The following assumptions are used: (1) Arco's cost of extracting enough oil to make a gallon of gasoline is $.10, (2) this oil can be sold on the open market for $.50, (3) it costs $.50 to refine the oil into gasoline, (4) Arco produces 1 million gallons of gasoline a month, and (5) there are no other relevant costs or revenues. The top panel shows Arco's income statement using standard

Accounting Profits

Selling price	$1.00/gallon	$.90/gallon
Sales	$1,000,000	$900,000
Extraction costs	$100,000	$100,000
Production costs	$500,000	$500,000
Profits	**$400,000**	**$300,000**

Economic Profits

Selling price	$1.00/gallon	$.90/gallon
Sales	$1,000,000	$900,000
Opportunity costs of oil	$500,000	$500,000
Production costs	$500,000	$500,000
Profits	**$0**	**($100,000)**

Table 8.1 Arco and Opportunity Costs

In this hypothetical example, Arco's cost of extracting enough oil to make a gallon of gasoline is $.10. This oil can be sold on the open market for $.50. It costs $.50 for refining the oil into gasoline. Arco produces 1 million gallons of gasoline a month. There are no relevant costs or revenues. The top panel shows Arco's income statement using standard accounting techniques assuming gasoline prices of either $1.00 or $.90. Here the cost of the oil is the $.10 per gallon production cost. Arco reports positive profits at both prices, $400,000 and $300,000, respectively. The bottom panel reproduces the income statements using the true opportunity cost of the oil (its current spot market price). In the latter case, it is better for Arco to get out of the production of gasoline and to sell the oil (or possibly the land) on the open market. It nets $400,000 by selling the oil compared to $300,000 producing gasoline. Arco is indifferent between the two alternatives when the price is $1.00 (in either case, Arco nets $400,000). This example emphasizes the basic point made in Chapter 5: Managers should make business decisions using opportunity costs, not accounting costs.

accounting techniques assuming gasoline prices of either $1.00 or $.90. Here the production cost of the oil is the $.10 per gallon. Arco reports positive profits at both prices—$400,000 and $300,000, respectively. Based on these accounting profits, it might appear that it is profitable for Arco to produce retail gasoline. The bottom panel reproduces the income statements using the opportunity cost of the oil: its market price. Using opportunity costs, Arco breaks even when the price of gasoline is a dollar but loses money when the price is $.90. In the latter case, it is more profitable for Arco to get out of the production of gasoline and enter the open market to sell the oil (or possibly the land—this choice depends on Arco's efficiency in extracting the oil). Arco is indifferent between the two alternatives when the price is $1.00; either way, it makes $400,000 over its production costs.[22] This example illustrates a basic point made in Chapter 5: Managers should make business decisions using opportunity costs—not accounting costs.[23]

---

[22]Whether it produces the gasoline or sells the oil directly, it captures the difference between the $.50 market price for oil and the $.10 production cost. At the $1.00 price, the difference between the market price of gasoline and the market price of oil is just sufficient to cover Arco's refining costs of $.50. At the $.90 price, the difference between the price of gasoline and oil is not sufficient to cover the refining costs. Arco makes only $300,000 producing gasoline, as opposed to $400,000 by simply selling the oil.

[23]In Chapter 17, we shall discuss how accounting costs can play an important role in helping to control incentive conflicts in organizations.

Producer Surplus at the Gap

The Gap is a retailer of casual clothing. Its annualized stock return for the 10-year period from mid-1988 through mid-1998 was a spectacular 38.8 percent. A primary reason for this success has been Mickey Drexler, the company's CEO. Outsiders regularly suggest that he has been the driving force behind the company. Indeed, the performance of Gap's core business slipped significantly in the middle 1990s when Drexler turned his attention to the company's Old Navy Division. Performance soon improved when Drexler refocused his attention on Gap's core business. To quote from *Fortune:*

> Everything at Gap depends on Drexler's eye; it isn't making turbine engines. If he's off the mark for one season, if he approves a line of clothes in colors that aren't just right, sales collapse and so does Gap's stock price.

But relying on its key manager as a major source of its competitive advantage placed the Gap in a tenuous position—for example, should he leave the company or become ill. Moreover, economic theory suggests Drexler should capture a large share of the gains from his talents. In 1998 his 1.8 percent stake in the company was valued at $465 million. In 1997, he was paid nearly $4 million in total compensation plus additional stock options.

If Drexler has been the major reason for the Gap's success, why have all the gains not gone to him (rather than being shared with stockholders)? The major factor that is likely to limit the gains Drexler could capture is that he is not entirely mobile in the sense that he is more valuable to the Gap than to other companies in the retail industry. For instance, his knowledge of the Gap's organization and personnel is valuable and not readily transferable to other companies. With a competitive managerial labor market, Drexler's compensation would be bid up to the value in his *next best* employment. So long as he is more valuable to the Gap than to competing companies, part of the remaining difference would go to shareholders.

Source: N. Munk (1998), "Gap Gets It," *Fortune* (August 3), 68–82.

Second-Price Auctions   Competition tends to take a differentiated asset to its highest-valued use, but at a price that reflects its *second-highest valued* use. In a competitive auction, no one has an incentive to bid more than the value they place on the asset. For example, if Lena Otis is the second-highest valued user of a piece of land, she will bid only up to her value, while José Ricardo, the highest valued user, can obtain the asset by bidding just slightly more. This principle implies that the producer surplus captured by the winning bidder is limited to the difference between the asset's first and second-highest valued use; the rest of the value will be reflected in the price of the superior asset.

Team Production   Firms consist of collections of assets. For example, at Microsoft their collection consists of Bill Gates, all his senior managers and employees, the company's physical assets, brand name and other intangible assets, as well as the installed base of existing Microsoft software. Because of the interdependencies among workers and assets, the value of the inputs as a "team"[24] sometimes can be greater than the simple sum of the values if each worker and asset were employed at its next best use across other firms. Thus, it is possible that the overall firm will be more valuable than the sum of its parts. We characterize such a firm as having *team production capabilities*. A firm can capture value by maintaining team production advantages only if competing firms cannot assemble comparably productive teams. If rivals can, then in a competitive marketplace the price of the product will be driven down so that the firm makes only a normal profit.

[24]The word *team* is used in a variety of contexts in the management literature (for example, to refer specifically to small work groups of people). Here, we use the term in a broader sense to refer to a combination of assets (both human and physical) used to produce a particular product or service.

How do firms create team production capabilities that are difficult to duplicate? Part of the answer is a natural consequence of differences in the past histories of firms and the now-sunk choices by managers about goods produced, markets entered, individuals hired, and capital acquired. Due to these differences, firms acquire unique combinations of assets, organizational processes, communication channels, collective learning, and so on. As environments evolve, some firms find themselves—either through luck or foresight—to be in the enviable position of having developed team capabilities that are especially productive in these new circumstances, whereas others do not. For example, Wal-Mart developed an efficient hub-and-spoke distribution network to serve its chain of successful rural stores. This system, along with its brand name and procurement advantages, also helped it compete successfully in larger urban areas.

Other firms can observe the team production capabilities of successful firms. Yet, duplicating these capabilities can be difficult because, from the outside, it is frequently difficult to pinpoint the exact source of synergies within the team: Many assets are combined in the typical firm. It also can be expensive to acquire the necessary assets (contracting/transaction costs), provide training to workers, and so on. In addition, as we shall discuss in Chapter 19, implementing significant changes within an existing organization presents daunting challenges. That team capabilities often are expensive to duplicate is consistent with the observation that many firms enter a new business by buying an existing firm in the industry, rather than by developing the new business within the firm.

Team Capabilities and Organizational Architecture   Part 3 of this book analyzes organizational architecture. A firm's architecture consists of its assignment of decision rights and its systems for evaluating and rewarding performance. Organizational architecture is important in contributing to team capabilities. For example, a decentralized firm can respond more quickly and effectively to a new opportunity that requires rapid "front-line" decision making (for instance, in competitive pricing to customers) than can a firm with a more centralized decision-making structure. Alternatively, other new opportunities that require detailed coordination of activities across several business units might favor the firm with the more centralized structure. As we shall discuss, it often is hard to copy another firm's architecture because multiple systems have to be changed in a coordinated manner. Implementing this type of major change in an organization can be surprisingly difficult (see Chapter 22).

Team Capabilities at Sharp Corporation

During the 1970s, Sharp began marketing electronic calculators with liquid crystal displays. As the company developed expertise with LCD technology, Sharp began to apply it to other products, such as television sets. Through these actions, Sharp developed a set of resources and capabilities that other companies did not have. With the large growth in consumer electronics and computers during the 1980s and 1990s, potential applications for LCDs expanded rapidly. Sharp profited from this growth. Other companies could not immediately overcome Sharp's competitive advantage because of time constraints and their lack of Sharp's accumulated assets and experience. Companies such as Matsushita, NEC, and Canon entered the industry. Yet, Sharp was able to maintain its dominant position because of its special team capabilities. This advantage was not completely captured by its individual assets in their market values; individual assets would not have allowed other firms to copy Sharp's advantage. Thus part of this advantage went to Sharp's shareholders and was reflected in its stock price.

Source: D. Collis and C. Montgomery (1997), *Corporate Strategy*
(Irwin: Chicago).

Flexible Manufacturing and Team Capabilities

Economists argue that often it is appropriate to view managerial policies as a system of complements—each policy is more valuable when it is adopted along with other complementary policies. For example, a fall in the costs of flexible manufacturing equipment can favor the following simultaneous changes in a firm's strategy and organizational architecture: investment in more flexible manufacturing equipment, increased output, more frequent product innovations, more continuous product improvements, higher levels of training, additional investment in more efficient production design procedures (computer-aided design), greater autonomy of workers and hence better use of local information, more cross-training, greater use of teams, additional screening to identify prospective employees with greater potential, and increased horizontal communication.

Changing only a subset of these policies might be less productive than changing them all at once because of the complementarities: More value is created when there are reinforcing changes across this collection of policies. For example, employee training is likely to add less value if employees are not given increased autonomy to employ their new skills. Yet, making rapid changes in many elements of a firm's strategy and organizational architecture is expensive.

Firms in which more of these policies are already in place are more likely to take advantage of a reduction in the cost of flexible manufacturing than firms without these policies in place. Because of their team capabilities, these firms are likely to generate economic profits that will not be competed away in the near term.

In this example, the unexpected change in the environment is a fall in the cost of flexible manufacturing technology. This change benefits some firms but not others. If a different environmental change occurred, a different group of firms might benefit.

Source: P. Milgrom and J. Roberts (1995), "Complementarities and Fit: Strategy, Structure, and Organizational Change in Manufacturing," *Journal of Accounting and Economics* 19, 179–208.

A Partial Explanation for Wal-Mart's Success

Sam Walton's initial strategy in the early 1960s was to establish stores in small towns (populations under 25,000) in rural Arkansas, Missouri, and Oklahoma. His intent was to place "good-sized stores in little one-horse towns, which everybody else was ignoring." As he increased the number of stores, he designed an extremely efficient distribution system—a hub-and-spoke system with regional distribution centers. He also cultivated key vendor relationships, a distinctive human-resource management system, and a nonunionized workforce. As his network of stores increased, he opened additional stores in nearby states, eventually expanding throughout the country and internationally.

As Wal-Mart continued to expand, its success became evident. Would-be competitors envied this success; yet, they did not have the capability to mimic Wal-Mart's strategy. First, it did not make economic sense for companies to construct competing stores in the small rural communities where Wal-Mart already operated. Surely, the resulting competition with Wal-Mart would drive prices down in these "one-horse" towns. Wal-Mart's first-mover advantage created an entry barrier and market power. Without a sufficient number of existing stores, it also did not make economic sense to copy Wal-Mart's distribution system in the rural Southeast. As Wal-Mart gained experience, it developed organizational processes and resources (team capabilities) that provided potential advantages over would-be competitors as it expanded into new geographic areas, such as the Pacific Northwest.

Economic Profits without Market Power: A Summary of the Key Concepts

Chapter 6 characterized competitive output markets in terms of four basic conditions: (1) many buyers and sellers, (2) product homogeneity, (3) rapid dissemination of accurate information at low cost, and (4) free entry into and exit from the product market. In this setting, firms have no market power and essentially are price takers in the output market: Firm demand curves are horizontal at the market price. The marginal firm sells the product at average cost and makes no abnormal profit.

In this chapter, we discuss how it is possible for some firms in a competitive market to make economic profits (produce at an average cost below the market price). Economists refer to these firms as being "inframarginal." To be inframarginal, two conditions must be met:

- Rivals cannot imitate the inframarginal firm and assemble teams of assets that produce the product at the same low cost—at least in the near term. If competitors can erode cost advantages through imitation, competition will drive the price down and eliminate above-normal profits.

- The full value of the firm's superior productivity cannot be captured by selling its assets to other firms—unless they are sold together. Otherwise the opportunity cost of production will be the same as for their rivals (even if they can't assemble equally productive teams).

The fact that firms have different histories and paths can help explain the existence of team capabilities and inframarginal firms. Nonetheless, staying inframarginal is not easy. Potential competitors have strong incentives to discover ways to imitate successful firms or otherwise counteract their advantages. Also, to the extent that an advantage is based on an identifiable asset, such as a talented manager or a prime location, the opportunity cost of the resource is likely to rise from competitive pressures in factor markets. Thus, competitive pressures in both the product and factor markets make sustaining economic profits difficult.

Wal-Mart could have sold some of its resources, such as individual stores, yet potential buyers would have limited incentives to bid up the price of these assets unless they could have purchased them all together. For example, the value of an individual store is lower when it is not coupled with Wal-Mart's distribution system.[25] Thus, although Wal-Mart faced an opportunity cost from not selling its individual assets piecemeal to other firms, the value of keeping these assets together within the same firm was likely to be far higher than this opportunity cost. If Wal-Mart were to construct an income statement based on its opportunity costs (as we did for Arco in the bottom panel of Table 8.1), it would show a positive economic profit.[26]

Even though Wal-Mart has had a competitive advantage in rural America, its advantage has been smaller in urban centers. Urban areas can support more than one discount store—thus promoting entry by Target, Kmart, and others. There also is more competition from nondiscount stores. Competing firms have copied many of Wal-Mart's innovations in distribution, vendor relationships, and so on. Thus, in urban areas Wal-Mart has had both less market power and a smaller productivity advantage. Wal-Mart also has had problems at some of its international locations, such as Brazil. Internationally, Wal-Mart's advantages from superior distribution and vendor relations are arguably smaller; also its brand name is less well known than in the United States.

[25]A reader might wonder why Wal-Mart couldn't sell the store to a buyer at a high price and contract with the buyer to allow it to use Wal-Mart's distribution system. This issue is addressed in Chapter 18. That analysis suggests that given the nature of the assets, Wal-Mart is better off owning them jointly.

[26]Recall that the opportunity costs of the individual resources are their next highest valued use outside of their current use.

Nomura Securities Company: It is not Easy to Remake a Business

Japan's Nomura Securities Company—whose roots go back to the nineteenth century rice exchanges of Osaka—was one of the world's most profitable securities firms in the 1980s. In 1997 following a serious scandal involving payoffs to racketeers, the company almost collapsed. The company also was hurt because it strongly recommended a set of stocks to customers that then fell significantly in value. The new president, Junichi Ujiie, vowed to remake the company. He wanted to deemphasize the selling of individual stocks to customers and focus more on asset gathering and portfolio advice. His objective was to become more like Merrill Lynch or Morgan Stanley Dean Witter & Company. By late 1999, Ujiie had failed to turn the company around. Indeed Nomura continued to lose out to smaller competitors in obtaining new business. Like many large companies, Nomura had trouble remaking itself to regain lost success and profitability.

Source: B. Spindle (1999), "Nomura Restructuring Falters; Can Mr. Ujiie
Still Remake the Firm?" *The Wall Street Journal* (September 3), A1.

All Good Things Must End

The business environment is constantly evolving with new technological innovations, changes in consumer tastes, new business concepts, new firms, and other developments. Given these changes, it is unlikely that any competitive advantage will last forever, unless the firm can find a succession of new value-increasing strategies. Just as the elements erode a mountain, persistent competition erodes firm profits over time. While entry may be limited, outside firms have strong incentives to devise methods of capturing profits from successful firms. Ultimately, one of these methods is likely to work. If one compares today's top firms with those of, say, 50 years ago, the lists are quite different. For example, today's top firms like Wal-Mart, Microsoft, and Intel did not exist 50 years ago, whereas many of the top firms from yesteryear have become less successful or gone out of existence.

Changing Fortunes

The fortunes of firms change over time. Due to competitive pressures, the top firms in one period are often not the top firms in subsequent periods. Below is a listing of the top ten firms in terms of market value in 1970 and 2000. The lists are different. Eastman Kodak, Sears, Texaco, Xerox, and Gulf Oil fell off the list between 1970 and 2000. New entrants to the list by 2000 include Ford, Wal-Mart, Citigroup, Philip Morris, and Boeing. (Standard Oil of NJ changed its name to Exxon in 1972 and merged with Mobil in 1999.)

Rank	1970	2000
1	IBM	General Motors
2	AT&T	Wal-Mart Stores
3	General Motors	Exxon-Mobil
4	Standard Oil of NJ	Ford Motor
5	Eastman Kodak	General Electric
6	Sears Roebuck	IBM
7	Texaco	Citigroup
8	General Electric	AT&T
9	Xerox	Philip Morris
10	Gulf Oil	Boeing

Consistent with this view, Wal-Mart's growth slowed significantly during the first part of the 1990s. Although its performance improved during the late 1990s, economic theory and experience suggested that continued superior performance should not be expected over the long run.

Economics of Diversification

Although some firms, such as Wrigley's gum, concentrate on a single major business, most large firms engage in numerous businesses: They are diversified. This raises the question: Is corporate diversification a productive strategy to create and capture value? *Economies of scope* are the primary reason that diversification might enhance value. In addition, combining businesses within the same firm can *promote complementary products*. But diversification also entails costs. Value maximization requires that firms consider both the benefits and the costs of diversification. In this section, we discuss these costs and benefits and analyze the circumstances under which diversification is most likely to create value. We also examine who is most likely to capture this value.

Benefits of Diversification

Economies of Scope   As discussed in Chapter 6, economies of scope exist when one firm could produce multiple products at lower cost than separate firms could produce the products. Economies of scope might occur anywhere along the vertical chain of production.[27] Consider the following examples: a diversified firm buys inputs at a discount reflecting its higher volume from using the same inputs in producing different products; a firm economizes on transportation costs because it delivers different products to the same customer; a firm uses salespeople more efficiently because they are able to offer customers an array of products; and a firm economizes on flotation costs because it raises capital to fund several businesses at once. Sometimes, producing one product unavoidably also produces others because of a jointness in the production process. For instance, if a firm produces beef by slaughtering cows, it also generally makes economic sense to produce other products with the bones and hides.

Combining activities inside the same firm is not the only way to achieve these types of economies. There are alternative ways to organize that also accomplish this objective. For example, an independent wholesaler might offer retailers an array of products produced by separate manufacturers, centralize the billing of retailers, and provide a more efficient inventory and distribution system. Which method of organization is best depends on contracting costs. For example, negotiating and enforcing contracts among independent firms can be expensive, as can organizing activities within the same firm (see below). Sometimes integrating activities within the same firm is less expensive than contracting among firms. In this case, diversification creates value. We discuss the trade-offs in choosing among organizational forms in greater detail in Part 3 of this book.

Promoting Complements   Another potential reason for diversification is to promote the supply of complementary products. For example, Ford and General Motors entered

---

[27]The vertical chain of production consists of the various steps in taking raw materials and transforming them into consumer products. These steps include research and development, purchasing, production, outbound logistics, marketing, sales, service, support activities, and so on. See Chapter 18 for a more detailed discussion of this chain of activities.

Wal-Mart Diversifies into the Traditional Grocery Store Business

In 1998, Wal-Mart opened three "experimental" 40,000 square foot grocery stores in Arkansas. The potential benefits of this diversification derive from economies of scope. Wal-Mart has a quite efficient distribution system that also can be used to stock the grocery stores. It has the potential to leverage its relationships with key vendors, which currently serve its discount stores and supercenters. Wal-Mart's management has significant experience in managing stores in a related business. This experience is likely to be helpful in choosing store locations, establishing and running management systems, and so on.

---

the consumer credit business in 1919 and 1959 respectively.[28] One potential benefit of auto manufacturers' entering the financing business would be to increase the demand for automobiles by offering low-interest-rate loans to customers (recall Figure 8.1).[29] Contracting/transaction costs also were reduced because the consumer could fill out the loan application while purchasing the automobile. Today, communication systems, computers, and sophisticated credit-scoring systems make it easy to apply for a car loan from a lender over the phone or the Internet. This was true neither in 1919 nor 1959. Again there may have been other ways of organizing to achieve these economies (for example, the automobile companies could have contracted to process loan applications for a bank). However, the costs of these organizational alternatives evidently were higher than combining the businesses within one company.

As another illustration, recall our example of PCs and printers. The companies benefited by coordinating the pricing of their products; another way of achieving this cooperation would be to merge the two firms.

Costs of Diversification

Although diversification has potential benefits, it also has potential costs. As firms grow, they often become bureaucratic and more expensive to manage. As we shall discuss in more detail in Part 3 of this book, it is difficult to devise compensation plans that motivate managers in large companies to behave like owners of smaller companies. Owners have a natural incentive to work hard and increase the value of their firms because they keep the profits of the firm, whereas salaried managers do not. If diversification occurs through the merger of two firms (as is often the case), it also can be quite expensive to develop common personnel, communication, information, and operating systems.

Management Implications

A Faulty Reason to Diversify   Some managers diversify to reduce earnings volatility. For example, the former CEO of Goodyear Tire justified diversification into the oil

---

[28]See G. Stigler (1966), *The Theory of Price,* 3rd edition (Macmillan Press: London).

[29]Offering low-interest-rate loans benefited Ford and GM only if their cost of providing credit to customers was lower than the prevailing market price for credit (for example, the loan market was noncompetitive or the auto company valued repossessed cars from bad loan customers more than other lenders). Otherwise, the companies could have obtained the same increase in sales by simply reducing the price of automobiles by the amount of the credit subsidy. (However, note that the credit subsidy might make it easier to price-discriminate between cash and credit customers. Low-interest rates might be used to hide price concessions to credit customers.) See S. Mian and C. Smith (1992), "Accounts Receivable Management Policy: Theory and Evidence," *Journal of Finance* 47, 169–200.

Proposed Megamerger Collapses in the Drug Industry

The planned $35 billion merger between American Home Products and Monsanto Company collapsed in late 1998. Monsanto's primary focus had been on biotechnology and drugs. For example, in the 1990s its strategy focused on being the first to cash in on patents for crops that make drugs and repel bugs. American Home Products brought a well-developed sales force to the deal that could have moved Monsanto's crop creations into drugstores and supermarkets. This merger of related companies had the potential to generate economies of scope.

The merger collapsed because of the costs of integrating the two companies. The two sides disagreed on many items ranging from which company should be assigned the corporate headquarters to how much compensation should be given to top executives. Especially problematic was merging the two management styles of the CEOs who planned to share the title of co-CEO. One of the CEOs was noted for tight-fisted cost cutting, whereas the other was known for more liberal spending and investment.

Upon the announcement of the merger collapse, Monsanto's stock closed at $37 per share, down $13.38 per share, or 27 percent. American Home Products' stock fell $5, or 10 percent. Apparently, the stock market thought that the merger would have created value and was disappointed when it collapsed.

Source: T. Burton and E. Tanouye (1998), "Another Drug Industry Megamerger Goes Bust," *The Wall Street Journal* (October 14), B1.

business because it was countercyclical to the tire industry. He reasoned that when gas prices were low, the company would do well in tires, since people would be driving more. When gas prices were high, the company might do poorly in tires but would do well in the oil business. Overall, earnings would be less volatile.

It is true that diversification can reduce earnings volatility. The problem with using this as a justification for diversification is that this reduction in volatility need not increase a firm's value. Shareholders (the owners of public companies) can diversify within their own investment portfolios at low cost. For example, it is easy for investors to purchase shares of both a tire company and an oil company. Through this diversification investors reduce return volatility on their overall portfolios. There is no reason for investors to pay a premium for a company simply to reduce return volatility, since they can achieve this same objective by purchasing stock in the two separate companies.[30] At the same time the costs of integrating diverse businesses within the same firm can be significant.

When Does Diversification Create Value? *Related diversification* occurs when the businesses serve common markets or use related technologies. For example, Disney Corporation operates theme parks, hotels, retail shops, and television stations. In each of these industries, Disney concentrates on employing its strong brand name to market family-oriented products. Their brand name reduces transaction costs to consumers in their search for quality products appropriate for children.

Net benefits are likely to be greater in related rather than unrelated diversification. If there is little interaction on either the production or demand side of the businesses, it is hard to envision where economies of scope might arise and by definition the two businesses would not produce complementary products.[31] An example of unrelated

[30]Although managers generally should be skeptical of the proposition that reductions in earnings volatility increase value, there are cases where the proposition is true, for example, if reducing earnings volatility reduces expected taxes or the costs associated with financial distress. See C. Smith and R. Stulz (1985), "The Determinants of Firms' Hedging Policies," *Journal of Financial and Quantitative Analysis* 20, 391–405.

[31]Some managers assert that their management skills are so good that they can create value in any business. Although this may be true, it is obvious that a given management team has limited capacity in the number of businesses the team can manage. Again, one might expect value to be maximized if the businesses are related.

Philips Electronics

A common view since at least the 1990s is that unrelated diversification can destroy value. In turn, many companies have streamlined their business portfolios to focus on core businesses. The decision to reduce the amount of diversification often has been motivated by pressures from stockholders and threats of corporate takeovers. If managers insist on remaining overly diversified, they can lose their jobs.

Philips Electronics NV is based in the Netherlands and is the world's biggest consumer-electronics company outside of Asia. In contrast to many other companies, Philips has remained "stubbornly diverse." Philips produces everything from toasters to televisions, software to computer chips, electric toothbrushes to traffic management systems—it even produces 13 different models of rice cookers. During the late 1990s, the company performed quite poorly; consequently, shareholders of the company suffered. For example, income from continuing operations fell by 50 percent in 1999, and return on equity was far below the industry average. Some analysts argued that Philips should sell off many of its businesses. Yet, they have failed to do so, in part, because of the lack of an active market for corporate control in Europe. Moreover, Dutch managers receive little incentive compensation tied to stock-price performance. Robert Lyon, president of Institutional Capital, which owns about 1.4 percent of Philips stock, has stated, "If Philips were an American company, it would have been acquired or busted up long ago."

Source: J. Flynn and G. Zachary (1999), "Philips, an Innovator in Electronics,
Proves Resistant to Change," *The Wall Street Journal* (September 10), A1.

diversification is KinderCare Learning Centers, a day-care management firm, which entered the savings and loan business; it subsequently entered bankruptcy.

Value is increased only when the benefits of diversification are larger than the costs. There is a significant body of research on the value consequences of diversification.[32] For the most part, diversified firms have not performed well. Indeed, many of the large conglomerates during the 1980s, such as ITT and Tenneco, increased their values by divesting units (through sales and spinoffs) and refocusing on a more narrow line of businesses. Research documents that 55.7 percent of exchange-listed firms had a single business segment in 1988, compared to 38.1 percent in 1979. More importantly, the research shows that this increase in focus was associated with higher stock returns.[33] Diversification has been most effective in the case of related diversification where there are potential economies of scope and opportunities to promote complements.[34]

Who Captures the Gains from Diversification?   Even if diversification creates value, the owners of the diversified firm do not always capture this value. Again, it depends on whether the firm brings some special resource or team capability to the transaction. If it does not, the value is likely to be captured by another party due to competition. Consider the potential benefits of merging a television cable company with a long-distance telephone company. Suppose that there is one cable company with the rights to operate in a specific area, whereas there are several long-distance telephone companies. Competitive bidding among the telephone companies would imply that the phone company that valued it the most would get the cable company at a price equal to its value to the

[32]See J. Barney (1997), *Gaining and Sustaining a Competitive Advantage* (Addison-Wesley: Reading, MA), 388–389, for a summary of this research. There are, however, examples of a few firms that appear to have created value through unrelated diversification.

[33]R. Comment and G. Jarrell (1995), "Corporate Focus and Stock Returns," *Journal of Financial Economics* 37, 67–87. This issue of the *Journal of Financial Economics* contains several other interesting articles on "corporate focus."

[34]There are some exceptions to this general finding. For example, General Electric is quite diversified and runs a variety of rather unrelated businesses. Nonetheless, it has performed extremely well.

Diversification Problems at Xerox

During the 1980s Xerox diversified into financial services. The company had gained experience in finance through the leasing of its copy machines, and management believed that by acquiring firms in the financial sector, it could leverage this experience. In late 1982, Xerox purchased a property/casualty insurance company, Crum and Foster, for $1.6 billion. This acquisition was followed by other acquisitions in life insurance, real estate, and investment banking.

With minor exceptions, this diversification turned out to be a financial drain on Xerox. The economies of scope were not as great as had been hoped and problems in the financial businesses distracted top management from Xerox's main business—copiers. In the 1990s Xerox repositioned itself as the "document company" and sold its financial businesses to other companies.

second-place phone company. This process would give most of the value gains to the owners of the cable company: They own the unique resource. Consistent with this example, substantial research documents the fact that target firms obtain most of the gains in corporate takeovers.[35] The average return to target firm shareholders around successful acquisitions over the past two decades has been in the neighborhood of 30 percent, whereas the average gain to the shareholders of bidding firms has been virtually zero.

Strategy Formulation

Developing and implementing strategies that increase a firm's value require an understanding of both the internal resources and capabilities of the firm and its external business environment.[36] Figure 8.5 displays these two factors.

Understanding Resources and Capabilities

An important first step in strategy development is understanding the firm's *resources and capabilities*. By resources and capabilities, we mean the firm's physical, human, and organizational capital. This includes both tangible and intangible assets; specifically, those activities which the firm can do better than other firms—its team production capabilities.

Faulty Analysis at Kodak

During the 1990s, Kodak executives decided to invest heavily to produce writable CD-ROMs. They knew they had the internal capability to produce this product. They, however, failed to consider the threats in the external business environment imposed by other potential competitors. Just because Kodak was a large producer of CD-ROMs did not necessarily mean that it had team capabilities to produce them less expensively than competitors. To quote CEO, George Fisher:

> [With regard to] the loss in writable CD-ROMs, I think we screwed up. A highly profitable business for us, No. 1 market share in the world, and I think we were wishing that it would stay that way. We let it get in the way of making objective decisions. We should have known that prices would fall as manufacturers worldwide ramped up production.

Source: *Rochester Democrat and Chronicle* (November 2, 1997).

[35]See G. Jarrell, J. Brickley, and J. Netter (1988), "The Market for Corporate Control: The Empirical Evidence Since 1980," *Journal of Economic Perspectives* 2, 49–68, for a summary of this research.

[36]A variety of approaches to strategic management are discussed in the strategy literature. The framework outlined in this section is most consistent with the "strengths, weaknesses, opportunities, and threats" approach. See J. Barney (1997), *Gaining and Sustaining a Competitive Advantage* (Addison-Wesley: Reading, MA).

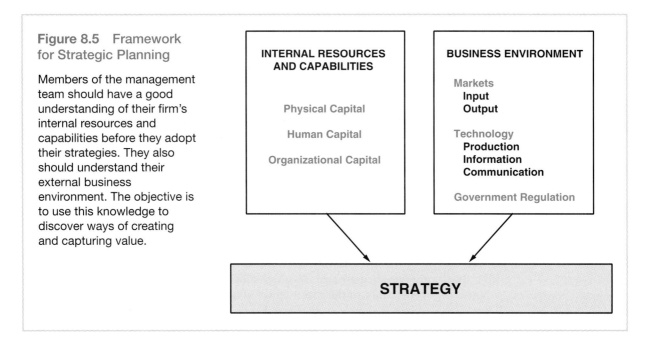

Figure 8.5 Framework for Strategic Planning

Members of the management team should have a good understanding of their firm's internal resources and capabilities before they adopt their strategies. They also should understand their external business environment. The objective is to use this knowledge to discover ways of creating and capturing value.

It also is important to understand the opportunity costs of using these assets within the firm. For example, how much would they be worth if they were sold to other firms?

Understanding the Environment

As depicted in Figure 8.5, important factors in the business environment include the firm's *markets* (both input and output), *technology* (production, information, and communications), and *government regulation.* Effective managers monitor the business environment to keep abreast of new developments in each of these areas.

Referring to Figure 8.1, managers *must* understand the business environment to identify opportunities for value creation. For example, what technological opportunities exist to reduce costs? It would be a poor decision to invest in an expensive technology to lower costs, if forecasted technological innovations are expected to make the investment obsolete soon. What opportunities exist to reduce consumer or producer transaction costs? Managers *must* have a detailed understanding of how transactions take place in the marketplace to discover ways of reducing transaction costs. What opportunities exist for improving consumer products? Are there ways of promoting complementary products? Are there potential industries in which the firm could leverage its resources and capabilities? Are there opportunities to create value through cooperating with other firms?

An understanding of the firm's environment also is important for identifying opportunities for, as well as threats to, capturing value. For example, what opportunities are there to block entry or the development of substitutes? What threats loom from potential substitutes, buyer power, supplier power, and industry rivalry?

Combining Environmental and Internal Analyses

Most resources and capabilities are finite—choices must be made. For example, firms have limited production capacity and human resources. Thus, they face trade-offs in

Strategy at Microsoft

Microsoft's market share has given it an advantage over competitors in the market for operating software for PCs. Consumers are reluctant to purchase competing operating systems because they want to be compatible with other users. Also, the many users of Microsoft products would have to learn new systems if they switched. Microsoft realizes this strength, but also realizes that the opportunities are limited in selling to first-time PC buyers. Microsoft's strategy, therefore, involves producing new upgrades of system software (for example, Windows 2000). These upgrades encourage existing users to buy new software. Microsoft also promotes hardware upgrades (to faster PCs) by developing new software that runs better on machines with faster processors. New hardware sales typically are associated with additional software sales.

deciding how to use these resources and in deciding whether it is worth the investment to supplement them. Also managers must decide whether it is best to use their marketable assets within the firm or whether to sell them to other firms. These strategic choices require managers to combine environmental and internal analyses: They must understand both their internal strengths and weaknesses, as well as the threats from and opportunities within their business environment. Typically, strategies do not remain constant, but evolve through time. It usually is important for managers to consider how other economic agents in the business environment will react to their strategic decisions (for example, rival firms, suppliers, and buyers). In Chapter 9 we examine this issue in detail.

In deciding how best to use special resources and capabilities, it is important to be forward-looking. Sometimes it is more profitable to invest in complementary resources and capabilities that allow the firm to exploit its unique position better in the future. For example, it might have been profitable for Sharp to invest in acquiring complementary knowledge about computers and other technologies to supplement the firm's skills in LCDs.

Strategy and Organizational Architecture

To be successful, a company must not only have a good strategy, but it also must have an appropriate architecture. Ultimately, both strategy and organizational architecture are key determinants of value. Part 3 of the book presumes that the strategy of a firm has been determined and presents a detailed analysis of how a firm's environment and

A Retail Success Story and Luck

IKEA, one of few retailers that has flourished on foreign soil, has 152 stores in 28 countries selling $7 billion a year worth of furniture. Its strategy is that well-designed furniture can be inexpensive without being ugly. IKEA entered international commerce by chance. Started in Sweden in the 1960s, local Swedish retailers pressured Swedish manufacturers to cut off supplies to the upstart IKEA. In response, IKEA turned to Poland for supplies and was surprised to find that it could buy well-crafted furniture more cheaply. This transformed IKEA into thinking about foreign suppliers and retail markets. The firm now has spread to Asia and North America. IKEA is a very patient firm. While trying to figure out how to please US shoppers, IKEA absorbed losses for years. They "had to learn that Americans expected jumbo beds and didn't think in centimeters."

Source: J. Hagerty (1999), "How to Assemble a Retail Success Story," *The Wall Street Journal* (September 9), A24.

Contemporary Approach to Strategy

A common approach to strategy in the 1990s has been to focus on *core competencies*. This popular term's meaning is closely related to the economic concept of team capabilities. Both terms are used to describe the ability of a firm to outperform other firms in some activity because of the firm's uniqueness as a team of productive resources. Core competencies are typically taken to mean team capabilities that can be extended or "leveraged" across different products and markets.

A common approach begins with identifying what, *if any*, are the firm's core competencies. The next step is to identify opportunities to leverage these competencies (for example, by entering a new industry). Sometimes it is important to invest in complementary assets and training to exploit the firm's core competencies effectively in the future.

An example is the Sony Corporation. Through its experience in producing solid-state AM radios, the company acquired a capability (competence) in electronic miniaturization. Arguably "team Sony" could create more value in producing miniaturized products than competing teams. Upon identifying this competency, Sony leveraged it by producing a wide range of electronic products—televisions, tape recorders, stereo equipment, and so on. In developing these new products, Sony acquired additional assets to supplement its team capabilities in electronic miniaturization.

Some consultants argue that most firms have core competencies. They simply need to identify them and decide how best to leverage them. A contrasting view presented in this chapter is that some firms have team capabilities at a point in time, whereas others do not. Trying to leverage core competencies when they do not really exist is a waste of resources.

Source: G. Hamel and C. Prahalad (1994), *Competing for the Future* (HBS Press: Boston).

strategy influence its organizational architecture. This approach is reasonable because the organizational design often is based on what the firm wants to do strategically. For example, if a firm adopts a strategy to react quickly to customer demands, it will probably have to design a decentralized decision system with accompanying performance evaluation and reward systems to motivate productive decisions. Figure 8.5, however, emphasizes that the effects are not all in one direction. A firm's architecture also can influence its strategy—it is an important part of the firm's internal resources. For example, if the firm has a well-functioning, decentralized decision-making system, it is more likely to enter markets for which this type of organizational design is well suited.

Can All Firms Capture Value?

Consultants often suggest that any firm can develop a strategy that produces economic profits, even if it does not begin with unique resources or team capabilities. What is necessary is that the manager be a "visionary" and make sound investments in developing the skills and capabilities to compete successfully in the future. (Of course, for a fee these gurus would be happy to help the manager accomplish this objective.)

Basic economics suggests that these consultants are wrong. Even if a manager is exceptional at predicting the future and seeing what resources and capabilities are important, abnormal profits will not be earned on a systematic basis so long as there are other managers who follow the same strategy.[37] Competition will bid up prices of the required resources in the factor markets and bid down prices in the output markets. As in any

---

[37]And even if no other manager were to have this skill, it still would not be clear that the firm would capture the gains: It is the manager who owns this unique resource.

CASE STUDY: *Wal-Mart.com*

Conventional wisdom holds that to succeed in electronic commerce, you have to get in early. But in late 1999, Wal-Mart decided to challenge that most sacred of web rules. After several years of tinkering with its web site, watching while others broke new Internet ground, the retailing giant was ready to flex some cyber muscle. Up to that point, Wal-Mart.com had realized modest success online, ranking forty-third among Internet shopping sites according to Media Metrix. It trailed web pioneers like eBay and Buy.com. For example, in May 1999 Amazon.com greeted almost 10 million online visitors; Wal-Mart.com saw only 801,000. For 1999, analysts expected Wal-Mart's e-commerce activities to produce sales of less than $50 million out of the company's total sales of $157 billion.

The company announced plans to expand its online store offerings before the end of 1999 to match more closely the breadth of its traditional outlets. To facilitate this expansion, Wal-Mart had penned deals with Fingerhut Business Services and Books-a-Million. Both had expertise in distributing individual orders directly to customers' homes— quite a different set of skills from bulk shipments, which had been Wal-Mart's forte.

Wal-Mart has done this before. When preparing to enter the grocery business with its initial supercenters, it scouted the competition and then signed deals with wholesalers to do much of the support work. As it worked through the details of its operating plan, Wal-Mart brought this work in-house and became a formidable competitor. It planned to implement the same approach online. "This process is not new for us as we begin new businesses," said Senior Vice-President Glen L. Hobern, the leader of Wal-Mart's e-commerce efforts.

Wal-Mart is facing direct competition from Amazon.com; in July 1999 Amazon announced its expansion from books, music, and videos into toys and consumer electronics. Wal-Mart already has become a powerhouse in these product categories through its traditional stores. It announced that it is planning to offer products from all 25 categories that are carried in a typical Wal-Mart discount store. Moreover, it expected to offer a broader array of higher-priced items than its traditional stores—for instance, DVD players and digital cameras. Moreover, customers would be able to return products ordered online to any of Wal-Mart's 2451 US discount stores. Like Amazon, it planned to provide tailored online specials to match the shopping habits of its repeat customers.

Demographic shifts that have been occurring in cyberspace offer the potential to help Wal-Mart. According to research from Jupiter Communication, e-commerce is expected to continue to grow from approximately $12 billion in 1999 to an estimated $41 billion in 2002. Much of this expansion would be concentrated in Wal-Mart's existing lower- and middle-class customer base. Jupiter analyst Kenneth R. Gasser noted, "Internet users are increasingly coming to resemble the population at large."

Discussion Questions

Placing yourself back in 1999, answer the following questions in a well-developed discussion.

1. What is the impact of Wal-Mart.com on customer-borne transaction costs?
2. Do you think that Wal-Mart.com is likely to create additional value?
3. Is it likely that Wal-Mart will capture any value created by Wal-Mart.com?
4. Should Wal-Mart have pursued e-commerce more aggressively sooner?
5. What do you think the potential impact of Wal-Mart.com will be on the parent company's efforts to expand internationally?

SOURCE: W. Zellner (1999), "When Wal-Mart Flexes Its Cybermuscles," *Business Week* (July 26), 82.

competitive market in equilibrium, the expected outcome is a normal rate of return—not sustained abnormal performance.

Although some managers may be better at systematically predicting the future, luck plays a key role in the acquisition of valuable resources. Under this view, many firms invest in projects that before the fact are expected to yield normal returns. These firms take somewhat different paths in their investment strategies, development of internal processes, hiring decisions, and so on. As time passes and environments change, some firms find themselves with superior resources and team capabilities, whereas others do not. It takes managerial talent to identify whether or not the firm has valuable resources and capabilities and to decide how best to use them to maximize returns. Managers easily might think they have unique resources and capabilities when in fact they do not.[38]

Firms without special resources or capabilities at best can expect to earn a normal rate of return on their investment. Firms whose resources and capabilities do not fit the changed environment should not expect to earn a normal rate of return and might prepare to go out of business.[39] In a competitive environment, it can take significant managerial effort and talent (devoted to decisions like choosing products as well as producing and marketing them efficiently) just to earn a normal return.

Summary	*Strategy* refers to the general policies that managers employ to generate value. Rather than focus on operational detail, a firm's strategy addresses broad, long-term issues facing the firm. Ultimately, along with its organizational architecture (to be discussed in Part 3), strategy is a key determinant of the success or failure of the enterprise. The ultimate objective of strategic decision making is to realize sustained profits. To achieve this objective, managers must devise ways to *create and capture value.* An essential first step in generating profits is discovering ways to create value. There are at least four general ways that managers can increase value: (1) They can take actions to lower production costs or producer transaction costs. (2) Managers can implement policies to reduce consumer transaction costs. (3) They can adopt strategies to increase demand. Demand might be increased by taking actions to increase perceived quality, lower the price of complements, or increase the price of substitutes. (4) They can devise new products or services. Sometimes more value is created by cooperating with firms than by competing against them. Creating value is a necessary first step in making profits. It is also necessary to capture value. A firm may have reduced its transaction/production costs or increased its consumer demand, but if other firms copy these changes quickly and enter the market, the competition will eliminate the profits. Chapter 6 indicates that the potential for firms to capture value increases with *market power.* Sometimes it also is possible to capture value without market power if the firm has *superior factors of production* that allow it to be more productive than competitors. The existence of effective *entry barriers* is required for market power. Entry barriers exist when it is difficult or uneconomic for a would-be entrant to replicate the position

[38]See M. Ryall (1998), "When Competencies Are Not Core: Self-Confirming Theories and the Destruction of Firm Value," working paper, University of Rochester.

[39]H. Kim and J. Schatzberg (1987), "Voluntary Corporate Liquidations," *Journal of Financial Economics* 19, 311–328. This article documents that, on average, shareholders incur significant financial gains around the announcements of voluntary liquidations. Apparently, the stock market is unsure that managers will make the tough decision to liquidate poorly performing firms and is happily surprised when liquidation announcements are made.

of industry incumbents. The existence of barriers, however, is no guarantee of market power or economic profits. At least four other factors are important: The *degree of rivalry within the industry, threat of substitutes, buyer power,* and *supplier power.*

Both human as well as physical assets vary in productivity. If an asset allows the firm to make a profit because of its superior productivity, other firms will compete for this resource and bid up its price. Thus, in a well-functioning market, gains from superior productivity go to the responsible asset. For example, if a firm owns a unique piece of equipment, its price will be bid up to reflect its superior productivity. The firm itself does not always have to use such assets to realize its values. It might earn more profits by selling or leasing the assets to other firms.

Competition tends to take a differentiated asset to its highest valued use, but at a market price that reflects its *second-highest valued* use. Because of the interdependencies among employees and assets, the value of the inputs as a *team* sometimes can be greater than the sum of their values if each were employed at their next best uses across other firms. Thus, it is possible that the overall firm will be more valuable than the sum of its parts. We characterize such a firm as having *team production capabilities.* A firm can maintain team production advantages only when competing firms cannot assemble teams that are equally productive. Firms develop different team capabilities because they have different histories and development paths.

The business environment is constantly evolving with new technological developments, changes in consumer tastes, new business concepts, new firms, and so on. Given these changes, it is unlikely than any competitive advantage will last forever.

Some firms concentrate on a single major business, but many large firms engage in multiple businesses: They are at least partially diversified. *Economies of scope* provide the primary reason why diversification might enhance value. In addition, combining businesses in the same firm can *promote complementary products.* Although diversification has potential benefits, it also has potential costs. As firms grow, they often become bureaucratic and more costly to manage. If diversification occurs through the merger of two firms (as often is the case) it also can be quite expensive to develop common personnel, communication, information, and operating systems.

Some managers diversify to reduce earnings volatility. This often is a poor reason to diversify because shareholders can diversify on their own account simply by owning the shares of multiple companies. *Related diversification* occurs when the businesses use related technologies or serve common markets. The net benefits are likely to be greater in related rather than in unrelated diversification. For the most part, highly diversified firms have not performed well. Diversification has been most effective in the case of related diversification where there are potential economies of scope and opportunities to promote complements. Even if diversification creates value, the owners of the diversified firm do not always capture this value. Again, it depends on whether the firm brings some special resource or team capability to the transaction. Historically, most of the gains in corporate acquisitions go to the shareholders of target firms.

Developing and implementing strategies that increase a firm's value require an understanding of both the internal resources and capabilities of the firm and the external business environment. A firm's *resources and capabilities* include its physical, human, and organizational capital. Important factors in the business environment include the firm's *markets* (input and output), *technology* (production, information, and communications), and *government regulation.* Managers monitor the external environment to identify threats and opportunities for creating and capturing value.

Most resources and capabilities are finite—choices have to be made. To make optimal choices, managers must consider the firm's resources and capabilities jointly, as well as threats and opportunities within the external business environment. Ultimately, the firm's strategy, along with its organizational architecture, is a key determinant of a firm's value.

Strategy consultants often suggest that all firms can develop strategies which deliver systematic economic profits even if they do not begin with unique resources or team capabilities. Basic economics suggests that this claim is false. Even if a manager were good at predicting the future and seeing what resources and capabilities were important, abnormal profits would not be earned on a systematic basis so long as a sufficient number of other managers adopt the same strategies. If multiple managers adopt the same strategy, there will be competition in the output markets as well as in input markets to obtain the necessary resources and capabilities. As in any competitive market, in the expected equilibrium outcome is a normal rate of return—not sustained abnormal performance. Firms whose resources and capabilities do not fit the changed environment will not expect to earn a normal rate of return; they should prepare to go out of business.

Suggested Readings

D. Besanko, D. Dranove, and M. Shanley (2000), *Economics of Strategy* (Wiley: New York).

A. Brandenburger and B. Nalebuff (1996), *Co-opetition* (Doubleday: New York).

D. Collis and C. Montgomery (1995), "Competing on Resources: Strategy in the 1990s," *Harvard Business Review*, 118–28.

M. Porter (1980), *Competitive Strategy* (Free Press: New York).

Review Questions

8–1. Choose a company that markets computer products over the Internet (for example, through a web search) In what ways does the company create value? Is it likely to capture much of this value? Explain.

8–2. Airbus and Boeing are two major producers of jumbo jets. Are these firms guaranteed to make high profits since there are only two large firms in the industry? Explain.

8–3. The Watts Brewing Company owns valuable water rights that allow it to produce better beer than competitors. The company sells its beer at a premium and reports a large profit each year. Is this firm necessarily making economic profits? Explain.

8–4. What are team capabilities? Give examples of firms that appear to have them.

8–5. Sun Resorts has a hotel on a Caribbean Island. It recently spent money to lobby the government to build a better airport and expand air service. Why did they do this? Do you think that Sun Resorts cares about how many airlines will serve the island? Explain.

8–6. Evaluate the following statement: "Business is war. Never consort with the enemy."

8–7. The Long-Drive Golf Company manufactures a new line of golf clubs. The Cushion Bag Company makes a special golf bag that protects the delicate shafts on these clubs. The respective prices are P_c and P_b for the clubs and bags. The marginal cost for producing either product is 100. Demand for each product is

$$Q = 1,000 - (P_c + P_b) \qquad \text{when } P_c + P_b \text{ is 1,000 or less, 0, otherwise}$$

How will the two companies price the products if they do not cooperate? What are the resulting quantities and profits? What are the prices, quantities, and profits if the two companies price cooperatively? Explain why there is a difference.

8–8. One CEO justified the merger of his soft-drink company with a machine tool company in the following manner: "This is a great merger. First the products are unrelated. Thus our company's earnings volatility is likely to decrease. Second, our management team has proved that we are better managers than the former management team of the tool company, and thus we are likely to discover new ways to create and capture value within the tool company." Evaluate this rationale.

8-9. Pepsi produces Fritos and Lays potato chips in addition to its basic soft-drink products. Discuss potential ways that this business combination might increase value.

8-10. The Strippling Drug Company has just obtained an important patent for a new drug that increases male virility and cures male pattern baldness at the same time. Does this imply that Strippling has a competitive advantage in producing the drug? Explain.

Chapter 9
Economics of Strategy: Game Theory

The Boeing Company and Airbus Industrie (a consortium of four European firms) manufactured most of the world's large commercial jetliners in the 1990s.[1] In 1998 Boeing, the long-standing market leader, had about a 60 percent market share and Airbus, about 30 percent. With just two major companies in the market, one might expect that the firms would cooperate regularly, avoiding competition to increase prices and profits. In actuality, these companies compete quite aggressively. During 1997 and the first part of 1998, prices of commercial jets dropped by about 20 percent. Boeing posted a $178 million loss in 1997, and earnings at Airbus fell by 61 percent to $147 million.

Many of the world's markets are like the commercial aircraft industry in that there are a few large firms who are the major players. Examples include soft drinks (Coke and

---

[1] Details for this example are from: A. Bryant (1997), "The $1 Trillion Dogfight," *The New York Times* (March 23), 3.1, and M. Freudenheim and J. Tagliabue (1998), "Regulators Investigating Price Increases by Boeing and Airbus," *The New York Times* (November 27), C.1.

Pepsi), US domestic airlines (American, United, and Delta), copy machines (Canon and Xerox), candy (Hershey and Mars), and film (Kodak and Fuji). Even small firms often compete with an identifiable set of rivals and can act as the major players within a given market area. Consider two competing gasoline stations in a small town.

In this type of market, it generally is important for managers to consider rivals' responses when making major decisions. For example, part of Airbus's marketing plan in the late 1990s was to be overtly negative toward Boeing. One Airbus brochure depicted the Boeing 777 as an aging stretch limousine painted like a yellow taxicab, while the Airbus craft was pictured as a Mercedes luxury sedan. In another ad, Airbus pointed out that the Boeing 737 entered service in 1968, the same year Richard Nixon first was elected President of the United States. Perhaps not surprisingly, Boeing produced negative advertisements of its own. In choosing its advertising policy, Airbus presumably had to consider whether a negative campaign was value-maximizing given Boeing's likely response. Similarly, Boeing had to consider Airbus's response in choosing its actions.

Game theory provides a useful set of tools for managers to use when considering rival responses in decision making. We briefly introduced these tools in Chapter 6. This chapter extends this introduction by presenting a more detailed discussion of the basic theory and by showing how managers might use these tools in decision making. This analysis also provides managers with a richer understanding of competition within different market settings. For example, it provides insights into why there is fierce competition in some concentrated industries (such as commercial aircraft), whereas in others the competition is more benign. Although we focus primarily on interactions among rival firms in product markets, these concepts also are useful to managers when dealing with other parties, such as suppliers, employees, or government officials.

Game Theory

Game theory is concerned with the general analysis of strategic interaction.[2] It focuses on optimal decision making when all decision agents are presumed to be rational, with each attempting to anticipate the likely actions and reactions of its rivals.[3] Although it began as a set of methods to analyze parlor games, this theory has evolved to the point where it is applied to study a wide variety of strategic interactions ranging from politics to competitive strategy. In this chapter, we introduce its basic elements and apply them in the context of managerial decision making.

[2] The terms *strategy* and *strategic* are used in at least three related yet slightly different ways in the economics literature. In all three contexts, the decision maker is assumed to interact with others in the environment. Thus the optimal decision is affected by the actions of others. The focus of the analysis, however, varies among the three uses. First, as in Chapter 8, the terms are employed to refer to the general policies that managers use to generate profits. The traditional strategy literature tends to use the terms within this context (for example, what businesses should the firm be in and how should they compete?). Even though rival responses are in the background in this literature, they are not explicitly treated in the analysis. Second, the terms are used to refer more specifically to decision-making contexts where it is essential for managers to consider the behavior of identifiable rivals in choosing their policies (for example, in setting prices in an industry with a few large firms). This is the primary use in this chapter. Third, they also are used in a more formal sense in game theory to describe the players' actions in a given game (for example, to describe a player's "strategy" in playing a game). We introduce this usage and related concepts in this chapter.

[3] Game theory is divided into two branches. In *cooperative games,* players can negotiate binding contracts that allow them to plan and implement joint strategies. In this chapter, we focus on *noncooperative games,* where negotiation and enforcement of binding contracts is not possible. This type of game theory generally is more useful for analyzing managerial decision making.

Sound managerial decision making often requires "putting yourself behind your rivals' desk." Assuming rivals are rational and acting in their self-interest, what decisions are they likely to make and how are they likely to respond to your actions? A complicating factor is that rivals' optimal choices typically will depend on their expectations of what you will do; their expectations, in turn, depend on their assessments of your expectations about them. This type of circularity or recursive thinking might appear to make the overall problem completely intractable. Yet, this situation is precisely where game theory is most useful.

Strategic interactions can take a variety of forms and involve many players who choose among a variety of potential actions. In this chapter, we limit ourselves to simple two-player, two-action cases. This limitation allows us to depict strategic problems using convenient diagrams. The fundamental intuition and concepts developed in these basic cases readily extend to multiple players and multiple actions. Some problems involve simultaneous decisions by rivals, whereas others involve sequential choices. We begin by examining strategic problems involving simultaneous choices. Later, we consider sequential problems. In some cases, interaction is expected to be repeated; in others, it is not. Throughout most of this chapter, we focus on problems where the interaction is not expected to be repeated. Toward the end of the chapter—and in the appendix—we consider implications of repeated interaction.

Simultaneous-Move, Nonrepeated Interaction

In strategic problems that involve *simultaneous moves,* rivals must make decisions without knowledge of the decisions made by their competitors. *Nonrepeated* means that the interaction is presumed to occur only once. As an example, suppose that Boeing and Airbus are asked to submit sealed bids on the price of 10 jet airliners to a foreign national airline. Both companies doubt that they will compete in similar ways in the future. Both companies can select either a high price or a low price. If one company bids high and the other bids low, the order goes to the low bidder; if both companies submit the same bid, they split the order. Each firm has the capacity to build all 10 airplanes.

Analyzing the Payoffs

Both companies privately choose their bids at the same time. The resulting payoffs (profits expressed in millions of dollars) depend on both firms' choices; they are

Figure 9.1 Strategic Form

In this case, Boeing and Airbus individually choose and simultaneously submit a bid price for 10 planes. They can submit either a high price or a low price. If one company bids high and the other bids low, the order goes to the low bidder; if both companies submit the same bid, they split the order. This diagram presents the possible profits from the interaction in strategic form (normal form). Each cell presents the payoffs (in millions of dollars) of a pair of decisions. The entry on the lower right of each cell is the payoff for Airbus, whereas the entry on the upper left is for Boeing. Both firms have a dominant strategy (shaded cell)—choose a low price.

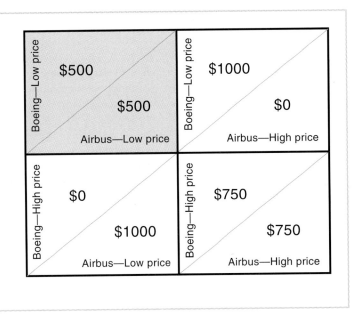

displayed in Figure 9.1. This type of diagram was first introduced in Chapter 6 and presents the potential payoffs from the interaction in what is called *strategic form* (also called *normal form*). Each cell presents the payoffs in millions of dollars for a pair of decisions. The entry on the lower right of each cell is the profit for Airbus, and the entry on the upper left is for Boeing.[4]

Dominant Strategies

A *dominant strategy* exists when it is optimal for a firm to choose that strategy no matter what its rival does. In Figure 9.1, both firms have a dominant strategy—choose the low price. To illustrate, consider Boeing's position. If Airbus chooses a high price (column 1), Boeing captures the entire order by submitting a low price. The resulting payoff of $1 billion is higher than the payoff of $750 million if both firms price high and split the order. If Airbus chooses a low price (column 2), Boeing is clearly better off to price low and split the order. Its alternative is to price high and sell no planes. The same logic holds for Airbus. Given these strong incentives, the likely outcome is for both firms to submit a low price. Note that the firms would be better off if they jointly were to submit high prices. But this outcome is unlikely without repeated interactions. This problem has the same structure as the *prisoners' dilemma* introduced in Chapter 6—we might call it the *rivals' dilemma*. As we shall see, a "cooperative" outcome where both firms submit high prices without explicit collusion is more likely if their interaction is expected to be repeated.

[4]This diagram has two primary columns and two rows. Boeing is the row firm in the sense that its strategies vary between the two rows. Airbus is the column firm in that its strategies vary across columns. We place the payoff to the row firm at the upper left of the cell and the payoff to the column firm in the lower right. An alternative way to picture the payoffs is a simpler 2×2 table with each row representing one of Boeing's potential actions and each column representing one of Airbus's potential actions. The entries in each cell of the table would list the payoff to Boeing and to Airbus, respectively (for example, 100, 0). Although this alternative is more common (possibly because it is easier to type), students seem to find diagrams like 9.1 easier to read. Both diagrams display the same information.

Stocklifting—A Dominant Strategy?

In the spring of 1998, Midwest Quality Gloves, Inc., paid about $700,000 to Lowe's Home Improvement Stores (the number-two home-center chain behind Home Depot) for 225,000 pairs of gloves produced by a competing firm, Wells Lamont. Midwest then sold the gloves for about $280,000 to a firm that specializes in liquidating closed-out merchandise. The motivation for this transaction was to clear shelf space, allowing Lowe's to restock the shelves with Midwest's gloves.

This practice, known as "stocklifting," is increasing in popularity. Makers of everything from bicycle chains to party napkins are lifting truckloads of competitors' products from large retail chains such as Kmart and Revco drugstores. Other stocklifting examples include cellular phones, power adapters, leather cases, pet toys, humidifiers, flashlights, faucets, and glue. The stocklifted merchandise is subsequently "dumped" for resale by faraway (sometimes foreign) retailers. The purpose in each case is to clear shelf space for the stocklifter's products. To quote one executive involved in this practice, "buybacks are a necessary evil in gaining market share."

From the standpoint of the manufacturer this costly practice is a potentially dominant strategy. To quote one product manager, "It costs a ton of money, however, if you want to land a major retail account, you're going to have to do it."

When competing manufacturers jointly engage in this practice, they can find themselves in a "rivals' dilemma" such as in our Boeing/Airbus example: They would each be better off if no one stocklifted. Given the private incentives of each firm, however, stocklifting is difficult to avoid. For instance, after purchasing stocklifted products from a company, one major liquidator makes "courtesy calls" to the victims, encouraging them to "return the favor" by working with his company.

Source: Y. Ono (1998), "Where Are the Gloves? They Were Stocklifted by a Rival Producer," *The Wall Street Journal* (May 15), A1.

This logic helps explain why Boeing and Airbus frequently compete aggressively on price. Airline orders frequently are measured in billions of dollars, so each sale is important. Further, customers (normally commercial airline companies) have economic incentives to deal with a single major supplier of aircraft since this policy reduces the required inventory of spare parts, technician training (maintenance personnel work only on one make of plane), and so on.[5] Thus if Boeing or Airbus lose an order, it implies the loss of potential future orders as well. Just as in Figure 9.1 the companies have strong economic incentives to submit low bids to capture orders.

Boeing and Airbus have particularly strong incentives to compete on price because each firm has the capacity to sell higher output. Boeing has stated that it wants to win two-thirds of all new orders (slightly above its current level), whereas Airbus wants to win about 50 percent (substantially above its current level). These conflicting goals promote price competition as each firm tries to take orders from the other. If the rivals faced tighter capacity constraints, it is likely that there would be less price competition. For instance in our simplified example, a firm clearly would not want to lower the price to capture the full order if it lacked the capacity to produce all 10 planes.

Nash Equilibrium Revisited

Firms do not always have dominant strategies. For instance, suppose in our example that the United States government places pressure on the foreign country to have its national

---

[5]Given these considerations, our assumption that if the bids are the same, the order is split between Boeing and Airbus should be questioned. Yet, if the buyer flips a coin and gives all the order to the lucky bidder whenever the bids are equal, the expected payoffs are the same as in Figure 9.1.

Figure 9.2   Nash Equilibrium

Boeing and Airbus individually submit prices for 10 planes. They either can choose a high price or a low price. If one company bids high and the other bids low, the order goes to the low bidder; if both companies make the same bid, they split the order. If Boeing loses the bid, it sells four planes at the high price through a side deal. The arrow technique provides a simple way to identify a Nash equilibrium. Start by assuming that Boeing will submit a low price (the top row). Draw an arrow pointing to the maximum payoff (in millions of dollars) that Airbus can achieve. This payoff (labeled #1) is in the cell where Airbus submits a low price (if the same payoff occurs regardless of whether Airbus submits a high or low price, the arrow would point to both cells). Second, move to the bottom row and assume that Boeing submits a high price; draw an arrow pointing to Airbus's highest payoff (#2). Third, assume Airbus will charge a low price (left column) and draw an arrow pointing to Boeing's highest payoff (#3). Fourth, move to the right column and assume Airbus submits a high price; draw an arrow pointing to Boeing's highest payoff (#4). If a Nash equilibrium exists, arrows will point to the payoffs in both halves of the cell. In this game, the Nash equilibrium is where Boeing submits a high price and Airbus submits a low price—shaded cell. (Note: Airbus has a dominant strategy— submit a low price—both arrows point left.)

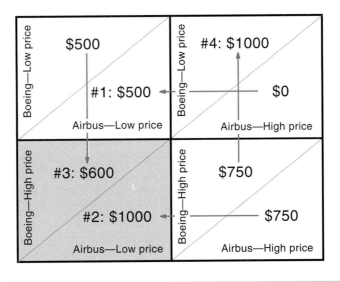

airline purchase planes from Boeing (governments actually have done this for their domestic producers). The airline still splits the order when the bids are the same and awards Boeing the entire order if Boeing is the low bidder. But due to this political pressure, if Boeing bids high and loses the bid, the airline will buy four planes from Boeing at the high price on a side deal after purchasing the 10 planes from Airbus at the low price. Figure 9.2 presents this new payoff structure. Choosing a low price is still a dominant strategy for Airbus. Boeing, however, does not have a dominant strategy. If Airbus prices high, it is optimal for Boeing to price low to capture the entire order, whereas if Airbus prices low, it is better for Boeing to price high and make the side deal.

Nash Equilibrium   When dominant strategies do not exist, the concept of a *Nash equilibrium* is useful in predicting the outcome. As defined in Chapter 6, a Nash equilibrium is a set of strategies (or actions) in which each firm is doing the best it can, given the actions of its rival. In Figure 9.2, the combination of a low Airbus price and a high

Are Nash Equilibria Likely?

Researchers have conducted many laboratory experiments on how people act in strategic situations. One particular question of interest is *Do they choose Nash equilibria?* The evidence suggests that the concept works relatively well in predicting behavior in simple single-move situations—especially if the individuals have prior experience interacting in similar ways with different partners in the past. It appears to work less well in more complex situations (for example, situations that involve sophisticated mathematical calculations) and in repeated situations (we discuss implications of repetition later in this chapter). Also it often fails where coordination is required and there are multiple equilibria, unless there is a natural focal point.

Source: D. Davis and C. Holt (1993), *Experimental Economics* (Princeton University Press: Princeton, NJ).

Boeing price is a Nash equilibrium. Neither firm would want to change its price given the price submitted by the other firm.

A particular problem might have multiple Nash equilibria. Nash equilibria are not necessarily the outcomes that maximize the joint payoff of the players. For instance, in Figure 9.1 the outcome where both firms submit low prices is a Nash equilibrium. Yet both firms would be better off if they jointly submitted high prices.

Identifying a Nash Equilibrium The *arrow technique*[6] provides a simple way to identify a Nash equilibrium in such a problem. Consider the case in Figure 9.2. Start by assuming that Boeing will charge a low price (this is in the top row). Draw an arrow pointing to the maximum payoff that Airbus can achieve. This payoff (labeled #1) is in the cell where Airbus submits a low price (if the same payoff were to occur regardless of whether Airbus submits a high or low price, the arrow would point to *both cells*). Second, move to the bottom row and assume that Boeing submits a high price; again draw an arrow pointing to Airbus's higher payoff (#2). Third, assume Airbus submits a low price (left column) and draw an arrow to Boeing's higher payoff (#3). Finally, move to the right column and assume Airbus submits a high price; draw an arrow to Boeing's higher payoff (#4). If a Nash equilibrium exists, arrows will point to the payoffs in both halves of the cell. In this problem, the Nash equilibrium is the shaded cell where Boeing submits a high price and Airbus submits a low price.

Dominant strategies also can be identified by this technique. If the firm has a dominant strategy, arrows will point to the strategy for all actions by the rival firm. In this example, submitting a low price is a dominant strategy for Airbus: For each of Boeing's possible actions the arrows point to submitting a low price.

Management Implications The power of a Nash equilibrium to predict the outcome in strategic situations stems from the fact that Nash equilibria are self-enforcing: They are stable outcomes. For instance, if Boeing can forecast Airbus's choice (perhaps because it understands that Airbus has a dominant strategy), it is optimal for Boeing to choose its equilibrium action, a high price. And Airbus has no incentive to avoid its equilibrium choice, a low price. Thus, even if both firms can forecast the outcome, neither firm has an incentive to choose any other action.

Although the idea of a Nash equilibrium is quite useful, it is not as powerful in predicting the outcomes of strategic interactions as is the concept of a dominant strategy. When dominant strategies exist, there are strong private incentives to choose them, regardless of what the other player does. Thus, it is quite predictable that rivals will

[6]This technique is described in I. Png (1997), *Managerial Economics* (Blackwell: London).

Figure 9.3 Coordination Game

Boeing and Airbus make simultaneous choices of new communication systems for their planes. Two technologies exist: Alpha and Beta (payoffs in millions of dollars). Both firms benefit if they choose the same technology. Applying the arrow technique, we can see that there are two Nash equilibria: Alpha/Alpha and Beta/Beta (shaded cells).

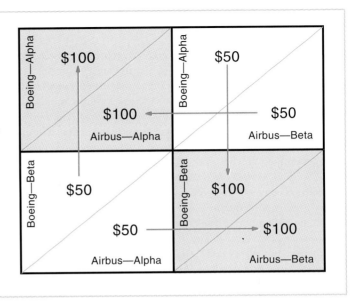

choose dominant strategies. With a Nash equilibrium, your best choice generally is contingent on what you expect your rival to do.

In many cases it is reasonable to expect that a Nash equilibrium will occur. This is more likely to be true when the rivals have more experience in similar strategic problems, have better information about each other, or when the Nash equilibrium is what is called a natural focal point.[7] For example, consider the problem in Figure 9.2. If Boeing has reasonable information about potential payoffs and Airbus's lack of political power within the specific country (it understands that there is a close working relationship between the local and US governments), it will realize that Airbus has a dominant strategy to submit a low price. Boeing correspondingly will choose a high price—the Nash equilibrium. When rivals know little about the game or each other and when there is not a natural focal point, outcomes other than Nash equilibria (nonequilibrium outcomes) are more likely to occur.

Competition versus Coordination

To this point, we have analyzed competitive interaction. In each case, at least one of the firms has an incentive to bid low to take sales from the other and garner additional profits. This potential gain comes at the expense of the other firm. Many strategic situations, however, involve coordination rather than competition.

---

[7]A focal point exists when there is a reasonable and obvious way to behave. To illustrate how a Nash equilibrium could be a focal point, consider a game where two strangers are asked to raise a hand. Both players receive a large payoff if they stick up the same hand (both left hands or both right hands) and nothing if they raise opposite hands. Two Nash equilibria exist: (1) both raising left hands, (2) both raising right hands. Nonequilibrium outcomes occur when the players raise opposite hands. The Nash equilibrium of both raising right hands is potentially a focal point. Most people are right-handed. If one player expects that the other is likely to raise his right hand because he is right-handed, she will have the incentive to raise her right hand as well. Reciprocally, it is reasonable for the other player to follow the same logic. Thus this outcome is potentially much more likely than either the nonequilibrium outcomes or the Nash equilibrium of two left hands.

Coordination Problems with HDTV

High-definition televisions are digital and capable of displaying images at very high resolution. When combined with a good sound system, HDTV can provide a theater-like experience. The introduction of HDTV into the marketplace was slowed by coordination problems between television networks and manufacturers. Both groups thought that they would benefit by the development of this product. However, neither wanted to be the first to commit. Network executives were quoted as saying that they were reluctant to move forward with plans for new programming until the television manufacturers committed themselves to producing enough affordable sets to receive it. Yet manufacturers did not want to commit until the networks indicated that there would be enough digital programming for consumers to want to buy the sets. The situation was summed up in 1997 by a senior executive at CBS, "The networks are waiting to see what the TV makers are going to do, and the TV makers are waiting to see what the networks are going to do." In this situation, there are two Nash equilibria: manufacturers and broadcasters both invest or neither invests. Due to coordination problems, firms may "get stuck" in the second equilibrium, even though both groups prefer the first. Although development of HDTV was slowed by coordination problems, it became a commercial reality by 1999. Manufacturers were selling the sets and broadcasting companies were providing more and more HDTV programming (the first equilibrium). Nonetheless, for HDTV to become a widely adopted product, available programming had to increase and set prices had to decline. Their initial prices for the sets ranged from about $5,000 to $10,000.

The coordination problems illustrated in this example arise frequently with new technologies. The overall value of a technology is usually higher when there are many users (there are network effects) and there is a common standard (for example, consider how much less valuable DVDs would be if there were several different incompatible formats and only a small number of users of any one type). Adopting a uniform standard can be difficult when there are numerous players with somewhat conflicting interests. Sometimes governments, joint ventures among firms, and industry trade groups play a constructive role in promoting common standards, thereby helping to realize a preferred equilibrium.

Source: J. Brinkley (1997), "Networks and Set Makers in Standoff over HDTV," *New York Times* (August 29), 5.

Consider the problem in Figure 9.3, in which Boeing and Airbus make simultaneous choices of new communication systems for their planes.[8] Two technologies exist: Alpha and Beta. Both firms benefit if they choose the same technology. A common technology standard allows producers to exploit scale economies and increases the likelihood that other companies will invest to develop new enhancements for the system because they can sell to both companies. Similarly, companies are more likely to develop service capabilities and stock larger inventories of spare parts. The overall demand for planes also might be higher because airlines would have lower costs in learning a single system.

Applying the arrow technique, we can see that there are two Nash equilibria: Alpha/Alpha and Beta/Beta. If precommitment communication is possible, it is quite likely that one of these equilibria will be reached. For instance, if both firms announce that they will choose Alpha, there is no private incentive to deviate from this choice. Coordination can prove more difficult in cases where precommitment communication is costly and/or there are many players.

Some strategic interactions involve elements of both competition and coordination. In the interactions problem in Figure 9.4, Boeing and Airbus benefit from choosing the

---

[8]For example, suppose each company is working to introduce a new intermediate-capacity plane at next year's Paris Air Show and each views its choice of communication technology as a critical selling point for its model. Each will have to commit to a technology at the design phase, and each might be reluctant to discuss such features with its rival before the new model is unveiled.

Figure 9.4   Coordination/Competition Game

Boeing and Airbus must make simultaneous choices of new communication systems for their planes. Two technologies exist: Alpha and Beta (payoffs in millions of dollars). Both firms benefit if they choose the same technology. Applying the arrow technique, we can see that there are two Nash equilibria (shaded cells): Alpha/Alpha and Beta/Beta. Boeing prefers the Alpha/Alpha equilibrium, whereas Airbus prefers the Beta/Beta equilibrium.

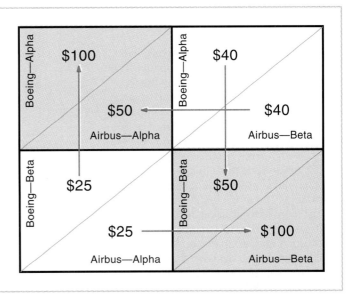

same technology; again, there are two equilibria. But the companies are not indifferent between the two. Boeing prefers the Alpha technology, whereas Airbus prefers the Beta technology (the technologies are better matches for their particular aircraft design). Coordination in this setting can be more difficult than in pure coordination problems, since the firms want different outcomes. Nonetheless, if one of the firms is convinced of the choice the other firm is going to make, it has an economic incentive to follow suit and choose the same technology. Below we discuss ways that firms might be able to make credible statements regarding their upcoming choices.

Mixed Strategies

In the strategic problems we have examined thus far, firms have chosen one specific action (for example, a high or low price). This type of choice is known as a *pure strategy*. Sometimes it can pay to randomize; for example, choose a high price with probability p and a low price with probability $1 - p$. The benefit of this so-called *mixed strategy* derives from the element of surprise. For example, a football team does not want its opposing team to forecast its plays with 100 percent accuracy because it will field defenses specifically designed to stop the predicted plays. The team wants to mix up its plays and surprise the other team. This same logic can hold in business.

Consider the strategic problem in Figure 9.5 where Boeing and Airbus simultaneously must commit to an advertising campaign. The advertising might focus either on the negatives of the other company's planes or the positive aspects of the company's own planes. Boeing is the market leader and benefits more when both firms choose the same strategy. Airbus does better when it can differentiate itself by choosing a different strategy. The arrow technique indicates that there is no equilibrium in pure strategies. If the campaigns match, Airbus wants to change. If the campaigns do not match, Boeing wants to change.

The problem has an equilibrium employing mixed strategies: Both firms randomize between the two actions with a probability of .5—they might base their actions on a

Figure 9.5 Mixed Strategy

Boeing and Airbus simultaneously must commit to an advertising campaign. The advertising either can focus on the negatives of the other company's planes or the positive aspects of the company's own planes (payoffs in millions of dollars). Boeing is the market leader and benefits when both firms choose the same strategy. Airbus does better when it can differentiate itself by choosing a different strategy. The arrow technique indicates that there is no equilibrium in pure strategies. There is a unique equilibrium in mixed strategies. In this equilibrium, each firm randomizes between the two campaigns (choosing each with a probability of .5).

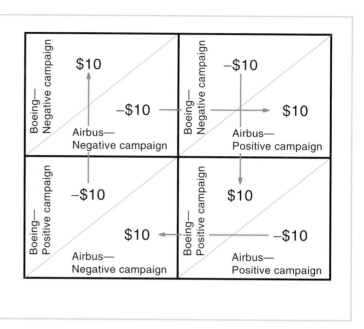

coin flip. To understand why this is an equilibrium, consider the following logic.[9] This problem is what is called a zero-sum game: If Boeing gains $10 (million), Airbus loses $10 and *vice versa*. Thus if one company has a positive expected value in the game, the other must have a negative expected value. If Boeing selects one of the campaigns with a probability greater than .5, Airbus can choose the other campaign with a probability of 1 and gain more than half the time. For instance, suppose Boeing chooses a positive campaign with a probability of .6, Airbus would gain 60 percent of the time by always choosing a negative campaign. Its expected payoff would be $.6(10) + .4(-10) = 2 > 0$. Boeing's expected payoff would be $.6(-10) + .4(10) = -2 < 0$. The only way that Boeing can assure an expected payoff of zero is by randomizing between the two actions with equal probabilities.[10] Symmetric logic holds for Airbus. The outcome of both firms randomizing with a probability of .5 is a Nash equilibrium. Neither firm has an incentive to change its strategy given the strategy of the other firm.

In equilibrium, a firm receives the same expected payoff regardless of which of the campaigns it actually chooses. Thus if Boeing flips a coin that indicates it should choose a positive campaign, there is no reason to deviate and choose a negative campaign. In either case it gets the same expected payoff (zero). By definition, it would not be an equilibrium if either firm had an incentive to alter its choice.

---

[9] All strategic interactions with a finite number of both players and actions have at least one Nash equilibrium in either pure or mixed strategies. In this chapter, we give examples of mixed strategies and discuss the general intuition behind the associated equilibria. More detailed discussion on how to solve for these equilibria can be found in Dixit and Nalebuff (1991), Chapter 7.

[10] If Boeing chooses each action with a probability of .5, the expected payoff is zero independent of Airbus's strategy. Suppose Airbus chooses the positive campaign with probability p. The probability of Boeing matching the positive campaign is $.5p$ (the probability of two independent events is the product of the individual probabilities of the events). Similarly the probability of matching a negative campaign is $.5(1 - p)$. Thus the likelihood of Boeing winning is $.5p + .5(1 - p) = .5$. It correspondingly loses .5 of the time and has an expected payoff of zero. This is true independent of the p Airbus actually chooses.

A Mixed Strategy at Wimbledon

Tennis players can serve either to an opponent's backhand or forehand. The receiver can choose to move left or right in anticipation of the serve. Both the opponent and receiver want to mix their choices to catch the other off guard. For example, if the server always serves to the backhand, the receiver will know that it is best to favor that side. The server would then want to mix it up and serve to the opponent's forehand. In a mixed-strategy equilibrium, the expected payoff to a given player is the same regardless of which action he actually ends up taking. Thus, if the server is mixing between serving to the receiver's backhand and forehand, the likelihood of winning the point should be the same. To test whether the concept of a mixed-strategy equilibrium actually explains the behavior of top tennis players, researchers recorded the results of serves in 10 matches at Wimbledon. There, data supported the theory—they could not reject the hypothesis that the success rates with serves to either the forehand or backhand were the same.

Source: M. Walker and J. Wooders (1999), "Minimax Play at Wimbledon," working paper, University of Arizona.

Managerial Implications

Managers often make decisions in circumstances where the decision is not expected to be repeated and the payoff depends on the simultaneous decisions of other parties, be they rival firms, customers, suppliers, or employees. Potential examples include making a large investment decision to enter a new market or industry, pricing a new product, or making an acquisition bid for a firm.

To summarize the managerial implications of our analysis, consider Valerie Black, who must submit the bid for Boeing in our example. Val should perform the following calculations:

- Estimate the payoffs given each of her potential actions as well as those of her rival, Airbus.[11]

- Examine whether she has a dominant strategy—if so, she should employ it.

- Without a dominant strategy, she should make her best estimate of what Airbus will do and identify her corresponding best action (which might be a mixed strategy).

- Check whether the resulting outcome is a potential Nash equilibrium: Does the forecasted action of Airbus appear optimal from their viewpoint, given her proposed action? If so, her proposed action appears reasonable; if not, Val should reexamine the underlying assumptions of her initial forecast.

Her forecast probably should be revised if it is based on the implicit assumption that Airbus is either dumb or irrational (for example, Airbus is unable to forecast a likely action on her part or does not know what is in its own best interests). In essence, Val should *place herself behind her rival's desk* and ask what she would do if she worked for Airbus. She should assume that Airbus undoubtedly is trying to forecast her actions, as well. Is there some reasonable set of beliefs that Airbus might have about her actions that would motivate the firm to choose the action in the initial forecast—can it be *rationalized*? If not, Val probably should revise the forecast. Since Val almost surely has less than perfect information about the factors affecting Airbus's choice, she may misforecast

---

[11]If she has many potential actions, she may wish to simplify the problem by focusing on a few key possibilities. Sometimes it is not feasible to quantify the payoffs. In these cases, managers can go through the following steps on a more qualitative basis.

Failure to Consider Strategic Interactions: The Paper Industry

Bennett Stewart of the Stern Stewart Company made the following point in a roundtable discussion with the CFO of International Paper:

> I'm kind of fascinated by your industry because it does go through these cycles, and some part of that cyclical market behavior seems to be self-inflicted. . . . When demand does rise, all the companies tend to throw piles of money into new capacity in attempts to maintain market share. . . . Then you all suffer together from excess capacity.

The CFO responded:

> If you're thinking about building a new paper facility, you're going to base your decision on some assumptions about economic growth—and, as the result of globalization, the relevant growth measure today is worldwide rather than just domestic or US growth. *What we never seem to factor in, however, is the response of our competitors.* Who else is going to build a plant or machine at the same time?

Managers generally will make better decisions if they incorporate the responses of competitors into their analysis.

Source: "Stern Stewart EVA Roundtable," *Journal of Applied Corporate Finance* (Summer 1994).

---

what Airbus actually does. Nonetheless, her goal is simply to do the best she can, given her imperfect information. Sometimes it will pay to collect additional information about a rival to make a better-informed choice (when the expected incremental benefits of the new information are larger than its incremental costs).

If Val is reasonably confident that Airbus will choose a nonequilibrium strategy (for example, Airbus has a track record of choosing a particular strategy in similar situations), it might be best for her to choose a nonequilibrium strategy as well. For instance, if she knows that Airbus will choose a particular action, she should choose the action that maximizes her payoff, even if the outcome is not a Nash equilibrium. The moral here is not that Val always should avoid nonequilibrium strategies, but that she should think carefully before selecting one.

If Val is extremely risk-averse and has little experience either dealing with this rival or managing in similar situations, one option is to choose a *secure strategy*—a strategy that guarantees the highest payoff given the worst possible case.[12] In other words, she forecasts the worst payoff that could arise for each of her potential actions and chooses the action that offers the highest payoff among the worst payoffs. But following such a strategy generally will not maximize the value of the firm (for example, if the primary benefit is to guard against an unlikely outcome), and often she could do better with additional analysis and thought.

Sequential Interactions

Thus far, we have limited our attention to simultaneous-move strategic problems. Yet in many business situations managers make decisions sequentially. For example, consider the problem in Figure 9.4 where Boeing and Airbus simultaneously chose new communication technologies. Decisions of this type often are made sequentially. For example, Boeing might choose the technology in one year, while Airbus chooses it in the next. As we shall see, the equilibrium outcome of strategic interactions can vary, depending on whether they occur simultaneously or sequentially. For instance, in this technology

---

[12]Another name for this type of strategy is *maximin*.

Figure 9.6 Extensive Form

In this sequential game, Boeing chooses the technology first and then Airbus makes a choice. This diagram shows the game in extensive form. A node indicates a point at which a firm must choose an action, whereas the branches leading from a node indicate the possible choices. The numbers at the end indicate the payoffs (in millions of dollars) for Boeing and Airbus, respectively. The game is solved by backward induction. Given the payoffs, Airbus will choose Alpha at node 2 and Beta at node 3. If Boeing forecasts these choices, it will choose Alpha at node 1. Bold lines indicate equilibrium choices.

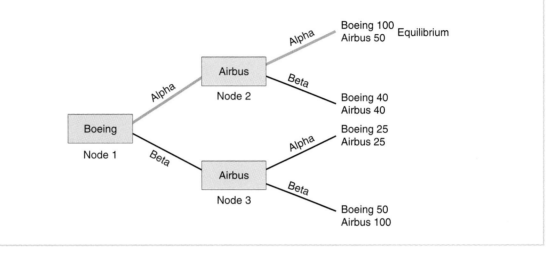

choice problem, there are two possible equilibria given simultaneous choices, but only one given sequential choices.

Extensive Form   Figure 9.6 displays this strategic interaction in *extensive form* assuming that Boeing moves first (for example, Boeing chooses the technology for the new model it introduces at this year's Paris Air Show, while Airbus will introduce its new model next year). The extensive form depicts the sequence of actions and the corresponding outcomes. A node indicates a point at which a firm must choose an action, while the branches leading from a node display possible choices at the node. At the first node (node 1) Boeing must choose between the Alpha and Beta technologies. Airbus makes the next move. Whether it is at node 2 or node 3 depends on Boeing's initial choice. At either node Airbus must choose whether to adopt the Alpha or Beta technology. The numbers at the end of the final branches indicate the ultimate payoffs to Boeing and Airbus, given the sequence of choices made by the two firms. (These payoffs are the same as in Figure 9.4.) If both firms choose the Alpha technology, the payoffs are 100 for Boeing and 50 for Airbus (as in the upper-left cell of Figure 9.4), while if they choose the Beta technology the payoffs are reversed (as in the lower-right cell). Payoffs are lower for both firms when they choose different technologies.

Backward Induction   We analyze this extensive form using *backward induction*— looking forward to the final decision nodes and reasoning backward. To illustrate, continue with the example in Figure 9.6. Begin at the final two nodes (2 and 3). At node 2, Airbus has an incentive to choose Alpha because it prefers the payoff of 50 to 40. At node 3, Airbus chooses Beta. Now move to the initial node. If Boeing foresees how

Airbus will act at the final nodes, Boeing will see that it is in its best interests to choose Alpha in the initial stage. If it chooses Alpha, Airbus will do so as well and Boeing will receive 100. In contrast if Boeing chooses Beta, Airbus will match that choice and Boeing will receive a final payoff of 50. Thus, the equilibrium outcome is for Boeing to choose Alpha in the first stage with Airbus matching that choice in the second stage.

The *equilibrium strategy* of a firm given sequential strategic interaction consists of a sequence of its best actions, where the actions are taken at the corresponding nodes. In this problem, Boeing's equilibrium strategy is to choose Alpha in the first stage, whereas Airbus's equilibrium strategy is to choose Alpha in the second stage if Boeing chooses Alpha and Beta if Boeing chooses Beta. The strategies of the two firms are a Nash equilibrium: Neither firm wants to change its strategy given the other firm's strategy.

First-Mover Advantage

In this example, Boeing has a *first-mover advantage*: By moving first, Boeing makes higher profits than Airbus, who moves second. If Airbus moves first, the advantage is reversed. Knowing Boeing's incentive to match the technology in the second stage, Airbus would choose Beta in the first round and receive higher profits. This example illustrates that managers must consider carefully the order of moves in strategic situations. When Boeing and Airbus make simultaneous choices, there are two potential equilibria. In the sequential game there is only one. The outcome, however, depends on who moves first.

The first mover does not always have a strategic advantage. In some situations, the follower has the advantage. Consider a firm that cuts its development costs by copying product innovations by pioneering firms (or a football quarterback who gains an advantage by observing the opponent's defense prior to calling a play).

Strategic Moves

Actions that are taken to influence the beliefs or actions of the rival in favorable ways are called *strategic moves*. Typically, they require individuals to restrict their own future actions. For example, prior to Boeing's choice, if Airbus could make a binding commitment to choose Beta no matter what Boeing did, it then would be in Boeing's interest to adopt the Beta technology in the first year.

Credibility Can Airbus offset Boeing's first-mover advantage by simply announcing that it will adopt the Beta technology next year no matter what Boeing does this year? Boeing would be clearly better off to adopt the Beta technology if it really believed that Airbus would carry out its announced plan. Yet Boeing probably should ignore such a

---

First-Mover Advantage: Wal-Mart

In Chapter 8, we discussed how Wal-Mart was the first company to place large discount stores in many small towns in the southeastern region of the United States (for instance, in Arkansas). Even though Wal-Mart has been quite profitable at these stores, other companies have been reluctant to place competing stores in the same towns. They realize that each town is big enough to support only one such store. If they did enter, they would have to compete with Wal-Mart and both would lose money. Thus Wal-Mart has a *first-mover advantage* in these communities.

statement by Airbus because it is not *credible.* The statement lacks credibility specifically because it would not be in Airbus's self-interest to carry out its announced plan if Boeing adopted the Alpha technology first. Airbus would be foolish to adopt the Beta technology after Boeing chooses the Alpha technology given its low payoff.

For a strategic move to be credible, it must consist of a sufficient commitment to convince the rival to change its beliefs. Merely announcing a planned future action typically is not enough—*talk is cheap.* As an example of a potentially credible action, suppose that Airbus signs a contract with the manufacturer of the Beta technology to pay the supplier a large sum of money whether or not Airbus employs its technology in the following year. This contract is legally binding and expensive to renegotiate. Now Boeing has a substantive reason to believe that Airbus will carry through with its announced plan to adopt the Beta technology even if Boeing were to choose the Alpha system. If it does not, it still will have to pay a large sum of money to the supplier and thus would be worse off than if it matches Boeing by choosing the Alpha technology. If Boeing decides this announcement is credible, Boeing should adopt the Beta system in the first year.

Managerial Implications

Many strategic situations involve a sequence of actions by the rivals. Examples include management negotiations with a labor union and the dissemination of a new product within an industry.

Strategic Behavior: NBA

There was a major labor dispute between National Basketball Association players and team owners in 1998. Issues included the percentage of revenues devoted to salaries, maximum salary caps, rookie salaries, maximum annual raises, as well as several other items. The players' union had delegated negotiating authority to a group of 19 players. The general membership of the union was to vote only on contract proposals endorsed by the negotiating group. The key negotiator on the owners' side was David Stern, commissioner of the NBA.

The first half of the season was canceled by a labor lockout as the two sides repeatedly exchanged contract proposals. By January 1999, the dispute had cost the league over a billion dollars in forgone revenue and the players over $500 million in salaries. Given the short life of the typical player's career (around five years) the cost borne by the players was particularly high. The dispute also created significant ill will among NBA fans. At the beginning of January, Stern informed the players that he would not consider their "final offer," would recommend to the owners that they cancel the rest of the season, and would begin looking for replacement players for the following year. The season, however, would be played if the players accepted the owners' "final" offer.

Stern's threat to end the season was a strategic move to motivate the players to settle the dispute. Was this move credible? After all, canceling the season also would impose significant costs on the owners. Apparently the players' negotiating group thought that the threat had merit. Following Stern's announcement, the negotiating group decided to allow the full 470 members of the union to vote on the owners' proposal. This action was something that Stern had wanted all along but the negotiating group had refused. However, Stern did back off on his commitment not to consider new proposals from the union. Prior to the final vote, a union attorney called the commissioner's office and indicated that the players were prepared to vote to cancel the remainder of the season. However, a last minute deal was still possible if the NBA owners "gave some ground." After an all-night bargaining session, a deal was reached and the labor dispute settled.

Source: S. Fatsis (1999), "NBA, Players Reach Accord, Saving Season," *The Wall Street Journal* (January 7), A3.

It Pays to Think Sequentially

According to a story that frequently has circulated over the Internet, two college students drove to an out-of-town basketball game the day before an important exam. The students drank too much and were unprepared to take the test. Rather than flunk the exam, they decided to tell the teacher that a flat tire delayed their return. Being the understanding type, the professor said, "No problem; take the test tomorrow." The students arrived the next day to take the exam; they were put into separate rooms. The first question, worth 5 points, was quite easy. But confidence turned to apprehension as each student turned to the next question, worth 95 points, that simply asked, "Which tire?" If the students had thought ahead more carefully, they would have behaved differently.

To illustrate the management implications of our analysis of sequential strategic interactions, consider Helmut Mueller, the manager who must choose the communication technology for Airbus in the communication technology problem. Helmut should begin by defining carefully the sequence of moves. For example, he may have enough information to know that Boeing will choose a new technology this year, whereas Airbus's production schedule will not allow it to make a choice until the following year. He then should work backward to predict the likely outcome of their interaction. Starting at the end of the process, he will realize that he will have a strong incentive to match Boeing's choice in the second period. Moving to the first node, he should place himself behind a Boeing desk. He should realize that Boeing is likely to understand that Helmut will have strong incentives to match Boeing's technology in the second period. Given this belief, Boeing will adopt the Alpha technology. Airbus is less profitable with this outcome and thus would prefer the joint adoption of the Beta system. As a final step, he should analyze whether he could make any strategic moves that would influence the beliefs of Boeing managers and thus motivate them to adopt the Beta technology. He must realize that Boeing's management is unlikely to believe a simple announcement that Airbus will choose the Beta technology in the future. Helmut might conclude that a contract with the

---

Boeing and Airbus Accused of Price Collusion

On July 21, 1998, Boeing raised prices on its aircraft by 5 percent, its first price increase in 23 years. Airbus followed with a 3 percent increase in September. Antitrust regulators in Washington and at the European Union in Brussels almost immediately began separate investigations of whether the two companies had engaged in price fixing. Both companies vehemently denied the allegations.

Game theory implies that a cooperative equilibrium is possible given repeated interaction without explicit communication or collusion. One interpretation of the price increases is that the two firms had moved from cutthroat competition where both firms were losing money to a more cooperative equilibrium. Experience suggests, however, that cooperative equilibria are not always easy to sustain. Consider the difficulties experienced by OPEC in trying to restrict output to maintain high oil prices or the American airline industry in avoiding price wars. It will be interesting to see if Boeing and Airbus engage in vigorous price competition in the future.

Source: M. Freudenheim and J. Tagliabue (1998), "Regulators
Investigating Price Increases by Boeing and Airbus," *The New York Times*
(November 27), C.1.

Beta manufacturer would provide sufficient commitment to alter Boeing's beliefs and choice. After entering this contract, it is important that Helmut make his action known to Boeing. For instance, Helmut might want to report the contract to the financial press.

Repeated Strategic Interaction

Many strategic situations involve repeated interaction among rivals. For example, Boeing and Airbus have many opportunities to compete against each other to supply commercial jet aircraft. Indeed many, if not most, companies deal with the same competitors, suppliers, employees, and regulators over extended periods of time.

When interaction is expected to occur repeatedly, more equilibria frequently are possible. For instance, recall the situation illustrated in Figure 9.1. In this problem, Boeing and Airbus make bids to produce 10 airplanes. The dominant strategy is for both to bid low, even though they would be better off if both bid high—a rival's dilemma. With repeated interaction, the equilibrium still might consist of both firms' pricing low. However, other equilibria, such as both firms' pricing high, are possible. The basic idea is that with repeated interaction, there is more to consider than the short-run payoffs. The decision maker also has to consider the potential benefits of establishing a long-term cooperative relationship.

The appendix to this chapter contains an example of how rivals' dilemmas (such as in the Boeing/Airbus problem) sometimes can be overcome given repeated interaction.[13] The likelihood of a "cooperative" outcome increases if (1) the long-run gains from cooperating are larger relative to the short-run gains from not cooperating (assuming the other firm does), (2) it is easier for the firms to recognize whether or not cooperation has occurred, and (3) the expected length of the repeated relationship is longer. Discount rates also are important (higher discount rates imply that the decision maker cares more about present payoffs relative to future payoffs). The appendix emphasizes the managerial implications of this analysis. In Chapter 21, we revisit this topic by discussing how reputational concerns can motivate managers to behave with integrity in economic transactions.

Strategic Interaction and Organizational Architecture

We have focused on competition between rival firms throughout this chapter, but the analysis of strategic interactions has much broader implications and can provide useful implications for managers when interacting with other parties within their own organization. Part 3 of this book examines organizational architecture. As an introductory example, consider the problem in Figure 9.7 between a manager, Kiana Ross, and a lower-level employee, Lenin Steenkamp. Len must decide whether to work or shirk. If he exerts effort, the value of his expected output is $25 (all numbers in this example are

---

[13]Generally, it is important to have an uncertain ending date in the repeated relationship. If there is a finite ending date, both you and your rival are likely to realize that there is no incentive for either of you to cooperate in the last interaction. Then both of you will have an incentive not to cooperate in the next to the last interaction (since your reputation for cooperating will not matter in the last round). Yet if this is true there is no incentive to cooperate in the interactions before. The final result can be no cooperation in the first interaction. If on the other hand the date of the final interaction is uncertain, there always can be some reason to cooperate.

Figure 9.7   Incentive Game

The employee, Len Steenkamp, decides to work or shirk, and the manager, Kiana Ross, decides whether or not to monitor (payoffs in thousands of dollars). Len would prefer to shirk than to work, whereas it is costly for the manager to monitor. As the arrow technique shows, there is no pure strategy equilibrium. If the employee works, the manager does not want to monitor; if the manager does not monitor, the employee shirks. There is a mixed strategy equilibrium where Len randomizes between working and shirking and Kiana randomizes between monitoring and not monitoring (all with a probability of .5).

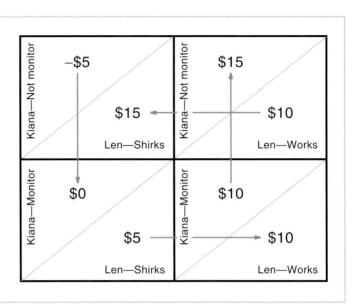

in thousands of dollars); if he shirks, the expected output is $5. Len does not like exerting effort and bears personal costs if he works that he values at $5, but no cost if he shirks. Kiana can monitor Len for a cost of $5 and can tell whether or not he has exerted effort.[14] The labor contract pays the employee $10, unless he is caught shirking—in which case, he is fired and receives no payment.

The arrow technique indicates that there is no pure-strategy equilibrium. The reason is that if Len always works, Kiana has no incentive to monitor, whereas if Kiana were never to monitor, Len always would shirk. This problem has an equilibrium in mixed strategies, where Len works some of the time and shirks others, and Kiana monitors some of the time and not others.[15]

Figure 9.7 indicates that the combined payoff is highest when Len always works and Kiana never monitors. Although this outcome is not a feasible equilibrium if the interaction is not repeated,[16] Kiana might be able to promote this equilibrium within an ac-

Auditing: A Mixed-Strategy Equilibrium

Independent accountants commonly audit firms. One of the reasons audits exist is to help ensure that managers are not embezzling funds. Accountants do not verify all economic transactions when they audit a firm. Rather, they review most of the large transactions and draw a random sample of the smaller ones. If accountants reviewed every transaction, there would be little or no fraud (since managers would know they would get caught if they were fraudulent). However, given the correspondingly small chance of fraud, it would not make economic sense to bear the high costs of auditing every transaction. The result is a mixed-strategy equilibrium. Auditors randomly select accounts to audit and managers sometimes engage in fraud.

[14]Kiana cannot tell for sure if Len has worked from simply observing his output. Although the expected output is $25 or $5, depending on whether or not Len works, output is also affected by random factors beyond Len control. Thus output can sometimes be high even if Len has not worked, and low even if he has.

[15]In this equilibrium, both Kiana and Len randomize between their two actions, choosing each action .5 of the time.

[16]It is achieved one-quarter of the time in the mixed strategy equilibrium (.5 × .5).

Aspartame is a low-calorie sweetener marketed by Monsanto under the name of NutraSweet. It was a major impetus to the rapid growth of Diet Coke and Diet Pepsi during the 1980s and 1990s. A scientist at the G. D. Searle & Co. first discovered aspartame in 1965; Searle received a patent for the product in 1970. US regulators did not approve its use in soft drinks until 1983. In 1985, Monsanto acquired Searle—and with it a monopoly on aspartame. Monsanto's patents expired in 1987 and 1992 in Europe and the United States, respectively.

In 1986, Holland Sweetener was formed through a joint venture of Tosoh Corporation and Dutch State Mines. Its sole purpose was to challenge Monsanto in the aspartame market. It began by building a plant in the Netherlands to compete in the European market. The "big prize," however, was the US soft-drink market, which was to open up at the end of 1992.

Initially, Holland Sweetener was quite optimistic about capturing a large share of the US market. To quote their vice president of marketing and sales in referring to Coke and Pepsi, "every manufacturer likes to have at least two sources of supply." To Holland Sweetener's surprise, they never became a big player in the US market. In 1992, just before Monsanto's patent expired, Coke and Pepsi signed long-term contracts with Monsanto for the continued supply of NutraSweet. The big winners in this contract negotiation were Coke and Pepsi, who realized about $200 million a year in savings. Monsanto remained the major supplier to these companies, while Holland Sweetener was "left pretty much out in the cold."

Envision a pricing problem between Monsanto and Holland Sweetener in 1992 that led to the Monsanto contract. Assume (1) the cost to Holland Sweetener of entering the US market, $25 million,

has been incurred; (2) Monsanto and Holland Sweetener simultaneously choose to quote either a high or low price to Pepsi and Coke for aspartame; (3) if both Monsanto and Holland Sweetener quote the same price, Pepsi and Coke contract with Monsanto because customers are familiar with the NutraSweet label—Holland Sweetener loses its initial investment; (4) if both firms submit a high price, Monsanto nets $300 million; (5) if both firms submit a low price, Monsanto nets $100 million; (6) if Monsanto prices high and Holland Sweetener prices low, Holland Sweetener nets $100 million (after the initial investment) and Monsanto nets $0.

Discussion Questions

1. Construct the strategic-form payoff matrix for this strategic pricing problem. Find the Nash equilibrium.
2. Now assume that the interaction is sequential where Holland Sweetener chooses to enter and if so they face the pricing problem in the second stage. Should Holland Sweetener enter?
3. Why do you think Holland Sweetener entered? Were they just dumb or were there other potential considerations?
4. Prior to Holland Sweetener's entry into the U.S. market, Pepsi and Coke began deemphasizing the NutraSweet label on their cans and bottles. Why do you think they did this?
5. Explain how Monsanto had a "first-mover's advantage."
6. Pepsi and Coke were the big winners in this case. Explain why.

SOURCE: A. Brandenburger and B. Nalebuff (1996), *Co-opetition* (Doubleday: Garden City, NY).

tual firm. For instance, one tool that Kiana has at her disposal is the structure of the labor contract. It might be possible to motivate Len to work in the absence of monitoring by paying him a share of total output, thus offering incentive compensation rather than a fixed salary. Altering the labor contract creates a new set of payoffs and potentially a more preferred equilibrium. Part 3 of the book analyzes in detail how managers can use compensation plans and other organizational arrangements to increase productivity and the firm's value.

This example is but one of many ways that managers might apply these methods to analyze business problems. The chapter appendix provides another example.

Summary

Game theory is concerned with the general analysis of strategic interaction. It focuses on optimal decision making when all decision makers are presumed to be rational, with each attempting to anticipate the likely actions and reactions of its rivals. These techniques can be employed to study a wide variety of phenomena ranging from parlor games to politics and competitive strategy. In this chapter, we introduce the basic elements of this theory in the context of managerial decision making.

In *simultaneous-move problems,* firms must make decisions without knowledge of the decisions made by their rivals. *Nonrepeated* means that the game is played only once. We diagram these interactions by showing the payoffs in *strategic (normal) form.*

A *dominant strategy* exists when it is optimal for the firm to choose a particular strategy no matter what its rival does. A firm should employ a dominant strategy if one exists.

Firms do not always have dominant strategies. When dominant strategies do not exist, we employ the concept of a *Nash equilibrium* to predict the outcome of the interaction. A Nash equilibrium is a set of strategies (or actions) in which each firm is doing the best it can, given the actions of its rival. A problem can have multiple Nash equilibria. Nash equilibria are not necessarily the outcomes that maximize the joint payoff of the firms. The *arrow technique* provides a simple method to identify Nash equilibria.

The power of a Nash equilibrium to predict the outcomes of strategic interactions stems from the fact that Nash equilibria are self-enforcing—they are stable outcomes. In many cases it is reasonable to expect that a Nash equilibrium will occur. This is particularly true when the firms have experience with similar problems, when they have information about each other, or when the Nash equilibrium outcome is a natural "focal point."

Some interactions are *competitive*—at least one of the firms has an incentive to take actions that benefit them at the expense of their rival. Other strategic situations involve *coordination* rather than competition. Some interactions have elements of both.

When a firm chooses one specific strategy or action, it is called a *pure strategy*. Sometimes it can pay to randomize—to use a *mixed strategy*. The benefit of a mixed strategy comes from the element of surprise; sometimes a firm is at a disadvantage if it is too predictable.

In many business situations, managers make decisions sequentially. Sequential interactions are pictured in *extensive form*. The extensive form displays the sequence of actions and corresponding outcomes. A node indicates a point at which a party must choose an action, and the branches leading from a node display the possible choices at the node. We solve the extensive form by *backward induction*—looking forward to the final decision nodes and reasoning backward.

In some interactions it is advantageous to move first: There is a *first-mover advantage*. In other cases it is better to move second.

Strategic moves are taken to influence the beliefs or actions of the rival in favorable ways. Typically, strategic moves involve a firm restricting its own future actions. For strategic moves to work, they must be *credible*. For a strategic move to be credible, it must include a commitment sufficient to convince its rival to change its beliefs.

Many strategic situations involve repeated interaction among rivals. When an interaction is expected to occur more than once, it is called *a repeated interaction*. Typically, more equilibria are possible with repeated interaction than in a nonrepeated problem. For instance, cooperation is a potential equilibrium in repeated rivals' dilemmas (see the appendix to this chapter for a more detailed analysis).

This chapter focuses primarily on competition between rival firms. The analysis of strategic interactions also provides managerial insights for interactions with other parties, such as suppliers and government regulators. It can be particularly useful in analyzing interactions with other employees within the firm.

Appendix

Repeated Interaction and the Teammates' Dilemma[17]

Prisoners' dilemmas occur when it is in the joint interests of the parties to cooperate but individual incentives motivate an equilibrium where they fail to cooperate. Situations of this type occur frequently both between and within business firms. This appendix provides an example of how cooperation sometimes can be achieved when the decision makers are confronted with this same dilemma on a repeated basis. The example highlights the factors that are important in determining whether cooperation will be achieved in a repeated setting. Managerial implications are discussed.

Much of the analysis in this chapter has focused on interaction between rival firms. This example focuses on the interaction between two employees assigned to a team and is chosen to illustrate the wide applicability of the analysis of strategic interactions.

The Example   Anne van Gastel and Bert Dijkstra work on a production team. They want to agree to a "contract" that both will work hard so that they can earn a bonus. They face a problem in that the contract is not legally binding and effort is not contractible. This problem is similar to the prisoners' dilemma introduced in Chapter 6 as well as several examples in this chapter (for example, the pricing problem between Boeing and Airbus).

Figure 9.8 displays the possible payoffs for this teammates' dilemma. If Anne and Bert both shirk, they receive salaries of $1,000. If both work hard, they receive a bonus. However, they experience disutility from the additional effort. The payoffs, net of this disutility, are $2,000 each. If Bert shirks and Anne works hard, they meet their production target and receive bonus payments. Bert, however, experiences no disutility from working hard and receives a payoff of $3,000. Anne also receives a cash bonus. However, being the only one to exert effort, she incurs a back injury. Her net payoff is $0. The opposite payoffs occur if Bert works and Anne shirks.

The Nash equilibrium in a single-period setting is for both to shirk. Given the payoffs, it is always in their *individual interests* to shirk. If Anne works, Bert is better off shirking since he receives $3,000 rather than $2,000. Similarly, if Anne shirks, Bert would rather receive the $1,000 from shirking than the $0 payoff from working. This same logic holds for Anne. This equilibrium outcome is not efficient. Both Bert and Anne would prefer the outcome where they both work—there, payoffs are $2,000 instead of $1,000. The problem is that they can't observe each other's effort until after the work is complete.

Now suppose that Bert and Anne expect to work together in the future. In particular, suppose that in a given period there is a probability p that they will work together in the next period.[18] Thus, the probability that they will work together through n periods is p^{n-1}. Now suppose that Bert and Anne each consider only two options in choosing their effort levels. One is to follow the strategy of *always shirking* every period. If both Bert and Anne select this strategy, the expected sum of each person's future earnings will be[19]:

$$E(\text{future earnings}) = \$1,000 + \$1,000p + \$1,000p^2 \ldots \qquad (9.1)$$

---

[17]This appendix modifies and extends an example in G. Miller (1992), *Managerial Dilemma: The Political Economy of Hierarchy* (Cambridge University Press: Cambridge), 184–186. It requires knowledge of basic statistics.

[18]In each period, Bert and Anne choose an effort level, observe output, and receive compensation from the firm.

[19]For simplicity, we ignore discounting future cash flows. Also, the formulation assumes that Bert and Anne have the possibility of living forever. Neither of these simplifications is crucial for our analysis.

Figure 9.8 Payoffs to Two Members in a Single-Period Setting

The payoff on the upper left in each cell is the payoff for Anne, and the payoff on the lower right is for Bert. If Bert and Anne both shirk, they receive salaries of $1,000. If they both work hard, they receive a bonus. However, they experience disutility from working hard. The payoff, net of this disutility, is $2,000. If Bert shirks and Anne works hard, they meet their production target and receive a payoff of $3,000. Bert also receives a cash bonus. However, being the only one to exert effort, Anne incurs a back injury. Her net payoff is $0. The opposite payoff occurs if Bert works and Anne shirks. The Nash equilibrium in this single-period setting is for both to shirk (shaded cell). Given the payoffs, it is always in their individual interests to shirk.

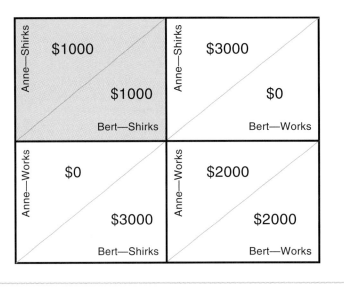

This expression is an infinite sum with a value of $1,000 $[1/(1 - p)]$. The other strategy, known as *tit-for-tat,* is to work hard the first period and thereafter mimic their teammate's previous choice. For instance, if Bert works hard in the first period and Anne shirks, Bert will shirk in the second period. If one person shirks in the first period, then in all future periods both people shirk (the person who selects to shirk in the first period has chosen the strategy of *always shirking*).

Both Bert and Anne want to maximize the expected sum of their individual future earnings from the working relationship. Figure 9.9 shows the generalized payoffs in the setting. Unlike the single-period case, it does not always pay a person to shirk. Clearly, if Anne expects Bert to shirk, she will shirk as well, since $1,000/(1 - p)$ is always greater than $-$1,000 + $1,000/(1 - p)$.[20] However, if Anne thinks that Bert is going to choose the tit-for-tat strategy, it *can be* in her interest to do so as well. Her expected payoff from selecting tit-for-tat is $2,000/(1 - p)$. Thus, she will select tit-for-tat whenever p is greater than $1/2$—since $2,000/(1 - p)$ is greater than $2,000 + $1,000/(1 - p)$. Symmetric logic holds for Bert's choice.

Figures 9.10 and 9.11 show the payoffs for Bert and Anne for the cases where $p = 1/3$ and $p = 3/4$. When $p = 1/3$, the Nash equilibrium is for both to shirk—the

---

[20]The payoff from tit-for-tat is $[\$0 + (\$1{,}000p + \$1{,}000p^2 \ldots)] = [-\$1{,}000 + \$1{,}000 + (\$1{,}000p + \$1{,}000p^2 \ldots)] = -\$1{,}000 + \$1{,}000/(1 - p)$.

Figure 9.9 Generalized Payoffs for Two Members in a Multiperiod Setting

Anne and Bert each consider two options in choosing their effort levels. One is to follow the strategy of always shirking every period. The other strategy, known as tit-for-tat, is to work hard for the first period and thereafter mimic their teammate's previous choice. For instance, if Bert works hard in the first period and Anne shirks, Bert will shirk in the second period. If one person shirks in the first period, then in all future periods both people shirk (the person who selects to shirk in the first period has chosen the strategy of always shirking). The upper-left payoff in each cell is Anne's, and the lower-right payoff is Bert's. In a given work period, there is a probability p that they will work together in the next period.

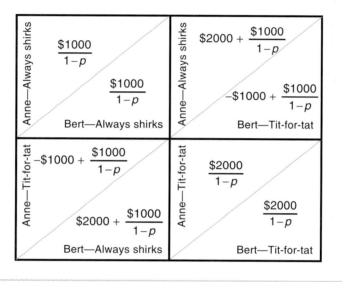

probability of repeated interaction is not large enough to promote cooperation. This example illustrates the general point that reputational concerns are unlikely to promote cooperation when the relationship is expected to be short-term. In the second case, two equilibria are possible: mutual shirking or mutual cooperation.

The existence of multiple equilibria when $p = 3/4$ suggests that Bert's and Anne's initial expectations are important. For instance, if Bert expects Anne to shirk, he will shirk as well. However, if he expects her to choose tit-for-tat, it makes sense for him to select the same strategy. Anne has similar incentives. Thus, the efficient outcome—for both to work—will occur when there is a mutual expectation that both will work hard. This example suggests that businesses might promote cooperation by fostering particular expectations among employees. For instance, suppose the company publicizes in a credible manner that its employees have a long record of mutual cooperation. Given this "corporate culture," it is reasonable for Bert to expect that Anne will select tit-for-tat. Anne will have similar expectations. Both will select tit-for-tat, and the corporate culture is reinforced.

We have shown that the expected length of the relationship is important in determining the level of cooperation. So are the expected payoffs. For instance, if the payoffs from mutual shirking are increased to $1,500, the probability of working together in the next period must be 2/3 to promote cooperation. Alternatively, if the payoffs from mutual cooperation are $2,500, the required probability falls to 1/3. These examples

Figure 9.10 Payoffs for Two Team Members of a Production Team When the Likelihood of Working Together in the Future is Low ($p = 1/3$)

Bert and Anne each consider two options in choosing their effort levels. One is to follow the strategy of always shirking every period. The other strategy, known as tit-for-tat, is to work hard for the first period and thereafter mimic their teammate's previous choice. For instance, if Bert works hard in the first period and Anne shirks, Bert will shirk in the second period. If one person shirks in the first period, then in all future periods both people shirk (the person who selects to shirk in the first period has chosen the strategy of always shirking). The payoff on the lower left in each cell is Anne's payoff, while the payoff on the lower right is Bert's. In a given work period, there is a probability p that they will work together in the next period. In this example, the probability of working together in the future is relatively small (1/3). The arrow technique indicates that the Nash equilibrium is for both to shirk (shaded cell).

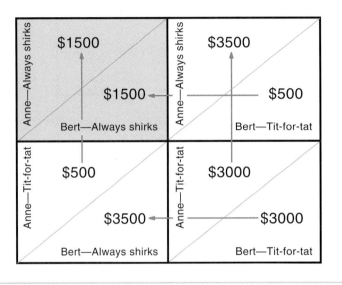

illustrate the general principles that reputational concerns will work best at resolving incentive problems when the short-term gains from cheating are small and when the gains from continued cooperation are large.

Another factor that is important is the likelihood of being caught shirking. In this example, shirking is observed perfectly before the next period. If Bert and Anne do not know for certain that the other person has shirked, they might continue to cooperate even if the other person has shirked. In this case, the temptation to shirk will be greater.

Managerial Implications Recently, managers have delegated more work assignments to teams. Problems like the one in this example can reduce team output and the firm's value. Managers can limit these problems and promote cooperation among team members by structuring rewards (for example, bonuses) that are high if team members cooperate and low if they do not. Also, managers must be careful not to change team composition too frequently: Incentive problems are larger when team members do not expect to work together in the future.

Appendix Problem The BQM Company frequently restructures. Employees regularly are transferred among departments and given different job assignments. Management argues that this action promotes a better trained and more responsive workforce.

Figure 9.11 Payoffs for Two Team Members of a Production Team When the Likelihood of Working Together in the Future is High ($p = 3/4$).

Bert and Anne each consider two options in choosing their effort levels. One is to follow the strategy of always shirking every period. The other strategy, known as tit-for-tat, is to work hard for the first period and thereafter mimic their teammate's previous choice. For instance, if Bert works hard in the first period and Anne shirks, Bert will shirk in the second period. If one person shirks in the first period, then in all future periods both people shirk (the person who selects to shirk in the first period has chosen the strategy of always shirking). The payoff on the lower left in each cell is Anne's payoff, and the payoff on the upper right is Bert's. In a given work period, there is a probability p that they will work together in the next period. In this example, the probability of working together in the future is relatively high (3/4). The arrow technique indicates that two Nash equilibria exist. One is mutual shirking; the other mutual tit-for-tat (both cells are shaded).

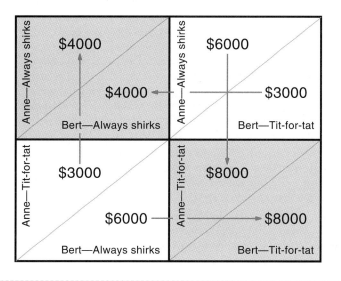

Do you see potential problems with this type of frequent restructuring? Does this mean that BQM is making a mistake? Explain.

Suggested Readings

A. Dixit and B. Nalebuff (1993), *Thinking Strategically* (W. W. Norton & Company: New York).

J. McMillan (1996), *Games, Strategies, & Managers* (Oxford University Press: New York).

Review Questions

9–1. Some manufacturers that contract with the United States government have *most favored nation clauses* in their contracts. This provision makes the firm sell to the government at the lowest price it charges to any other customer. On the surface this provision seems to be advantageous to the government because it assures them the lowest price charged to any customer. Others argue, however, that the clause gives manufacturers more power in bargaining with other buyers. Explain how this increased bargaining power might occur.

9–2. Suppose Microsoft can produce a new sophisticated software product. However, it wants to do so only if Intel produces high-speed microprocessors. Otherwise, the software will not sell. Intel, in turn, wants to produce high-speed microprocessors only if there is popular software on the market that requires high-speed processing. Is this a game of competition or coordination? What is the equilibrium?

9–3. What is the relation between a dominant strategy and a Nash equilibrium?

9–4. In this chapter we gave an example of coordination problems in the market for HDTVs. Show the game in strategic form using hypothetical payoffs of your choice. Use the arrow technique to identify the equilibria.

9–5. Some foolish teenagers play "chicken" on Friday nights. Two teenagers drive their cars at each other at high speeds. The first to swerve to the side is the "chicken" and loses. If both swerve out of the way, they are both chickens and both lose. Neither of the drivers wants to get into an accident. It causes a significant loss in utility (possibly death). However, both do not want to be known as a chicken. This causes some loss in utility. What is the equilibrium of this game? Do you think the two drivers will necessarily produce an equilibrium outcome? Do you think the chances are better or worse for achieving an equilibrium outcome if the two players know each other? Explain. Do you think it matters whether the two players have played the game before? Explain.

9–6. Two basketball players, Barbara and Juanita, are the best offensive players on the school's team. They know if they "cooperate" and work together offensively—feeding the ball to each other, providing screens for the other player, etc.—they can each score 12 points. If one player "monopolizes" the offensive game, while the other player "cooperates," however, the player who monopolizes the offensive game can score 18 points, while the other player can only score 2 points. If both players try to monopolize the offensive game, they each score 8 points. Construct a payoff matrix for the players that captures the essence of the decision of Barbara and Juanita to cooperate or monopolize the offensive game. If the players play only once, what strategy do you expect the players to adopt? If the players expect to play in many games together, what strategy do you expect the players to adopt? Explain.

9–7. General Electric has frequently placed managers together to work on teams. Often the work assignment is only for a short period of time. General Electric makes sure that the quality of an employee's performance on a given assignment is recorded and shared with future teams. Why do you think they do this?

9–8. Some managers commit undetected fraud in producing financial statements. Presumably, if the auditors were really diligent and the penalties for fraud were high enough, there would be no fraud. Does this mean that the accounting firms are not doing a good enough job in auditing? Explain.

9–9. A labor leader has announced that her union will go on strike unless you grant the workers a significant pay raise. You realize that a strike will cost you more money than the pay raise. Should you concede to the wage increase? Explain.

9–10. Suppose you are one of two producers of tennis balls. Both you and your competitor have zero marginal costs. Total demand for tennis balls is

$$P = 60 - Q$$

where $Q =$ the sum of the outputs of you and your competitor.
  a. Suppose you are in this situation only once. You and your competitor have to announce your individual outputs at the same time. You expect your competitor to choose the Nash equilibrium strategy. How much will you choose to produce and what is your expected profit?
  b. Now suppose that you have to announce your output before your competitor does. How much will you choose to produce? What is your expected profit? Is it an advantage or a disadvantage to move first? Explain.

9–11. You are considering placing a bid over the Internet in an eBay auction for a rare oriental rug. You are not a dealer in these rugs, and you do not have a precise estimate of its market value. You do not want to buy the rug for more than its market value. However, you would like to buy it if you can get it below the market value. You expect that many people will participate in the auction (including rug dealers). eBay asks that you give them the maximum bid you are willing to make. They will start low; whenever you are outbid, they will raise your bid just enough to lead the auction. eBay quits bidding on your behalf once your maximum price is reached. Your best guess at the market value is $1,000. What should you bid?

Chapter 10
Incentive Conflicts and Contracts

One of the largest takeovers in history occurred in 1988—the purchase of RJR-Nabisco by Kohlberg, Kravis, Roberts & Company. Public accounts report lavish expenditures and decisions of questionable merit by RJR executives preceding the takeover. For example, Burrough and Helyar in their best seller, *Barbarians at the Gate,* write,

> *It was no lie. RJR executives lived like kings. The top 31 executives were paid a total of $14.2 million, or an average of $458,000. Some of them became legends at the Waverly for dispensing $100 tips to the shoeshine girl. [Ross] Johnson's two maids were on the company payroll. No expense was spared decorating the new headquarters, highlighted by the top-floor digs of the top executives. It was, literally, the sweet life. A candy cart came around twice a day dropping off bowls of bonbons at each floor's reception areas. Not Baby Ruths but fine French confections. The minimum perks for even lowly middle managers was one club membership and one company car, worth $28,000. The maximum, as nearly as anyone could tell, was Johnson's two dozen club memberships and John Martin's $105,000 Mercedes.*

In addition, it appears that major investment decisions at RJR often were driven by the preferences of managers rather than by value maximization. For instance, Ross Johnson, chief executive officer of RJR, reportedly continued to invest millions of dollars in developing a smokeless cigarette long after it was obvious that the project would never be profitable.

The behavior of RJR executives raises at least four interesting issues:

- In previous chapters, we assumed that managers *always* maximize profits. Apparently, they do not. To understand management problems *within the firm,* we need a richer characterization of the firm and managerial decision making.

- RJR suggests that material conflicts of interest can exist between owners and managers: Shareholders are interested in the firm's value, whereas the managers are interested in their own utility. What other conflicts of interest exist within firms?

- RJR suggests that owner-manager conflicts can result in reduced productivity and waste. Unchecked, such conflicts of interest can destroy a firm. How do firms limit unproductive actions to enhance value and avoid failure?

- If techniques to limit unproductive actions exist, why did the owners (shareholders) at RJR allow the managers to engage in such dysfunctional behavior?

In this chapter, we examine these and related issues. We begin by enriching our understanding of the definition of a firm. We then use this more explicit understanding to discuss various conflicts of interest that exist within firms. Next, we examine how contracts help reduce or control these conflicts. We focus particular attention on the problems created by costly information. Finally, we discuss how reputational concerns can control incentive conflicts within firms.

Firms

In Chapter 3, we characterized the firm in terms of administrative decision making: Markets use prices to allocate resources; firms use managers. This prompted a discussion of the relative efficiency of firms and markets. Throughout our analysis thus far in the book, we have treated the firm as if it had one central manager who acts to maximize the firm's value. This characterization is employed widely in economics and has proved quite useful in explaining production and pricing decisions of firms.

The actual decision-making process within firms, however, is extremely complex and differs from this simple characterization in at least three ways. First, there are many decision makers within firms. In large corporations, the board of directors makes major policy decisions such as naming the CEO. The CEO, in turn, retains certain important decision rights while delegating many operating decisions (for instance, pricing, production, and financing decisions) to lower-level managers. Even the lowest-paid employee in the firm usually has some decision-making authority. Second, the primary objective of most of these decision makers is not to maximize the value of the firm: The investment behavior of the RJR executives certainly suggests interests in things other than value maximization. Third, firms often use internal pricing systems (transfer prices) to allocate internal resources.

> **Definition**
>
> The *firm* is a focal point for a set of contracts.

Analyzing organizational issues *within the firm* requires a richer concept of the firm. Several useful definitions have been developed by economists.[1] We focus on one definition that is particularly useful for our purposes[2]: The firm is a focal point for a set of contracts. This definition focuses on the fact that the firm ultimately is a creation of the legal system; it has been granted the legal standing of an individual (it can enter contracts, sue, be sued, and so on). The term *focal point*

---

[1]O. Hart (1989), "An Economist's Perspective on the Theory of the Firm," *Columbia Law Review* 89, 1757–1774.

[2]M. Jensen and W. Meckling (1976), "Theory of the Firm: Managerial Behavior, Agency Costs and Ownership Structure," *Journal of Financial Economics* 3, 305–360.

Figure 10.1 The Firm as a Focal Point for a Set of Contracts

The firm is a creation of the legal system that has the standing of an individual in a court of law. The firm serves as one party to the many contracts that make up the firm.

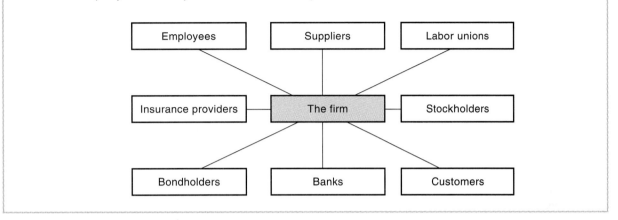

indicates that the firm always is one of the parties to each of the many contracts that constitute the firm. Examples of these contracts are employee contracts, supplier contracts, customer warranties, stock, bonds, loans, leases, franchise agreements, and insurance contracts. This contract view of the firm is illustrated in Figure 10.1.

Some contracts are explicit legal documents, whereas many others are implicit. And even within a relationship that has been formalized with an explicit contract, there is a broad array of aspects of the relationship that are not spelled out within the written agreement—they are implicit. An example of an implicit contract is an employee's understanding that if a job is done well, it will result in a promotion. Implicit contracts are often difficult to enforce in a court of law. Later in this chapter, we discuss how reputational concerns can help ensure that individuals honor implicit contracts.

Incentive Conflicts within Firms[3]

Economic theory characterizes individuals as creative maximizers of their *own utility.* Thus, the collection of individuals that contract with the firm are not likely to have objectives that are automatically aligned. The owners of the firm have title to the residual profits (what is left over after other claimants are paid) and are likely to be interested in maximizing the present value of these profits. Other individuals within the firm do not share this goal necessarily. We now discuss some of the more important incentive conflicts that arise within firms. We then discuss how contracts can be used to reduce and control these conflicts.

Owner-Manager Conflicts

Owners often delegate the management of firms to professional managers. For instance, in large corporations, the residual profits are owned by shareholders who delegate

[3]This section draws on M. Jensen and C. Smith (1985), "Stockholder, Manager, and Creditor Interests: Applications of Agency Theory," in E. Altman and M. Subrahmanyam (Eds.), *Recent Advances in Corporate Finance* (Irwin Professional Publishers: Burr Ridge, IL), 95–131.

Enforceability of Implicit Contracts

While implicit contracts are common, some lawyers argue "they aren't worth the paper they are not written on." Even though such contracts are hazy, most companies strive to avoid breaches because of their threat to productivity and the resulting employee turnover such breeches can engender. Lawyers advise that if you are offered an implicit contract, beware of managers promising something they cannot guarantee, such as lifetime employment. Also, try to document meetings where expectations are discussed and implicit promises are made. Such records can prove a useful paper trail if future litigation results.

Source: M. Culp (1998), "Implicit Contracts: 'Not Worth the Paper They Are Not Written On,'" *Democrat and Chronicle* (August 16), 1G.

significant decision authority to top executives. At least five sources of conflict arise between owners and managers:

- **Choice of effort.** Additional effort by managers generally increases the value of the firm, but since the managers expend the effort, additional effort reduces their utility.

- **Perquisite taking.** It is in the interests of owners to pay sufficient salaries and bonuses to attract and retain competent managers. However, owners do not want to overpay managers. In contrast, managers are likely to want not only higher salaries but also perquisites such as exclusive club memberships, lavish office

The Spectrum of Organizations

The firm can be viewed as a focal point for a set of contracts. One particularly important feature of these contracts is the distribution of the residual profits. Organizations vary remarkably along this dimension. In a sole proprietorship like Esptein's Deli, the owner/manager is the residual claimant. In a partnership like the law firm of Nixon-Peabody, the claims are shared by the partners. In a large public corporation like Amazon.com, these claims often are held by thousands of shareholders who take little direct interest in managing the company. In a mutual like the Prudential Insurance Company, ownership and customer claims are merged. In a cooperative like Ocean Spray, supplier and ownership claims are merged. In an employee-owned firm like United Airlines, the claims are owned by the employees. Finally, in a not-for-profit institution like the American Red Cross there are no owners of the residual cash flows. In most of these large organizations, management authority is delegated to professional managers, who often have small or no ownership positions in the organization. According to Coase, individuals have incentives to select the form of organization that minimizes total contracting costs (see Chapter 3).

Our discussion of conflicts between owners and managers suggests that problems arise in public corporations because of the separation of ownership and control. These problems are costly to resolve. Given these costs, what are the offsetting benefits that promote the prominence of large corporations? One of the most significant benefits is that capital is raised from many investors who share in the risk of the company. Individual shareholders place only a small amount of their wealth in a given company, and thus avoid "placing all their eggs in one basket." This diversification makes risk-averse investors (see Chapter 2) willing to supply capital to corporations at a lower cost. This benefit, however, comes at the cost of having to control the incentive conflicts between managers and owners. Thus, in smaller operations, where raising large amounts of capital is less of an issue, one should expect to find sole proprietorships and small partnerships (where there is less separation of ownership and control). Indeed, this is what is observed.*

*Note: There are also tax-related reasons that affect the choice of organizational form. See M. Scholes and M. Wolfson (1992), *Taxes and Business Strategy* (Prentice-Hall: Englewood Cliffs, NJ).

Perquisite Taking at MasterCard

In 1994, Eugene Lockhardt made his first big decision as CEO of MasterCard International: He moved MasterCard's operations out of the 450,000 square feet Manhattan skyscraper to the suburbs. The new location, close to Greenwich, Connecticut, was predicted to save the company between $11 and $15 million a year. Instead, the direct savings were only between $8 and $10 million. Further, more than one-fifth the workforce quit. There has been no demonstrable increase in employee productivity, and relocation expenses of $26 million were 24 percent higher than expected. Operating costs also were 12 percent higher than expected.

Why did Mr. Lockhardt make this decision? Purportedly, it was to save an estimated $250 million over 20 years. However, 3 years after the move and after Mr. Lockhardt had left MasterCard for a new job in California, some concede that the move was motivated by Mr. Lockhardt's desire to be "an eight-iron shot from Greenwich," where he was an avid golfer. This example suggests that perquisite taking often can take quite subtle forms and thus is hard to monitor and control.

Source: S. Frank (1997), "MasterCard's Suburban Adventure," *The Wall Street Journal* (August 20), B6.

furniture, luxurious automobiles, stimulating day care for children, and expensive French confections.

- **Differential risk exposure.** Managers typically have substantial levels of human capital and personal wealth invested in the firm. This large investment can make managers appear excessively risk-averse from the standpoint of the owners, who (at least in a large public corporation) typically invest only a small fraction of their wealth in any one firm.[4] Hence, managers might forgo projects that they anticipate would be profitable simply because they do not want to bear the risk that the project might fail, and lead to a reduction in their compensation.

- **Differential horizons.** Managers' claims on the corporation generally are limited by their tenure with the firm. Therefore, managers have limited incentives to care about the cash flows that extend beyond their tenure. Owners, on the other hand, are interested in the value of the entire future stream of cash flows, since it determines the price at which they can sell their claims in the company.

- **Overinvestment.** Managers can be reluctant to reduce the size of a firm, even if it has exhausted available profitable investment projects; they prefer to empire-build. Also, managers often are understandably reluctant to lay off colleagues and friends in divisions that are no longer profitable. Managers who fire their colleagues bear personal costs (disutility), whereas shareholders receive most of the benefits.

Other Conflicts

Similar types of incentive conflicts are likely to arise among most contracting parties in the firm. For example, top managers worry about effort and perquisite-taking problems with lower-level employees. The firm's creditors and shareholders can have disputes over the optimal dividend, financing, and investment policies of the firm. Firms can have

---

[4]To be more precise, we do not assume that the underlying preferences (utility functions) of owners and managers differ. Rather we focus on the fact that the risk of owners' claims on public firms can be managed more easily through diversification than can those of managers. The most valuable component of most managers' wealth is their human capital, and managers typically have but one job.

Buyer-Supplier Conflicts

Large firms have become increasingly aggressive at demanding price concessions from suppliers. A survey by the National Association of Purchasing Management of 300 large manufacturers indicates that the average price paid to suppliers decreased by about 1 percent in 1992. This price decline contrasts with price increases ranging from 2 to 5 percent over the previous 5 years. Large manufacturers also have become more likely to switch suppliers in an attempt to decrease costs. Such activities have increased the strain between buyers and suppliers and have made small suppliers less likely to enter into exclusive contracts with large firms. The co-owner of a small aerospace-industry supplier that derives two-thirds of its sales from Boeing says, "Pressure from Boeing to reduce prices has gotten worse in the past couple of years. They haven't learned to cut costs internally so they are beating up on the vendors. We are looking for new customers wherever we can." In some industries, the conflicts are particularly severe. According to a survey in 1992 by *Ward's Auto World* (a trade publication) more than half of 154 auto-industry suppliers say GM's cost-cutting reorganization was unfavorable to them. GM has been aggressive especially in demanding price cuts from suppliers.

Source: M. Selz (1993), "Some Suppliers Rethink Their Reliance on Big Business," *The Wall Street Journal* (March 29), B2.

incentives to default on warranties with customers. Managers often quarrel with labor unions. For example, Alcatel-Alsthom SA, a French conglomerate, was unable to divest any of its low-margin plants without engendering an uproar from its unions.[5]

Owners of firms would like to acquire high-quality inputs at low prices, whereas owners of supplying firms would like to provide inexpensive inputs at high prices. This tension produces conflicts between buyers and suppliers. Supplying firms worry about buying firms demanding price concessions, and buying firms worry that suppliers will either shirk on quality (to reduce cost) or raise prices. In Chapter 18, we provide a detailed analysis of buyer-supplier relationships.

Incentive conflicts also arise with joint ownership. For example, in a large accounting firm, the actions of each partner affect the profits of the organization, which are shared among the partners. This arrangement can motivate partners to *free-ride* on the efforts of others. Each partner hopes the other partners will work diligently to keep the firm profitable. However, each partner has an incentive to shirk: Individuals gain the full benefit of their shirking but bear only part of the costs (their share of the reduced profits). Free-rider problems are common in most group activities and, if left unchecked, greatly reduce the output of teams. (We shall refer to such free-rider problems throughout this book.)

Controlling Incentive Problems through Contracts

What keeps these incentive conflicts from undermining cooperative undertakings and destroying all organizations? For example, might the fear that managers will use all company resources for their personal benefit dissuade owners from delegating operating authority to managers?[6] Fortunately, there are mechanisms that help control incentive conflicts. Among the most important are contracts.[7]

---

[5]D. Lavin (1998), "Union and Regulators Restrain Alcatel's Restructuring," *The Wall Street Journal* (August 7), A8.

[6]In fact, some authors suggest that this concern ultimately will cause the collapse of the public corporation. See A. Berle and G. Means (1932), *The Modern Corporation and Private Property* (Macmillan: New York).

[7]Other important mechanisms are the market for corporate control and the product market. Managers have incentives to increase a firm's profits because firms with inefficient managers can be taken over by other firms and the management team replaced. Indeed, this is what happened at RJR-Nabisco. Also, inefficient firms eventually go out of business in a competitive market.

Experimental Evidence on Free-Rider Problems

More than 50 years ago a German scientist named Ringelmann asked workers to pull as hard as they could on a rope attached to a meter that measured the strength of their efforts. Subjects worked alone and in groups of two, three, and eight.

While the total amount of force on the rope increased as group size rose, the amount of effort by each person seemed to drop. While one person pulling alone exerted an average of 63 kg of force, this dropped to about 53 kg in groups of three and was reduced to about 31 kg in groups of eight. The greater the number of people performing the task, the less effort each one expended.

The impact of any social force directed towards a group from an outside source (for example, a manager) is divided among its members. Thus, the more persons in the group, the less the impact such force will have upon each. Because they are working with others, each group member feels [that others] will take up any slack resulting from reduced effort on their part. And since all members tend to respond in this fashion, average output per person drops sharply.

Source: A. Furnham (1993), "Wasting Time in the Board Room," *Financial Times* (March 10).

Contracts (both implicit and explicit) define the firm's organizational architecture—its decision right, performance evaluation, and reward systems. This architecture provides an important set of constraints and incentives that helps resolve incentive problems. For instance, if a contract specifies that Erin O'Malley, the firm's Chief Financial Officer, will receive an annual salary of $200,000, she can be fired if she unilaterally pays herself more: She does not have the decision right to set her own compensation.[8] If Erin is evaluated on firm profits and rewarded with a large bonus for good performance, she has incentives to care about the firm's profits.

Costless Contracting

Under some circumstances, contracts can resolve incentive problems at low cost. As an example, consider Jerold Concannon, CEO of the Bagby Printing Company. Jerry gains utility U, both from his monetary compensation C and perquisites P such as company expenditures on luxury cars and club memberships:

$$U = f(C, P) \qquad (10.1)$$

If the firm provides no perquisites to Jerry, it must pay him a salary S in cash compensation; otherwise, he will work for another firm. The owners of the firm are willing to pay Jerry S if he consumes no perquisites. However, as CEO, Jerry has numerous opportunities to consume company resources. These opportunities present an incentive problem: Jerry wants to spend company resources on himself, whereas the owners do not want Jerry to reduce the firm's value by consuming excess perquisites. As we will see, some amount of perquisites actually increases value. But beyond this level of perquisite consumption, value falls.

Suppose for now that the owners of the firm have precise knowledge of the profit potential of the firm, Π_P (if Jerry is paid S and consumes no perquisites). In this case, realized profits of the firm, Π_R (if he is paid S and consumes perquisites, P) are the difference between potential profits and Jerry's excess perquisite consumption:

$$\Pi_R = \Pi_P - P \qquad (10.2)$$

---

[8]Restricting an agent's decision-making authority can reduce incentive problems. However, it also can mean that authority has not been granted to the individual with the best knowledge to make the decision. This tension is a fundamental concern in designing organizational architecture and is a central focus of Chapter 11.

Incentive Conflicts throughout the World

Incentive conflicts are not just an American business phenomenon, nor do they occur only in private firms. Rather, these conflicts exist throughout the world in both the private and public sectors. For example, government officials taking bribes is an example of a basic incentive conflict between government officials and the people they represent.

In 1999, Indonesian President B. J. Habibie's political party, Golkar, allegedly siphoned off $66 million from a nationalized bank, PT Bank Bali, to help fund the president's reelection campaign. After the allegations were made, the government hired PriceWaterhouseCoopers to audit the transactions. They cited "numerous indications of fraud."[a]

A similar event occurred in China where a bureaucrat confessed to using a safe-deposit box in Hong Kong to stash away more than $1.2 million in cash bribes from companies attempting to get pieces of real-estate deals she controlled. Meanwhile, in the banking sector, the premier of China is attempting to change the common practice by bankers of ignoring credit standards and awarding loans to people "with connections." In one case, eight bankers received stiff sentences, including the death penalty, for accepting bribes in return for loans.[b]

[a] J. Solomon (1999), "Bali High Jinks: In Indonesia, Crisis and Corruption
Create Financial Vigilantes," *The Wall Street Journal* (September 21), A1.

[b] J. Barnathan (1993), "A Crackdown—Of Sorts," *Business Week* (July 26), 47.

With this information, the owners can solve the potential incentive problem by offering Jerry the following compensation contract:

$$C = S - (\Pi_P - \Pi_R) \tag{10.3}$$

This contract, which reduces Jerry's salary by the difference between realized and potential profits, is equivalent to charging Jerry the full cost of his perquisites—that is, $C = S - P$.

Figure 10.2 displays Jerry's choice of perquisites. His objective is to maximize his utility subject to the constraint that he is paid according to his compensation plan. Jerry chooses the combination (C^*, P^*), which occurs at the tangency point between his indifference curve and the compensation constraint. This combination places Jerry on the highest indifference curve possible given the compensation plan. This choice is Pareto-efficient. The owners are indifferent to Jerry's choice: They always pay the equivalent of S (they pay him $S - P$ in cash and P in perquisites). Jerry, however, is better off being able to choose the combination of salary and perquisites that he prefers. For example, Jerry had a back injury and prefers a more expensive, ergonomically designed desk chair to the company's standard office furniture, even though he knows that his compensation is reduced to reflect the additional expense. Also, Jerry might prefer a combination of salary and perquisites to a pure salary because perquisites frequently are untaxed.[9]

Note how the compensation plan aligns Jerry's and the owners' incentives. Jerry is given the decision right to choose how much the firm spends on his perquisites. The contract, however, charges Jerry the full cost of his perquisite consumption. In essence, he is rewarded for consuming fewer perquisites. This reward structure gives him private incentives to limit his perquisite consumption.

This example suggests that some perquisite taking by managers is likely to be efficient (from the standpoint of both the managers and the firm) because some perquisites increase productivity and because of the differential tax treatment for perquisites and

---

[9]This tax effect is reflected in Jerry's indifference curves. Over some range, Jerry is willing to trade more than a dollar of cash for a dollar's worth of perquisites because on an after-tax basis, he is better off. Over this range, the slope of the indifference curve has a slope with an absolute value greater than one. The optimal choice of salary and perquisites occurs at the point where the indifference curve's slope is -1.

Figure 10.2 Optimal Perquisite Taking

The manager is paid a cash salary *S*, as long as the manager maximizes profits. If the manager fails to maximize profits by taking perquisites (for example, too many club memberships, paying excessive salaries to top subordinates, or buying expensive company cars), the owners reduce the compensation by the amount of the lost profits. Given this compensation scheme, the manager chooses the combination (*C**, *P**). This choice is Pareto-efficient.

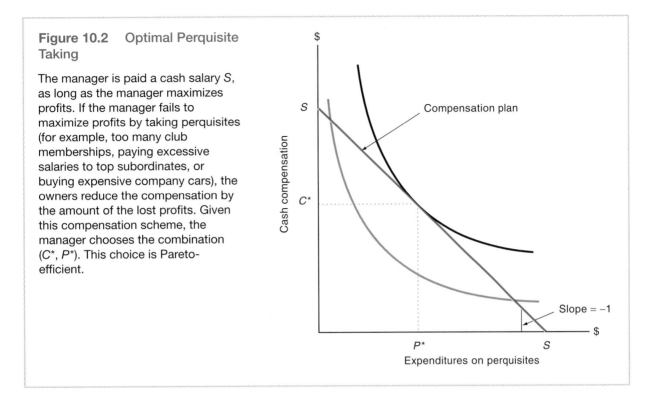

salary. Thus, the perquisite taking by RJR executives was not necessarily inconsistent with the shareholders' objective of value maximization. Without the perquisites, the shareholders might have had to pay higher salaries to attract and retain the management team. Evidence from the stock market, however, suggests that the behavior of RJR executives was excessive. The stock price of RJR went from about $55 per share at the

Agency Problems with Owner-Managers

Baan Co., a leading provider of enterprise business software that competes with SAP and Oracle, was founded in 1978 by brothers Jan and Paul Baan in Holland. In 1998 the brothers owned 39 percent of the public company and also owned several private companies. Headquartered in a nineteenth century chateau with a moat and decorated with Dutch master paintings, the Baan Co. did not own the building. It paid an undisclosed amount of rent to the Baan brothers' private company that owned the building. The private Baan company bought software from the public company and resold it. Because the public had little access to the private companies' operations or financial status, it was extremely difficult for investors to assess the health of the combined operation accurately. Investor concerns about potential conflicts of interest and stagnating software sales caused the stock price to drop from a high of $49 at the start of 1998 to a low of about $10 per share at the end of 1998. One day in July 1998 after the Baan brothers disclosed the extent of some of the ties between the public and private companies and after announcing steps to separate the parts of their empire, Baan Co. stock jumped 11 percent to $41. The brothers since have sold or donated much of their stock in the public company and are no longer actively involved in management. This example illustrates several important lessons. First, managers with large controlling ownership interests in their firm have opportunities to enrich themselves at the expense of shareholders. Second, the capital market anticipates this behavior and discounts the stock price to reflect the expected amount of this self-dealing.

Source: M. Maremont and M. Rose (1998), "Dutch Software Firm Has Extensive Links to Founder's Interests," *The Wall Street Journal* (July 10), A1.

beginning of the takeover contest in October 1988 to about $110 per share when the company was taken over. Furthermore, the management team subsequently was replaced. Thus, the old RJR management team does not appear to have been maximizing the firm's value.

Costly Contracting and Asymmetric Information

We have shown how, in some cases, well-designed contracts can resolve incentive problems at low cost. Yet the example of RJR suggests that contracts often are unsuccessful in accomplishing this objective.

Unlike our hypothetical example, contracts in practice are not costless to negotiate, write, administer, or enforce. For instance, suppose that the owners of Bagby Printing delegate executive compensation decisions to its board of directors. In this case, Jerry might be able to convince board members not to enforce his contract to reduce his salary for perquisite consumption. (Indeed, Ross Johnson at RJR apparently attempted to keep board members loyal and supportive by paying them large retainers.) Board members participating in such collusion with senior managers can be replaced, but only at a cost. Legal fees alone can be substantial for writing and enforcing contracts (the legal profession's total receipts were estimated at $124.8 billion in 1996[10]).

A major factor limiting the ability of contracts to resolve incentive conflicts is costly information. In contrast to our example, it is unlikely that the owners of Bagby Printing actually would know the profit potential of the firm. Information is likely to be *asymmetric:* Jerry simply knows more than the owners about the firm's profit potential as well as his perquisite taking. Given this distribution of information, controlling Jerry's perquisite taking by using a compensation contract that requires perfect information about the profit potential of the firm clearly is infeasible.

There are two general types of information problems that arise in contracting. The first problem is informational asymmetries before the contract is negotiated. The second is the problem of informational asymmetries during the implementation of the contract. Below, we elaborate on each of these problems. We begin with the postcontractual problems because of their importance in this text.

Postcontractual Information Problems

Agency Problems   An *agency relationship* consists of an agreement under which one party, the *principal,* engages another party, the *agent,* to perform some service on the principal's behalf. Many agency relationships exist within firms. Shareholders appoint boards of directors as their agents to oversee the management of firms. Boards delegate much of the operating authority to senior executives; they, in turn, assign tasks to lower-level employees. As we have discussed, there is good reason to believe that the incentives of principals and agents are not aligned automatically. There are *agency problems:* After the contract is set, agents have incentives to take actions that increase their well-being at the expense of the principals. For instance, as in the case of RJR, managers might shirk, consume perquisites, and choose investment and operating policies that reduce profits but increase the managers' expected well-being.

Asymmetric information typically precludes costless resolution of these contracting problems. Since the principal cannot observe the actions of the agent costlessly, the

---

[10]US Census Bureau (1998), *Statistical Abstract of the United States,* 780.

Pilots of Private Jets

Corporate jets often have to refuel on intercontinental flights, usually in Kansas or Nebraska. A typical refueling costs $1,800. Refuelers at the same airport compete by offering pilots frozen steaks, wine, or top-of-the-line golf gear. These freebies are usually offered only if the pilot forgoes discounts on fuel and almost always are bestowed so that the corporation owning the plane never knows why the pilot chose to refuel at that particular place. Suppose the pilot chooses a refueler who charges $150 more than the least-cost option because the pilot gets $80 worth of gifts. There is a wealth transfer from the shareholders to the pilot (unless the behavior is anticipated) and a wealth reduction by the shareholders of $150, and hence a residual loss of $70.

Source: S. McCartney (1998), "We'll be Landing So the Crew Can Grab a Steak," *The Wall Street Journal* (September 8), A1.

agent generally can engage in activities such as shirking and perquisite taking without those activities invariably being detected by the principal. Nonetheless, the principal usually can limit such behavior by establishing appropriate incentives for the agent through the contract and by incurring *monitoring costs.* Also, agents might incur *bonding costs* to help guarantee that they will not take certain actions or to ensure that the principal will be compensated if they do. (For example, agents might bond themselves by purchasing insurance policies that pay the principal in the case of theft.) The agent is willing to incur these expenses to increase the amount paid to the agent by the principal for the agent's services. If it is costly to control these contracting problems, then it generally will not pay for either party to incur sufficient costs to ensure that the agent will follow the wishes of the principal completely (at some point marginal cost exceeds the marginal benefits of additional expenditures to increase compliance). The dollar equivalent of the loss in gains from trade that results from this divergence of interests within the agency relationship is known as the *residual loss. Total agency costs* are the sum of the *out-of-pocket costs* (monitoring and bonding costs) and the residual loss.[11]

Example of Agency Costs   To illustrate the concepts of agency costs and asymmetric information, consider Good Tire Company and the Brown & Brown law firm. Good Tire wants outside legal counsel for contracting and litigation, as well as for general legal advice. Brown & Brown is capable of supplying these services.

Good Tire's marginal benefit, MB, for hours of legal services is

$$\text{MB} = \$200 - 2L \tag{10.4}$$

where L equals the hours per week of legal services provided to the firm. Good Tire faces some important legal issues, and thus the marginal benefits for legal services are quite high for the first few hours. But as these fundamental issues are resolved, the company receives advice on successively less important issues. Therefore, the marginal benefit of additional hours of legal services declines with the total number of hours provided.

Brown & Brown's marginal cost (MC) for providing additional hours of legal services is constant at $100 per hour:

$$\text{MC} = \$100 \tag{10.5}$$

---

[11]Thus, agency costs consist of that component of total contracting costs that arises from postcontractual information problems. M. Jensen and W. Meckling (1976), "Theory of the Firm: Managerial Behavior, Agency Costs and Ownership Structure," *Journal of Financial Economics* 3, 305–360.

Value is maximized—all potential gains from trade between Good Tire and Brown & Brown are realized—at the point where the marginal benefits of legal services equal their marginal costs:

$$MB = MC$$

$$200 - 2L = 100$$

$$L^* = 50 \text{ hours} \tag{10.6}$$

It is not optimal to provide more than 50 hours of legal services because the marginal benefits would be lower than the marginal costs. Correspondingly, it is suboptimal to provide fewer than 50 hours because the marginal costs of providing additional hours would be lower than the marginal benefits.

Assuming no contracting costs, the optimal contract simply might specify 50 hours per week of legal services. For example, Good Tire could agree to pay Brown & Brown $6,250 a week for 50 hours of legal work. This outcome is pictured in the left panel in Figure 10.3. The total gain from the exchange (surplus) is $2,500, as depicted by the triangle labeled *S*. At a price of $6,250 for legal services, the gains are split evenly between the two companies.[12] The fee covers Brown & Brown's costs of $5,000 (50 × $100) and provides it with a profit of $1,250. Good Tire receives gross benefits of $7,500. However, it pays a fee of $6,250, yielding net benefits of $1,250. If the two firms negotiate other prices for the 50 hours of legal services, the split in gains would be different. If the market for legal services is perfectly competitive, the price would be $5,000 ($100 per hour), and all gains would go to Good Tire. But as long as total hours are set at 50, the agreement is efficient and total surplus is $2,500.

A potential incentive problem can confound this relationship: It is costly for Good Tire to observe how many hours of legal work Brown & Brown actually provides to the firm (there is asymmetric information). Thus, Brown & Brown might work fewer than 50 hours but still claim it worked the full amount. Indeed, the problem might be so severe that Good Tire does not hire Brown & Brown at all. In this case, the total potential gains from trade are lost. This contracting cost is a residual loss: The lost surplus that results because it is simply too costly to resolve this incentive problem.

More generally, the two firms might be able to promote a mutually advantageous exchange by controlling this incentive problem through expenditures on monitoring and bonding. For example, Good Tire might spend $400 per week to hire a manager specifically to oversee Brown & Brown's work, and Brown & Brown might spend $400 per week to document that it is actually conducting legal work for the firm. But it is unlikely that it will pay the two parties to expend sufficient resources to guarantee that Brown & Brown will do no overbilling. For example, the end result might be that, after the $800 expenditures on monitoring and bonding, Brown & Brown provides 40 hours of legal service and bills for 50 hours. Both parties anticipate this outcome and might negotiate a price of $5,200 for the legal service.[13] This price is lower than in the case where information is costless and there are no incentive problems: Good Tire is unwilling to pay as much for the anticipated 40 hours as it would if it were sure it would receive 50 hours of legal services.

---

[12]Recall that total benefits (TB) are equal to the area under the marginal benefit curve, while total costs (TC) are the area under the marginal cost curve. Thus, at 50 hours of legal service, the total surplus is $S = \text{TB} - \text{TC}$.

[13]Good Tire cannot observe the actual hours worked by Brown & Brown. Nonetheless, it can have *rational expectations* (an unbiased forecast given the information that it does have) that Brown & Brown will work 40 hours, yet bill for 50. Note that the $5,200 price is chosen somewhat arbitrarily in this example; as we will see, it is the price that splits the surplus.

Figure 10.3 Agency Costs in Legal Contracting

The left panel shows the marginal benefit (MB) to Good Tire for hours of legal services (L) and the marginal cost (MC) to Brown & Brown for providing these services. Assuming no incentive problems, the optimal number of hours is 50. The total gains from trade, $2,500, are shown by the triangle labeled S. The right panel reflects the contracting costs between the two firms—Brown & Brown might bill for more hours than hours worked. The two firms spend $400 each for monitoring and bonding costs. These out-of-pocket costs are shown by the rectangle labeled O. Since it does not pay to solve the incentive problem completely, we assume that Brown & Brown ends up providing only 40 hours of legal services. The triangle R represents the residual loss of $100. The original surplus S is reduced by the sum of the out-of-pocket costs and the residual loss. The resulting surplus, labeled S', is $1,600. How this surplus is split depends on the price charged for the legal services.

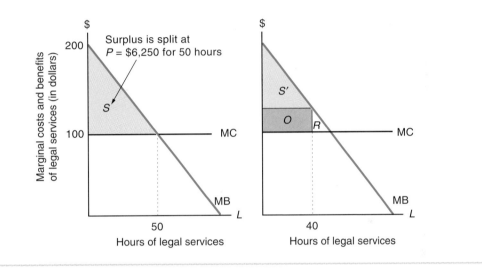

The right panel in Figure 10.3 illustrates this outcome. The triangle, labeled R, is the residual loss of $100—the lost surplus that results because it is not efficient to resolve the incentive problem completely. In addition, the two companies pay $400 each for monitoring and bonding. These payments reduce the surplus by $800, as shown by the rectangle labeled O.[14] The remaining surplus is $1,600. This surplus is equal to the original surplus of $2,500 minus the total contracting costs of $900—the sum of the out-of-pocket costs (monitoring and bonding costs) and the residual loss. In the end, Brown & Brown earns a net profit of $800 [= $5,200 − (40 × 100) − 400]. Good Tire obtains net benefits of $800 [= $6,400 − $5,200 − $400].[15] Both firms are $450 per week worse off than in the case where there was neither asymmetric information nor incentive problems.

Precontractual Information Problems

Information normally is asymmetric at the time of contract negotiations, as well. For example, in negotiating a labor contract, the prospective employee typically has superior

[14]The placement of this rectangle is arbitrary. All that is important is that the area of the original surplus be reduced by the $800 out-of-pocket expenses.

[15]The $6,400 is the gross surplus for Good Tire. It is the area under the marginal benefit curve between zero and 40 hours.

Do Firms Really Have Incentive Problems with Their Law Firms?

Our example of incentive problems with law firms illustrates a real problem faced by businesses every day—figuring out whether their lawyers are "playing it straight." According to *Business Week*,

> The task is time-consuming and often unpleasant, but for companies battling ever diminishing budgets can be fruitful. General Dynamics, for example, lopped off $186,000, or 42 percent from just one bill when it discovered a law firm charging for what ended up to be useless research. Motorola Inc. saved a pocketful when it confronted counsel for billing it for hours spent preparing documents that, because of a statute passed a year earlier, were no longer required.

In addition to doing useless research to pad their bills, some lawyers fraudulently increase the number of hours worked. For example, William Duker was ordered to pay $2.6 million to the Federal Deposit Insurance Corp. Mr. Duker's law firm was hired by the FDIC to seek damages from junk-bond king Michael Milken. Mr. Duker personally took home between $1 million and $5 million a year for this work. But in addition he added hours each day for work performed by other lawyers in his firm, typically inflating the firm's overall bills by more than 10 percent. In addition to the fines and penalties, Mr. Duker also faced a prison term of 1 to 4 years.

Sources: L. Himmelstein (1993), "The Verdict: Guilty of Overcharging," *Business Week* (September 6), 62. P. Barrett (1997), "Lawyer Was a Critic of Law Firm Fraud; Now He Faces Prison," *The Wall Street Journal* (September 30), A1.

information on what wage is acceptable, whereas the employer knows more about what the firm is willing to pay. Precontractual informational asymmetries also generate contracting costs and can cause at least two major problems—bargaining failures and adverse selection.

Bargaining Failures   Asymmetric information can prevent parties from reaching an agreement even when in theory a contract could be constructed that would be mutually advantageous. Suppose that Sheri Merriman is willing to accept a job for as little as $2,500 per month and Jon Park, the human resources manager, is willing to pay as much as $3,000 per month. In principle, a mutually advantageous contract could be negotiated at any price between $2,500 and $3,000. Neither side, however, is likely to know the other side's reservation price (the highest price that Jon is willing to offer and the lowest price that Sheri is willing to accept). In an attempt to get the best price possible, both parties might overreach, resulting in a bargaining failure. In her initial interview, Sheri might ask for $3,500. Hearing this, Jon might discontinue negotiations because he doubts that he can hire Sheri for less than $3,000 (his reservation price). This phenomenon helps to explain the existence of labor strikes that end up hurting both labor and the company. (Strikes result in lower productivity and sales; thus there are fewer profits to be divided between labor and the company.)

Adverse Selection   A second problem caused by precontractual informational asymmetries is *adverse selection*. Adverse selection refers to the tendency of an individual with private information about something that affects a potential trading partner's costs or benefits to extend an offer that would be detrimental to the trading partner.

As an example, consider the market for health insurance.[16] Table 10.1 displays three individuals and their expected medical costs for the year. Angela is the healthiest and

[16]Managers often are involved in designing or modifying fringe-benefit policies. Understanding the following problem is important in this activity. We discuss this issue in greater detail in Chapter 11.

	Expected Annual Medical Expenditure
Angela Wilson	$100
Bruno Lopez	$500
Cindy Lo	$900
All three individuals	$500 per person

Table 10.1 **Example of Adverse Selection in Insurance Markets**

This table shows the expected annual medical expenditures for three individuals. If an insurance company sells insurance to all three at a price above $500 per year, it expects to make a profit. However, if the company prices insurance at $500, Angela is unlikely to purchase the insurance. Bruno and Cindy have average expected expenditures of $700 per person. Thus, if Bruno and Cindy are the sole purchasers, the company must sell the insurance at above $700 to break even. In this case, Bruno might not buy the insurance. The end result can be a market failure, where the company prices the insurance at $900 and sells only to Cindy.

expects to spend only $100 on medical expenses, whereas Cindy is the least healthy and expects to spend $900; Bruno is in the middle with expected expenditures of $500. The average expected expenditure for all three individuals is thus $500 per person.

It is likely that each individual knows more about his or her health than an insurance company does: Individuals know how they have been feeling and their health habits, whereas an insurance company is likely to have information that is restricted to the typical expenditures for readily observed categories within the population (for example, age and gender categories). In this spirit, suppose that each individual knows his or her expected expenditure whereas the insurance company knows only the expected expenditure for the three individuals as a group—$500 per person. If the company expects to make a profit, it must sell insurance policies at premiums that exceed the expected expenditures of the buyers.

The information structure in this example can dissuade some potential customers from transacting in the market, thereby reducing the gains from trade. For instance, assume that the insurance company tries to sell insurance at $510. If all three parties bought the insurance, the company would expect to make a profit. However, at this price, Angela might not want to purchase insurance. She expects to spend only $100 on medical expenses; from her perspective, the insurance appears extremely expensive.[17] At a premium of $510, if only Bruno and Cindy bought the insurance, the company on average would lose money: Expected losses would be $190 per policyholder since their expected expenses would be $700. The insurance company might anticipate that healthy individuals will not buy the insurance at $510 and attempt to raise the price. For example, if it offered the insurance policies to both Cindy and Bruno and they purchased at $710, it would make a profit. However, at this price Bruno is less likely to buy the insurance because the price is substantially above his expected expenditure of $500. In the end, the insurance company might price insurance at a cost above $900 and sell only to Cindy—the least healthy of the three.

The company might be able to sell insurance to all three parties by becoming better informed about the individual health status of each of its applicants so that it could

---

[17]Since Angela is risk-averse, she would be willing to spend more than $100 for insurance (see Chapter 2). However, suppose she concludes that $510 is too expensive.

Battling Informational Problems in the Automobile Insurance Industry

Robert Plan Corporation specializes in providing automobile insurance to high-risk customers in urban areas. Most insurance companies have stayed away from this market because of high risks from both adverse selection and fraud. Robert Plan has been successful in this market by addressing both problems aggressively. The company carefully scrutinizes applications to assess the proper premium. It claims that virtually 100 percent of its applications are "misstated," with applicants fibbing about items such as whether they drive to work or where their primary residence is. Robert Plan uses its own private investigators to check out potential fibs. They may visit applicants' homes and follow them as they drive their cars (to determine if they are driving to work).

The company also is concerned about the problem of excessive claims. The company is notorious for being aggressive in ensuring that it does not pay excessive claims. Company investigators say one maneuver that "works well" is letting the air out of a tire to see if someone claiming a back injury "feels well enough to change it." Senior management of the company does not "condone this action and says if it is going on it will stop it." However, the company recognizes that if it is going to survive while serving this market, it must conduct "hand-to-hand combat with fraud."

Source: S. Woolley (1993), "Smile, Cheater, You're on Candid Camera,"
Business Week (October 4).

quote more customized rates. For example, it might require a medical exam of all applicants, as well as access to their medical records. In this case, different rates could be charged, depending on the health of the individual. Collecting information, however, is costly, and thus there is an incentive to consider these costs in the design of the organization and its policies.[18] For instance, since the cost of the additional information is fixed, the insurer might require exams of applicants requesting broader coverage limits but not for those willing to accept narrower coverage.

In some cases, adverse-selection problems can be reduced by the clever design of contracts. An insurance company might be able to offer a menu of contracts with different deductibles, coinsurance requirements, and prices that would motivate these individuals to *self-select* based on their private information. For example, Angela might choose a low-priced insurance contract with a high deductible, whereas Cindy might choose a high-priced contract that provides full insurance. In this case, the company might be able to sell insurance to all three customers at a profit.

Sometimes, it is possible for individuals to communicate, or *signal,* their private information to other parties in a credible fashion. For example, Angela might be able to convince the insurance company that she is quite healthy and should be sold insurance at a low rate. (She might document that she participated in six marathon races during the year.) Angela's communication to the company will be convincing to the company only if the cost to Bruno and Cindy for sending the same signal is higher than Angela's. (For example, because they are not in excellent health, they are unable to participate in marathons.) Otherwise, they could take the same action to claim they were healthy, and then there would be no reason for the company to believe any of their claims.

Adverse-selection problems are not limited to insurance markets; they occur in many settings. Prospective employees are likely to know more about their talents and productivity than employers. Similarly, the seller of a used car knows more about the quality of the car than the buyer. Thus, at a given price, sellers are more likely to offer "lemons"

---

[18]The company also might overcome the problem by selling group insurance to a company that employs all three individuals. In this case, the individuals do not select whether or not to be covered. Thus, the insurance company can make a profit at a premium above $500 per person.

Coke's Implicit Contract

Coke, one of the most valuable brand names in the world, has an implicit contract with its consumers for high quality and consistency. Thus, Coca-Cola faced a big problem when in June 1999, 200 people in Belgium and France, many of them children, came down with nausea and dizziness after drinking Coke. A number of European countries immediately banned Coke. Coca-Cola identified poor-quality carbon dioxide and a fungicide to treat wooden pallets in the warehouse as the source of the smell and taste that might have caused the illness.

Coke's Chairman and CEO M. Douglas Ivestor immediately flew to Europe and published a personal apology in the leading newspapers in an attempt to restore consumer confidence. Coca-Cola said it would charge earnings $60 million related to the 14-million-case recall. In the seven trading days following the incident, Coke's stock price fell about 8 percent from $66 to $61.

Source: "Coke's Hard Lesson in Crisis Management," *Business Week* (July 5, 1999), 102.

---

than high-quality cars.[19] In these settings, traders often develop mechanisms that help reduce adverse-selection problems. Used-car dealers offer warranties that guarantee that if the car is a lemon, the dealer will repair or exchange it at the dealer's expense. Also, there are diagnostic mechanics that provide prospective buyers with a professional assessment of the quality of a car.

Implicit Contracts and Reputational Concerns

Implicit Contracts   Many of the contracts that constitute the firm are implicit: They consist of promises and understandings that are not formalized by legal documents. Examples include promises of promotions and salary increases for a job well done and informal understandings that suppliers will not shirk on quality. By definition, implicit contracts are difficult to enforce in court; they depend largely on private incentives of individuals to honor their terms. Given the incentive conflicts that we discuss in this chapter, why would individuals ever expect others to honor terms of implicit contracts? Specifically, why would an employee ever trust an unwritten promise by a manager to give the employee a raise for a job done well? Doesn't the manager always have incentives to abrogate the contract after the job is complete? After the task is complete, the benefits are sunk. Not granting the raise would appear to reduce costs, increase profits, and thereby increase the manager's bonus.

Reputational Concerns   The answer to these questions is that reputational concerns act as a powerful force to motivate contract compliance. In particular, the market can impose substantial costs on institutions and individuals for unscrupulous behavior. Thus, market forces can provide powerful private incentives to act with integrity. (Chapter 21 contains an extended discussion on promoting ethical behavior within corporations.)

As an example, consider a firm that has a long-term contract to provide a metal part to a manufacturing firm each month at a price of $10,000. The cost of producing this product is $9,000, so the profit per unit is $1,000. It is possible for the supplier to produce a low-quality product for $2,000. However, it has agreed to provide a high-quality product. Suppose the quality of the part is known to the buyer only after the

[19]G. Akerlof (1970), "The Market for Lemons: Quality Uncertainty and the Market Mechanism," *Quarterly Journal of Economics* 84, 488–500.

purchase; it would be possible for the supplier to make a profit of $8,000 by producing a low-quality part, yet claiming it to be high-quality. The buying firm, however, will detect the quality of the part after purchase and will cancel future purchases if it is cheated. The supplying firm thus faces a trade-off. It can gain an additional $7,000 in the short run by cheating. However, it loses a $1,000 per month future profit stream. The supplier has a strong incentive to be honest so long as the present value of the future profit stream is greater than the short-run gain from cheating.

Typically, the costs of cheating on quality are higher if the information about such activities is more rapidly and widely distributed to potential future customers. Within a market like the diamond trade in New York, misrepresenting quality to another merchant is quite rare. This market is dominated by a close-knit community of Hasidic Jews; information about dishonest behavior spreads rapidly throughout this market. In other broader markets, specialized services that monitor the market help ensure contract performance. *Consumer Reports* evaluates products from toasters to automobiles, the *Investment Dealer's Digest* reports on investment bankers, and *Business Week* ranks MBA programs. By lowering the costs for potential customers to determine quality, these information sources increase the costs of cheating.

More generally, reputational concerns are more likely to be effective in promoting contract compliance when (1) the gains from cheating are smaller, (2) the likelihood of detecting cheating is higher, and (3) the expected sanctions imposed if cheating is detected are higher. (For instance, sanctions are likely to be higher if the relationship is anticipated to extend over a longer period.) When these conditions are not met, reputational concerns are less effective in motivating contract compliance. In many settings, reputational concerns are extraordinarily important in promoting cooperation and integrity. The ability to enter into self-enforcing agreements can reduce the costs of contracting within an organization materially: Fewer resources are used for negotiating and enforcing formal contracts.

Incentives to Economize on Contracting Costs

It is important to understand that everyone has incentives to resolve contracting problems in the least costly manner. By so doing, there are additional gains from trade to share among the parties. In the Good Tire example, if their incentive problems could be resolved costlessly, there would be an additional $900 of surplus to split between Good Tire and Brown & Brown. (If they didn't have to spend money on auditors and compliance, they could divide the resulting savings between themselves.)

Can the SEC Reduce Contracting Costs?

Audit committees, a group within a company's board of directors, oversee and provide a check on the firm's financial controls. Audit committees hire and supervise the independent CPA firm engaged to conduct the audit. The outside auditor reports its findings to the audit committee. Audit committees thus perform an important monitoring function within public corporations.

In response to a number of recent corporate accounting frauds, the Securities and Exchange Commission appointed a blue-ribbon panel. Their recommendations involve a tougher set of requirements for audit committee members. Directors are disqualified from audit committees if family members work for or do business with the firm. At least one member of the audit committee must have an accounting or finance background. These proposals are aimed at preventing unqualified members or those too close to the company from serving on audit committees.

The question arises as to how these proposals can increase the level of monitoring and thereby control incentive problems. The contracting parties already have incentives to minimize total contracting costs. If they fail to do this, the value of the firm is lower. Government regulation might lower contracting costs if there are externalities in the sense that financial frauds lower investor confidence in capital markets. (Chapter 20 further discusses various aspects of government regulation.)

Source: J. Lublin and E. MacDonald (1999), "More Independent Audit Committees Are Sought," *The Wall Street Journal* (February 8).

> **Basic Principle: Value Maximization**
>
> Incentive problems generate costs that reduce value. It is in the interests of all parties to a contract to develop efficient solutions to agency problems. More value is created, which can be shared among the contracting parties.

It is in the self-interest of individuals to minimize total contracting costs in any relationship.[20] Incentives exist to negotiate contracts that provide monitoring and bonding activities to the point where their marginal cost equals the marginal gain from reducing the residual loss. This means that incentives exist within the contracting process to produce an efficient utilization of resources (at least from the standpoint of the contracting parties).

Viewing contracts as efficient responses to the particular contracting problem can be an extremely powerful tool in explaining observed organizational architectures. As a simple example, consider the difference between the way fruit pickers are paid compared to the way employees who assemble airplanes are paid. Agricultural workers usually are paid on a piecework basis: The more fruit they pick, the more pay they receive. Alternatively, employees who assemble airplanes often are paid a straight salary (the same salary is paid independent of output). What accounts for this difference in observed contracts? In general, output increases if people are paid on a piecework basis. A person will pick more pieces of fruit per hour if paid by the piece than by the hour. However, piecework payments generate their own set of incentive problems. These payments motivate people to focus more on output and less on quality. In fruit picking, a supervisor can monitor the quality of the output inexpensively through direct inspection of the harvested fruit. In the case of airplanes, quality problems may not be detected until after the employee leaves the job (for example, after the plane is delivered, put into service, and—in the most extreme case—crashes). In this situation, the contracting costs of piecework payments are larger than the benefits. We apply this type of logic throughout the book to explain the design of organizations.

[20]Technical note: For this statement to be strictly true, production costs must be separable from agency costs and there must be no wealth effects. (The choices of the principal and agent are independent of their individual wealth levels.) When these conditions are violated, the individuals might not want to minimize total agency costs. Nonetheless, they still have strong incentives to consider these costs in designing contracts. For our purpose, it is reasonable and convenient to ignore these technical considerations.

CASE STUDY: *eBay.com*

eBay is the world's largest online auction. In late 1999, the service listed over 2,000 categories of items from sports memorabilia to automobiles. In total, eBay hosted more than 2.5 million auctions a day. Sellers pay a few dollars to eBay to list their items. They provide a description of the item, photographs, the minimum acceptable bid, accepted forms of payment, and other relevant information. Bidders submit electronic bids over the Internet. After the auction closes (auctions usually last several days), the high bidder receives an e-mail. The high bidder must contact the seller within 3 business days to claim the item as well as arrange for payment and delivery of the item. eBay provides other support services.

- *The Feedback Forum* is a place where eBay users leave comments about each other's buying and selling experiences. If you're a bidder, you can check the seller's Feedback Profile easily before you place a bid to learn about the other person's experience with previous buyers. If you're a seller, you can do the same with your bidders.

- Every eBay user is covered by *insurance* at no additional charge under the terms of eBay's program. If a buyer pays for an item and never receives it (or receives the item, but it was less than expected), eBay reimburses the buyer up to $200, less a $25 deductible.

- *SafeHarbor,* eBay's safety staff, investigates alleged misuses at eBay such as fraud, trading offenses, and illegally listed items. Potential resolutions include things like banning a person from future trading on eBay.

- Buyers and sellers can use an *escrow service* in transactions involving expensive items. eBay's escrow partner, i-Escrow, holds a buyer's payment and sends it to the seller only after the buyer has inspected the merchandise and gives approval. Sellers have the same opportunity to inspect and approve a returned item before the buyer gets a refund.

To obtain more detailed information, go to www.ebay.com.

Discussion Questions

1. How does eBay create value?
2. What potential contracting problems exist on eBay?
3. How does eBay address these problems?
4. What are the contracting costs at eBay?
5. eBay claims that it has only a small problem with fraud and misuse of the system. Does this imply that it is overinvesting in addressing potential contracting problems? Underinvesting? Explain.

Summary

Treating a firm as if it were an individual decision maker who maximizes profits is a useful abstraction in some contexts. For example, this characterization has been used in previous chapters in analyzing output and pricing decisions. But to analyze organizational issues within the firm requires a richer definition. A particularly useful definition for our purposes is that the *firm is a focal point for a set of contracts.*

Since individuals are creative maximizers of their own well-being, there are likely to be incentive conflicts among the parties that contract with the firm. Examples include owner-manager, buyer-supplier, and free-rider conflicts. Contracts (explicit and implicit) specify a firm's *organizational architecture* (its decision right, performance evaluation, and reward systems). This architecture establishes a set of constraints and incentives that can reduce the costs of incentive conflicts. Contracts are unlikely to resolve incentive problems completely because they are costly to negotiate, administer, and enforce. *Asymmetric information* causes particularly important problems.

An *agency relationship* consists of an agreement under which one party, the *principal,* engages another party, the *agent,* to perform some service on behalf of the principal. Many agency relationships exist within firms. Agents do not act in the best interests of principals automatically—there are *incentive problems.*

Asymmetric information usually implies that incentive problems cannot be resolved costlessly by contracts. The principal usually can limit the divergence of interests by structuring the contract to establish appropriate incentives for the agent and by incurring *monitoring costs* aimed at limiting dysfunctional activities by the agent. Also, agents might incur *bonding costs* to help guarantee that they will not take certain actions or to ensure that the principal will be compensated if they do. Generally, it does not pay to resolve incentive conflicts completely. The dollar equivalent of the loss in the gains from trade that results due to the divergence of interests in the agency relationship is known as the *residual loss.* Total agency costs are the sum of the *out-of-pocket costs* (monitoring and bonding costs) and the opportunity cost of the residual loss.

Precontractual informational asymmetries can cause breakdowns in bargaining and *adverse selection.* Adverse selection refers to the tendency of individuals, with private information about something that affects a potential trading partner's costs or benefits, to make offers that are detrimental to the trading partner. Costs of adverse selection reduce the gains from trade and can cause market failures. Precontractual information problems can be mitigated by information collection, clever contract design, credible communication, and mechanisms such as warranties.

Many of the contracts within firms are *implicit contracts* rather than formal legal documents. Implicit contracts are difficult to enforce in a court of law and depend largely on the private incentives of individuals for enforcement. *Reputational concerns* can provide incentives to honor implicit contracts. These concerns are more likely to be effective when (1) the gains from cheating are smaller, (2) the likelihood of detecting cheating is higher, and (3) the expected sanctions imposed if cheating is detected are higher. It sometimes is possible to structure organizations in ways that increase the likelihood that reputational concerns will be more effective in encouraging individuals to behave with integrity.

Parties to a contract have incentives to resolve contracting problems in the least costly manner. By so doing, there are additional gains from trade to share among the parties. Viewing observed contracts as efficient responses to the particular contracting problem provides a powerful tool for explaining organizational architecture.

Suggested Readings

O. Hart (1989), "An Economist's Perspective on the Theory of the Firm," *Columbia Law Review* 89, 1757–1774.

M. Jensen and W. Meckling (1976), "Theory of the Firm: Managerial Behavior, Agency Costs and Ownership Structure," *Journal of Financial Economics* 3, 305–360. Pay particular attention to the first 11 pages.

M. Jensen and C. Smith (1985), "Stockholder, Manager, and Creditor Interests: Applications of Agency Theory," in E. Altman and M. Subrahmanyam (Eds.), *Recent Advances in Corporate Finance* (Richard D. Irwin: Burr Ridge, IL), 93–131.

J. McMillian (1992), *Games, Strategies, and Managers* (Oxford University Press: New York).

G. Miller (1992), *Managerial Dilemmas: The Political Economy of Hierarchy* (Cambridge University Press: Cambridge).

Review Questions	**10–1.** What is a firm?

10–1. What is a firm?

10–2. Give examples of incentive conflicts:
    a. Between shareholders and managers
    b. Between coworkers on teams

10–3. What is asymmetric information? How can it limit contracts from solving incentive conflicts?

10–4. Name the two parties involved in an agency relationship.

10–5. What potential problems exist in agency relationships?

10–6. Is it worthwhile for shareholders to seek to completely eliminate incentive problems with managers and directors through means such as monitoring? Why or why not?

10–7. What is adverse selection? Give an example.

10–8. How do reputational concerns aid in the enforcement of contracts?

10–9. Schmidt Brewing Company is family-owned and -operated. The family wants to raise some capital by selling 30 percent of the common stock to outside shareholders. The company has been profitable, and the family indicates that it expects to pay high dividends to shareholders. The family will maintain 70 percent ownership of the common stock and continue to manage the firm. The rights of shareholders are specified in the company's corporate charter. The charter specifies such items as voting rights (procedures and items subject to a vote), meeting requirements, board size, rights to cash flows, and so on. Once adopted, a charter can only be changed by a vote of the shareholders. What types of provisions in the corporate charter of Schmidt Brewing might motivate minority shareholders to pay higher prices for the stock? Explain.

10–10. Which of the following examples is an adverse-selection problem and which is an incentive problem? Explain why. In each case, give one method that the restaurant might use to reduce the problem.
    a. A restaurant decides to offer an all-you-can-eat buffet that is sold for a fixed price. The restaurant discovers that the customers for this buffet are not its usual clientele. Instead, the customers tend to have big appetites. The restaurant loses money on the buffet.
    b. A restaurant owner hires a manager who promises to work long hours. When the owner is out of town, the manager goes home early. This action results in lost profits for the firm.

10–11. Sears recently indicated that it is planning to reinstate commissions for salespeople in their Auto Centers. It even plans on paying commissions for selling customers brake jobs and wheel alignments. These two products were the core of the 1992 scandal (see Chapter 2). Sears says that it has taken steps to prevent a recurrence of past problems. In particular, the decision right to recommend repairs is granted to mechanics who are paid a straight salary. Sales consultants are paid commissions for selling repair services but are not authorized to recommend repairs. Under the old system that caused problems, these individuals diagnosed repair problems and sold the corresponding service to customers. Why do you think Sears wants to reinstall commissions for its salespeople? Do you think that the new safeguard that separates diagnosing problems from selling services will prevent a recurrence of past problems? Explain.

10–12. The Sonjan company currently purchases health insurance for all of its 1,000 employees. The company is considering adopting a flexible plan whereby employees either can have $2,000 in cash or purchase an insurance policy (which currently costs $1,000). Do you see any potential problems with the new plan? Explain.

Part 3
Designing Organizational Architecture

Chapter 11
Organizational Architecture

In 1984, ITT Corporation was the largest manufacturer of telecommunications equipment in the world. Operating in over 80 different countries, it also was diversified broadly with operations in industrial and consumer products, insurance, automotive parts, telephone service, natural resources, food processing, and utilities. Yet ITT faced a variety of market pressures that made 1984 an especially difficult year. To quote *Moody's Handbook of Common Stocks* (Winter 1984–85):

> ITT's telecommunications operations continued to suffer from soft market conditions in the United States, a personal computer glut, and competitive pricing. European operations are being hurt by the strength of the US dollar.

ITT's 1984 earnings were only $2.97 per share; they had been $4.50 a year earlier. Dividends were cut by nearly $1.00 per share. ITT was rumored to be a potential takeover target.

Part of ITT's problem was that it had become too large, too diversified, too unfocused. Decision making within the organization was formalized and bureaucratic. This system made it difficult for ITT to respond rapidly either to changing customer demands or to competitive pressures. The inability to act quickly was especially troublesome given the dramatic changes occurring in both telecommunications and computers.

ITT responded by announcing that it planned to sell over $2 billion in assets to focus on its major lines of business and core strengths. As one example of this "asset redeployment program," ITT sold O. M. Scott & Sons Company in a divisional leveraged buyout in December 1986.[1] Scott, the largest producer of lawn care products in the United States, originally had been acquired by ITT in 1971.

The buyout was accompanied by organizational changes at Scott that were designed to enhance performance. These changes involved three important aspects of the organization—aspects that we refer to as the firm's *organizational architecture*[2]:

- The assignment of decision rights within the firm
- The methods of rewarding individuals
- The structure of systems to evaluate the performance of both individuals and business units

While part of ITT, Scott managers often had to seek approval from executives across a number of levels at ITT headquarters; moreover, approval frequently was denied. After the buyout, managers at Scott were given substantial authority to make and implement decisions. To motivate value-enhancing decisions, coverage under the bonus plan was expanded to encompass additional managers. Payouts for exceeding performance targets were raised materially from the company's old plan. For example, average bonuses as a percent of salary for the top 10 managers increased from 13 percent in the 2 years before the buyout, to 52 percent in the 2 years after. In addition, employees had substantial financial interests in the firm through stock ownership. Before the buyout, employees had owned virtually no stock in the company; after the buyout, employees owned 17 percent of Scott's equity. Correspondingly, the performance-evaluation system was changed to place a heavy emphasis on financial performance, with specific targets for corporate, divisional, and individual performance.

These changes in the organization were accompanied by a dramatic increase in Scott's operating performance. In the 2-year period following the buyout, sales increased by 25 percent and earnings before interest and taxes increased by 56 percent. These increases were not caused by a reduction in either R&D expenditures or expenditures on marketing and distribution; expenditures in both categories increased, as did spending on capital projects. In addition, there were no major layoffs of employees—although employment fell from 868 to 792 over the period. One explanation for the improved performance is that the changes in Scott's organizational architecture provided managers with both the authority and incentives to implement value-increasing decisions.

This example of O. M. Scott illustrates that organizational architecture is an important determinant of the success or failure of firms. The purpose of this chapter is to introduce the concept of organizational architecture and to provide a broad overview of the factors that are likely to be important in designing the optimal architecture for a particular organization. The remaining six chapters of Part 3 contain a more detailed discussion of each of the three components of organizational architecture.

---

[1]Details of this example are from G. Baker and K. Wruck (1989), "Organizational Changes and Value in Leveraged Buyouts: The Case of the O. M. Scott & Sons Company," *Journal of Financial Economics* 25:2, 163–190.

[2]The importance of these three features of organizations has been recognized by a number of authors in economics and management. For instance, see M. Jensen and W. Meckling (1995), "Specific and General Knowledge, and Organizational Structure," *Journal of Applied Corporate Finance* 8:2, 4–18; P. Milgrom and J. Roberts (1992), *Economics, Organization & Management* (Prentice Hall: Englewood Cliffs, NJ); and D. Robey (1991), *Designing Organizations* (Richard D. Irwin: Burr Ridge, IL).

Understanding organizational architecture provides managers with powerful tools for affecting the firm's performance. As we shall see, managers must be careful and thoughtful in their use of these tools or the results can be counterproductive. This book presents material designed to help managers employ these tools more effectively.

We begin by discussing the fundamental problem facing firms and markets. We then examine how organizational architecture can help solve this problem.[3]

The Fundamental Problem

The primary goal of any economic organization is to produce the output customers want at the lowest possible cost. The challenge of discovering customer demands while reducing costs, both for economic systems and within individual firms, is complicated by the fact that important information for economic decision making is generally held by many different individuals. Furthermore, this information often is expensive to transfer (that is, the information is *specific* as opposed to *general*). For example, a scientist is likely to know more about the potential of a specific research project than are executives higher in the firm. Similarly, individual machine operators normally know more about how to use their particular machines than do their supervisors. In both cases, communicating such information to headquarters for approval is likely to be cumbersome, resulting in many lost opportunities.

A second complication is that decision makers might not have appropriate incentives to make more effective decisions even if they have the relevant information. As discussed in Chapter 10, there are *incentive problems*. For example, a scientist might want to complete a research project out of scholarly interest even if convinced the project is unprofitable. Similarly, machine operators might not want to use machines efficiently if this means additional work for them.

In sum, the principal challenge in designing both firms and economic systems is to maximize the likelihood that decision makers have both the relevant information to make good decisions and the incentives to use the information productively.

There are many alternative ways of organizing economic activity to try to achieve these objectives. Economic transactions can occur within markets or firms. Firms can be organized as corporations, mutuals, partnerships, supplier cooperatives, employee-owned companies, or sole proprietorships. In each case, there are many different possible organizational architectures. All these alternatives involve costs as well as benefits. As we have discussed in previous chapters, individuals have incentives to select value-maximizing forms of organization. By maximizing the "size of the pie," there is more to share among the parties to the transaction. To achieve this objective, it is important to have a detailed understanding of the architectures of both markets and firms.

Architecture of Markets

The price system helps solve information and incentive problems in markets. In market economies, individuals have private property rights. If Jorge Ortega owns a building, he decides how it will be used. If Aldo Deng knows how to make better use of the building, Aldo can bid more for the building than it is worth to Jorge. Jorge can sell it and pocket the proceeds. He has strong incentives to use the building productively because he bears the wealth effects.

[3]The first part of this chapter draws on M. Jensen and W. Meckling (1992), "Specific and General Knowledge, and Organizational Structure," *Journal of Applied Corporate Finance* 8:2, 4–18.

Spontaneous Creation of Markets: Evidence from Prisoner-of-War Camps

One interesting feature of markets is how they often arise with limited human direction. As an example, economist R. A. Radford studied economic activity inside prisoner-of-war camps during World War II. In these camps, prisoners obtained rations from the Red Cross consisting of food, cigarettes, and other items. Of course, not all prisoners valued individual items the same. The English preferred drinking tea to coffee, whereas French prisoners preferred coffee to tea. Some prisoners smoked heavily, whereas others were nonsmokers. Potential gains from trade quickly motivated exchanges among prisoners. Before long, an organized market evolved. Cigarettes became the common currency. Prisoners quoted prices for goods in terms of the number of cigarettes. The price of individual items depended on supply and demand. For example, the price of chocolate would drop dramatically if a new Red Cross shipment increased supply substantially. The markets at the prisoner-of-war camps were quite active and emerged without a central planner saying, "let's create a market." The welfare of the prisoners was significantly enhanced by the presence of these markets—although they benefited significantly more when they were liberated!

Source: R. Radford (1945), "The Economic Organization of a P.O.W. Camp," *Economica* 12, 189–201.

Hence, the market provides an architecture that promotes efficient resource use. First, through market transactions, decision rights for resources are rearranged so that they tend to be held by individuals with the relevant specific knowledge for using those resources most productively. Individuals with the relevant specific knowledge will profit the most by owning the resources and thus are likely to be willing to pay a higher price to own them. Second, the market provides a mechanism for evaluating and rewarding the performance of resource owners: Owners bear the wealth effects of their actions. This mechanism generates important incentives to take efficient actions. A valuable feature of the price system in a market economy is that this architecture is created spontaneously, with little conscious thought or human direction.

Architecture within Firms

Within firms, there are no automatic systems either for assigning decision rights to individuals with information or for motivating individuals to use information to promote a firm's objectives. Organizational architecture is created by executives through the implicit and explicit contracts that constitute the firm (see Chapter 10). For instance, decision rights are granted to employees through formal and informal job descriptions, whereas performance evaluations and rewards are specified in formal and informal compensation contracts. At both ITT and O. M. Scott, the architectures were designed and implemented by senior management.

Decision Rights   Although transfer prices are used to allocate selected resources in some firms, most resources are allocated by administrative decisions.[4] For example, the CEO of a company typically transfers a manager from one division of the company to another by a simple command. Similarly, the utilization of a plant can be changed by administrative order. A critical responsibility of senior management is to decide how to assign decision rights among employees of the firm.[5] For instance, does the CEO make

---

[4]In Chapter 17, we discuss the economics of transfer pricing.

[5]In small firms, senior management and owners often are the same. In large firms, owners (the shareholders) delegate most decision rights to the board of directors and the CEO. These parties are charged with developing the architecture for the firm. In this chapter, we treat senior managers and owners as the same. In subsequent chapters, we expand our analysis to discuss potential contracting problems between senior management and owners.

most major decisions, or are these decisions delegated to lower-level managers? Can machine operators deviate from procedures outlined in company manuals?

Controls   Through the delegation of decision rights, employees are granted authority over the use of company resources. Employees, however, are not owners: They cannot sell company property and keep the proceeds. Therefore, employees have fewer incentives to worry about the efficient use of company resources than do owners. To help control these incentive problems, managers must develop a *control system*. That is, managers must structure the other two basic pieces of the organization's architecture, the reward and performance-evaluation systems that help align the interests of the decision makers with those of the owners. As we discuss below, an optimal control system depends on how decision rights are partitioned in the firm, and vice versa.

Trade-offs   Once the firm grows beyond a certain size, the CEO is unlikely to have the relevant information for all major decisions. Consequently, the CEO faces three basic alternatives in designing organizational architecture. First, the CEO can make most major decisions, despite lacking relevant information. In this case, there are limited incentive problems and the development of a detailed control system is less critical.[6] However, the CEO is likely to make suboptimal decisions. Second, the CEO can attempt to acquire the relevant information to make better decisions. This option can enhance decision making. Yet obtaining and processing the relevant information can be both costly and time-consuming. Third, the CEO can decentralize decision rights to individuals with better information. This choice assigns decision-making authority to employees with the relevant information. But delegating decision rights gives rise to increased incentive problems, which requires that control systems be developed. Another potential drawback of decentralization involves the costs of transferring information between the CEO and other decision makers in coordinating efforts across the organization.

Of course, CEOs can choose a mix of these basic alternatives. For example, executives are likely to choose to retain some decisions while delegating others. The optimal choice, as we discuss below, depends primarily on the business environment and strategy of the firm. In some cases—especially in smaller firms in relatively stable industries—senior managers are likely to have most of the relevant information for decision making, and thus decision rights are more likely to be centralized at headquarters. In other cases—especially larger firms experiencing rapid change—senior managers and their corporate staff often will not be in the best position to make a broad array of decisions. In such cases, decision rights are more likely to be decentralized, with corresponding control systems adopted and implemented.

This discussion indicates that the CEO plays a major role in framing the basic architecture for the firm. Organizational decisions, however, are made by managers throughout the organization. For example, when the CEO delegates a set of decision rights to middle-level managers, these managers must decide what decisions to make themselves and what decisions will be delegated to lower-level managers. These lower-level managers then are faced with similar organizational questions. The overall architecture of a firm is determined through this process, ultimately involving managers throughout the organization.

---

[6]The manager still has a contracting problem in motivating lower-level employees to follow detailed instructions. However, this contracting problem is likely to be less severe than when the manager gives the lower-level employees considerable discretion in making decisions.

Organizational Architecture at Century 21

Century 21 International is the largest residential real estate firm in the world. In 1990, Century 21 brokers and sales associates assisted over 800,000 families in buying or selling properties, translating into an estimated $80 billion in real estate worldwide and approximately $2.2 billion in commissions. By 1999, its system consisted of 6,300 independently owned and operated offices with 110,000 brokers and agents worldwide—Century 21 operates throughout the United States and in 24 other countries, including Japan, the United Kingdom, and France.

Given the geographic and cultural diversity facing Century 21, it would not be productive for the US headquarters to make all major decisions. Such centralized decision making would be especially problematic for the international operations, where laws and cultures may be far different than in the United States. To quote Century 21's management,

> We provide the international regions with whatever knowledge we possess on how they can help their franchisees develop better offices. What they use is basically up to them and will reflect their housing market and real estate traditions. We allow our master subfranchisors a great deal of flexibility in running their regions, and internationally we want them to be able to accommodate their services to their culture. We are not going overseas with our system and saying, "This is the way it is, you can't change it." We wouldn't get very far that way. There has to be some flexibility.

Decentralized decision making requires a control system that promotes productive effort. At Century 21, most of the local operators are franchisees. Franchisees essentially are owners of their units and keep a large share of their units' profits. This ownership provides strong incentives to increase sales and value. Also, Century 21 reserves the right to terminate individual franchises that fail to maintain acceptable levels of service.

Sources: C. Shook and R. Shook (1993), *Franchising: The Business Strategy That Changed the World* (Prentice Hall: Engelwood Cliffs, NJ) and Century21.com (1999).

Architectural Determinants

As suggested above, optimal architectures will differ across companies. Such structural differences are not random but vary in *systematic* ways with differences in certain underlying characteristics of the companies themselves. To illustrate the point, companies operating in the same industry tend to develop similar architectures. If an important aspect of an industry's environment changes, most companies in that industry will react by readjusting their decision rights and internal control systems.

In Figure 11.1, we summarize those factors which are likely to be most important in designing the optimal architecture for a given firm. At the top of the figure are three aspects of the firm's *external business environment: technology, markets,* and *regulation.* For any firm, these three factors—technologies that affect the production of or demand for its products, its methods of production, and its information systems; the structure of its markets (competitors, customers, and suppliers); and the regulatory constraints on its activities—are likely to have the greatest influence on its *strategy.* By *strategy,* we mean that broad set of issues discussed in Chapters 8 and 9, including the firm's primary goals—nonfinancial as well as financial, the firm's sources of comparative advantage, its choice of industry, products and services, its target customers, and pricing policies.

Take the case of AT&T in the early 1980s, before it was separated into a long-distance carrier and regional operating companies called the Baby Bells. Regulation dictated many aspects of the firm's strategy—what services it could offer, what customers it could serve, and how much it could charge them. After the breakup of AT&T and the accompanying deregulation of the telecommunications industry, both the Baby Bells and the new AT&T were forced to devise new strategies to provide new products, serve new customer bases, and develop new pricing structures.

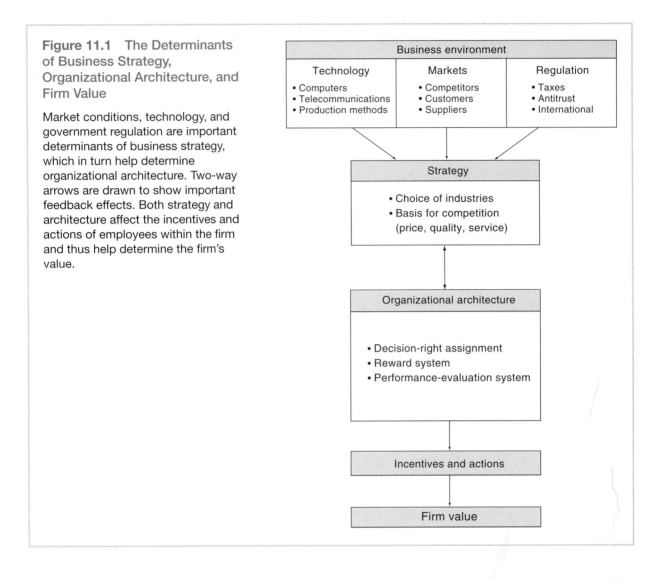

Figure 11.1 The Determinants of Business Strategy, Organizational Architecture, and Firm Value

Market conditions, technology, and government regulation are important determinants of business strategy, which in turn help determine organizational architecture. Two-way arrows are drawn to show important feedback effects. Both strategy and architecture affect the incentives and actions of employees within the firm and thus help determine the firm's value.

As depicted in Figure 11.1, the ultimate goals of the firm, as reflected in its strategy, in turn affect its optimal organizational architecture. As the celebrated architect Louis H. Sullivan—designer of the first skyscraper and founder of the American school of architecture—once observed, "Form ever follows function." Applying the same principle within organizations, we see that significant changes in the business environment and hence in strategies typically call for major changes in decision-making authority, performance measures for evaluating employees, and incentive-compensation systems.

Returning to our telecommunications example, in the early 1980s a regulated AT&T faced little competition or pressure for technological innovation. It operated within a reasonably stable environment—one where it made sense for a huge formal bureaucracy to make the most important decisions from the top down. Since the breakup of the company, the telecommunications industry has experienced almost continuous upheaval, with deregulation, increased competition, and rapid technological change. In 1992, after a nearly decade-long series of incremental moves toward decentralization, AT&T established a large number of fairly autonomous profit centers run by managers

Cell Phones Reduce Demand for Manual Transmissions

Cell phones may be the last nail in the coffin for the stick shift. Certain car buffs would only buy models with manual transmissions because of the sense of control and power they provide. However, trying to use cell phones while eating breakfast and shifting during the morning commute is too arduous for most drivers. As Americans are bringing more nondriving activities into their cars (Cadillac has announced Internet connections for some of its 2000 models), automobiles are being turned into minihomes. Something had to give, and the big loser is manual transmissions. The percentage of cars with stick shifts fell from 17.5 percent in 1989 to 13.6 percent in 1997. (Some high-end specialty autos like the Audi offer an automatic transmission that lets the driver shift gears with a stick but without a clutch.) This example illustrates how new technology in an apparently unrelated market (cell phones) can affect the strategy of companies in other markets.

Source: S. Goo (1998), "Americans Shift Down and Out of Manual Transmissions," *The Wall Street Journal* (August 19), B1.

on pay-for-performance plans tied to their units. In 1995, AT&T broke itself into three separate publicly traded companies and laid off 40,000 employees. And by 1999, following a series of acquisitions, AT&T had expanded its scope and served more cable subscribers than any other cable company (including Time Warner).[7]

Although in our discussion we have emphasized the effects of strategy on architecture, the effects are not all in one direction—note the two-headed arrow in Figure 11.1. Strategy also can be influenced by organizational architecture. A company might decide to enter a new market in part because its decision and control systems are especially well-suited for this new undertaking (see Chapter 8). For instance, before the 1980s, Atlanta, Georgia, was widely acknowledged as the banking center of the South. Yet at the beginning of the twenty-first century, Charlotte, North Carolina, claims the title. Bank branching historically was regulated by the states. Georgia limited the banks' ability to branch, while North Carolina permitted statewide branching. As restrictions on interstate banking fell in the 1980s, the North Carolina Banks—especially NCNB (now Bank of America), First Union, and Wachovia—exploited their experience acquired in establishing and managing statewide systems to create regional and then national banks. These banks have been quite successful, in part because their organizational architectures were better-suited to the new regulatory environment.

As another example of how changes in the environment can affect organizational architecture, consider the case of increased foreign competition in the 1980s and 1990s. For years, many large American companies (for example, ITT, IBM, General Motors, Eastman Kodak, and Xerox) faced limited competition in their product markets. Many of these companies had substantial market power and had little external impetus to focus on rapid product development, high-quality production, or competitive pricing. Their organizations were highly bureaucratic, with quite centralized decision making and limited incentive compensation. Many of these firms experienced a dramatic increase in foreign competition over the past two decades—especially from the Japanese. This competition forced these large firms to rethink their basic strategies and increase their emphasis on quality, customer service, and competitive pricing. To accomplish these objectives, firms often had to change their architectures. They frequently pushed decision rights lower in the organization, where specific knowledge about customer demands was located (recall the example of O. M. Scott). They also increased their use of

[7]D. Lieberman (1999), "AT&T Tries to Keep Balance," *USA Today* (October 7), B1–2.

Accelerating Technological Change

In 1996, when Denver-based Qwest Communications began laying 96-strand optical cable, each fiber was designed to carry 8 WDM (wavelength-division multiplexing) channels. With technology changing so fast, 2 years later it had been upgraded to 16 channels, doubling capacity. In 1995, optical technology used an 8-color 2.5-gigabit laser in each color to send data at 20 gigabits per second. In 1996, throughput doubled by using 16-color bands. In 1997, 40-color rainbows and 10-gigabit lasers pumped out 400 gigabits a second, 20 times more than 2 years earlier. In 1998, the company announced plans for 80-band and 160-band systems to be installed in 1999 and 2000. This doubling of bandwidth reduces cost and price, and increases the quantity of data demanded by consumers. Some experts forecast that the entire contents of the Library of Congress can be delivered to a customer every single second. This rapid technological change is altering the way information is flowing to consumers.

Source: O. Port (1998), "Through a Glass Quickly," *Business Week*
(December 7), 96–98.

incentive compensation and developed performance-evaluation systems that focused on quality and customer service.

In some ways, Figure 11.1 provides an overly simplistic view of the determinants of strategy, architecture, and firm value. The figure admittedly ignores potential feedback effects among the environment, business strategy, and architecture. Consider, for example, how Microsoft invests resources to develop software that, in turn, alters the basic technology facing the firm. Large firms also often have political power that can be used to influence government regulation. Even though these types of feedback effects at times can be important, in most circumstances managers must take the business environment essentially as given. This environment, in turn, largely determines what the firm can expect to accomplish (its strategy) and its architecture. Figure 11.1 provides managers with a structured way of thinking about the factors that are likely to affect their firm's architecture. We use this structure throughout the book for analyzing organizational decisions.

Changing Architecture

Although changes in market conditions, technology, or government regulation can affect appropriate organizational design, organizational change is by no means a costless

Changing Organizational Architecture at JC Penney

Purchasing decisions at JC Penney used to be relatively centralized. Buyers in New York would decide on the company's clothing lines for the year. Unfortunately, this procedure did not incorporate much of the relevant specific information about what products would sell best at particular stores in different parts of the country. During the 1980s, Penney's invested in satellite communications that provided the firm with closed-circuit television. This technology allowed central buyers in New York to display goods to local store managers, who could stock their stores based on their specific knowledge of local tastes and fashions. This type of decentralized decision making was feasible because of the new communications technology.

Source: H. Gilman (1986), "J.C. Penney Decentralizes Its Purchasing:
Individual Stores Can Tailor Buying to Needs," *The Wall Street Journal*
(May 8), A1.

Changing Organizations Too Frequently: Not a New Phenomenon

We trained hard, but it seemed that every time we were beginning to form into teams we would be reorganized. I was to learn later in life that we tend to meet any new situation by reorganizing, and what a wonderful method it can be for creating the illusion of progress while producing confusion, inefficiency, and demoralization.

Petronius Arbiter, 210 BC

process. It is important to assess the costs as well as the benefits in evaluating the merits of an organizational restructuring. Organizational change should be undertaken only when the expected incremental benefits exceed the expected incremental costs.

First, there are direct costs. The new architecture has to be designed and communicated to employees throughout the company. Moreover, changes in architecture frequently require costly changes in the firm's accounting and information systems. Sometimes, what appears to be a straightforward change in the performance-evaluation system is a major and costly project for the firm's data processing and accounting departments. Literally hundreds of computer programs might have to be modified to alter the accounting and information systems.

Second, and perhaps more important, are indirect costs. Changes in architecture are likely to affect some employees positively—for example, by increasing their responsibility and possibilities for rewards—but others negatively. Thus, the attitudes toward change are likely to vary among employees. Dealing with the associated incentive problems of implementing change in a firm can be expensive (see Chapter 19). In addition, frequent changes in architecture can have undesirable incentive effects. Increasing the likelihood that workers will change assignments in the near future reduces their incentives to invest in learning current job assignments, devising more efficient production processes, and developing effective relations with coworkers. Frequent restructuring within a firm causes

Changing Organizational Architecture Requires Careful Analysis

At any point in time, a particular set of prominent management techniques is touted as the key to success. Popular techniques in the 1990s included reengineering, benchmarking, total quality management, broadbanding, worker empowerment, the learning organization, and skill-based pay. Most of these techniques involved fundamental changes in organizational architecture. For example, advocates of total quality management commonly recommended delegating decision rights to teams and not paying incentive compensation based on individual performance.

Adopting the most recent business trend or fad can get a firm in trouble unless the change is warranted by the actual circumstances facing the firm. Unfortunately, many firms appear to adopt changes without careful analysis of the relevant costs and benefits. To quote *The Wall Street Journal,* "Many companies try management fads, only to see them flop."* In fact, surveys indicate that a majority of companies are dissatisfied with the results of organizational changes.

Managers should not change their organization simply because it is the current fad. Certainly, some organizational changes can enhance value. However, managers should consider carefully whether the benefits of a change are larger than the costs, given their particular circumstances. (See Chapter 22 for a detailed analysis of management innovations.)

*F. Bleakley (1993), "The Best Laid Plans: Many Companies Try Management Fads, Only to See Them Flop," *The Wall Street Journal* (July 6), A1.

uncertainty about job assignments and will promote actions that focus more on short-run payoffs and less on long-run investments (see Chapters 9 and 10).

Interdependencies within the Organization

It is important to understand that the components of organizational architecture are fundamentally interdependent. The appropriate control system depends on the allocation of decision rights, and vice versa. For example, if decision rights are decentralized, it is important to have a control system that provides incentives for employees to make value-enhancing decisions. Reward and performance-evaluation systems have to be developed that compensate employees based on performance outcomes. Similarly, if a firm adopts a compensation plan to motivate employees, it is important to grant employees decision rights so that they can respond to these incentives. In this sense, the components of organizational architecture are like *three legs of a stool*. It is important that all three legs be designed so that the stool is balanced and functional. Changing one leg without careful attention to the other two is typically a mistake. For example, it is unlikely that O. M. Scott would have been as successful after the buyout if managerial decision rights had been changed without accompanying changes in the firm's compensation plan.

Organizational architecture interacts with an array of other interrelated policies and systems within the firm. For example, incentive-compensation schemes for lower-level managers often are based on accounting performance for their particular business units. Changing business-unit structure and associated compensation plans therefore can require changes in the firm's accounting system. Similarly, it might be effective to pay the manager of a subsidiary based on the stock market performance of the subsidiary. But, for this policy to be implemented, shares in the subsidiary must be publicly traded. Thus, there can be interdependencies between the organizational architecture and the firm's financing policies. As another example, consider the design of the firm's organizational architecture and its computer/information systems. New computer programs provide expert systems that allow low-skilled workers to complete complicated tax returns, assess the qualifications of mortgage applicants, and perform other tasks that previously required extensive training and experience. These programs have allowed

---

When the Legs of the Stool Don't Balance

A major airline had a plane grounded for repairs at a particular airport. The nearest qualified mechanic was stationed at another airport. The decision right to allow the mechanic to work on the airplane was held by the manager of the second airport. The manager's compensation was tied to meeting his own budget rather than to the profits of the overall organization. The manager refused to send the mechanic to fix the plane immediately because the mechanic would have had to stay overnight at a hotel and the hotel bill would have been charged to the manager's budget. The mechanic was dispatched the next morning so that he could return the same day. A multimillion-dollar aircraft was grounded, costing the airline thousands of dollars. However, the manager avoided a $100 hotel bill. Presumably, the mechanic would have been dispatched immediately had the manager been rewarded on the overall profit of the airline or, alternatively, if the decision right had been held by someone else with this objective.

Source: M. Hammer and J. Champy (1993), *Reengineering the Corporation* (Harper Business: New York).

financial services companies to decentralize additional decision rights to lower-level employees. For example, lower-level employees in some financial institutions now have the rights to approve mortgage applications without supervisor approval if the computer program indicates that the applicant is qualified.

Corporate Culture

Corporate culture is one of the more frequently used terms in the literature on organizations. Corporate culture usually encompasses the ways work and authority are organized, the ways people are rewarded and controlled, as well as organizational features such as customs, taboos, company slogans, heroes, and social rituals. Managers are exhorted to develop high-powered, productive cultures. Yet, little concrete guidance is provided on how to accomplish this goal.

Our focus on organizational architecture is consistent with this concept of corporate culture. Indeed, our definition of organizational architecture corresponds to key aspects of what frequently is discussed as corporate culture. For example, the architecture specifies how authority (decision rights) is distributed among employees and how rewards are determined. An advantage of our approach is that it defines the key components of a firm's corporate culture and analyzes how managers might affect culture through identifiable actions.

As an example, recall our discussion of Sears Auto Centers in Chapter 2. The old corporate culture at Sears Auto Centers could be characterized as an environment where dishonest salespeople regularly misled customers. After the scandal became public, Sears had to find a way to change this corporate culture. Our approach provides direct guidance on how this change might be accomplished—in this case, by changing the compensation scheme.

Some dismiss the "softer" elements of corporate culture—for example, role models, company folklore, and rituals—as being unimportant. Rather, they stress formal architecture as being the primary, if not sole, determinant of a firm's value.[8] Economics, however, suggests at least two important roles for these elements of corporate culture: enhancing communication and helping to set employee expectations.

Corporate Culture and Communication   Most organizations do not write down all important features of their organizations in detailed procedures manuals. Rather, these features typically are communicated to employees in less formal yet frequently more effective ways. Aspects of the corporation such as slogans, role models, and social rituals can be methods of communicating organizational architecture to workers in a particularly memorable way. A slogan like *At Ford, Quality Is Job 1* emphasizes that workers are expected to focus on quality and customer service and that this focus will be rewarded by the company. Given this slogan and other reinforcing signals from top management, employees at Ford have a reasonably clear idea of how respond to situations such as angry customers even without formal policies to follow. Similarly, social rituals, such as training sessions and company parties, can help disseminate information by increasing the interaction among employees who might not see each other on a frequent basis.

---

[8]For instance, managers that subscribe to the teachings of Frederick Taylor believe that the designs of work processes and incentive systems are the primary determinants of firm value. F. Taylor (1923), *The Principles of Scientific Management* (Harper & Row: New York).

Changing Culture: Continental Airlines

For years morale at Continental Airlines was low due to layoffs, bankruptcies, and wage cuts. Colleagues bickered with one another as planes departed half-loaded. People had lost trust in management.

A turnaround occurred when Continental hired a new CEO, Gordon Bethune. Since then the airline has ranked first or second in measures such as on-time performance, baggage handling, and customer satisfaction. Bethune eliminated 20 of 60 vice presidents. He brought employees into downsizing decisions, established a phone line to handle employee complaints, and invited employees to call his personal voice mail. Mechanics began fabricating their own noncritical parts. Boeing 737 jets, which had never fit into Continental's maintenance facility, began to be serviced by mechanics who found that by jacking up the nose to lower the tail, they could slide them in for service. Bethune also began to measure every department on what mattered to customers.

Bethune says, "If I tell you how I'll measure success, I can change your behavior." He paid every employee $65 every month Continental finished in the top half of the federal rankings of on-time flights and $100 if it finished first. And these checks were sent home—not part of the employee's regular pay. Instead of arguing over whose job it was to deliver wheelchairs to the gate, ramp workers and gate agents began to cooperate and help customers. One employee remarked, "Getting the plane off the gate isn't my job or your job, we act like it's everybody's job."

In 1998 *Fortune* magazine named Continental one of the best 100 companies to work for and the most improved company of the decade. This example illustrates that changing corporate culture involves changing all three legs of the stool along with supporting employee communication programs.

Source: S. McCartney (1996), "Piloted by Bethune, Continental Air Lifts Its Workers' Morale," *The Wall Street Journal* (May 15), A1.

Singling out role models or heroes for special awards is another way of communicating explicitly what the company values.

Less tangible features of organizations, such as rituals and role models, can be important in reinforcing and communicating organizational architecture. However, they also can increase the costs of changing architecture. Managers can change formal evaluation and compensation schemes and clearly communicate these changes to the relevant employees. But getting employees to change their heroes, customs, and social rituals can be more time-consuming and difficult. These features often are created through informal communication channels: They take time to dismantle as well as to create.

Corporate Culture and Employee Expectations   In the appendix to Chapter 9, we illustrated how the decisions of employees to exert effort and to cooperate with other employees can depend on their expectations about how other individuals will respond. In this example, employees work hard only if they think that other employees will work hard as well. Expectations of how other individuals will behave are shaped, in part, by the formal architecture of the firm. If Ehud Rabin observes that Colleen O'Shea is paid a commission on sales, it is reasonable for Ehud to forecast that Colleen will exert some effort in trying to increase sales. Expectations, however, also are affected by less formal aspects of corporate culture. For example, Microsoft has developed a reputation for hiring creative, hard-working individuals. If two Microsoft employees are placed together on a team, it is reasonable for each to expect that the other is clever and industrious. This analysis suggests that it generally will be advantageous for managers to use both the formal architecture as well as the less formal aspects of corporate culture to foster expectations that promote productive choices by employees. For instance, suppose that employees are most likely to focus on quality if they think other employees have the same focus. A manager interested in increasing manufacturing quality might supplement changes in the formal evaluation and reward systems with slogans, executive speeches, employee relations campaigns, and clever use of the media, all aimed at creating a "quality-centered" culture.

A System of Complements Features of organizations like rituals and role models can be effective in reinforcing and communicating the goals of the firm, and they possess the potential to produce influential aspects of a coherent architecture. Their effectiveness in specific cases has led some management gurus to claim that a productive corporate culture can be molded with no attention to formal evaluation and compensation schemes. Some people—for instance, quality expert W. Edwards Deming— argue that incentive pay actually is detrimental to a productive organization. Our analysis suggests that it is a mistake to think of these hard and soft aspects of the organization as mutually exclusive or in competition with each other; both can play a valuable role in increasing firm value. The various elements of the organization are more likely to be *complements* than substitutes. In Chapter 19, we present a detailed discussion of Xerox's early efforts to increase product and service quality. Xerox CEO, David Kearns, initially focused on softer elements—slogans, speeches, and media campaigns—in his efforts to foster a quality culture within his organization. He soon realized that to be effective, he also had to change the company's formal evaluation and reward systems.

Corporate Culture at Mary Kay Cosmetics

Total sales at Mary Kay Cosmetics increased from about $198,000 in 1963 to over $1 billion in 1999. Mary Kay has built a sales force of more than 500,000 in 29 countries around the world. In the United States more than 100 women have obtained the status of Independent National Sales Director with incomes well into six figures.

The organizational structure at Mary Kay focuses directly on sales. All sales consultants purchase products directly from Dallas at the same price. Rewards are based solely on sales and recruiting additional sales consultants. There is no cap on what sales consultants earn. As sales and the recruiting of consultants rise, so do commissions. Past résumés and credentials are unimportant—"You say you were a brain surgeon in your last job? Fine. Get a beauty case and start dialing."

What is interesting about Mary Kay is how many features of the firm's culture reinforce one another in a consistent manner. Stories of role models are prevalent throughout the organization. Almost every employee knows the story of Mary Kay Ash, who started out as a young salesperson for Stanley Home Products. She was so poor that she had to borrow $12 to travel from her Houston home to Stanley's 1937 convention in Dallas. Through hard work, she built the Mary Kay Cosmetic Company and amassed a family fortune of over $300 million. Stories of other successful sales consultants permeate the organization. These stories reinforce the architecture and help motivate hard work and increased sales. The company also is famous for rewarding its successful sales consultants lavishly in a very public manner. The annual sales meeting is an extravaganza where individuals are rewarded with complementary pink Cadillacs, jewelry, color-coded suits, badges, emblems, and being crowned as "queens."

The message at Mary Kay is clear. Success is measured by sales and recruiting efforts. Do these things well and you will be rewarded, both financially and through public recognition. This message is consistently communicated through compensation plans, stories of role models, company rituals, and ceremonies.

Sources: A. Farnham (1993), "Mary Kay's Lessons in Leadership," *Fortune* (September 20) 68, and MaryKay.com (1999).

When an Architecture Fails

Sometimes, managers either are unable or unwilling to design value-increasing architectures or strategies. Consider the management at RJR-Nabisco in the late 1980s, as highlighted in Chapter 10. In cases such as RJR-Nabisco, value can be created by replacing existing management with new managers who are willing and able to choose architectures and strategies that increase value.

Firing the Manager In public corporations, the board of directors has the decision rights to hire, fire, and compensate senior managers. Evidence indicates that boards are most likely to fire managers when firm performance is poor (as measured by stock returns and accounting earnings).[9] Consider Eastman Kodak in 1993. The company was performing poorly, and senior managers acknowledged that a poorly designed architecture was among the company's most significant problems. These managers were unable to design a better one. The board of directors fired the CEO and hired a new one. The new CEO, George Fisher, rapidly changed both the architecture and the strategy of the company. The stock market greeted these actions with a substantial increase in the Kodak stock price. At the end of this chapter, we present a case study of this example.

Although firing the CEO is a relatively rare event, firings at other management levels are more common. When middle managers perform poorly by implementing ineffective strategies and inappropriate architectures for their business units, they can be fired or reassigned by senior managers. Middle managers, in turn, have decision rights to replace lower-level managers.

Market for Corporate Control Another mechanism for replacing poor management is the market for corporate control—for example, tender offers and mergers. During the last few decades, the wealth of shareholders has increased by billions of dollars due to corporate takeovers. Typically, when a poorly performing company is acquired by another company, its management is replaced.[10] The architecture and strategy also are changed as a result. ITT's poor performance in 1988 motivated takeover speculation. Existing management took actions to increase the firm's value, and a takeover did not materialize. In contrast, the former management team at RJR-Nabisco did not make the necessary changes to increase its firm's value, and the company was acquired by Kohlberg, Kravis, Roberts & Company. KKR subsequently replaced the management team and implemented significant changes in RJR's architecture and strategy.

Product Market Competition When all else fails, inefficient firms eventually go out of business. In Chapter 6, we discussed how competitive pressures tend to drive prices toward marginal cost. If a firm is inefficient and cannot cover its total costs at these prices, it eventually has to shut down. As discussed in Chapter 1, this competitive process resembles natural selection in biology—*the strong survive.* It is a process we refer

---

[9]J. Warner, R. Watts, and K. Wruck (1988), "Stock Prices and Top Management Changes," *Journal of Financial Economics* 20, 461–492; and M. Weisbach (1988), "Outside Directors and CEO Turnover," *Journal of Financial Economics* 20, 431–460. Similar evidence is observed in the non-profit sector; see J. Brickley and L. van Horn (2000) "Incentives in Nonprofit Organizations: Evidence from Hospitals" (Working paper, University of Rochester).

[10]For a summary of the evidence on corporate takeovers, see G. Jarrell, J. Brickley, and J. Netter (1988), "The Market for Corporate Control: The Empirical Evidence Since 1980," *Journal of Economic Perspectives* 2, 49–68. For evidence on management turnover after takeovers, see K. J. Martin and J. J. McConnell (1991), "Corporate Performance, Corporate Takeovers, and Management Turnover," *Journal of Finance* 46, 671–688.

to as economic Darwinism. Barings Bank is a dramatic example of a firm that became insolvent due to the poor design of its architecture.

Managerial Implications

Organizational architecture provides a powerful framework for addressing management problems throughout the organization. In many cases, a problem can be traced directly to defects in organizational architecture (consider O. M. Scott and Sears Auto Centers). By using this framework, managers can identify problems more quickly and craft solutions more effectively. In analyzing business problems and cases, students and managers often find it useful to refer to Figure 11.1 and ask themselves the following set of questions:

- Does the strategy fit the business environment (technology, market conditions, and regulation) and the capabilities of the firm?
- What are the key features of the current architecture?
- Does the current architecture fit the business environment and strategy? In particular, does the architecture link *specific knowledge* and decision rights in an effective manner and provide *incentives* to use information productively?
- Are the three legs of the stool mutually consistent? Given the decision-right system, does the control system fit, and vice versa?
- If the answers to any of the previous questions suggest a problem, what changes in strategy and architecture should the firm consider?
- What problems will the firm face in implementing these changes?

Marmots and Grizzly Bears

Business writers, consultants, and government regulators frequently claim that existing business practices are inefficient, and they propose changes that allegedly would improve productivity. The principle of economic Darwinism, however, suggests that many of these claims are likely to be misguided. In a competitive world, if organizations survive over the long run with a particular architecture, it is unlikely that there is some *obvious change* that could be implemented to increase profits. Sometimes the reasons for survival of a particular practice might not be clear to an outside observer. Existing practices, however, should not be deemed inefficient without careful analysis.

The interaction between marmots and grizzly bears serves to illustrate this point. Marmots are small groundhogs and are a principal food source for certain bears. Zoologists studying the ecology of marmots and bears observed bears digging and moving rocks in the autumn in search of marmots. They estimated that the calories expended searching for marmots exceeded the calories obtained from consuming marmots. Thus, searching for marmots appeared to be an inefficient use of the bear's limited resources. Given Darwin's theory of natural selection, bears searching for marmots should become extinct. A well-meaning consultant or government regulator, therefore, might recommend that bears quit searching for marmots.

Fossils of marmot bones near bear remains, however, suggest that bears have been searching for marmots for quite a long time. An explanation is that searching for marmots provides benefits to bears in addition to calories. For instance, bears sharpen their claws as a by-product of the digging involved in hunting for marmots. Sharp claws are useful in searching for food under the ice after winter's hibernation. Therefore, the benefit of sharpened claws and the calories derived from marmots offset the calories consumed gathering the marmots. The moral is that in biology or business, an outside observer should be cautious in concluding that long-standing practices are inefficient without careful study.

Source: J. McGee (1980), "Predatory Pricing Revisited," *Journal of Law & Economics* 23:2, 289–330.

Evaluating Management Advice

In a competitive marketplace, surviving firms tend to be those firms with the most productive strategies and architectures, given their business environments. This principle suggests that architectures are not random. There are sound economic explanations for the existing architectures within most industries. Consultants, however, frequently argue that long-standing practices obviously are inefficient and that companies would be better off by following their advice in changing the architecture. For example, many recent books on *empowerment* argue that most firms have made mistakes over a long time period in not delegating more decision rights to lower-level employees. Correspondingly, profits would be improved by further empowering workers. Although this advice clearly makes sense for some firms in some environments (especially if the environment recently has undergone some fundamental change that favors decentralization of decision rights), our analysis suggests that managers should be cautious in condemning prevailing organizational architecture without careful analysis. The discussion in the subsequent chapters provides important material to help conduct this analysis.

Benchmarking

Firms frequently *benchmark* other firms in an attempt to determine value-increasing policies. For example, a firm considering a change in its executive compensation plan is likely to collect information on the compensation plans of other firms. This practice has obvious merit. Firms that survive in the marketplace tend to have strategies and architectures that fit their environment, and studying these firms has the potential to yield valuable insights. Our analysis has at least three implications for effective benchmarking. First, different architectures are appropriate for different environments. It is important to benchmark firms facing similar environments. Second, since it is unusual to find firms in identical environments, it is important to

---

Qwerty versus Dvorak

Most keyboards are arranged using the QWERTY system—named for the first five letters on the third row. Invented in 1867 by Christopher Sholes, he devised the layout to reduce key jamming. The Sholes layout placed the most commonly used keys in the third row and under the left hand rather than on the second (home) row where typists keep their fingers. As a result, typing on a QWERTY keyboard can be tiring.

Once typewriter design evolved to reduce key jamming, a new keyboard layout was designed by August Dvorak in 1932. He placed the most frequently used keys under the right hand on the home row. Dvorak typists' fingers travel less and they can achieve higher speeds than QWERTY typists. Then why do QWERTY keyboards remain so prevalent today? The survival of QWERTY technology illustrates that the costs of change are potentially enormous. If a company converts all its computers to Dvorak keyboards, which would not be very expensive, then everyone has to be retrained, including all new hires.

Source: J. Diamond (1997), "The Curse of QWERTY," *Discover* (April) 34–42. (For additional discussion of these issues, see S. Leibowitz and S. Margolis (1990), "The Fable of the Keys," *Journal of Law and Economics* 33, 1–25.)

understand any differences in the environments of the benchmarked firms and to take these differences into account when analyzing the data on firms' policy choices. Third, it is important to view the architecture of other firms as a system of complements. Studying a single feature of another firm's architecture, without considering how it fits with other complementary elements of its architecture, can produce erroneous conclusions.

Overview of Part 3

The next six chapters provide a detailed discussion of the three components of organizational architecture—the three legs of the stool. Chapters 12 and 13 analyze the assignment of decision rights. Through the assignment of decision rights, firms define jobs. Two important characteristics of jobs are the variety of the assigned tasks and the authority in making decisions on how to complete these tasks. Chapter 12 examines the issue of decision authority, and Chapter 13 focuses on the assignment of tasks.

Once jobs are created, firms must design reward systems that will attract and retain qualified individuals. Chapter 14 analyzes the level of pay and the components of the compensation package—the mix between salary and fringe benefits. The focus in this chapter is how to design pay packages that allow firms to attract and retain qualified employees at the lowest cost. Although the level of pay attracts individuals to jobs, incentive compensation generally provides a primary motivation for employees to complete the assigned tasks. Chapter 15 provides a detailed analysis of incentive compensation.

Incentive plans base their payoffs on measures produced by the performance-evaluation system. Chapter 16 focuses on performance measurement of individual employees, while Chapter 17 examines performance measurement of subunits within the firm—for example, divisions and subsidiaries.

Benchmarking the Lincoln Electric Company

Lincoln Electric company has had a long history of delivering large profits. Often, this record is attributed to Lincoln's unique reward system, which places a heavy emphasis on incentive compensation (we describe this system in detail in Chapter 13). Managers from all over the world come to the Lincoln Electric headquarters at Cleveland, Ohio, to study the system. Our analysis suggests that these managers should consider Lincoln's business environment, strategy, and other elements of organizational architecture (for instance, its decision-right system) in their benchmarking. Lincoln's success should not be attributed to its reward system alone but to how well this feature fits with its environment and overall architecture.

Interestingly, Lincoln managers made the costly mistake of ignoring these considerations themselves. During the 1980s, the management at Lincoln decided to export its incentive system internationally through a series of mergers throughout Europe, Asia, and Latin America. Unfortunately, the system did not fit the business environments at many of their new locations. For instance, the influence of unions in Germany and labor laws in Venezuela made it impossible for Lincoln to implement its compensation system successfully. Lincoln ended up losing millions of dollars on these ventures. Lincoln might have avoided these mistakes if in its decision-making process it had applied carefully the framework discussed in this book.

CASE STUDY: *Eastman Kodak*

For many years, Eastman Kodak had a virtual monopoly in film production. This market power resulted in large profits. It also permitted Kodak to control the timing for introducing new products to the marketplace and responding to changes in consumer demands.

By the 1980s, Kodak's market environment had changed materially. The Fuji Corporation produced high-quality film that eroded Kodak's market share. Increased competition also came from generic store brands. In addition, the 1980s witnessed a technological explosion. Improved communications, design capabilities, and robotics allowed companies to bring new products to market within months rather than years.

These changes in the market environment placed significant pressure on Kodak. Kodak's stock price dropped from over $85 per share in 1982 to just over $71 in 1984. This 16 percent decline in stock price appears particularly dramatic when it is compared to the substantial increase in stock prices for the market as a whole. Earnings per share at Kodak also dropped substantially. The company realized it had to change its organization to regain profits and market share. To quote Colby Chandler, former CEO of Kodak, at the 1984 annual meeting:

Like many companies, we are not used to working in an environment where there is rapid technological transfer from laboratory to the marketplace. But we know that will be important in our future.

During 1984, Kodak undertook a major corporate restructuring. Prior to the restructuring, decision making at Kodak was quite centralized. Top-level approval was required for most major decisions. The restructuring created 17 new business units with profit-and-loss responsibility. Business-unit managers were given increased decision-making authority for new products, pricing, and other important policy choices. By decentralizing decision rights, senior management hoped to make the company more responsive to changing customer demands and market conditions. To quote the 1984 annual report:

In short, Kodak is finding new ways to stimulate the innovative nature of its people. The result: a spirit of independence, new ideas and a quickened pace in the process which turns new ideas into commercial realities.

Unfortunately for Kodak, changing the *assignment of decision rights* did not have a significant impact on the company's performance. In response, Kodak adopted the Management Annual Performance Plan (MAPP) in 1987. Under this plan, the base salary of management employees was reduced by 10 percent and replaced with a variable bonus. The bonus was to average 10 percent, ranging from 0 to 20 percent. Bonus payments were based on individual, unit, and company objectives.

The idea behind MAPP was that changing the *performance-evaluation and reward systems* would motivate managers to be more creative and industrious. The plan, however, did not have a large impact on managerial incentives or corporate profits. In 1993, Kodak officials were quoted as saying (1) that management had not really been held accountable for its failure to deliver results, (2) that management had to develop tougher work standards and demote failing employees, and (3) that in the past, managers who advanced at Kodak had excelled in office politics but not necessarily leadership.* Frustrated by the continued lack of success, Kodak's board of directors fired its CEO in late 1993.

Discussion Questions

1. What factors motivated Kodak to change its organizational architecture?
2. What mistakes did Kodak make in changing its architecture?
3. What might it have done differently?
4. How does this example relate to the concept of economic Darwinism?

*Democrat and Chronicle (June 27, 1993).

Summary

Organizational architecture includes three important components of organizational design that are major determinants of the success or failure of firms:

- The assignment of decision rights
- The methods of rewarding individuals
- The structure of systems to evaluate the performance of both individuals and business units

The fundamental problem facing both firms and economic systems involves trying to ensure that decision makers have the relevant information to make good decisions and that these decision makers have appropriate incentives to use their information productively. The price system provides an architecture that helps solve this problem in markets. Through market transactions, decision rights tend to be transferred to individuals with the relevant knowledge to make productive use of the resources. The market also provides a mechanism for evaluating and rewarding the performance of resource owners—owners bear the wealth effects of their actions. A valuable feature of markets is that this architecture is created spontaneously with little conscious thought or human direction.

Markets are not always the most efficient method for organizing economic activity—frequently, firms are more efficient. Within firms, there is no automatic system for either assigning decision rights to individuals with information or motivating individuals to use information to promote the firm's objectives. Organizational architecture has to be created. The appropriate architecture depends on the environment facing the firm. In some firms, senior management will have most of the relevant information for decision making, and relatively centralized decision making is more likely to be adopted. In firms where lower-level employees have the relevant information, decision rights are more likely to be decentralized. In this case, reward and performance-evaluation systems must be developed to control incentive problems and to promote better decision making.

Market conditions, technology, and government regulations interact to determine the firm's appropriate strategy and architecture. The strategy and architecture, in turn, are major determinants of the firm's value.

Changes in the external business environment can motivate changes in the firm's organizational architecture. Changing architecture, however, is costly. In addition to the direct costs of designing and implementing new procedures, there are potentially important indirect costs. Thus, changing architecture should be done only following careful analysis.

The components of organizational architecture are highly interdependent. They are like three legs of a stool. Changing one leg without careful attention to the others is usually a mistake. Organizational structure also is related to other policies and systems within a firm, including the accounting and information systems, marketing, and financial policy.

Corporate culture is a frequently used term. Corporate culture usually is meant to encompass the ways work and authority are organized and the ways people are rewarded and controlled, as well as organizational features such as customs, taboos, company slogans, heroes, and social rituals. Our focus on organizational architecture is consistent with this concept of corporate culture. Indeed, our definition of organizational architecture corresponds to key aspects of what is frequently defined as corporate culture. The advantage of our approach is that it defines the key components of corporate culture and analyzes how managers might affect culture through conscious action. It also helps explain why corporate cultures of firms vary systematically across industries—different environments motivate different architectures. Elements of corporate culture like customs, social rituals, folklore, and heroes perform at least two important roles: enhancing communication and fostering more productive expectations among employees. These elements, however, are likely to be less effective unless they are reinforced by the formal architecture of the firm.

Sometimes, managers are unable or unwilling to adopt value-maximizing architectures or strategies. In such cases, value can be created through management replacement. Management replacement occurs through firings and corporate takeovers. If a firm remains inefficient, it eventually will go out of business in a competitive marketplace.

This chapter introduces the concept of organizational architecture and provides a broad overview of the factors that are likely to be important in determining the optimal architecture for a particular organization. The next six chapters contain a more in-depth discussion of each of the three components of organizational architecture: the assignment of decision rights, the reward system, and the performance-evaluation system.

Suggested Readings

M. Jensen (1983), "Organization Theory and Methodology," *The Accounting Review* 58, 319–339.

M. Jensen and W. Meckling (1995), "Specific and General Knowledge, and Organizational Structure" *Journal of Applied Corporate Finance* 8:2, 4–18.

D. Kreps (1990), "Corporate Culture and Economic Theory," in J. Alt and K. Shepsle (Eds.), *Perspectives on Positive Political Economy* (Cambridge University Press: Cambridge).

P. Milgrom and J. Roberts (1995), "Complementarities and Fit: Strategy, Structure and Organizational Change in Manufacturing," *Journal of Accounting and Economics* 19, 179–208. Focus particular attention on pages 191–208.

Review Questions

11–1. Describe the three aspects of organizational architecture.

11–2. What is a major difference between the architectures of markets and firms?

11–3. Suppose that a manager decides that a company's decision making is too centralized. Will simply delegating more decisions to lower-level employees solve the problem? Explain.

11–4. Traditionally, many public utility companies (such as telephone and electric companies) have been highly regulated by the government. Thus, they have operated in stable environments, shielded from competition and rapid change. Recently, deregulation has substantially altered the environments of some of these companies. For the first time, they are being exposed to intense competition from other companies. Discuss how this change in the environment is likely to affect the optimal organizational architecture of utility companies.

11–5. In most restaurants, waiters receive a large portion of their compensation through tips from customers. Generally, the size of the tip is decided by the customer. However, many restaurants require a 15 percent tip for parties of eight or more. Using the concepts from this chapter, discuss (a) why the practice of tipping has emerged as a major method of compensating the wait staff, (b) why the customer typically decides on the amount of the tip, and (c) why restaurants require tips from large parties.

11–6. How might the softer elements of corporate culture help increase productivity in an organization? Give some examples of how managers might foster these elements to implement desired change in an organization.

11–7. Prominent management consultants sometimes argue that decision making in teams is usually more productive than decision making by individuals (important synergies arise when teams operate that are absent when individuals work by themselves). These consultants suggest that most companies have long failed to make proper use of teams. Their advice is that most firms should increase their use of teams significantly. Critique this advice.

11–8. Suppose that you are an executive at ITT in 1984, prior to the leveraged buyout of O. M. Scott. Analyze the problems facing the company.

11–9. Assume that some firms within the same industry are observed to be multidivisional whereas others are functionally organized. Assume further that all firms are about the same size and have existed for a long period of time in their current organizational structures. Is this observation inconsistent with the "survival of the fittest" concept discussed in class? Explain.

11–10. Evaluate the following argument:

> *Management fads make no sense. One day it's TQM. The next, it is empowerment or business-process reengineering. There is no economic justification for these fads. Management are just like sheep following each other to the slaughter.*

11–11. Some of the electric generating plants of the Tennessee Valley Authority are powered by coal. Coal is purchased by a separate procurement division and is transferred to the plants for use. Plant managers often complain that the coal is below grade and causes problems with plant maintenance and efficiency. What do you think is causing this problem? What changes would you make to help correct this problem?

Chapter 12
Decision Rights: The Level of Empowerment

Honda Motor Company was founded in 1948 by Soichiro Honda.[1] Initially, decision making within the company was quite centralized. Mr. Honda made virtually all product and design decisions, whereas finance and marketing decisions were made by his partner, Takeo Fujisawa.

In 1973, Honda retired. Successors adopted a more decentralized decision system. Major decision-making authority was spread among nearly 30 senior executives, who spent much of their time gathered at conference tables hammering out policies in informal sessions called *waigaya*—a Honda word meaning "noisy-loud." Engineers in research and development had significant control of the design of new automobiles. Under this so-called Honda System, the company grew and prospered.

[1]Details of this example are from C. Chandler and P. Ingrassia (1991), "Just as U.S. Firms Try Japanese Management, Honda Is Centralizing," *The Wall Street Journal* (April 11), A1; M. Williams (1993), "Redesign of Honda's Management Faces First Test with Unveiling of New Accord," *The Wall Street Journal* (September 1), B1; E. Thornton, L. Armstrong, and D. Woodruff (1998), "Honda: A Heckuva Time to Switch Drivers," *Business Week* (August 31), 42–44.

By the late 1980s Honda's growth had stalled and profits declined. Honda lost market share in the Japanese auto market, falling from third to fourth behind Mitsubishi, Nissan, and Toyota. Part of Honda's problem was that it failed to respond to changing tastes in the Japanese auto market. Many Japanese consumers wanted to purchase sporty cars with distinctive styling, yet Honda concentrated on producing four-door family sedans.

In April 1991, the new CEO, Nubuhiko Kawamoto, announced that he was changing the decision-making system at Honda radically by taking direct control of the company's automotive operations in Japan. He reasoned that the company had grown too large for group decision making. To quote Kawamoto,

> *We'd get the people from research, sales, and production together and everyone would say "not this" or "not that." We'd talk but there would be no agreement. Product planning would be on a tight schedule but we would have another discussion, another study and more preparation. Finally, the decision would come months later.*

The centralization of decision rights at Honda was seen as a cultural revolution. Even after Kawamoto obtained the retired Honda's support for this radical change, Honda employees resisted. Yet in spite of this resistance, the system was changed. In 1993, powerful "car czars" ran the development of new models, middle managers had clear job responsibilities, and according to some insiders, Kawamoto's power exceeded even that once held by Honda.

The first real test of the new management structure was the unveiling of the 1994 Accord in fall 1993. The vehicle was priced competitively and was widely acclaimed a success. The Accord was named one of the Top 10 Cars of 1994 by *Car and Driver* magazine and Import Car of the Year by *Motor Trend* magazine. In 1998 a new CEO, Hiroyuki Yoshino, took over at Honda. The Accord was still the top-selling car in the United States, and Honda reported record profits of $1.8 billion on revenues of $41 billion.

Honda is just one of many firms that changed the assignment of decision rights within their organizations in the 1990s. In contrast to Honda, many firms decentralized decision rights—for example, through *empowering* employees. An example, again from the automobile industry, is Fiat. In 1992, Fiat announced that it was decentralizing certain decision rights, assigning them to the operating levels and reducing management positions. Other firms that decentralized decision rights in the 1990s include General Electric, Motorola, and United Technologies to name but a few. A common action has been to decentralize decision rights to teams of employees rather than to individuals. The financial press is replete with stories about how companies have improved profits, quality, and customer satisfaction through employee empowerment and other changes in their decision-making systems.

These examples raise a number of important organizational questions:

- Can altering the assignment of decision rights really have an important impact on productivity and value?
- What factors affect the optimal allocation of decision rights within the firm?
- When is it optimal to delegate decision rights to a team of employees rather than to specific individuals?

The purpose of Chapters 12 and 13 is to address these and related questions. This chapter focuses on a single decision right and asks where that right should be located within the firm. Chapter 13 considers multiple decision rights and examines how combinations of rights are bundled into jobs and subunits (for example, divisions) of the firm.

This chapter begins by providing a more detailed discussion of the problem of assigning tasks and decision rights within the firm. We then present a simple example that illustrates some of the factors that are important in determining the optimal assignment of a specific decision right—in this case, pricing a product. We use this example to discuss centralization versus decentralization, as well as the placement of a right among employees within the same hierarchical level. We also use this example as a springboard to discuss the trade-offs between assigning a decision right to an individual versus a team of individuals. Next, we consider the decision process in more detail and define the terms *decision management* and *decision control,* terms that are especially helpful in making the concept of empowerment more precise. Finally, we examine how the incentives of employees trying to influence decision makers can affect the optimal assignment of a decision right within the firm. The appendix to this chapter provides a more detailed analysis of some of the problems that can arise in team decision making.

Assigning Tasks and Decision Rights

Firms transform inputs into outputs, which are sold to customers. This *process* typically involves many *tasks.* For example, at Honda Motor Company, vehicles have to be designed, assembled, sold, and delivered. An important element of organizational architecture is partitioning of the totality of tasks within the organization into smaller blocks and assigning them to specific individuals and/or groups.

Through the process of designing the organization, specific *jobs* are created. For example, if a set of clerical tasks is bundled together and assigned to an individual, a secretarial job might be created. Jobs have at least two important dimensions: the *variety of tasks* that the employee is asked to complete and the *decision authority* to determine when and how best to complete those tasks.

Jobs vary substantially in terms of the variety of tasks and decision authority. Figure 12.1 pictures four possibilities. Point 1 displays a combination of few tasks and limited decision authority. An example is a typist in a typing pool who concentrates on a single task and has limited discretion as to what to do or how to do it. Point 2 shows a combination of many tasks and limited decision authority. For instance, clerical jobs typically involve numerous tasks (filing, typing, answering the phone, and scheduling meetings, for example) but limited decision authority. Point 3 pictures a narrow set of tasks with broad decision authority. As an example, consider a sales representative who has broad decision rights concerning which customers to call, what sales pitch to make, what prices to charge, and so on. Yet the person concentrates on one principal task—selling products to customers. Recently, there has been a trend toward creating jobs like point 4 that are less specialized and where employees have broader decision authority. Reasons for this trend will become evident as we proceed through the next two chapters.

As a manager moves up in the corporation, design issues consume larger amounts of the person's time. For example, the manager of a purchasing department plays an important role in defining the tasks each employee within the department performs. Unfortunately, the problem of partitioning tasks into jobs is extremely complex. It involves the assignment of literally thousands of tasks and decision rights. It also involves simultaneous consideration of other corporate policies such as performance evaluation and compensation policy—the other two legs of the organizational architecture stool. Although current theory is not sufficiently well developed to provide a detailed solution to

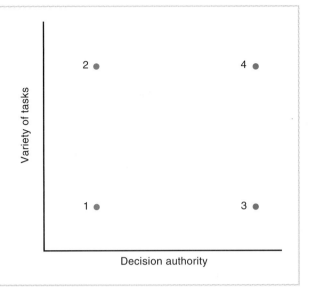

Figure 12.1   Dimensions of Job Design

Two important dimensions of job design are the variety of tasks and decision authority. This figure illustrates four possible combinations. Traditionally, many firms have created jobs like point 1, which involve few tasks and limited decision authority. Lately, there has been a trend toward jobs like point 4, which involve many tasks and broad decision authority. However, it is easy to give examples of jobs like point 2, which involve many tasks and limited decision authority—for instance, certain clerical jobs. Similarly, it is easy to point to examples of jobs like point 3, which involve few tasks and broad authority—for instance, certain sales jobs.

this general problem, through some relatively simple examples we can derive important insights. In this chapter, we present such an example to explore the issue of decision authority. The next chapter considers the problems of *bundling* tasks into jobs and jobs into subunits of the firm. Thus, this chapter concentrates on the horizontal axis in Figure 12.1 (decision authority), whereas Chapter 13 concentrates on the vertical axis (variety of tasks).

Our primary example in this chapter involves AutoMart, a firm selling automobiles in two cities. As pictured in Figure 12.2, the management of the firm consists of Roberto (Bob) Cruz, the CEO, and two local managers, Pekka Sahlstrom and Colleen O'Hagan. The local managers oversee the operations in the two cities. We concentrate on one specific task/decision right, pricing. Assigning an individual the right to set prices at a local unit increases that person's decision authority. If Bob grants local managers the right to set prices, he reduces his decision authority and correspondingly increases the decision authority of the local managers. Initially, we assume that either Bob sets the prices at the local units or he grants the right to set prices to the local managers. In reality, Bob can grant the local managers some decision authority without giving them full pricing rights. For example, Bob might allow the managers to set prices within a given range. We consider these additional possibilities later in this chapter.

The issue of *centralization versus decentralization* focuses on which level of the firm's hierarchy to place the decision right. The firm is said to have centralized decision making if the right is assigned to Bob and decentralized decision making if the right is assigned to the local managers. A second issue is *choosing where in a given hierarchical level a decision should be made.* The decision authority of both local managers is increased if both are given decision rights for pricing. Alternatively, Bob might decide to increase the decision authority of only one of the local managers—for example, by letting Colleen make all pricing decisions. We begin by discussing centralization versus decentralization. We subsequently consider the lateral issue of where across a hierarchy to place the right.

Figure 12.2   Organizational Structure of AutoMart Company

AutoMart markets automobiles in two cities. Roberto (Bob) Cruz is the CEO. The two local managers oversee the operations in the two cities. The one important decision right in this example is the pricing decision. The first question involves centralization versus decentralization. Should Bob make the pricing decisions or should they be decentralized to Colleen and Pekka? The second question involves horizontal placement of decentralized decision rights. If pricing decisions are decentralized, Bob could (1) grant each manager the pricing right for that manager's own location, (2) grant both decision rights to one manager who would make all pricing decisions, or (3) grant the decision rights for the two locations to both managers and ask them to work as a team.

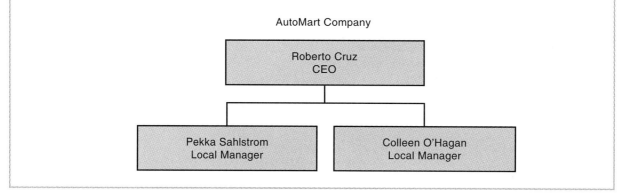

Centralization versus Decentralization

Most of the analysis of assigning decision rights has focused on the question of whether to centralize or decentralize decision rights.[2] We employ AutoMart to illustrate the major implications of this analysis. The basic question is should Bob set the prices at the two locations or should the pricing decisions be decentralized to the local managers? The answer to this question depends on the benefits and costs of decentralized decision making (relative to centralized decision making).

Benefits of Decentralization

Effective Use of Local Knowledge   Local managers are likely to have important information about local markets. For example, they are likely to have better information than Bob about the demands and price sensitivities of particular customers. They are also likely to know more about the quality and condition of their used cars. This

[2]As an example of the standard treatment of this topic, see R. Kaplan and A. Atkinson (1989), *Advanced Management Accounting* (Prentice Hall: Englewood Cliffs, NJ). Also see M. Jensen and W. Meckling (1995), "Specific and General Knowledge, and Organizational Structure," *Journal of Applied Corporate Finance* 8:2, 4–18, and A. Christie, M. Joye, and R. Watts (2000), "Decentralization of the Firm: Theory and Evidence," working paper (University of Rochester: Rochester, NY). For a more technical discussion of these issues, see. S. Athey, J. Gans, S. Schaefer, and S. Stern (1994), "The Allocation of Decisions in Organizations," working paper (Stanford University: Palo Alto, CA); M. Aoki (1986), "Horizontal vs. Vertical Information Structure of the Firm," *American Economic Review* 76, 971–983; J. Cramer (1980), "A Partial Theory of the Optimal Organization of Bureaucracy," *Bell Journal of Economics* 11, 683–693; J. Marshak and R. Radner (1972), *The Economic Theory of Teams* (Yale University Press: New Haven, CT); and R. Sah and J. Stiglitz (1988), "Committees, Hierarchies and Polyarchies," *Economic Journal* 98, 451–470.

Improving Performance through Decentralization: The Zebra Team

Eastman Kodak manufactures about 7,000 black-and-white film products that are used for a variety of purposes such as printing, X rays, and even spy satellites. Annual sales of these products are about $2 billion. Prior to 1989, Kodak used a very centralized decision-making process for manufacturing film. Manufacturing was divided into functions such as emulsion mixing (used for coating film), film coating, and film finishing. People in each of these functions reported up the line to functional managers.

In the late 1980s, poor performance motivated Kodak to reorganize the manufacturing of black-and-white film. Primary responsibility for the entire flow of the process was decentralized to a team of managers. A key feature of the new organization was the use of self-directed work teams.

The results of this reorganization were impressive. The "Zebra Team" cut production costs by some $40 million and inventory by about $50 million. In film finishing, what had taken 4 to 6 weeks was accomplished routinely in 2 days. In film coating, what had taken 42 days now was done in less than 20. New products were brought to market in half the time.

A good example of how the Zebra Team made effective use of local specific knowledge is the development of Cholach's Chariot. *Accumax* is a film product used in the manufacturing of circuit boards. Any dust on the film translates into a broken wire on a circuit board and thus makes the film worthless. Accumax is finished and slit into final products in a high-tech, ultraclean room. Unfortunately, the old supply cart used to transport the film to storage was not dust-free and thus much film was wasted. Bob Cholach was a slitter operator with specific knowledge about how the problem could be fixed—an airtight transport cab. Through his efforts, such a cab was designed and built, resulting in significant benefits to the company. Comparing the new empowered work environment with the old system, Cholach noted,

In the old days I'd have been told, "That's not your job—don't worry about it." But here I was given the power and finances to design and build something that would help my teammates. It wasn't like dropping a piece of paper into a suggestion box, either. They let me run with it from start to finish.

Source: S. Frangos with S. Bennett (1993), *Team Zebra* (Oliver Wight Publications: Essex Junction, VT).

---

information is potentially costly to transfer. If Bob makes all pricing decisions, either the firm incurs information transfer costs or bears the cost of making decisions absent relevant knowledge. Decentralizing decision rights links decision-making authority with local specific knowledge and can reduce the costs of information transfer and processing. More effective use of local knowledge is thus one of the major benefits of decentralized decision making.

Centralized decisions require local managers to seek permission to change prices. Local information has to be transferred to Bob or be ignored. Subsequently, Bob has to deliberate and convey his decisions back to local managers for implementation. This process takes time, and decision making is slower as a result. Such delays can lead to lost sales. Granting decision rights to the local managers promotes more rapid decision making and quicker responses to changing market conditions.[3]

Conservation of Management Time   If Bob makes local pricing decisions, substantial opportunity costs might be incurred: Using top-management time for pricing decisions means that time cannot be used for other decisions. Often, it is better to decentralize operating decisions to local managers and focus senior managers' attention on strategic

---

[3]In the Honda example, decentralized decision making was slower than centralized decision making. However, in Honda's case, decision rights were decentralized to a team of employees rather than to an individual. Thus, the bottleneck was in the centralized coordination of the inputs from a number of team members. Later in this chapter we discuss how team decision making can be time-consuming.

Railroads Decentralize after Centralizing

Union Pacific Corp. centralized its railroad management by moving operating managers and train dispatchers out of local offices to Omaha, Nebraska. Relying on computers and technology to link operations with the field, centralization was aimed at cutting cost. Burlington Northern Santa Fe Corp and CSX also spent millions of dollars to build network operations centers.

When service problems began developing in the field after Union Pacific took over Southern Pacific, Union Pacific concluded that it had lost touch. Service delays and freight jams began in Texas and spread to the western United States. Customers cut production and had to pay higher freight costs. Union Pacific poured additional crews and locomotives into the area. It cut its dividend and raised $1.5 billion for infrastructure. Union Pacific announced it was reorganizing into three regional groups, each with a vice president, and acknowledged, "The railroad is too large to operate from one location." Each railroad dispatcher will report to one of the three teams. Burlington and CSX also pushed managers back into the field.

Source: D. Machalaba (1998), "Union Pacific to Reverse Centralization," *The Wall Street Journal* (August 20), A3.

decisions (for example, which car lines to sell and how to promote them). As Alfred Sloan, former CEO of General Motors and an early proponent of decentralization, described,

> *My office force is small. That means we do not do much routine work with details. They never get up to us. I work fairly hard, but it is on the exceptions . . . not on routine or petty details.*[4]

Training and Motivation for Local Managers   It is important for firms to attract talented employees and to train them as eventual replacements for senior management. Decentralizing decision rights promotes both objectives. Granting responsibility helps attract and retain talented, ambitious local managers who are likely to value this aspect of the job. It also provides experience in decision making that is important training for more senior positions. Finally, with the power to choose projects, lower-level managers can have stronger incentives to exert effort in finding and evaluating new projects, assuming they gain utility from implementing their projects.

Costs of Decentralization

Incentive Problems   Decentralizing decision rights marries authority with local specific knowledge. However, the local managers do not necessarily have strong incentives to act to maximize a firm's value. For example, the managers might sell cars to their friends at low prices or obtain kickbacks from customers in return for selling at low prices. Developing an effective control system to motivate desired actions is not always easy or inexpensive. Also, there is a residual loss because it generally does not pay to resolve incentive problems completely. Incentive problems usually are larger the further down in the organization decision rights are placed.[5]

Ideally, Bob would like to measure the effect of the local managers' decisions on the value of the firm. If Bob could, it would be relatively easy to use compensation schemes

---

[4]A. Sloan (1924), "The Most Important Thing I Ever Learned about Management," *System*, 124.

[5]There are incentive problems even with centralized decision making—the decision maker is concerned that employees might not follow orders. These incentive problems usually are less severe than the incentive problems from decentralized decision making.

Technology Spurs Centralization in Financial Services

John Meyer, president of Diversified Financial Services unit of the consulting firm EDS, argues that advanced networks are creating huge operational changes in financial service firms, in particular, centralization. Call centers and loan processing used to be distributed (decentralized). Electronic networks are centralizing and consolidating these services. Some credit-scoring applications are being handled remotely with no human involvement, and others can be run from kiosks in shopping centers connected via video conferencing to central locations.

Source: "ROI for Networks," *CFO* (March 1999), 75.

to motivate value-maximizing behavior. Unfortunately, observing the effect of individual decisions within the firm on the value of the firm is usually impossible. Compensation schemes can be based on performance measures such as internal accounting numbers. For example, the local managers might be paid based on total profits for their units. However, as we will discuss in Chapters 14 through 17, developing effective compensation schemes and performance measures is difficult. The firm can use other mechanisms—for example, direct monitoring—to reduce incentive problems, but none of these techniques is costless and none will resolve these problems completely.

Coordination Costs and Failures   If the two local managers set prices independently, they might ignore important interaction effects. For instance, lowering the price in one city might divert sales from the other city, especially if they are nearby and share local media. It also might be wasteful for both managers to conduct the same type of market analysis to decide on their pricing policies if their markets are similar. For instance, most of the information might be obtained by conducting only one survey, or more precise estimates might be derived by pooling the data.

Less Effective Use of Central Information   Local managers do not necessarily have all the relevant information to make good pricing decisions. Bob might have important information about product costs, upcoming promotions, and new products from the automobile manufacturer. Bob also might have important knowledge and expertise for solving pricing problems. Often, central managers obtain important information from

Centralization and New Product Innovations

In 1997, Haagen-Dazs began serving a new ice cream flavor in Buenos Aires called *dulce de leche,* named after a popular local flavor in Argentina. Within weeks it was the store's best seller. One year later, consumers from Paris to Los Angeles could find the same flavor. In stores that carry *dulce de leche,* only vanilla sells better. To promote more effective transfer of the knowledge of hot products in one local market to other markets, firms are reorganizing decision rights. American companies such as Nike and Levi Strauss are reorganizing so that hot products in one region are spotted more readily and introduced into other regions. This often requires added centralization. Haagen-Dazs consolidated its international division, which offers seminars for its US and foreign-based executives to swap ideas. Quaker Oats cut a layer of management and merged some foreign divisions to build better communications across regions. McDonald's reorganized its US structure to resemble its foreign organization to encourage ad campaigns and tie-ins to cross borders better in the future.

Source: D. Leonhardt (1998), "It Was a Hit in Buenos Aires—So Why Not Boise?" *Business Week* (September 7), 56–57.

observing the effects of various policies implemented through time and across multiple locations. In contrast, local managers generally have more limited experience and obtain direct information from only one location. There also can be economies of scale in having Bob make pricing decisions for all units within the firm (some decisions only have to be made once, rather than multiple times). And if industry conditions are such that rapid decision making involving central information is important, the benefits of centralization of decision rights are even greater.

This discussion implies that an important role of central management in a decentralized decision system is to promote information flows and coordination among decision makers in the firm. These activities are likely to be costly. For instance, transferring information to local decision makers can be expensive. The value of coordination and central information will be lower when the product demands and costs for the local units are more independent (for example, the locations are further apart) and more of the relevant knowledge for decisions is held by the local managers. The benefits and costs of decentralized decision making are summarized in the accompanying chart.

The Benefits and Costs of Decentralized Decision Making

Benefits	Costs
More effective use of local knowledge	Incentive problems
Conservation of the time of senior management	Coordination costs and failures
Training and motivation for local managers	Less effective use of central information

Illustrating the Trade-offs

To illustrate the basic trade-offs in this example, assume that the pricing decision can be decentralized to the local managers in varying degrees. We use D to represent the degree of decentralization of the pricing decision. When $D = 0$, all pricing decisions are made by Bob; as D increases, the local managers are granted more decision rights. For example, at a low level of D, the managers might have the authority to alter centrally determined prices within a 5 percent band. At a sufficiently high D, the local managers have full authority to set prices. For simplicity, assume that D is continuous. Also, suppose that the benefits of decentralization can be written:

$$\text{Benefits} = B \times D \tag{12.1}$$

where B is a positive constant. The benefits include better use of local knowledge, conservation of senior management time, and training/motivation for local managers.

There are, however, costs associated with decentralization. For instance, there are increased incentive problems, and the decisions of the local managers have to be coordinated. Also, there are the increased costs of having to transfer central information to local decision makers. Assume the costs of decentralization are

$$\text{Costs} = (A \times D) + (C \times D^2) \tag{12.2}$$

where A and C are positive constants. The first term, AD, represents the contracting costs that arise from resolving the incentive problems of decentralization; the second

Figure 12.3   A Graphical Illustration of the Trade-offs between Centralization and Decentralization of Decision Making at AutoMart

In this example, the local managers have important specific knowledge that is valuable for decision making, and timeliness of response is important. The benefits of decentralization are given by Benefits = BD, where D is the level of decentralization of pricing decisions and B is a positive constant. These benefits include better use of local knowledge, increased response times, conservation of the time of senior management, and training/motivation for local managers. The costs are given by Costs = $AD + CD^2$, where the first term, AD, represents the increased contracting costs from decentralization and the second term, CD^2, represents the increased coordination costs (A and C are positive constants). The optimal level of decentralization is $D^* = (B - A)/2C$. At this point, the marginal benefits and the marginal costs of decentralization are equal. (The slopes of the total benefit and cost curves are the same.)

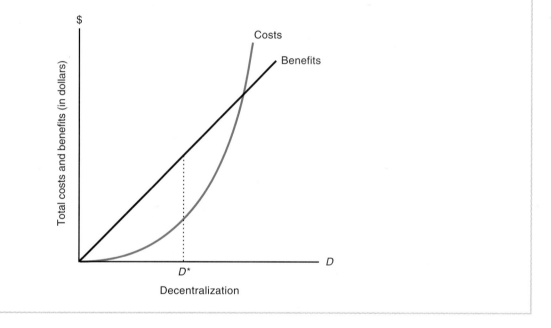

term, CD, represents the coordination/central information costs. This formulation assumes that coordination/information costs increase at an increasing rate with decentralization.[6] For example, it becomes more and more difficult to coordinate decisions as decision rights become more decentralized.

The objective of the firm is to choose D to maximize the net benefits, where

$$\text{Net benefits} = \text{Benefits} - \text{Costs} = BD - AD - CD^2 \qquad (12.3)$$

Figure 12.3 depicts the benefits and costs of decentralization. Net benefits are maximized where the vertical distance between the benefits and the costs is greatest. This condition occurs at

$$D^* = (B - A)/2C \qquad (12.4)$$

---

[6]Coordination and central information costs do not have to be quadratic, and the other benefits and costs do not have to be linear. We use these functional forms to produce convenient solutions in our example. The basic principles of our analysis do not depend on these assumptions.

Local Content Rules and Decentralization

Bombardier Inc., the Canadian railcar company, has 12 factories in Europe, is buying more, but could save millions by consolidating operations. But it won't. "Local presence is very important," says one manager. Although formal local-content rules, which require foreign companies to use local workers, are banned in Europe, informal practice exists. Public authorities fear political fallout from awarding contracts to companies with workers elsewhere. One venture capitalist remarks, "If you look at who wins orders, local content is still very important." These political pressures are causing companies like Bombardier to be more decentralized than they would without the pressures. However, Bombardier is trying to centralize engineering and purchasing in Europe to reduce costs.

Source: S. Steinmetz and C. Chipello (1998), "Local Presence Is Key to
European Deals," *The Wall Street Journal* (June 30), A15.

As is standard in problems of this type, D^* is the level of decentralization at which the marginal benefits of decentralization equal the marginal costs.[7] At this point, the additional benefits from more decentralized decision making just offset the additional costs. (The slopes of the cost and benefit curves are equal.)

Over time, it is likely that the costs and benefits of decentralization will change. For example, the importance of local knowledge can change with changes in competition in the industry or shifts in consumer demand. Also, the costs of transferring information and controlling incentive problems can fall due to new technologies (for example, consider fax machines and network computers). Changes in the benefits of decentralization can be represented by changes in B, the coefficient in the benefits equation. For example, if the importance of local knowledge increases with more global competition, B increases. Equation (12.4) and Figure 12.3 indicate that increases in B are associated with increases in the optimal amounts of decentralization. Changes in the contracting and coordination/information costs of decentralization can be represented by changes in A and C, respectively. Both Equation (12.4) and Figure 12.3 indicate that an increase in these costs is associated with a decrease in the optimal level of decentralization.

Our analysis of centralization versus decentralization can help us understand the changes in the assignment of decision rights at Honda Motor Company in 1991. Recall that after Soichiro Honda retired in 1973, the relevant specific knowledge for decision making was spread among many executives, making the benefits of decentralization high. In the context of our example, Honda could be viewed during this period as operating with an appropriately high level of decentralization. By 1991, however, Honda had grown tremendously and consensus decision making was no longer effective. Also, Nubuhiko Kawamoto, the new CEO, had been a Honda engineer and had detailed specific knowledge about designing automobiles. Thus, the benefits of decentralization were smaller than in the past (when senior management possessed less of the relevant knowledge). In response to these changing conditions, Kawamoto decreased the level of decentralization. In the context of our example, there had been a reduction in the ben-

---

[7]Technical note: The solution to this maximization process can be obtained through elementary calculus. Alternatively, Equation (12.3) is quadratic, and thus you can use the quadratic formula to solve for the roots of the equation. The two roots, 0 and $(B - A)/C$, are where net benefits equal 0. The parabola is at a maximum midway between the two roots: $(B - A)/2C$. Note that the optimal point D^* is where the vertical distance between the benefits and costs is greatest. This point occurs where the slope of the benefit curve is equal to the slope of the cost curve. The slope of the benefit curve is the marginal benefit, whereas the slope of the cost curve is the marginal cost. Thus, the optimal point is where the marginal benefit of decentralization equals the marginal cost.

Not Everyone Likes Empowerment

An Eaton Corp. small forge plant in Indiana adopted worker-empowered teams. Many workers liked the idea of being their own boss, not having time clocks or supervisors. Self-directed work teams were responsible for hiring and firing, disciplining their members, and organizing production. Managers now are called "vision supporters" and perform more the functions of coaching than directing. Everyone wears the same blue uniforms. New hires undergo a grueling interviewing process, often requiring 13 interviews—some with team members. Employees are careful about endorsing people because if that person fails, it reflects badly on the endorser.

However, many employees had difficulty adapting to the subtle control mechanisms of self-directed teams. Instead of one boss, employees now had a hundred bosses—everyone on their team. When one team mistakenly produced a batch of faulty parts, the entire team had to explain the mistake to the rest of the factory. Disciplining coworkers in open meetings turned out to be extremely uncomfortable for some people. One employee in discussing such disciplinary team meetings remarked, "I'd rather a 'vision supporter' dealt with stuff like that." This has produced one of the highest turnover rates among all of Eaton's factories, 10 percent annually.

Source: T. Aeppel (1997), "Empowerment Doesn't Suit All Workers," *The Wall Street Journal* (September 8), A1.

efits of decentralization as well as an increase in the costs, resulting in a lower optimal level of decentralization.

Our graphical illustration simplifies the centralization/decentralization decision in many ways. For example, the analysis is much more complicated if the assignment of more than one decision right is considered. Also, the example takes the divisional structure of the firm as given (two operating divisions and a headquarters). More generally, the unit structure is determined along with the assignment of decision rights. (We discuss this issue in the next chapter.) It is particularly important to emphasize that when a firm changes its decision system, it typically is necessary to make corresponding changes in other organizational features, such as the performance-evaluation and reward systems. As we noted in Chapter 11, these aspects of organizational architecture are like three legs of a stool, and it is important to keep them in balance. It often is desirable to accompany decentralization with an increased emphasis on performance and incentive compensation to motivate the empowered decision makers. Our illustration is incomplete in that it does not incorporate simultaneous changes in these other organizational variables. (We discuss these issues in Chapters 14 through 17.) Despite these limitations, the example highlights some of the important trade-offs in deciding on the degree of decentralization.

Management Implications

Our analysis indicates that decentralization involves both costs and benefits. These costs and benefits are likely to vary across firms and time. We now examine how the optimal level of decentralization is likely to vary across firms. We then discuss factors motivating recent trends toward decentralization in many firms.

Across Firms   In Chapter 11, we discussed how the firm's business environment and strategy are major determinants of organizational architecture. We focused particular attention on three aspects of the environment: technology, market conditions, and regulation. We expect that the net benefits of decentralization will be highest in rapidly changing environments. In unregulated industries where market conditions and production technologies frequently change, the timely use of local knowledge is likely to be particularly important. In more stable environments, companies can use centralized decision making and concentrate on gaining economies of scale through large-scale standardized production.

We expect that the benefits of decentralization are likely to increase as the firm enters more markets. If a firm offers a broad array of products, it is less likely that senior managers have the specific knowledge to make good operating decisions across its various businesses. Although not always the case, decentralization frequently will be more important for firms following a strategy in which they develop differentiated products that command price premiums. Such a strategy requires effective use of information on customer demands and competitor offerings. Often, this information is held by people lower in the organization. With cost strategies that focus on low-cost production of standardized products, local knowledge frequently is less important.

Another element of strategy is the degree of vertical integration; for instance, whether a manufacturing firm should make its own inputs or provide its own retail distribution and service network—see Chapter 18. In general, we expect as the firm becomes larger, either through vertical integration or through geographic expansion, that the appropriate level of decentralization will increase. As a firm's size increases, more decisions have to be made. Time and mental-processing constraints simply will preclude central managers from making all major decisions.

Centralized decision making has particular advantages when coordination of activities within the firm is important. For instance, hub-and-spoke airlines schedule short-haul flights from the spokes to arrive at roughly the same time at a central hub. Passengers connect to their next flights that leave later. Airlines using centralized scheduling are able to coordinate the flight schedules and arrange baggage connections at lower cost, offering greater convenience to customers, than if schedules were determined by multiple decentralized decision makers (for example, the pilots). Similarly, it is important for large banks to coordinate the development of automatic teller machines centrally, so that all branches use the same system.

Information Transmission: The Rapid Response Team at McKinsey

Decentralized decision making takes advantage of local specific knowledge. However, local decisions require coordination. Also, these decisions often can be enhanced by providing local decision makers with useful information from other parts of the organization. An example of the importance of computers in transferring information to local decision makers involves McKinsey & Company.

McKinsey is one of the most prominent management-consulting firms in the world. In 2000, it had over 8,500 professionals working at over 80 offices spread across five continents. It is important for McKinsey to have relatively decentralized decision making because of the vast amounts of local specific knowledge held by on-site professionals. Nonetheless, for McKinsey to deliver consistent, state-of-the-art products, it is important to communicate througout the organization.

In 1989, McKinsey formed their Rapid Response Team. The purpose of this team was to respond to requests about the best current thinking and practice by providing ready access to both documents and experienced consultants. This activity requires a computerized database that catalogs printed material and the experience profiles of consultants throughout the organization. In 1991, the Rapid Response Team responded to over 1,000 requests for information and assisted nearly a quarter of the firm's consultants and clients throughout the world.

Sources: J. Katzenbach and D. Smith (1993), *The Wisdom of Teams* (Harvard Business School: Boston) and McKinsey.com (2000).

Technology and Bureaucracy: Cypress Semiconductors

Computer technology has allowed senior managers to communicate more directly with lower-level employees. As a result, this technology makes it less expensive for senior managers to control and coordinate the actions of individuals. Thus, it has reduced the demand for middle managers, who traditionally have played an important role in transmitting information from the top of the organization to lower levels. An example of the use of computer technology in this context is Cypress Semiconductors. T. J. Rodgers, CEO of Cypress, uses a computer system to track the daily objectives of every company employee. The company essentially has no middle management. To quote from *Fortune,*

> The computer system allows the CEO to stay abreast of every employee and team in his fast-moving organization. Each employee maintains a list of 10 to 15 goals like "Meet with marketing for new product launch," or "Make sure to check with Customer X." Noted next to each goal is when it was agreed upon, when it's due to be finished and whether it's finished yet or not.
>
> This way, it doesn't take layers of expensive bureaucracy to check who's doing what, whether someone has got a light enough workload to be put on a new team, and who's having trouble. Rodgers says he can review the goals of all 1,500 employees in about 4 hours, which he does each week.

Source: B. Dumaine (1991), "The Bureaucracy Busters," *Fortune* (June 17), 46.

Empirical evidence on some of these arguments is provided by Christie, Joye, and Watts, who examine decentralization of decision making between the CEO and the next layer of senior management (general managers) for a sample of 121 firms.[8] They find that larger firms with more local specific knowledge, higher diversification, and less regulation are more likely to have a greater degree of decentralization.

Recent Trends   In contrast to Honda Motor Company, the general trend over the last two decades has been toward greater decentralization. In Chapter 11, we suggested that changes in organizational architecture are motivated by changes in the basic economic environment. We now examine those factors which have changed in the environment to promote decentralization.

In the past two decades, global competition has increased tremendously in many industries. Consider, as examples, the automobile, film, and computer industries. This competition has placed pressures on firms to cut costs, produce higher-quality products, and meet the demands of customers in a more timely fashion. The information for improving quality, customer service, and efficiency often is located lower in the organization. Thus, these competitive pressures have increased the benefits of decentralization for many firms.[9]

Technology has motivated changes in the level of decentralization for two reasons. First, the rate of technological innovation has increased dramatically. Firms either must respond quickly to the resulting changes in market conditions and production technologies or lose profits. This innovation can prompt firms to decentralize decision rights when important aspects of the knowledge of new technologies are not held by the

---

[8]A. Christie, M. Joye, and R. Watts (2000), "Decentralization of the Firm: Theory and Evidence," working paper (University of Rochester: Rochester, NY).

[9]Foreign competition also has weakened the power of labor unions in the United States to enforce inefficient work rules (for example, contract restrictions limiting the tasks that specific employees can perform). When competition largely was restricted to domestic, heavily unionized firms, there was limited pressure to change work assignments and decision rights in American firms. Competition from more efficient foreign and nonunion competitors altered this environment.

central corporate office. Second, new technologies have altered the costs of information transfer significantly (for instance, cellular phones and e-mail). In some cases, these changes have worked to promote decentralization. For example, computers and telecommunications systems (satellites and fiber optics) have reduced the costs and time of transferring central information to local decision makers to coordinate and enhance decentralized decisions. Computers also have made it less expensive to track the sales and production costs of individual products. This reduction in costs has increased the feasibility of developing more precise performance standards for local decision makers to use in incentive compensation plans.

In other cases, the effect has been in the opposite direction: Local information has become less expensive to transfer to central headquarters, thus favoring more centralized decision making. For example, computerized cash registers allow central tracking of inventory and can increase the benefits of centralized purchasing. Many of the restocking decisions within Wal-Mart now are handled by an automated system through which suppliers restock items at individual stores whenever the computer system indicates that inventories have fallen to a specified level. Managers at individual stores have few decision rights over inventory levels.

Technological advances also have allowed many firms to flatten their management structures. Traditionally, firms have relied on middle managers to transmit information and instructions from senior management to lower-level employees. Middle managers also have played an important role in coordinating and monitoring the actions of these lower-level employees. Internet-based technology, by facilitating communication between senior management and lower-level employees, has reduced demands for middle managers. Technology also has motivated changes in the roles of middle managers. In many firms middle management's role has shifted from being a conduit in the information flow to one that more closely resembles the coach of a sports team—assembling the optimal set of players, helping them design winning strategies, providing motivation, and so on.

Lateral Decision-Right Assignment

Although discussion of decision rights often focuses on centralization versus decentralization, lateral issues also can be important. In our AutoMart example, if Bob decentralizes decision rights, he can

- Grant the two managers the pricing decisions for their own locations, or
- Grant both decision rights to one manager who makes all pricing decisions, or
- Grant the decision rights for pricing at the two locations to both managers and ask them to work as a team in deciding on the pricing policy

As in the centralization versus decentralization problem, the relevant factors in making this choice include the distribution of knowledge and the costs of coordination and control. For example, granting decision rights to the managers separately takes greater advantage of local specific knowledge. But pricing at the two locations will not necessarily be well coordinated. Alternatively, granting all decision rights to one manager promotes coordinated decision making and takes advantage of any economies of scale in having one person make both decisions. But it comes at the potential expense of less effective utilization of the other manager's local knowledge. There also might be differences in contracting costs between these two alternatives. For example, it might be less expensive to monitor the decisions of one person than two. The value of the third option, granting decision rights to a team of managers, depends on a number of factors that we discuss in the next section. Which of the three options is best depends on the specific circumstances facing the firm. For instance, having the two managers make independent decisions is likely to dominate when the two markets are more independent and more of the relevant knowledge for pricing is at the individual unit level.

Questions relating to the lateral placement of decision rights frequently arise within organizations. For example, should personnel decisions be made within each individual division, or should these rights be granted to a separate human resources department? Should a divisional manager be in charge of R&D, or should this function be performed elsewhere in the organization? Can the college of business operate its own career services center, or must it rely on centralized career services of the university?

Assigning Decision Rights to Teams

Our analysis of AutoMart suggests that a firm might want to assign a decision right to a team of employees rather than to one individual. In this discussion, we use the term *team* to refer broadly to the many different types of work groups that have decision-making authority (teams, committees, task forces, and so on); for our purposes, more refined definitions are unnecessary. Firms grant decision rights to teams of employees for at least three basic purposes[10]: to manage activities, to make products, and to recommend actions. Teams that manage activities often are composed of several individuals from different functional areas (for example, marketing and finance). Teams that make products frequently are located at the plant level. For instance, some firms have granted to teams of production employees the decision rights to set their own work schedules and assignments and to organize the basic production process. Both types of teams tend to be reasonably permanent. The assignment is to manage some particular business or process. Teams that recommend actions focus on specific projects and normally disband when the task is complete. An example is the Silver Bullet Team formed at Eastman Kodak to reduce the use of silver—the most expensive ingredient in making film. Kodak is the world's largest user of silver. We now discuss the benefits and costs of group decision making relative to assigning the decision right to one individual.

Benefits of Team Decision Making

Improved Use of Dispersed Specific Knowledge   The relevant specific knowledge for decision making often is dispersed among many people within an organization. For instance, the relevant knowledge for designing new products often is held by a variety of employees, including scientists, engineers, and sales personnel. Through the use of teams, those individuals with specific knowledge are involved directly in the decision-making process. By definition, specific knowledge is expensive to assemble and transfer to a single decision maker. Also, it can be important for the individuals with the relevant knowledge to share information among themselves. By sharing information in a group setting, new ideas might be generated that would not occur in a sequence of bilateral communications between a central decision maker and each of the individuals. By sharing information, employees also become better informed for future decisions and actions. Granting decision rights to a team encourages the members to communicate and to brainstorm. Final decisions are made through consensus or some type of voting mechanism.

[10]Katzenbach and Smith (1993).

Employee Buy-In   Employees often are suspicious that management-initiated decisions benefit managers at the expense of other employees; managers frequently suggest that they grant decision rights to groups of employees specifically to increase employee "buy-in." It is asserted that employees who take part in a decision process are more likely to support the final decision and be more active in its implementation. This occurs for at least three reasons: First, asymmetric information and uncertainty, in turn, prevent employees from knowing the full consequences of a decision. Second, a group of employees has less to fear if they make the decision themselves or if the decision is made by employees with similar interests (see also Chapter 19). Reduced concerns about the effects of the decision increase employee buy-in, even when the same decision might have been made by the central manager. Third, employees have stronger incentives to invest in implementing decisions that they recommend because their reputations depend on the ultimate outcomes of the decisions.

Costs of Team Decision Making

Collective-Action Problems   Collective decision making often is slower. Recall how senior executives at Honda Motor Company took months to reach a consensus on policy decisions. Also, group decisions are not always efficient or rational.[11] (Consider the old saying that a camel is a horse designed by a committee.) Group decision making also can be subject to manipulation and political influence. In the appendix to this chapter, we illustrate how the common decision rule of majority voting can be subject to manipulation; management implications of this analysis are highlighted.

Free-Rider Problems   Team members bear the full costs of their individual efforts but share the gains that accrue to the team. This arrangement encourages team members to free-ride on the efforts of others (see Chapter 10). As we discuss in subsequent chapters, free-rider problems can be reduced through appropriate performance-evaluation and reward schemes. However, these schemes are costly to design and administer.

Management Implications

When Will Team Decision Making Work Best?   Some managers and consultants suggest that team decision making is virtually always better than individual decision making.[12] Our discussion indicates that this suggestion is not correct. Team decision making is optimal only if the benefits exceed the costs. Team decision making is more likely to be productive in environments where the relevant specific knowledge for the decision is dispersed among individuals and where the costs of collective decision making and controlling free-rider problems are lower.

Team decision making is a common component of total quality management programs. Many firms have increased their use of team decision making in the last few years through the implementation of TQM programs. Yet experience indicates that the *indiscriminate use* of teams in TQM programs can be counterproductive—in such cases, the costs exceed the benefits.

Optimal Team Size   Increasing the size of the team enhances the knowledge base of the team. However, it also increases the incentives to free-ride, as well as other costs

[11]K. Arrow (1963), *Social Choice and Individual Values* (John Wiley & Sons: New York).

[12]For example, Katzenbach and Smith (1993).

Monsanto Uses Two-Person Teams

CEO Robert Shapiro of Monsanto Inc., a chemical conglomerate, believes he can generate a competitive edge over his biotech rivals by bringing new genetic technologies to market faster than competitors. How?—By forming two-person teams that merge R&D and commercial skills. By genetically reengineering seeds, disease and pest-resistant plants can be produced. The team model consists of a scientist and a marketing or financial specialist who as codirectors oversee a Monsanto business, such as global cotton seed. The two work in adjoining cubicles and are called "box buddies." They jointly share all decision-making responsibilities, and earn the same pay, benefits, and bonuses. In Monsanto's giant agricultural sector, 30 box buddies lead most of the crop teams. This is the way Monsanto tries to assemble relevant knowledge for decision making. But constant communications and good relationships are necessary. Besides adjacent offices, box buddies use advanced pagers, e-mail, and video conferencing. Most teams travel together. However, when Monsanto and American Home Products tried to merge, the deal fell through. The two CEOs were to be co-CEOs. The two simply could not agree on how to share the top job and become box buddies.

Source: T. Schellhardt (1998), "Monsanto Bets on 'Box Buddies,'" *The Wall Street Journal* (February 23), B1.

associated with collective decision making. For instance, as team size grows, it can become difficult to make decisions and work in a coordinated fashion. Team size is optimal at the point where the marginal costs of adding a new member equal the marginal benefits. The research of Katzenbach and Smith indicates that virtually all the effective teams they observed had no more than 25 members and most were much smaller (ranging from 2 to 25).

Decision Management and Control[13]

Thus far, our characterization of decision making has been rather simplified. In particular, we generally have assumed that an employee either has a decision right or does not. In reality, some aspects of a decision can be decentralized whereas others can be maintained at a higher level. For example, at AutoMart, the managers might be granted the right to set prices within some range but have to obtain approval from Bob for larger price changes. Thus, the decision authority of an employee can be increased (see Figure 12.1) without granting the employee all rights to a particular decision.

A useful characterization divides the decision-making process into four steps:

- **Initiation.** Generation of proposals for resource utilization and structuring of contracts
- **Ratification.** Choice of the decision initiatives to be implemented
- **Implementation.** Execution of ratified decisions
- **Monitoring.** Measurement of the performance of decision makers and implementation of rewards

> **Definition**
> **Decision management:** The initiation and implementation of decisions.
> **Decision control:** The ratification and monitoring of decisions.

Often, firms assign initiation and implementation rights to the same employees. Fama and Jensen refer to these functions as *decision management;* they use the term *decision control* to refer to the ratification and monitoring functions.

[13]This section draws on E. Fama and M. Jensen (1983), "Separation of Ownership and Control," *Journal of Law & Economics* 26, 301–326.

Team-Based Organization: Hallmark Greeting Cards

It used to take about two years for Hallmark to bring a new card to market. A new card had to move through the various functional areas (for example, art, design, production, and marketing). Some of these functions were located in separate buildings. This all took time. Now Hallmark uses teams and organizes around specific holidays. For example, one team might work on cards for Mother's Day and another for Valentine's Day. Teams are given most of the decision rights for the design and marketing of particular cards. Through this process, Hallmark has cut its time to market new cards in half. For Hallmark, team decision making has proved more productive than centralized decision making.

Source: T. Stewart (1992), "The Search for the Organization of Tomorrow," *Fortune* (September 22), 92–98.

Basic Principle: Allocating Decision Rights

If decision makers do not bear the major wealth effects of their decisions, decision management and decision control will be held by separate decision makers.

Employees normally do not bear the full wealth effects of their actions—there are incentive problems. Granting an employee decision management and decision control rights for the same decision typically will lead to dysfunctional behavior. In the case of AutoMart, if the local managers make pricing decisions and there is no monitoring or other control, the managers are more likely to use the decision rights for their own benefit. For instance, the managers might sell cars to family and friends below cost. Whenever decision makers are not owners, decision management and decision control will be separated. Only when the decision maker also is the major residual claimant—the person with the legal rights to the profits of the enterprise once all the other claimants of the firm (for example, bondholders and employees) are paid—does it make sense to combine decision management and control.

Separation of Decision Management and Control   A prominent example of separating decision management and decision control is the presence of a board of directors at the top of all corporations. In large corporations, the residual claimants are shareholders. The management of the firm is largely the responsibility of the CEO, who typically owns less than 1 percent of the firm's stock. To mitigate potential incentive problems, shareholders grant major decision-control rights to the board of directors. The board ratifies major decisions initiated by the CEO. The board also has monitoring authority and the rights to fire and compensate the CEO. However, since board members often are not major shareholders, there still is a role for other parties to "monitor the monitor." This role is performed by large blockholders (such as public pension funds) and takeover specialists. If board members do a poor job, they can be replaced through a proxy fight or corporate takeover.

The principle of separation of decision management and control helps explain the frequent use of hierarchies in organizations. In hierarchies, decision management is formally separate from decision control—that is, decisions of individuals are monitored and ratified by individuals who are above them in the hierarchy. The same employee might have both decision-control and decision-management functions. For example, divisional managers might have approval rights over certain initiatives of lower-level employees while at the same time have to request authorization for the division's capital expenditure plan. The important thing is that one employee not have the rights in both decision management and decision control for the *same decision.* In smaller organizations, where one person (or a small number) has the relevant knowledge to make

---

Investigating Sexual Harassment at Compuware

In the spring of 1998, Sheila McKinnon charged her boss, Peter Karmanos, CEO of Compuware, with sexual harassment. Karmanos, with a 12 percent stake worth $656 million in Compuware, founded the company and built it into a $1.1 billion software company. At a May 29, 1998, meeting of the board of directors, Karmanos informed the board of McKinnon's allegations. Compuware's general counsel Thomas Costello presented an 18-page report from an outside investigator hired to look into the allegations. It concluded that there was "no independent support for McKinnon's claims." Within 90 minutes the board decided to terminate McKinnon. Two days later she was fired. And four days after that, McKinnon sued Karmanos and Compuware alleging sexual harassment and retaliation. In March 1999 the suit was settled out of court for an undisclosed amount.

The investigation of McKinnon's charges was supervised by Compuware's general counsel, Costello—one of the CEO's subordinates. The outside directors failed to take control of the investigation. They allowed Karmanos to retain the decision rights over an investigation into his own alleged behavior. Experts in employment law say, "Get out of the way. When such explosive charges reach all the way to the top, it's crucial that the board, not the CEO or other senior executives, take control of the matter immediately." The board has a fiduciary responsibility to the company and to the shareholders to ensure a thorough investigation. To meet this responsibility the outside directors should exercise the decision rights over the investigation, including hiring outside counsel and investigators. And they should report back to the board, not to the CEO.

Source: J. Muller (1999), "How Compuware Mishandled Its Explosive Sexual Harassment Case," *Business Week* (July 5), 74–84.

---

decisions, it is expensive to separate decision management from decision control. In this case, the two functions often are combined. In such cases the decision maker also tends to be the major residual claimant to avoid incentive problems. (For example, the company is organized as a sole proprietorship, partnership, or corporation where the managers own much of the stock.)

Although management and control rights for a decision often are granted to individuals at different levels in the organization, they sometimes are granted to separate individuals at the same level of the corporate hierarchy. For example, the quality of the output of a manufacturing division sometimes is monitored by a quality unit with equal status within the organization. Similarly, internal auditors often monitor units on the same hierarchical level.

Empowerment   The concepts of decision management and decision control also are useful in making the term *empowerment* more precise. Managers sometimes are unclear about what rights are being granted when they announce that they are empowering employees. This ambiguity can lead to disputes and conflicts between management and employees—for example, when management reverses the decisions of employees who thought they were empowered. The principle of separation of decision management and control suggests that empowerment should not mean that an employee has all rights to a particular decision. An empowered employee might have explicit rights to initiate and implement decisions; however, there is still an important role for managers to ratify and monitor decisions. Ratification does not necessarily mean that an employee must seek approval for every decision. In some cases, managers might want to preratify decisions within a particular range—*boundary setting*. For instance, we discussed how the managers at AutoMart might be given authority to set prices within some range. In any case, Bob would want to maintain monitoring rights over the decision. Often, conflicts over empowerment can be avoided by a careful discussion about what rights actually are being delegated to the employee.

Should CEO and Board Chair Be Separate?

Many commentators complain that boards of directors of US companies fail to provide adequate discipline of senior managers. Of particular concern is the common practice of combining the titles of CEO and chair of the board. On the surface, this practice seems to violate the principle of separating decision management and decision control. Benjamin Rosen, chairman of Compaq Computer, voiced this concern succinctly:

> When the CEO is also Chairman, management has *de facto* control. Yet the board is supposed to be in charge of management. Checks and balances have been thrown to the wind.*

Large shareholder associations and pension funds in recent years have sponsored proposals at Sears, Roebuck and other large firms calling for separation of the titles. Government officials have considered regulations to force this change.

Contrary to the allegations of reformers, combining the CEO and chair titles does not necessarily violate the principle of separation of decision management and decision control. The extreme case of no separation exists only when the CEO is the board's sole member. Indeed, the boards of several large US companies, including American Express, Eastman Kodak, General Motors, IBM, and Westinghouse, have fired their CEOs/chair in the 1990s.

Estimates indicate that the titles are combined in over 80 percent of US firms. In the vast majority of the remaining cases, the chair is the former CEO. Typically, when a new CEO is appointed, the old CEO/chair retains the position as board chair for a probationary period; with acceptable performance, the new CEO also receives the title of board chair and the old chair often retires. Proponents of regulations to force firms to appoint outsiders as chair essentially argue that almost all major firms in the United States are inefficiently organized. Although this assumption might be correct, reformers have presented no cogent argument for how such an important corporate control practice can be wealth-decreasing and still survive in the competitive marketplace for so long across so many companies.

*USA Today (April 22, 1993).

Source: J. Brickley, J. Coles, and G. Jarrell (1997), "Leadership Structure: Separating the CEO and Chairman of the Board," *Journal of Corporate Finance* 3, 189–220.

Influence Costs[14]

To this point, we have assumed that decision-making authority is granted either to an individual or to a team within the firm. Once the right is granted, the employee or team is involved actively in decision making (subject to ratification and monitoring from others). Sometimes, firms use bureaucratic rules that purposely limit active decision making. For example, airlines allocate routes to flight attendants based on seniority—there is no supervisor who decides who gets which route. Similarly, some firms base promotions solely on years worked with the firm. Some universities do not permit grade changes once the grade is recorded.

One potential benefit of limiting discretion in making decisions is that it reduces the resources consumed by individuals trying to influence decisions. Employees often are quite concerned about the personal effects of decisions made within the firm. For example, flight attendants care about which routes they fly. Employees are not indifferent to which colleagues are laid off in an economic downturn. These concerns motivate politicking and other potentially nonproductive *influence activities.* For instance, employees might waste valuable time trying to influence decision makers. In vying for promotions, employees might take dysfunctional actions to make other employees look bad.

---

[14]This section draws on P. Milgrom (1988), "Employment Contracts, Influence Activities and Efficient Organization Design," *Journal of Political Economy* 96, 42–60.

Separate Decision Management and Control: Not a New Idea

The English merchant guilds were formed during the twelfth century. These precursors to the modern corporation were chartered by the crown and given a monopoly to conduct trade within their own towns, usually in return for a payment to the crown. Each guild would specialize in a particular trade (carpenters, stone cutters, pewterers, etc.). The guilds held property and elected officials to manage the trade and property. Incorporation by the crown created a legal entity that could conduct business.

In order to protect the members of the guild from embezzlement and mismanagement by their elected officers, charters of the guilds contained provisions for election of auditors from the general membership to audit the financial records of the guild. For example, The Worshipful Company of Pewterers of the City of London was audited by its members. The Book of Ordinances of 1564 contains the following "order for ye audytors":

> Also it is agreed that there shalbe foure Awdytours Chosen euery yeare to awdit the Craft accompte and they to parvese it and search it that it shall be perfect. And also to accompt it Correct it and allowe it So that they make an ende of the awdet therof between Mighelmas and Christmas yearely and if defaute made of ffenishings thereof before Christmas yearly euery one of the saide Awdytours shall paye to the Craft box vj s. viij d. pece.

Audits by members of the guild are early examples of separating decision management from control. The guild officers had decision management rights, but decision control rights in the form of annual monitoring of financial transactions were vested in member auditors.

Source: E. Boyd (1968), "History of Auditing," in R. Brown (Ed.), *History of Accounting and Accountants* (A.M. Kelley: New York), 79. Also, R. Watts and J. Zimmerman (1983), "Agency Problems, Auditing, and the Theory of the Firm: Some Evidence," *Journal of Law & Economics* 26, 613–633.

Not assigning the decision right to a specific individual lowers *influence costs*—there is no one to lobby. But such a policy can impose costs on an organization. Consider individuals who are competing for a promotion. These individuals have incentives to provide evidence to their supervisor that they are the most qualified for the promotion. This information often is useful in making better promotion decisions. However, this information comes at a cost: Employees spend time trying to convince their supervisor that they are the most qualified rather than focusing on other activities such as selling products. It makes sense to run a "horse race" so long as the incremental benefits from better information are larger than the incremental costs of the influence activity. But the race should be stopped at the point where the value of the additional information about individual qualifications is equal to the cost of the additional influencing activity.

Influence Costs at Reynolds Tobacco

After a century of "one-for-all," the scramble to succeed Sticht as CEO split Reynolds into warring camps. People no longer pulled together for the company. Now they looked after the interests of the executive to whom they hitched their star: Wilson, Horrigan, or Abely. Preparing for a financial analysts' meeting, Wilson and Abely quarreled over who would speak first—a squabble Sticht finally had to settle. At a rehearsal for presentations to a companywide conference, Abely had run over his allotted time when Horrigan stomped into the room. "What's that . . . doing up there?" he stormed. "It's my time." Abely ordered a feasibility study on spinning off Sea-Land. Wilson, to whom Sea-Land reported, got wind of it and confronted John Dowdle, the treasurer, who was doing the study. "I'm sorry, I can't tell you about that," Dowdle said. "Abely will fire me if I tell you." Horrigan hired a public relations firm to get him nominated for the right kinds of business and humanitarian awards to enhance his résumé. Horrigan's big score: a Horatio Alger award.

Source: B. Burrough and J. Helyar (1990), *Barbarians at the Gate* (Harper Perennial: New York), 58.

CASE STUDY: *Medford University*

Medford University is a research university with about 10,000 students. It has a good liberal arts undergraduate program, a top-rated medical school, and a fine law school. It employs about 12,000 people. A majority of these employees work at the university hospital. Lately, the university has faced significant financial pressures. It is in intense competition for quality students with other colleges. Recent financial donations have been small. The hospital is under intense pressure to reduce costs because of changing health care regulation and insurance coverage.

The university currently spends about $100 million annually on fringe benefits (health insurance, retirement plans, and so on). It also faces large future payments of promised medical benefits to current and future retirees. The president of the university, Hiromi Kobayashi, has appointed a task force to design a new fringe benefit package. The task force consists of faculty and staff from departments throughout the university. The task force has been asked to consider the university's tenuous financial condition. President Kobayashi wants to reduce expenditures on fringe benefits (while maintaining the quality of the faculty and staff). The president has appointed the chief administrator of the hospital as the chair of the task force. The president also has appointed one of her key assistants, the vice provost, to serve as secretary of the task force (to take minutes and coordinate meeting schedules).

Discussion Questions*

1. Why did President Kobayashi appoint a task force to consider the issue of fringe benefits? She could have asked the university's human resources department to design a plan.
2. Should the president anticipate that all members of the task force will strive to cut university expenses? What actions can the president take to increase the likelihood that the task force members have this objective as a major priority?
3. Why did the president appoint the administrator of the hospital as the chair of the task force? The chair, in turn, has delegated much of the work to subcommittees (a health insurance committee, a retirement committee, and so on). What advice would you offer the chair in appointing subcommittee chairs? Explain.
4. Does the president want to commit to accepting the committee report or does she want to reserve the right to make modifications? Explain.
5. Why did the president appoint a key assistant as secretary of the task force?

*More complete answers to these questions can be developed by incorporating the material in the appendix to this chapter.

In some cases, the firm's profits largely are unaffected by decisions that have an enormous impact on individual employee welfare. For example, firm profits might be totally unaffected by which flight attendant gets the Hawaii route versus the Sioux Falls route. It is in such settings that bureaucratic rules for decision making are most likely. The firm benefits from a reduction in influence costs but is little affected by the particular outcome of the decision process. (There still is a potential cost to the firm; by not taking individual employees' preferences into account in making job assignments, the firm may have to pay higher wages to attract and retain employees—we discuss this idea in Chapter 14.)

Summary

Firms transform inputs into outputs, which are sold to customers. An important element of organizations is partitioning the totality of *tasks* of the organization into smaller blocks and assigning them to individuals and/or groups within the firm. Through the design process, jobs are created. Jobs have at least two important dimensions: *variety of tasks* and *decision authority.* This chapter focuses on decision authority. The next chapter focuses on the bundling of tasks.

In *centralized decision systems,* most major decisions are made by individuals at the top of the organization. In *decentralized systems,* many decisions are made by lower-level employees. Decentralized decision making has both benefits and costs. Potential benefits include more effective use of local knowledge, conservation of senior management time, and training/motivation for lower-level managers. Potential costs include contracting and coordination costs and less effective use of central information. The optimal degree of decentralization depends on the incremental benefits and costs, which vary across firms and over time. There has been a recent trend toward greater decentralization, motivated in part by increased global competition and changes in technology.

Decision rights are not assigned just to a hierarchical level but to particular positions within the hierarchical level. Similar to the centralization versus decentralization problem, relevant factors in making this horizontal choice include the distribution of knowledge and the costs of coordination and control.

Sometimes, firms assign decision rights to *teams* of employees rather than to specific individuals. Firms assign decision rights to teams for at least three basic purposes: managing activities, recommending actions, and making products. The use of team decision making sometimes can increase productivity; but this is not always the case. Team decision making is most likely to be productive when the relevant information is dispersed and the costs of collective decision making and controlling free-rider problems are low.

Decision management refers to the initiation and implementation of decisions, whereas *decision control* refers to the ratification and monitoring of decisions. When individuals do not bear the major wealth effects of their decisions, it generally is important to separate decision management from decision control. This principle helps explain the presence of *hierarchies* in most organizations. It also can help make the concept of empowerment more precise.

Sometimes, firms adopt rules that limit the discretion of decision makers; for example, airlines assign routes to flight attendants based on seniority. One benefit of limiting discretion is that it reduces incentives of individuals to engage in excessive *influencing activities.* Some influencing activity is valuable in that it produces information that improves decision making. Firms are, therefore, most likely to limit discretion when the firm's profits are not very sensitive to the decisions, yet the decisions are of considerable concern to employees.

Appendix

Collective Decision Making[15]

Managers commonly delegate decisions to groups of employees through the use of teams, committees, and task forces. The presumption is that team members have important specific knowledge to make the decisions and that they are more likely to buy in to decisions when they participate in the decision-making process. Manager should realize that team members' interests are unlikely to be aligned either with each other or with the interests of the owners. Also, group decision processes sometimes can be manipulated by team members. It is critical to understand these potential problems with teams; they are the topic of this appendix.

The Example of Majority Voting   Suppose that Hassan Ragab, a senior executive, appoints a team of three managers to recommend a new marketing strategy. Patrick Stefan,

[15]This appendix draws on K. Arrow (1963), *Social Choice and Individual Values* (John Wiley & Sons: New York). See also Chapter 19.

	Preferences		
	Most Favored	**Second Favored**	**Least Favored**
Pat	A	C	B
Maria	B	A	C
Sean	C	B	A

	Pairwise Votes		
	A versus B	**A versus C**	**B versus C**
Pat	A	A	C
Maria	B	A	B
Sean	B	C	C
Winner*	B	A	C

	Sequence of Pairwise Votes		
Round 1	**Round 2**		**Ultimate Winner**
A versus B	B† versus C		C
A versus C	A† versus B		B
B versus C	C† versus A		A

* Majority-voting rules.
† Winner of the first round.

Table 12.1   Majority Voting and the Order of Consideration

This table presents an example of how the outcome of a series of pairwise votes can depend on the order in which the votes are taken. The top section shows the preferences of the three managers who are voting on the proposals, A, B, and C. The middle section shows the outcomes of all possible pairwise votes. The example assumes that the managers vote their preferences in each election. A majority voting rule is used. The bottom section displays the ultimate outcome of a sequence of pairwise votes (the winner of the first vote is run against the remaining proposal). Any outcome is possible, depending on the order of consideration. In contrast to this example, the order of consideration does not always matter in majority voting—it depends on the individual preferences of the voters.

Maria Lopez, and Sean MacDonald are from the finance, marketing, and sales departments, respectively. Hassan wants the three managers to recommend the strategy that would maximize the value of the firm. However, given their current compensation schemes and positions within the company, they are more closely aligned with the interests of their particular departments than with the firm as a whole. For instance, Sean is evaluated by the vice president of sales. Sean knows that his vice president will be unhappy with any recommendation that reduces the size or influence of the sales department. Sean thus has incentives to represent the vice president's views on the task force.

The managers are considering three options, labeled Plans A, B, and C. The top panel of Table 12.1 shows the preferences of the three managers. Each prefers a different plan. The managers decide to select a plan through a majority vote. When all three plans are considered together, each receives one vote and there is no winner. The managers, therefore, decide to conduct pairwise votes. The middle panel of Table 12.1 displays the outcomes of all possible pairwise votes. The bottom panel shows the ultimate outcomes from the three possible sequences of pairwise votes. Any one of the three plans can win, *depending on the order* in the election! This example suggests that agenda control can be critically important. If Maria has the right to select the order of voting (for instance, if she is appointed the team leader), she can manipulate the voting outcome in her favor.[16]

Majority voting is commonly used in group decision making—especially when the group is large. For instance, task forces of 20 or more people commonly vote on issues. Sometimes, other voting rules are used. For instance, some groups require unanimity for passage (each person has a veto). Others require a supermajority (for example, two-thirds of the votes). Small groups often do not vote on issues formally. Rather, they make decisions by consensus. Nonetheless, the basic points of our analysis continue to hold—the outcome need not be efficient, can be subject to manipulation, and can depend on the order in which proposals are considered. Indeed, Nobel prize–winner Kenneth Arrow has demonstrated that any collective decision-making mechanism, other than granting the decision right to an individual, is subject to the types of problems illustrated in this example (depending on the preferences of the individuals in the group).

The analysis in this appendix has several important implications for managers who delegate decisions to groups of employees:

- Managers should not presume that members of a team always will have the interests of the company as their primary objective—there are incentive problems. These problems must be considered in forming a team. Sometimes, people with important information should be excluded from a team if the contracting costs of including them on the team are substantial.

- Managers often can reduce the incentive problems on teams through incentive compensation plans. In our example, the existing compensation scheme motivated the managers to focus on their own departments rather than on the firm as a whole. Compensating the managers based on the firmwide valuation effects of the team's recommendation would alter these incentives. If all three managers were concerned about the overall value of the firm, there would be no problem.[17]

- Agenda control can be a powerful device in group decision making. Not only can the outcome be affected by the order of the voting (as in Table 12.1) but it also can be affected by the timing of the election. For instance, the vote might be set when it is known that a particular manager will be absent. Senior executives, therefore, have an interest in who is appointed to positions such as team leaders and committee chairs. In this example, the senior executive should favor a team leader who cares about firm-value maximization—agenda control would be used to benefit the overall firm.

---

[16]Our example assumes that the managers vote their preferences in each round of the voting. Managers might choose to vote *strategically:* They might vote in a manner that is inconsistent with their preferences in the first round to achieve a preferred outcome in the final round of voting. (For example, some Democrats voted for John McCain in the 2000 Republican primary in Michigan, even though they planned to vote for Al Gore in the general election; the longer George W. Bush had to campaign against McCain, the more likely Gore would be successful in the general election.) Although strategic voting is a strong possibility in this setting, the basic point of our analysis remains: Managers can influence the outcome if they have agenda control. See Appendix Problem 2. Note also that majority voting does not always result in this type of order-dependence outcome. It depends on the preferences of the individual team members.

[17]It is difficult to develop incentives schemes that completely resolve incentive problems within teams. As we discuss in the text, it is difficult to design schemes that hold individuals fully responsible for their own actions. Thus, there often are incentives to free-ride in teams. We discuss this issue in greater detail in subsequent chapters.

Appendix Problems

1. What factors should a manager consider when deciding on the composition of a team charged with making an important decision?

2. Suppose the managers in the example in this appendix do not necessarily vote according to their preferences in each round of the voting. Rather, they might vote for a less preferred option in the first round to obtain a preferred outcome in the final round. Suppose that Patrick has agenda control. How should he manipulate the agenda to achieve his preferred outcome?

Suggested Readings

E. Fama and M. Jensen (1983), "Separation of Ownership and Control," *Journal of Law & Economics* 26, 301–326.

M. Jensen and W. Meckling (1995), "Specific and General Knowledge, and Organizational Structure," *Journal of Applied Corporate Finance* 8:2, 4–18.

R. Kaplan and A. Atkinson (1998), *Advanced Management Accounting* (Prentice Hall: London).

G. Miller (1993), *Managerial Dilemmas: The Political Economy of Hierarchy* (Cambridge University Press: Cambridge).

Review Questions

12–1. Discuss the costs and benefits of decentralized decision making relative to centralized decision making.

12–2. Mark Wilson, chief of personnel, has been instructed to increase the hiring of women at the Morton Cement Company. Mark will be evaluated by the company president Josh Cohen on his success or failure in meeting this goal. Mark does not evaluate the performance of any of the division chiefs, and each chief must approve all new division employees. Do you expect Mark to succeed in this endeavor? Why or why not? Explain your reasoning.

12–3. Define the terms *decision management* and *decision control*. Under what circumstances might it be optimal to make one individual responsible for both decision management and decision control? What do you expect the ownership of common stock to look like in such a firm? Explain.

12–4. Jan van der Schmidt was the founder of a successful chain of restaurants located throughout Europe. He died unexpectedly at the age of 55. Jan was sole owner of the company's common stock and was known for being quite authoritarian. He personally made most of the company's personnel decisions. He also made most of the decisions on menu selection, food suppliers, and advertising programs. Employees throughout the firm are paid fixed salaries and were closely monitored by van der Schmidt. Jan's son, Karl, spent much of his youth driving BMWs around Holland and Germany at high speeds. He spent little time working with his father in the restaurant business. Nonetheless, Karl is smart and just received his MBA degree from a leading business school. Karl has decided to follow his father as the chief operating officer of the restaurant chain. What advice about organizational architecture for the company would you offer Karl now that he has taken over?

12–5. Discuss the positive and negative effects of a university rule that would not allow professors to change a grade once recorded.

12–6. United Airlines assigns flight attendants to routes using the following procedure: Once a month, the attendants request the routes they prefer, with conflicts resolved strictly on the basis of seniority. Why does United use this procedure rather than simply let the supervisor of the attendants assign the flights?

12–7. Many companies have been experimenting with organizing their manufacturing around teams of employees. The employees are given decision rights on such things as how to organize the work and employee schedules. Often the employees are paid based on team output. Sometimes, this organizational arrangement has worked well. In other cases, it has not. Discuss the conditions under which you think that this type of team organization is most likely to succeed.

12–8. A leading business school currently uses study teams in the MBA program. Each team has five members. Some of the work in the first year is assigned to study teams and graded on a group basis. Discuss the trade-offs involved with enlarging student study groups in the MBA program from five to six people.

12–9. It is frequently argued that for empowerment to work, managers must "let go of control" and learn to live with decisions that are made by their subordinates. Evaluate this argument.

12–10. It is sometimes argued that empowerment can be successful only if managers learn to live with decisions made by lower-level employees. Managers are to set clear boundaries within which employees can make decisions (for example, allowing a salesperson to set prices between $15,000 and $20,000). Managers should never overturn a decision if it is within the boundaries. Rather, good decision making should be encouraged through proper incentives and training. Do you agree that for empowerment to work, managers should always set clear boundaries and live with decisions within these boundaries? Explain.

12–11. Several Fortune 100 companies have nominated members of the clergy to be members of their boards of directors. Discuss the advantages and disadvantages of such a proposal.

12–12. An organizational consultant evaluates your division. She indicates that she does not like the divisional manager's top-down management style. She recommends setting up a board that consists of the divisional manager and his top 10 department managers. The consultant suggests that all major policy decisions be made by the board by a majority voting rule. She argues that this process will make for better use of information within the organization. She also argues that our political system is a democracy, which works well, and that the same concept could be applied beneficially within the corporation. Evaluate the recommendation.

12–13. The Colorado Symphony Orchestra (CSO) was formed after the Denver Symphony was no longer financially viable. CSO's corporate charter requires that it cannot have an operating deficit in any year. Revenues, donations, grants, and other income must equal or exceed operating expenses. CSO balances its budget each year by adjusting the musicians' salaries. For example, in 1999 the musicians were not paid for the last 2 weeks of the year.

CSO's board of directors and executive management committees are composed of one-third each of musicians, full-time CSO staff, and community supporters of the CSO.

In most organizations, it is unusual for labor to have representation on the board of directors and management committees. Explain why you would expect musicians to have seats on the CSO board and management committees.

12–14. Discuss the trade-offs involved with enlarging student study groups in the MBA program from around five people (the current number) to ten people.

12–15. Recently a number of companies have adopted what is known as *open-book management.* Under this concept lower-level employees are given training to help them understand the company's financial statements and how their individual actions affect financial performance. They are given access to information previously known only to more senior management. They are also given detailed revenue and cost data as it relates to their jobs. For instance, one company gave delivery drivers information about the maintenance costs of the company's vans, whereas a building company gave employees detailed cost information on such items as a spoiled batch of glue. Why do you think this management trend is occurring now, rather than say 20 years ago? Does this policy fit with other changes that are occurring in organizations? Explain. Do you think all companies should "open their books" to lower-level employees? Explain.

12–16. Microsoft's Encarta is a multimedia encyclopedia on CD-ROM. It has nine different editions. Examples include editions in British English, American, German, and Italian. The North American version alone has 40 million words and 45,000 articles. Microsoft has delegated major editorial decisions to teams of local experts, mostly academics and specialists "who know their stuff." For example, a team of experts primarily from Italy have been given editorial decisions for the Italian edition. Encyclopedia Britannica uses a different policy. Its central staff has decision rights to ensure a standard presentation is presented in all editions. Discuss the pluses and minuses of Microsoft's policy relative to Encylopedia Britannica's.

12–17. Blue Cross Blue Shield of Rochester is Rochester's largest health insurance provider. In exchange for the insurance premiums they pay, families insured by BCBS receive all their health care needs from a group of approximately 500 doctors approved by BCBS. (Families must choose their doctors from among these 500 doctors.)

When a patient insured by BCBS visits a doctor for a consultation, the patient pays a small copayment (usually $10). The doctor is reimbursed for the difference between the cost of the consultation and the copayment by RCIPA Corp. RCIPA Corp. is a firm owned by the 500 doctors who are BCBS-approved. At the beginning of each fiscal year, BCBS and RCIPA agree on a total dollar amount that BCBS will pay to RCIPA for medical services provided to patients covered by BCBS. BCBS further agrees that this dollar amount will not be adjusted for higher- or lower-than-expected medical care required by BCBS patients. RCIPA in turn pays member doctors, based on a fee schedule, for the medical services they provide to BCBS-insured patients. If, at the end of the year, there is any money left over, it is distributed to RCIPA members. If there is not enough money to pay for all the services provided by the member doctors, then the shortfall is allocated among the member doctors who must contribute cash to make up the shortfall.

Why do you think RCIPA serves as an intermediary between BCBS and the doctors who care for BCBS's clients? Why would BCBS risk paying "too much" for the medical care of their customers? Why would RCIPA and its members risk being "underpaid" for their services? Is one of the two parties forcing the other to agree to such an arrangement? If so, who is forcing whom? Why?

12–18. In the past several years, General Motors, a large auto manufacturer, and Levi Strauss, a major apparel manufacturer, have implemented team-based production processes. Under team-based production, each employee is assigned to a team, and each employee is evaluated and compensated based on the productivity of their team.

General Motors implemented team-based production at its new Saturn car plant. No other GM plant has implemented team-based production (at least not nearly to the same extent). The Saturn plant is a new facility (i.e., not a converted existing GM facility), and team-based production processes have been in place since the plant began production. Saturn employees were generally new hires; few, if any, came from other GM facilities.

Levi Strauss adopted team-based production processes at its existing plants. Employees who had been previously paid on a piece-rate basis were put on a team-based process.

a. In general, what are the advantages and disadvantages of team-based processes?

b. Team-based production at the General Motors Saturn division is widely regarded as a success. Saturn cars are some of the best-built cars in the GM product line. Workplace morale is high at the Saturn plant. By contrast, the Levi Strauss team-based initiative is widely regarded as a failure. Worker productivity has declined and employee morale is low.

What factors caused the Saturn experiment with team-based production to be a success and the Levi Strauss experiment to be a failure? Why?

12–19. Joan Zimmerman owns a local CPA firm. The company employs 10 CPAs and some additional staff employees. Joan sets her own pay and makes most of the major decisions facing the firm. Joan often initiates new ideas and implements them. The company has no board of directors, and no one is responsible for monitoring Joan's actions. Does this organizational arrangement contradict the basic principle concerning the value of separating decision management and control? Explain.

12–20. Traditionally, lending decisions at financial institutions were made by people relatively high up in the organization. For instance, a senior loan officer might have to approve even a small loan. Recently, some financial institutions have decentralized this decision, sometimes to people without college degrees. Discuss why it might have historically made sense to centralize the lending decision. Discuss potential factors that might have motivated the decentralization of these rights in certain organizations.

Chapter 13
Decision Rights: Bundling Tasks into Jobs and Subunits

IBM Credit Corporation is a wholly owned subsidiary of IBM. Its major business is the financing of installment payment agreements for IBM products. If IBM Credit were a stand-alone company, it would rank in the Fortune 100 finance companies with assets valued at over $10 billion. In 1993, IBM Credit was touted in the financial press for decreasing the time required to process a credit application from six days to four hours.[1] This decrease in cycle time was achieved through a substantial rebundling of the tasks performed by individual employees. Prior to *reengineering,* individuals performed narrowly assigned tasks. For example, one employee would check the applicant's credit and another would price the loan. Employees were grouped based on functional specialties to form the basic subunits of the firm (for example, the credit and pricing departments). After reengineering, applications were handled by "case workers"

---

[1]Details of this example are from M. Hammer and J. Champy (1993), "The Promise of Reengineering," *Fortune* (May 3), 94–97.

who were assigned most of the tasks involved in processing the application. The basic subunit structure of the company was altered correspondingly.

The results at IBM Credit suggest that the bundling of tasks into jobs and subunits can affect a firm's productivity dramatically. This chapter examines these important managerial decisions. We begin by analyzing the problem of how to bundle tasks into jobs. We then consider the problem of combining jobs into subunits of the firm. We conclude the chapter by discussing recent trends in the assignment of decision authority (the topic of Chapter 12) and the bundling of tasks (the topic of this chapter). We expand on the example of IBM Credit to illustrate these trends. The appendix to this chapter uses a simple game-theoretic example to illustrate some of the basic principles from this chapter.

Bundling Tasks into Jobs

In Chapter 12, we discussed how jobs have at least two important dimensions—decision authority and variety of tasks. We then analyzed the topic of decision authority in greater detail. We now turn to the second dimension, the bundling of tasks. The problem of how to bundle tasks obviously is quite complex; unfortunately, limited formal analysis of the topic exists. Nonetheless, the problem is economic in nature: Managers face a set of *economic trade-offs* when they bundle tasks. As in the case of decision authority, important insights into the nature of these trade-offs can be gained through simple examples.

Specialized versus Broad Task Assignment

FinWare Inc. is a distributor of financial software. Its customers include individual consumers and businesses. Within FinWare, there are two primary activities or *functions,* selling software and after-sales service (helping customers install the software on their systems and managing its interface with other programs). Thus, as displayed in Figure 13.1, FinWare must perform four basic tasks—sales and service for each of its two customer groups. Of course, these four basic tasks could be subdivided into a much larger number of smaller tasks. To keep the analysis tractable, we ignore this finer partitioning and assume that the firm has but four tasks. Our analysis readily extends to more general cases.

FinWare operates at multiple locations throughout the country. At its planned new Greensboro office, each of the four tasks is expected to take four hours per day to complete. Thus, the firm must hire two full-time employees in this office. In structuring the two jobs, the most obvious alternatives are to have each employee specialize in one function (either selling or service) that is performed for both customer groups or have one employee provide both sales and service to individual consumers and the other employee perform both functions for business customers. We refer to the first alternative as *specialized task assignment* and the second as *broad task assignment.* We now examine the relative benefits and costs of these two groupings.

Benefits of Specialized Task Assignment   There are at least two important benefits that can arise from using specialized rather than broad task assignment:

- **Exploiting Comparative Advantage.** Specialized task assignment allows the firm to match people with jobs based on skills and training and correspondingly has employees concentrate on their particular specialties. For example, FinWare can

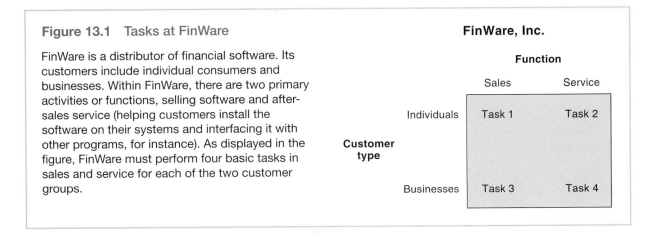

Figure 13.1   Tasks at FinWare

FinWare is a distributor of financial software. Its customers include individual consumers and businesses. Within FinWare, there are two primary activities or functions, selling software and after-sales service (helping customers install the software on their systems and interfacing it with other programs, for instance). As displayed in the figure, FinWare must perform four basic tasks in sales and service for each of the two customer groups.

hire salespeople to sell and technicians to provide service. The principle of comparative advantage suggests that this specialization often will produce higher output than having individuals perform a broad set of tasks—there are potential economies of scale in concentrating on a smaller number of tasks.

· **Lower Cross-training Expenses.** With specialized task assignment, each employee is trained to complete one basic function. With broad task assignment, employees are trained to complete more than one function, which can be expensive. For instance, suppose at FinWare the service function requires a skilled technician with an advanced college degree, whereas the sales function requires an individual with only a high school diploma. Specialized task assignment allows FinWare to hire one person with an advanced degree and one person without an advanced degree. With broad task assignment, the level of education required is usually the highest level across the assigned tasks. Thus, broad task assignment requires FinWare to hire two people with advanced degrees and train them to perform both functions. Because it costs more for FinWare to hire a person with an advanced degree than a person with only a high school diploma, broad task assignment is more expensive than specialized task assignment.

Adam Smith on the Economies of Specialization

With specialized task assignment, employees concentrate on performing a narrow set of tasks. Adam Smith, an important eighteenth-century economist and philosopher, was among the first to recognize the potential gains from this type of specialization. In his classic book, *The Wealth of Nations,* he argued how a number of specialized employees, each performing a single step in the manufacturing of pins, could produce far more output than the same number of generalists making whole pins. Smith presents the following description of a pin factory using specialized employees:

> One man draws the wire, another straightens it, a third cuts it, a fourth points it, a fifth grinds it at the top for receiving the head; to make the head requires two or three distinct operations; to put it on is a peculiar business, to whiten the pins is another; it is even a trade by itself to put them into the paper.

Smith argues that a small factory with 10 specialized employees could produce about 48,000 pins a day, while 10 employees working independently could not have produced 20 pins per day.

Source: A. Smith (1776), *The Wealth of Nations* (Modern Library: New York, 1937), 4.

Costs of Specialized Task Assignment Specialized task assignment has advantages relative to broad task assignment, but it also has drawbacks. Some of the costs of specialized task assignment include

- **Forgone Complementarities across Tasks.** Sometimes, performing one task can lower the cost of having the same person perform another task. For example, important information about a customer's service requirements might be gained through the sales effort. This information is less likely to be utilized if sales and service are conducted by separate people: It can be costly to transfer the information to the other individual. As another example, consider the case of two employees on an automobile assembly line. The first attaches the door to the car frame; the second attaches the latching mechanism and makes sure the door latches to the frame. If the first does not align the door properly, the second will have more difficulty getting the door to latch properly. Combining both tasks into one job increases the care with which the person attaching the door checks for proper alignment before the latch is attached.

- **Coordination Costs.** The activities of specialized employees have to be coordinated. For instance, FinWare would have to establish procedures for transferring sales orders to service technicians. Also, it might have to appoint a manager to handle exceptions to these procedures (for instance, before committing to the purchase of the software, a customer might demand authorization for specialized installation). Developing procedures and coordinating activities can be expensive.

- **Functional Myopia.** With specialized task assignment, employees tend to concentrate on their individual functions rather than on the overall process of providing good sales and service to customers. For example, a salesperson who is compensated primarily through commissions will have incentives to sell software to customers even if the sale imposes large service costs on the company, such as when the software is not well matched with the customer's existing computer system.

- **Reduced Flexibility.** Failure to cross-train employees has costs as well as benefits. For example, if only one person is trained to perform a particular function, what happens if the person is sick or on vacation? Also, having only one person trained to do a job in a firm can place the firm at a disadvantage when bargaining with the employee over salary and other benefits.[2] These problems are likely to be greatest in small companies, since large companies are more likely to have several people trained to perform any given task.

Incentive Issues Our discussion of the costs and benefits of specialized versus broad task assignment has focused on informational and technological considerations. Incentive issues also can be important. From an incentive standpoint, sometimes it is better to have employees concentrate on a narrow set of tasks, while in other circumstances, a broad set of tasks is preferred.

With broad task assignments, the firm not only is concerned with how hard employees work but also with how they allocate effort among the tasks.[3] For instance, senior

---

[2]L. Stole and J. Zwiebel (1996), "Organizational Design and Technology Choice with Nonbinding Contracts," *American Economic Review* 86, 195–222.

[3]B. Holmstrom and P. Milgrom (1991), "Multitask Principal-Agent Analyses: Incentive Contract, Asset Ownership and Job Design," *Journal of Law Economics and Organization* 7, 24–52.

managers at FinWare would be concerned with the way employees balance their efforts between sales and service. Designing an evaluation and compensation scheme that motivates an appropriate balance of effort is complicated by the fact that the effort exerted on some tasks often is more easily measured than for other tasks. At FinWare, the sales effort might be estimated easily by sales volume, while it might be quite difficult to measure the quality of after-sales service—there are no good direct indicators of service quality, and poor quality might reveal itself very slowly over time (primarily as customers fail to make repeat purchases). If FinWare pays a sales commission, employees will concentrate on sales at the expense of providing good after-sales service to customers: Selling increases their incomes, whereas providing better service has a small impact (it affects income only through its effect on repeat purchases). FinWare can reduce this incentive to misallocate effort by not paying a sales commission. But this provides employees with relatively low incentives to exert effort on either task. One potential response to this problem is to use specialized task assignments. The salesperson could be provided high-powered incentives to concentrate on sales. The service person would not be evaluated on quantifiable output measures, but on more subjective measures, such as customer-satisfaction surveys. We discuss these issues in greater detail in Chapters 15 and 16.

In some cases, producing output requires the coordinated execution of several separate tasks that individually are difficult to assess. Here, it can make sense to assign all the tasks to one individual who is accountable for the final product. For instance, in the example of attaching doors and latches to automobiles, assigning both tasks to one employee makes it easy to identify who is to blame if the door does not latch properly. Similarly, at FinWare the failure of a customer to make a repeat purchase might be due to either poor sales effort or service. Having one employee conduct both sales and service facilitates identification of the employee responsible for the unhappy customer.

Costs and Benefits of Specialized Task Assignment*

Benefits	Costs
Comparative advantage/economies of scale	Forgone complementarities across tasks *can't do more than 1 job*
Lower cross-training expenses	Coordination costs
	Functional myopia *narrow focus*
	Reduced flexibility

*Incentive issues can favor either specialized or broad task assignment, depending on the nature of the production technology and information flows.

Productive Bundling of Tasks

The choice between specialized and broad task assignments depends on the technological, informational, and incentive issues discussed above. One variable that is likely to be of particular importance in making this decision is the relative degree of complementarity among tasks within, versus across, functional areas. At FinWare, the magnitude of the benefits of specialized task assignment depends largely on how related the selling efforts are between the two customer groups. If there are only minor differences between selling to individuals and businesses, training employees to do one makes them well prepared to do the other. In contrast, if the selling tasks are quite different between individuals and businesses, little is gained by training one employee to perform the two selling tasks compared to training separate employees. In addition, any economies of scale that result from specializing in sales are likely to be small. Similarly, the costs of specialized task assignment at FinWare depend on the importance of complementarities across functional areas. When these complementarities are low (for instance, little valuable information is gained about service through the selling effort), little is lost by having employees concentrate on a single function. It also is relatively easy to coordinate the individual specialists through the use of routine procedures. Ultimately, the degree of complementarity among tasks depends on how specialized knowledge is created and the costs of transferring knowledge. It also depends on the technology used in the production process.

Our FinWare example is quite simplified, and in most settings, more complicated task divisions are feasible. For instance, the selling function might have two phases—initial contact and closing the deal. The initial contact requires less specialized product and service knowledge than closing the deal but is potentially more time-consuming. Here, it might be better for a salesperson to handle the initial contact and have a joint call by both the salesperson and service person to close the deal. As another example, at some locations, more complete specialization might be feasible. For instance, an employee at an office with a larger sales volume could concentrate solely on selling to individuals or to businesses. While our basic FinWare example abstracts from these more complicated considerations, it nevertheless isolates some of the key considerations in deciding on how to divide tasks into jobs.

Bundling of Jobs into Subunits

Our discussion of specialized versus broad task assignment highlights the economic trade-offs of bundling tasks into jobs. Managers are confronted with a similar set of trade-offs when they bundle jobs into subunits (for example, departments, divisions, and subsidiaries).

Grouping people together within a subunit lowers the communication and coordination costs among the people *within the subunit*. For instance, they often report to the same manager, who facilitates information flows and coordination. Employees also are more likely to form closer working relationships if they share the same workspace—especially if they are evaluated and compensated on subunit performance. Managers, however, must devise methods of coordinating activities *across the subunits*. For instance, rules and procedures must be developed for coordinating activities among interdependent subunits, managers must be appointed and granted the authority to rule on exceptions to these procedures, and liaison staff and coordinating committees often must be appointed to address interunit issues. In summary, there is a trade-off between the benefits that come from grouping people together and the costs of coordinating their activities with those performed within other subunits. In addition, it is important to consider incentive issues: Some groupings make it easier to devise productive performance-evaluation and reward systems than other groupings (we elaborate on such incentive issues in Chapter 17).

In what follows, we begin by describing two standard methods of grouping jobs into subunits—by function and by product and/or geography. We then discuss the economic trade-offs between these two subunit designs. This discussion is followed by an examination of other methods that firms use to group jobs into subunits.

Figure 13.2   **FinWare as a Functional Organization**

This figure displays an organizational chart for FinWare when jobs are grouped by functional specialty. These jobs are characterized by specialized task assignment. All the sales jobs in the organization are grouped together to form a sales department, and the service jobs are grouped together to form a service department. These departments are charged with managing their particular functions across the firm's entire product line. Senior management plays an important role in defining organizational architecture, coordinating activities across departments, and making key operating decisions.

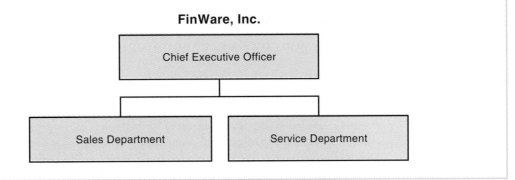

Grouping Jobs by Function

One common method of grouping jobs is by functional specialty (engineering, design, sales, finance, and so on). This organizational arrangement sometimes is referred to as the *unitary form (U form)* of organization because it places each primary function in one major subunit (rather than in multiple subunits). Figure 13.2 displays an organizational chart for FinWare under this type of functional grouping. Individual jobs are characterized by specialized task assignment. All the sales jobs in the organization are grouped

---

Concentrating on Functions at Cadillac

Some of the coordination problems that can arise within a functional organization are highlighted by the process that Cadillac formerly used for developing new products. Under this process, engineers were grouped by narrow functional specialty and charged with completing a related set of tasks:

> The designer of the car's body would leave a hole for the engine, then the power-train designer would try to fit the engine into the cavity, then the manufacturing engineer would try to figure out how to build the design, and finally the service engineer would struggle to invent ways of repairing the car. The results were predictable. On one model, the exhaust manifold blocked access to the air-conditioning compressor, so seasonal maintenance meant removing the exhaust system. On another model, the connection between the spark plugs and the spark plug wires was so tight that mechanics tended to break the wires when they pulled them off to check the spark plugs.

Automobile companies have been able to reduce problems of this type by moving to a system of "concurrent engineering" where everyone affected by design participates in the process as early as possible. Often, companies use development teams that are charged with the entire process—these development teams group jobs by product rather than by function.

Source: W. Davidow and M. Malone (1993), *The Virtual Corporation* (Harper Business: New York).

together to form a sales department, and the service jobs are grouped together to form a service department. These departments are charged with managing their particular functions across the firm's entire product line. Senior management plays an important role in defining the architecture, coordinating activities across departments, making key operating decisions, and setting strategy. Rules and procedures are established for coordinating the activities across the functions. For example, detailed procedures are established to transfer sales orders to the service department. Exceptions and special cases are handled by the senior management and/or coordinating committees (which often include senior division managers and corporate staff).

Grouping Jobs by Product or Geography

Another prominent subunit design is the *multidivisional form (M form)* of organization, which groups jobs into a collection of business units based on product or geographic area. Operating decisions such as product offerings and pricing are decentralized to the business-unit level. Senior management of the firm is responsible for major strategic decisions, including organizational architecture and the allocation of capital among the business units. Figure 13.3 shows how FinWare would look organized around product or geography. In the first case, the company is divided into a business products division and a consumer products division. Each of these divisions has its own sales and service departments that focus on the particular products of the division (often, jobs within the business units are grouped by functional area). Organized geographically, the company is divided into a West Coast division and an East Coast division. In this case, sales and service departments within each business unit serve both individual and business customers within their geographic areas.

Trade-offs between Functional and Product or Geographic Subunits

Benefits of Functional Subunits   At least three major benefits stem from grouping jobs by function. First, this grouping helps promote effective coordination within the functional areas. For instance, a supervisor in service can assign employees to specific projects based on current workload and expertise. It also is frequently easier for functional specialists to share information if they work within the same department. For example, if a service technician develops a new solution to a problem, that employee's supervisor can help promote its use by training other technicians within the department. Second, this grouping helps promote functional expertise. Individuals focus on developing specific functional skills and are directly supervised by knowledgeable individuals who can assist and support this development. Third, there is a well-defined promotion path for employees. Employees tend to work their way up within a functional department—for example, from salesperson to local sales manager to district sales manager. Having a well-defined promotion path can reduce employee uncertainty about career paths and thus can make it less expensive to attract and retain qualified employees (recall our discussion of risk aversion in Chapter 2).

Problems with Functional Subunits   Although functional grouping has advantages, it also has disadvantages. First, there is the opportunity cost of using senior management's valuable time coordinating functions and making operating decisions. This time

Figure 13.3 FinWare as a Product and Geographic Organization

This figure shows how FinWare would look organized around product or geography. In the first case, the company is divided into a business products division and a consumer products division. Each of these divisions has its own sales and service departments that focus on the particular products of the division. (Often, jobs within the business units are grouped by functional area.) Organized geographically, the company is divided into a West Coast division and an East Coast division. In this case, the sales and service departments within each business unit serve both individual and business customers within their geographic areas.

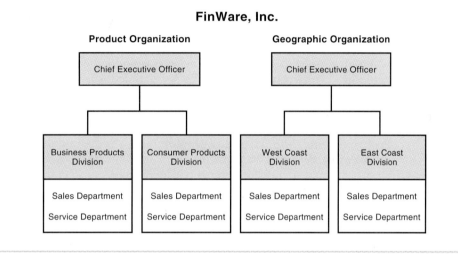

might be focused more productively on activities such as strategic planning—deciding in which businesses the company should compete and how to be successful in those businesses (see Chapter 8). Second, there can be significant, time-consuming coordination problems across departments. At FinWare, when a sale is made by the sales department, the order has to be communicated to the service department, which in turn must schedule the required customer service. This process can cause lengthy delays in serving the customer. Moreover, important information can be lost in these transfers between departments. Third, employees sometimes concentrate on their functional specialties

The Formation of Multidivisional Firms in the Oil Industry

In the 1950s, most of the Fortune 500 oil companies were organized into functional departments. These companies were not performing well in competition with smaller corporations. Oil companies began experimenting with their organizational architectures. The design that appeared to work best was the multidivisional form of organization. Some of the firms organized around geographic areas, whereas other firms organized around product lines. Companies that switched to the M form early outperformed other companies that switched later. By the middle 1970s, most large oil companies had switched to the multidivisional form of organization. Those which did not switch tended to be smaller companies that performed well using the old structure.

Source: H. Armour and D. Teece (1978), "Organizational Structure and
Economic Performance," *Bell Journal of Economics* 9, 106–122.

rather than on the process of satisfying customers. For instance, the sales department might focus on achieving department goals, even if that focus imposes costs on other departments in the firm. A salesperson might promise rapid installation to a customer even though the workload of the service department already is high.

Benefits of Product or Geographic Subunits   An advantage of the M form of organizing large corporations—especially within dynamic environments—is that decision rights for operations are assigned to individuals lower within the organization, where in many cases the relevant specific knowledge is located. Managers of business units are compensated based on the performance of their units; this provides incentives to use this specific knowledge more productively. Decentralizing decision rights to business-unit managers also frees senior management to concentrate on other, more strategic issues. The separation of the corporate office from operations focuses senior executives' attention on the overall performance of the corporation rather than on specific aspects of the functional components. A product or geographic focus promotes coordination among the functions that must be completed to produce and market a particular product or to serve a given geographic area.

Problems with Product or Geographic Subunits   Business-unit managers tend to focus on the performance of their own units. This focus is consistent with the maximization of a firm's value so long as product demands and costs are independent across business units. In this case, firm value is simply the sum of the values of the individual units. Frequently, there are important interdependencies among units that must be taken into account if a firm's value is to be maximized. For example, there is likely to be some overlap in customers, intermediate products often are transferred between subunits, and the units share common resources. If managers focus on their own units and do not consider these interdependencies, the overall value of the firm is reduced. For example, the West and East Coast divisions of FinWare might compete against each other for a national customer and reduce overall profits by selling products at a lower price than if they coordinated their marketing. This problem can be mitigated by forming *groups* of interrelated business units and basing a component of unit managers' compensation on overall group performance. However, as we discuss in Chapters 14 and 15, developing a compensation scheme that appropriately motivates unit managers is not easy. Splitting functional personnel among business units also forgoes potential economies that might result from combining similar specialists within one subunit.

Benefits and Costs of Functional Organization as Opposed to Product or Geographic Organization

Benefits	Costs
Improved coordination among functional specialists	Less effective use of local product or geographic information
Promotes functional expertise	Opportunity cost of senior management time
Provides a well-defined promotion path	Coordination problems among subunits
	Functional focus: It is difficult to design compensation plans that promote a focus on profits and customers

Where Functional Subunits Work Best   Functional grouping works best in small firms with homogeneous products and markets. In these firms, it is easier for senior managers to coordinate operating decisions across departments. For large firms with more diverse product offerings, senior executives are less likely to possess the relevant specific knowledge for making operational decisions for the company. In addition, the opportunity cost of having senior management concentrate on operating and coordination issues rather than on major strategic issues for the firm can be enormous.[4] In such cases, grouping by product or geography often will be the preferred alternative.

Another variable that is likely to affect the desirability of functional subunits is the rate of technological change in the industry. Here, we consider technological change broadly to include new products, new production techniques, and organizational innovations. Functional subunits are more effective in environments with a more stable technology, since frequent communication across functional departments and specialists is less important and interactions can be handled through routine rules and procedures. In addition, senior management is likely to possess more of the relevant specific knowledge to coordinate functional areas.

In less stable environments, direct communication across functional areas is more important and new situations are more likely to arise that will challenge established coordination procedures. In turn, senior managers are less likely to have all the relevant specific knowledge to address these challenges. Rather, the specific knowledge is more likely to be spread across employees throughout the firm. For example, the frequent introduction of new products increases the benefits of communication among salespeople and design engineers about customer demands and preferences. Similarly, it is important for development and manufacturing personnel to share information when production techniques and technologies are changing more frequently.

Finally, in a rapidly changing environment, there is likely to be more uncertainty about the appropriate organizational architecture. With divisions organized around products or geography, different divisions can experiment with different architectures. For example, when Citibank began offering swaps, it opened trading desks in New York, Toronto, London, and Tokyo. The different operations competed not only with other financial institutions for business but also with one another. By encouraging experimentation with the architecture of these businesses, Citibank exploited the benefits of economic Darwinism within the firm. As experience mounted, the best procedures were made standard across the bank. Thus, when an environment is more dynamic, the desirability of a product or geographic organization increases.

Environment, Strategy, and Architecture

In Chapter 11, we discussed how appropriate organizational architecture is influenced by the firm's business environment and strategy. Our discussion of the appropriate subunit configuration highlights this influence. Both environmental factors (such as the rate of technological change) and the firm's business strategy (whether the firm produces multiple products, chooses to operate in multiple locations, and so on) affect the desirability of functional versus product or geographic organization.

An important illustration of the influence of the environment and strategy on subunit design is the experience of large United States firms at the beginning of the twentieth century. The first large firms in the United States were the railroad companies, which emerged around 1850.[5] These firms initially organized around basic functions

---

[4]O. Williamson (1975), *Markets and Hierarchies* (Free Press: New York).

[5]A. Chandler, Jr. (1977), *The Visible Hand: The Managerial Revolution in American Business* (Belknap Press: Cambridge, MA).

such as finance, pricing, traffic, and maintenance. As the incidence of large firms increased in other industries in the late 1800s (such as steel, tobacco, oil, and meatpacking), most followed the lead of the railroads and organized around basic functions. As companies like Du Pont, General Motors, and General Electric continued to expand—both geographically and in the number of product lines—in the early 1900s, they began faring poorly in product markets where they faced smaller competitors. Their organizational architectures did not fit their changing environments or strategies. In response, these companies began experimenting with different organizational forms. After significant experimentation, many large companies adopted the M form of organization. Economic historian, Alfred Chandler concludes[6]:

> *The inherent weakness in the centralized, functionally departmentalized operating company . . . became critical only when the administrative load of the senior executives increased to such an extent that they were unable to handle their entrepreneurial responsibilities efficiently. This situation arose when the operations of the enterprise became too complex and the problems of coordination, appraisal, and policy formulation too intricate for a small number of top officers to handle both long-run, entrepreneurial, and short-run, operational administrative activities.*

Matrix Organizations

Some firms attempt to capture the benefits of both functional and product or geographic organization by using overlapping subunit structures.[7] These *matrix organizations* have functional departments such as finance, manufacturing, and development. But employees from these functional departments also are assigned to subunits organized around product, geography, or some special project. Matrix organizations are characterized by intersecting lines of authority—the term *matrix* refers to the intersecting lines resulting from such an organizational arrangement. Individuals report both to a functional manager and a product manager. Functional departments usually serve as the primary mechanism for personnel functions and professional development. The functional managers typically have the primary responsibility for performance reviews (since they have better technical knowledge for evaluating an employee's performance). Product managers provide input into these reviews. For example, in hospitals, nurses work with physicians and medical technicians in the delivery of health care in "product line" hospital units such as pediatrics or orthopedics. Much of the nurses' specific directions in caring for a particular patient comes from physicians. Yet in many hospitals, nurses are hired, supervised, and evaluated by other nurses who ultimately report to the director of nursing. Physicians are assigned only advisory authority in this process.

Matrix organization often is used in industries such as defense, construction, and management consulting. These industries are characterized by a sequence of new products or projects (for example, building a new airplane or a new shopping mall). Individuals are assigned to work in teams on a particular project and when that project is completed, they are reassigned to new project teams. Given the nature of the projects in these industries, it is important for individuals across functional areas to communicate and to work together closely. For example, a successful airplane design must meet the demands of the customer; thus, there are benefits from the use of product-oriented teams. However, it is critical that the plane be aerodynamically sound. Thus, these

[6]A. Chandler, Jr. (1966), *Strategy and Structure* (Doubleday: Garden City, NY) 382–383.

[7]For a more detailed discussion of matrix organizations, see W. Baber (1983), *Organizing for the Future* (The University of Alabama Press: Tuscaloosa, AL).

Figure 13.4   FinWare as a Matrix Organization

This figure shows how FinWare might look organized as a matrix organization. The firm maintains functional divisions of sales and service. Individuals from these divisions simultaneously are assigned to either the business-products or consumer-products subunits (teams). These teams are indicated by the shaded rectangles. The functional managers focus on managing the particular function across both products, while the product managers focus on managing particular products across functions.

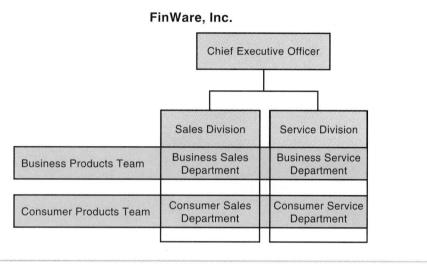

projects also benefit from a high level of functional expertise, which is promoted by maintaining functional areas.

Figure 13.4 shows how FinWare might look if it were organized as a matrix organization. The firm maintains functional departments for sales and service. Employees from these departments are assigned simultaneously to either the business-product or consumer-product subunits (teams). Functional managers focus on managing their particular function across both products, whereas product managers focus on managing particular products across functions.

A potential advantage of a matrix organization, as opposed to a functional organization, is that employees are more likely to focus on the overall business process rather than on their own narrow functional specialty. However, in contrast to a pure product or geographic organization, functional supervision is maintained; there is a mechanism

Intel Corporation: A Matrix Organization

Intel Corporation's organizational structure in 1992 provides an example of a matrix organization. The company organized around five major product groups, including entry-level products, Intel products, microprocessor products, multimedia and supercomputing components, and semiconductor products. Intel staffed these groups with people from the basic functional groups of corporate business development, finance and administration, marketing, sales, software technology, and technology and manufacturing. Thus, individual workers were members of both product and functional groups.

Source: A. Dhebar (1993), "Intel Corporation: Going into OverDrive,"
Harvard Business School Case 9-593-096.

for helping ensure functional excellence and for providing clearer opportunities for advancement and development.

While matrix organizations look good on paper, in practice they often are difficult to implement. Potential problems with the matrix form of organization arise from the intersecting lines of authority. Employees who are assigned to product teams do not automatically have strong incentives to cooperate or be concerned about the success of the team. Rather, individuals might be more concerned about how their functional supervisors view their work, since functional supervisors are responsible for their primary performance reviews. Moreover, employees often see their roles as being representatives of their functional areas. Employees might be concerned excessively about how the decisions of a product team impact their particular area. These problems sometimes can be reduced by appropriate design of the performance-evaluation and reward systems (discussed in Chapters 14 to 17). Individuals will be more concerned about the output of a product team if their compensation depends on team output. A related problem with matrix organizations is the potential for disputes between functional and product managers and the cost of resolving such disputes. Having both a functional and product manager also can increase influence costs—there are two supervisors to influence, not one. For instance, nurses might lobby with both their nursing supervisors as well as physicians to give them good performance reviews or specific assignments.

Mixed Designs

Often, firms use more than one method to organize subunits. Chase Manhattan Bank uses three types of subunits for different activities within the bank. Some are organized by product, some by geography, and some by customer. For example, Chase Delaware handles all the bank's credit card business. The business for individuals and middle-market firms is organized geographically. Large business customers are served by specific teams that generally operate out of New York City. Frequently, these teams are set up by industry. As another example, large multinational corporations often organize their international divisions around the matrix concept (with overlapping country and product managers), whereas their domestic subunits are organized around function, product, or geography.

Network Organizations

Firms (and groups of firms) have experimented with other methods of organizing subunits. One example is the network organization. *Network organizations* are divided into work groups based on function, geography, or some other dimension. The relationships among these work groups are determined by the demands of specific projects and work activities rather than by formal lines of authority. These relationships are fluid and frequently change with changes in the business environment.[8] The Japanese *keiretsu,* which is an affiliation of quasi-independent firms with ongoing, fluid relationships, is another example of a network organization. Networks can facilitate information flows and cooperative undertakings among work groups. However, their heavy reliance on implicit understandings and informal relationships also can lead to misunderstandings or opportunism.

---

[8]W. Baker (1992), "The Network Organization in Theory and Practice," in N. Nohria and R. Eccles (Eds.), *Networks and Organizations* (Harvard Business School: Boston), 397–429.

Figure 13.5   Functions at IBM Credit

This figure lists the basic functions that IBM Credit must perform in order to complete the process of transforming credit applications into formal credit offers.

IBM Credit Functions
- Credit checking
- Contract preparation
- Pricing
- Document preparation

Organizing within Subunits

We have examined the topic of partitioning the firm into major subunits. The same analysis applies to grouping jobs within subunits (for example, departments). Grouping jobs into functional departments at a business-unit level is most likely to be effective when the unit is small and has a limited range of products. In contrast, in large business units with diverse product offerings, organizing by product or geography can be a more productive alternative. Product or geographic organization is also likely to be more effective in rapidly changing business environments, since senior management is less likely to have the relevant specific knowledge to make operating and coordination decisions.

Recent Trends in Assignments of Decision Rights

Traditionally, many firms have created jobs that specify limited decision authority (the topic of Chapter 12) and narrow task assignments. In turn, these jobs have tended to be grouped by functional specialty—either at the overall firm level or at the business-unit level. During the 1990s, there was a significant shift toward granting employees broader decision authority and less specialized task assignments. Many companies also have shifted from functional subunits toward more product-oriented organizations. As we discuss below, these changes have been motivated by increased global competition and various technological changes.

To illustrate some of the factors that have motivated such organizational changes, we examine IBM Credit Corporation in more detail. Figure 13.5 lists the basic functions that IBM Credit must perform to process a credit application.[9] The credit of the applicant has to be checked; the deal must be priced (an interest rate must be chosen); formal contracts drafted; and final documents compiled and sent to the applicant.

Prior to reengineering, IBM Credit was organized around these four basic functions; it was divided into functional departments, including credit, pricing, contracts, and documents. Figure 13.6 shows an organizational chart for IBM Credit under this functional structure. Employees typically were assigned a specialized set of tasks within their functional areas and given limited decision authority on how to

---

[9]Details of this example are from M. Hammer and J. Champy (1993), *Reengineering the Corporation* (Harper Business: New York). Our discussion of IBM Credit abstracts from many of the details of the actual operation of the company. For example, we do not consider the company's credit collection activities, and the organizational chart is extremely simplified. This simplification allows us to illustrate the main points of our analysis without becoming enmeshed in less relevant detail.

Figure 13.6   IBM Credit with Functional Organization

Under a functional organization, the firm is divided into functional departments, including credit, contracts, pricing, and documents. Employees typically are assigned a specialized set of tasks within their functional areas.

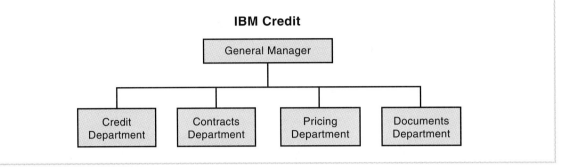

complete them. For example, a clerk in the credit department might have the simple task of logging applications using prescribed procedures. Coordination across functional departments was accomplished by senior management, often through formal rules and procedures. For example, IBM Credit had procedures for transferring credit applications among the various functional departments. Department heads served together on committees to assist in this coordination process. With this architecture, customers received relatively poor service. IBM Credit took about six days to process a credit application, and it was difficult to provide timely information to the customer about the status of an application. However, each application was subject to a careful credit check and each stage of the process was conducted by functional experts.

An Executive Perspective on Increased Foreign Competition

Over the past few decades, competition has increased in many industries. This increased competition has been motivated by such things as reduced transportation costs, deregulation, lost patent protection, and improved technology throughout the world. David Kearns was CEO of Xerox during the 1980s. During his tenure, Xerox faced a substantial increase in foreign competition. This increased competition motivated Xerox to improve customer service and the quality of its products. To achieve this objective, Xerox substantially reassigned decision rights by empowering workers and moving away from functional organization. In Kearns's words,

> About the only consoling factor was that I knew we weren't the only ones in the soup. Global competition had set upon this country, and everyone was vulnerable. American business was threatened not only by Japan and Korea. Europe was mobilizing into a potent force that demanded serious consideration. And yet, as I looked around me, I saw that so many great and admired companies were doing nothing but sitting on their hands. Like us, they were kissing away their businesses and laying the groundwork for their own destruction.
>
> After my string of trips to Japan and after deep introspection about Xerox's strengths and flaws, the solution began to point in one direction. Our only hope for survival was to urgently commit ourselves to vastly improving the quality of our products and service. This was something a lot of corporations talked about, but it was extraordinarily difficult to do. It meant changing the very culture of Xerox from the ground up. Everyone from the cleaning people to the chairman would have to think differently.

Source: D. Kearns (1992), *Prophets in the Dark* (Harper Business: New York), xv–xvi.

Recent Trends in Organization: GTE

During the 1990s, there was a trend toward more product-oriented organizations. An example of a firm that reorganized along these lines is the telephone company GTE. Traditionally, GTE had been organized into functional departments such as repair, billing, and marketing. This structure often frustrated customers, who had difficulty locating which person in the company was responsible for addressing particular problems. Due to increased competitive pressures, GTE decided that it had to offer dramatically better customer service to its telephone customers. Rather than make incremental improvements in each of its functional departments, GTE decided to reorganize around the basic process of providing customer service. In particular, customers wanted one-stop shopping—for example, one number to fix an erratic dial tone, question a bill, sign up for call waiting—or all three—at any time of the day. GTE began meeting this demand when it set up its first pilot "customer care center" in Garland, Texas, in 1992. GTE management stated that preliminary data from these pilot projects indicated a 20 to 30 percent increase in productivity. Customers also obtained better service.

Source: T. Stewart (1993), "Reengineering: The Hot New Management Tool," *Fortune* 128 (August 23), 40–48.

When IBM Credit was the only major producer of mainframe computers, few customers were lost due to delays in processing finance applications. Rather, it could focus on careful and deliberate application procedures. The emergence of Japanese competitors—for example, Hitachi—increased pressure on IBM to change its strategy to focus more on customer service and to shorten the time required to process a credit application. Otherwise, it faced a substantial decrease in sales.

New information and computer technologies enabled IBM Credit to develop internal systems to support an organizational change. For instance, some of the necessary information for processing a credit application previously was stored in a manual filing system. Given this system, it made sense to assign certain tasks to individuals who had both familiarity with and proximity to this data. Computerizing this database allowed employees throughout the firm to access this information directly—a change that

F.W. Taylor on Iron Workers

Frederick Winslow Taylor, an industrial engineer at the beginning of the twentieth century, is known as the father of scientific management. His views were quite influential in affecting the assignment of decision rights in many firms. In particular, he argued that the attributes of lower-level employees dictated that they be granted limited decision authority and a narrow set of tasks. In his words,

> Now one of the very first requirements for a man who is fit to handle pig iron as a regular occupation is that he shall be so stupid and so phlegmatic that he more nearly resembles in his mental make-up the ox than any other type. The man who is mentally alert and intelligent is for this very reason entirely unsuited to what would, for him, be the grinding monotony or work of this character. Therefore the workman who is best suited to handling pig iron is unable to understand the real science of doing this class of work. He is so stupid that the word "percentage" has no meaning to him, and he must consequently be trained by a man more intelligent than himself into the habit of working in the accordance with the laws of this science before he can be successful.

Many modern managers do not think that this view of lower-level employees is accurate, especially in today's environment. The workforce of today is better educated than in Taylor's time, and modern production technologies often call for increased education and less brawn. Correspondingly, many managers have empowered lower-level employees by giving them broader decision authority and a less specialized set of tasks.

Source: F. Taylor (1923), *The Principles of Scientific Management* (Harper & Row: New York), 59.

Figure 13.7   **IBM Credit's Revised Organization**

Under the revised structure, individual caseworkers have the primary decision rights and responsibility for completing all the steps in the credit-granting process. Each financing request is assigned to a caseworker, who checks the applicant's credit, prices the deal, completes the contracts, and so on. There are some functional specialists in the firm (not shown on the chart) who help the caseworkers when difficult or unusual circumstances arise.

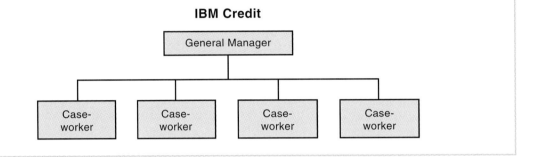

permitted the firm to reassign tasks more easily. Similarly, IBM Credit was able to develop computer programs to assist less skilled personnel in pricing loans. Such expert systems made functional expertise less important, thereby diminishing the importance of one of the advantages of their old organizational architecture.

Given these competitive pressures and new technologies, IBM Credit completely changed its assignment of decision rights. Under the new structure, pictured in Figure 13.7, individual *caseworkers* have the primary decision rights and responsibility for completing all the steps required in the credit-granting process. Each financing request is assigned to one caseworker, who checks the applicant's credit, prices the deal, and draws the contracts. Employees have substantial decision authority in completing these tasks, and the functional subunits of the firm largely have been abandoned.[10] Performance-evaluation and reward systems correspondingly were changed to focus more

The Importance of Informal Communications

A 1993 movie, *Six Degrees of Separation,* popularized the famous Harvard University experiment where randomly selected people in Kansas were handed a letter addressed to people they did not know in Massachusetts. They were asked to forward the letter to an acquaintance who might bring it closer to the "target." On average, it took only five intermediaries before the letter reached the recipient. Social scientists believe that we are all connected to each other by six people or less. In a large global corporation, if communications require on average moving through six people (even with e-mail) before finding the right person who can respond to the query, the delay and distortion of the message could be quite costly. Two researchers at Cornell University developed a mathematical model to show that a few well-placed individuals in the organization that cut across traditional boundaries can increase the speed of communication greatly.

Source: N. Andreeva (1998), "Do the Math—It *Is* a Small World," *Business Week* (August 17), 54–55.

[10]Some functional specialists remained in the organization to help the caseworkers with difficult or unusual circumstances.

specifically on processing times and customer service. With this new organizational architecture, IBM Credit is able to process a credit application in about four hours. Customer satisfaction has increased as a result.

IBM Credit and GTE are but two examples of the many firms that undertook similar restructurings during the 1990s. The success stories from these restructurings have led some management consultants to advocate widespread change for all firms throughout the world. The analysis in Chapters 12 and 13, however, indicates that a firm should not restructure without carefully considering whether a reassignment of decision rights is warranted given its particular business environment and strategy.

Although changes in technology and competition have changed the optimal assignment of decision rights in many firms, these shifts have not occurred in all industries. The benefits of narrow task assignment and functional specialization are still likely to be high for many firms in relatively stable industries. Consider, for example, a small coal-mining operation. Here, it is likely to continue to make sense to have some employees concentrate on mining the coal, while other employees sell it, and still other employees deliver it.

CASE STUDY: *Bagby Copy Company*

Bagby Copy Company is a worldwide producer of copy machines. It manufactures 10 different copiers, ranging from low-end desktop copiers that sell for a few hundred dollars to high-volume document machines that retail for over $200,000.

Each copy machine requires a wiring bundle. Each bundle contains several hundred wires and connectors that provide circuits connecting the paper-flow units, scanner, and photoreceptor to the internal computer logic. The wire harness is plugged into various components during the assembly process. It is possible to assign each major task in this process to different employees. For example, a given employee might focus on one of the many connectors or on testing the completed wire harness. Alternatively, one individual might be assigned the task of producing and testing a completed harness.

In either case, there are a group of employees that are assigned individual tasks to produce a wire harness for a particular copier. In total, there are 10 subgroups of wire harness makers. One alternative is to place all 10 groups in one wire harness department. Another alternative is that each of these 10 subgroups can be assigned to and report to a manager responsible for a particular copier.

Bagby operates in five European countries. Currently, it has separate subunits in each country, where a country manager handles the manufacturing and marketing of all 10 copiers. The company is considering two alternatives. One would be to organize its foreign operations around products. In this case, there would be 10 international product managers with decision rights for managing the manufacturing and sale of a particular copier throughout Europe. The company also is considering a matrix organization, organized around product and country.

Discussion Questions

1. What are the trade-offs that Bagby faces in choosing between specialized and broad task assignment?

2. What are the trade-offs between these two methods of grouping wire-harness makers into subgroups?

3. Which trade-offs does Bagby face in choosing among the country, product, and matrix forms of organizing its international operations?

Summary

The bundling of tasks into jobs and subunits of the firm is an important policy choice that can affect a firm's productivity dramatically. The primary purpose of this chapter is to examine this bundling decision.

We distinguish between two types of jobs: those with *specialized task assignment* and those with *broad task assignment*. With specialized task assignment, the employee is assigned a narrow set of tasks concentrated within one functional specialty—for example, sales. With broad task assignment, the employee is assigned a broader variety of tasks. The benefits of specialized task assignment relative to broad assignment include exploiting comparative advantage and lower cross-training expenses. The costs of specialized task assignment include forgone complementarities from not performing multiple functions, coordination costs, functional myopia, and reduced flexibility. Incentive issues might favor either specialized or broad task assignment, depending on the production technology and information flows. The appropriate bundling of tasks depends on the magnitude of the costs and benefits of each alternative. One variable that is likely to be of particular importance is the relative degree of complementarity among tasks within, versus across, functional areas. Specialized task assignment is favored when the complementarity of tasks within a functional area is relatively high.

Firms can group jobs into subunits based on functional specialty, geography, product, or some combination of the three. *Functional subunits* group all jobs performing the same function within one department (for example, a sales department). Senior management plays a major role in coordinating these departments and in making operating decisions. Benefits of functional organization are the promotion of coordination and expertise within functional areas and provision of a well-defined promotion path for employees. Problems with functional organization include the high opportunity cost of employing senior management time to coordinate departments and make operating decisions, handoffs across departments that can take significant time, coordination failures across departments, and employees concentrating on their own functional specialties rather than on the customer. Functional subunits are likely to work best in smaller firms with a limited number of products operating in relatively stable environments.

Larger, more diverse firms often find it desirable to form subunits based on product or geography. In the *multidivisional (M form) firm,* operating decisions are decentralized to the business-unit level. Senior management of the firm is responsible for major strategic decisions, including finding the optimal organizational architecture and allocating capital among business units. A primary benefit of the M form corporation is that decision rights for operations are assigned to individuals lower in the organization where relevant specific knowledge often is located. Managers of business units are compensated based on the performance of their units so as to provide incentives to use this specific knowledge productively. Decentralizing decision rights to business-unit managers also frees senior executives to concentrate on other issues. Problems with the M form of organization arise because business-unit managers often have incentives to take actions that increase the performance of their business units at the expense of other units within the firm. These problems can be controlled through careful design of business units and by basing a component of business-unit managers' compensation on *group performance*—where the group consists of profit centers with interrelated costs and demands. It is usually difficult, however, to control this problem completely. Multidivisional firms also forgo potential economies that might result from combining similar functional specialists within one unit.

Some firms maintain an overlapping structure of functional and product or geographic subunits. These *matrix organizations* have functional departments such as finance and marketing. Members of these departments are assigned to cross-functional product teams (subunits). Team members report to both a product manager and a functional supervisor. Generally, performance evaluation is conducted by the functional supervisor. Matrix organizations are common in project-oriented industries such as defense, construction, and consulting. An advantage of a matrix organization, in contrast to a pure functional organization, is that individuals are more likely to focus on the overall business process rather than just on their own narrow functional specialty. Potential advantages over a pure product organization are that the functional departments help ensure functional excellence and provide more clearly identified opportunities for advancement and development. Potential problems with the matrix organization arise from the intersecting lines of authority. An employee is likely to have loyalties divided between the goals of the project team and the goals of the functional department. This problem can be mitigated by appropriate design of the performance-evaluation and reward systems. However, as we shall see in subsequent chapters, accomplishing this objective can be difficult.

Firms often use more than one method for organizing subunits. They also use other less standard ways of organizing subunits. One example is a *network organization*.

Decisions on how to group jobs must be made at many levels in the organization. Our analysis of the costs and benefits of alternative groupings of jobs focuses on the overall firm level—how to form major subunits. This same basic analysis applies to the grouping of jobs at lower levels within the firm.

Historically, many firms have created jobs that are low in decision authority and narrow in task assignment. Recently, there has been a trend toward granting employees more decision authority and broader task assignments. Many companies also have shifted away from functional subunits toward more product-oriented organizations. These trends can be explained by specific technological changes and increases in global competition, along with accompanying changes in business strategies.

Appendix

Battle of the Functional Managers[11]

This appendix uses a simple game-theoretic example to illustrate some of the trade-offs that firms face in grouping jobs into subunits. Currently, the Quick Motorcycle Company is functionally organized. Two of its main departments are design and marketing. Pino Pentecoste is the manager of the design department, while Lan Nguyen manages marketing.

Pino has two options for designing a new product. One design focuses on speed, and the other design focuses on safety. Lan has two options for the corresponding marketing campaign. One option concentrates on magazine advertising and reaches older consumers, whereas the other option focuses on television and reaches younger audiences more effectively. Figure 13.8 displays the payoffs that Pino and Lan face for each combination of design and marketing programs (for example, from their respective bonus plans or personal preferences). The payoffs indicate that coordinating the design and marketing is important. If Pino chooses design option 1, and Lan undertakes marketing plan 2, both Pino and Lan receive low payoffs ($100 each). A similar outcome exists if Pino chooses design option 2 and Lan chooses marketing plan 1. In this setting, two Nash equilibria are possible. One is design option 1 and marketing plan 1; the other is

[11]This example is based on the "battle of the sexes" game. For example, see R. Gibbons (1992), *Game Theory for Applied Economists* (Princeton University Press: Princeton, NJ).

Figure 13.8 Battle of the Functional Managers

Quick Motorcycle Company is functionally organized. Pino Pentecoste, the manager of the design department, selects from two designs for a new product. Lan Nguyen, the market manager, selects from two marketing plans. There are two Nash equilibria: Design option 1 and marketing plan 1; design option 2 and marketing plan 2. Both Pino and Lan prefer to coordinate their actions rather than not coordinate (and end up on the off diagonal). However, they disagree on the preferred equilibrium.

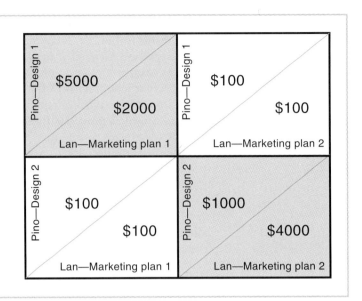

design option 2 and marketing plan 2. Pino and Lan have a conflict over which equilibrium each prefers. Pino receives a higher payoff in the first case, whereas Lan receives a higher payoff in the second case. Nonetheless, both Lan and Pino prefer either equilibrium to cases where they fail to coordinate.

Suppose total firm profits are correlated with the combined payoffs for both Pino and Lan. In this case, the CEO of the firm prefers the combination of design option 1 and marketing plan 1. With complete information about the payoff structure, the CEO selects this option and then allows the design and marketing departments to focus on their specialties in implementing this program. This focus on specialization would allow each department to take advantage of its relative strengths. It also allows Pino and Lan to coordinate the new program with other design and marketing projects in their respective departments. Thus, this example illustrates that functional organization can work well if the CEO has the specific knowledge to coordinate the activities of the functional managers at low cost. This specific knowledge, in turn, is most likely to be held by the CEO in small firms within relatively stable environments.

In a rapidly changing environment it is unlikely that the CEO will know the payoffs facing the managers for each of the options (or even know all the available options). In this case, the CEO does not have the knowledge to order the profit-maximizing alternative. Both Pino and Lan prefer coordination to noncoordination. However, they do not agree on the preferred alternative. There is no guarantee that they will choose the value-maximizing equilibrium. Indeed, they might fail to reach either equilibrium. Pino and Lan have to make concurrent decisions.[12] In an attempt to achieve their preferred equilibrium, they might fail to coordinate and both will suffer. In any case, they will consume resources bargaining (battling) over which options to choose. In this environment, the CEO might want to reconfigure the subunits around products (the firm produces multiple products). The decisions on the design and marketing of each

[12]Both design and marketing require long lead times before a final product is brought to market. It obviously takes time to design and test a product. Similarly, in marketing, an advertising agency must be chosen, a marketing/advertising campaign must be developed, contracts with the media have to be negotiated, and so forth. In Lan's and Pino's case, both must commit to a specific option at about the same time.

product would be made within one subunit. Profit-maximizing choices could be motivated through profit-based bonus plans. In choosing this organizational option, the CEO forgoes any efficiencies that come from combining a given functional activity (across all products) within one unit. If the benefits of functional grouping are high, rather than changing the subunit structure, the CEO might want to foster coordination through the formation of coordinating committees and changes in performance-evaluation and reward systems that promote value-maximizing choices.

Appendix Problem In the early 1900s, General Motors had separate divisions that manufactured Buicks, Cadillacs, Chevrolets, Oaklands, and Oldsmobiles. Decision rights were highly decentralized, and there was little direction or coordination from the central corporate office. As a result, the divisions often failed to coordinate decisions on design standards, which prevented them from taking advantage of economies of scale in buying or making common components (for example, spark plugs). Discuss potential organizational changes that GM might have adopted to reduce this coordination problem.

Suggested Readings	A. Chandler, Jr. (1977), *The Visible Hand: The Managerial Revolution in American Business* (Belknap Press: Cambridge, MA).
	A. Chandler, Jr. (1966), *Strategy and Structure* (Doubleday: Garden City, NY).
	M. Hammer and J. Champy (1993), *'Reengineering the Corporation* (Harper Business: New York).
	O. Williamson (1983), *Markets and Hierarchies* (Free Press: New York).

Review Questions

13–1. Discuss the costs and benefits of specialized task assignment relative to broad task assignment. What variables are likely to be particularly important in determining the optimal choice between these two alternatives?

13–2. Define the following: functional organizations, product organization, geographic organization, matrix organization, and network organization.

13–3. Discuss the circumstances under which you think functional organizations will work best.

13–4. Discuss the pluses and minuses of matrix organizations.

13–5. Why do you think many US firms have reorganized their international divisions from a country focus to matrix organizations focusing on both country and product?

13–6. In the early 1990s, Chrysler Corporation placed nearly all decisions about the development of a new vehicle in the hands of a single, cross-functional product team. In contrast, General Motors used an approach that placed a stronger emphasis on functional specialties. Small teams were established that consisted of experts from the same functional field. Each team was charged with a particular assignment that related to its area of specialization. For example, one team might have had the primary responsibility for the design of the body of the vehicle, whereas another team might have been charged with developing the drive train. The teams worked simultaneously on their specific tasks. Some individuals on these teams also served on additional cross-functional teams that were charged with coordinating the development process across the functional areas. Discuss the relative advantages and disadvantages of these two approaches to product development.

13–7. For many years, your firm has been protected by patents. Technological change and the introduction of new products have been slow. Soon, these conditions will change. Your patent protection is expiring, and the rate of technological change and innovation has increased substantially. Discuss how these changes are likely to affect your firm's optimal bundling of tasks into jobs and subunits.

13–8. Johnson & Johnson (J&J) is one of the largest medical products companies in the world. In 1994, it had 33 major lines of business, with 168 operating companies in 53 countries. Decision rights in J&J were quite decentralized. For instance, in 1993, the baby oil manager in Italy ran his own factory and got to decide such things as package size, pricing, and advertising. Similarly, other country managers had considerable discretionary authority for similar products sold in their countries. This type of decentralized decision making has served J&J well: Its returns to shareholders have been very good. Significant changes, however, are occurring in J&J's environment. In particular, trade barriers have been significantly reduced in Europe.

    a. Describe the advantages of J&J's decentralized decision making that have helped to explain the success of the company.

    b. What organizational changes do you think J&J should consider given the change in the environment? Explain. Draw a new organizational chart for J&J's international operations (based on your suggestions).

13–9. AutoMart Repair Shop is currently organized as follows: a repair manager meets with the customer to discuss the problems with the car. A repair order is completed. The mechanics specialize in particular types of repairs (for example, air conditioning, body work, etc.). Typically, a car in the shop requires work by several specialists. The manager plans the sequence of service among the specialists. The car is then serviced by each of the necessary specialists in turn. Discuss how AutoMart Repair Shop might look if it reorganized around the process of fixing an automobile. Discuss the pluses and minuses of the current structure compared to the more product-oriented structure.

13–10. Many companies are making increased use of telecommuting, which consists of employees working out of their homes, linked to the central office by telephone, computer, and fax machine. Discuss the benefits and costs of telecommuting. What types of occupations are likely to be best suited for telecommuting? Explain why.

13–11. Evaluate the following statement: "It is usually best to organize as a matrix organization. Matrix organizations combine the best of both worlds, functional excellence and product focus."

13–12. Stable Inc. is in a relatively stable environment in terms of technology, competition, and regulation. Variance Inc. is in a relatively unstable environment with more frequent changes in technology, competition, and regulation. Both produce the same number of products. Which firm is more likely to be functionally organized? Explain why.

13–13. Professors Brickley and Smith are writing two chapters for a new book. Two primary tasks are involved. First, someone has to write each of the chapters. Second, someone has to copyedit the chapters. The second step involves making sure that the writing is good, that there are no typographical errors, etc. They are considering two alternative ways to organize the work. In one case, one of the professors would write both chapters, and the other professor would copyedit both chapters. In the other case, each professor would select one chapter and be responsible for all writing and copyediting. The two professors have equal abilities and knowledge. Discuss the trade-offs between these two methods of organizing the work. What factors do you think will be most important in deciding how to organize?

13–14. Jog PCS is a wireless telephone company. It sells portable digital phones to three customer groups: (1) business users, (2) high-volume individual users, and (3) low-volume individual users. Currently, the company is functionally organized. Primary functions include product development, marketing, sales, and customer service. The organizational chart is as follows:

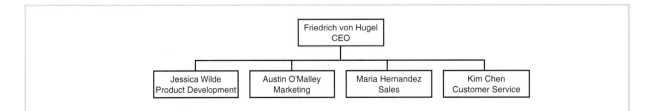

a. The CEO, von Hugel, is considering reorganizing the company as a multidivisional firm organized around customer type. Draw the revised organizational chart.

b. Discuss the pros and cons of the proposed reorganization, relative to the current structure.

c. Jessica Wilde, vice president of product development suggests that a matrix organization might be better. Draw the organization chart implied by her proposal.

d. Discuss the pros and cons of the matrix proposal relative to the multidivisional proposal.

Chapter 14
Attracting and Retaining Qualified Employees

RKO Warner Video sells and rents prerecorded videotapes.[1] In 1988, RKO owned and operated 24 video stores; it was one of the larger video chains in the New York City area. It had an enormous inventory and specialized in high-quality service and attractive decor.

Although the company had been reasonably successful, senior management was concerned about two human resource problems. First, the turnover of employees was "unacceptably high." Second, "the quality and consistency of performance by store managers varied considerably across the chain." In structuring the store manager positions, senior management had bundled specific tasks and decision rights into jobs (see Chapters 12 and 13). For instance, store managers had key responsibility for making sure the racks were alphabetized, keeping the store clean, opening on time, returning tapes to racks promptly, ordering product from the warehouse, and keeping checkout

[1]Details of this example are from S. Shimer, under the supervision of G. Baker (1993), "RKO Video, Inc.: Incentive Compensation Plan," Harvard Business School Case 9-190-067.

times short. RKO, however, had not designed a complementary reward system to motivate appropriate effort on these tasks—RKO's *organizational architecture* was poorly designed.

To address these concerns, RKO adopted a new bonus plan for store managers. The aims of the plan were twofold. First, the company wanted to raise the level of compensation to "attract and keep qualified store managers." Second, RKO wanted to structure the compensation package in a manner that would motivate managers to "be more conscientious and take pride in their work."

The plan suffered from some design flaws, but it accomplished these two objectives—at least in part. The plan had a substantial impact on the level of pay and made RKO more competitive in the local labor market. In early 1988, RKO store managers received annual salaries ranging from $21,000 to $28,000. The new bonus plan was targeted at increasing these base salaries by about 15 percent, depending on performance. In fact, during the first quarter under the bonus plan, two store managers received substantially more in bonus pay than in base pay. Although the incentive effects of the plan are harder to document, there is some evidence that the plan also had a positive impact on managerial performance.

The example of RKO highlights two important objectives of compensation policy: (1) *to attract and retain qualified employees,* and (2) *to motivate employees to be more productive.* This chapter concentrates on the first of these objectives—attraction and retention. We postpone a detailed discussion of incentive compensation until Chapter 15. Since the two topics are interrelated, we also discuss some incentive-related issues in this chapter. In particular, we examine how the level of pay can be used not only to attract and retain employees but also to motivate them.

We begin by providing a more detailed discussion of the objectives of compensation contracting. We then present a benchmark economic model of employment and wages. Subsequently, we extend the basic model and examine the implications of investments in human capital, compensating differentials, costly information about market wage rates, internal labor markets, and the choice between salary and fringe benefits.

Contracting Objectives

In Chapter 10, we emphasized that it is in the joint interests of contracting parties to maximize the value created by their relationships. By exploiting fully the business opportunities the firm faces and maximizing value, the size of the overall "pie" is maximized and all parties can be made better off. This general principle holds for labor contracts. By designing compensation contracts that maximize the value of employees' output net of costs, the firm's value is maximized and hence both the owners of the firm and their employees can be made better off.

Individuals will not participate in an employment relationship unless they expect to receive at least their opportunity cost. If they do not receive their *reservation utilities*—the utility they could obtain in their next best alternative—they will quit and go to work for another firm (or withdraw from the labor force). Since individuals gain utility from compensation, the level of compensation is a key factor in attracting and retaining qualified employees. Owners also must receive an adequate return on their investment, or they will close the business and reinvest elsewhere. In a competitive market, paying employees more than the competitive rate results in a cost disadvantage that in the long run could drive the company out of business. Owners have incentives to design compensation packages that allow them to attract and retain employees with the required skills at the lowest possible cost.

The Level of Pay
The Basic Competitive Model

In this section, we present a benchmark model of employment and compensation; it is patterned after the standard competitive model that we discussed in Chapter 6. This model is a useful starting point for analyzing issues related to the level of pay. Subsequently, we extend the analysis to consider other important issues.

Suppose the labor market is characterized by the following conditions:

- The labor market is *competitive.* Firms have no discretion over the wages they pay to employees; rather, wages are determined by supply and demand in the marketplace.
- Market wage rates are costlessly observable.
- Individuals are identical in their training and skills.
- All jobs are identical. They do not vary in their risk, location, level of intellectual challenge, travel opportunities, and so on.
- There are no long-term contracts. Rather, all labor is hired in the "spot" market for a single period.
- All compensation comes from monetary compensation. The firm does not provide any fringe benefits such as vacation pay or health insurance.

Figure 14.1 depicts the hiring decisions of individual firms within this market setting. Each firm continues to hire employees to the point where the marginal revenue product equals the market-determined wage rate. Until this point, hiring additional employees produces more revenue than it costs to hire the individuals. Past this point, the costs of hiring additional individuals are larger than their benefits. The hiring decisions of all firms in the market determine the demand curve for labor. The supply curve is determined by the decisions of individuals on whether to accept the given wage rate or stay out of the labor force. The market wage rate equates supply and demand.

The implications of this analysis are that if a firm pays too little (below the market wage rate), it will be unable to attract qualified employees or it will have high turnover. This principle motivated RKO to raise its level of pay. On the other hand, a firm that pays too much will have long queues for job openings and low turnover. However,

---

Setting the Wrong Level of Pay at Salomon Brothers

In the first year out of the training program, 1983, Howie Rubin made $25 million for Salomon Brothers in the new activity of mortgage-backed securities. The several-hundred million-dollar question was first raised by Howie Rubin: Who really made the money—Howie Rubin or Salomon Brothers? Salomon Brothers decided it was the company and refused to pay Rubin more than the normal pay scale. In his first year, Rubin was paid $90,000, the most permitted a first-year trader. In 1984, his second year, Rubin made $30 million trading. He then was paid $175,000, the most permitted a second-year trader. In the beginning of 1985 he quit Salomon Brothers and moved to Merrill Lynch for a 3-year guarantee: a minimum of $1 million a year, plus a percentage of his trading profits.

After 1985, Salomon Brothers lost much of its market share in mortgage-backed securities to other firms such as Merrill Lynch.

Source: M. Lewis (1989), *Liar's Poker* (Norton Press: New York), 126.

Figure 14.1 How Firms Choose Employment and Wages: The Basic Competitive Model

In our basic model, firms have no discretion over the wages they pay to employees; rather, the wages are determined by supply and demand in the marketplace. As shown in the figure, individual firms continue to hire employees up to the point E^*, where the marginal revenue product equals the market-determined wage rate. Until this point, hiring additional employees brings more revenue into the firm than it costs to hire the employee. Past this point, the costs of hiring additional individuals are larger than the benefits.

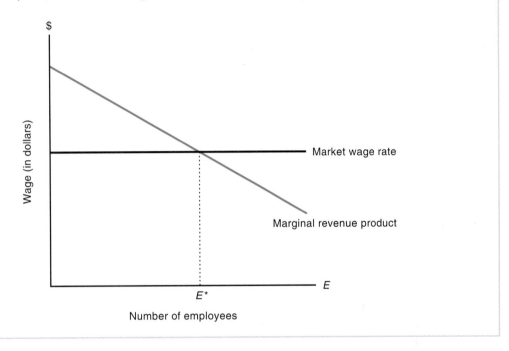

the firm will incur higher costs and thus will report lower profits than firms that do not overpay. Given a competitive market for its products, it eventually will go out of business.

Human Capital[2]

In our benchmark model, all individuals are alike. Yet employees often vary in their abilities, skills, and training. *Human capital* is a term that characterizes individuals as having a set of skills that can be "rented" to employers. The value of human capital is determined by supply and demand in the marketplace. Individuals invest in their human capital through education and training, migration, and search for new jobs. The return on this investment consists of higher wage rates that come from having more valuable human capital—hence college graduates typically earn more than high school graduates.

It is useful to distinguish between *general* and *specific* human capital. General human capital consists of training and education that is equally useful to a broad array of different firms. Investments in general human capital include obtaining an MBA degree, mastering general principles of engineering, or learning popular word-processing programs.

[2]This section draws on G. Becker (1983), *Human Capital* (University of Chicago Press: Chicago).

Paying for Specific Human Capital

The Pratt & Whitney North Berwick plant, Maine's largest factory, manufactures parts for jet engines. In 1993 it was about to be closed, due to high operating costs and inefficiencies. A new plant manager overhauled operations. There were 129 job classifications, 90 containing only one or two people. He broadened job descriptions, so that 18 inspectors do 15 percent more work than 28 did 5 years ago.

A new pay scheme links pay to the amount of training a worker has, not seniority. Automatic raises were out. The new pay structure has three levels tied to the workers' level of skills—"automatic" (basic requirements for holding a job), "conscious" (keeping parts flowing through their machining operations), and "creative" (lead projects to cut costs or improve quality). As workers receive training for each level and as they shoulder more responsibility, their pay increases. Shop-floor wages vary between $9 and $19 per hour with the most money going to people running special cost studies or quality projects—tasks previously held by managers. The plant's overall operating costs per hour have fallen 20 percent in 2 years, without the employees taking a pay cut.

Source: J. White (1996), "How a Creaky Factory Got Off the Hit List, Won Respect at Last," *The Wall Street Journal* (December 26), A1.

Specific human capital, on the other hand, is more valuable to the current employer than to alternative employers. Investments in specific capital include such things as learning the details of a particular firm's accounting system or product information.

In our benchmark model extended to allow for differences in training, firms would not invest in general training. The gains from general training go to the employees, not firms: If a firm does not pay the employee the market price for the new skills, the individual moves to another firm that is willing to pay. Thus, employees pay for their own general training. Correspondingly, employees are reluctant to invest in specific training, since it does not increase their market values. Thus, in our benchmark model, firms must pay for specific training.

Compensating Differentials[3]

Our benchmark model does not consider differences in working conditions across jobs. In reality, jobs vary in many dimensions, including quality of the work environment,

---

Investments in General Human Capital

Livingston County deputy sheriff Ray DiPasquale received a $10,000 raise to bring his salary to $45,000 by moving to the larger Greece town police force. Rural and small departments generally pay no more than $34,000 annually, whereas larger departments pay about $46,000 and offer better benefits. By offering a more attractive compensation package, they get to hire better qualified, more experienced police officers. In fact, 80 percent of Greece police have been transfers. Small, usually rural police departments hire untrained officers and train them. Training a cadet with no experience costs nearly $25,000 and ties up personnel for up to 35 weeks. This example illustrates that general human capital (policing) is captured by the employee, not the firm making the investment.

Source: M. Daneman and K. Breen (1999), "Big Bucks Lure Cops to Bigger Towns," *Democrat and Chronicle* (September 20), A1.

---

[3]In this section, we discuss the key points of the theory of compensating differentials as they relate to managerial decision making. For an expanded discussion of compensating differentials, see R. Ehrenberg and R. Smith (1988), *Modern Labor Economics,* third edition (Scott, Foresman: Glenview, IL), Chapter 8.

Compensating Differentials for Working at Night

Many production employees in the United States work night shifts. Since most employees prefer to work during the day, firms have to pay compensating differentials to attract enough employees to staff their night shifts. Research suggests that in 1984, night employees in manufacturing plants received about $.30 more per hour than day employees. The average manufacturing wage in 1984 was $9.18.

Source: S. King and H. Williams (1985), "Shift Work Pay Differentials and Practices in Manufacturing," *Monthly Labor Review* 108 (December), 26–33.

geographic location, length of commute, exposure to danger, characteristics of coworkers, and the degree of monotony associated with the tasks. Facing equal salary levels across job offers, an individual will choose the job with the most desirable characteristics (such as low risk of injury and attractive location). To attract employees to less desirable jobs, firms must increase the level of pay.[4]

The *extra* wage that is paid to attract an individual to a less desirable job is called a *compensating wage differential*. For instance, RKO probably has to pay more to attract a manager to work at night at a more dangerous location than it does to attract a manager to work during the day at a safer location.

Labor Secretary's Bid for Plant Safety Runs into Skepticism

In the summer of 1994, Labor Secretary Robert Reich charged a Bridgestone Tire subsidiary with 107 safety violations. He also levied a fine of $7.5 million. The labor secretary ostensibly took this action on behalf of the employees at the tire plant. To quote the secretary, "American workers are not going to be sacrificed at the altar of profits." The secretary, however, was "amazed" when the employees and local community did not support his action. Indeed, employees were generally skeptical and nonsupportive of his claims. For example, one employee indicated that the secretary "didn't know what the hell he was doing."

The lack of employee support for this action might reflect two considerations. First, employees might worry about layoffs if it is too expensive to comply with the regulations. Second, the theory of compensating differentials implies that dangerous jobs offer a premium over jobs in safer environments. Employees who accept dangerous jobs generally consider themselves better off than if they were working at lower wages in safer environments. Thus, regulations that force firms to provide safer work environments and lower wages (wages have to be reduced to remain competitive) can make employees worse off. Thus employees potentially are harmed by this type of regulatory action.

Nonetheless, there are at least two arguments that might justify government intervention. First, the employees might not have good information about the level of danger. For example, they might think that a plant is safer than it really is. (Yet, why the government would be better informed about the level of safety at a plant than the employees is not obvious.) Second, there are other parties that have to be considered. For example, employees who get injured on the job can impose costs on society through subsidized medical care and disability payments. Although the overall costs and benefits of this type of regulation are hard to estimate, it is clear that employees do not always believe that they benefit.

Source: A. Nomani (1994), "Muffed Mission: Labor Secretary's Bid to Push Safety Runs into Skepticism," *The Wall Street Journal* (August 19), 1.

[4]This prediction assumes that employees can obtain reasonably good information about important characteristics of the job either before or shortly after employment. This assumption is likely to be valid in many cases. For instance, applicants for a firefighter position in an arid location are likely to know that the job is hazardous. They also can observe the quality of the fire station and equipment. Applicants can collect other information about the work environment from current or past employees.

Tight Labor Markets Increase Competition

With intense competition for skilled employees, especially managers, companies are resorting to a variety of tactics other than raising the level of pay. Key employees receive retention bonuses of 15 to 50 percent of 1 year's pay spread over 3 years if they stick around. After NYNEX and Bell Atlantic merged, top managers received retention bonuses above $1 million if they stayed at least 3 years. No one left.

Often under the guise of "increasing corporate loyalty" firms seek ways to attract and retain managers. To reduce turnover rates that can run as high as 1.1 percent a month, employers are revamping rigid pay systems to make it easier for employees to move laterally to enhance their skills. New career-development programs help employees plan their next moves up the corporate ladder. Citibank's program for 10,000 managers reviews each manager twice a year to see what their next step should be. International Paper requires managers to discuss career desires with employees annually, separate from their annual performance review. Booz Allen has a rotation program for its consultants. By creating more flexible workdays, this program allows employees to balance work and family life better. One consultant whose parents developed health problems assigned him a stint as a college recruiter. This flexibility gave him the time to help his parents. When head hunters now call him he says, "I made a commitment to the firm, and they made a commitment to me." Many of these programs are nonpecuniary forms of compensation that particular employees value enormously.

Sources: A. Bernstein (1998), "We Want You to Stay. Really," *Business Week* (June 22), 67–72. B. Wysocki (1997), "Retaining Employees Turns into a Hot Topic," *The Wall Street Journal* (September 8), A1.

The prediction that unpleasant jobs pay more than pleasant jobs *holds other factors constant.* Variation in job requirements for education, skills, and training also account for differences in pay. For example, an office job in a pleasant work environment might pay more than the relatively unpleasant job of garbage collector because the skills required for the office job are higher. However, garbage collectors will be paid more than similar unskilled labor engaged in more pleasant tasks.

Some of the most compelling evidence of the existence of compensating wage differentials is provided by studies that relate wages to the risk of fatal injury on the job.[5] Using data from around the world, wages were found to be positively associated with the risk of being killed on the job, holding other factors constant. The estimates of the magnitude of the compensating differential are relatively imprecise and vary across studies, but they indicate that employees receive between $20 and $300 more per year for every 1 in 10,000 increase in the risk of being killed on the job. These estimates imply that a firm with 1,000 employees could reduce wage costs between $20,000 and $300,000 per year by increasing the level of safety enough to save one life every 10 years.

Compensating wage differentials have two important effects. First, all societies have unpleasant tasks that must be completed—for instance, most require morticians and garbage collectors. Compensating differentials attract people to these jobs and reward them for their efforts. Individuals who accept unpleasant tasks tend to be the ones who bear the lowest cost for performing them. For example, if a wage premium is offered for working in a noisy factory, the people most likely to apply are those least bothered by noise. Individuals who are particularly noise-averse would choose to work in a quiet environment at a lower wage. Second, compensating differentials cause employers who offer unpleasant work environments to have higher labor costs. Employers thus can reduce their labor costs by enhancing their work environments. This possibility implies that the firms providing better work environments will be those firms which can do so

---

[5]For a more detailed summary of this empirical work, see Ehrenberg and Smith (1988), 266–270.

Compensating Differentials

A number of professionals, lawyers, dentists, accountants, and managers are forgoing six-figure incomes to earn a third that much as personal trainers. Fitness trainers advise clients on exercise techniques and diet. In the gym, trainers are celebrities—everyone knows them and they usually look great. Their clients like them. One trainer said, "You wouldn't believe the warm and fuzzies I get helping a gal into a pair of jeans she never thought she could fit into." A former software programmer became the official trainer for the Indianapolis Colts Cheerleaders. Trainer Bob says, "Every morning I wake up, I think: It's good to be me." Most trainers typically earn between $20,000 and $40,000 a year with no benefits. But they do it because they make their own hours, they wear shorts and T-shirts all day, and they work out. A big part of their pay, maybe 80 percent in some cases, is the compensating differential they receive from the life style.

Source: K. Helliker (1999), "They Left Professions for a True Calling as Personal Trainers," *The Wall Street Journal* (February 25), A1.

at low cost (since the marginal cost of providing a pleasant environment is low relative to the marginal benefit of reducing the penalty).

This discussion suggests that there is a job-matching process in labor markets where firms offer and individuals accept jobs in a manner that makes the most of their strengths and preferences. Organizations have incentives to reduce the risk of injury in order to reduce wage premiums. In turn, the people who take risky jobs are likely to be the most tolerant toward risk—individuals *self-select* based on their risk preferences. For example, fishing companies often find it too expensive to reduce the risk of injury beyond some level, and thus they must offer wage premiums to crews of fishing boats. Individuals applying to work on these boats are likely to be among those most willing to place their lives at risk on the job. Because of this self-selection, the compensating differential is lower than if the firm attempted to hire a randomly selected person from the population. A firm that can provide a safe environment at a low cost will offer low-risk jobs and lower wages; these positions will be filled by more risk-averse employees.

Costly Information about Market Wage Rates

In contrast to our benchmark model, compensation in many labor markets is not readily observable. Individuals vary in characteristics and generally are not perfect substitutes. Thus, observing the wage for one individual does not provide full information on what it would require to hire another. In addition, firms do not share complete information about their levels of compensation. The difficulty in observing the market price for labor means that it is not always easy to tell if a firm is underpaying or overpaying its employees.

Two important indicators of whether a firm is paying the market wage rate are the number of applications it receives for job openings and the quit rate among existing employees. If a firm is inundated by *qualified applicants* when it advertises a job opening and its quit rate is low, the firm probably is paying above the market wage rate.[6] In contrast, if the applicant rate is low and turnover is high, the firm probably is paying below the market.

[6]Paying above the market wage rate typically will place the firm at a competitive disadvantage. As we discuss below, however, there are several reasons why some profit-maximizing firms might want to pay above the market wage rate.

Paying Too Much at Nucor?

When Nucor's mill in Darlington, South Carolina, advertised to fill eight openings last fall, over 1,300 applicants showed up, creating such a traffic jam that state police had to be called out. Unfortunately, the force was a bit thin—three officers were already at Nucor applying for jobs.

It is possible that the number of applications at Nucor included many unqualified candidates. But the size of the applicant pool certainly prompts the questions of whether Nucor is paying too much and whether it wants to pay more than the market wage rate for particular jobs.

Source: N. Perry (1988), "Here Come Richer, Riskier Pay Plans," *Fortune* (December 19), 58.

In choosing the rate of pay, it is important to consider the trade-offs between incremental compensation and turnover costs. Turnover costs include the costs of recruiting employees, training expenses, and reduced productivity from employing inexperienced employees. In addition, if employees expect that they will work for the firm for only a short time, they are less likely to be concerned about how their actions affect the long-run cash flows of the firm. For instance, a salesperson might push to make a sale to collect a commission, knowing that the customer will be unhappy with the product and will reduce future purchases. Sometimes, employees who leave a firm take customers and trade secrets to competing firms. Nonetheless, turnover also has beneficial effects on the firm—for example, it adds "new blood" and fresh ideas to the organization.

Outside job offers made to existing employees also are indicative of market rates. Although these offers provide important information about the market value of existing employees, firms must be careful in deciding whether to match these offers. Failure to match can result in losing valued employees. But a policy of matching all outside offers can encourage employees to invest in generating such offers. This activity might take time away from work and also might increase the likelihood that employees will receive offers that entice them to leave the firm.

Internal Labor Markets

While our benchmark model provides a reasonably good description of some labor markets, such as the market for unskilled agricultural workers, it does a poor job describing employment and wages in many other cases. In contrast to the model, many firms rarely reduce employee compensation and frequently invest in general training—such as paying tuition for an employee to obtain an MBA. Also, employees often invest their time and effort in developing firm-specific skills.

Many firms are better characterized as having *internal labor markets,* wherein outside hiring focuses primarily on filling entry-level jobs and most other jobs are filled from within the firm. Firms with internal labor markets establish *long-term relationships* with employees. It has been estimated that in 1991, the typical employee between 45 and 54 had been with his or her current employer for 10 years. Another study found that over half of all men and one-fourth of all women in the United States work for the same employer for at least 20 years.[7]

[7]J. Aley (1994), "The Myth of the Job Hopper," *Fortune* (September 19), 32; and R. Hall (1982), "The Importance of Lifetime Jobs in the US Economy," *American Economic Review* 72, 716–724.

Established career paths and the prospect for promotions play important roles in firms with internal labor markets. These firms interact with outside labor markets only on a limited basis. Rather than simply reflecting outside market conditions, the rates of pay (discussed in more detail below) and job assignments in internal labor markets often are determined by administrative rules and implicit understandings. Firms can have more than one internal labor market. For example, the internal market for white-collar employees might have little interaction with the internal market for blue-collar employees. In addition, firms with internal labor markets typically offer some jobs that are well described by our basic model—for instance, certain low-skilled positions.

Agreements between employers and employees concerning compensation and responsibilities are contracts. Firms generally do not enter into formal written agreements (*explicit contracts*) with nonunion employees. Rather, most employees work under *implicit contracts*—a set of shared, informal understandings about how firms and employees will respond to contingencies.[8] Implicit contracts differ from explicit contracts in that they normally are unwritten and more difficult to enforce in a court of law. Firms and employees, however, often have strong economic incentives to honor implicit contracts to protect their reputations (see Chapter 10). A primary reason for the frequent use of implicit contracts is that it would be quite costly to detail all possible contingencies and associated responses in formal documents.

Reasons for Long-Term Employment Relationships

In Chapter 3, we discussed how all methods of organizing economic activity involve contracting costs. Firms have incentives to consider these costs and to organize economic exchanges in an efficient manner.[9] Spot-market exchange is not always the most efficient way to organize firm-employee relationships. There are at least three factors that help promote the widespread use of the long-term employment relationships found in internal labor markets. These factors include specific human capital, employee motivation, and information about employee attributes.

Firm-Specific Human Capital   Long-term relationships provide incentives for employers and employees to invest in specific training. If employers and employees expect that their relationships will be of short duration, limited incentives exist to make these investments. In contrast, long-term relationships allow firms and employees to capture the benefits of accumulated specific human capital.

Employee Motivation   The prospect of a long-term relationship with a firm provides powerful incentives for employees to work on behalf of their employers. Employees who consider shirking, stealing, or other dysfunctional activities must weigh their potential benefits of these actions against the costs of losing future benefits should they be caught and dismissed. Since there is more to lose in long-term relationships than in short-term relationships, the incentives both to engage in productive activities and to avoid dysfunctional activities are higher within long-term relationships.[10] Also, as we discuss

---

[8]S. Rosen (1985), "Implicit Contracts," *Journal of Economic Literature* 23, 1144–1175.

[9]R. Coase (1988), *The Firm, the Market, and the Law* (University of Chicago Press: Chicago).

[10]This statement assumes that an employee cannot costlessly replicate the same stream of benefits by changing to a new employer. For example, the new job might pay lower compensation, the individual might incur moving costs, there might be a period of unemployment, and so on.

Internal Labor Markets in Japan

Large companies in Japan make extensive use of internal labor markets. Many Japanese executives spend their entire careers with the same firm. Senior executives virtually never move from one major firm to another. Firms rarely go outside to hire for any position other than entry-level jobs. Turnover is extremely low. Pay is tied largely to seniority, and the differences in pay among employees are small relative to the differences in American companies.

Small pay differentials would be difficult to maintain if there were an active outside labor market in Japan. Market pressures would tend to bid up the salaries of the strong performers. Recently, poor performance has placed pressures on Japanese firms to reconsider their policies of lifetime employment guarantees. If many firms abandon this policy, the outside labor market is likely to become more active.

Source: M. Aoki and R. Dore (Eds.), (1994), *The Japanese Firm* (Oxford University Press: Oxford, UK).

below, long-term relationships increase the flexibility that a firm retains in designing compensation packages to motivate employee effort.

Learning Employee Attributes   Over time, managers receive much information about the skills, work habits, interests, and intelligence of individual employees. Employers then can use this information in matching employees and jobs within the firm. For example, firms with internal labor markets have fewer surprises in filling higher-level jobs than firms that rely on outside labor markets.

Costs of Internal Labor Markets

Not all firms have internal labor markets. Some firms rely heavily on outside markets to fill positions at all levels. The observation that some firms do not operate internal labor markets suggests that the costs of these markets can be larger than their benefits. One potentially important problem with internal labor markets is the restricted competition for higher-level jobs within the organization. If a firm considers only internal candidates for higher-level jobs, it will not always hire the most qualified person— who may be from outside the firm. The likelihood of finding a desirable candidate in

Hiring an Outside CEO at Kodak

Eastman Kodak had a long history of filling senior positions exclusively with long-time employees. An advantage of this policy is that senior executives have significant experience with the firm and detailed specific knowledge of the company. The prospect of promotion and long-term employment also provides important motivational effects. A disadvantage, however, is that sometimes the best people for senior jobs are outsiders.

During the late 1980s and early 1990s, shareholders placed intense pressure on Kodak's board to appoint outsiders to senior positions. Many shareholders thought that hiring outsiders was necessary to bring new skills and vision into the firm. In late October 1993, Kodak announced that it had hired George Fisher, CEO of Motorola, as the new CEO. The stock market greeted this announcement with an 8 percent increase in Kodak's stock price (from the close of the market on October 26th to the close on the 28th). This reaction represented a $1.6 billion increase in the overall value of the company. After serving as CEO for 6 years, Fisher announced his retirement effective January 1, 2000. This time Kodak decided to fill the position with a long-time employee, Daniel Carp.

the outside labor market is highest when the job does not require specific training (since experience with the firm does not create an advantage in the job). Thus, firms are more likely to use internal labor markets where specific training is important. Indeed, firms in the steel, petroleum, and chemical industries, where complicated production technologies take significant time to learn, tend to rely on internal labor markets, whereas firms in the shoe and garment industries do not.[11] Firm-specific skills are arguably less important in garment and shoe manufacturing than in steel, petroleum, or chemicals.

Pay in Internal Labor Markets
Careers and Lifetime Pay

Employees who take jobs at firms with internal labor markets often expect that they will spend much of their *careers* at the same firm. Thus, in considering an entry-level job, prospective employees generally will focus on the entire stream of earnings over their anticipated career path. For example, an individual might accept a job at Firm A that pays less than another job offered at Firm B because the individual anticipates faster compensation growth at Firm A.

The fact that individuals tend to base employment decisions on career earnings gives firms with internal labor markets more flexibility over choosing the level and time profile of pay. In contrast to our basic model, firms do not need to pay the market wage rate (or equivalently, in equilibrium, the marginal revenue product) at each point in time. Rather, firms can vary compensation over a career path, as long as the overall value of the remaining stream is competitive at each point in time (valued as highly by employees as streams offered by competing firms in the labor market).

Economists have identified at least three ways that firms can use their flexibility in setting the level and time profile of pay to enhance employee motivation. These methods include the payment of efficiency wages, upward-sloping earnings profiles, and tying major pay increases to promotions. As we discuss below, however, influence costs can limit the extent to which firms exploit this potential flexibility.

Competition for the Top Job

In April 1999, the stock price of Black & Decker Corp., the $4.5-billion power-tool maker, fell 8 percent on the announcement that Joseph Galli had quit. Galli, age 41, ran 65 percent of the business and was responsible for the new products that had turned B&D around. He was viewed as the heir apparent to the CEO. Galli had pressed B&D's CEO, 13-year B&D veteran Nolan Archibald, 55, to step down before 65 so that Galli could fill the position. Archibald was afraid Galli would quit, and so Archibald found a replacement and announced that Galli had quit. When pressed on the matter, Archibald disclosed, "I chose the timing." This vignette is not unusual. It illustrates the importance of succession planning and the often large nonpecuniary income some managers receive from the power of the top job.

Source: A. Barrett (1999), "How to Keep Rising Stars from Straying," *Business Week* (June 7), 80.

---

[11]P. Doeringer and M. Piore (1971), *Internal Labor Markets and Manpower Analysis* (D. C. Heath: Lexington, MA).

Lifetime Employment Collapses at Mitsubishi

During its peak, Mitsubishi employees were like lords of the universe. Hired from the top universities and treated like the elite, they had good jobs, security, and lifetime employment. But then the bubble burst. Using huge capital gains from real estate to make numerous bad investments in 1980s created huge losses in the 1990s. Mitsubishi is actually a group of associated companies called a *keiretsu*. The main Mitsubishi companies (autos, banks, heavy industries) had a return on equity of 4 percent in contrast to the United States where anything less than 15 percent is considered poor. Now, recent hires quit and look for new jobs. There is no longer the same sense of security as before.

Source: B. Bremner and E. Thornton (1999), "Mitsubishi: Fall of a Keiretsu," *Business Week* (March 15), 86–92.

Efficiency Wages   In many jobs, it is difficult to monitor employee actions. It also is difficult to devise incentive compensation schemes that motivate desired behavior. For example, manufacturing companies want production employees to work hard. In most cases, it is difficult to measure employee effort with much precision. In addition, the payment of piece rates or other output-based compensation can discourage employees from paying enough attention to quality.

One potential way of motivating employees in such cases is to pay compensation *above* the market rate. Paying a premium for employees obviously increases labor costs. However, it can have the desirable effect of motivating them not to shirk. Individuals who are paid a wage premium are likely to reduce their shirking because they understand that if they are caught and fired, they will have difficulty finding another job that offers such a premium. This effect will be greater for employees who have longer time horizons with the firm, since they have more to lose. Wage premiums of this type often are referred to as *efficiency wages*. Efficiency wages also provide incentives for employees to stay with the firm. These incentives can be particularly important when the employee

Motivating Honesty in the Local Police Force

Economists Gary Becker and George Stigler were asked to consider ways of reducing corruption within the Chicago police force. The recommendation of these Nobel laureates was to pay the police more than the market wage rate. With sufficiently high premiums, the police would have incentives not to take bribes from criminals. For this condition to hold, the immediate gains from taking bribes must be offset by the expected loss in wage premiums given the possibility of being caught and fired. Thus, the required premium to prevent cheating depends on the size of the bribes and the likelihood of getting caught. Higher bribes and lower likelihood of getting caught translate into higher required premiums.

Paying wage premiums will entice a large number of people to apply for job openings. To reduce the surplus of applicants, Becker and Stigler suggested that the jobs be sold to officers. The price of jobs would reflect the expected premiums. Under this plan, the payment for a job can be considered as a bond posted by an officer not to cheat. If the officer is honest, the officer gets the bond back in the form of the premium wage. If the officer cheats and gets caught, the bond is lost.

The suggested wage premiums are very similar to the concept of efficiency wages. In more modern theories of efficiency wages, however, employees do not purchase jobs. The concept of buying jobs may seem unusual. However, this originally was the practice among yeoman warders—the beefeaters who guard the tower of London. And today many people essentially do this when they purchase the right to manage an outlet of a franchise company.

Source: G. Becker and G. Stigler (1974), "Law Enforcement, Malfeasance, and Compensation," *Journal of Legal Studies* 3, 1–18.

has specific human capital (the firm does not want to replace the employee with a person with less training and experience).[12]

Economists debate whether the use of efficiency wages is widespread. Although the empirical evidence is inconclusive, some studies suggest that firms in particular industries use efficiency wages with reasonably high frequency. The authors of one study find systematic wage differences across industries after controlling for many job and employee characteristics. In addition, they find a negative correlation between turnover and industry wage differentials, suggesting that employees in high-wage industries receive wage premiums. The authors interpret this evidence as consistent with the hypothesis that efficiency wages are paid in certain industries.[13]

Job Seniority and Pay[14] Compensation typically increases with seniority within the firm. Part of this increase is explained by increases in productivity that come from experience. In many firms, however, compensation increases faster than productivity as the employee ages. Firms frequently offer attractive retirement packages to encourage older employees to retire and (unless precluded by law) often have mandatory retirement. For example, the employee must retire at age 65.[15]

One explanation for these age-related policies is that they establish stronger incentives to employees to work in the interests of the firm. To see how, consider the example

---

The Costs of Wage Compression

In tight labor markets it is not uncommon for new hires to be paid more than people recruited a few years earlier. At Price Waterhouse (now PriceWaterhouseCoopers) in 1998, Scott Sanster, a strategy consultant said, "This year, M.B.A.s are being offered salaries and sign on bonuses nearly 30 percent higher than what I got. It can be a real morale buster." A company spokesman contends, "We are keeping pay increases at a level roughly equal to the increase in starting salary." Employees often feel frustrated that new hires earn more than experienced workers. Some managers believe they can pay current employees slightly below their market wage because it is costly for employees to search and investigate employment opportunities. Someone who has been at the firm for around a year is unlikely to move to a new company for a 5 to 10 percent pay increase. To keep their best and brightest, some companies with high turnover are bumping up those employees' pay semiannually or even quarterly.

Source: T. Schellhardt (1998), "Rookie Gains in Pay Wars Rile Veterans," *The Wall Street Journal* (June 4), B1.

---

[12]For a more detailed analysis of efficiency wages, see G. Akerlof (1984), "Gift Exchange and Efficiency Wages: Four Views," *American Economic Review* 74, 78–83; C. Shapiro and J. Stiglitz (1984), "Equilibrium Unemployment as a Worker Discipline Device," *American Economic Review* 74, 433–444; and J. Yellen (1984), "Efficiency Wages Models and Unemployment," *American Economic Review* 74, 200–208. If all firms in an industry pay efficiency wages, there will be unemployment. (The supply of labor will exceed demand.) The threat of unemployment can provide incentives for employees not to shirk. Note that in our basic model, marginal revenue product and the wage rate are independent. The efficiency-wage concept, however, suggests that they can be related: Employees' marginal products can be affected by their wage rates due to incentive effects from potential dismissal for cause.

[13]A. Krueger and L. Summers (1988), "Efficiency Wages and the Inter-Industry Wage Structure," *Econometrica* 56, 259–293. Another empirical paper that supports the notion of efficiency wages is P. Osterman (1994), "Supervision, Discretion, and Work Organization," *American Economic Review* 84, 380–384.

[14]This section draws on E. Lazear (1979), "Why Is There Mandatory Retirement?" *Journal of Political Economy* 87, 1261–1284.

[15]Amendments made to the Age Discrimination Employment Act in 1978 and 1986 have precluded mandatory retirement for most workers in the United States.

Figure 14.2   An Example of an Upward Sloping Earnings Profile

This figure displays both the marginal revenue product and compensation for a representative employee in a given firm. Within this particular firm, both marginal revenue product and compensation increase as the employee becomes more experienced. Compensation, however, increases at a faster rate. In the early years, the employee is paid below the marginal revenue product, whereas in later years the employee is paid more. The employee is underpaid in early years yet still is willing to work for the firm because of the expectation of being overpaid in subsequent years. Under this compensation plan, young employees have incentives to work hard to avoid both being fired and losing future wage premiums. Older employees, in turn, do not want to be dismissed because they receive more than they could earn at other firms.

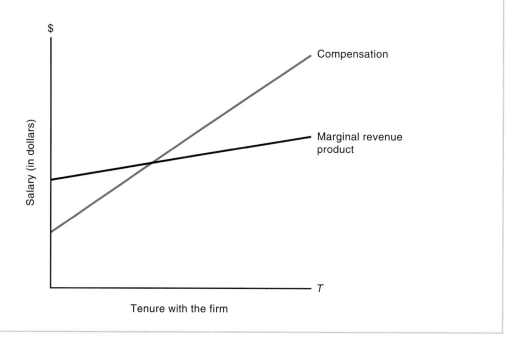

depicted in Figure 14.2. This figure displays the growth patterns of the marginal revenue product and compensation for a representative employee within a particular firm. Both the marginal revenue product and compensation increase as the employee becomes more experienced. (The analysis does not change if we allow for declines in productivity in later years.) Compensation, however, increases at a faster rate. In the early years, the employee is paid below the marginal revenue product, whereas in later years the employee is paid more. The employee is underpaid in early years but is willing to work for the firm because of the expectation of being overpaid in subsequent years. Under this compensation plan, younger employees have incentives to make firm-specific human capital investments and to work hard to avoid being fired and losing future wage premiums. Older employees do not want to get fired because they are being paid more than they could earn at other firms.

Firms that employ this type of compensation policy have short-run incentives to fire older employees, since older employees are paid more than they are worth. Unjustified dismissals of older employees, however, are not in the long-run interests of firms because they reduce the incentive effects of the compensation plan: Younger employees will not believe that hard work will lead to wage premiums when they get older. Firms cannot pay premiums to all older employees for an indefinite period and stay in business. Thus, these firms will adopt policies that help ensure that older employees will retire when they reach a specified age. For example, if legally allowed a mandatory retirement age might be established where the present value of the underpayments in the early years offsets the overpayments in the later years. Thus, over their entire careers, employees are still paid their marginal revenue products (as in our basic model). Such a condition helps the firm survive in a competitive marketplace.

Promotions[16]   Firms are typically partitioned into hierarchical levels, where the jobs at a given level pay more than positions at lower levels. Employees move up this hierarchy through promotions. Since employees compete for promotions, promotions can be viewed as contests or tournaments among employees. Employees' productivity is higher as they try to win these contests.

Promotions obviously play an important role in providing incentives within many organizations.[17] One benefit of using a promotion-based incentive scheme is that it commits the firm to serious performance reviews of its employees. Promoting the wrong person to a job can impose material costs. Employers have incentives to conduct in-depth performance reviews to reduce the likelihood of making such mistakes. Another primary benefit is that promotion contests help filter out random shocks in evaluating performance. Typically, the employee with the best *relative performance* is chosen for promotion. As we discuss in Chapter 16, potential risk-sharing benefits come from using relative performance measures rather than absolute performance measures.[18] In particular, employees are less likely to be rewarded or penalized for factors beyond their control—common shocks that affect all the contestants in the promotion contest are filtered out of the decision.

Promotion-based systems can have several significant drawbacks.[19] First, judging people on relative performance can undermine employee cooperation, and employees might even sabotage the work of others. Second, promotions can be a rather crude tool for providing incentives. Promotions occur only at discrete intervals, and either the employee is promoted or not. Monetary incentives, such as bonus payments, are more flexible. Third, there can be serious conflicts between matching people for jobs and providing incentives. The so-called Peter principle argues that employees keep getting promoted until they reach jobs that they cannot handle. Fourth, employees do not always value promotions. For example, research scientists and professors often do not want administrative positions. Fifth, promotion contests can subject decision makers to significant influencing activities.[20]

Despite these drawbacks, promotions are a widely employed method for motivating employees throughout the world. Lately the prospect for promotion in many firms has

---

[16]This section draws on E. Lazear and S. Rosen (1981), "Rank Order Tournaments as Optimal Labor Contracts," *Journal of Political Economy* 89, 841–864.

[17]Promotions also play an important role in matching people with jobs based on skills and ability.

[18]Relative performance measures are based on how an employee performs compared to a peer group. Absolute performance measures compare the employee's performance to some predetermined standard.

[19]G. Baker, K. Murphy, and M. Jensen (1988), "Compensation and Incentives: Practice and Theory," *Journal of Finance* 43, 593–616.

[20]Promotions are typically based on the subjective judgments of people rather than on objective output measures (such as pieces produced). As we discuss in more detail in Chapter 16, subjective performance evaluation can motivate nonproductive actions to influence the supervisor's rating.

A Horse Race at General Electric

Sometimes, firms "run horse races" among internal candidates. Under this procedure, the candidates are notified that they are competing for a job with higher pay and prestige. The contest provides significant incentives for the candidates to perform since the prize for winning can be very large. General Electric ran such a horse race to fill the CEO position when Reginald Jones retired in 1981. The winner was Jack Welch. In 1999, Welch was paid $13.3 million in salary and bonuses. The next highest paid person in the firm received $4.2 million.

Sources: R. Vancil (1987), *Passing the Baton* (Harvard Business School: Boston) and GE Proxy (2000).

---

fallen due to an overall reduction in middle-management positions and a slowing in growth rates. This development reduced the incentives for many employees, who think that the chances for promotion are low even if they do a good job. In response, many firms have tried to restore employee incentives by adopting more explicit pay-for-performance plans. The American Productivity and Quality Center reports that 75 percent of employers in the United States have an incentive plan (such as a profit- or gain-sharing plan) for rank-and-file employees and that roughly 80 percent of these plans have been adopted since 1983.[21]

Influence Costs

Teammates frequently compare compensation levels. Differences in pay among coworkers motivate employees to seek explanations for compensation decisions. Employees also use information about the pay of other employees to lobby for pay increases. It frequently is conjectured that firms limit the differentials in pay to reduce this type of influence activity. Such a policy, however, comes at a cost; underperforming employees are likely to be paid too much, whereas more productive employees are likely to be undercompensated and leave the firm. Influence costs also help explain why many firms try to keep their compensation decisions confidential. In many cases, however, it is difficult to prevent teammates from sharing information on compensation.

Firms often expend substantial resources on evaluating and comparing jobs within the organization. One popular method is the Hay System.[22] Under this system, each job within the organization is evaluated on factors such as required know-how, problem-solving skills, the number of people supervised, and accountability. Based on this evaluation, each job is assigned a total number of points and placed in a position within the firm's hierarchy. Jobs at a given level in the hierarchy have similar ranges in compensation. For example, jobs included in the same level might pay from $20,000 to $25,000, depending on experience and qualifications. Although salaries reflect external market rates to some extent, a major emphasis is placed on internal consistency among jobs (equal pay for equal work). Internal consistency appears to reduce employee complaints about compensation policies and helps protect the firm against liability in discrimination suits. However, if pay is related to the number of employees supervised, such a plan can lead to empire building by managers.

[21]N. Perry (1988), "Here Come Richer, Riskier Pay Plans," *Fortune* (December 19), 50–58.

[22]For a more detailed discussion, see G. Milkovich and J. Newman (1993), *Compensation* (Richard D. Irwin: Burr Ridge, IL), Chapter 4.

Influence Costs and Pay in Universities

The potential for influence activity is especially high in firms where employees have common knowledge about one another's pay. Our discussion suggests that these firms might limit the differences in pay to reduce influence costs. One study provides empirical evidence on this issue by examining compensation levels in academic departments at about 2,000 colleges. Common knowledge about pay is more likely in small departments, in departments where the members frequently interact on a social basis, and in public institutions (where public disclosure of pay often is required). Consistent with the influence-cost arguments, this study found that all three factors were associated with reductions in the dispersion of pay.

Source: J. Pfeffer and N. Langton (1988), "Wage Inequality and the Organization of Work: The Case of Academic Departments," *Administrative Sciences Quarterly* 33, 588–606.

The Salary–Fringe Benefit Mix[23]

In our benchmark model, individuals receive their compensation in the form of cash payments. Most employees, however, receive a substantial amount of their compensation in the form of *fringe benefits*—compensation that is either in kind or deferred.

Examples of in-kind payments are health insurance and membership in a company recreation center, where the employee receives an insurance policy or a service rather than cash. Payments to pension plans and Social Security are examples of deferred compensation. For the typical American employee, about 75 percent of the total compensation package is pay for time worked, while about 25 percent is fringe benefits. Based on the cost to the employer, the most important fringe benefits are pensions and insurance, paid leave time (vacations and sick or other leave), and mandated contributions to Social Security and Workers' Compensation. Many employees also receive benefits such as company-paid education, dental care, discounted meals, and subsidized recreation programs. A 1998 survey of 2,120 college grads found the following ranking as the most important job benefit: medical insurance, pension benefits, annual salary raises, and dental and life insurance.[24]

Employment Market Niches

WRQ in Seattle develops connectivity software. To attract scarce engineers and programmers, WRQ, with 700 employees, must make its recruiting appeal heard over the "giant sucking sound" of crosstown rival Microsoft (with over 12,000 employees). Microsoft offers an alluring stock plan that has transformed employees into millionaires. WRQ offers a work environment with employee-friendly policies: team management, reasonable and flexible hours, time off for volunteer work, natural light from a 10-story atrium, massage, napping and breast feeding rooms, and balconies overlooking the lake. Such policies have allowed WRQ to recruit more experienced people, especially more women, and to experience only half the turnover of other software companies. A former Microsoft employee, age 31 with a wife and new baby, used to enjoy his work at Microsoft, but now with WRQ, he does not miss the 13-hour days and being on call around the clock. By taking advantage of certain employee preferences for a less stressful job environment, WRQ is able to compete effectively for talent.

Source: S. Shellenbarger (1997), "Rooms with a View and Flexible Hours Draw Talent to WRQ," *The Wall Street Journal* (August 13), B1.

[23]This section draws on Ehrenberg and Smith (1988), Chapter 11.

[24]A. Karr (1998), "Special News Report about Life on the Job—and Trends Taking Shape There," *The Wall Street Journal* (May 5), A1.

Employee Preferences

Silicon Valley has more than its share of programmers—those who do much of the heavy lifting in this information age. Given to marathon sessions in front of their computer screens, programmers tend to be an eccentric bunch. One programmer reasoned with his supervisors that he preferred to work in the buff. He noted that he worked alone, was most productive late at night, and that the building was locked after 11 P.M. Well, good programmers are difficult to find, so after some discussion, he was given permission to strip after 11 P.M.

Of course there is more to the story—apparently things went well until one evening when this programmer misread the clock in his cubicle. He was not the only one surprised when he wandered into what he had assumed would be a deserted workroom.

Source: P. Bronson (1999), *The Nudist on the Late Shift* (Random House: New York).

Employee Preferences

Salary and fringe benefits typically are not perfect substitutes from an employee's viewpoint. One reason is taxes: Certain fringe benefits (such as health insurance) are not subject to income taxes when received by the employees. For example, an employee who wants to purchase an insurance policy that costs $5,000 would prefer that the firm provide the policy rather than $5,000 in cash. Since insurance premiums are not counted as taxable income, an employee in a 33.33 percent tax bracket would have to receive $7,500 in salary to purchase the policy. The employee also might want the firm to purchase fringe benefits because the benefits can be purchased by the firm at lower prices. For example, a firm might be able to provide group insurance at a lower cost per employee than if employees individually purchased the insurance. The potential cost advantage of employee group health and life insurance has two main components: It reduces the adverse selection problems and lowers administrative and selling expenses. On the other hand, employees often prefer $5,000 in cash to $5,000 in fringe benefits, since the cash gives them more flexibility in selecting their purchases.[25]

In our initial analysis, we do not break fringe benefits into finer categories. Rather, we consider the choice between salary and overall fringe benefits. Later, we discuss the mix of fringe benefits. Figure 14.3 displays an employee's preferences for salary and fringe benefits using indifference curves. The convexity of the curves implies that this employee is willing to substitute a relatively large amount of salary for additional expenditures on fringe benefits when the employee is paid primarily cash (possibly due to tax considerations). However, this willingness to substitute declines as the employee receives more fringe benefits (the employee prefers cash for other purposes).

The employee, of course, would like to be on as high an indifference curve as possible. A firm, however, will be able to hire the individual so long as the compensation package meets the individual's reservation level of utility. If the compensation package provides this level of utility (or more), this person is at least as well off working at the firm as working for alternative employers or not working at all. For example, the reservation utility of the individual in Figure 14.3 might be depicted by the indifference curve labeled U_2. (Note that the reservation utility of the individual would increase if the compensation packages offered by other employers were increased so that other alternatives become more attractive.)

[25]D. Mayers and C. Smith (1981), "Contractual Provisions, Organizational Structure, and Conflict Control in Insurance Markets," *Journal of Business* 54, 407–434.

Figure 14.3 Employee Preferences for Salary and Fringe Benefits

This figure displays an employee's preferences for salary and fringe benefits using indifference curves. The convexity of the curves implies that this employee is willing to substitute a relatively large amount of salary for additional fringe benefits when the employee receives few fringe benefits (possibly due to tax considerations). However, this willingness to substitute declines as the employee receives more fringe benefits (the employee wants cash for other purposes).

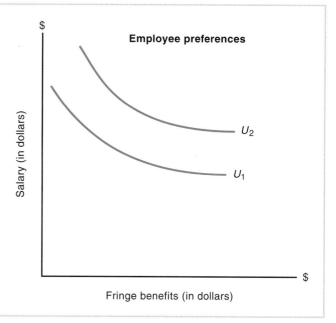

Employer Considerations

Initially, suppose that the firm's managers do not care whether they pay an employee cash or use the same amount of cash to provide fringe benefits. For instance, both expenditures might be deductible for corporate tax purposes, and so it costs the firm the same amount in either case. Figure 14.4 displays isocost curves for a representative firm under this assumption. Each curve is a straight line with a slope of -1; firm value is unaffected by the split between salary and fringe benefits. Along any isocost curve,

Figure 14.4 Employer Preferences for Paying Salary or Fringe Benefits

This figure displays isocost curves for a representative firm, under the assumption that the firm's value is unaffected by whether it pays the employee cash or uses the same amount of cash to provide fringe benefits. Each curve is a straight line with a slope of -1; firm value is unaffected by the split between paying a dollar for salary or a dollar for fringe benefits. Along any isocost curve, the labor expenses for the firm are the same. The firm's value is highest on the lowest isocost curve possible (since lower isocost curves mean lower labor expenses and higher profits).

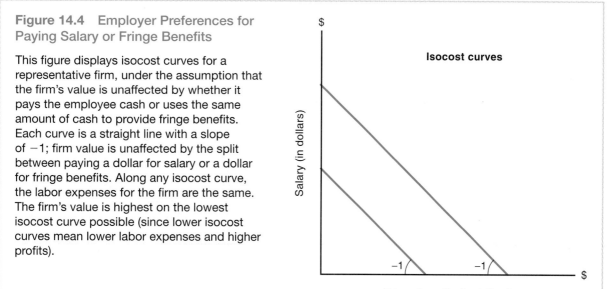

Figure 14.5 The Optimal Mix between Salary and Fringe Benefits

The figure pictures an indifference curve *U* for the reservation utility of a representative individual that the firm is trying to hire. The firm can hire the individual using any compensation package along this curve. The figure also shows selected isocost curves for the firm. To maximize the firm's value, choose the compensation package that meets the reservation utility of the individual at the lowest cost. This optimal choice is *S**, *F**, where the indifference curve is tangent to the isocost curve. Management could choose other combinations along the indifference curve. However, these combinations are more expensive. Although the firm could offer combinations that are less expensive than *S**, *F**, these combinations would not meet the individual's reservation utility.

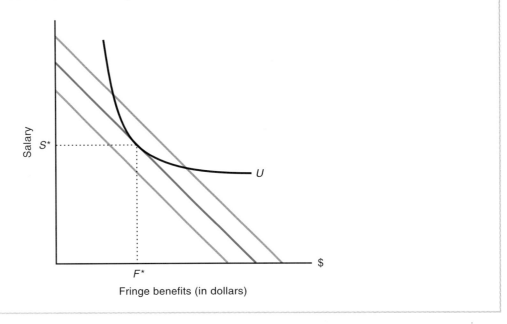

Fringe benefits (in dollars)

expenditures to attract and retain employees are the same. The firm's value would be highest with the lowest isocost curve possible (since lower isocost curves imply lower employee expenses and higher profits).

The Salary–Fringe Benefit Choice

Suppose that all individuals the firm might hire have similar preferences for wages and fringe benefits. Figure 14.5 pictures an indifference curve for the reservation utility of a typical employee. The firm can hire this individual using any compensation package along this curve. The figure also shows selected isocost curves for the firm. Management's objective is to choose the compensation package that meets the reservation utility of the employee at the lowest cost. The optimal choice is *S**, *F**, where the indifference curve is tangent to the isocost curve. Management could choose other combinations along the indifference curve. However, these combinations are more expensive. Although management could offer combinations that are less expensive than *S**, *F**, these combinations would not meet the individual's reservation utility.

This analysis suggests that it is in management's interest to heed employee preferences about fringe benefits. If employees prefer that the company buy a dental policy rather than pay them the same amount in cash, the firm should offer the dental policy.

Figure 14.6 Optimal Choice of Salary and Fringe Benefits with Payroll Taxes

This figure illustrates how payroll taxes can affect the optimal choice of salary and fringe benefits. In the first case, the firm does not pay payroll taxes (such as Social Security) on wages or fringe benefits. The optimal choice is S^*, F^*. In the second case, the firm pays payroll taxes on wages, but not fringe benefits. This tax flattens the isocost curves for the firm, and the optimal choice is S', F'. In the second case, the firm pays lower salaries and higher fringe benefits.

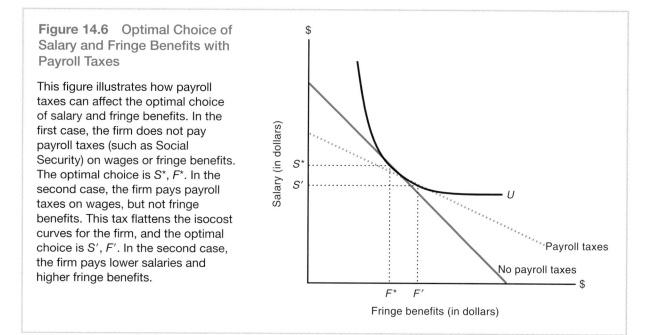

Offering the dental policy makes the employees better off and the value of the firm no lower. Indeed, if the change would result in paying employees more than their reservation utilities, the firm can lower cash compensation further and share in these gains. (The firm might do this by giving lower raises in the subsequent years.) Designing more efficient contracts allows the firm to attract and retain employees at a lower cost.

We have assumed that the firm's value is unaffected by the split between paying a given amount of cash to employees and spending the same amount on fringe benefits. This assumption is likely to be valid in many cases, but there are at least two complicating factors. First, taxes at the firm level can be important. For example, the firm generally has to pay Social Security taxes on wages but not fringe benefits. This tax changes the slope of the firm's isocost curves. For example, assuming a Social Security tax rate of 6 percent, managers would be indifferent between paying $1.00 for salary or $1.06 for fringe benefits. The slope of the isocost curve is -0.943. As depicted in Figure 14.6, it is better to offer higher fringe benefits and lower salary than without the tax. Note that personal taxes are incorporated in the shape of employees' indifference curves, whereas the firm's taxes are incorporated in the slope of the firm's isocost curves. Thus,

Paying for Fringe Benefits at Lincoln Electric

The willingness of firms to listen to the preferences of employees suggests that employees pay for their own fringe benefits. For instance, most companies would be willing to pay higher salaries if employees did not want health insurance. Employees, therefore, face an opportunity cost of lost salary when they receive fringe benefits. Lincoln Electric, a manufacturing company in Cleveland, makes this trade-off quite clear to employees. Employees at Lincoln receive about half their compensation in the form of annual bonus payments. Fringe benefit costs are taken out of this bonus payment and are shown on the employees' pay stubs. On several occasions, Lincoln employees have voted against dental plans because the majority of employees prefer cash.

Ford and Volvo Perk Parity

When Ford purchased Volvo AB's car division in 1999, they had to decide what to do about the differences in the fringe benefits received by the employees. Although Ford plants have fitness centers, these centers do not have the amenities offered at the Volvo plants such as Olympic-size pools, badminton and tennis courts, tanning beds, and saunas. One reason for the high level of fringe benefits at Volvo is the extremely high tax rates in Sweden. Company-supplied services such as plush health facilities are not taxed by the government. However, Ford employees in the United States might be tempted to argue for "perk parity" especially during union contract negotiations.

Source: A. Latour (1999), "Detroit Meets a 'Worker Paradise,'" *The Wall Street Journal* (March 3), B1.

our analysis suggests that in designing compensation packages, management should consider the *total* tax bill for the employee and the firm.[26] Reducing the joint tax liabilities imposed on both the firm and its employees means that there is more money to split between the firm and its employees. It is generally inappropriate to focus only on the taxes of one party (for example, the firm's taxes).

The second complication is that fringe benefits can affect employee behavior in ways that affect the firm's profits. For example, sick leave can motivate absenteeism. Similarly, liberal insurance coverage can reduce employee incentives to worry about prices for medical care. These types of incentive effects can affect the appropriate compensation package. For example, some firms have reduced insurance coverage to employees for the express purpose of providing employees with stronger incentives to negotiate with doctors over price. Presumably, employees do not like to bargain with doctors and must be offered higher wages to offset this increased cost in addition to the higher wages to offset the reduced insurance coverage in the fringe benefit package. However, the cost to the firm will be reduced if the increase in wages is less than the reduction in insurance costs. These considerations can shift the slope of the isocost curves in either direction and thus can either increase or decrease the optimal amount of fringe benefits.

Trend Toward Temporary and Part-Time Workers

Part-time workers make up a growing portion of the workforce at United Parcel Service (UPS). If UPS has a peak load in the morning and another in the afternoon, hiring part-time employees offers UPS more flexibility than taking on more full-time employees. Many part-time employees like working a part-time schedule.

In contrast to part-time jobs, temporary jobs are full-time (40 hours per week) jobs, but not necessarily permanent. Many companies hire temps through employment agencies to fill in when permanent employees are on extended leave or if the job is temporary. These positions usually provide fewer fringe benefits. Microsoft and Time Warner have been in court over whether temps who have been in the position for several years are entitled to the same benefits as permanent employees. Who is the real employer—the employment agency or the company employing the "permatemps"? If it is the company, it owes the temp pension benefits. An IRS complaint against Microsoft claims that many of Microsoft's 6,000 temps are really common-law employees and entitled to company pension benefits,

Sources: M. Phillips (1997), "Part-Time Work Issue Is Greatly Overworked," *The Wall Street Journal* (August 11), A1; A. Bernstein (1998), "When Is a Temp Not a Temp?" *Business Week* (December 72), 67–72.

[26]M. Scholes and M. Wolfson (1992), *Taxes and Business Strategy* (Prentice Hall: Englewood Cliffs, NJ).

Figure 14.7 Using the Mix between Salary and Fringe Benefits to Attract Particular Types of Employees

The figure displays an isocost curve for the firm and indifference curves representing the reservation utilities of a person who is single and a person who has a family. In this example, people with families have a higher preference for fringe benefits (for example, health insurance) than single people who prefer cash. If management wants to attract individuals with families, it will offer high fringe benefits and low wages, ($\$_M$, F_M). In this case, only people with families will apply for the job. Single individuals will not apply because the package does not meet their reservation utilities. If, instead, management wants to hire single people, it will offer high salary and low fringe benefits, ($\$_S$, F_S).

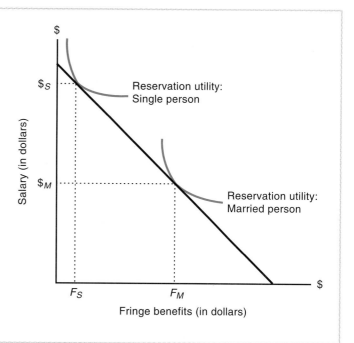

Using Fringe Benefits to Attract Particular Types of Employees   Employers often care about the personal characteristics of the individuals they hire. For example, firms facing higher costs of turnover might favor hiring people with families since they might be less likely to quit. Alternatively, firms with intense work environments, such as investment banks in New York City, might favor hiring single people because they are more likely to be willing to work longer hours. Firms are constrained in using salary offers to attract a particular type of labor force. For example, firms are likely to violate discrimination laws if they offer people with families more money than they offer single people. Firms, however, sometimes can use the mix between fringe benefits and salary to attract particular types of employees.[27] Figure 14.7 depicts an example. The figure displays an isocost curve for the firm and indifference curves representing the reservation utilities of people who are single and people who have families. In this example, people with families have a higher preference for fringe benefits (for example, health insurance) than single people. If management wants to attract individuals with families, it will offer higher fringe benefits and lower wages ($\$_M$, F_M). In this case, people with families are more likely to apply for the job. Single individuals are less likely to apply because the package does not meet their reservation utilities. If, instead, management wants to hire single people, it will offer higher salary and lower fringe benefits ($\$_S$, F_S).

The Mix of Fringe Benefits   Our basic analysis of the choice between fringe benefits and salary also applies to the choice of the mix of fringe benefits. For example, it will make sense to provide employees with disability insurance rather than dental insurance whenever the employees prefer the disability insurance—assuming the same cost to the company. In this spirit, some companies have adopted menu or *cafeteria-style* benefit

---

[27]Our objective in this section is to describe how firms use the salary and fringe benefit mix to attract particular types of individuals. We are not arguing that such a policy is ethical, just, or legal in all cases.

plans, where individual employees allocate a fixed fringe benefit allowance among a variety of choices. The potential benefit of these plans is that not all employees value specific benefits equally. By allowing them to choose, they will be more willing to work for the firm at a lower overall cost. Note that a cafeteria plan is more likely to be valued by two-career families since, for example, one spouse can acquire dental insurance while the other obtains health insurance.

Cafeteria plans entail costs that can limit their desirability. First, they are more expensive to administer. For example, employees must be informed of all their options and an administrative system has to be established to record choices, make the appropriate payments to suppliers, allow for changes in choices, and complete the appropriate tax forms.

Second, cafeteria plans can generate adverse-selection problems that increase the cost of the benefits. Adverse selection is likely to be a particular problem with health, life, and disability insurance. As discussed in Chapter 10, individuals know more about their likelihood of getting sick than an insurance company. This asymmetric information is less a problem if the insurance company provides the benefits to all employees as a group. When free to choose, the people who are most likely to buy insurance are those who find it a good deal at the quoted price. Thus, at any given price, the insurance company is likely to attract a clientele that causes it to lose money. To reduce the likelihood of losing money, the insurance company can do things like demand physical examinations and investigate past medical records before agreeing to insure an applicant. However, these actions increase the costs of supplying the coverage. To reduce the adverse-selection problem, companies often allow employees to opt out of health insurance only if they can document that their spouse has coverage at another firm. This policy limits the amount of discretion that employees have on whether to buy health insurance and helps ensure that the insurance company will have a reasonable cross-section of health risks in the pool.

| Summary | Chapters 12 and 13 discussed how firms assign decision rights. A second important component of organizational architecture is the reward system: Productive firms design compensation plans that *attract and retain* qualified employees and *motivate* them to exert effort and make decisions that exploit the business opportunities faced by the firm. This chapter examines how firms attract and retain qualified employees and how the level of pay can be used to motivate employees. The next chapter focuses on incentive compensation. |

In our benchmark model of wages and employment—patterned after the standard competitive model—firms have no discretion over the wages paid to employees; rather, wages are determined by supply and demand in the marketplace. If a firm pays too little, it will have difficulty attracting employees to job openings and will experience high turnover. A firm that pays too much will have numerous job applicants and low turnover. In addition, the firm will have high costs and will compete poorly in the product market.

Human capital is a term that characterizes individuals as having a set of skills that can be "rented" to employers. We distinguish between *general* and *specific* human capital: General human capital consists of training and education that is equally useful to many different firms; specific human capital is more valuable to the current employer than to alternative employers. In our benchmark model, employees would be expected to pay for their own general training, and employers would pay for specific training.

Our benchmark model does not consider differences in working conditions across jobs. Yet actual jobs vary in many dimensions, such as geographic location and the level of danger. Holding other factors constant, unpleasant jobs must pay a *compensating differential* to attract employees. Compensating differentials attract employees to unpleasant tasks; they also provide employers with direct financial incentives to enhance the work environment whenever it is cost-effective.

In some settings, it can be difficult to tell whether a firm is paying the market wage rate to employees. Important indicators are the application and quit rates and the nature of outside job offers made to existing employees.

Our benchmark model provides a good description of some labor markets, such as the market for unskilled agricultural workers. It is less useful in describing employment and wages in many other cases. Many firms are better characterized as establishing *internal labor markets,* where outside hiring is done primarily for entry-level jobs; most other jobs are filled from within the firm. Internal labor markets are characterized by *long-term relationships* between the employee and the firm. Long-term relationships can be beneficial because they provide both employers and employees incentives to invest in specific training, offer incentives for employees to work to exploit the business opportunities facing the firm, and allow firms to take greater advantage of information about employee attributes. One cost of using internal labor markets is that it sometimes is undesirable to limit the search to the firm's current employees, especially when filling higher-level positions.

Employees accepting jobs with firms that employ internal labor markets evaluate *career earnings.* Thus, firms with internal labor markets have more flexibility in setting the level and career profile of pay. Firms can vary compensation over the career path, so long as the overall remaining stream of earnings is competitive at each point in time relative to the streams offered by other firms within the same labor market. Economists have identified at least three ways in which firms can use their flexibility in setting the level and sequencing of pay to enhance employee motivation. These methods include the payment of *efficiency wages, upward-sloping earnings profiles,* and the tying of major pay increases to *promotions.* However, influence costs can affect the desirability of exploiting this potential flexibility. Firms might reduce the dispersion of pay among coworkers to limit influence costs.

The typical American employee receives about 25 percent of total compensation in the form of *fringe benefits* such as vacation time, insurance coverage, and contributions to retirement plans. Salary and fringe benefits are not perfect substitutes for most employees. Tax benefits and the fact that the company often can purchase fringe benefits more cheaply favor fringe benefits. The desire for flexibility in making purchases can favor cash payments. Employers have incentives to heed the preferences of employees when it comes to the choice between salary and fringe benefits. By responding to their preferences, firms can design compensation packages that attract and retain qualified employees at the lowest cost. Firms sometimes can use the salary–fringe benefit mix to attract particular types of employees. For example, offering liberal insurance coverage is more likely to attract people with families than single individuals, who are more likely to prefer cash payments. Firms also have incentives to heed employee preferences when it comes to choosing the mix of fringe benefits. This incentive has motivated many firms to consider *cafeteria-style* benefits. Use of these plans is limited due to administrative costs and *adverse-selection problems.*

Suggested
Readings

M. Aoki (1988), *Information, Incentives, and Bargaining in the Japanese Economy* (Cambridge University Press: Cambridge).

G. Becker (1983), *Human Capital* (University of Chicago Press: Chicago).

P. Doeringer and M. Piore (1971), *Internal Labor Markets and Manpower Analysis* (D. C. Heath: Lexington, MA).

R. Ehrenberg and R. Smith (1999), *Modern Labor Economics: Theory and Public Policy,* seventh edition (Addison-Wesley: Reading, MA), Chapters 8, 9, and 11.

Review
Questions

14–1. Explain the following quotation: "My employer doesn't determine my salary, he determines where I work."

14–2. In the basic competitive model, why do employees pay for general training and firms pay for specific training?

14–3. Why do firms form internal labor markets?

14–4. Evaluate the following statement: "Firms are free to set salaries in any manner they want in an internal labor market."

14–5. Present an economic argument to explain why firms often have mandatory retirement (where allowed by law).

14–6. How do influence costs affect pay within internal labor markets?

14–7. The United States Congress has considered proposals that would limit the level of top executive pay to some multiple of the lowest-paid employee in the company (for example, executive pay must be less than 10 times the lowest-paid employee). Do you think this type of proposal is a good idea? Explain what effect the proposal would have on the involved companies.

14–8. President Clinton proposed eliminating the tax deduction for all compensation over $1 million for CEOs unless the pay is tied to company performance. Proponents argue that this proposal will benefit shareholders. "Everyone knows that CEOs are overpaid and that their pay is not appropriately tied to performance. This legislation helps solve both problems." Present an argument against this proposal.

14–9. The Brown Tool Company is a multidivisional firm with offices throughout the country. The company sets the salaries of most of its positions at the central level. For example, secretaries are paid $8 per hour throughout the company. Discuss two important reasons why the firm might adopt such a policy. Discuss two important problems that the policy might cause.

14–10. A recent study concluded that many employees fake sickness to avoid going to work. The authors argue that through unwarranted sick leave, employees "steal" about $150 billion a year from firms. This amount is three times larger than the estimated loss from shoplifting. One proposal is for Congress to outlaw the granting of sick leave to employees. The argument is that companies would be much better off because they would not incur the giant losses associated with sick leave. Further, the costs of taking sick leave would be internalized with the employees. Comment on this proposal.

14–11. The University of Rochester used to pay all faculty a 10 percent bonus as a substitute for a retirement plan. Individuals could either place this money in a retirement fund or keep the cash. Placing money in the fund deferred taxes on the income until the point of withdrawal. Changes in the United States tax code forced the university to change this policy. In particular, employees cannot be given options of this type but must either be covered or not covered as a group. The university now has the following policy: All new faculty members without prior service at another university are given a 10 percent bonus in cash. This payment is treated as ordinary income for tax purposes. Most new faculty are young people fresh out of graduate school. All faculty members with more than 2 years of service must place the bonus in a retirement account. Taxes are deferred until withdrawal from the account. Explain why it might make economic sense for the university to have such a two-group plan, rather than treat all employees (old and new) the same.

14–12. The University of Medford pays the full tuition for the children of faculty members at any university in the world. Recently, this policy has received bad publicity. The argument has been made that people in other occupations have to pay the tuition costs for their children and so should college professors. According to this argument, it is not fair to have these relatively well-paid people get subsidized in this manner. The board of trustees of the University of Medford has been asked to reconsider this policy. Provide an economic argument to explain why the board of trustees might want to continue this policy.

14–13. Payments under some retirement plans are based on the average earnings in the last few years of employment. Discuss the potential incentive effects of this policy.

14–14. Suppose UAW negotiations argue for upgraded perquisites for Ford's US employees to match those available in the Swedish plants Ford acquired from Volvo.
  a. Ford might achieve perk parity by upgrading US facilities or by reducing Swedish facilities. What would be the implications of each policy?
  b. Ford might live with different levels of perks. What would be the implications?
  c. Suppose the difference in perks between US and Swedish employees is reduced following the merger. What are the efficiency implications for the merger?

14–15. Companies can often gain if they listen to employees about what they prefer in the way of a fringe benefit package—a more preferred package serves to attract and retain employees at a lower cost. Nevertheless, many firms have shunned "menu plans" where each employee would be completely free to choose their own fringe benefit package. (For instance, those wanting health insurance could buy it through the company, whereas those who want some other benefit or cash would make different choices.) Why do you think many firms have avoided this type of menu plan?

14–16. The Good Beer Brewing Company currently purchases health insurance for its 10,000 employees. The company is considering a flexible plan where employees can have either $2,000 in cash or insurance coverage (the insurance costs $2,000). The company figures it will expend the same amount of money either way. However, employees will be better off because they can choose the option that is most preferred. Do you see any potential problems with this idea? Explain.

14–17. Public accounting firms have traditionally paid low starting salaries to new employees. Nevertheless, these firms have been able to hire and retain qualified employees (even though these employees could obtain higher salaries elsewhere). Is this observation inconsistent with economic theory? Explain.

14–18. Parkleigh Pharmacy is a small department store in Rochester, NY, specializing in upscale, expensive personal accessories (e.g., sunglasses, beauty aids, leather goods) and home decorations (e.g., crystal, china, table lamps). Kaufmann's is a large department store chain, based in Pennsylvania, with several stores in the Rochester area. Kaufmann's carries a broader range of products and caters more to middle-income consumers.

    Salespeople at Parkleigh are paid a straight hourly wage (i.e., no sales commissions). In addition, they are entitled to a 30 percent discount on anything they buy at the store. By contrast, salespeople at Kaufmann's are paid an hourly wage (lower than the hourly wage paid at Parkleigh) plus a commission of 5 percent on sales they make. They receive no discount on products they buy at Kaufmann's.
  a. Why do you think the compensation plans differ at the two firms? In particular, why do you think Kaufmann's pays commissions to salespeople, while Parkleigh does not? Why does Parkleigh offer employees discounts on purchases, while Kaufmann's does not?

b. Assume, for the moment, that neither store pays sales commissions. Parkleigh offers an hourly wage plus the employee discount. Kaufmann's offers only an hourly wage. Do you expect Kaufmann's hourly wage to be higher or lower than Parkleigh's? Why?

14–19. Critically evaluate the following statement:

> *At Lincoln Electric, workers must pay for their own fringe benefits (for example, health insurance). The payment for these benefits is taken out of the annual bonus checks. At other firms, the firm pays for fringe benefits. Therefore, the workers at Lincoln are worse off than at other firms.*

14–20. People buying disability insurance on an individual basis are often required to take physical exams. Physical exams are typically not required when employees acquire disability insurance through a company-sponsored plan (which covers all employees in the firm). Provide an economic rationale for the different policies relating to physical exams.

14–21. Marks & Spencer is a large, established British retailer of apparel, housewares, and food products. The company has a large workforce. As part of the company's benefits package, employees receive a discount of 30 percent off all purchases of apparel.
   a. What are the advantages and disadvantages of offering a 30 percent discount off company merchandise?
   b. What are the advantages and disadvantages of offering a 30 percent discount off apparel, but not housewares and food products? Why do you think the company differentiates between apparel and other products?

14–22. Consultants often spend much of their time away from home. Deloitte and Touche recently implemented a policy that curbs its consultants' travel time. Instead of spending five days a week at a client's office, consultants spend three nights and four days, fly home and work a fifth day at their home cities. One observer argued that Deloitte and Touche is putting employee concerns ahead of good business. Deloitte and Touche should focus on company profits, not employee comfort. Do you agree that the firm is necessarily wasting company profits? Explain using concepts from class. In answering this question assume that employees would be more productive if they stayed at the client's office.

14–23. A recent study found that CEOs in Europe are paid substantially less than CEOs in America, even after controlling for a firm's size and industry. Does this necessarily imply that American CEOs are overpaid? Explain.

14–24. You work in the human resource office of a major cruise line that offers cruises in various locations around the world (the Caribbean, the Mediterranean, Asia, etc.). The CEO of your company has recently proposed that all employees in the corporate office (i.e., those employees who do not actually work on a ship) be offered free passage on your firm's cruises as a fringe benefit. The CEO has asked for your thoughts on this proposal.
   a. If this proposal is adopted, what will happen, if anything, to employee salaries? Why?
   b. What are the advantages and disadvantages of this proposal? What factors should be considered when evaluating the proposal?

14–25. Consider two states that are nearly identical in terms of such factors as income, climate, and population. There are public universities in both states. One state has a law which specifies that all professors of a given rank (assistant, associate, and full professor) have to be paid the same. Thus an assistant professor, whether in history or in law, has to be paid the same. Associate professors are paid more than assistant professors. However, all associate professors have to be paid the same. The same is true for full professors. The other state does not have such a law. In this state, law professors are paid substantially more than history professors within each rank. The laws in both states allow the universities to choose their own teaching loads for faculty. These loads can vary across faculty members.
   a. How do you expect the teaching loads to vary across the two states (you can focus on history and law departments)? Explain the economic reasoning behind your answer.

      b. Are either history or law professors in the state with the law necessarily better or worse off than their counterparts in the state without the law? Explain.

      c. Discuss how the residents of the state might be made worse off by such a law.

14–26. Some companies base promotions solely on seniority. Discuss the negative and positive aspects of such a policy.

Chapter 15
Incentive Compensation

In October 1988, Du Pont's fibers division announced "one of the most ambitious pay-incentive programs in America."[1] Its plan covered nearly all of the division's 20,000 employees, including both management and rank-and-file employees. Under the plan, a portion of employees' pay would be placed into an "at-risk pool." If the business exceeded its profit goals for the year, the employees would receive a multiple of the at-risk monies as a bonus. If not, the employees stood to lose the money in the pool. The intent was eventually to place as much as 6 percent of annual pay at risk. The plan was adopted initially for a 3-year trial period. Many companies indicated that they were watching this experiment carefully to see what they could learn about incentive pay. "The attention that the American business community has given to the Du Pont program is tremendous," said Robert C. Gore, a vice president at Towers Perrin Company—a major compensation consulting firm.

The largest of Du Pont's chemical businesses, the fibers division comprised departments ranging from automobile seat covers to apparel. In 1990, the division had to achieve a target of 4 percent real-earnings growth for its employees to recover their

---

[1]Details of this example are from L. Hays (1988), "All Eyes on Du Pont's Incentive Program," *The Wall Street Journal* (December 5), B1, and R. Koening (1990), "Du Pont Plan Linking Pay to Fibers Profit Unravels," *The Wall Street Journal* (October 25), B1.

at-risk pay. But profits for the first 9 months were off 26 percent, due largely to a poor economy and unexpectedly high input prices. Demand for the division's products had declined substantially due to weak housing and automobile markets, and oil prices had risen materially because of the Gulf War. By fall 1990, it was obvious that the employees were likely to lose all the monies placed in the bonus pool. Employee discontent was quite high: Employees were facing significant financial losses, largely due to factors beyond their control. In October 1990, Du Pont precipitously canceled the incentive program with more than a full year left in the trial period. In the words of the fibers division chief, "I have to conclude it was an experiment that didn't work."

Given the widespread interest in this experiment, it is important to understand why the Du Pont plan failed. Incentive pay, as some critics claim, simply might be a bad idea. If so, any firm adopting a large-scale incentive plan is making a mistake and should expect to experience a fate similar to Du Pont's. Alternatively, the failure of this plan might be traced to basic design flaws that could have been avoided by more careful planning. In this chapter, we examine the economics of incentive compensation. Our analysis suggests that Du Pont's failure was due largely to problems with the structure of the plan. Correspondingly, our analysis provides insights into how companies might design more effective compensation plans.

We begin this chapter by providing a more detailed discussion of incentive problems. We then examine how ownership can resolve some of these problems by providing strong incentives for individuals to take efficient actions. Next, we consider a critical limitation of ownership in controlling incentive problems—inefficient risk bearing. We then detail the implications of risk bearing for the design of compensation contracts. Next, we review some of the key insights about incentive compensation contained in the economics literature. We begin by discussing the standard principal-agent model. We then extend this basic analysis by considering the informativeness principle, group incentive pay, multitask principal-agent problems, alternative forms of incentive pay, and the role of incentive pay in the process of matching individuals with jobs. Toward the end of the chapter, we discuss the debate on whether incentive pay works, and we provide a case study on CEO compensation to allow the reader to apply some of the concepts we develop on compensation policy. In the appendix we examine multitask principal-agent problems in greater detail.

The Basic Incentive Problem

As described in Chapter 10, incentive problems exist within firms because owners and employees have fundamentally different objectives. For example, the owners of an insurance company want its salespeople to sell insurance policies to customers, but salespeople might prefer to play golf. Similarly, stockholders of a research company want its scientists to develop marketable products, whereas scientists might prefer to work on more interesting but less marketable ideas. Presumably, employees at Du Pont's fibers division have other interests than simply making and selling fibers products.

Consider the example of AssemCo, a small company that assembles components for several large electronics firms. As in most companies, there is a basic conflict between the aims of the owners and the aims of the employees. The owners would like employees to work diligently, but the employees would prefer longer coffee breaks and working at a more leisurely pace.

To add concreteness to our discussion, we focus on the problem of motivating a particular employee at AssemCo, Ian MacLeod. For simplicity, we focus on a given time period (for example, motivating Ian over a single week). Ian's preferences with respect to income and work are portrayed by the following utility function[2]:

$$U = I - e^2 \tag{15.1}$$

where I is his income for the period and e is the number of units of effort exerted (for example, hours spent actually assembling components). This utility function, which measures utility in dollar equivalents, indicates that he is better off as his total income increases, but becomes worse off as he exerts more effort on component assembly. As Ian exerts effort, he suffers decreased utility because he would rather engage in other activities. His reservation utility is equivalent to $1,000. AssemCo must meet this level of utility or Ian will not work for the firm.

The firm benefits from Ian's effort, since more components are assembled. The benefits to AssemCo from his effort are

$$B = \$100e \tag{15.2}$$

Suppose that his effort is costlessly observable and verifiable—hence, effort is contractible. In this case, the firm offers Ian a compensation contract that would pay him a sum of money if, and only if, he provides a specified level of effort, $\hat{e}$. He will accept this contract, so long as he is paid his reservation utility. To meet this condition, the firm must pay him a wage of $\$1,000 + \hat{e}^2$. If he delivers that level of effort and is paid $\$1,000 + \hat{e}^2$, then his utility is $U = (\$1,000 + \hat{e}^2) - \hat{e}^2 = \$1,000$ and he receives his reservation utility. The profits to the firm P from his efforts are

$$P = \$100\hat{e} - (\$1,000 + \hat{e}^2) \tag{15.3}$$

The firm then chooses the $\hat{e}$ that maximizes the firm's value.

Figure 15.1 provides a graphical illustration of this problem. The figure displays both the benefits to the firm ($\$100e$) and the costs ($\$1,000 + e^2$). Profits are the difference between the two. As the figure indicates, maximum profits occur at $e^* = 50$. At this effort level, Ian is paid $3,500 and the profits for AssemCo are $1,500. This outcome is the efficient bargaining solution. Ian is indifferent among the feasible effort choices—he is paid his reservation wage in all cases—and the firm's profits are maximized at 50. The firm could induce him to provide additional effort by paying him more. However, the additional costs to the firm would exceed the incremental benefits. At the optimal effort level of $e^* = 50$, the marginal costs of effort are equal to the marginal benefits; hence relevant benefits and costs to both parties are considered.[3]

Thus far, we have assumed that Ian's effort is costlessly observable. But this is rarely the case. Effort will be observable neither by the firm nor by a court of law—effort is not contractible. In addition, the firm is unlikely to be able to tell whether Ian worked hard simply by observing his output. Often, output is difficult to measure and is affected by factors beyond the employee's control.[4] In this case, there is a standard incentive

---

[2]We chose this particular utility function (as well as the firm's benefit function, discussed below) to simplify the calculations. Our basic results, however, are quite general and are not specialized to this particular example.

[3]Technical note: Recall that the marginal benefit at a point is equal to the slope of the total benefit at that point. The same relation holds between marginal cost and total cost. Using elementary calculus, the slope of the total cost curve is $2e$, whereas the slope of the total benefit curve is 100. The optimal effort level is $2e = 100$; thus $e^* = 50$.

[4]In our simple example, the firm can infer e from observing Q, Ian's output. More generally, Q would be affected by factors that are beyond the control of the employee. For example, the following relation might hold: $Q = \$100e + \mu$, where μ is a random error. Random factors that might affect his output include the quality of raw materials and equipment failures. With the random error term, the firm cannot infer e simply from observing Q.

Figure 15.1 The Optimal Effort Choice at AssemCo

This figure pictures both the benefits and the costs to the AssemCo from the efforts of a given employee. Profits are the difference between the two. Maximum profits occur at $e^* = 50$. This example assumes that the employee will exert the agreed-upon effort as long as he is paid his reservation utility. To meet this constraint, the firm must pay a wage of $\$1,000 + e^2$. This payment meets the reservation wage of $\$1,000$ and reimburses the employee for his disutility of effort. Benefits to the firm are $\$100e$. At the optimal effort level, $e^* = 50$, $\$5,000$ in gross benefits are generated. The employee is paid $\$3,500$ and the firm's profits are $\$1,500$. The firm could induce the employee to exert more effort by paying him more. However, the costs are larger than the benefits. The effort choice of 50 is efficient. The employee is indifferent among the possible choices (since he is paid his reservation utility in each case), and the profits for the firm are maximized at this level.

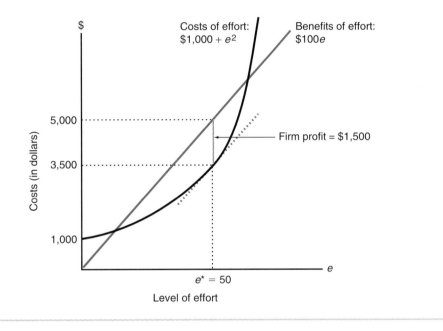

problem. If Ian promises to provide 50 units of effort and is paid a fixed salary of $\$3,500$, he has the incentive to renege on his promise and provide less effort. He gets paid anyway and benefits from exerting less effort. The firm might suspect that Ian did not work hard. However, it would not know for sure. In this case, a straight salary of $\$3,500$ fails to provide Ian with appropriate incentives. Rather, AssemCo must devise some other type of contract that motivates him to provide additional effort.

This simple example illustrates three important points about incentive problems:

- Incentive problems exist basically because of conflicts of interest between employers and employees. If the interests of employees and employers were aligned perfectly, there would be no reason to worry about incentives.
- Incentive conflicts do not cause problems when actions are contractible. Firms can identify the most efficient actions and pay employees only if those actions are taken. For instance, if the actions of employees at Du Pont were costlessly observable, there would be no reason for the firm to adopt a profit-based plan for

employees. Rather, the employees could be motivated appropriately by contracts based directly on their actions.

- In a competitive labor market, employees must be compensated for undertaking undesirable actions—there are compensating differentials. It normally is not sensible to have employees work as hard as physically possible. In choosing the optimal action, there is a trade-off between the benefits of the action for the firm and the personal costs borne by the employees.

Incentives from Ownership

In some cases, there is a simple way to resolve incentive problems, even when the actions of employees are unobservable. This solution is to sell each employee the rights to his or her total output. The incentive problem is caused by the fact that most of the costs of exerting effort are borne by employees, while much of the gains go to the owners. By selling employees their output, both the benefits and costs of exerting effort are internalized by employees and thus employees will make more productive choices. For instance, in our AssemCo example, the firm could sell Ian the rights to the value of his output ($100e$) for a price of $1,500. AssemCo makes the same profits as when effort was costlessly observable. Ian's objective, in turn, is to maximize his personal utility given by

$$U = (\$100e - \$1,500) - e^2 \tag{15.4}$$

where the first term represents the income from exerting effort (the value of the output minus the $1,500 payment to the company) and the second term represents the disutility of effort. Given this problem, Ian will choose to exert 50 units of effort and will have utility of $1,000.[5] This outcome is the same as in the perfect information case. It is achieved even though the employer cannot observe Ian's effort.

This discussion highlights the strong incentive effects that come from ownership. In practice, ownership often is used as an incentive mechanism. For example, a majority of the businesses in the United States are private. Moreover, the 1980s witnessed a large number of managerial buyouts of public firms and divisions of public firms, where the managers went from the status of employees to owners. Although some aspects of these buyouts might be controversial, the evidence indicates that the managers operated the units more efficiently when they became owners.[6] Furthermore, about one-third of all retail sales in the United States are made through franchised outlets (including car dealers and gas stations). In franchising, the future profits of each unit are sold to franchisees, who as owners have strong incentives to maximize value.[7]

---

[5]Technical note: This solution can be found using elementary calculus (see footnote 3) or a graphical analysis, as in Figure 15.1. We present a more detailed analysis of the employee's effort choice later in this chapter.

[6]S. Kaplan (1989), "The Effects of Management Buyouts on Operating Performance and Value," *Journal of Financial Economics* 24, 217–254.

[7]P. Rubin (1978), "The Theory of the Firm and Structure of the Franchise Contract," *Journal of Law & Economics* 28, 223–233; J. Brickley and F. Dark (1987), "The Choice of Organizational Form: The Case of Franchising," *Journal of Financial Economics* 18, 401–420. In many franchise agreements, the central company receives an ongoing sales royalty from the franchisee. This royalty provides incentives to the central company to honor commitments on training and promoting the brand name. The franchisee's claim on future profits is typically limited to some time period—for example, 20 years. The contract often is renewable.

At least three important factors limit the use of ownership in resolving incentive problems:

- **Wealth Constraints.** Limited wealth can make the ownership solution infeasible. For instance, although senior managers at Du Pont might have stronger incentives if they owned the company, few management groups have access to sufficient capital to finance this purchase.

- **Risk Aversion.** Typically, employees do not have full control over their outputs. Rather, output depends on random outside events in addition to employee efforts. For example, Du Pont's profits are affected by changes in the oil, housing, and automobile markets. In making employees fully accountable for their actions, ownership also exposes them to random events that affect their output, but are beyond their control. Given that employees do not like to bear risk, employee ownership entails a risk-bearing cost (see Chapter 2). As we discuss below, this cost must be considered in designing incentive contracts.

- **Team Production.** In most firms, there are production synergies; total output is greater than the sum of what each employee could produce individually. Identifying the separate contributions when there is this type of team production is problematic. Even if the firm were owned jointly by the employees, it would not solve this incentive problem—there still would be the standard free-rider problem discussed in Chapter 10.

Optimal Risk Sharing

To illustrate some of the basic principles of efficient risk sharing, consider the example of Abby Ross and Jess Rodgers. Abby receives a monthly income from a trust fund. Depending on the performance of the fund, this income can be either $0 or $10,000, each with a probability of .5. Abby's expected income is $5,000.[8] However, the income stream is risky—half the time, Abby gets $0. Jess also has a trust fund with the same income possibilities. Half the time he gets $0; the other half, $10,000. The income flows for Abby and Jess are *independent*. (That is, regardless of the outcome for Abby, the probability is still .5 that Jess will get $0.)[9] The left column of Table 15.1 displays the joint distribution of outcomes for Abby and Jess.[10] The probability of each outcome is given in the middle column.

Assuming that Abby and Jess are *risk-averse* (holding expected income constant, the person prefers less dispersion in outcomes), they both can be made better off by agreeing to split the combined income. The possible payoffs for each individual are given in the right column of Table 15.1. The expected income per individual is still $5,000. By sharing the risks, however, the variability of their individual incomes has been reduced. The variability is reduced because the likelihood that both Jess and Abby will be lucky

---

[8]The expected income is the *average* amount that Abby will receive in a month. It is calculated by adding together each possible income multiplied by the respective probability: ($10,000 × .5) + ($0 × .5) = $5,000.

[9]We assume that the flows are independent to simplify the calculations in the example. The basic insights of this analysis hold as long as the two flows are not perfectly positively correlated.

[10]A joint outcome ($X, $Y) refers to Abby receiving X dollars while Jess receives Y dollars. Since the events are independent, the probability of any joint outcome is the probability of the first event (that Abby receives $X) multiplied by the probability of the second event (that Jess receives $Y). For example, the probability that both will receive $0 is .5 × .5 = .25.

Joint Outcomes	Probability	Individual Payoffs from Splitting
($0;$0)	.25	$ 0
($0;$10,000)	.25	5,000
($10,000;$0)	.25	5,000
($10,000;$10,000)	.25	10,000
		E(Income) = $ 5,000

Table 15.1   Example of Risk Sharing

In this example, two people receive incomes from different trust funds. Each fund pays either $0 or $10,000, each with a probability of .5. The two funds have independent payoffs. The left column displays the possible joint payoff outcomes, and the middle column shows the probability of each outcome occurring. For instance, ($0;$0) is the outcome where both funds pay $0 for the period. The probability of this outcome is .25. The right column shows the individual incomes if the two people agree to split the payoffs from the two funds. Splitting the payoffs makes both better off, compared to relying solely on the payoffs from their individual funds. The expected income in either case is $5,000. However, risk is reduced by the pooling of the funds. For instance, each person has a .5 chance of receiving no income when keeping all the income from his or her own fund. The two people only have a .25 chance of receiving no income when they pool the funds.

or unlucky is less than the likelihood that only one of them is lucky or unlucky. For example, by sharing the risks, the probability of getting nothing is only .25, compared to .5 with no risk sharing. Being risk-averse, they prefer the less volatile income stream. (Ideally, they would like income streams that are certain.) It is this reduction in volatility from pooling risks that drives individuals to purchase insurance, as well as to invest in diversified portfolios—for example, mutual funds.

People often differ in their attitudes toward risk. Some people are more willing to tolerate large financial risks, whereas others are not. An efficient allocation of risk takes these differences in preference into account. For example, suppose that Jess is *risk-neutral,* whereas Abby is risk-averse. (A risk-neutral person cares only about the expected payoff and does not care about the dispersion in potential values around that expected value.) Jess will value each of the two random income flows at $5,000 (the expected value), whereas Abby will not. For example, Abby might be willing to accept a certain payment of $4,000 for her risky income flow. Here, there are gains from trade by having Jess buy Abby's income. A payment of $4,500 would split the potential gains of trade between the two parties. Each party would be better off by $500.

The common stock of large corporations typically is owned by many investors, each holding well-diversified portfolios. Because of this diversification, investors are less concerned about the fortunes of any one company. (Things that are specific to individual firms tend to average out over their entire portfolios; that is, one firm is lucky, whereas another firm is unlucky.)[11] Employees, in contrast, receive large fractions of their incomes from their individual employers (each generally has but one job), and thus they care greatly about the fortunes of individual firms. This difference in outlook simply reflects the fact that employees of a firm have less effective methods to manage firm-specific risk than the firm's shareholders. (Note that we are not saying that employees

[11]For example, H. Markowitz (1959), *Portfolio Selection* (John Wiley & Sons: New York), and W. Sharpe (1964), "Capital Asset Prices: A Theory of Market Equilibrium under Conditions of Risk," *Journal of Finance* 19, 179–211.

have different preferences than owners; rather, it is their ability to manage risk through well-diversified portfolios that makes shareholders in large corporations more willing to bear such risk.)

Assuming that the shareholders of the firm can manage firm-specific risks more effectively than employees, they will be willing to bear these risks at a lower price. Thus, it is better from a risk-sharing standpoint to pay employees fixed salaries and let the total risk of random income flows be borne by the shareholders. By paying fixed salaries, the firm avoids having to pay a compensating differential for risk bearing to attract and retain the desired workforce.

Effective Incentive Contracts

> **Basic Principle**
> Trade-offs between incentives and risk sharing

Our discussion to this point suggests that compensation contracts serve at least two important functions. First, they are used to motivate employees. Second, they are used to share risk more efficiently. Unfortunately, there is a trade-off between these two objectives. Efficient risk sharing suggests that it is better to pay employees fixed salaries, while incentive considerations suggest that it is better to tie pay to performance. A compensation contract strikes an appropriate balance between these two considerations.

- When the owners of a firm have a comparative advantage in bearing firm-specific risks, it is better from a *risk-sharing standpoint* to offer employees more fixed salaries and let more of the risk of random income flows be borne by owners (for example, shareholders in large corporations).
- Fixed salaries do not provide strong incentives. Incentives are provided by basing pay on performance.
- The first two points indicate that there is a trade-off between paying incentive compensation to increase effort and the associated costs of inefficient risk bearing. Often, an effective contract consists of a fixed salary and one or more variable components based on performance.

Economists have devoted significant resources to studying how to design effective compensation contracts. In this section, we summarize some of the more important findings from this research. We begin with the most basic model in the economics literature, the standard principal-agent model. This model considers a contracting situation that closely resembles our example of Ian MacLeod of the AssemCo. However, the model generalizes this example and focuses on choosing the optimal contract when the employer cannot observe the employee's effort. Following the introduction of the basic model, we extend the analysis by considering the informativeness principle, group incentive pay, multitask principal-agent problems, types of incentive pay, and the role of incentive pay in self-selection.

Principal-Agent Model

The Basic Model Economic analysis of incentive compensation begins with the basic principal-agent model.[12] This model presents a relatively simple characterization of the contracting process, illustrates the trade-offs between risk sharing and incentives, and

---

[12]One of the first presentations of this model is B. Holmstrom (1979), "Moral Hazard and Observability," *Bell Journal of Economics* 10, 74–91.

provides a number of useful insights for designing more effective compensation plans. In this single-period model, there is an employer (the principal) who wants the employee (the agent) to work on the employer's behalf. The employer is risk-neutral, while the employee is risk-averse. The most basic analysis focuses on an individual employee. Concerns about teamwork do not arise within the basic model.

Consider the example of Erica Olsson of a biotech firm, DNAcorp. Erica's output Q is a function of her effort, plus some random effect, μ (with expected value 0 and variance, σ^2):

$$Q = \alpha e + \mu \tag{15.5}$$

where output is defined as the market value of her production. The model does not consider the possibility that Erica might manipulate the observed output level (for example, by "cooking the books"). Both Erica and her supervisor, Jon Chang, can observe her output.

If Erica increases effort by one unit, output goes up by α dollars. Thus, α is Erica's marginal productivity—the higher the α, the higher her marginal productivity. The random effect μ reflects factors that can affect output but are beyond Erica's control (for example, equipment failures). The higher σ^2, the more likely it is that the output will experience larger random shocks.

Optimal risk sharing suggests that there are benefits from having the owners of the DNAcorp bear the output risk and pay Erica a fixed salary. For example, Erica might agree to put forth effort level $\hat{e}$ and be paid a fixed salary W for this effort. The owners of DNAcorp receive the difference between the value of the output and W.

$$\text{Owners' profits} = (\alpha \hat{e} + \mu) - W \tag{15.6}$$

There is, however, an incentive problem with this arrangement if Erica's supervisor can observe neither her effort level nor μ, the random shock. Erica has the incentive to agree to $\hat{e}$ as an effort level but then exert less effort. Jon will tend to observe lower output when she shirks. However, Erica always can claim this result was due to bad luck—that is, μ was negative.

Employee's Effort Problem   Incentives can be provided to Erica by basing part of her compensation on realized output. For example, consider Erica's incentives under the following contract:

$$\text{Compensation} = W_0 + \beta Q \tag{15.7}$$

where $0 \le \beta \le 1$. This contract pays Erica a fixed wage W_0, plus a proportion β of the output Q.[13] To illustrate Erica's effort choice, suppose $W_0 = \$1{,}000$, $\beta = .2$, $Q = \$100e + \mu$, and $C(e) = e^2$, where $C(e)$ is Erica's cost of effort in dollar equivalents. Given these values, the compensation contract is

$$\text{Compensation} = \$1{,}000 + .2(\$100e + \mu) \tag{15.8}$$

The benefit to Erica from exerting effort is that it increases compensation—each unit of effort increases her compensation by \$20 (.2 × \$100). Random shocks μ affect total

---

[13]For simplicity, we restrict our attention to linear compensation contracts. One justification for focusing on linear contracts is that in practice they are observed commonly. For instance, salespeople and real estate agents often are paid commissions, while factory employees frequently are paid piece rates. Linear contracts have the advantage of providing consistent incentives to the employee that do not depend on past output (the marginal payoff for increasing output by one unit is constant). In contrast, lump-sum bonuses that are paid once some threshold is reached lose their incentive effects once the target is met. For a technical justification for linear contracts, see B. Holmstrom and P. Milgrom (1987), "Aggregation and Linearity in the Provision of Intertemporal Incentives," *Econometrica* 55, 303–328.

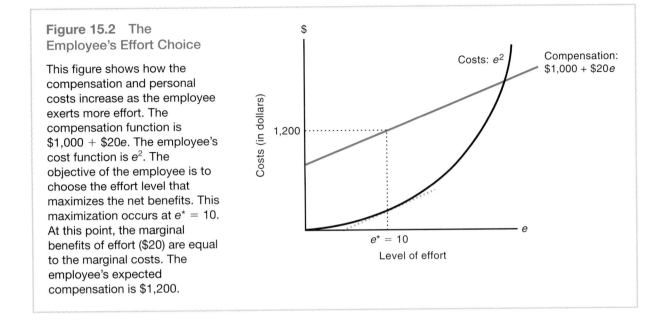

Figure 15.2 The Employee's Effort Choice

This figure shows how the compensation and personal costs increase as the employee exerts more effort. The compensation function is $1,000 + $20e. The employee's cost function is e^2. The objective of the employee is to choose the effort level that maximizes the net benefits. This maximization occurs at $e^* = 10$. At this point, the marginal benefits of effort ($20) are equal to the marginal costs. The employee's expected compensation is $1,200.

compensation but do not affect the benefits of exerting effort. For any realization of μ, compensation is always $20 higher for every extra unit of effort provided. Thus, in choosing the optimal effort level, Erica can ignore μ. (It does not affect the costs or benefits of her effort.)[14] Erica's cost from exerting effort is e^2. Her objective is to choose the effort level that maximizes her net benefits.

Figure 15.2 depicts how Erica's compensation and personal costs increase as she exerts more effort. As shown in the figure, the optimal effort choice is 10. Note that this figure displays total costs and benefits. The marginal benefits and marginal costs at any effort level are equal to the slopes of the total curves at that point. The difference between total costs and benefits is greatest when the slopes of the total curves are equal. Thus, at the optimal choice ($e^* = 10$), the marginal costs of effort are equal to the marginal benefits, and net benefits are maximized. If Erica exerts more than 10 units of effort, the extra income is insufficient to compensate her for the extra disutility she experiences from exerting more effort. When e is less than 10, Erica is made better off by exerting more effort, since the additional compensation is more than sufficient to cover the added costs of her additional effort.

Figure 15.3 depicts how Erica's effort choice changes with changes in the fixed wage W_0 and the incentive coefficient β. Changing the fixed wage from $1,000 to $2,000 results in a parallel shift in compensation, but Erica still chooses $e^* = 10$. The higher fixed wage *provides no incentives* for her to work harder since it does not affect the *marginal benefits* of effort. Marginal benefits are $20, regardless of the fixed wage. In contrast, when the incentive coefficient is increased, Erica selects a higher effort level. For instance, with $\beta = .3$, Erica selects 15 units of effort. In this case, marginal benefits increase to $30 and she exerts more effort.

[14]Technical note: Throughout our analysis, we assume that Erica's attitude toward risk does not change with her level of wealth. Relaxing this assumption means that she will consider an additional effect in choosing the effort level. In particular, the effort choice will affect her utility by altering the costs imposed on her from bearing risk. We ignore this potential effect because it complicates the analysis without providing substantially more insights.

Figure 15.3   How the Employee's Effort Choice Changes with Changes in the Fixed Wage and Incentive Coefficient

The initial contract is Compensation = $1,000 + .2($100e). The picture shows that increasing the fixed wage from $1,000 to $2,000 causes a parallel shift in the compensation function but does not alter the optimal effort choice (it stays at 10). Changing the incentive coefficient β from .2 to .3 changes the slope of the line and increases the optimal amount of effort to 15.

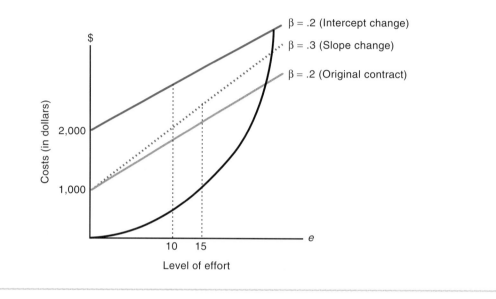

The implications of this analysis should be contrasted with the common argument that well-paid employees work harder because they are happier on the job. In our analysis, higher pay does not provide incentives unless it is tied to good performance. It is important to note that our analysis focuses on a single time period. In a multiperiod setting, a high level of pay can motivate employees if the *likelihood of being fired is contingent on performance.* (See the discussion in Chapter 14 on efficiency wages—in this case, the threat of dismissal effectively ties pay to performance.) But high pay and guaranteed tenure with the firm would provide no incentive effects.

Motivating Employees at Allen-Edmonds Shoe Company

Theory argues that tying pay to performance motivates employees more than fixed salaries. Allen-Edmonds Shoe Company learned this principle the hard way. Allen-Edmonds is a manufacturer of high-priced shoes. For years, it paid its factory employees based on individual output through a piece-rate system. In 1990, following the advice of quality gurus, the company abandoned the piece-rate system and started paying employees fixed hourly wages. The intent was to encourage employees to focus on quality and teamwork. But productivity plummeted as employees were observed taking more breaks and "fooling around." After the company lost $1 million in 1990, it reinstated piecework payments. Productivity and profits immediately "shot back up." An executive of the company stated, "Our people needed the discipline that the piecework system gives to them."

Source: B. Marsh (1993), "Allen-Edmonds Shoe Tries 'Just-In-Time' Production," *The Wall Street Journal* (March 4), B2.

Factors That Favor High Incentive Pay

1. The value of output is sensitive to the employee's effort.
2. The employee is not very risk-averse.
3. The level of risk that is beyond the employee's control is low.
4. The employee's response to increased incentives is high (the employee exerts substantially more effort).
5. The employee's output can be measured at low cost.

Table 15.2   Implications of the Principal-Agent Model

The model suggests that the five factors listed are likely to be particularly important in determining how strongly to base pay on performance.

The Optimal Contract   We have shown how Erica will choose effort under different compensation contracts. The firm's problem is to choose the specific compensation contract that maximizes expected profits, given Erica's anticipated effort choice. The primary choice variable is the incentive coefficient, β. Given this choice, W_0 can be adjusted up or down to meet Erica's reservation utility. Selecting a contract with a high β benefits the owners of the firm because it increases Erica's effort. However, choosing a high β also imposes costs on the firm. The expected compensation that the firm must pay to Erica increases with β for two reasons. First, as discussed above, Erica must be compensated for exerting more effort. Second, increasing β imposes additional risk on her—the variable portion of her compensation increases. As risk increases, so does the compensating differential that must be paid to induce Erica to remain with the firm. The optimal contract involves an appropriate balancing of these costs and benefits.

Implications   Employees normally are offered an incentive contract that implies less effort than would be required if the employer could costlessly observe the effort choices. When effort is contractible, the effort level $\hat{e}$ that would maximize the firm's value could be elicited without imposing risk on the employee. When effort is unobservable, the employer could elicit $\hat{e}$ by paying sufficiently high incentive pay. Yet costs of inefficient risk bearing normally make this an undesirable choice.[15]

Our analysis suggests five factors that are likely to be important in selecting how strongly pay should be tied to performance. These factors are summarized in Table 15.2. The first factor is the sensitivity of the value of the output to additional effort from the employee. In our example, this factor is captured by α—Erica's marginal productivity. A high α implies that incentive pay (holding other factors constant) is effective because the benefits of motivating effort are high. A second factor is the risk aversion of the employee. Higher risk aversion implies a higher cost from inefficient risk bearing and thus lowers the use of incentive pay. The third factor is the level of risk that is beyond the employee's control (σ^2). When the level of risk is low, output is determined primarily by the employee's effort and it makes sense to pay higher levels of incentive compensation. But when this risk is high, incentive compensation imposes high costs for inefficient risk bearing. The fourth factor is how much additional effort the

---

[15]The basic model assumes that the employer has the relevant knowledge to solve this problem, including knowledge of the production function, the employee's utility function, and the variance of the random error term. For a mathematical derivation of the results in this section, see Chapter 7 of P. Milgrom and J. Roberts (1992), *Economics, Organization, and Management* (Prentice Hall: Englewood Cliffs, NJ).

Incentive Pay and Expected Compensation

A study of earnings of employees in 500 US firms in the footwear and clothing industries found that piece-rate employees on average were paid 14 percent more than employees paid straight salaries. This premium was found after controlling for union status, sex, and other variables that might affect compensation. Economic theory suggests at least three reasons for this wage premium. First, people work harder under piece rates than under fixed salaries and must be compensated for the extra effort. Second, piece rates impose risk on employees; output is affected by random factors such as equipment failures. Thus firms using piece rates must pay a compensating differential for risk. A third reason—which we have not discussed in this chapter—is that piece rates are likely to attract more highly skilled and productive employees, since they will earn more under piece rates than under fixed salaries. Firms have to pay more for more talented employees.

Source: E. Seiler (1984), "Piece Rate vs Time Rate: The Effect of Incentives on Earnings," *Review of Economics and Statistics* 66, 363–376.

---

employee exerts as incentives are increased. If the employee is unresponsive to increased incentives, high incentive compensation imposes more risk on the employee while inducing little additional effort. Thus, there is less reason to provide high incentive pay. The responsiveness to incentive pay depends on the personal costs to the employee for exerting additional effort. For instance, changing the cost function in Figure 15.3 from e^2 to e^3 would make Erica less responsive to changes in incentives. With the original cost function, Erica increases effort by 5 units as β is increased from .2 to .3. But the increase is only .58 under the second cost function.[16] Finally, our analysis presumes that Erica's output can be observed costlessly. This is not always the case. The more expensive it is to measure her output, the less likely that she will be offered incentive pay. We discuss these measurement cost issues further in Chapter 16.

Du Pont Revisited   The principal-agent model suggests at least two problems with the Du Pont plan. Both problems stem from using divisional profits as an output measure. First, under the plan, individuals bear the full costs of their own effort but realize only a small fraction of the output of their effort—it is shared with 19,999 other employees (β is quite small for individual employees). The limited incentives are due to the basic *free-rider problem* discussed in Chapter 10. We discuss this issue in greater detail below under the topic of group incentives. The second problem is that divisional profits are affected by many random factors (σ^2 is high) as well as the effects of other employees throughout the division. Thus the compensation plan imposes substantial uncontrollable risk on the employees. Du Pont would have provided more effective incentives if it had paid the employees based on disaggregated output measures over which they had greater control—in the limit, their own output.

Informativeness Principle[17]

As we have seen, incentive problems exist because of imperfect information. If the actions of employees were observable at zero cost, it would be easy to write contracts to

---

[16]Technical note: It is the second derivative of the cost function that is important in determining the response rate. Larger second derivatives (or equivalently steeper marginal cost curves) translate into lower response rates.

[17]Material in this section draws on B. Holmstrom (1982), "Moral Hazard in Teams," *Bell Journal of Economics* 13, 324–340.

> **Basic Principle: Informativeness Principle**
> In designing compensation contracts, theory suggests that it is productive to include all performance indicators that provide additional information about the employee's effort (assuming the measures are available at low cost). Measuring the employee's effort with more precision reduces the costs of inefficient risk bearing and leads to a more efficient effort choice.

motivate appropriate behavior. It follows that the inefficiencies that result from incentive problems can be reduced by improvements in information. The standard principal-agent model assumes that there is only one indicator of an employee's effort, the employee's output. In many cases there are other sources of information that can be used to determine whether or not the employee worked hard. For instance, Du Pont was able to tell that the decline in profits in 1990 was not due entirely to a lack of effort on the part of divisional employees by observing the increase in the price of oil and the performance of other companies as well as by gathering information such as government reports on general business conditions. Appropriate use of this type of information increases the precision by which employee effort is measured, and when included in the compensation contract (with the appropriate weights) reduces the costs of inefficient risk bearing. In theory, it is optimal to include all indicators that provide additional information about the employee's effort in the compensation contract—assuming the measures are available at low cost. This basic idea is called the *informativeness principle*.

One important source of information about an employee's effort level is the output of coworkers performing similar tasks. For instance, if a salesperson's performance is poor in a given year, was the person unlucky or lazy? If average sales in the company declined substantially over the same time period, it is more likely that the employee was simply unlucky. If other salespeople had great years, the salesperson is more likely to have been lazy. The informativeness principle implies that information about other employees' sales should be included in the compensation contract as a benchmark—that is, the firm should employ a *relative performance contract*. Chapter 16 provides an extended discussion of relative performance evaluation and highlights several potential problems that can make relative performance evaluation undesirable.

The informativeness principle indicates that it typically is beneficial to include low-cost indicators in the compensation contract that improve the employee's performance measure. It also can be desirable for the firm to expend additional resources on developing even more precise measures of performance. Here, there is a trade-off between the costs of developing as well as implementing better performance measures and the benefits of improved effort motivation and more effective risk sharing.

The informativeness principle suggests that Du Pont could have reduced the risk imposed on the employees by including other indicators in the contract. For instance, rather than use an absolute performance standard (such as 4 percent of real earnings growth), the target could have been set relative to the growth of other firms in the same industry. This type of contract might have avoided some of the problems that the company faced in 1990, when employees were likely to lose money under the plan due to circumstances beyond their control.

The informativeness principle also suggests that Du Pont could have reduced the uncontrollable risk imposed on its employees by adjusting earnings to reflect external changes in market conditions. For example, the company could have adjusted division profits for the change in oil prices from the Gulf War. In fact, the firm might want to enter financial contracts (for example, futures, forwards, swaps, or options) to transfer this risk from the fibers division to external markets to reduce the risk imposed on the division's employees and hence the required compensating differentials in their compensation packages.[18]

[18]C. Smith (1995), "Corporate Risk Management: Theory and Practice," *Journal of Derivatives* 2, 21–30.

Group Incentive Pay

In the basic principal-agent model, employees are motivated by being paid based on their *own output.* Many firms, however, base incentive pay on *group performance*—Du Pont is an example. For instance, of 735 publicly traded companies responding to a 1998 survey by the American Compensation Association, 73 percent offered performance-related variable pay in addition to base salary for nonexecutive employees. In addition, 46 percent offered company stock options to nonexecutive employees.[19]

There are at least three reasons why firms might favor group incentive plans over individual plans:

- Individual performance generally is difficult to measure, while the performance of a group of employees often can be measured at reasonably low cost. For example, most firms' cost accounting systems measure the performance of business units for control purposes. Hence, at little additional cost these measures also can be used in administering compensation plans. However, further disaggregation—in the limit, providing a personalized measure of the performance of each employee—would be much more difficult and expensive.

- Group pay encourages cooperation and teamwork, whereas some individual incentive plans (depending on design) motivate more self-centered actions.

- Group plans can motivate employees to monitor each other for bad performance. Mutual monitoring is beneficial because the specific knowledge about individual performance often is held by teammates.

Nonetheless, standard free-rider arguments provide a strong reason to question whether group plans provide effective incentives, particularly when the group is quite large. In Du Pont's fibers division, with its 20,000 employees, contributions of individual employees have little discernible effect on the overall bottom line (profits are an incredibly noisy measure of each employee's output). Also individual employees receive only a small fraction of the value each creates (it is shared with 19,999 other divisional employees and the owners of the firm). Thus, profit-sharing plans would appear to produce limited incentive effects. Yet this is not surprising. Should one really expect that paying a janitor on overall company performance would motivate that person to push the broom harder or to complain when other janitors shirk on their jobs?[20] These arguments suggest that large-group incentive plans (like Du Pont's) impose risk on employees but produce limited benefits.

Although many economists find the free-rider arguments to be quite compelling, there are some offsetting considerations that potentially help explain the widespread popularity of group plans—despite the fact that free-riding is a problem. First, it might be beneficial to increase the awareness of employees about the stock-price performance and profitability of the company. By focusing on these measures, employees learn how managerial and employee actions affect the bottom line. For instance, employees might be less likely to complain about a corporate restructuring when they see that it increases the firm's stock price. Indeed, it probably takes little stock ownership to motivate most employees to monitor the stock price on a frequent basis. Hence, these benefits can be obtained while shifting little risk to the employees. Second, employees might be less

---

[19]We thank Kevin J. Murphy for providing these estimates based on his analysis of the ACA data.

[20]This example was suggested by K. J. Murphy.

likely to take actions that harm other members of a group with whom they identify closely. Thus, when the group receives incentive pay, employees might not want to harm teammates by shirking on the job. In this case, attempting to avoid feelings like guilt or shame might motivate employees, even if they face limited direct financial consequences from shirking.[21] Third, paying employees on stock-price performance and profits sends signals to employees about what is valued within the company. These signals serve to reinforce a performance-based corporate culture (see Chapter 11). To be most effective, however, they must be complemented by other features of organizational architecture that provide more direct incentives.

Multitask Principal-Agent Problems[22]

In the standard principal-agent model, effort is one-dimensional—the firm cares only about how hard the employee works. But most jobs involve a variety of tasks. For instance, employees on an assembly line can spend time increasing output, improving quality, performing preventative maintenance, or helping teammates. Similarly, professors at universities allocate their time among teaching, research, consulting, and administrative duties. Thus, managers usually have to be concerned not only with how hard employees work but also with how they allocate their time among assigned tasks; university officials are not indifferent to how professors allocate their time.

Motivating an employee to strike the appropriate balance among tasks is not easy. A complicating factor is that in some tasks, effort is more easily monitored and output more easily measured than in others. For instance, university officials can observe teaching ratings, whereas the quality of administrative service is harder to measure. Compensating employees based on what is measurable encourages them to exert effort on the compensated tasks but to shirk on the others. For example, paying professors based solely on teaching ratings would encourage effort on teaching at the expense of administrative service and research. Similarly, paying an assembler based on output would encourage the employee to produce more units but to ignore quality or helping teammates. These multitask considerations suggest that firms often might want to avoid paying employees based solely on measurable outputs. The appendix to this chapter provides a more detailed analysis of these considerations.

Given enough time, managers are likely to obtain information about the overall performance of employees. For example, deans have the opportunity to observe the service of professors on committees; they hear comments on faculty research from colleagues; they talk to students about teaching quality. Incentives can be provided to employees by basing promotions, terminations, and periodic pay adjustments on this type of information. Indeed, universities rely heavily on these mechanisms to motivate faculty. Evaluating this information usually requires *subjective judgments* on the part of managers. To provide proper incentives to employees, managers must develop reputations of being impartial and objective. To be most effective, firms must establish performance measures and rewards that motivate managers to develop these reputations. Chapter 16 provides an expanded discussion of subjective performance evaluation.

---

[21]E. Kandel and E. Lazear (1992), "Peer Pressure and Partnership," *Journal of Political Economy* 100, 801–817.

[22]This section draws on B. Holmstrom and P. Milgrom (1991), "Multitask Principal-Agent Analysis: Incentive Contracts, Asset Ownership, and Job Design," *Journal of Law, Economics and Organization* 7, 24–52.

Incentive Compensation Means Pay Cuts for Poor Performance

Imposing risk on employees means that poor performance gets penalized. Take the case of Stephen Wiggins, former CEO of Oxford Health Plans. Oxford, the once high-flying managed-care company, suffered large losses of $291 million in 1997. The stock price fell 80 percent from its high a year earlier. Wiggins, who founded the company and still owned about 5 percent of the stock in the firm, took a 61 percent pay cut. All but one of the other six highest-paid executives took pay cuts and only two of the seven executives at Oxford in 1997 were there in 1998. And Wiggins, although still chairman of the board, was replaced as CEO. In 1998, he resigned as chairman.

Source: R. Winslow (1998), "Wiggins, Ex-CEO of Oxford Health, Took 61% Cut in Total Pay Last Year," *The Wall Street Journal* (May 4), B8.

Forms of Incentive Pay

The term *incentive pay* frequently evokes images of piece rates, commissions, and cash bonus plans, where employees are paid based on measurable output. This image is not surprising given that more than a quarter of the employees in the US manufacturing sector receive at least part of their income through such incentive plans.[23] Our discussion in this chapter suggests that mechanisms like tying promotions and salary adjustments to performance also are forms of incentive pay. Broadly speaking, any compensation contract (explicit or implicit) that rewards employees for good performance or punishes employees for poor performance can be considered incentive pay. (Recall the Mary Kay Cosmetic Company's innovative use of incentives discussed in Chapter 11.) Under this definition, all the following are forms of incentive compensation[24]:

- Piece rates and commissions
- Bonuses for good performance
- Prizes for winning contests (for example, vacations)
- Salary revisions based on performance
- Promotions and titles for good performance
- Preferred office assignments for good performance
- Stock ownership and profit-sharing plans
- Firings and other penalties for poor performance
- Deferred compensation and unvested pensions that are forfeited on dismissal

It is important to note that rewards *do not have to be monetary*. Rewards can consist of anything that employees value. For example, managers in some organizations have little flexibility in what they pay employees. Nonetheless, incentives can be provided by rewarding more productive employees with desirable job assignments, better offices, preferred parking spaces, special honors, and trips to training sessions in attractive locations.

---

[23]J. McMillan (1992), *Games, Strategies, and Managers* (Oxford University Press: New York), 93.

[24]G. Baker, M. Jensen, and K. Murphy (1988), "Compensation and Incentives: Practice versus Theory," *Journal of Finance* 43, 593–616.

Imaginative Incentives to Reduce Absenteeism

At an automobile company, employees were awarded points for each day that they were present at the factory. The points could be redeemed for prizes, such as tickets to popular vacation attractions. The interesting feature of the plan was that the points were not given to the employee but to the employee's spouse! Reports indicate that with the spouse helping to monitor employee attendance, the absenteeism rate declined significantly.

In a second plan, Dawson Personnel Systems attributes the double-digit increase in sales in the last 2 years to its practice of giving employees time off for exceeding targets. Any salesperson could leave work at 2:00 PM for the rest of the month after hitting sales targets.

Sources: R. Ehrenberg and R. Smith (1988), *Modern Labor Economics* (Scott, Foresman: Glenview, IL), 417; S. Shellenbarger (1999), "Work and Family," *The Wall Street Journal* (December 29), B1.

Incentive Compensation and Information Revelation

The basic principal-agent model assumes that the employer and employee have the same information at the time of initial contract negotiations. In some contracting situations, precontractual information is asymmetric.[25] For example, prospective employees generally know more about their likelihood of quitting over the next year than the prospective employer. Similarly, sales representatives are more likely to know about the sales potential of their territories than are higher-level managers.

Sometimes it is possible for the firm to induce employees to reveal their private information by clever design of the compensation contract. Consider the example of Onex Copy Company. This company uses sales representatives throughout the country to sell copy machines to customers. Each salesperson is assigned a specific territory. Some territories have greater sales potential than others. For simplicity, suppose that there are only two types of territories, good and bad. Good territories have the potential to generate $2 million in sales, while bad territories have the potential to generate only $1 million in sales. The sales representatives know the quality of their own territories. Central managers do not have the information to distinguish which territories are good and bad.

The firm would like to use information about whether specific territories are good or bad to evaluate the performance of the sales representatives. The company also wants accurate forecasts to plan production cycles. The company simply could ask the sales representatives to state the quality of their territories. But the sales representatives with good territories are likely to be less than completely truthful: If the firm thinks that a good territory is bad, the representative will look good when sales are high. (Alternatively, the salesperson can generate the expected poor sales with only limited effort.)

In this example, the firm can induce the salesperson to tell the truth by offering the following menu of contracts. Sales representatives who state that their territories are good receive compensation contracts that pay 2.6 percent of sales. Sales representatives

---

[25]In Chapter 10, we divided asymmetric information into two categories—precontractual and postcontractual. Thus far, in this chapter, we have focused on postcontractual information problems (also called *moral-hazard* or agency problems). In this section, we discuss precontractual information problems (also called *adverse-selection* problems).

Providing Incentives to Work and Tell the Truth at IBM Brazil

There is no systematic evidence on how frequently firms design compensation contracts to provide incentives for truthful information revelation and hard work. We are aware of one example, IBM Brazil. During the 1970s, this company experimented with a compensation plan that rewarded its salespeople for accurate sales forecasts and actual sales performance. At the start of each period, headquarters would provide salespeople with forecasts of future sales in their territories. Each salesperson would then indicate what proportion of this forecast he thought he could meet. For instance, a value of 1 would indicate that the salesperson expected to meet the forecast, and a value of 1.5 would indicate that he thought he could beat it by 50 percent. The bonus payments under the plan rewarded salespeople for actual sales, relative to the company forecasts, and sales relative to their own forecasts. The payments were set in a manner that encouraged both hard work and accurate forecasts.

According to IBM's management, the plan seemed to work relatively well. The company did encounter some unanticipated problems in implementation. For instance, salespeople quickly learned how the plan could be "gamed" by shifting sales between sales periods. For example, a salesperson might delay a sale in one period in order to promote higher sales and improve personal sales forecasts in the future. IBM, however, implemented penalties that discouraged this type of behavior. The difficulties that IBM encountered in implementation might help explain why these types of plans are not used more frequently by other companies.

Source: G. Jacob (1978), "Tie Salesmen's Bonuses to Their Forecasts," *Harvard Business Review* 56 (May–June), 116–123.

who state that their territories are bad receive a flat wage of $50,000. Given this choice, it is in the interests of all salespeople to tell the truth: Those with bad territories would prefer the $50,000 wage contract (2.6 percent of $1 million = $26,000), whereas those with good territories would prefer the contract that pays 2.6 percent of sales (for them, a $52,000 payout). The key to making the plan work is that the compensation for each type of employee is higher when the information is correctly reported than when it is not.

In this example, there are many potential compensation plans that can induce truth telling. The problem for the firm is to choose the most profitable contract. Onex is likely to want the compensation contract to provide strong performance incentives, as well as to induce truth telling. Thus, it might choose to pay commissions to both types of employees but structure different commission rates to induce truth telling.

Does Incentive Pay Work?

Throughout this chapter, we have argued that compensation plans motivate employees. Although this argument is readily accepted by many people, it is not without controversy. Quality guru W. Edwards Deming has gone so far as to assert that "pay is not a motivator." In the same spirit, psychologist Alfie Kohn, in a controversial article on the merits of incentive pay states, "Bribes in the workplace simply can't work."[26]

Critics of incentive pay generally rely on two basic arguments. The first is that money does not motivate employees. As support for this view, it is pointed out that employees usually rank money relatively low when it comes to factors that make a job attractive. Factors such as the nature of work and quality of colleagues appear more

[26]A. Kohn (1993), "Why Incentive Plans Cannot Work," *Harvard Business Review* (September–October), 54–63.

The Power of Incentives: Evidence from Chinese Agriculture

One especially interesting piece of evidence on the effectiveness of incentive pay comes from one of the largest economic experiments in history—reforms in Chinese agriculture in the early 1980s. Between 1952 and 1978, the Maoist period, Chinese agriculture revolved around the commune system. Under this system, employees were divided into production teams. There were some attempts to tie pay to performance. However, these incentives were relatively weak, and there was a tendency to base pay on family size, independent of effort. From 1980 to 1984, under the rule of Deng Xiaoping, the commune system was gradually replaced by the "household-responsibility system." Under this system, each peasant family was given a long-term lease on a plot of land. The family had to deliver a quota of agricultural products to the government each year, but it could keep any production in excess of the quota. This additional output could be consumed by the family or sold to others.

Economic theory argues that the ownership of residual claims on output provides strong incentives. Thus, this theory predicts higher productivity under the household-responsibility system than the commune system. Empirical studies support this prediction. For instance, one study estimated that productivity in Chinese agriculture increased by nearly 50 percent over the period of the Dengist reforms.

Source: J. McMillan (1992), *Games, Strategies, and Managers* (Oxford University Press: New York), 96–98.

important. The second, more prominent criticism is that it is difficult (if not impossible) to design an effective incentive compensation plan. Support for this argument is provided by the many examples of flawed compensation plans that have produced unwanted behavior (for example, the case of Sears Automotive Centers discussed in Chapter 2). Interestingly, these two lines of criticism are somewhat at odds with one another. If money did not motivate people, incentives plans would not produce the dysfunctional behavior that proponents of the second argument cite. In making a

Teachers Gaming Student Test Scores

To improve public education, a number of school districts reward teachers with cash bonuses if their school's test scores rise. However, such systems have spawned cheating among teachers to boost their ratings. Kentucky, for example, created an annual test, heavy on essay questions. Schools were rated on how well their students did along with attendance and dropout rates. The essays were graded by the students' own teachers. If a school's rating dropped, sanctions were imposed—consultants were hired, and in extreme cases a new principal was brought in with the power to dismiss teachers. Schools performing well received rewards that, at the discretion of teachers, were used to buy supplies or pay teachers bonuses. In 98 percent of the time, the teachers paid themselves a bonus, as much as $2,602 in extra cash or 7 percent of the average salary.

Problems surfaced quickly. In 96 percent of the schools surveyed, auditors found that grades assigned to the writing portion of the exam—which counted for 14 percent of each school's total score—were too generous by an average of 35 points on a 140-point scale. Teachers were found typing students' essays. Students received advance copies of the test and tip sheets. Teachers explained questions to students during the exam. Students admitted to being coached by teachers during the test.

The tests are distributed to schools three weeks before the exam so that school officials can prepare for the exam. Ed Reidy, state deputy commissioner for assessment, states, "I operate under the assumption most people are ethical and what we need are procedures in place to catch folks when they're not." This example demonstrates that poorly designed incentive plans can induce dysfunctional behavior.

Source: B. Stecklow (1997), "Kentucky's Teachers Get Bonuses, but Some Are Caught Cheating," *The Wall Street Journal* (September 2), A1.

CASE STUDY: *The Debate over CEO Compensation*

The most visible and highly paid person in most corporations is the chief executive officer. CEO compensation is particularly important to firms for three reasons. First, the compensation package is likely to be important in attracting and retaining good CEOs. Second, the form of the pay contract is likely to help determine whether the CEO focuses on value maximization or some other objective. Third, employees throughout the organization carefully follow their CEO's pay. Important morale problems can occur when employees think that the CEO is overpaid. For instance, employees complain bitterly when they are asked to take pay cuts because the company is in trouble, yet at the same time the CEO gets a big raise.

Controversy over CEO pay has increased substantially in recent years. One charge is that the *level* of CEO pay is too high. It is easy to point to many CEOs who report compensation in the millions of dollars (reported compensation figures typically include salary and bonus payments, as well as gains from the exercise of stock options). For example, in 1991, Stephen Wolf was paid over $18 million as CEO of UAL. To quote Edward Lawler, "CEO pay just seems to get more absurd each year. What is outrageous one year becomes a standard for the next."

The second major criticism of CEO pay concerns *how* CEOs are paid. Critics argue that CEOs are agents of stockholders and that CEO pay should be based heavily on stock-price performance. Michael Jensen and Kevin Murphy provide the most detailed evidence on this topic. They estimate that for the

typical CEO, a $1,000 change in the value of the company stock results in about a $3.25 change in CEO wealth. They argue that this relation (which is equivalent to the CEO owning .325 percent of the common stock) is too small and that most companies would be better off if they increased incentive pay for CEOs. Some support for this view seems to come from studies that document an increase in stock price when companies announce that they are increasing incentive pay for CEOs.

Discussion Questions

1   Do you think the fact that most American CEOs are paid so much more than rank-and-file employees suggests CEOs are overpaid? Explain.
2. Japanese CEOs generally receive much lower levels of compensation than CEOs in the United States. Does this imply that US CEOs are overpaid?
3. Is it obvious that $3.25 per thousand is too low incentive pay for CEOs? Explain.
4. Does the observation that the stock price increases when firms increase incentive pay for CEOs suggest that most CEOs do not receive enough incentive compensation? Explain.

SOURCES: J. Byrne (1991), "The Flap over Executive Pay," *Business Week* (May 6), 90–112; M. Jensen and K. Murphy (1990), "CEO Incentives—It's Not How Much You Pay, but How," *Harvard Business Review* (May–June), 138–153; J. Haubrich (1994), "Risk Aversion, Performance Pay, and the Principal-Agent Problem," *Journal of Political Economy* 102, 258–276; and J. Brickley, S. Bhagat, and R. Lease (1985), "The Impact of Long-Range Compensation Plans on Shareholder Wealth," *Journal of Accounting and Economics* 7, 115–129.

similar point, economist George Baker notes, "The problem is not that incentives can't work but that they work all too well."[27]

Certainly, it is easy to point to many examples of compensation plans that have caused dysfunctional behavior among employees. We have done so throughout this book. Incentive plans also involve administrative costs, such as tracking output and explaining the system to employees. The important question is not whether incentive plans entail costs—they certainly do. Rather, is it possible to design incentive plans where the benefits exceed the costs? Examples like the Lincoln Electric Company

[27]G. Baker (1993), "Rethinking Rewards," *Harvard Business Review* (November–December), 44–45.

(discussed in Chapter 16) suggest that the answer is yes. Also, the fact that incentive plans—commissions, piece rates, bonus plans, and stock options—have survived so long in a competitive marketplace suggests that the net benefits of incentive pay often are positive.

Unfortunately, the scientific evidence on this debate is limited.[28] Numerous studies indicate that tying pay to performance has a positive impact on employee performance. Other studies reach the opposite conclusion. Since many of these studies have serious flaws, it is difficult to draw strong conclusions from the evidence. Our overall reading of this literature indicates that incentive compensation is value-enhancing if properly designed and implemented. Our focus has been on providing insights into how managers might accomplish this task.

Summary	Incentive problems exist because of conflicts of interest between employers and employees. These problems are easily resolved when actions are costlessly observable. Firms can identify the most efficient actions by employees and pay employees only if these actions are taken. In most situations employee actions are not observable at low cost. Here, firms can motivate employees through incentive compensation.

In a competitive labor market, employees must be compensated for undertaking actions they find undesirable—there are compensating differentials. Thus, it is not sensible to have employees work as hard as possible. In eliciting particular actions, there is a trade-off between the benefits of the action for the firm and the personal costs to the employees.

Incentive problems arise because most of the costs of exerting effort are borne by employees, whereas most of the gains go to their employers. Sometimes, there is a simple way to resolve this incentive problem even when the actions of employees are unobservable. The solution is to sell each employee the rights to his or her total output. By selling employees their output, both the benefits and costs of exerting effort are internalized by employees and thus employees will make more productive choices. We observe this solution being approximated in private firms as well as in franchising. There are at least three important factors that limit the use of ownership in solving incentive problems: wealth constraints, team production, and costs of inefficient risk bearing.

Risk-averse individuals do not like to bear financial risks; they prefer income flows with less volatility. Risk-averse individuals can benefit from sharing risks because it lowers the volatility of the individual cash flows. People often vary in their attitudes toward risk. For instance, some people are more willing to tolerate financial risks than others. An efficient allocation of risk takes these differences in preferences into account. If one party is risk-neutral whereas another party is risk-averse, it is better to have the risk-neutral party bear all the risk and the other party to receive a fixed payment.

Stockholders of firms often hold diversified portfolios and act as if they are essentially risk-neutral with respect to firm-specific risks. Employees, in contrast, have much of their human capital invested in a single firm and hence have fewer opportunities to manage risk through diversification. Thus, from a risk-sharing standpoint, it is better to pay employees more through fixed salaries and to let the risk of random income flows be borne more by the shareholders. Yet fixed salaries provide limited incentives for employees to exert effort: *Therefore, there is a trade-off between optimal risk sharing and optimal incentives.*

Economic analysis of incentive compensation begins with the basic principal-agent model. This model presents a relatively simple characterization of the contracting

---

[28]G. Milkovich and J. Newman (1993), *Compensation* (Richard D. Irwin: Burr Ridge, IL), Chapter 8.

process. However, it illustrates the trade-offs between risk sharing and incentives and provides a number of useful insights for designing better compensation plans. In particular, the model suggests that firms should pay more performance-based pay when (1) the sensitivity of the value of output to additional effort by the employee is higher, (2) the employee is less risk-averse, (3) the level of risk that is beyond the employee's control is lower, (4) the employee response to increased incentives in terms of exerting additional effort is more pronounced, and (5) employee output is more easily measured.

According to the *informativeness principle,* it is useful to include all indicators that provide additional information about employee effort into the compensation contract—provided that these indicators are available at low cost. Including these indicators in the contract reduces the randomness of payouts and thus the costs of inefficient risk bearing. One important source of information about an employee's effort is the output of coworkers performing similar tasks. The informativeness principle suggests that it is useful to employ *relative performance evaluation.* In Chapter 16, however, we discuss several factors that can limit the desirability of relative performance evaluations.

In the basic principal-agent model, employees are motivated by basing compensation on their own output. But many firms base incentive pay on *group performance.* Common reasons offered for group incentive pay are that group performance can be less expensive to monitor than individual performance, group performance emphasizes teamwork, and group plans motivate employees to monitor one another's performance. Standard free-rider arguments provide a strong reason to question whether group plans provide effective incentives—particularly when the group is large. At least three factors might help explain the widespread popularity of these plans, even though free-riding is a potential problem. First, it can be beneficial to increase employee awareness of stock-price performance and profitability (assuming employees can be motivated to monitor these measures by relatively modest plans that do not impose much risk on employees). Second, employees might feel guilty from shirking and imposing costs on teammates who are compensated on group performance. These feelings might motivate employees, even if the direct financial consequences are small. Third, paying employees on firm performance sends a strong signal to employees about what is valued within the company. To be most effective, however, these signals must be reinforced by other parts of the organizational architecture that provide more direct incentives.

Most jobs involve a variety of tasks. Motivating an employee to strike the appropriate balance among tasks is not easy. A complicating factor is that some tasks are more easily measured than others. Compensating the employee based on what is measurable will encourage the employee to exert more effort on the compensated tasks but shirk on other tasks. These *multitask considerations* suggest that firms often want to avoid paying employees based solely on measurable outputs. Given enough time, managers are likely to obtain information about the overall performance of employees. Incentives can be provided by basing promotions, terminations, and periodic pay adjustments on this information. Often, this information is not easily quantifiable but is based on the subjective opinions of supervisors.

The term *incentive pay* conjures up images of piece rates, commissions, and cash bonus plans, where the employee is paid based on measurable output. Broadly speaking, however, any compensation contract (explicit or implicit) that rewards employees for good performance or punishes employees for poor performance can be considered incentive pay. *Rewards do not have to be monetary.* Rather, rewards consist of anything that employees value.

The basic principal-agent model assumes employers and employees have the same information at the time of initial contract negotiations. In many contracting situations precontractual information is asymmetric. Sometimes it is possible for the firm to induce employees to reveal their private information by clever design of the compensation contract. For such a plan to work, the payoffs to employees must be higher when they are honest than when they misrepresent information.

Throughout this chapter, we have argued that compensation plans motivate employees. Although this argument is accepted by many, it is not without controversy. Critics of incentive pay rely on two basic arguments. The first is that money does not motivate people. The second, more prominent criticism is that it is difficult (if not impossible) to design an effective incentive compensation plan. The first argument seems inconsistent with the many examples where monetary incentives have dramatically affected employee behavior. The second argument is correct: Developing an appropriate incentive plan rarely is easy. The important question is whether plans can be designed where the benefits exceed the costs. Examples such as Lincoln Electric suggest it can be done. Our intent is to provide insights into how managers might design value-maximizing contracts.

Appendix

Multitask Principal-Agent Theory[29]

This appendix provides a more detailed example of the multitask principal-agent model. It also uses this framework to analyze the corporate practice of *telecommuting*—employees working out of their homes and communicating with the central office via fax, computer, or telephone. This application illustrates how principal-agent theory can provide insights into specific managerial policy decisions.

Multitask Model   Adel el Gazzar is a production employee at the Bijar Dye Company. He works 10 hours per day. His job consists of two tasks, assembling parts and checking the quality of his output. He is paid a piece rate for each part that he assembles. He also receives a bonus that is based on the quality of his output. Denote t_1 and t_2 as the hours per day he devotes to producing output and checking quality, respectively. Adel's incentives are high enough so that he will not shirk: He works the full 10 hours. Therefore, $t_2 = (10 - t_1)$.

Suppose that Adel's compensation translates into the following relation between compensation and the time allocated to each activity:

$$\text{Compensation} = \alpha_1\left(6t_1^{1/2}\right) + \alpha_2 t_2$$
$$= \alpha_1\left(6t_1^{1/2}\right) + \alpha_2(10 - t_1) \qquad (15.9)$$

where the α's are the weights that the compensation plan places on quantity and quality (the *incentive coefficients*).[30] Adel's objective is to maximize his compensation. He chooses t_1 to meet the following first-order condition:

$$\alpha_1\left(3t_1^{-1/2}\right) = \alpha_2 \qquad (15.10)$$

This condition has a straightforward interpretation. The left-hand term is the marginal benefit for allocating time to producing higher quantity, whereas the right-hand term is the marginal benefit for allocating time to producing higher quality. At an interior solution, these marginal returns must be equal. If the marginal benefits are not equal, Adel

---

[29]This appendix requires knowledge of elementary calculus. This appendix draws on Milgrom and Holmstrom (1991).

[30]The terms in this equation are chosen to simplify the calculations and yield reasonable values for the time allocated to the two activities. Our basic results, however, are quite general and are not specialized to this particular example.

Figure 15.4   Optimal Allocation of Effort

In this example, Adel must allocate his time between two activities, producing quantity and checking its quality. The number of hours devoted to quantity is t_1. Since he puts in 10-hour workdays, he devotes $t_2 = (10 - t_1^*)$ hours to quality. This figure illustrates the case where there is an interior optimum. At this optimum, the marginal benefit MB from allocating additional time to either activity is the same. Adel spends t_1^* hours on quantity and $(10 - t_1^*)$ hours on quality. But if the marginal benefits for quantity are higher than the marginal benefits from quality over the relevant range $(0 \leq t_1 \leq 10)$, Adel allocates all his time to producing output—there is a corner solution.

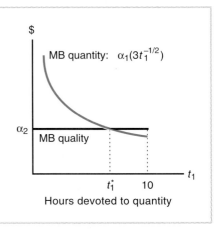

is better off devoting more time to the activity with the higher value and less time to the activity with the lower value. Figure 15.4 provides an illustration. When t_1 is small, the returns for devoting extra time to quantity are high relative to the returns from allocating time to quality. Here, it makes sense to increase the time devoted to quantity and correspondingly reduce the time spent on quality. As Adel continues to increase the amount of time he spends on quantity, the marginal benefit declines.[31] At the optimum t_1^*, the marginal returns are equal. Beyond t_1^*, the marginal returns from allocating time to quantity are less than for allocating time to quality.

If Adel's supervisor chooses α_1 and α_2 so that the marginal return for one of the activities is always higher over the relevant range, $0 \leq t_1 \leq 10$, Adel will devote all 10 hours to the activity with the higher marginal return (there is a corner solution).

Solving Equation (15.10) for t_1 yields

$$t_1 = 9(\alpha_1/\alpha_2)^2 \qquad (15.11)$$

This equation shows that when $\alpha_1 = \alpha_2$, Adel will spend 9 hours producing output and 1 hour checking its quality. Observing how t_1 and t_2 change with changes in the α's provides two important insights:

- A manager can motivate an employee to devote more time to a task in two ways: First, the manager can increase the incentive coefficient for that task. Second, the manager can reduce the incentive coefficient for the alternative task. In our example, Adel will devote more time to quantity if either α_1 is increased or α_2 is decreased. Increasing α_1 increases the direct return from investing in quantity, while decreasing α_2 reduces the opportunity cost (the compensation that is lost from not investing in quality).

- If an incentive coefficient for a given task is sufficiently small, relative to the other incentive coefficient, an employee will devote no time to the task. In our example, if $(\alpha_1/\alpha_2)^2 > 1.12$, Adel will devote no time to quality $(1.12 \times 9 > 10$ hours). This result indicates that if a manager wants an employee to devote time to multiple tasks, the manager must be careful to provide balanced incentives. Setting too strong an incentive for one task can undermine effort on other tasks.

[31]Technical note: For simplicity, we assume that time devoted to producing quantity is more strenuous than that devoted to quality. Thus, with more time devoted to quantity, he becomes tired and less productive. We have assumed that the marginal benefit from allocating time to quality is constant. This assumption is not necessary.

An Application: Telecommuting Recently, there has been an increase in the use of telecommuting by large firms—working out of an office in the employee's own home. The asserted benefits of this practice are (1) companies can reduce office expense—it can be less expensive to reimburse an employee for a home office than to provide office space in an urban center, (2) employees avoid wasteful commutes to work, (3) firms can hire higher-quality employees at lower wages by offering them the flexibility to work out of their homes (for instance, employees can balance child care and career demands more easily), and (4) employees can be closer to customers (for example, salespeople frequently have homes in their sales territories).

One potential drawback with telecommuting is the lost synergy that results from having employees work at separate locations. For instance, there is likely to be less information sharing, team production, and so on. While computer technologies (such as e-mail) reduce these concerns, they frequently are still important and limit the viability of telecommuting in many occupations. For instance, it would simply be infeasible for a dental assistant to telecommute. Another is the reduced ability to share specific equipment when individuals work from different locations. Our focus is on a third potential concern with telecommuting—the problem of motivating employees to exert effort on their jobs.

In analyzing telecommuting, it is useful to envision the employee being at home and choosing how to allocate time between two activities, home and work. The incentive coefficient for home activities (α_1) is the personal benefit the employee obtains from spending extra time playing with children, watching television, working in the garden, and so on. The incentive coefficient for working on company activities (α_2) depends on the compensation plan.

Viewed in this context, the multitask model has at least two important points relating to telecommuting. First, it usually is important to provide incentive compensation to telecommuters.[32] Without sufficient incentives, employees tend to shirk and devote too much of their time to home activities rather than work. Second, the most viable jobs for telecommuting are those where output is easily measured, and thus incentive compensation can be used most readily. For instance, sales jobs often are good candidates for telecommuting, since incentives can be provided by sales commissions. (Synergies from having salespeople work out of a central location also are likely to be relatively low.) If it is difficult to measure employee output, it can be better to *require the employee to come*

Some Costs and Benefits of Telecommuting

Cisco Systems, the computer-networking company, claims that telecommuters improve their productivity 25 percent and save the company $1 million of overhead. Telecommuters tend to be in high-tech or knowledge-driven industries. In 1998 about 20 percent of IBM's 270,000 global employees spent at least two days a week at home or visiting clients. However, not all companies enthusiastically endorse telecommuting programs. One consultant estimates that 20 percent of the programs fail—causes include resistant managers, isolated employees, and insufficient opportunities for teamwork. Telecommuters have fewer opportunities to talk shop. Informal communications are reduced. IBM decided to schedule meetings and other social interactions that used to happen automatically. Arthur Andersen hosts informal lunches. Other companies require telecommuters to spend at least a day or two at the office.

Source: A. Tergesen (1998), "Making Stay-at-Homes Feel Welcome," *Business Week* (October 12), 155–156.

---

[32]As discussed in the text, this incentive pay need not take the form of a commission or a piece rate. Rather, it can be a bonus plan, a promotion based on performance, and so on.

to work at a central location. This requirement has two effects. First, it is easier to monitor the employee's efforts. Second, it is equivalent to reducing the incentive coefficient on home activities to zero (the employee is unable to devote time to home activities and thus cannot gain from these activities). Since there are fewer activities that compete for their time, employees spend more time on work-related activities.

Appendix Problem

Life insurance agents focus on selling policies. The company expects little follow-up in terms of providing ongoing customer service. In contrast, auto insurance agents often are expected to provide ongoing customer assistance after a policy is sold (answering questions about the policy, providing assistance in filing claims, and so on).

Some insurance companies use independent agents to sell their policies. These agents are paid solely on commission and are often allowed to sell the products of other companies (the agent presents the customer with a choice of plans across multiple companies). Other insurance companies hire their own agents. These employees are restricted from selling other companies' products and are sometimes paid a salary in addition to any commission they might receive.

1. Which type of insurance company, life or auto, is more likely to use the in-house agent? Explain. (Be sure to discuss why the in-house agent faces product restrictions and is not always paid on a pure commission basis.)

2. Some auto insurance companies separate the tasks of selling and customer service and assign them to different people. Why do you think they do this?

Suggested Readings

G. Baker, M. Jensen, and K. Murphy (1988), "Compensation and Incentives: Practice versus Theory," *Journal of Finance* 43, 593–616.

J. McMillan (1992), *Games, Strategies, and Managers* (Oxford University Press: New York), 91–129.

P. Milgrom and J. Roberts (1992), *Economics, Organization, and Management* (Prentice Hall: Englewood Cliffs, NJ), 206–247.

Review Questions

15–1. Evaluate the statement: "Employers want employees to work as hard as possible."

15–2. Two employees are assigned to work overseas for a 2-year period. One person sells his house in the United States, whereas the other leases it for 2 years to another family. Which house do you think will be in better condition after the 2 years? Explain.

15–3. Explain why an investor is usually better off if she holds a diversified portfolio rather than investing all her resources in the stock of one company.

15–4. Discuss trade-offs between efficient risk bearing and incentives in compensation plans.

15–5. Some companies reward salespeople based on their performance relative to other salespeople in the company. Why would a company want to do this?

15–6. Evaluate the statement: "Profit-sharing plans are good; they encourage teamwork."

15–7. Some school districts have compensated teachers based on the performance of students on standardized tests. Do you think this is a good idea? Explain.

15–8. Evaluate the following statement: "John is paid a straight salary with no bonus pay. Obviously, he has no incentives to do a good job."

15–9. Mrs. Fields' Cookie Company is a very successful company out of Salt Lake City, Utah. The company sells freshly baked cookies to customers in shopping malls. The company has expanded and opened outlets in other cities such as San Francisco. Debbie Fields has been on the cover of several business magazines. The articles stress that Mrs. Fields works very long hours and is often at the stores monitoring the quality of the product and making sure the cookies are produced with "tender loving care." The Fields have earned millions of dollars from this business. In 1986, they were planning to open new outlets throughout the country. They had a policy that they would not franchise units. To quote Mrs. Fields, "We do not want to turn into just another fast-food franchise company. Our success is based on high-quality products produced with great care and love. We do not want to lose this quality by expanding through franchises. Rather, we prefer to maintain ownership of all units to ensure continued good service and quality." Evaluate the Fields' franchising policy.

15–10. The Roman Empire taxed many faraway provinces. Rome would auction the rights to tax collection to the highest bidder. The winning bidder was given the right to set the tax rate for the province and the right to collect (and keep) the taxes. In turn, the winner would pay the bid amount to the Roman government. Assume (1) that the Emperor is a young man interested in maximizing the present value of all future revenues to Rome from auctioning off the tax rights, and (2) that the auction for the rights to each province is conducted annually.
   a. Give two reasons why Rome would auction off the rights to tax collection rather than simply send a Roman soldier to collect the taxes.
   b. Discuss two problems this system might generate for the Emperor.

15–11. There has been an increased emphasis on compensating employees through incentive pay. High incentive pay, however, is not likely to be productive in all settings. Discuss the factors that are likely to favor paying high incentive pay to employees.

15–12. In 1995, Philip Morris Company ratified a new labor pact that gave employees stock in lieu of pay increases. The agreement covered 7,800 employees, with each employee being given 94 shares (1994 value of about $60 per share). Employees cannot sell the stock for at least a year and forfeit the stock if they quit or are fired before the year expires. *Business Week*[33] argued that the "deal was good for Philip Morris" because the employees' base pay and fringe benefits did not rise. Also "current shareholders' shares won't be diluted, since employees probably will get less than 500,000 shares out of 850 million outstanding." Discuss the pros and cons of this policy compared to a policy of simply giving a cash bonus to employees of a similar dollar value.

15–13. Two successful firms are observed with quite different compensation plans for their salespeople. One firm pays its salespeople on a commission basis, whereas the other firm pays its salespeople fixed salaries. Do you think that one of the two companies is making a mistake? Explain.

15–14. You work for a compensation consulting firm. You are designing a pay package for the CEO of a major corporation. The board has asked you to choose the parameters *a, b,* and *c,* in the following pay contract:

$$\text{Pay} = a + b[(\text{company stock return}) - c(\text{industry stock return})]$$

Discuss the key factors that will influence your recommendation for each of these three parameters.

15–15. You are a sales manager at the XYZ Corporation. You want to hire a new sales representative. You plan to make an offer to Sally Gomez. You can pay Sally a fixed salary of $20,000 per year or a 10 percent sales commission plus α (a fixed component in the compensation formula). She has a competing offer at another company for $20,000. You anticipate you can hire her if you meet the $20,000 fixed salary offer.
   Sally's sales will either be high or low depending on whether she gets a corporate account. If she gets the account, sales will be $100,000. If she does not, sales will be $10,000. The probability of getting the account is .7. This probability is beyond Sally's control. Sally's utility function can be represented by

$$u(\text{compensation}) = (\text{compensation})^2 \tag{1}$$

[33]A. Bernstein (1995), "At Philip Morris, Blue Chips for Blue Collars," *Business Week* (March 27), 38.

She seeks to maximize *expected utility*. Expected utilities under the two plans are

$$\text{Fixed salary: } u = (20{,}000)^{1/2} \tag{2}$$

$$\text{10 percent plan: } u = .7(\alpha + 10{,}000)^{1/2} + .3(\alpha + \$1{,}000)^{1/2} \tag{3}$$

a. Sketch the graph of the function $u(x) = (x)^{1/2}$.
b. Is Sally's utility function convex or concave? Is she risk-loving or risk-averse?
c. What α makes Sally indifferent between the two plans?
d. As the sales manager, which plan do you select? Give an explanation that shows why this plan is optimal.

15–16. Susan Jones is a salesperson at Radex Co. Her utility function can be represented by $U = C^2$, where C is her compensation.
    a. The company is considering paying her a sales commission rather than a straight salary. The sales manager, however, is concerned that he will have to pay her a compensating differential for imposing risk on her that is beyond her control (sales at Radex are heavily dependent on macroeconomic factors and central company policies). Is the sales manager's concern about paying Susan higher compensation justified? Explain.
    b. Is this example representative of the typical worker in most companies? Explain.

15–17. Top executives of European firms are typically paid substantially less than the top executives of American firms. They are also paid differently. For example, stock options are much more common among American than European executives. Do these differences imply (**a**) that American executives are overpaid, and (**b**) that the form of the compensation in either America or Europe is suboptimal? Explain.

15–18. American accounting rules do not require firms to expense stock options on their accounting statements. Thus, firms can grant executive stock options without impacting "bottom-line performance." Correspondingly, some people argue that the primary reason firms pay executives in the form of stock options is that they are free. Do you agree (1) that stock options are free and (2) that this is the primary reason for paying executives in options? Explain.

15–19. Bobby's Burgers is a large restaurant chain with nearly 10,000 units worldwide. It is experiencing incentive problems among its outlet managers. The managers are not working very hard and are letting quality deteriorate at their units. CEO, Bobby Jones, is considering a stock plan where each unit manager would be given 500 shares of stock in Bobby's Burgers. He reasons that making the managers part owners of the company will motivate better service.
    a. Critically evaluate the proposed stock plan.
    b. Discuss other ways that Bobby Jones might motivate increased effort at the units.

15–20. How does the concept of a *risk premium* in incentive compensation relate to the concept of a *compensating differential* in compensation policy?

15–21. Consider two successful sales companies. One company pays its salespeople a high commission, whereas the other pays its salespeople a straight salary. Assume that both companies are paying their salespeople in an optimal manner. Explain potential differences in the firms that might help to explain the difference in pay policy.

Chapter 16
Individual Performance Evaluation

Lincoln Electric Company, headquartered in Cleveland, Ohio, was founded in 1895 to manufacture electric motors and generators.[1] In the early part of the twentieth century, the firm became the premier supplier of electric arc welding machines and welding disposables (electrodes). It 1999, Lincoln manufactured welding and cutting supplies and industrial electric motors in 20 plants across 14 countries. Prior to expanding manufacturing operations outside the United States in the

[1] Details of this example are from N. Fast and N. Berg (1975), "The Lincoln Electric Company," Harvard Business School Case 376-028 and Lincoln Electric's financial reports.

1980s, Lincoln Electric had an almost unbroken string of profitable operations and often was cited as a model of productivity gains and cost savings.

At the heart of Lincoln Electric's success has been a strategy of building quality products at a cost lower than that of its competitors and passing these savings to customers by continuously lowering prices. Lincoln has been able to implement this strategy, in part, through an employee incentive system that fosters labor productivity increases arising from a pay-for-performance compensation plan. For production employees, wages are based entirely on piecework. In addition, they receive a year-end bonus which averages approximately 100 percent of regular compensation.

A key element of Lincoln's organizational architecture, and the topic of this chapter, is its performance-evaluation system. There are two components of Lincoln's performance evaluation: pieces produced and merit rating. The first component is an objective, readily quantifiable performance measure for each production employee—the number of good units produced. The employee's wage is equal to a piece rate times the number of good units produced. (Employees are not paid for defects.) The piece rates, set by the time study department, allow employees producing at a standard rate to earn a wage comparable to those for similar jobs in the local labor market. However, by working hard—in some cases even through meal and coffee breaks—employees can double and sometimes triple their pay. Moreover, Lincoln's policies prohibit piece-rate changes simply because an employee is making "too much" money. Finally, any employee who has been at Lincoln for at least 2 years is guaranteed employment for at least 75 percent of the standard 40-hour week.

The second component of Lincoln's evaluation system is the employee's merit rating. These ratings are used to determine the employee's share of the bonus pool. Although there is substantial annual variation, the size of the bonus pool approximately equals total wages and is about twice Lincoln's net income after taxes. Each employee's merit evaluation is based on employee dependability, quality, output, ideas, and cooperation—all of which are assessed primarily by the employee's immediate supervisor.

Two important observations emerge from Lincoln Electric. First, the reward system uses as an input the output from the performance-evaluation system—the two systems are linked. Second, as measures of performance, firms use items that range from quite objective and explicit (units produced) to extremely subjective (dependability and cooperation).

Employee performance is evaluated for at least two reasons. First, performance evaluation provides employees with feedback on job achievement that provides important information on how they might improve performance. For example, additional training in particular areas might be indicated. Second, performance evaluation is used

Japanese Car Makers Adopt Performance Evaluations

The large Japanese automobile companies are adopting traditional Western performance-evaluation systems to link compensation and promotion more closely to individual performance. Honda and Toyota have been examples of lifetime employment in Japan's auto industry. But in 1993 and 1994, both companies announced plans to change this practice. In 1993, Honda became the first Japanese car company to adopt a merit-pay plan that ties the manager's pay to achieving performance goals. In 1994, Toyota announced that it would depart from its seniority-based pay and promotion system. Mazda and Nissan announced they were adopting merit-pay systems for their managers in the summer of 1994.

Source: R. Johnson (1994), "Advance or Perish, Honda Tells Managers,"
Automotive News (March 18).

in determining rewards and sanctions—wages, raises, bonuses, promotions, reassignments, and dismissals. These two purposes create somewhat different incentives. For example, if evaluations were used exclusively to provide feedback, employees would have fewer incentives to distort their evaluations to make themselves look better. But distortions to improve reported performance are more likely if employees are rewarded based on measured performance.

In this chapter, we focus primarily on the second reason for performance evaluation—as input for setting rewards and sanctions for employees. This chapter as well as the next describes the performance-evaluation system, the third leg of our three-legged stool that constitutes the firm's organizational architecture. Performance evaluation involves evaluating both individual employees and subunits of the firm. This chapter focuses on individual performance evaluation. Chapter 17 examines issues in evaluating subunits within the firm.

To organize our discussion of individual performance evaluation, we return to the basic principal-agent model presented in Chapter 15. In that model, the employee's output Q depends on effort e and a random component μ:

$$Q = \alpha e + \mu \tag{16.1}$$

where α is the employee's marginal productivity. For every unit of effort, α units of output are expected. In this model, e and μ are unobservable by management, but α is known by both management and the employee. If the employee is paid a fixed wage, independent of output Q, the employee has incentives to shirk because low Q can be blamed on negative μ, which is not observable. (Remember, effort is costly to the employee.) To limit such shirking, the firm bases employee compensation on output:

$$\text{Employee compensation} = W_0 + \beta Q \tag{16.2}$$

where β represents the sensitivity of pay to performance. Such compensation contracts create incentives for employees to reduce their shirking on effort. But these contracts also impose risk on employees because pay is now a function of μ, the random component in the production of output. Since the employee is risk-averse, the firm must compensate the employee for bearing this risk or else the employee will work someplace else. This additional compensation for bearing such risk is called a *compensating differential*. Thus, owners of firms must trade off the additional effort the employees will exert from more powerful incentives with the larger compensating differential to bear this risk.

In this basic principal-agent model, output is assumed contractible; Q is an *objective performance measure*. The employee and the firm can execute compensation contracts based on Q at relatively low cost. Hence, compensation and performance evaluation (two legs of the stool) are explicitly linked.

The basic model leading to Equation (16.2)—and Equation (16.3), which follows—implicitly includes the following assumptions:

- The principal knows the employee's production function ($Q = \alpha e + \mu$), but not the actual values for e and μ.
- Output can be observed at zero cost.
- There is a only one quantitative measure of performance—output.
- The employee produces a single output.
- The employee cannot game the performance measure.
- The employee works independently; there is no team production.
- Any mutually beneficial contract is feasible; labor markets are unregulated.

Clearly in practice, managers must implement performance-evaluation systems in situations that do not conform to some or all of these assumptions. The remaining sections of this chapter describe various issues that arise when these assumptions are relaxed.

Setting Performance Benchmarks

Solving for the optimal β in Equation (16.2) requires management to know α in Equation (16.1). Since the employee's marginal productivity is not readily observable, management must estimate it. To illustrate the issues involved in estimating the employee's marginal productivity, consider the following simplified example. Conrad Mueller can assemble a particular model of welder at the following daily rate:

$$\text{Units assembled} = 5e_c + \mu_c \qquad (16.3)$$

where e_c is the number of hours of normal effort worked, and μ_c is a random error term. If Conrad worked 8 hours at a normal effort level, $e_c = 8$, then on average he would assemble 40 welders (5 $\times$ 8). On average, the error μ_c is zero. If Conrad worked 8 hours but at a faster, more strenuous pace ($e_c > 8$)—the equivalent of, say, 12 hours at a normal effort level ($e_c = 12$)—then 60 units per day would be assembled on average. If he slacked off and took numerous short breaks, e_c might only be 5, and 25 units on average would be assembled.

While the average error μ_c is zero, the number of units assembled is subject to potentially large shocks; this means that the variance of μ_c is not zero. For example, if Conrad were to receive low-quality parts or subassemblies, the number of units assembled would be down even if Conrad were to expend normal amounts of effort ($e_c = 8$) because more time would be required to fit together each slightly out-of-specification part. Or perhaps Conrad might be idled for a few minutes each hour waiting for parts delivery. In these cases, μ_c would be negative. Alternatively, he might get lucky and assemble more than $5e_c$ units because of an unusually well produced set of parts, ample parts inventory, productive tools, or few distractions.

The assembly department in the preceding example might establish a benchmark of 40 welders assembled per employee per day. Production above 40 then would be considered good performance and less than 40 considered poor performance. The standard of 40 is absolute in the sense that it is fixed and known before the employee exerts effort. Management, however, might know neither the exact relation between effort and production (welders assembled = $5e + \mu$) nor that the average employee exerted 8 units of effort a day. Thus, the output of the average assembler must be estimated. There are at least two ways to do this: time and motion studies and historical production data analysis.

Time and Motion Studies

In time and motion studies, industrial engineers estimate how much time a particular task requires, with the goal of determining the most effective work method. Motion studies involve the systematic analysis of work methods, considering the raw materials, the design of the product, the process, the tools, and the activity at each step. Besides focusing on how long a particular activity should take, industrial engineers often are able to redesign the product or process to reduce the time required. Time studies employ a wide variety of techniques for determining the duration a particular activity requires under certain standard conditions. Work sampling (one type of time study) involves selecting a large number of observations taken at random intervals and observing how long employees take performing various components of the job. Time and motion studies often are expensive in terms of engineering time used in the studies. They usually must be redone whenever product design changes or new equipment is introduced. They also suffer from potential bias because of employees' incentives to establish lower quotas by underperforming during the study period.

Past Performance and the Ratchet Effect

Another common mechanism for setting performance goals uses historical data on past performance. Unfortunately, this method often leads to a perverse incentive called the *ratchet effect*.[2] The ratchet effect refers to basing next year's standard of performance on this year's actual performance. But performance targets usually are adjusted in only one direction: upward. A poor year usually causes subsequent years' targets to be reduced not at all, or to be reduced by very little. This "ratcheting up" of standards discourages employees from exceeding the quota substantially to avoid raising the standard for future periods by too much.[3] Many illustrations of dysfunctional behaviors induced by the ratchet effect exist:

- Companies often base a salesperson's bonus on meeting target sales where the target is based on last year's sales. If salespeople expect an unusually good year, they often will try to defer some sales into the next fiscal year. For instance, they might take the customer's order but delay processing it until the next fiscal year.

- In the old Soviet Union, central planners would set a plant's production quota based on past experience. Plant managers meeting their targets received various rewards, and those missing the target were punished. This created incentives for managers to exceed the quota just barely.

- In one automobile engine assembly plant, a labor productivity performance goal was mandated each year. Each department's target was based in part on last year's performance plus an increase. This created incentives for managers to defer making big productivity improvements in any one year, preferring instead to spread them over several years.[4]

Lincoln Electric avoids the dysfunctional problems of the ratchet effect by its policy that the piecework rate cannot be changed even if the employee is making too much money. Once a piecework rate is set by the time study department, it is never changed until production methods or processes are changed, or unless the employee challenges the rate and a new time study is conducted.

Another way to reduce problems caused by ratcheting up each year's performance targets is more frequent job rotation. If you know that next year someone else has to meet the sales figures you achieve this year, you will sell more now. However, job rotation can destroy job-specific human capital such as customer-specific relationships.

[2]A. Leone and S. Rock (2000), "Empirical Tests of Budget Ratcheting and Its Effect on Managers' Discretionary Accrual Choices," University of Rochester.

[3]Some of the incentive not to exceed the target by a large amount is reduced if the employee's bonus is a function of the amount by which output exceeds the target. The actual dysfunctional incentives created by the ratchet effect depend on the precise form of the incentive compensation contract. For example, if past performance is used to set β in Equation (16.2), very different incentives are created than if past performance is used to set a target performance and a fixed bonus is paid so long as actual output exceeds this target.

[4]R. Kaplan and A. Sweeney (1993), "Peoria Engine Plant (A)," Harvard Business School Case 9-193-082.

Measurement Costs

When it is costly to observe the employee's output, performance evaluation becomes much more complicated—and interesting. For example, your server at the restaurant might appear to have performed well. But you only begin to suspect that you were served caffeinated instead of decaffeinated coffee at 2 AM when you still cannot sleep. The quality of a patent attorney's work is not known until a challenge to the patent is filed. Measuring an elementary teacher's output is complex. Relying on standardized test scores captures only a part of student learning. Or, a research scientist's output is difficult to quantify and observe. "Observability," "verifiability," and "contractibility" ultimately are questions of cost. Almost everything is observable—even effort—at some cost. For example, in jobs where physical effort is required, how hard an employee works might be measured by attaching heart-rate monitors or videotaping the person. But, such measurements frequently are quite costly.

Costs are incurred in generating performance measures. For example, accounting systems must be developed and maintained to keep track of sales, costs, quality, or divisional profits. Computer systems and software capable of producing detailed reports are more complicated. And if the measures are used for performance evaluation, additional management and clerical time must be spent ensuring the accuracy of the performance measures. High measurement costs can lower the net benefits of tying pay to performance.

In our simple principal-agent model, the employee's output is used in setting compensation. However, output depends on random factors. Even if output were costlessly observable, it still can be optimal to expend additional resources to measure the employee's effort level more precisely. To the extent the firm can reduce the employee's exposure to the variance of these random factors via more sophisticated performance measures, the lower the compensating differential the firm must pay the employee to bear this risk. As we noted in Chapter 15, the informativeness principle implies that whenever low-cost information is available that allows a more accurate assessment of the employee's effort, such information should be used in assessing performance. A value-maximizing firm will go to the point where the incremental cost of increasing the precision of its performance measurement (through more sophisticated accounting and information systems, for instance) equals the incremental benefits. These benefits include the reduction in the risk premium that must be paid to employees.

In general, the more incentive pay in the employee's compensation package, the more risk the employee bears and the more the firm should spend on measurement systems to quantify the impact of these random factors. Thus, the choice of the optimum β in Equation (16.2) and the choice of how much to spend measuring performance are jointly determined. These two legs of the stool are complements. Increasing the

---

Measuring What Counts

Determining the weight of an orange may be a low cost, accurate operation. Yet what is weighed is seldom what is truly valued. The skin of the orange hides its pulp, making a direct measurement of the desired attributes costly. Thus the taste and amount of juice it contains are always a bit surprising.

Source: Y. Barzel (1982), "Measurement Cost and the Organization of Markets," *Journal of Law & Economics* XXV, 27–48.

Lowering Measurement Costs in Self-Service Laundries

Most coin-operated laundries are grungy, hot, and generally unattractive operations. They also tend to be mom-and-pop operations. But that is beginning to change. New national chains are beginning to emerge. Duds 'n Suds offered cocktails along with clothes cleaning. SpinCycle and Laundromax are national chains twice as large as most laundries, with full-time attendants, industrial-strength machines, air conditioning, plenty of televisions, and other amenities. At the heart of this change of ownership is the use of debit cards. Coin-operated laundries are ripe for employee theft of the cash. As a result, the stores typically were operated by the owners. Debit cards eliminate coins altogether, thereby lowering measurement costs and facilitating the transformation of mom-and-pop stores into corporate chains.

Source: R. Ho (1998), "Is There a Place for the Blockbuster of Coin
Laundries?" *The Wall Street Journal* (July 7), B1.

---

employee's incentive compensation β should be accompanied by increasing the precision with which effort is measured.[5]

In some cases, observing and measuring the employee's output becomes so expensive that the firm begins to look for alternative proxy variables that capture employee performance. For example, managers often are evaluated on the accounting profits of their divisions, even though the firm ultimately is interested in the total value created by its managers. This value includes not only short-term divisional profits (as measured by the accounting system) but future expected profits, as well as the effects of the manager's efforts on other divisions' profits. Similarly, schoolteachers often are evaluated on their students' performance on standardized tests, even though the school ultimately is interested in broader, harder-to-measure indicators of learning. Whether or not a particular proxy variable is good for purposes of performance evaluation depends on whether the employee's actions have similar effects on both the proxy variable and the underlying output variable.[6] For example, if paying a manager on divisional profits motivates more diligent effort as well as actions that increase underlying value, then divisional profits would be a productive performance measure. Alternatively, to the extent divisional profits motivate actions that do not enhance value (for example, sacrificing substantial future profits to achieve only a modest increase in near-term profits), divisional profits are a poor performance measure. Ill-designed performance measures promote opportunism and gaming.

Opportunism

Employees often behave opportunistically in ways that affect their performance evaluation. This section describes two examples of such opportunism: gaming and the horizon problem.

Gaming

Our basic principal-agent model assumes that the employee shirks only in the amount of effort exerted this period. If measured output is not perfectly correlated with firm value, employees endeavoring to increase reported output might cause the firm's value to

[5]For a more formal treatment of this principle, see P. Milgrom and J. Roberts (1992), *Economics, Organizations, and Management* (Prentice Hall: Englewood Cliffs, NJ), 226.

[6]G. Baker (1992), "Incentive Contracts and Performance Measurement," *Journal of Political Economy* 100, 598–614.

Gaming Objective Performance-Evaluation Systems

This example illustrates how members of one local management team, who did not want to lose their jobs, successfully gamed the performance-evaluation system their company used in deciding when to close unprofitable mines.

In this particular company, mines were shut down after the yield per ton of ore dropped below a certain level. One old marginal mine managed to stay open for several years because of the strategic behavior of its management. It happened that the mine contained one very rich pocket of ore. Instead of mining this all at once, the management used it as its reserve. Every time the yield of the ore it was mining fell below an acceptable level, it would mix in a little high-grade ore so the mine would remain open.

Source: E. Lawler and J. Rhode (1976), *Information and Control in Organizations* (Goodyear Publishing: Santa Monica, CA), 87–88.

decline. Thus, objective measures of output can motivate employees to engage in dysfunctional activities to improve their evaluations. Recall the costs Sears incurred when its mechanics overcharged customers for unneeded car repairs (Chapter 2). Doing so increased the mechanics' incomes but was extraordinarily damaging to Sears. Other examples include the following: A salesperson offers customers discounts to shift sales from one evaluation period to another. An employee paid based on output reduces quality to increase output. A refuse hauler, compensated on the weight of trash delivered to the landfill, uses a fire hose to top off his load with water before weighing in at the truck scales. Finally, Lincoln Electric installed counters on typewriters to record the number of characters typed by their secretaries who were paid on this basis. But piecework for secretaries was abandoned when one secretary, who earned much more than the others, was found staying at her desk during lunch and coffee breaks depressing a repeating key on her keyboard, thus typing totally useless pages quite rapidly. Hence, seemingly objective measures of performance such as sales or output often create incentives for employees to take value-reducing actions (such as lowering product quality) if such actions increase their measured performance.

Horizon Problem

Objective output measures frequently focus on the near term because of the difficulty of objectively measuring consequences that might occur in the future. Short-run, objective performance measures can cause employees—especially those about to change jobs or

Gaming Compensation Plans

Insurance agents, sales managers, and some executives at Prudential Insurance Company are paid commissions based on sales volume. To boost sales, agents engaged in "churning." Agents would convince customers who had life insurance policies with large cash values built up to use the cash balance to buy bigger policies on the promise that it wouldn't cost them anything. Some customers weren't even told the cash value was being used this way. Once the cash values were exhausted paying the premiums on the new policies, many policyholders, some elderly, were hit with big, unexpected premium bills. Those customers who couldn't pay lost their insurance coverage. The technique kept the new policies in force long enough for the agents to collect large commissions. In 1997, Prudential agreed to pay $410 million to settle a class-action suit related to deceptive sales practices.

Source: L. Scism and S. Paltrow (1998), "Prudential's Auditors Gave Early Warnings about Sales Abuses," *The Wall Street Journal* (July 7), A1.

Relative Performance Evaluation in Banking

Research suggests that firms use relative performance evaluation. One study focuses on subsidiary bank managers in multibank holding companies. Turnover of these managers is greater when their own bank's performance is poor and when the median bank's performance in the same holding company is high. This study's findings are consistent with market and industry risk being filtered out in making compensation and retention decisions.

Source: D. Blackwell, J. Brickley, and M. Weisbach (1994), "Accounting Information and Internal Performance Evaluation: Evidence from Texas Banks," *Journal of Accounting and Economics* 17, 331–358.

leave the firm—to concentrate their efforts on producing results that will influence their appraisals favorably over their remaining horizon with the firm (see Chapter 10). For example, a 64-year-old salesperson, paid on commission and expecting to retire at age 65, has little incentive to work at developing long-term customer relationships.

Relative Performance Evaluation

Multiple employees performing similar tasks potentially can provide useful additional signals about the random errors affecting individual employees. For example, if in addition to Conrad, Dina van den Brink also assembles welders and her output is

$$\text{Units assembled by Dina} = 5e_d + \mu_d \qquad (16.4)$$

where e_d is the number of hours of normal effort worked by Dina, and μ_d is her random error term. In assembling welders, both Conrad and Dina expect that if they exert average effort of $e = 8$, each expects to produce 40 units. If Conrad's and Dina's error terms, μ_c and μ_d, are positively correlated because they depend on many of the same conditions (raw material quality and working conditions), then in evaluating Conrad's performance, management can look at Dina's output for information about uncontrollable factors affecting Conrad's production. If Dina were to have unusually low output, it is likely that there was some shock that would have lowered Conrad's output, as well.

More generally, suppose that in addition to Conrad and Dina, a number of other employees also assemble the same welders. As we noted in Chapter 15, the informativeness principle implies that an important source of information about an employee's effort is the output of coworkers performing similar tasks. Thus to reduce the risk of noncontrollable factors, management uses information about the average number of welders assembled by all these employees. Forty units per employee per day is the expected number of welders, given normal quality and no unusual events. Suppose the average number of welders across all the employees on a given day was 43. Then for this day, average $\mu = 3 (43 - 40)$. And if Conrad produced 41 welders that day, his compensation would be adjusted by some part of his two-unit shortfall (41–43). Using the output of other employees to adjust the employee's output in the compensation contract is called *relative performance evaluation*. (The appendix to this chapter discusses methods to estimate the optimal adjustment.)

Within-Firm Performance

Using other employees' output within the same firm to estimate the average error is a useful method of reducing risk if they all sell or manufacture the same products and face the same competitors and economywide factors. However, forming a reference

Relative Performance Evaluation for CEOs

CEO compensation (salary plus bonus) and turnover likelihoods depend on relative performance evaluation. Gibbons and Murphy examine 2,214 CEOs serving in 1,295 large, publicly traded, US corporations from 1974 to 1986. They find that CEOs' compensation is positively related to their own stock return performance and negatively related to the stock return in the market and industry. That is, compensation is higher when the CEO's own firm's stock return is higher and when the market or industry stock return is down. Finally, they study the likelihood that the CEO is replaced. Executive turnover is lower the larger the firm's own stock price return and the lower the industry return. If the industry is performing poorly, the CEO is more likely retained, holding everything else constant. However, CEOs also are compensated using awards of stock and options. The realized values of these awards are adjusted for overall market or industry performance only rarely. Thus, although some of the incentives of executives are based on relative performance, others are based on absolute performance.

Source: R. Gibbons and K. Murphy (1990), "Relative Performance Evaluation for Chief Executive Officers," *Industrial and Labor Relations Review* 43, 30S–51S.

group from employees inside the firm also can have drawbacks. Only in rare cases are employees' jobs identical. For instance, some salespeople have large established territories—others, small developing ones. Customer types can vary dramatically across sales territories.

If an internal reference group is formed and its group average is used to assess normal performance, the group has incentives to punish "rate busters"—extremely productive employees who raise the average. In a classic research study known as the Hawthorne experiments, employees were observed hitting colleagues who exceeded the commonly accepted output rate.[7] Thus, explicit employee collusion to hold down the benchmark can occur. Also, instances of sabotage are observed in relative performance evaluations. Instead of working diligently and increasing their own performance, coworkers sabotage their peers within the reference group. Alternatively, employees might try to get themselves classified into a reference group that has weak performance so they will appear above average.

Relative performance evaluation also affects recruiting incentives. Employees often are involved in interviewing and selecting potential colleagues. If paid based on relative performance, such employees have the incentive to recommend hiring less competent new employees. This improves the relative performance of the current employees.

Across-Firm Performance

The Securities and Exchange Commission requires publicly traded firms when describing their executive compensation to select a benchmark reference group of other firms and report how their firm has performed relative to that benchmark. This is an example of selecting a reference group outside the firm. Some firms also employ external benchmarking to overcome the lack of an internal reference group or to avoid the pernicious actions of sabotage and collusion. Firms exchange information directly or do so through a trade association that aggregates information across several firms to mask individual firm data. Thus, average performance in other firms is used as the reference group.

---

[7]H. Parsons (1974), "What Happened at Hawthorne?" *Science* 183 (March 8), 927.

Potential Costs of Relative Performance Evaluations

Individuals gaming performance-evaluation systems are not uncommon. This example illustrates the lengths to which some people will go to sabotage others when their advancement is based on relative performance evaluations:

> I was recently talking to a friend of mine who works at a big bank. When I asked him about his new promotion, he told me how he got it. He managed to crack the network messaging system so that he could monitor all the memos. He also sabotaged the work group software and set back careers of a few company-naive souls who didn't realize that someone was manipulating their appointment calendars. They would miss important meetings and be sent on wild-goose chases, only to look like complete buffoons when they showed up for appointments that were never made. By the time any of these bumpkins knew what hit them, they had a new vice president.

Source: J. Dvorak (1988), "New Age of Villainy," *PC Magazine* (September 27).

There are several disadvantages to external benchmarking. Use of this method often is precluded by a lack of data: Other firms view their performance data as proprietary and thus are unwilling to share it. Even if firms are willing to share data, for firms in the same industry such cooperation is potentially illegal under antitrust laws. Moreover, employees in outside firms may not be subject to the same common shocks as the benchmarking firm's employees. Thus, with external benchmarking the risk to employees might be increased, rather than decreased.

Subjective Performance Evaluation

Most jobs contain numerous dimensions. For example, baseball players have to field the ball, get hits (ranging from bunts to home runs), run the bases, and generally support the team. It is difficult to specify and measure all aspects of the job. If explicit measures are used only for some aspects, employees will deemphasize the unmeasured job attributes. For instance, if a veteran ballplayer is evaluated solely on his hitting, he has fewer incentives to spend time mentoring young ballplayers. Often, the firm augments its use of objective, explicit measures of output and uses more subjective yet comprehensive measures of performance.

Subjective performance reviews are conducted primarily because it is expensive to measure accurately all the dimensions of the employee's output that are valued by the firm. In fact, most employees are not evaluated exclusively based on objective measures. Rather, their performance evaluations tend to include subjective elements. For example, most employees receive annual performance reviews from supervisors. These reviews often form the basis for setting salaries and promotions. Even when compensation is based entirely on objective measures (piece rates in agriculture), the firm reserves the right to fire employees for low-quality production, tardiness, inability to get along with coworkers, or other dysfunctional behavior. Lincoln Electric bases factory employees' wages entirely on piecework—an objective measure. But in addition to this objective measure, Lincoln also uses a subjective merit evaluation to set the employee bonus, which is approximately the same magnitude as wages.

We first describe an important reason firms use subjective performance measures—namely, assigning multiple tasks to employees. Then various subjective evaluation systems are described. Finally, problems with subjective evaluations are summarized.

Multiple Tasks and Unbalanced Effort

As discussed in Chapter 13, multiple tasks often are assigned to one employee because there are efficiency gains from bundling the tasks. For example, secretaries answer phones, word process, file, schedule appointments, and make travel plans. Or, an employee might be expected to sell products to existing customers, contact potential new customers, and fill out sales reports. These tasks all are complementary to selling the product.

Suppose Conrad Mueller performs two tasks, assembling welders and training new employees to assemble welders. Some activities are more easily measured, such as counting the number of welders Conrad assembles; others, like training new assemblers, are more difficult to assess. If Conrad's evaluation is based primarily on the easily measured tasks (welders assembled), he has incentives to concentrate his efforts on these activities. Conrad will not allocate the optimal amount of time to the other unmeasured tasks (see Chapter 15). Remember: *You get what you pay for—and frequently, that is all you get.*

Recall from Chapter 13 that this multitask problem can affect optimal job design. For example, a firm might want to have certain employees concentrate only on assembling welders when complementarities among tasks are low. These employees then could be evaluated on their output of assembled welders. Other employees would concentrate on training new assemblers and correspondingly be evaluated on their training. By separating the tasks, each employee can be given more focused incentives to perform their single task.

Subjective reviews evaluate an employee's performance on a more comprehensive basis. Aspects of the job that are measured less easily can be considered along with more easily measured activities. For example, the supervisor might consider the employee's efforts at being cooperative, being part of a team, being responsive to potential customers, or filling out reports accurately. Conrad's supervisor can observe how he instructs new hires, how patient he is, and how they ultimately perform as assemblers in assessing Conrad's performance as a trainer. Moreover, if Conrad games the performance measure—takes firm-value reducing actions that increase the objective performance measure—his supervisor (if aware of these dysfunctional actions) can penalize Conrad through his subjective performance evaluation.

Subjective Evaluation Methods

There are two widely used subjective performance-appraisal systems: standard-rating-scale systems and goal-based systems. Goal-based systems tend to be more explicit and less subjective than standard-rating-scale systems.

Standard-Rating-Scale Systems   Standard rating scales require the evaluator to rank the employee on a number of different performance factors using, for example, a five-point scale: far exceeds requirements, exceeds requirements, meets all requirements, partially meets requirements, does not meet requirements. The different performance factors judged vary across firms and positions within firms but often include the following:

- Achieves forecasts, budgets, objectives
- Organizes effective performance through oral and written communications
- Sets and attains high performance goals for self and group
- Updates knowledge of job-related skills
- Emphasizes teamwork among subordinates
- Identifies and resolves problems

- Evaluates subordinates objectively
- Ensures equal opportunities for all subordinates

After ranking the employee on each of these narrow criteria, the evaluator then assigns a rating for the overall job: excellent, better than satisfactory, satisfactory, needs further improvement, and unsatisfactory. Most subjective performance appraisals contain a section where the supervisor provides detailed comments on the employee's strengths and weaknesses and offers specific recommendations for improvement and further development.

Goal-Based Systems   In a goal-based system, each employee is given a set of goals for the year. For example, goals might be "hold training sessions for all employees in the department by November 1," or "hire four additional qualified members of minority groups." These goals tend to be more objective and easier to measure than the more vague performance factors used in the standard rating scales such as "emphasizes teamwork." Nonetheless, these goals still are more subjective than standard piecework measures. At the end of the year, the supervisor writes a memo detailing the extent to which each goal has been met. An overall evaluation of the employee is based on the extent to which the goals are achieved.

After evaluators have rated their employees using either a standard rating scale or a goal-based system, evaluators usually then review the evaluations with their supervisors. This helps ensure the accuracy of the review and promotes consistency of criteria across employees. Next, supervisors give copies of the evaluations to the employees and meet with them to review the evaluations. Employees can respond to the evaluation in writing, including the expression of formal disagreement with any of the specifics in the appraisal. Finally, the evaluators and their supervisors review the feedback provided by the evaluators and the employees' responses.

In the majority of cases, the employee's immediate supervisor does the performance evaluation. In some cases, firms have experimented with peer evaluations—especially in situations where teams are important. The benefit of peer evaluations is that peers have information about typical performance in group assignments and the actual contribution of the individual to the team. Offsetting the better specific knowledge of peers is the added costs of training everyone in the team to do evaluations. Moreover, peer evaluation can increase the tensions within the team. For example, some team members might

---

360-Degree Performance Reviews

Privately held W. L. Gore & Associates employs 5,600 employees and manufactures Gore-Tex waterproof fabric. All employees are called associates. There are no "bosses," but each employee is assigned a "sponsor" who acts as a mentor. Gore has been using 360-degree evaluation as part of its performance feedback since 1958. Under this system, annual evaluations are gathered on all associates from the individual's peers, subordinates, and superiors. The evaluations are anonymous and rate employees on their contributions to the success of the business during the past year. All ratings on each employee receive equal weight. Compensation committees composed of sponsors with specialized knowledge of the area use the rankings to award pay increases or performance warnings. Thus, such review systems are not new; much of what is new is the jargon invented to make these performance-evaluation systems appear to be a recent innovation.

Source: J. Lopez (1994), "A Better Way?" *The Wall Street Journal Supplement*
(April 13), R6.

systematically lower everyone else's ratings to make themselves look better. Or, friends may be rated highly to increase their chance of being promoted to supervise their former colleagues. Finally, teammates might decide to collude to give everyone higher performance ratings.

Frequency of Evaluation   Most subjective performance evaluations are conducted yearly, primarily because most salary adjustments are made annually. The benefits of more frequent evaluations (say quarterly) unlikely offset the higher costs. However, there are some examples of more frequent review. For example, new hires typically receive more frequent evaluations; often a new employee is evaluated at the end of 3 months. During this probationary period, the firm must decide whether to keep the individual. Also during this period, frequent feedback helps the employee learn and improve performance. As another example, consultants are evaluated after each professional assignment by the partner-in-charge of the engagement. Especially where team composition changes from project to project, capturing performance-evaluation information on a timely basis is important. The person's performance is known, and there is no reason to wait until the end of the year. Moreover, the evaluation provides more timely information to base subsequent project assignments.

Problems with Subjective Performance Evaluations

There are several potential problems with subjective performance evaluation.

Shirking among Supervisors[8]   Disciplining employees and informing them of their shortcomings often are unpleasant tasks. Supervisors do not capture the full wealth effects of these actions. Hence, potential shirking among supervisors leads to the provision of inaccurate performance evaluations. For example, a supervisor might be reluctant to give adverse ratings to avoid conflict with subordinates. In other cases, supervisors compress ratings around some norm rather than distinguish good and poor performers. Or, a supervisor might rank employees based on personal likes and dislikes rather than on job performance. Bias adds noise to the performance-evaluation system; it typically reduces morale and consequently the employees' incentives to work diligently, thereby lowering overall firm performance.

Indirect empirical evidence suggests that managers tend to assign relatively uniform performance ratings to employees. In a study of 7,000 performance ratings of managers and professionals in two firms, the researchers report that 95 percent of all appraisals were in just two categories: Good and Superior (Outstanding).[9] A survey of employee attitudes at Merck & Co., a large United States pharmaceutical firm, reported the following attitudes[10]:

- Managers are afraid to give experienced people a 1, 2, or 3 rating. It's easier to give everyone a 4 and give new people a 3.

[8]C. Prendergast and R. Topel (1993), "Discretion and Bias in Performance Appraisals," *European Economic Review*, (June), 355–365; C. Prendergast and R. Topel (1996), "Favoritism in Organizations," *Journal of Political Economy* 104 (October) 958–978.

[9]J. Medoff and K. Abraham (1980), "Experience, Performance, and Earnings," *Quarterly Journal of Economics* 95, 703–736.

[10]Quotes excerpted from a 1985 Merck report by K. Murphy (1992), "Performance Measurement and Appraisal: Motivating Managers to Identify and Reward Performance," in W. Bruns (Ed.), *Performance Measurement, Evaluation, and Incentives* (Harvard Business School: Boston), 37–62.

- Charlie's been in that job for 20 years. He hasn't done anything creative for the last 15 years. Do you think my manager would give him a 3 rating? No way! Then he'd have to spend 12 months listening to Charlie complain.
- What's the use of killing yourself? You still get the same rating as everyone else, and you still get the same 5 percent increase. It's demoralizing and demotivating.

This evidence suggests that low-rated, disgruntled employees can impose costs on supervisors. In response, supervisors bias their evaluations. Hence, performance ratings are inaccurate appraisals of the employee's true performance. Biased, inaccurate appraisals reduce the incentive of employees to improve their performance by working harder and can lead to the promotion of less qualified people. Here, the problem lies not in the evaluation system *per se,* but rather in the incentives for the evaluators.

At Lincoln Electric, supervisors have incentives to do a good job because they are evaluated and compensated on the job they do in evaluating lower-level employees. Also, employees can discuss their ratings with senior management. Problems of bias are likely to be lower if the supervisor is held accountable for the future performance of individuals that are promoted based on the supervisor's recommendation.

Forced Distributions   To overcome the tendency to rate all employees "above average," some firms impose a forced distribution where a fixed fraction of employees are assigned to each category (that is, the supervisor must rank a certain percentage of the employees as poor). However, forced distributions may not reflect the true distribution of performance accurately in each work group. Forced ranking systems can cause problems, especially when the size of the group to be evaluated is small. For example, having to rank one of four employees as poor might force the supervisor to rate a good-performing employee as poor; inaccuracies from the forced distribution might be larger than those from a biased supervisor. Moreover, forced distributions do not necessarily reduce the costs imposed on the supervisor. Under a forced distribution, supervisors might assign ratings based on the potential costs employees will impose on them—not based on the employees' true performances.

Performance Reviews under Attack

A survey by the Society for Human Resource Management concluded that more than 90 percent of subjective appraisal systems are unsuccessful. One management consultant described annual job-performance reviews as a "deadly disease." He asserts that virtually every survey finds that most employees who get them and most supervisors doing them rate the process a resounding failure. Consulting firms now find advising companies on how to improve their appraisal process a lucrative and fast-growing business. Some managers find performance appraisals an annual ritual: They pull out last year's review and update it quickly. Consultants disagree about the cause of the problems. Some claim the process does not work because the forms used are outdated or were designed by personnel specialists with limited input from managers who use the forms. Others argue that supervisors are poorly trained to conduct appraisals and give feedback. Or, that supervisors hate giving negative feedback and employees have a hard time accepting any criticism. One consultant recommends that companies should teach "everyone how to give and receive good feedback." Other consultants suggest at least twice-a-year reviews and more frequent informal feedback. Formal written appraisals often are used to combat wrongful-discharge lawsuits. However, such systems can backfire when employees are let go in spite of the fact that they have received acceptable reviews. While universally criticized, subjective performance systems also are pervasive—suggesting that few better alternatives exist.

Source: T. Schellhardt (1996), "It's Time to Evaluate Your Work, and All Involved Are Groaning," *The Wall Street Journal* (November 19), A1.

Influence Costs   Influence costs (discussed in Chapter 12) include those nonproductive activities employees engage in to influence outcomes—in this case, politicking for higher ratings by their supervisor. One potential method of reducing these costs is to rotate supervisors or employees more frequently (getting on the good side of one supervisor is of limited benefit). Rotation of employees, however, can limit potential synergies and cost reductions that arise with repeated interaction between a given manager and employee. New supervisors have limited knowledge of employees' specialized skills. Also, more frequent rotation potentially increases total influence costs, since the employee has more lobbying opportunities.

Reneging   There is the potential that the firm will renege on promises to employees to reward good performance.[11] For example, management might promise to give raises to those who perform well. Afterward, management might unjustifiably say that work was poor to avoid higher payments. It is less likely that an employee will be successful in a lawsuit involving subjective performance measurement than when the employee can document that a firm reneged on an explicit contract involving objective performance measures.

As discussed in Chapter 10, managers in healthy firms generally have incentives to maintain good reputations for honoring implicit contracts. However, reneging on implicit contracts will appear most attractive to firms in financial difficulty (near bankruptcy). Reneging also can occur when a supervisor has a short horizon with the firm and is compensated on business-unit profits. (Unit profits might be increased in the short run by not granting raises to employees.) We discuss these issues further in Chapter 21.

Combining Objective and Subjective Performance Measures

Performance-evaluation systems generally fall on a continuum between the two extremes—objective and subjective evaluation systems. Objective measures consist of items like output and sales that can be quantified easily and thus explicitly measured. Objective measures can be used in formal contracts between the employee and the firm. Subjective measures consist of noncontractible judgments about employee performance (the year-end evaluation from a supervisor). Subjective measures are used in implicit contracts. Few job-performance measures are purely objective or purely subjective; most measures involve mixtures of both. In most cases, organizations that use objective measures also use subjective measures to evaluate the same employee (as does Lincoln Electric, for example). Investment bankers pay bonuses based on fees generated by the employee but also use subjective measures such as the "quality of the deals."[12]

Both objective and subjective performance measures can be inaccurate measures of the employee's contribution to the firm's value. As the accuracy of either measure decreases, more weight will be placed on the other in determining performance (holding its accuracy constant). As the accuracy of each measure decreases, the risk the employee bears increases, as does the compensating differential the employee must be paid.[13]

Besides being inaccurate, both objective and subjective measures can induce various dysfunctional behaviors. We indicated earlier that objective measures can create

---

[11]G. Baker, R. Gibbons, and K. Murphy (1994), "Subjective Performance Measures in Optimal Incentive Contracts," *Quarterly Journal of Economics* CIX, 1125–1156.

[12]Baker, Gibbons, and Murphy (1994).

[13]See C. Prendergast (1999), "The Provision of Incentives in Firms," *Journal of Economic Literature* 37 (March), 7–63, for a survey of the relevant papers.

incentives for gaming, which reduces the firm's value, as in the case of the Sears auto repair business. If supervisors shirk when writing subjective performance reviews, employees' incentives to work diligently are reduced. Also, employees will generate influence costs lobbying for higher subjective ratings. Finally, implicit contracts using subjective measures are more easily abrogated by the firm than formal contracts based on objective measures. Employees must trust that the firm will not renege on implicit contracts. An important constraint on the firm from reneging is its reputation. Thus, firms facing a greater likelihood of financial distress will find subjective evaluations more costly to use.

Because the costs and benefits of objective and subjective measures vary across jobs, in some situations only objective measures are observed, others are mixtures of both, and in other cases, only subjective performance measures are observed. Each firm will face specific costs and benefits of objective and subjective measures and will tailor its performance measures to its circumstances. Moreover, the costs and benefits are likely to vary over various divisions of the firm and jobs. However, employees performing similar tasks in similar industries tend to have similar performance-evaluation systems because the costs and benefits of alternative evaluation methods will be similar.

Both objective and subjective performance measures are costly. The larger these costs, the less firms tend to rely on performance evaluations for setting rewards and punishments. Paying employees straight salary and giving simple cost-of-living raises to all employees will lead to predictable shirking and other incentive problems. Yet these costs still might be lower than the costs of implementing a performance-based incentive plan.

Team Performance

As we discussed in Chapter 12, teams frequently are used at all levels of the organization. Teams are formed because they are more successful at assembling specialized knowledge for decision making than are alternative methods that might be used to pass the knowledge through the traditional hierarchy. As discussed below, teams also can prove useful particularly when one employee's productivity affects the productivity of other employees. For instance, one complaint by employees at Lincoln Electric is that their pay suffers when employees ahead of them on an assembly line are unable to keep them supplied with work.

Team Production

To illustrate the performance problems of teams, again consider welder assemblers Conrad Mueller and Dina van den Brink. To simplify the notation, assume they exert a common effort level *e,* whether in a team or not. If they work independently, their individual output is

$$\text{Individual output} = 5e + \mu \qquad (16.5)$$

where *e* represents the individual effort of either Conrad or Dina and μ is a random error term with zero mean and positive variance. If Conrad and Dina work as a team, they produce

$$\text{Team output} = 4e^2 + \mu \qquad (16.6)$$

For *e* > 2.5, the expected output working as a team is higher than the output of working independently:

$$\text{Expected team output} = 4e^2 > \text{Expected individual output} = 5e + 5e \qquad (16.7)$$

Objective and Subjective Performance Evaluation at Fiat

This example illustrates how one very large company combines both objective and subjective performance reviews into a single, integrated system.

The Italian firm, Fiat, is one of the world's largest corporations, with over 250,000 employees in 16 operating sectors. Although automobiles are its largest product, Fiat also has operating units in railway systems, aviation, publishing and communications, and financial and real estate services. In the 1980s, Fiat introduced a formal management by objectives (MBO) evaluation program for its 500 highest-level managers. Under the MBO program, annual bonuses of up to about 30 percent of base salary were awarded for meeting objectives. Managers had a set of objectives tailored to the specific situations. Managers in charge of profit centers had profit and debt objectives. Profit targets were defined in terms of net profit before taxes. Because Fiat had an extremely high level of debt in the 1980s, profit center managers also were given objectives to lower their group's borrowings. Besides these specific financial objectives, managers had other performance indicators such as increasing sales in particular markets, completing an acquisition, improving quality or customer service, and introducing new products or processes.

Even though managers might meet their particular objectives, unless the larger group also achieved its goals, no bonus would be paid. For example, the Fiat Group has 16 sectors headed by a manager. If the entire Fiat Group failed to meet its objectives, none of the 16 sector managers would receive their bonuses, even though some of them achieved their goals. Each manager had a set of weightings attached to each objective. Unless the manager achieved a minimum level of profits before taxes, no bonus would be paid. Once this threshold profit level was achieved, the weights attached were 20 to 40 percent profits, 10 to 20 percent reducing debt, and 10 to 15 percent for each of three or four other performance targets. Each objective was scored on a 5-point scale, with 3 being the minimum acceptable score. Superiors would set the targets for each objective. In setting the performance targets, the following probabilities of achieving each target were supposed to be used:

Performance Level	Ideal Probability of Achievement
3 (threshold)	90–99%
4 (good)	50–60%
5 (excellent)	10–20%

For example, suppose "install new production-control system" was an objective that had a weighting of 20 percent. If the system was installed by November, it is judged as a 3 threshold. To achieve a 4, installation must be completed by October. And a 5 is earned if completed by September. If actual completion is October, a 4 is earned with a weighting of 20 percent and 0.80 (4 × 20%) was added to the manager's other performance objectives to compute an overall grade—say, 3.69. A performance rating of 3 would receive a bonus of 12 percent of salary. Ratings below 3 would receive no bonus. A rating of 4 would receive an 18 percent bonus, and a 5 would receive a 30 percent bonus. Fractional ratings are scaled (e.g., a 3.69 receives 12% + 0.69 × [18% − 12%] or 16.14%). The median manager's rating was between 4.1 and 4.4. In any given year about 10 percent of the managers were rated below 3.0 and about 15 percent were rated 4.9 or better.

This performance-evaluation system at Fiat is similar to those used by many large United States corporations.

Source: K. Merchant and A. Riccaboni (1992), "Evolution of Performance-Based Management Incentives at the Fiat Group," in W. Bruns (Ed.), *Performance Measurement, Evaluation, and Incentives* (Harvard Business School: Boston), 63–96.

As displayed in Figure 16.1, Conrad and Dina's team output always is larger than the sum of their individual outputs whenever they each exert 2.5 units of effort (they jointly exert 5 units of effort).

In this example, there are team-production effects: Output is potentially higher when Dina and Conrad work as a team. Team output can be larger because Dina and Conrad

Figure 16.1 Comparing Individual and Team Outputs

When Conrad and Dina each exert at least 2.5 units of effort, their team output is greater than their outputs working independently.

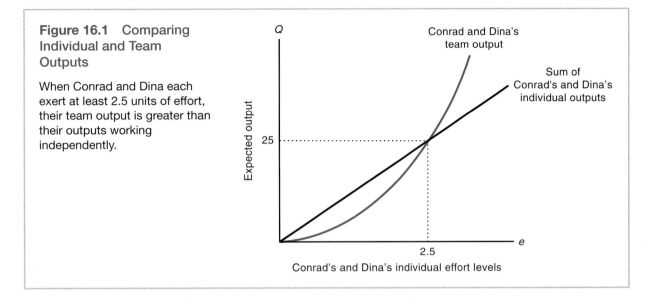

help each other. Large, awkward pieces can be attached in less than half the time by two people assisting each other than if they worked independently. In other cases, team output is larger than individuals working separately because the team makes better use of the knowledge of its members.

Evaluating Teams

Teams are formed because of their joint production effects.[14] These team production effects make evaluating the performance of individual team members quite complicated. Although often there is no measure of individual output—only team output is observed—it normally is optimal to evaluate team members, at least in part, on team output. Using team output focuses team members on a common objective and helps promote cooperation. However, paying team members on group output provides individuals with incentives to free-ride. These incentives are less pronounced in smaller teams. But as team size grows, these free-rider problems can become enormous.

Free-rider problems can be controlled by evaluating team members not only on team output but on other measures as well. For instance, the following factors might be used to assess performance by Conrad and Dina: the number of hours worked, a supervisor's subjective evaluation as to how hard they are working, the condition of their tools, and peer evaluations. Peer evaluations consist of Dina's evaluation of Conrad's work and Conrad's evaluation of Dina's work. Peer reviews often are important in evaluating the individual performance of team members because it is teammates who have the specific information about how each team member has performed.

Sometimes the costs of controlling free-rider problems within teams exceed the benefits that come from team production. In this case, it is better to work individually

[14]A. Alchian and H. Demsetz (1972), "Production, Information Costs and Economic Organization," *American Economic Review* 62, 777–795.

Peer Review Performance Ratings of Teams

This example describes the specific areas and skills evaluated for individuals working on teams. One small company is organized around nine management teams. Using a five-point scale, each team member rates all other team members on each of the following ten topics:

- Expresses opinions freely
- Comes to meetings prepared
- Takes initiative
- Accepts criticism
- Listens to others
- Delegates authority
- Shares information freely
- Bases decisions on sound data
- Values all customers
- Recognizes others' contributions

These individual peer ratings then are averaged across the ten topics and team members to arrive at an overall peer evaluation for each team member. Pay and promotion decisions as well as future team assignments are based on these evaluations, along with the team's overall performance.

Peer Pressure within Teams

Levi Strauss, maker of Levi jeans, installed multitask teams in its US plants, replacing the old piecework system. Each team had 20 to 30 employees responsible for completing individual orders by assembling full pairs of pants, instead of each employee specializing as a zipper sewer or a belt-loop attacher. In essence, jobs were redesigned from being functional to being more multitask and process-oriented (recall Chapter 13's discussion). The much touted move was designed to empower workers, cut down on monotony, reduce stress, and increase productivity.

Employee incentive compensation was based on team output, which created free-rider problems, which in turn led to absenteeism and shirking, which caused tempers to flare. Supervisors on the plant floor spent more time intervening to prevent "big fights." One plant manager reported, "Peer pressure can be vicious and brutal." Before installing the multitask teams, each employee received 2 weeks of training in group dynamics and an additional 1-day seminar in "let's-get-along sessions" with private consultants. These training sessions did not resolve the conflicts. In fact, productivity dropped and costs rose. The quantity of pants produced per hour worked fell in 1993 to 77 percent of preteam levels. At one plant the cost of stitching a pair of Dockers went from $5 before teams to $7.50 with teams.

Then, Levi's share of the domestic men's denim-jeans market fell from 48 percent in 1990 to 26 percent in 1997. In 1997, Levi closed 11 US plants and laid off 6,400 employees. While vowing to preserve the team strategy at its remaining US plants, many of them unofficially are going back to individual piecework. Robert Haas, Levi's CEO, admits, "Teams created pressures and tensions and a lot of unhappiness, and some people would rather go back. Ours is a culture of experimentation and novelty, and we're not always successful."

Sources: R. Mitchell (1994), "Managing by Values," *Business Week* (August 1),
50; R. King (1998), "Levi's Factory Workers Are Assigned to Teams and
Morale Takes a Hit," *The Wall Street Journal* (May 20), A1.

rather than as a team. For instance, if evaluating Dina and Conrad on team output provides low incentives to exert effort and the costs of monitoring individual performance of teammates (for example, through supervisor or peer reviews) are high, the net value of their combined output might be higher with individual production and performance evaluation.

One of the key tasks for new teams is to develop the internal architecture for the team. Decision rights (task assignments) must be partitioned among the team members. Accordingly, members must decide how to evaluate the work efforts of team members. Finally, members must decide on the rewards and punishments for members of the group. Sometimes the rewards and punishments are social; for example, a shirking member may be ostracized.

As another example of evaluating team output, consider the case of student project teams in business school courses. Such projects build leadership skills and teach students how to work more effectively in teams. These projects also enhance learning by allowing students to share their understanding and by helping all students on the team to learn more than if they each did the project individually. Instructors assigning projects to study teams frequently give the same grade to all members of the team. Thus, the team is evaluated based on the team's joint output.

Rather than assign all the members of the team the same project grade, some instructors apportion the total project grade among the team members based on peer reviews where unequal team grades are possible. Thus, although the overall project's grade might be a B+, some team members might receive an A− and others a B so long as the average across the team is a B+. Providing the team with the decision rights to evaluate one another reduces the free-rider problem and increases team production. But it can also reduce morale and lead to increased influence costs as team members lobby one another for better evaluations. In the worst case, some team members might downgrade a team member unfairly to raise their own grades. These dysfunctional incentives are likely to be greater if the team is formed for a single project. As described in Chapter 10, free-rider problems are smaller if the team spans several courses and students have more incentives to invest in their reputations.

Why Teams Fail

Along with Mom and apple pie, teamwork has become a sacred cow to American businesses. Yet, one survey by Mercer Management found that only 13 percent of 179 teams received high ratings. "Somehow, we have to get past this idea that all we have to do is join hands and sing *Kum Ba Yah* and say, 'We've moved to teamwork.'" Many companies are narrowing the focus and time horizon of teams. A team manger at Texas Instruments counsels that not everyone has to be on a team and that only 5 percent of its workforce are on self-directed teams.

Teams fail for several reasons including:

- The mental opt-out. Busy managers feel compelled to sit through endless team meetings and frequently "surrender by withholding any real effort." Thus half the decisions reached by teams never get implemented.

- Dueling advice. "Teams start out with everyone very polite. Then they start to storm." Several months can pass before things settle down.

- Old-fashioned pay scales. Often when companies move to teams, they keep individual performance measures and pay systems. Team-based pay systems are not used to reward the entire team for meeting goals.

Source: E. Neuborne (1997), "Companies Save, But Workers Pay," *USA Today* (February 25), 1B.

Government Regulation of Labor Markets

The basic principal-agent model assumes that both parties are free to arrive at any mutually agreeable contract and that labor markets are unregulated. However, government regulates labor markets and hence constrains the agreements employees and firms might otherwise reach. Since the 1960s, federal laws in the United States dealing with affirmative action and equal employment opportunity (EEO) have had a profound effect on both performance-evaluation systems and reward systems. Federal and state legislation and court actions have forced companies to document their compensation and promotion decisions to demonstrate that their actions are related to performance and are not influenced by the employee's race, religion, sex, age, or national origin.

Labor laws and court decisions have had a material impact on the performance-appraisal systems. In deciding cases involving alleged discriminatory employment practices, courts look more favorably at companies with the following characteristics[15]:

- The firm's job descriptions are clearly written and well defined.

- The appraisal system has clear criteria for evaluating performance such as written objective scales and dimensions.

- There are specific written instructions on how to complete the performance appraisal.

- Employees are provided feedback about their performance appraisal.

- Higher-level supervisors' evaluations are incorporated into the appraisal system.

- Individuals who receive similar evaluations in the firm are treated equally and consistently.

Although these characteristics appear sensible, even worthwhile for many firms, government regulation has negative side effects. The law does not permit companies and employees to "opt out" of these regulations. Even if these characteristics were appropriate and would be adopted voluntarily by the majority of firms, they are imposed on all firms and hence impose costs on that minority that would not have chosen them voluntarily.

The presence of potential legal scrutiny of the firm's performance-evaluation systems pushes these systems to become more formal, more objective, with less reliance on subjective appraisal. Every action and appraisal must be documented. The firm's human resources department typically assumes the role of ensuring that the firm is complying with the labor laws.

The performance-appraisal system that meets these regulatory criteria would not necessarily maximize the firm's value absent the regulation. For example, many Japanese managers try "to make everybody feel that he is slated for the top position in the firm"[16] by delaying differentiating among cohorts and performance appraisals for 12 to 15 years after joining the firm. Such limitations on annual feedback to employees potentially would run afoul of affirmative-action laws in the United States and thus would be opposed strenuously by human resources departments at most large corporations. Hence, US firms find it more difficult to use less formal, more subjective performance-evaluation systems than their foreign competitors, even though such systems might be value-enhancing for some firms if they could operate in a less regulated setting.

---

[15]Major federal legislation includes the Equal Pay Act of 1963, Title VII, and the Civil Rights Act of 1964. A. Barnes, T. Dworkin, and E. Richards (1994), *Law for Business* (Richard D. Irwin: Burr Ridge, IL), Chapter 23; G. Milkovich and J. Newman (1993), *Compensation* (Richard D. Irwin: Burr Ridge, IL), 316–318.

[16]N. Hatvany and V. Pucik (1981), "Japanese Managerial Practices and Productivity," *Organizational Dynamics* 13, 4. Also, M. Aoki (1988), *Information, Incentives and Bargaining in the Japanese Economy* (Cambridge University Press: Cambridge).

Government regulations cause US firms to spend more money than they would otherwise on appraisal systems that, to a court's satisfaction, document the firm's compliance with affirmative-action regulations. Thus, regulations likely cause some US firms to adopt different performance-appraisal systems. This is another example of how regulation affects the firm's optimal choice of organizational architecture. (Chapter 20 describes government regulation more generally and provides additional organizational architecture examples.)

Summary	In the previous four chapters, we have examined the first two components of organizational architecture: the assignment of decision rights and the reward systems. In this chapter, we began to examine the third component: the performance-evaluation system.

Performance evaluation is conducted for both individuals within the firm and subunits of the firm: How did Taylor perform? How did Morgan's team perform? Such questions require individual and team performance evaluations. Also, Morgan and Taylor are in the automotive products division. How did this division perform? Answering this last question requires divisional performance measures. This chapter focuses on individual performance-evaluation systems; divisional performance evaluation is discussed in Chapter 17.

The simple principal-agent model in Chapter 15 suggests that part of the employee's compensation should be based on performance (output). But basing pay on output requires that output is observable at low cost and is difficult to manipulate by the firm or the employee. Among the costs of performance measures are the *compensating differentials* employees must be paid for bearing the additional risks of incentive pay. Moreover, the model assumes that the firm and employee are free to contract in an unregulated labor market. This chapter explores how individual performance evaluation is affected when these conditions are violated.

To set the optimum compensation package, management must know the employee's marginal productivity of effort. One way managers estimate these marginal productivities is to use time and motion studies or data on past performance. If past performance is used, dysfunctional incentives due to the *ratchet effect* can result; employees will limit output if they anticipate that the next period's target benchmark will be raised. To reduce the dysfunctional consequences of the ratchet effect, some firms set performance estimates at the beginning of the period and do not adjust them simply because employees are making high earnings.

In some cases, measuring output can be extremely costly. For example, accurately measuring the output of a teacher is likely to be quite costly. Firms will select performance evaluations based on the direct cost of the measure, the cost of employee opportunism induced by the performance measure, and the indirect cost incurred by imposing more risk on the employee.

Another assumption of the model is that the employee shirks only on effort. If output is not correlated perfectly with the firm's value, employees attempting to increase output might cause the value of the firm to decline. Such dysfunctional results can occur when employees game the system—as in the Sears auto mechanics case of overcharging customers.

Often a manager has multiple signals available regarding the employee's output. The informativeness principle from Chapter 15 suggests that the manager should use all these signals (so long as they are available at low cost) because they allow the firm to reduce the risk the employee bears and hence lower the compensating differential the employee must be paid. The informativeness principle suggests that when several employees are performing similar tasks, their combined output provides information about common random shocks affecting all their outputs. Thus, the employee's compensation should be adjusted relative to peers. This is called *relative performance evaluation.* Relative performance evaluation requires the firm to establish a reference group of employees to use as a benchmark. But relative performance evaluations can lead employees to collude or sabotage coworkers to improve their evaluations. Moreover, establishing the appropriate reference group and measuring its performance is costly.

In some cases, the measurement costs or the costs from employees' dysfunctional attempts to maximize explicit performance measures become so great that alternative measures of performance are sought. *Subjective performance evaluations* are periodic reviews by supervisors that usually incorporate a comprehensive examination of all the employee's outputs. Subjective evaluations can be based on either standard rating scales for a number of different areas or goal-based systems. Standard rating scales have the appearance of objectivity but entail subjective judgments by the evaluator. Goal-based systems set performance targets at the beginning of the period that the evaluator uses at the end of the period to determine an overall, subjective evaluation.

Subjective performance measures also involve costs. It becomes easier for a manager or the firm to renege on the promise to reward good performance because it is harder to define "good." There is more latitude to exercise favoritism and introduce bias in subjective measures. Finally, subjective systems often generate greater influence costs as employees try to lobby for better ratings.

Subjective and objective performance evaluations usually complement each other. Subjective evaluations often are used to reduce the incentives of employees to engage in opportunistic behaviors that increase the costs of objective measures. For example, the Lincoln Electric secretary who typed meaningless characters during lunch could be penalized using a subjective system: The supervisor could dismiss the secretary or give the secretary a poor subjective evaluation.

When employees work in teams, each individual's marginal contribution to the team's output depends on others' efforts. There are synergies or interdependencies among employees. Measuring individual output is difficult, and it is costly to disentangle individual shirking from others' effort. Evaluating teams of employees usually requires a measure of team performance while still recognizing individual contributions to the team. Individual performance (possibly measured using peer reviews) is rewarded to overcome free-rider problems. In some cases, each team member's bonus is based on individual performance, but the bonus is paid only if the entire team reaches its goals.

The principal-agent model assumes that the parties are free to contract, yet labor laws constrain their choices. The equal employment opportunity laws in the United States have had a pronounced effect on performance-evaluation systems. For example, defending against affirmative-action lawsuits has encouraged firms to adopt more explicit, objective appraisal systems than they otherwise might have chosen voluntarily.

Appendix

Optimal Weights in a Relative Performance Contract[17]
In this chapter, we argued that it can be optimal to base an employee's pay on performance *relative* to some benchmark group such as employees within the same organization who perform similar tasks. The advantage of this type of system is that it filters out common shocks in the evaluation of employees and thus reduces the costs of inefficient risk bearing. In this appendix, we consider how a risk-neutral firm might optimally weight the performance of such a benchmark group in a compensation contract.

[17]Technical note: This appendix requires elementary knowledge of statistics, decision theory, and calculus. Material in this appendix draws on the analysis in Milgrom and Roberts (1992), Chapter 10.

For simplicity, we restrict our attention to simple linear compensation contracts of the following form:

$$\text{Compensatoin} = W_0 + \beta(Q - \lambda\overline{Q}) \tag{16.8}$$

where W_0 and β are fixed parameters, Q is the employee's own output, and $\overline{Q}$ is the average output of the benchmark group (for example, similar employees within the firm). W_0 is the employee's fixed wage under a relative performance contract. We are interested in how to choose the optimal λ. Note that if $\lambda = 0$, average output receives no weight and thus is left out of the contract. In contrast, if $\lambda = 1$, then compensation is based on a simple difference between own output and average output.

In the discussion that follows, we show that expected compensation can be held the same by simply adjusting W_0. Second, under certain assumptions, the employee's effort choice is independent of λ. Third, we show how to choose λ to minimize the risk the employee bears. Since expected compensation can be the same for any λ and if the effort choice isn't affected by λ, then the efficient contract is the one that minimizes the risk borne by the employee.

Expected Compensation   Rewriting Equation (16.8) yields

$$\text{Compensation} = W_0 + \beta Q - \beta\lambda\overline{Q} \tag{16.9}$$

Expected compensation in Equation (16.9) is $W_0 + \beta E(Q) - \beta\lambda E(\overline{Q})$. Expected compensation can be held constant at any level of λ by adjusting W_0 by $+\beta\lambda E(Q)$.

Effort Choice   Under certain assumptions, the employee's effort choice is independent of λ. In this case, the firm can choose λ without being concerned about how it might affect employee productivity. In particular, suppose that the employee's cost of exerting effort is given by the function $C(e)$, which expresses the disutility of effort in dollar equivalents. The employee's certainty equivalent can be approximated by the following formula[18]:

$$\text{Certainty equivalent} = E[W_0 + \beta E(Q - \lambda\overline{Q})] - .5rs^2 - C(e) \tag{16.10}$$

where E denotes the expectation operator, r is the coefficient of absolute risk aversion, and s^2 is the variance of compensation. In this expression, the first term on the right-hand side represents expected compensation, the second term is the risk premium (employees discount the expected value because they are risk-averse), and the last term is the cost of effort. We make two additional assumptions: (1) the effort of the employee does not affect the average output of other employees of the benchmark group, and (2) r is a constant. Employees want to maximize their certainty equivalent with respect to the effort choice e—which is equivalent to maximizing their utility. Conceptually, the maximizing effort level is found by taking the partial derivative of the certainty equivalent with respect to effort e and setting it equal to zero. The first-order condition is therefore

$$\beta Q' = C'(e) \tag{16.11}$$

where Q' and $C'(e)$ are partial derivatives with respect to e. This expression indicates that the employee chooses the effort level that equates marginal benefits and marginal costs. The marginal benefit is the extra compensation that the employee receives from

---

[18]Technical note: A certainty equivalent is the amount of cash that employees would require with certainty to make them indifferent between this certain sum and the uncertain income stream. The approximation of the certainty equivalent in Equation (16.9) is a basic result from decision theory. It holds when the risk is small and the utility function is sufficiently smooth. J. Ingersoll (1987), *Theory of Financial Decision Making* (Rowman & Littlefield: Totowa, NJ), 38.

Figure 16.2   Choosing the Optimal Weight in a Relative Performance Contract

This figure reflects a simple linear contract of the form Compensation $= W_0 + \beta(Q - \lambda\bar{Q})$, where W_0 and β are fixed parameters. Q is the employee's own output, and $\bar{Q}$ is the average output of the benchmark group (for example, similar employees in the firm). Pictured is the variance of compensation as a function of λ. Given the assumptions in the analysis, the optimal weight, $\lambda^* = \text{Cov}(Q, \bar{Q})/\text{Var}(\bar{Q})$. This is the value that minimizes the variance of compensation.

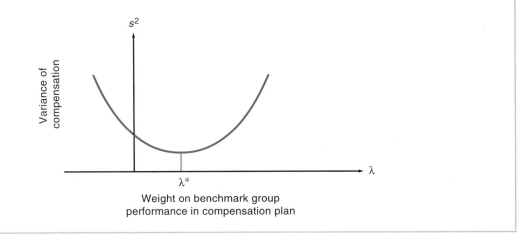

Weight on benchmark group
performance in compensation plan

---

exerting more effort, and the marginal cost is the extra disutility that he experiences from working harder. Note that λ does not enter into this equation, since the average output of other employees does not depend on this employee's effort. Thus, in this case, the firm can choose any value for λ without affecting the employee's effort level.

Minimizing Employee Risk   Note from Equation (16.10) that the employee is made better off by reducing the variance of compensation (it lowers the discount for risk). The firm, on the other hand, is not harmed by this choice because the employee exerts the same effort level under any λ and W_0 can be adjusted to keep expected compensation the same. Indeed, the firm potentially can share in the gains from the risk reduction to the employee by paying a lower expected level of compensation—since the firm can meet the employee's reservation wage with a lower expected level of payout.

Basic statistics allows us to express the variance of compensation [Equation (16.8)] as

$$\text{Var(Compensation)} = \beta^2[\text{Var}(Q) + \lambda^2\,\text{Var}(\bar{Q}) - 2\lambda\text{Cov}(Q, \bar{Q})] \quad (16.12)$$

Figure 16.2 shows a picture of this quadratic function. The optimal weight is λ^* at the bottom of the parabola. Using basic calculus, we can show that

$$\lambda^* = \text{Cov}(Q, \bar{Q})/\text{Var}(\bar{Q}) \quad (16.13)$$

Equation (16.13) has a quite intuitive interpretation. The numerator of the expression $\text{Cov}(Q, \bar{Q})$ is a measure of the association between this employee's own output and the average output of other employees. The higher this association, the more information average output contains about random shocks that affect the employee's output (the better is the "signal"). For example, if this covariance is zero, average output contains no information about these shocks and should not be included in the compensation contract. The denominator of the expression is the variance of average output. The higher this variance, the more noise there is in average output and the less information it contains about the employee's effort. The optimal weight λ^* can be estimated using a time series of observations on own output and average output.[19]

Firms sometimes base compensation on the simple difference between the employee's output and average output. This measure is equivalent to choosing $\lambda = 1$. Our analysis indicates that this choice is not always optimal and in some cases can be worse than excluding average output in the contract (for example, when the covariance between the two variables is small). Indeed, the optimal weight could be negative if the two variables were negatively correlated.

Appendix Problem   Assume that a salesperson, Edwynn Phillips, has the following annual compensation package:

$$C = \$15{,}000 + .2(\text{own sales})$$

This compensation plan induces Ed to exert a given level of effort in selling. Given this effort level, expected sales are $30,000 per year.

Below are 10 years' worth of data for Ed's sales and the average sales for other employees in the company (Ed's own sales are excluded in calculating this average). The expected value of average sales is also $30,000. However, in any given year, average sales might rise or fall, depending on general economic conditions, and so on. Some of these same conditions affect Ed's sales. Ed has no impact on the average sales for other employees.

Year	Ed's Sales	Average Sales
1	30,000	30,000
2	24,000	27,000
3	36,000	28,500
4	27,000	27,000
5	33,000	36,000
6	30,000	33,000
7	25,500	27,000
8	24,000	24,000
9	34,500	30,000
10	36,000	36,000

1.   Based on the 10 years of data, calculate Ed's average annual pay and standard deviation under the existing compensation plan.

2.   Calculate Ed's average pay and standard deviation under the alternative plan:

$$\$21{,}000 + .2(\text{own sales} - \text{average sales})$$

Note: We adjust the intercept of the pay plan by $6,000 to reflect Ed's average loss imposed on the employee by subtracting .2 (average sales) from the compensation. This adjustment keeps the expected pay the same as before. Also, the sample mean of average sales over a 10-year period need not equal the expected value of $30,000.

[19]Technical note: Readers familiar with linear regression analysis should note that the right-hand side of Equation (16.12) is the formula for the slope coefficient in a simple linear regression, where the employee's output is the dependent variable and average output of other employees is the explanatory variable. Thus, this formula can be estimated through a simple regression.

3. Does including the average sales in the pay package alter Ed's incentives to work hard? Explain. (Assume that Ed cannot affect the average by collusion, sabotage, etc.)

4. Is this pay plan superior to the original plan from a risk-sharing standpoint?

5. Devise an even better plan using the more general form:

$$C = a + .2(\text{own sales} - \lambda \text{ average sales})$$

(Remember to adjust the intercept to keep expected compensation the same.)

6. Calculate the average pay and standard deviation for this plan.

<table>
<tr>
<td>Suggested
Readings</td>
<td>

A. Alchian and H. Demsetz (1972), "Production, Information Costs and Economic Organization," *American Economic Review* 62, 777–795.

G. Baker, R. Gibbons, and K. Murphy (1994), "Subjective Performance Measures in Optimal Incentive Contracts," *Quarterly Journal of Economics* CIX, 1125–1156.

Y. Barzel (1982), "Measurement Cost and the Organization of Markets," *Journal of Law & Economics* XXV, 27–48.

E. Lazear and S. Rosen (1981), "Rank Order Tournaments as Optimal Labor Contracts," *Journal of Political Economy*, 89, 841–864.

G. Milkovich, J. Newman, and C. Milkovich (1999), *Compensation* (Irwin/McGraw-Hill: Burr Ridge, IL).

G. Milkovich and A. Wigdor (1991), *Pay for Performance* (National Academy Press: Washington, DC).

C. Prendergast (1999), "The Provision of Incentives in Firms," *Journal of Economic Literature* 37 (March) 7–63.

</td>
</tr>
</table>

<table>
<tr>
<td>Review
Questions</td>
<td>

16–1. Discuss some of the costs and benefits of 360-degree evaluation systems.

16–2. Semco S.A. in São Paulo, Brazil, has 500 employees and manufactures capital goods. The employees elect their managers and evaluate them every 6 months. Managers rated poorly are transferred or fired. There are 100 nonunion employees who set their own performance standards and arrange their own work schedules. Twice a year, the nonunion employees receive a market salary survey and are asked to set their own pay for the next 6 months. Employees setting their pay too low receive that amount, as do employees requesting too high a salary. If management decides after 1 year that the employees' salaries were above what they were worth to the company, these employees are fired. The 400 unionized employees' pay is set by union contract. Critically evaluate Semco's performance-evaluation system.[20]

16–3. In 360-degree performance review programs, personnel evaluations are collected anonymously from employees knowing the manager being evaluated (superiors, subordinates, and coworkers). These are tabulated and a consensus summary is provided to the manager. Each manager being evaluated also does a self-evaluation, and this is used to benchmark how closely the manager and the coworkers' assessments match. About one-third of the managers match their coworkers, one-third have an inflated view, and one-third rate themselves lower. Those who overrate themselves tend to be judged "least effective" as perceived by their coemployees. However, these overraters are more common higher up in the organization.[21]
   a. What does the breakdown of three one-thirds indicate?
   b. Offer some plausible explanation of why overraters are higher up in the organization.

</td>
</tr>
</table>

[20]J. Lopez (1994), "A Better Way?" *The Wall Street Journal Supplement* (April 13), R6.
[21]B. O'Reilly (1994), "360 Feedback Can Change Your Life," *Fortune* (October 17), 93–100.

16–4. The following quote is based on statements made by quality expert W. Edwards Deming:

> *If by bad management the components of a company become competitive, the system is destroyed. . . . A common example lies in the practice of ranking people, divisions, teams, comparing them, with reward at the top and punishment at the bottom. Jobs and salaries are based on comparisons. Teams naturally become competitive; divisions become competitive. Each tries to outdo the other in some competitive measure. The result is higher costs, battle of market share. Everybody loses.*[22]

Do you agree with Deming that performance evaluations based on comparative rankings always reduce company value? Explain.

16–5. The United States Navy recently revamped its officer fitness report system.[23] Under the old system, officers were ranked into one of four categories, where 4.0 was the highest grade. This old system had been used for 20 years and grade inflation had become rampant. Eighty percent of all sailors routinely were ranked a perfect 4.0. One officer remarked, "Let's face it, 85 percent of the people are 4.0 and 80 percent [of those] have every mark in 4.0." A retired admiral commented, "The old system wasn't entirely broke, it was just deteriorating over time and became less and less useful."

The Navy decided to change the evaluation system because of the natural tendency for senior officers to promote their own subordinates over unknown sailors. Not everyone deserved a 4.0, but to get their own people promoted, senior officers had to play along because that's what everyone else was doing.

The new system requires each officer to be rated on a 1–5 scale in seven areas: professional expertise, leadership, support for equal opportunity programs, military bearing and appearance, teamwork, mission accomplishment, and interpersonal skills. The total points out of 35 possible are then used to provide an overall promotion recommendation:

- Clearly promote
- Must promote
- Promotable
- Progressing
- Don't promote

The number of ratings in the top two categories—"clearly promote" and "must promote"—will be severely restricted to at most 20 percent of the evaluations. If an officer is evaluating 10 junior officers, at the most only 2 can receive the top two ratings.

What are the expected consequences of this new system? What are the likely outcomes? What are the pros and cons of the new system?

16–6. Evaluate the following statement:

> *The overarching purpose of a measurement system should be to help a team, rather than senior managers, gauge its progress. A team's measurement system should primarily be a tool for telling the team when it must take corrective action.*[24]

16–7. The Green Shoe Company is considering going to a piece rate system, where manufacturing employees are paid based on their level of output. Discuss what factors the firm should consider in deciding whether this idea should be implemented. How should the initial piece rate be set? Under what circumstances should the company alter the piece rate once it is adopted?

16–8. Your company currently has a bonus plan for its sales managers. If annual sales for a manager's unit exceed $1 million, the manager receives a $10,000 bonus. In a typical year, about 5 of the 10 managers in the firm meet the target and receive the bonus. However, the number

---

[22]R. Aguayo (1990), *Dr. Deming: The American Who Taught the Japanese about Quality* (Fireside Simon & Schuster: New York), vii–viii.

[23]E. Blazar (1995), "The New Standard of Excellence," *Navy Times* (March 20), 12–14.

[24]C. Meyer (1994), "How the Right Measures Help Teams Excel," *Harvard Business Review* (May–June), 96.

receiving the bonus varies from year to year due to the state of the economy, which in turn has an effect on sales. The company is considering replacing the bonus plan with a plan that rewards the top-five selling managers each year with a $10,000 bonus. Discuss the potential benefits and costs of the new plan relative to the old plan.

16–9. Communities are frequently concerned about whether police are vigilant in carrying out their responsibilities. Several communities have experimented with incentive compensation for police. In particular, some cities have paid members of the police force based on the number of arrests that they personally make. Discuss the likely effects of this compensation policy.

16–10. A consultant does not like the fact that you use subjective performance measures in your firm. He argues that they are arbitrary and should be replaced with objective measures. He stresses that objective measures provide a clear target for employees, but mentions none of the potential costs. What are the potential problems associated with using objective performance measures?

16–11. Some firms have recently adopted 360-degree performance evaluations. Under this evaluation system, the employee is evaluated not only by supervisors and peers but also by employees who report to the employee being evaluated. Discuss why a firm might want to adopt 360-degree reviews. What are the likely problems with this type of performance evaluation?

16–12. Evaluate the following quote:

> *Teams do not spring up by magic. Nor does personal chemistry matter as much as most people believe. Rather, we believe that . . . most people can significantly enhance team performance. And focusing on performance—not chemistry or togetherness or good communications or good feelings—shapes teams more than anything else.*[25]

16–13. A basic principle in accounting is that of "responsibility accounting." Under this principle, it is inappropriate to base performance evaluation on measures that are beyond the control of the employee. Do you think that you should ever include variables in a workers' compensation plan that are not under at least partial control of the employee? Explain.

16–14. Once again, the Eastman Kodak Company has altered the determinants of pay raises for US employees. Whereas in the past pay increases for managers, professionals, and hourly workers had been automatic, starting in 1996 the company began determining the size of an annual bonus pool and then allocated lump-sum bonuses to employees on the basis of performance. Hourly workers were to be evaluated within their annual performance appraisals; professional-level employees would work with their supervisors to establish personal goals against which they would be measured.

    a. What problems do you foresee with the implementation of this arrangement? Be specific about who will be affected by the problems you've identified.

    b. What recommendations would you offer to top management at Kodak to preempt or minimize problems with the new reward system?

16–15. Agricultural workers are often paid piece rates. For example, pear pickers are paid a fixed amount for each box of pears they pick. Pear companies, however, pay tree thinners on an hourly basis. These thinners remove excess fruit from trees so that the remaining fruit can grow larger. (Each piece of fruit must be at least 6 inches apart on the tree.) Why do you think these companies pay thinners by the hour? Presumably, they would work harder if they were paid by the tree.

16-16. Evaluate the following statement:

> *I am a manager at a governmental agency. I have no control over compensation policy. All workers are paid the same salary, and I cannot fire them. Therefore, an understanding of the basic principles of organizational architecture will not help me be more effective in my job.*

16-17. The JAB Gold Mining Company observes that some firms pay their CEOs based on performance *relative* to the S&P 500. Most firms, however, have stock prices that are positively

---

[25]J. Katzenbach, and D. Smith (1993), *The Wisdom of Teams* (Harvard Business School: Boston), 61.

correlated with the S&P 500. JAB has a *negative beta*! (Its stock returns are negatively correlated with the index.) Does this mean that JAB would be wrong in paying its CEO based on performance relative to the S&P 500? Explain.

16–18. Martina Genser sells copiers for Xerox. Her sales are a function of her effort *e*, and can be expressed in the following manner:

$$Sales = 100e + \mu$$

where μ is a random error term with expected value of zero. Martina's personal cost of exerting effort is

$$C(e) = e^2$$

She is paid a straight salary plus a commission:

$$Compensation = \$1,000 + .10 \text{ sales}$$

Her personal objective is to maximize

$$U = E(Compensation) - C(e)$$

the difference between the expected value of her compensation and her cost of effort.

a. Find Martina's optimal effort level.

b. Now assume that Xerox compensates Martina based on her sales relative to the average sales for salespeople in the company. Assume that Martina's sales are not included in the calculation of this average and that she cannot affect the average sales through her effort. The expected value of average sales is 500. Her compensation is now

$$Compensation = \$1,000 + .10(\text{sales} - \text{average sales})$$

Calculate Martina's optimal effort level under this compensation plan.

c. Including average sales in the contract affects expected compensation. What adjustment must be made in the salary to keep expected compensation the same as before?

d. Does including average sales in the compensation contract affect the variance of Martina's compensation? Assume that her sales and average sales are positively correlated. Give a brief verbal explanation to support your answer.

16–19. The Quantum Division of Nextel Corp., based in San Jose, California, manufactures semiconductors that convert analog signals to digital signals. Lynn Kraft is the division manager. Her compensation consists of a base wage of $50,000 plus a bonus of 2 percent of division profits above $10 million. Last year's division profits were $12 million, and so Kraft received a bonus of $40,000.

This year two things happened that adversely affected division profits. First, the price of gold, a key ingredient in Quantum's chips, increased dramatically, causing the division's costs to be higher than expected. Second, an earthquake in the San Jose area caused Quantum's plant to be closed for 6 weeks and to require $1 million in repairs. Division profits for this year were $9 million.

Kraft believes her compensation plan should be adjusted for these events. She believes that, but for these events, division profits would have been $13 million for the year.

What issues should the CEO of Nextel consider when deciding whether to adjust Kraft's bonus plan? Do you think the plan should be adjusted? Why?

Chapter 17
Divisional Performance Evaluation

CHAPTER OUTLINE

CSX is a large freight railroad with fleets of locomotives, railcars, and containers.[1] CSX's primary business is transporting freight in containers connecting trucks and cargo ships. In 1988, CSX changed the way it evaluated its internal divisions: It adopted Economic Value Added, which is the after-tax operating profit of the division minus the total annual opportunity cost of the capital invested in the division. The total annual cost of capital is calculated as the product of the division's per dollar cost of capital times the amount of capital employed within the division. The EVA of one of CSX's major division's was a negative $70 million—which means that within this division, the opportunity cost of the capital employed exceeded its operating profits by $70 million. The CEO of CSX informed the managers of this division that if they were unable to raise their EVA to break even by 1993, their division would be sold.

By 1993, after reorganizing and evaluating their managers' performance using EVA, freight volume increased by 25 percent, the number of freight trailers was reduced from

[1]Details of this example are from S. Tully (1993), "The Real Key to Creating Wealth," *Fortune* (September 20), 38–50. EVA is a registered trademark of Stern Stewart.

18,000 to 14,000, and its locomotive fleet fell from 150 to 100. Rather than permitting trailers and containers just to sit idle, managers now had incentives either to use them or to reduce their numbers. Under the old performance-evaluation system, managers were not charged for the opportunity cost of the capital employed by their business units, and they treated the existing stock of containers and trailers essentially as "free." By 1993, containers and trailers were loaded and back on the tracks in five days rather than sitting idle for two weeks. This division's 1993 EVA was about $30 million. CSX's stock price rose from $28 in 1988 when EVA was adopted to $75 in 1993. Since 1994 CSX stock has underperformed the S&P 500, due in part to a costly $10 billion purchase of Conrail, excessive costs of absorbing 10,700 miles of track, and increased competition for freight.[2]

In Chapter 16, we described individual performance-evaluation systems. Our discussion is extended in this chapter to evaluating the performance of business units within the firm. As described in Chapter 13, firms are organized in a variety of ways: by function, by product line, or by geography. Most organizations partition decision rights among subunits within the firm. This chapter describes different ways organizations measure the performance of their various businesses. The next section describes commonly used arrangements—cost centers, expense centers, revenue centers, profit centers, and investment centers. These subunits are assigned different sets of decision rights and accordingly use different performance-evaluation metrics—for instance, costs, revenues, profits, or EVA. Because business units within the organization interact with one another and often exchange goods or services among themselves, reported performance of each center involved in an exchange depends on the rules used to value the exchange. Performance evaluation of business units exchanging goods or services requires establishing an internal transfer price for these exchanges. The following section discusses these transfer-pricing issues. Finally, because most firms rely on their accounting systems to measure the performance of their business units, we discuss general issues involving use of the accounting system in measuring performance.

Measuring Divisional Performance[3]

All but the smallest organizations invariably are divided into subunits, each granted some decision rights and then evaluated based on performance objectives for that subunit. Rewards typically are based on these performance evaluations. In effective organizations, performance-evaluation and reward systems are consistent with the decision rights granted the unit manager—the three legs of the stool are balanced. Chapter 13 described alternative organizational structures: U form, M form, and matrix organizations. In the U form, one unit might be responsible for manufacturing, another for R&D, another for marketing, and so forth. These basic building blocks of the organization are the work groups that define what each part of the firm does. Senior management attempts to evaluate the performance of these various subunits both for setting rewards for lower-level managers as well as for making business decisions—for instance, which businesses to expand.

Chapter 12 pointed out that teams often produce more than individuals working independently. The business units of the organization are, in effect, production teams. For example, the maintenance department maintains facilities; the marketing group

[2]W. Zellner (1999), "Steep Grade for a Rail Deal," *Business Week* (July 5), 29.

[3]This section draws on M. Jensen and W. Meckling (1998), "Divisional Performance Measurement," in M. Jensen (1998), *Foundations of Organizational Strategy* (Harvard University Press: Cambridge MA), 345–361.

structures and implements marketing plans; research and development explores potential new products; support groups provide products and services to customers. Each unit generally can be characterized into one of five categories based on the decision rights it has been granted and the way its performance is evaluated: cost centers, expense centers, revenue centers, profit centers, and investment centers. For instance, CSX changed from evaluating some of its divisions as profit centers to evaluating them as investment centers.

Cost Centers

Cost centers are assigned the decision rights to produce a stipulated level of output; in achieving this objective, the unit's efficiency is measured and rewarded. Cost center managers are granted decision rights for determining the mix of inputs—labor, materials, and outside services—used to produce the output. Managers of cost centers are evaluated on their efficiency in applying these inputs to produce output. Since they are not responsible for selling their output, they are not judged on revenues or profits.

To evaluate the performance of a cost center, its output must be measurable. Moreover, because it retains the decision rights to specify the department's output or budget, central management must possess the requisite specialized knowledge. Manufacturing departments like the welder assembly department at Lincoln Electric normally are cost centers. The output of the welder assembly department is measured by counting the number of welders completed. Besides manufacturing settings, cost centers also are used in service organizations such as CSX's railcar maintenance department (where output is measured as the number of railcars serviced), check processing by a bank (number of checks processed), or food services in a hospital (number of meals served). In addition to measuring the quantity of output, its quality must be monitored effectively. If not, unit managers evaluated on costs have incentives to meet their targets by cutting quality. Thus, Lincoln Electric must have mechanisms to ensure that assembled welders meet quality standards, which requires that quality must be reasonably observable.

Various objectives are used for evaluating cost center performance. Two of the more widely used are

- Minimize costs for a given output.
- Maximize output for a given budget.

In Chapter 5, we indicated that to maximize value, managers must select the optimal output Q^*, and produce this output at minimum cost. Cost center managers focus primarily on the second of these activities—cost minimization. Their task is to choose the efficient input mix. For example, if Anthony Mancuso, the manager of the railcar maintenance department, is told to service 100 railcars per day, he is evaluated on meeting this production schedule and controlling the cost of servicing the 100 railcars. The quantity decision tends to be made by central management. The first potential evaluation criterion focuses directly on cost minimization. Minimizing costs given a prespecified quantity (and quality) is consistent with value maximization, so long as Q^* is selected as the target output.

The second potential evaluation criterion, maximizing output for a specified budget, provides incentives equivalent to the first criterion, given that the specified budget is the minimal budget necessary for producing Q^*. For example, Tony might be given a fixed budget ($27,500 per week) and evaluated based on the number of railcars serviced that meet quality specifications within his fixed budget. In either case, Tony has incentives to select the cost-minimizing input mix for producing Q^*.

Quantity	Price	Revenue	Total Cost	Total Profits	Average Cost
1	$35	$ 35	$ 78	$−43	$78.0
2	33	66	83	−17	41.5
3	31	93	90	3	30.0
4	29	116	99	17	24.8
5	27	135	110	25	22.0
6	25	150	123	27	20.5
7	23	161	138	23	19.7
8	21	168	155	13	19.4
9	19	171	174	−3	19.3
10	17	170	195	−25	19.5

Table 17.1 Example Demonstrating That Minimizing Average Cost Does Not Yield the Profit-Maximizing Level of Sales

Minimizing average unit cost is not the same as maximizing profits. Maximum profits occur where marginal costs and marginal revenues are equal, which need not be where average unit costs are lowest. This simple example shows that profits are maximized by selling 6 units. However, minimum average cost occurs by producing 9 units.

For both objectives, the manager is constrained either by total output or by budget. Effective implementation requires that central management choose either the value-maximizing output level or the appropriate budget for efficient production of this output level. Nonetheless under both cost center arrangements, Tony has incentives to reduce costs (or increase output) by lowering quality—again, the quality of production in cost centers must be monitored.

Cost center managers sometimes are evaluated based on minimizing average cost. In this case, the manager has the incentive to choose the output at which average costs are minimized and to produce this output efficiently. It is important to understand that value maximization need not occur at the point where average costs are minimized. In general, minimizing average unit cost is not the same as maximizing value. For example, in Table 17.1, profits are maximized by selling 6 units; yet, average cost is minimized by producing 9 units. Maximum profits occur where marginal costs and marginal revenues are equal—this need not be where average unit costs are lowest. As another example, suppose a cost center has fixed costs in addition to constant marginal costs. Then average unit costs fall with increases in output. To illustrate, assume that total costs are

$$\text{TC} = \$6\,Q + \$300{,}000 \qquad (17.1)$$

Fixed costs are $300,000, and marginal costs are a constant $6 per unit. Given the equation for total costs, average costs are derived by dividing both sides of the equation by Q to get

$$\text{AC} = \frac{\text{TC}}{Q} = \$6 + \frac{\$300{,}000}{Q} \qquad (17.2)$$

With constant marginal cost, as quantity produced increases, AC falls. In this situation, a cost center manager who is evaluated based on minimizing average unit costs has incentives to increase output, even as inventories mount. Focusing on average costs can provide incentives for cost center managers to either overproduce or underproduce; it will depend on how the value-maximizing output level compares to the quantity where average costs are minimized.

Cost centers work most effectively when central managers have a good understanding of the business unit's cost structure, can determine the value-maximizing output level, can monitor quantity as well as quality, and can establish appropriate rewards; in addition, the cost center manager has specific knowledge of the optimal input mix. Table 17.2 summarizes the measures used to evaluate performance for the different types of centers, the decision rights the various centers are granted, and circumstances under which particular centers are used most effectively.

Expense Centers

Cost centers are a common way of organizing manufacturing units. However, activities such as personnel, accounting, patenting, public relations, and research and development, often are organized as expense centers. As in cost centers, expense center managers are given fixed budgets and asked to maximize service/output. The fundamental difference between expense centers and standard cost centers is that output in expense centers is measured more subjectively than objectively. Thus, an expense center is basically a cost center that does not produce an easily measurable output.

The difficulty in observing the output of an expense center has several implications. As director of personnel, Salman Abassi is given a total budget and told to provide as much service as possible. Because the cost per unit of output is difficult to measure, the users of this expense center typically are not charged directly for the center's services.[4] Hence, his users tend to overconsume the services, and Sal regularly requests larger budgets. The central corporate budget-setting organization has difficulty determining the budget that maximizes the firm's value, again because output is not easily observed. Expense center managers frequently derive additional benefits from managing larger staffs (empire building), which reinforces the tendency of these centers to grow faster than the firm as a whole. If the central budget office tries to cut the personnel department's budget, Sal might threaten to reduce those services that are most highly valued by users to enlist their help lobbying against the proposed budget cuts. This behavior is yet another example of influence costs (see Chapter 12).

A number of devices are employed to control expense centers. One is to benchmark their budgets against those of comparable centers in similar-sized firms. Another is to reorganize the firm and place the expense center under the control of their largest user, who then not only has more specialized knowledge of the expense center's value but also the decision rights to set the expense center's budget. Yet, this reorganized structure frequently supplies too little of the service to other units. If these other users are charged more than marginal cost, they demand too little of the services. Alternatively, without a charge-back system for the expense center's services, the controlling user might ration resources provided to other business units and again other users would receive too little of its services.

---

[4]In some cases, firms indirectly charge for these services through a cost allocation system. For example, human resources does not charge for services provided; rather, other business units are charged based on head count.

Unit Type	Performance Measures	Decision Rights	Typically Used When
Cost center	Minimize total cost for a fixed output Maximize output for a fixed budget	Input mix (labor, material, supplies)	Central manager can measure output, knows the cost functions, and can set the optimal quantity and appropriate rewards. Central manager can observe the quality of the cost center's output. Cost center manager has knowledege of the optimal input mix.
Expense center	Minimize total cost for a fixed level of services Maximize service for a fixed budget	Input mix (labor, material, supplies)	Output is difficult to observe and measure.
Revenue center	Maximize revenues for a given price (or quantity) and operating budget	Input mix (labor, material, supplies)	Central manager has the knowledge to select the optimal product mix. Central manager has the knowledge to select the correct price or quantity. Revenue center managers have knowledge of the demand curves of the customers in their sales districts.
Profit center	Actual profits Actual profits compared to budgeted profits	Input mix Product mix Selling prices (or output quantities)	Profit center manager has the knowledge to select the correct price/quantity. Profit center manager has the knowledge to select the optimal product mix.
Investment center	Return on investment Residual income EVA	Input mix Product mix Selling prices (or output quantities) Capital invested in center	Investment center manager has the knowledge to select the correct price/quantity. Investment center manager has the knowledge to select the optimal product mix. Investment center manager has knowledge about investment opportunities.

Table 17.2 Summary of Cost, Expense, Revenue, Profit, and Investment Centers

Performance measures and decision rights are balanced across the various subunits of the organization. Their use depends on the distribution of specific knowledge.

Revenue Centers

To organize the marketing activities of selling, distributing, and sometimes servicing finished products received from manufacturing, revenue centers are used. The idea behind a revenue center is to compensate the manager for selling a set of products. For example, a regional sales office might be evaluated as a revenue center. The regional sales manager, Eva Szabo, is given a budget for personnel and expenses and has decision rights as to how to deploy the budget to maximize revenue. Eva has limited discretion in setting the selling price; typically, she must keep the price within a prescribed range.

As with a cost center, various objectives can be used to evaluate revenue centers. One objective is to maximize revenue for a given price (or quantity) and budget for personnel and expenses. That is, the revenue center is told the price of each product it sells and is given a fixed operating budget. This objective is consistent with value maximization so long as central management chooses the correct price-budget combination for each product sold by the revenue center.

Giving Eva decision rights over product pricing or quantity and then evaluating her based on maximizing total revenue usually is inconsistent with value maximization. To maximize revenue, Eva goes to the point where marginal revenue equals zero—not to where it equals marginal cost. Since marginal cost usually is greater than zero, Eva's firm loses money on units sold at prices below marginal cost.

Revenue centers work best if sales managers have specialized knowledge of the demand curves of the customers within their sales district and understand how to sell products effectively while central managers understand aggregate market conditions—for instance, they need to be able to select the correct price-quantity combination as well as the optimal product mix (otherwise, salespeople might shift effort toward selling higher revenue-generating products rather than selling products that generate greater value).

Profit Centers

Profit centers often are composed of several cost, and possibly expense and revenue, centers. Profit center managers are given a fixed capital budget and allocated decision rights for input mix, product mix, and selling prices (or output quantities). Profit centers are most appropriate when the knowledge required to make the product mix, quantity, pricing, and quality decisions is specific to the division and this information is costly to transfer.

Managers rely on their internal accounting systems to provide performance measures for profit centers. Profit centers usually are evaluated on the difference between actual and budgeted accounting profits for their division. Although measuring the profits of profit centers is seemingly straightforward, two complications often consume managers' attention: how to price transfers of goods and services between business units (transfer pricing) and which corporate overhead costs to allocate to specific business units. In every large firm, managers constantly debate these two issues. (We examine the transfer-pricing problem in the next section.)

When there are interdependencies among business units, motivating managers of individual profit centers to maximize the profits of their business units normally fails to maximize the value of the firm as a whole. For instance, individual units focusing on their own profits frequently ignore how their actions affect sales or costs of other units.[5]

---

[5]Conceptually, other units could offer side payments to take these effects into account. However, in the presence of transaction costs, these offers are likely to be limited.

One division might free-ride on another division's quality reputation, thereby reaping short-run gains at the expense of the other division and the whole firm. For example, Chevrolet and Buick are two profit centers within General Motors. Suppose Chevrolet, in pursuit of higher profits, decides to raise its car quality. This might affect consumers' perceptions of the average quality of all General Motor cars—including Buick's perceived quality. An enhanced reputation for all General Motors cars helps Buick. But if Chevrolet receives no credit for additional Buick profits, it is likely to ignore this positive externality that it generates for Buick and will tend to underinvest in quality enhancements. To help managers internalize both positive and negative externalities that their actions impose on other profit centers, firms often base incentive compensation not just on the profits of the manager's own business unit but also on a group of related profit centers' profits and/or firmwide profits. Unless the group and/or the entire firm makes a certain profit target, no individual profit center manager receives a bonus.

Investment Centers

Investment centers are similar to profit centers. However, they have additional decision rights for capital expenditures and are evaluated on measures such as return on investment. Investment centers are most appropriate where the manager of the unit has specific knowledge about investment opportunities as well as information relevant for making the unit's operating decisions.

Investment centers often comprise several profit centers. They have all the decision rights of cost and profit centers, as well as decision rights over the amount of capital to be invested. For example, suppose Lars Erikssen manages the consumer electronics group of an electronics firm that comprises three profit centers: the television division, the DVD division, and the stereo division. Lars has decision rights over the amount of capital invested in consumer electronics and is evaluated based on the return on the capital invested. There are two commonly used measures of performance for investment centers: return on investment and residual income (EVA).

Accounting ROA   The most commonly used investment center performance measure is *return on assets*. ROA is the ratio of accounting net income generated by the investment center divided by total assets invested in the investment center. It has intuitive appeal because ROA can be compared to external market-based yields to provide a benchmark for a division's performance.[6] However, using ROA creates potential problems. ROA is not a measure of the division's economic rate of return because accounting income (the numerator) is not a measure of economic profit and assets (the denominator) is not the market value of the division's assets. Economic profit is the change in value over the period. Accounting rules tend to be conservative: They dictate that accounting net income excludes some value increases and includes some value declines. For example, accounting net income excludes any appreciation in land value until the land is sold but recognizes permanent declines in market value even though the land has not been sold. Also, accounting depreciation, which is deducted from accounting profits, does not necessarily reflect the change in the economic value of the depreciable assets.

Lars has an incentive to reject profitable projects with ROAs below the mean ROA for the consumer electronics group because accepting these projects lowers the group's ROA.

---

[6]For levered firms, it is important to add back interest expense to accounting income before comparing ROA to the firm's external market-based yields.

For example, suppose the group has an average ROA of 19 percent, 4 percent above its 15 percent cost of capital.[7] A new investment project that is 10 percent the size of the existing group investment is available. Its ROA is 16 percent, which also is above its cost of capital of 15 percent; thus, taking this project would increase firm value. But if this project is accepted, the group's ROA falls to 18.7 percent (.90 × 19% + .10 × 16%). If his group is evaluated based on increasing ROA, Lars will reject the project, even though its returns exceed the opportunity cost of capital.

Riskier projects require a higher cost of capital to compensate investors for bearing additional risk. If managers are rewarded solely for increasing their ROA without being charged for any additional risk imposed on the firm, they have incentives to plunge the firm into risky projects. Finally, a manager near retirement who is evaluated based on ROA might take projects that boost ROA immediately, even if they were expected to be unprofitable projects—this is just a specific case of the horizon problem (see Chapter 16).

Accounting Residual Income   To overcome some of the incentive deficiencies of ROA, such as divesting projects with ROAs above their cost of capital but below the division's average ROA, some firms use *residual income* to evaluate performance.[8] Residual income measures business-unit performance by subtracting the opportunity cost of capital employed from the profits of the business unit. For example, suppose Amita Singal manages a division that has profits of $20 million (after tax but before interest expense) and investment (total assets) of $100 million. Furthermore, her division has a required cost of capital of 15 percent. Its ROA is 20 percent, which is in excess of its opportunity cost of capital (15 percent). Residual income is $5 million ($20M − 15% × $100M). Under the residual income approach, divesting a project with an ROA of less than 20 percent but above 15 percent lowers residual income, although it raises average ROA.

Nonetheless, residual income has its own problems. Residual income is an absolute number; thus, larger divisions typically have larger residual incomes than smaller divisions. This makes relative performance-evaluation comparisons across investment centers of different sizes more difficult. To implement residual income measures requires that senior managers estimate the opportunity cost of capital for each division. In principle, each division will have a different required cost of capital to allow more precise performance evaluations by controlling for risk differences. However, these risk adjustments also potentially lead to greater influence costs as divisional managers lobby to lower their required capital costs.

Like ROA, residual income measures performance over a single year. It does not measure the impact of actions taken today on a firm's value in the future. For example, by cutting maintenance, current period residual income (and ROA) is increased, but future cash flow and hence the value of the firm might be jeopardized. Managers with short-term horizons will have incentives to avoid projects that have negative EVAs in early years even if they are quite profitable in the long run. Thus, the use of EVA is not sufficient for making investment decisions.

Table 17.2 summarizes our discussion of the various types of subunits of the firm. Notice that performance-evaluation measures and decision-right assignments are balanced: Decision rights assigned to the center and performance measures are matched.

---

[7]Cost of capital is the rate of return the firm must pay the market to raise capital. If the firm can raise money at 15 percent and invest in projects earning 16 percent, the value of the firm increases.

[8]For a more detailed discussion of residual income, see D. Solomons (1968), *Divisional Performance: Measurement and Control* (Richard D. Irwin: Burr Ridge, IL).

Note also the linkage between decision rights assigned to each center and the location of the specific knowledge. For example, if a center does not have knowledge of customer demand curves, it does not have decision rights for pricing and hence is evaluated as a cost center.

Although not explicit in Table 17.2, to ensure that our three-legged stool remains balanced, performance rewards must be tied to the performance evaluations. For example, besides introducing EVA in 1988, CSX also changed its management compensation plan. In 1991, CSX introduced a stock incentive program whereby 160 managers

---

EVA Often Is Linked to a Change in the Compensation Plan

At the beginning of this chapter, CSX's use of economic value added was described as a performance measurement plan that is being widely heralded and adopted by such companies as AT&T, Briggs & Stratton, Coca-Cola, Equifax, and Quaker Oats. EVA is a variant of residual income. The formula for EVA is

$$\text{EVA} = \text{adjusted accounting earnings} - (\text{weighted average cost of capital} \times \text{total capital})$$

This is the same formula as residual income, but variables used in computing EVA are measured more carefully than historically has been done. Instead of using the same accounting procedures that are used in reporting to shareholders, different accounting procedures are used to arrive at "adjusted accounting earnings." For example, standard United States accounting rules require that the entire amount spent on research and development each year be deducted from earnings. This creates incentives for managers with a short time horizon to cut R&D spending. One adjustment to accounting earnings is to add back R&D spending and treat it as an asset to be amortized, usually over 5 years. Total capital, in the above formula, consists of all the firm's assets, including the amount invested in R&D and other adjustments made to earnings.

EVA uses a weighted average cost of capital, which reflects the cost of equity and debt. The cost of equity is the price appreciation and dividends the shareholders could have earned in a portfolio of companies of similar risk. This is the opportunity cost the shareholders bear by buying the company's stock. The cost of debt is the current market yield on debt of similar risk. The costs of debt and equity are weighted by the relative amounts of debt and equity. Suppose the cost of equity is 18 percent, the cost of debt is 10 percent, and the firm's capital structure is 40 percent debt and 60 percent equity. Then, the weighted average cost of capital is 14.8 percent $(0.60 \times 18\% + 0.40 \times 10\%)$.*

EVA, like residual income, measures the total return after deducting the cost of all capital employed by the firm. It estimates the economic profits of the firm in the period (usually a year). Many of the firms adopting EVA to measure divisional performance did so as part of a corporate reorganization. AT&T was organized as a huge corporate monolith providing balance sheets only for a few large groups such as long-distance services. In 1992, AT&T reorganized into investment centers, each resembling an independent company. The long-distance service function now has 40 units selling products like 800 service, telemarketing, and public telephones. Each is measured using EVA. Besides decentralizing decision rights and adopting EVA as the performance measure, firms also change the third leg of the three-legged stool, the reward system. Manager bonuses are based on EVA.

* EVA is calculated on an after-tax basis using adjusted accounting earnings before interest but net of income taxes. The weighted average cost of capital is computed as follows. The after-tax cost of debt is computed using 1 minus the marginal corporate tax rate times the market yield on debt of similar risk. For example, suppose the market yield on equivalent debt is 15 percent and the marginal corporate tax rate is 38 percent. The after-tax cost of debt is 9.3 percent $[15\% \times (1 - 0.38)]$. If the cost of equity is 20 percent and the proportions of debt and equity are the same, the after-tax weighted average cost of capital is 14.65 percent $(0.50 \times 9.3\% + 0.50 \times 20\%)$.

Sources: B. Stewart (1991), *The Quest for Value* (Harper Business: New York); and S. Tully (1993), "The Real Key to Creating Wealth," *Fortune* (September 20), 38–50.

accepted a plan to purchase CSX stock at the market price of $48. They paid 5 percent in cash, and CSX loaned them the balance at 7.9 percent interest. If the stock price were above $69 per share in July 1994, CSX would forgive the loan's interest and 25 percent of the principal. If the stock were below $69, the managers would pay all the interest and principal. With the stock selling at about $77 at the end of July 1994, the managers made a substantial profit—but so did the shareholders. Therefore, besides linking pay to the performance measure, EVA, CSX also changed the performance reward system.

Transfer Pricing[9]

As discussed above, firms organize into business units. Whenever business units transfer goods or services among themselves, measuring their performance requires that a *transfer price* be established for the goods and services exchanged. For example, suppose a large chemical company is organized into profit centers. Besides producing for and selling to outside customers, these profit centers also sell intermediate products to other profit centers within the company. In order to measure the performance of these profit centers, each of these internal transactions requires a transfer price. The purchasing division pays the transfer price; the producing division receives the transfer price.

Some executives do not view the transfer-pricing problem as important from the overall firm's perspective. They think that changing transfer-pricing methods merely shifts income among divisions and that, except for relative performance evaluation, little else is affected. But this is a mistake: *The choice of transfer-pricing method does not merely reallocate total company profits among business units, it affects the firm's total profits.* Think of the firm's total profit as a pie. Choice among transfer-pricing methods not only changes how the pie is divided among the business units, it also changes the size of the pie to be divided.

Managers make investment, purchasing, and production decisions based on the transfer prices they face. If from the firm's perspective these transfer prices do not reflect resource values accurately, managers will make inappropriate decisions and the value of the firm will be reduced. For example, if the opportunity cost to the firm of producing an intermediate chemical is $20 per kilogram but the transfer price is $30, the purchasing division will consume too little of the chemical and total firm value will be reduced. Purchasing division managers will have the incentive to shift away from using the chemical to other inputs that in reality are more expensive. Also, because transfer prices affect managers' performance evaluations, incorrect transfer prices can result in inappropriate promotion and retention decisions.

Transfer prices are more prevalent in organizations than many managers realize. Firms often have extensive charge-back system for internal service departments. Consider the charges that the advertising department receives from the maintenance department for janitorial service, as well as charges for telephones, security services, data processing, legal, or personnel services. Most firms charge inside users for these internally provided services. Such charge-back systems also exist in hospitals, universities, and other nonprofit organizations. These charge-back systems are internal transfer prices.

Because the use of transfer prices (including charge-back systems) is widespread and because transfer pricing affects performance evaluation and hence the rewards managers receive, fighting over the transfer price between divisions is virtually inevitable. Transfer pricing is a continuing source of tension within firms. Many managers in

---

[9]This section draws on J. Brickley, C. Smith, and J. Zimmerman (1995), "Transfer Pricing and the Control of Internal Corporate Transactions," *Journal of Applied Corporate Finance* 8, 60–67.

Transfer Pricing and Taxes

DHL, the package delivery and courier service, lost a transfer-pricing dispute with the Internal Revenue Service and had to pay $32 million more in US taxes. In fact, 30 percent of all US corporate tax adjustments made each year involve transfer-pricing disputes. Beginning in the late 1980s, the US began imposing penalties of between 20 percent and 40 percent of the tax underpayment caused by transfer-pricing issues and strict record-keeping requirements. As a result, corporate tax departments quickly realized that if they underpaid their US taxes, they could be exposed to huge penalties; if they underpaid other countries, they would face less severe penalties. But other countries quickly followed suit. Canada doubled the size of their staff of transfer-pricing examiners. Australia, Brazil, Japan, and France put new penalties in place.

To attempt to streamline the transfer-pricing dispute-resolution process, the IRS instituted an Advanced Pricing Agreement (APA) Program. A taxpayer team and IRS team work together prospectively to develop the transfer-pricing method the taxpayer will use. As long as the taxpayer complies with the agreement, the IRS will not challenge subsequent years' transfer prices. The IRS had negotiated about 350 APAs by the end of 1999.

Source: S. Wrappe, K. Milani, and J. Joy (1999), "The Transfer Price Is Right," *Strategic Finance* (July), 39–43.

multidivisional firms are involved in a parade of transfer-pricing disputes over the course of their careers.

A potentially important factor in determining an optimal transfer price is taxes. If the producing and purchasing divisions are in different countries and subject to different tax rates, then taxes affect the opportunity cost of the product and thus the optimal transfer price. The producing division pays income taxes on the difference between its costs and what it receives for each unit, which is determined by the transfer price. In general, to minimize the sum of the two taxes, the firm should set the transfer price so as to allocate as much of the profit as possible to the division in the country with the lower tax rate.[10] To simplify the analysis, this section focuses on the organizational economics of transfer pricing and ignores these important tax issues.

Economics of Transfer Pricing

The transfer-pricing rule is quite simple to state: The optimal transfer price for a product or service is its opportunity cost—it is the value forgone by not using the product transferred in its next best alternative use. Unfortunately, as we will see, this rule, although simple to state, often is difficult to implement in practice.

Transfer Pricing with Costless Information   To illustrate the concept of opportunity cost, we focus on two of a multinational firm's profit centers—US manufacturing and European distribution. Senior management is considering making a product in the US division and transferring it to its European division. Assume also that marginal cost of production is $3 per unit, and that the US division has excess capacity. If the product is transferred to Europe, they can sell it and receive $5 for each unit, net of their own marginal cost. Also, everyone knows each division's cost and revenue data.

[10]International tax treaties and local regulation constrain the transfer-pricing methods firms can use for tax purposes. See M. Scholes and M. Wolfson (1992), *Taxes and Business Strategy* (Prentice Hall: Englewood Cliffs, NJ).

Dual Transfer Pricing Systems?

Some consultants advocate using two separate transfer pricing systems, one aimed at satisfying tax reporting and another directed at internal decision making. Jay Tredwell, director of CEO Solutions for Answer *Think* Consulting Group, says, "Having a separate system can give senior managers a better view of . . . real profitability [as opposed to] their 'tax profitability.'" However, Michael Patton, a partner at Ernst and Young, counters,

> An essential problem with separated reporting is that transfer prices already reflect the profitability of a division or project. If you are trying to make decisions about new activities or facilities, and trying to judge their returns on invested capital, you need good benchmarks to judge these by, and good transfer prices provide part of that. Basically, then the question is whether your current transfer prices reflect economic reality or not. If they do, there's little need for a new system. If not, the tax authorities may have a question or two for you on audit in a few years' time.

Case Corp., a $6 billion farm and construction equipment maker, opposes separate transfer-pricing systems for statutory and internal reporting. They argue dual systems are costly. Case keeps all accounts around the world based on US accounting practice and bases management results and compensation on actual transfer prices used by divisions for tax purposes.

Source: I. Springsteel (1999), "Separate but Unequal," *CFO* (August), 89–91.

If the unit is not manufactured, the firm saves $3 in US manufacturing costs but forgoes $5 in European revenue, hence reducing profit by $2. If the unit is manufactured and transferred, the firm forgoes $3 (marginal cost to produce) and receives $5, for a net receipt of $2. The better alternative is to manufacture and transfer the unit. The resources forgone by transferring it from the United States to Europe—and hence the opportunity cost of such a transfer—are $3 per unit, the same as US manufacturing's marginal cost of production.

As this example is meant to suggest, the marginal cost of producing the unit often is its opportunity cost. But this is not always the case. Sometimes, the opportunity cost is the marginal revenue of selling the intermediate good externally. For example, suppose the US division can produce one unit for $3, and can either transfer that unit to Europe or sell it for $6 in the United States, but, because of limited capacity, it cannot do both. In this case, by having the US division transfer the unit to Europe, the firm forgoes selling the intermediate good in the US market. And even though the marginal cost of producing the unit still is $3, the opportunity cost of making the transfer now is $6. Thus, it now is optimal to sell it externally rather than to transfer it to Europe.

More generally, the US division will produce to the point where the marginal cost of the last unit equals the transfer price. Likewise, the European division will buy units from the US division so long as their net receipts just cover the transfer price. When opportunity cost is used to set the transfer price and both divisions are maximizing their respective profits, total firm profits are maximized, assuming no other interdependencies between the divisions (we consider the case of dependencies among units later). Thus, in this simple example, the transfer price represents the marginal cost to the European division. If the transfer price is too high or too low relative to opportunity cost, Europe purchases too few or too many units and the firm's profits are not maximized.

Transfer Pricing with Asymmetric Information   The preceding discussion assumes that everyone knows that the US division's marginal production cost is $3, that the intermediate product has an external price of $6, that Europe's marginal revenue is $5, and whether the US division has excess capacity. Yet if all this knowledge were readily

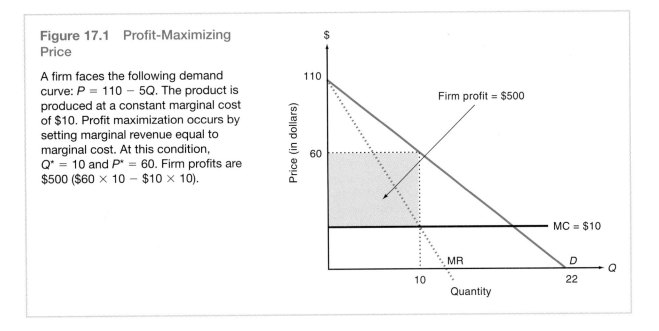

Figure 17.1 Profit-Maximizing Price

A firm faces the following demand curve: $P = 110 - 5Q$. The product is produced at a constant marginal cost of $10. Profit maximization occurs by setting marginal revenue equal to marginal cost. At this condition, $Q^* = 10$ and $P^* = 60$. Firm profits are $500 ($60 $\times$ 10 − $10 $\times$ 10).

available, there would be no reason to decentralize decision making within the organization. Central management would have the knowledge to make the decision and could retain the decision rights or, if the decision rights were delegated, closely monitor the process at low cost. In reality, much of this information is not readily available to central management. Especially in large, multidivisional firms, such knowledge generally resides at lower levels within the firm where it is private knowledge, costly to either transfer or verify by senior management. In some circumstances, lower-level managers have incentives to distort the information they pass to senior managers. To illustrate these incentives, we consider a firm with market power (see Chapter 6).

Consider the situation where Hiroshi Komada, the manager of manufacturing, is the only person with detailed knowledge of his division's marginal costs, and assume that Hiroshi seeks to maximize the profits of his division. Even if distribution is allowed to purchase the product on the outside, if manufacturing has market power in setting the transfer price, it will attempt to set the price above marginal cost to increase its *measured* profits. When this happens, the firm manufactures and sells too few units of the product. This is another example of unexploited gains from trade from monopoly that we described in Chapter 6. The manufacturing division possesses what amounts to monopoly rights in information and hence behaves like a monopolist. Just as monopolists earn "monopoly profits" by raising prices and restricting output, manufacturing's higher profits lead to lower-than-optimal production levels and reduced total firm value.

This problem can be illustrated by example. For simplicity, consider a firm that produces one product and faces the following demand:

$$P = 110 - 5Q \qquad (17.3)$$

Assume that the product is produced at a constant marginal cost of $10. Profit maximization occurs by setting marginal revenue equal to marginal cost. At this condition, $Q^* = 10$ and $P^* = 60$. Firm profits are $500 ($60 $\times$ 10 − $10 $\times$ 10). Figure 17.1 depicts this situation.

The Successive Monopoly Case

A basic principle in economics says that to maximize the value of the firm, a monopoly price should be charged only once whereas all other transfers are charged marginal cost. To illustrate, suppose a paper box company has both a patented technology for making boxes and a patented box design. The production technology belongs to the manufacturing division and the unique box design is sold by the distribution division. Distribution buys the boxes from manufacturing, and both divisions are run as profit centers. Further assume that manufacturing has enough capacity to sell both internally and externally. Thus, the opportunity cost of manufacturing's transfer is its marginal production cost.

Transfer-pricing theory implies that the profit-maximizing solution in this case is to set the price to external customers at the price where the firm's marginal revenue is equal to the combined marginal costs of manufacturing and distribution. This result obtains if distribution buys the boxes from manufacturing at marginal cost. In this case, to maximize its own profits, distribution will set the external price at the point where the marginal revenue from customers equals the sum of distribution's own marginal cost and the transfer price, which is manufacturing's marginal cost.

However, if the transfer price is marginal cost (and assuming marginal cost is less than or equal to average cost), manufacturing reports no profit. If manufacturing tries to report a profit by charging distribution a transfer price above marginal cost, the firm's profits are lower than in the original case. For, if manufacturing is able to set the transfer price above marginal cost, then when distribution sets the final price to the customer, it will equate marginal revenue to a now-higher marginal cost—that is, its own marginal cost plus the transfer price. To maximize its own profits, distribution will thus set the price "too high," buy fewer units from manufacturing, and hence fewer units will be sold than under the profit-maximizing case above.

The transfer-pricing rule thus holds that when two divisions inside the same firm have market power (that is, when they are able to charge prices above long-run marginal cost), both divisions should not be allowed to charge prices above their own costs. When there are such successive monopolies within firms, only one division should be permitted to charge a price above cost. If monopoly prices are charged at both stages of the production process, a firm's profits will not be maximized.

Assume that manufacturing produces the good at $MC = 10$ and transfers it to distribution at a transfer price, P_t. Suppose the only cost to the distribution division is the transfer price. (For simplicity, additional distribution costs equal zero.)

Distribution sells the product externally and thus the demand curve for its product is the firm's demand curve. How many units of the good will the manager of this unit want to buy at each possible transfer price? Note that distribution's marginal cost is the transfer price $MC_d = P_t$. Distribution maximizes division profit by setting $MC_d = MR_d$. Hence, in this case, the firm's marginal revenue curve represents distribution's demand for the good and thus is the derived demand curve facing manufacturing: $P_t = 110 - 10Q$ (the marginal revenue curve in Figure 17.1).

Next, assume that manufacturing sets the transfer price. It has monopoly power, and because of costly information, senior management cannot monitor the decision. What price will manufacturing set and what quantity of the good will be produced? Our manager of manufacturing, Hiroshi, sets marginal cost equal to marginal revenue: $MC_m = MR_m$. As discussed above, manufacturing faces a *derived demand curve* equal to the marginal revenue curve for the firm: $P_t = 110 - 10Q$. The marginal revenue for the manufacturing division is, therefore, $P_t = 110 - 20Q$. Profit maximization for manufacturing will involve setting the transfer price at $60 and selling 5 units of the good. (See the left panel in Figure 17.2.) Facing a transfer price of $60, distribution in turn will sell the 5 units to the external market at a price of $85 (right panel in Figure 17.2).

Figure 17.2 Decentralized Firm

In the decentralized firm, manufacturing produces the good at MC = 10 and transfers it to distribution at a transfer price, P_t. Distribution's demand curve for the product is the firm's demand curve. Distribution's marginal cost is the transfer price $MC_d = P_t$. Distribution maximizes profit (for the unit) by setting $MC_d = MR_d$. The firm's marginal revenue curve represents distribution's demand for the good and is, therefore, the demand curve facing manufacturing: $P_t = 110 - 10Q$. The manager of manufacturing sets marginal cost equal to marginal revenue: $MC_m = MR_m$. The marginal cost = 10. The marginal revenue for the manufacturing division is $P_t = 110 - 20Q$. Profit maximization for manufacturing will involve setting the transfer price at $60 and selling 5 units of the good (see the left panel). Facing a transfer price of $60, distribution will in turn sell the 5 units to the external market at a price of $85 (right panel). Total firm profits are $375 (5 × $85 − 5 × $10), which are lower than at the firm profit-maximizing output of 10 units ($500). Manufacturing has profits of $250, and distribution has profits of $125.

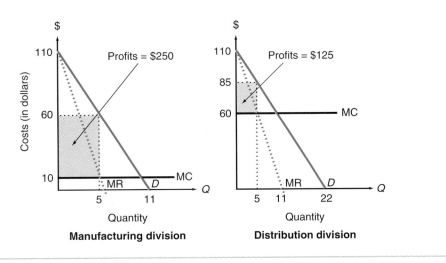

Manufacturing division | Distribution division

Total firm profits are $375 (5 × $85 − 5 × $10), which are lower than at the profit-maximizing output of 10 units—$500. Manufacturing reports profits of $250, and distribution books profits of $125. Both divisions are reporting profits, but total firm profits are lower in Figure 17.2 than in Figure 17.1.

The basic problem is that distribution, facing a transfer price of $60, is overestimating the *opportunity* cost to the firm of producing extra units of the good ($10). Hence, from the firm's standpoint, distribution stops short of the optimal quantity to be sold to the external market. The transfer price that ensures firm profit maximization in this example is the marginal production cost of the unit. Note, however, that Hiroshi does not want to set that transfer price because manufacturing would report a lower profit—in this example, $0.

The above discussion thus illustrates the basic incentive problems associated with internal transfers when information is held privately by divisional managers. Opportunity cost is the transfer price that maximizes a firm's value. But because business-unit managers tend to have better knowledge of opportunity costs than senior management and because transfer prices frequently are used in performance evaluation and in setting managerial rewards, divisional managers have incentives to distort information to influence the transfer price.

Complicating matters further, getting the information necessary to calculate opportunity costs is especially difficult for senior management because opportunity costs depend on the firm's next best alternative use of the good or service. Central management is likely to know less about the next best use of a product, and about the resources used to make the product, than the manager of the division that produces it. Moreover, the next best alternative will change as the firm's business opportunities change. For example, sometimes the division has excess capacity and manufacturing can sell the good both internally and externally. At other times, manufacturing has only enough current capacity to produce for either the inside or outside user. This specialized knowledge of the alternatives is held primarily by the division managers.

Problems arise whether distribution or manufacturing has the decision rights to set the price of the goods or services transferred and the other division cannot purchase or sell outside. Manufacturing sets a price above opportunity cost to capture some monopoly profits, and distribution purchases fewer units than if the appropriate (lower) transfer price were set. But, if given the decision rights to determine the price, distribution would set a transfer price below the opportunity cost and manufacturing would supply too few units. Again, the number of units transferred is below the profit-maximizing level. If central management knew the opportunity cost, it would not have to decentralize decision making to the profit centers and could dictate both price and quantity decisions.

The economics of transfer pricing is summarized well by the following quote:

The economist's first instinct is to set the transfer price equal to marginal cost. But it may be difficult to find out marginal cost. As a practical matter, marginal cost information is rarely known to anybody in the firm, because it depends on opportunity costs that vary with capacity use. And even if marginal cost information were available, there is no guarantee that it would be revealed in a truthful fashion for the purpose of determining an optimal transfer price.[11]

Common Transfer-Pricing Methods

The correct transfer price, then, is opportunity cost. But as we also have noted, determining opportunity costs is expensive—in part because the information necessary to calculate such costs resides with operating managers who have incentives to distort it. To address this problem, companies sometimes commission special studies of the firm's cost structure by outside experts. Such studies, however, are not only costly, but their findings become outdated whenever the firm's business opportunities or productive capacities change. On the other hand, if senior management simply vests the right to set the transfer price with either manufacturing or distribution, prices are likely to be set too high or too low, resulting in too few units transferred and the firm's value lower than it could be.

Because determining opportunity costs is itself an expensive undertaking, managers resort to various lower-cost approximations. There are at least four different methods for setting transfer prices that firms regularly use to approximate the opportunity cost of the units transferred: market price, marginal production cost, full cost, and negotiated pricing. As discussed below, each of these four methods is better than the others in some situations, but not in others. For example, if the divisions operate in different countries with different tax rates, then the choice of method will be driven in part by tax considerations. If manufacturing faces lower tax rates than distribution, full-cost prices will allocate more of the profit

---

[11]B. Holmstrom and J. Tirole (1991), "Transfer Pricing and Organizational Form," *Journal of Law, Economics, and Organizations* 7, 201–228.

to the lower-taxed division than marginal-cost prices. Our aim in the rest of this section is to describe these basic alternatives and set forth their advantages and disadvantages so that managers can select the best transfer-pricing method for their particular circumstances.

Market-Based Transfer Prices   The standard transfer-pricing rule offered by most textbooks is this: Given a competitive external market for the good, the product should be transferred at the external market price. If manufacturing cannot make a long-run profit at the external price, then the company is better off not producing internally and instead should purchase in the external market. If the purchasing division cannot make a long-run profit at the external price, then the company is better off not processing the intermediate product and instead should sell in the external market.

In short, the use of market-based transfer prices often is assumed to produce the correct make-versus-buy decisions. In many situations, however, market prices will not provide an accurate reflection of opportunity costs. If the firm and the market both are making the intermediate good, the fundamental question arises, *Can both survive in the long run?* If one can produce the good at a lower, long-run average cost than the other, the high-cost producer should not be producing the intermediate product.

Yet it is important to keep in mind that transactions generally take place inside rather than outside firms whenever the cost of repetitive internal contracting is cheaper than outsourcing.[12] For example, production of different kinds of goods tends to take place inside the same firm when there are important interdependencies or synergies among those products. And, of course, the more valuable such synergies, the more likely the firm will continue producing internally.[13]

At the same time—and this is what makes the issue of transfer pricing so difficult—in circumstances where the firm is most likely to produce a good internally, the external market price is least likely to provide an accurate reflection of the opportunity cost of internal production. For example, it is often the case that an intermediate good is either not being produced by other firms or that the good produced externally is not identical to the good produced internally. In one case, there is no market price; in the other, the market price often will be an unreliable guide to opportunity cost. And, even when there are virtually identical "cheaper" external products, producing internally still can make sense insofar as it provides greater quality control, more assurance of timeliness of supply, or better protection of proprietary information. When these factors are included in the analysis, the external market may no longer be "cheaper."

In such cases, use of the market price as the transfer price may understate the profitability of the product and its contribution to the value of the firm.[14] Suppose, for

---

[12]Advantages to internal transactions include the elimination of credit risk, lower marketing costs, and learning from production. Chapter 3 and R. Coase (1937), "The Nature of the Firm," *Economica* 4, 386–405. For a summary of the arguments for the types of costs that are lowered by firms, see R. Watts (1992), "Accounting Choice Theory and Market-Based Research in Accounting," *British Accounting Journal* 24, 242–246. These arguments include economies of scale in contracting, team production and monitoring, postcontractual opportunism, and knowledge costs. Chapter 18 discusses these topics.

[13]Interdependencies or synergies that cause production to occur inside the firm are classic economic externalities. If interdependencies in production or demand functions exist, the market price does not capture these interdependencies. The same occurs inside the firm and causes the external price to mismeasure the opportunity cost of one more unit being transferred.

[14]This point has been recognized by others. As one notes, "observed market prices cannot directly guide the owner of the input to perform in the same manner as if every activity he performs were measured and priced." In S. Cheung (1983), "The Contractual Nature of the Firm," *Journal of Law & Economics* 26 (April), 5; R. Ball (1989), "The Firm as a Specialist Contracting Intermediary: Applications to Accounting and Auditing," working paper (University of Rochester: Rochester, NY).

Controlling Quality by Internal Production at Kodak

Eastman Gelatine buys 80 million pounds of cow bones annually. In their plant in Peabody, Massachusetts, the company turns these bones into gelatine. Trucked to Kodak headquarters, it is mixed with other chemicals to create a photosensitive emulsion on strips of film. The gel-making process is complicated and is affected by the bone used. (Male is better than female; young is better than old; longer is better than shorter; drier is better than wet.) Kodak founder George Eastman started the plant in 1930 to provide better control over the gel-making process. He nearly had been ruined after buying a batch of bones from cattle fed mustard seed, causing his gel to overexpose the film. Kodak, like many companies, has outsourced an array of activities from its cafeteria to plant security. Yet it has kept Eastman Gelatine, in part to control quality of a critical input.

Source: A. Klein (1999), "Who Knew Kodak Would Keep So Many Skeletons in Its Closet?" *The Wall Street Journal* (January 18), A1.

example, an intermediate product can be purchased (but not sold) externally for $3 per unit. Synergies such as high transaction costs of using the market make it effective to produce the item internally. Internal production avoids the costs of writing and enforcing contracts. Suppose there are $.50 worth of synergies, so that the correct transfer price is $2.50 in the sense that $2.50 is the opportunity cost to the firm. But, if the market price of $3.00 is used as the transfer price, distribution will purchase fewer units than if $2.50 were used, and the value of the firm will not be maximized.

Marginal-Cost Transfer Prices   If there is no external market for the intermediate good or if large synergies among business units cause the market price to be an inaccurate measure of opportunity cost, then marginal production cost may be the most effective alternative transfer price. As we saw earlier, marginal cost represents the value of the resources forgone to produce the last unit.

As with other transfer-pricing methods, there are problems with marginal production cost as a measure of opportunity cost. One is that manufacturing does not necessarily recover its fixed costs. If all manufacturing's output is transferred internally and marginal cost is below its average total cost, manufacturing's fixed costs are not recovered. Thus, manufacturing appears to be losing money.[15]

One variant of marginal-cost transfer pricing is to use a two-part price—to price all transfers at marginal cost while also charging distribution a fixed fee for these services. Distribution pays marginal cost for the additional units and buys the number of units that maximize the firm's profits. Unlike straight marginal-cost pricing, this variant allows manufacturing to cover its full cost and earn a profit. The fixed fee represents the rights by distribution to acquire the product at marginal cost, and it is set to cover manufacturing's fixed cost plus a return on equity.

Another problem with marginal-cost transfer pricing occurs in situations where the marginal cost per unit is not constant as volume changes. Suppose the marginal cost per unit increases as volume expands (say, a night shift is added with higher wages per hour). If marginal cost is greater than average cost and all users are charged the higher marginal cost, the total charged to all the users is greater than

[15]Of course, if central management knows the magnitude of the fixed costs, it can budget for this loss. But, once again, if central management knew the magnitude of the fixed costs, then it would know marginal cost, and thus there would be little reason to have a separate business unit and transfer-pricing system in the first place.

the total cost incurred by the firm. Users who did not expand their volume will still see their costs increase. In such cases, conflicts are likely within the firm over the appropriate measure of marginal cost and whether all users should pay marginal cost or just those users who expanded output, thereby prompting the addition of the night shift.

A similar problem arises when manufacturing approaches capacity. To illustrate the problem, let's assume that manufacturing is considering a $2.5 million outlay to add more capacity. These capacity additions costs of $2.5 million are variable in the long run but become short-run fixed costs (depreciation and higher utilities and maintenance). Thus, conflicts arise between manufacturing and distribution as to whether these additional capacity costs should be included in the transfer price or not. What makes such conflicts so difficult to resolve is that there is no indisputably objective method for calculating marginal costs. They are not reported in *The Wall Street Journal.* Instead, they have to be estimated, normally as "variable costs," from accounting records. Although most of the components of marginal cost are easily observed, such as the cost of direct labor and direct material, some components are quite difficult to estimate. For example, it is not easy to estimate the additional costs imposed on the purchasing department when additional units are manufactured.

Marginal-cost transfer pricing also creates incentives for manufacturing to distort marginal cost upward, perhaps by misstating some fixed costs as variable. For example, how much of the electricity bill is fixed and how much is variable? Since these classifications are to some extent arbitrary, resources are wasted as managers in manufacturing and distribution debate various cost terms and their applications—and as senior managers are forced to spend time arbitrating such disputes.

Moreover, under marginal-cost transfer pricing, manufacturing can have an incentive to convert a dollar of fixed costs into more than a dollar of marginal costs—for example, by using high-priced outsourcing of parts instead of cheaper internal manufacturing—even though this clearly reduces the value of the firm. For manufacturing, the use of outsourcing can remove the burden of any fixed costs while distribution, as well as the firm as a whole, bears the extra cost of such decisions.

Full-Cost Transfer Prices   Because of the information and incentive problems described above, simple, objective, hard-to-change transfer-pricing rules can lead to higher firm value than transfer-pricing rules that give one manager discretion over the transfer price. Objective transfer-pricing rules such as those based on full accounting cost often are adopted primarily to avoid wasteful disputes over measuring marginal costs. Since full cost is the sum of fixed and variable cost, full cost cannot be changed simply by reclassifying a fixed cost as a variable cost.

The problem, however, is that full-cost transfer pricing frequently causes distribution to purchase too few units. Full-cost accounting generally overstates the opportunity cost to the firm of producing and transferring one more unit internally. And so distribution usually will buy too few units internally. Full cost also allows manufacturing to transfer any of its inefficiencies to distribution. Thus, manufacturing has less incentive to be efficient under a full-cost transfer-price rule.[16]

Despite all these problems, however, full-cost transfer pricing is quite common. In various surveys of corporate practice, full-cost transfer prices are used 40 to 50 percent

---

[16]J. Zimmerman (2000), *Accounting for Decision Making and Control* (McGraw-Hill/Irwin: Burr Ridge, IL) Chapter 5.

Transfer Pricing at Hewlett-Packard

Jon Flexman, CFO at Hewlett-Packard, oversees a mish-mash of interdivisional transfer-pricing mechanisms based on both financial and tax-accounting regulations. "We currently reward managers based on their product margins, as they are created by our transfer-pricing system." Managers "often get caught up in negotiations with each other" to produce profits for their division and themselves personally. This produces a set of final output prices that hampers what sales representatives charge end users. Another manager at Answer *Think* Consulting Group complains, "The biggest problems are when the measured profitability of a business unit has more to do with the skill of its manager in negotiating his transfer prices within the company than [it does with] its economic profits and the factors that drive shareholder-value creation."

Source: I. Springsteel (1999), "Separate but Unequal," *CFO* (August), 89–91.

of the time.[17] In most cases, moreover, the definition of *full cost* includes both direct materials and labor as well as a charge for overhead.

One reason for the popularity of full-cost transfer prices is their ability to deal with the problem of changes in capacity. As a plant begins to reach capacity, opportunity cost is likely to rise because of congestion and the cost of alternative uses of now-scarce capacity. Hence, opportunity cost is likely to be higher than direct materials and labor costs. In this case, full cost might be a closer approximation to opportunity cost than just the cost of materials and labor.

Perhaps the most important benefit of full-cost transfer pricing, however, is its simplicity and hence its low cost of implementation. Because of its simplicity and objectivity, full-cost transfer pricing reduces influence costs. That is, because operating managers have less ability to manipulate full-cost than marginal-cost calculations, senior management faces fewer calls to arbitrate disputes over calculating the transfer price. Nonetheless, managers should consider carefully whether full-cost pricing is optimal for their particular situation. If the opportunity cost differs from full cost materially, the firm's forgone profits can be substantial.

Negotiated Transfer Prices   Transfer prices can be set by negotiation between manufacturing and distribution. This method can result in transfer prices that approximate opportunity cost because manufacturing will not agree to a price that is below its opportunity cost and distribution will not pay a price above that for which it can buy the product elsewhere.

With negotiated transfer prices, the two divisions have the incentive to set the number of units so as to maximize the combined profits of the two divisions. Once the value-maximizing number of units is established, the transfer price determines how the total profits are divided between the two divisions. In terms of Figure 17.1, if the two divisions negotiate over both price and quantity, they have the joint incentive to set $Q = 10$ because this maximizes the total profit to be split—$500. Yet if the two divisions just negotiate over price, there is no guarantee they will arrive at the transfer price that maximizes the firm's value.

[17]Technical note: To be sure, marginal-cost transfer prices also allow the selling division to export some of its inefficiencies to the purchasing division, but the problem is not as pronounced as under full cost. Nevertheless, the problem of exporting inefficiencies to the buying division through cost-based transfer prices is reduced if the purchasing division can purchase externally as well as from the selling division. This forces the selling division to remain competitive.

While negotiation is a fairly common method, it too has drawbacks. It is time-consuming and can produce conflicts among divisions. Divisional performance measurement becomes sensitive to the relative negotiating skills of the two division managers. Moreover, if the two divisions negotiate a transfer price without at the same time agreeing on the quantity to be transferred at that price, there is no guarantee that they will arrive at the transfer price that maximizes the firm's value.

Reorganization: The Solution If All Else Fails

In some cases, transfer-pricing conflicts among profit centers can become sufficiently divisive to impose large costs on the firm. These costs take the form of both influence costs and the opportunity costs that arise when other than firm-value-maximizing transfer prices are chosen. Costly transfer-pricing disputes usually occur when the relative volume of transactions among divisions is large. In such cases, a small change in the transfer price can have a large effect on the division's reported profits. Hence, the potential for (and destructive effects of) opportunistic transfer-pricing actions by operating managers is substantial.

If transfer pricing becomes sufficiently dysfunctional, reorganize the firm. For example, senior management could combine two profit centers with a large volume of transfers into a single division. Alternatively, it might make more sense to convert manufacturing into a cost center rather than a profit center and compensate the operating head based on efficiency of production. Or, senior management might even organize both divisions as cost centers and keep the pricing and quantity decisions at the central office.

A final possibility is to give distribution the right to produce the input—that is, change the allocation of decision rights and allow both manufacturing and distribution the rights to make the transferred good. However, this alternative can be expensive due to the duplication of resources and effort.

Internal Accounting System and Performance Evaluation[18]

Accounting costs, revenues, profits, return on investment, and residual income usually are used as performance measures of cost, expense, revenue, profit, and investment centers. Accounting costs frequently are used as transfer prices. The accounting system is an important component of the firm's performance-evaluation system and thus is an integral part of the firm's control system—the performance-evaluation and reward systems. This section elaborates on accounting's role within the firm.

Uses of the Accounting System

Many people think of the firm's accounting system in terms of its external financial reports—balance sheets and income statements—to the shareholders, taxing authorities, regulators, and lenders. These external financial reports (both quarterly and annual) are an incredibly aggregated view of the enormous amount of data produced internally. Internally, managers rely on detailed, often computer-accessible, operating reports of expenses, product costs, and customer account balances from the accounting system.

These internal reports are used by management for two general purposes: decision management and decision control. As discussed in Chapter 12, the decision-making process can be divided into decision management (initiation and implementation) and

---

[18]This section draws on analysis in Zimmerman (2000).

Internal Auditing in Law Firms

Law firms, scared of adverse publicity from billing errors, are turning to internal auditors to catch problems before others do. The fear of embarrassment provides incentives for firms to check their bills more carefully. The firm of Bartlit, Beck, Herman, Palenchar & Scott caught an error before the bills went out. In two out-of-town trials, one client was almost billed $8,000 for a hotel in which its attorneys didn't stay. Before Winston and Strawn in Chicago hired its internal auditor, its former managing partner went to jail for cheating the firm and several clients of more than $750,000. Some of these internal auditors report to the head of the finance department. Other firms, fearing a conflict of interest, have the auditor report directly to the firm's executive director or to the firm's executive committee (which would be equivalent to the board of directors in a corporation).

Source: E. White (1998), "More Law Firms Are Auditing Themselves to
Catch Billing Errors," *The Wall Street Journal* (July 14), B8.

decision control (ratification and monitoring). Managers frequently have both decision-management and control rights, but normally not for the same decisions. More senior managers in the firm tend to hold more decision-control rights, whereas decision-management rights tend to be delegated to managers lower in the firm. To exercise either decision-management or decision-control rights, managers require information. Some of that information is provided by the accounting system. Thus, although the accounting system is used for both decision management and decision control, its primary function within most firms is decision control.

Decision management requires estimates of future costs and benefits. Initiating an investment decision to build a new plant requires that the manager forecast future alternative uses of this plant; designing a marketing campaign requires judgments of likely future sales and competitors' responses. Managers frequently use accounting-based data as inputs to these decisions. Accounting numbers provide a starting point in forecasting future consequences of proposed actions. Most firms have accounting-based budget systems. Managers forecast costs and revenues for the next year in preparing their budgets. This process encourages managers to be forward-looking, to coordinate their operations with those managers most directly affected by their decisions and to share specialized knowledge of their markets and production technologies. Accounting-based budgets provide the framework for such coordination and knowledge sharing.

Although helpful for decision management, accounting systems generally are more useful for decision control (ratification and monitoring). In fact, this is the primary reason they evolved. Accounting systems are based on historical costs and historical revenues. Historical costs record what the firm paid for its current resource base and in this sense are backward-looking. Internal accounting systems protect against theft of company assets, fraud, and embezzlement. They also provide a scorecard to show how a business unit did historically by measuring costs, profits, or residual income. Monitoring is by definition an historical function, one well served by the accounting system. Since accounting systems are primarily used for decision control—to prevent malfeasance and to measure past performance—when it comes to providing managers with information for decision management, accounting systems often are found wanting.

Trade-offs between Decision Management and Decision Control

Considering how the accounting system is used for both decision management and decision control leads to a number of important insights. First, accounting measures, to

---

Massive Financial Fraud at Cendant

In the vast majority of cases, there are sufficient controls such as internal and external auditors to ensure that the firm's accounting reports accurately reflect the organization's financial performance. However, in rare situations, the managers have "cooked the books." Take the case of Cendant, the result of the $14 billion merger between HFS Inc. and CUC in 1997. HFS had been a franchising powerhouse with brands such as Ramada, Howard Johnson, Coldwell Banker, and Avis. CUC had been a hodgepodge of businesses including software, advertising, publications, and an online venture. Most of CUC's revenues came from selling memberships in discount shopping, travel, and entertainment clubs.

Four months after the merger, two former CUC managers who stayed on with Cendant after the merger disclosed to Cendant's CFO that they had been instructed to record millions of dollars of phony orders. They were told to adjust revenue up or expenses down. Further investigation concluded that about $500 million of revenue reported between 1995 and 1997 was simply invented and 61 percent of 1997 reported net income was fraudulent. Investors have filed at least 71 lawsuits. The US attorney's office and the Securities and Exchange Commission are investigating. The former CEO of CUC resigned and his CFO was fired. The day Cendant announced it had uncovered extensive alleged accounting irregularities that would force it to cut 1997 earnings by about 13 percent, Cendant's stock plunged 46.5 percent. The former CEO of HFS and current CEO of Cendant lost $800 million of personal wealth because of Cendant stock's plunge.

Source: E. Nelson (1998), "How Whistle-Blowers Set Off a Fraud Probe That Crushed Cendant," *The Wall Street Journal* (August 13), A1.

---

the extent that they are used for monitoring purposes, are not under the complete control of the people being monitored—the operating managers.

Second, managers with decision-management rights tend to be dissatisfied with financial measures for making operating decisions. The data often are at too aggregate a level and hence do not provide sufficient detail for the decision. In response, operating managers develop their own, often nonfinancial, information systems to provide more of the knowledge required for decision management. But at the same time, they rely on accounting-system output to monitor the managers who report to them.

Third, nonaccounting measures frequently are more timely than accounting measures. Not every decision requires ratification or monitoring. Decision monitoring can be based on aggregate data to average out random fluctuations. Instead of monitoring every machine setup, it usually is more effective to aggregate all setups occurring over the week or month and make sure the average setup cost is within acceptable levels.

One survey reports that managers rely on nonfinancial data (labor counts, units of output, units in inventory, units scrapped) to run their day-to-day operations. But when they are asked about their "most valuable report in general," they say it is the monthly income or expense statement because this is one of the measures used to judge their performance.[19]

In choosing among alternative accounting systems, managers often must make trade-offs between decision management and decision control. Consider the transfer-pricing decision. The transfer-pricing method that most accurately measures the opportunity cost to the firm of transferring one more unit inside the firm might not be the transfer-pricing method that gives internal managers the most effective incentives to maximize the firm's value. For example, if the transfer-pricing method that most accurately measures the opportunity cost of units transferred (decision management)

---

[19]S. McKinnon and W. Bruns (1992), *The Information Mosaic* (Harvard Business School: Boston).

CASE STUDY: *Celtex*

Celtex is a large, quite successful, decentralized specialty chemical producer organized into five independent investment centers. Each of the five investment centers is free to buy products either inside or outside the firm and is judged based on residual income. Most of each division's sales are to external customers. Celtex has the general reputation of being one of the top two or three companies in each of its markets.

Leopoldo Garcia, president of Synchem, Celtex's synthetic chemicals division, and Walid Murad, president of the consumer products division, are embroiled in a dispute. It all began 2 years ago when Wally asked Leo to modify a synthetic chemical for a new household cleaner. In return, Synchem would be reimbursed for out-of-pocket costs. After Synchem spent considerable time perfecting the chemical, Wally solicited competitive bids from Leo as well as several outside firms; he then awarded the contract to one of the outside firms which was the low bidder. This annoyed Leo, who expected his bid to receive special consideration because he developed the new chemical at cost, yet the outside vendor took advantage of his division's R&D.

The current conflict has to do with Synchem's producing chemical Q47, a standard product, for consumer products. Because of an economic slowdown, all synthetic chemical producers have excess capacity. Synchem was asked to bid on supplying Q47 for consumer products. Consumer products is moving into a new, experimental product line and Q47 is one of the key ingredients. Although the magnitude of the order is small relative to Synchem's total business, the price of Q47 is quite important in determining the profitability of the experimental line. Leo bid $3.20 per gallon. Meas Chemicals, an outside firm, bid $3. This time, Wally is annoyed because he knows that Leo's bid contains a substantial amount of fixed overhead and profit. Synchem buys the base raw material, Q4, from the organic chemicals division of Celtex for $1 per gallon. Organic chemical's out-of-pocket costs (i.e., variable costs) are 80 percent of the selling price. Synchem then further processes Q4 into Q47 and incurs additional variable costs of $1.75 per gallon. Allocated fixed overhead adds another $.30 per gallon.

Leo argues that he has $3.05 of cost in each gallon of Q47. If he turned around and sold the product for anything less than $3.20, he would be undermining his recent attempts to get his salespeople to stop cutting their bids and start quoting full-cost prices. Leo has been trying to enhance the quality of the business he is getting, and he fears that if he is forced to make Q47 for consumer products, all of his effort the last few months would be for naught. He argues, "I already gave away the store once to consumer products and I won't do it again." He questions, "How can senior managers expect me to return a positive residual income if I am forced to put in bids that don't recover full cost?"

Wally, in a chance meeting at the airport with Diana Philapados, senior vice president of Celtex, described the situation, and asked Philapados to intervene. Wally believed Leo was trying to get even after their earlier clash. Wally argued that the success of his new product venture depended on being able to secure a stable, high-quality source of supply of Q47 at low cost.

Diana has hired you as a consultant and has asked you to do the following:

Discussion Questions

1. Prepare a statement outlining the cash flows to Celtex of the two alternative sources of supply for Q47.
2. Offer advice regarding how she should handle the issues raised by Wally.

also requires manufacturing to reveal privately held and hard-to-verify knowledge of costs, then manufacturing has substantial discretion over the transfer prices. If these prices are important in rewarding managers (decision control), manufacturing can distort the system to its benefit. Given the reward system, a transfer-pricing method that is less subject to managerial discretion might in the end be a more accurate measure of opportunity costs than one that requires managers to disclose private, hard-to-verify knowledge.

All accounting (as well as nonaccounting) performance measures are prone to managerial opportunism in the form of accounting manipulations and dysfunctional decisions. Managers can choose depreciation methods that reduce expenses and increase reported earnings (straight-line depreciation). These accounting choices artificially raise ROA. Investment center managers can increase ROA by rejecting (or divesting) profitable projects with ROAs below the average ROA of the division. Most accounting measures are short-term measures of performance. They all suffer from the horizon problem, whereby managers emphasize short-term performance at the expense of long-term returns. Therefore, any accounting-based performance-measurement system requires careful monitoring by senior managers to control dysfunctional behavior by lower-level managers.

In the United States, accounting methods are regulated and managers must choose accounting methods from *generally accepted accounting procedures* (GAAP). Yet managers still have considerable discretion. External, third-party auditors ensure the accuracy and consistency of the accounting reports. Most firms employ a single accounting system for multiple purposes: reporting to shareholders, taxes, internal decision management and control, and regulation.[20] Debt agreements, management compensation plans, and financial reports all use these accounting-based numbers. Using the same numbers for many purposes helps control the incentives to distort the numbers for any single purpose.

Finally, no performance-measurement and reward system works perfectly; no system eliminates all managerial decisions that will increase the manager's welfare at the expense of the firm's other claimholders. The key question is: Does the system outperform the next best alternative after all the costs and benefits are included? One should avoid the "nirvana fallacy," which suggests discarding a system because it fails to eliminate all managerial opportunism. The nirvana fallacy arises when one compares a real system to a hypothetical but unachievable "perfect" system.[21]

Summary

Chapter 16 described individual performance-evaluation systems; this chapter extended the discussion to evaluating divisional performance.

Decision rights are allocated to cost, expense, revenue, investment, and profit centers. These centers often are evaluated and rewarded based on accounting-based performance measures. Cost centers are delegated decision rights over how to produce the output, but not over price or quantity. Cost centers are evaluated either on minimizing total cost for a fixed output, or maximizing output for a fixed total cost. Expense centers such as personnel departments are like cost centers except that their output is not easily

---

[20]Even though the firm has "one" accounting system, the accounting numbers often are adjusted for special purposes. For example, the system may use straight-line depreciation for shareholders but adjust these numbers to accelerated depreciation for taxes.

[21]H. Demsetz (1969), "Information and Efficiency: Another Viewpoint," *Journal of Law & Economics* XII, 1–22.

quantifiable. This difficulty in quantifying output means users often are not charged for the expense center's output; hence the demand for expense center services tends to grow faster than the firm's output.

Revenue centers also are similar to cost centers, with the difference that they are responsible for marketing the products. They have decision rights over how to sell or distribute the product, but not over the price-quantity decision. Revenue centers are evaluated on maximizing revenue for a given price or quantity and a fixed budget for operating expenses.

Profit centers have all the decision rights of cost centers plus product mix and pricing decisions. They do not have decision rights over the level of investment in their profit center. Profit centers are evaluated based on total profits. Finally, investment centers are like profit centers except that they also have decision rights over the amount of capital invested in their division. Evaluating performance of investment centers involves adjusting profits for the amount of capital invested. Two commonly used investment center measures are return on assets and residual income (or economic value added). Both measures create incentives for managers to eliminate assets that are not covering their opportunity cost of capital. However, ROA gives incentives to eliminate profitable projects with returns below the average ROA for the division. Residual income avoids this incentive problem, but as a performance measure it makes comparing divisions of different sizes more difficult.

Large companies, particularly those operating across multiple lines of business, typically are organized into multiple business units or divisions. Such an organizational architecture is intended to furnish senior managers with information about the profitability or efficiency of different businesses and to provide accountability and incentives for the operating managers charged with running those businesses.

Nonetheless, when there are significant interdependencies among different business units, often involving internal transfers, motivating individual profit centers to maximize their own profits generally will not maximize profits for the firm as a whole. Individual units focusing on their own profits often will ignore how their actions affect the sales and costs of other units.

One valuable role of a transfer-pricing method, then, is to lead managers to allocate resources internally in ways that take account of such interdependencies among divisions. But transfer pricing is a quite complicated undertaking. The likelihood of getting the wrong answer is high, and the consequences of so doing—primarily in the form of poor pricing and output decisions—can be substantial. Transfer prices not only change how total profits are divided among business units, they affect total firm profits.

The opportunity cost of a transferred resource is the correct transfer price. But accurate information about opportunity cost usually is known only by local divisional managers. If either the buying or selling division can set the transfer price unilaterally, it has incentives to behave opportunistically. The selling division will set too high a price trying to capture monopoly profits, and too few units will be transferred. If the buying division is allowed to set the transfer price, a price below the true opportunity cost is likely to be chosen; in this case, too few units will be produced and transferred.

Because accurate information about opportunity costs is quite expensive to obtain (or at least to verify), managers generally rely on approximations such as market values, marginal costs, full costs, or negotiated prices. Each of these approximations works better than others in certain circumstances. Market-based transfer prices are most useful when competitive external markets exist. But if an external market is employed, why is the firm producing the good or service? If there are important synergies favoring internal production, the external market price is unlikely to capture them. For example, if there are transaction costs of using the market, such as writing and enforcing contracts, then the transfer price is the market price less these transaction costs. Marginal cost is another popular transfer-pricing method. But marginal cost is expensive to estimate and can generate influence costs as managers debate whether certain expenditures are "marginal" or not. Full-cost transfer prices are objective, simple-to-compute transfer prices. They also are used widely in practice. However, full-cost transfer prices likely suffer from setting the transfer price above opportunity cost. Negotiated transfer prices, although time-consuming to establish, give both parties to the contract the incentive first to negotiate the quantity that maximizes the firm's profits and then negotiate the transfer price that determines how the total profits will be divided.

No matter what transfer-pricing method is used, it normally is important to permit both buying and selling divisions access to the external market. In this case, the external market acts as a check on opportunistic managerial behavior. But again, if the external market is employed regularly, one must examine whether the firm should be producing the intermediate product at all.

Finally, most divisional performance-evaluation systems rely on internally generated accounting-based numbers. These accounting-based performance metrics are for decision control (decision ratification and decision monitoring). Besides exercising decision-control rights, employees also exercise decision-management rights (decision initiation and implementation). Exercising decision-management rights requires information; often managers turn to their accounting systems for this information. But the accounting systems of most firms are designed for decision control—not necessarily for decision management. This leads to a trade-off between these two uses and to the general conclusion that most managers find their accounting systems wanting when it comes to providing information for decision management.

Suggested Readings	

R. Eccles (1985), *The Transfer Pricing Problem: A Theory for Practice* (Lexington Books: Lexington, MA).

J. Gould (1964), "Internal Pricing in Firms When There Are Costs of Using an Outside Market," *Journal of Business* 37, 61–67.

J. Hirshleifer (1964), "Internal Pricing and Decentralized Decisions," in C. Bonini, P. Jaediecke, and R. Wagner (Eds.), *Management Controls: New Directions in Basic Research* (McGraw-Hill: New York).

B. Holmstrom and J. Tirole (1991), "Transfer Pricing and Organizational Form," *Journal of Law, Economics, and Organizations* 7, 201–228.

D. Solomons (1985), *Divisional Performance: Measurement and Control,* 2nd edition (Richard D. Irwin: Burr Ridge, IL).

B. Stewart (1991), *The Quest for Value* (Harper Business: New York).

J. Zimmerman (2000), *Accounting for Decision Making and Control* (McGraw-Hill/Irwin: Burr Ridge, IL), Chapters 5 and 8.

Review Questions	

17–1. Auto-fit is a multidivisional firm that produces auto parts. It has the capacity for annual production of 100 units of a particular part. The marginal cost of producing each unit is $10. These units can be sold internally either to other divisions or to external customers. The external market price is $20. The allocated share of corporate overhead for each part produced is $5. Total corporate overhead expenditures do not vary with the production of the part. How many units of the part should the company produce? What is the theoretically correct transfer price (should the company decide to transfer the part internally)? Explain.

17–2. High Tech, Inc., has strong patent protection on a particular type of computer chip. High Tech uses the chip for the internal production of PCs. It also sells the chip to other manufacturers on the open market. Does High Tech necessarily want to charge the same price to both external and internal customers? Explain.

17–3. A firm has a demand curve: $P = 50 - Q$. Its total costs are

$$TC = 110 + Q + 3Q^2$$

Prepare a table that computes the profit-maximizing quantity. What quantity minimizes average cost? (Hint: Prepare a table similar to Table 17.1 for $Q = 1, 2, \ldots 10$.)

17–4. Assume that a firm faces a demand curve: $P = 6,600 - 10Q$. The total cost of production is $TC = Q^2$ and marginal cost is $MC = 2Q$. What are the optimal output, price, and profits for the firm?

Now assume that the firm is divided into 2 profit centers. One division manufactures the product at a total cost of $TC = Q^2$ and then transfers it to a selling division that faces the firm's demand curve. The selling division has no costs other than the transfer price for the product. Assume that the manufacturing division has the power to set the transfer price and that the selling division can only buy internally. The selling division, however, can select the quantity to purchase. What transfer price will the manufacturing unit select? What are the resulting profits for the 2 units? From the firm's standpoint, what is the optimal transfer price?

17–5. Chips Computer Company assembles personal computers and sells them in the retail marketplace. The company is organized into two profit centers: the assembly division and the distribution division. The demand curve facing the company (and the distribution division) is $P = 3,000 - 10Q$. The marginal cost for assembly (which includes purchasing the parts) is constant at $500. The distribution division faces constant marginal distribution costs of $50 per unit. What is the profit-maximizing retail price and output for the firm as a whole? If the assembly division has monopoly power to set the transfer price, what transfer price will it select (assuming it knows all the information above)? Calculate the profits for the two divisions in this case.

17–6. The Xtrac Computer Company is organized into regional sales offices and a manufacturing division. The sales offices forecast sales for the upcoming year in their territories. These figures are then used to set the manufacturing schedules for the year. Prices of the computers are determined by corporate headquarters, and the salespeople are paid a fixed wage and a commission on sales. The regional sales offices are evaluated as revenue centers. The regional sales manager is paid a small wage (about 30 percent of total pay) and a commission on all sales in her territory (about 70 percent of total pay) that exceeds the budget.

Xtrac has a notoriously bad track record for forecasting computer sales. Its budgets always underforecast sales, and then, during the year, manufacturing scrambles to produce more units, authorizes labor overtime, and buys parts on rush orders. This drives up manufacturing costs. At first, management thought the underforecasting problem was due to high unexpected growth in the computer industry. But Xtrac even underforecasts sales when the economy is slow and the industry growth is below its long-run average.

a. What is the likely reason Xtrac persistently underforecasts sales?
b. What are some likely explanations for the reason in part (a)?
c. Propose three likely solutions, and critically evaluate each of them.

17–7. Scoff Division of World-Wide Paint is currently losing money, and senior management is considering selling or closing Scoff. Scoff's only product, an intermediate chemical called Binder, is used principally by the latex division of the firm. If Scoff is sold, the latex division can purchase ample quantities of Binder in the market at sufficiently high quality levels to meet its requirements. World-Wide requires all of its divisions to supply product to other World-Wide divisions before servicing the external market.

Scoff Division Profit/Loss Last Quarter (in thousands of dollars)

Scoff's statement of operations for the latest quarter is as follows:

Revenue:		
Inside	$200	
Outside	75	$275
Operating expenses:	$260	
Variable costs		
Fixed costs	15	
Allocated corporate overhead	40	315
Net income (loss) before taxes		$ (40)

Notes:
1. World-Wide Paint has the policy of transferring all products internally at variable cost. In Scoff's case, variable cost is 80 percent of the market price.
2. All of Scoff's fixed costs are avoidable cash flows if Scoff is closed or sold.
3. Ten percent of the allocated corporate overhead is caused by the presence of Scoff and will be avoided if Scoff is closed or sold.

Calculate the annual net cash flows to World-Wide Paint of closing or selling Scoff.

17–8. Suppose a firm has two different accounting systems. For example, suppose it uses EVA to measure and reward management performance. To calculate EVA, annual spending on research and development is recorded as an asset and then depreciated in calculating earnings. In reporting earnings to shareholders, R&D spending in any given year is expensed against earnings.

Describe some of the likely consequences that can arise if the firm tries to maintain two different accounting systems.

17–9. An organizational consultant does not like the way your company compensates profit center managers (currently a large part of their pay is based on the center's profits). He argues that you should compensate the managers based on whether or not they made "reasonable decisions" and not based on the outcome of the decisions, which is partly beyond the control of the managers. The consultant argues that the managers will then have incentives to make good decisions but will not be subject to undue levels of risk. Evaluate this argument.

17–10. Below is a suggestion from a leading economics text on how to set optimal transfer prices. In this context, both the manufacturing and distribution divisions are profit centers. Do you think it would work? Explain.

The manufacturing division could be supplied data on the net marginal revenue curve for the distribution division and told to use this as its relevant marginal revenue curve in determining the quantity it should supply. By choosing the output where marginal revenue equals marginal cost, firm profits are maximized. The transfer price should be the marginal cost at this output level.

17–11. Xerdak Inc. has a corporate jet, which it uses to fly managers from Rochester to Chicago. The associated costs (monthly) of maintaining and flying the jet are as follows:

Pilot:	$10,000
Depreciation:	10,000
Overhead	10,000

In addition, each round trip to Chicago costs $10,000 in fuel. Commercial airlines (for example, United) charge $600 for a round trip to Chicago. Managers consider the commercial service and the company service to be identical. The company plane flies a maximum of 20 times each month and has 50 seats. There are always more managers wanting to fly on the plane than there are seats. The company wants to buy some more planes. Unfortunately, they are back-ordered, and so the company will not be able to obtain additional capacity in the near future. According to economic theory, what is the optimal transfer price for a round trip to Chicago? Explain why.

17–12. Geriatrics Inc. has a patent on a new type of hospital bed. The marginal cost of producing each bed is $400. The company has significant production capacity. Geriatrics sells the beds to customers on the open market and also uses them internally throughout its nursing home chain. The external demand for the product is given by $P = 5,000 - Q$. Assuming that Geriatrics wants to profit-maximize, what is the optimal external market price? What is the optimal internal transfer price?

17–13. Biotech Inc. is a new company that invests in technologies relating to the use of plants in drugs. The stock market perceives that the company has the potential to generate large profits once it develops a line of products. To date, however, the company has not reported positive profits and does not anticipate doing so over the next 5 years or more. The owners of Biotech are particularly concerned about the investment choices of the managers. They are concerned that the managers do not have the right incentives to choose value-maximizing investments. They are considering adopting an EVA evaluation and compensation plan for the managers. Do you think this is a good idea? Explain.

17–14. Speed Company sells printers. It is divided into a manufacturing unit and a sales unit. The marginal cost of producing a printer is $200. External demand is given by $P = 1,000 - .01Q$. Selling and distribution costs total $150 per unit.
    a. What is the profit-maximizing retail price and quantity? What are firm profits?
    b. Suppose the manufacturing unit has monopoly power to set the transfer price and knows all the information in this problem. What transfer price will it charge? What are the resulting retail price, quantity, and firm profits?

17–15. Do you agree with the following statement? Explain.

> *Obviously the correct transfer price is the opportunity cost of the resource. Any firm that uses full cost (which includes an allocation of corporate overhead) is doing it wrong.*

17–16. You are the owner and CEO of a large divisionalized firm, with operations in a number of diverse industries. Reporting to you are a number of division managers. Division managers have considerable decision-making responsibility with respect to the day-to-day operations of their divisions, but you must approve any capital investments above $100,000 before they are made.
    a. As owner, what type of capital investments would you like your division managers to be proposing to you?
    b. Is there a potential agency problem between you, as owner, and your division managers with respect to capital investments? What is the nature of that problem? Why is it a problem?
    c. How might you attempt to solve that agency problem?
    d. Do you think you can solve the problem entirely? Why or why not?

17–17. The Jameson Company has recently formed a subsidiary, Bright Ideas, to manufacture and sell household appliances.
    a. What is the difference between an investment center and a profit center?
    b. What factors should Jameson consider in deciding whether to evaluate Bright Ideas as a profit or investment center?

Part 4
Applications of Organizational Architecture

Chapter 18
Vertical Integration and Outsourcing

In 1989, Eastman Kodak sold its mainframe computers to IBM and contracted with IBM to do much of Kodak's data processing for the next 10 years.[1] Under the contract with Kodak, IBM was responsible for operating Kodak's data center. IBM provided the operating software and hardware and was responsible for backups and file protection. Kodak retained its own staff for developing applications software and was responsible for most data entry. For example, Kodak provided IBM with the basic data for running its sales-forecasting models and had developed much of the specific software for this application. IBM was responsible for running Kodak's programs on its operating system.

This *outsourcing* of computer services was newsworthy specifically because no company of Kodak's size or prominence had turned over its computers to outsiders before. Other large companies began considering similar moves. In 1990, US businesses spent $7.2 billion on outsourced computer operations. According to Standard & Poor's, worldwide outsourcing of all types will exceed $170 billion by 2003.

In 1998, IBM developed and managed a procurement system for United Technologies (UT)—makers of Pratt & Whitney aircraft engines, Carrier air conditioners, and Otis elevators. UT expected to save $750 million of purchasing costs within 2 years. IBM assumed responsibility of some of UT's purchasing operations and created a procurement system (online purchasing and payments) involving negotiating and handling contracts with suppliers. IBM procured goods and services from office supplies to temporary help. However, IBM would not be responsible for procuring parts for manufacturing.

Outsourcing has not been limited to information and procurement systems. Among the services most often outsourced are trucking, catering, copying, and accounting. For example, in 1992, Du Pont sold its copy machines to Lanier and contracted with the company to provide copying services. Kodak used to operate its own kitchens to provide meals for the 40,000 employees at its headquarters in Rochester, New York. In 1992, Kodak sold this operation to the Marriott Corporation. Reebok, one of the leading athletic shoe companies in the world, owned no plants. Rather, it contracted out all footwear production to suppliers in various Asian countries. Moreover, Chrysler bought about 70 percent of its parts from external suppliers in 1999.

Outsourcing involves a fundamental change in organizational architecture. First, it reassigns decision rights relating to certain assets and employees from one firm to another. For instance, to staff its new data center, IBM hired about 300 people who formerly had worked for Kodak. IBM now owns the mainframes that serve Kodak and has the decision rights on the utilization, maintenance, and replacement of these machines. Second, performance-evaluation and reward systems also generally change with outsourcing. Kodak previously evaluated its data processing units as cost centers. By contrast, the senior managers at the new IBM-run data center are evaluated on business growth, operational efficiency, and satisfaction of Kodak users. Overall, the IBM unit more closely resembles a profit center than a cost center. Since Kodak pays scheduled fees for computer services, IBM benefits directly if it can improve efficiency and cut costs.

---

[1]Details of these examples are from W. Richmond, A. Seidmann, and A. Whinston (1992), "Incomplete Contracting Issues in Information Systems Development Outsourcing," *Decision Support Systems* 8, 459–477; D. Kirkpatrick (1991), "Why Not Farm Out Your Computing?" *Fortune* (September 23), 103–112; S. Tully (1993), "The Modular Corporation," *Fortune* (February 8), 106–114. R. Narisetti (1998), "IBM Picked to Develop, Run a System for United Technologies Procurement," *The Wall Street Journal* (June 29), B5; *Standard & Poor's Industry Surveys* (1999), "Computers: Commercial Services" (December 16), 1–5.

This discussion of outsourcing raises a number of important questions:

- What are the costs and benefits in choosing between the alternative architectures that are implied by within-firm production versus outsourcing?

- What activities make the most sense to outsource? Why are data processing, catering, copying, and trucking among the most frequently outsourced services? Why did Kodak outsource the operation of its data center to IBM but maintain the responsibility for developing applications software?

- When a company outsources, what are the determinants of the specific contract provisions? Why did Kodak and IBM negotiate a 10-year contract instead of a 1-year contract? Why do some firms grant distributors exclusive rights to particular territories?

- What has motivated the recent trend in increased outsourcing?

We begin by discussing the process of producing and marketing products. We then discuss trade-offs among alternative ways of organizing the steps in this process (market transactions, long-term contracts, and vertical integration), the appropriate length of a contract, contracting with independent distributors, and reasons for the recent increases in outsourcing. In the appendix to this chapter, we provide a more detailed example that highlights some of the trade-offs between company ownership and outsourcing.

Vertical Chain of Production

Consumer goods are produced through a series of steps described by the *vertical chain of production.*[2] Figure 18.1 pictures this vertical chain for personal computers. At the top of the chain are the raw materials such as chemicals, metals, and rubber that are used as inputs to produce PCs. These inputs are transported to processors that make the intermediate products used in the final construction of PCs (for instance, plastics manufacturers, chip makers, and operating software producers). The intermediate goods are transported to companies that assemble them into PCs. Finally, the PCs are transported to retail stores, which sell them to consumers and provide after-sales servicing. Each step of this vertical chain is supported by administrative services such as accounting, finance, and marketing. Firms can locate at different positions along the vertical chain. Intel is an intermediate-goods processor that manufactures computer chips; Dell Computers, which sells IBM-compatible PCs, concentrates on final assembly and distribution. Firms also can specialize in providing support services (for instance, shipping and accounting firms).

When a firm participates in more than one successive stage in the vertical chain, it is said to be *vertically integrated.* Firms vary dramatically in their degree of vertical integration. Dell Computers leases much of its manufacturing space and makes virtually none of its component parts. It does not make or even stock the many software products that it sells. IBM is much more vertically integrated, producing many of its component parts and much of its software in-house. IBM also maintains its own sales force for mainframe computers.

Firms change their degree of integration over time. An organization that begins to produce its own inputs is engaging in *backward,* or *upstream,* integration, whereas an

---

[2]D. Besanko, D. Dranove, and M. Shanley (1995), *The Economics of Strategy* (John Wiley & Sons: New York), 71.

Figure 18.1 The Vertical Chain of Production for Personal Computers

At the top of the chain are the raw materials, such as chemicals, metals, and rubber, that are used as inputs to produce PCs. These inputs are transported to intermediate-goods processors. These processors (for instance, plastics manufacturers, chip makers, and operating software producers) make the intermediate products used in the final construction of the PCs. These intermediate goods must be transported to the companies that assemble them into the final consumer products. Finally, these products are transported to retail stores, which sell them to consumers. Each step of the vertical chain is supported by administrative services such as accounting, finance, and marketing.

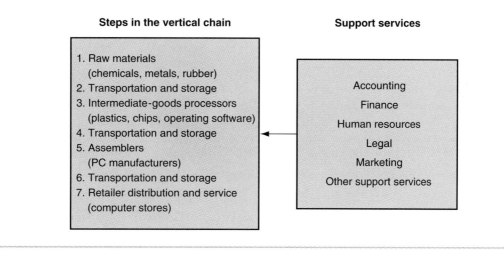

Steps in the vertical chain

1. Raw materials
   (chemicals, metals, rubber)
2. Transportation and storage
3. Intermediate-goods processors
   (plastics, chips, operating software)
4. Transportation and storage
5. Assemblers
   (PC manufacturers)
6. Transportation and storage
7. Retailer distribution and service
   (computer stores)

Support services

Accounting

Finance

Human resources

Legal

Marketing

Other support services

Long-Term Contracts

In this chapter, we do not differentiate among the various types of long-term contracts. Rather, we focus on how firms choose among spot markets, contracts, and vertical integration. Long-term contracts, however, can take a variety of forms. First, there are *standard supply and distribution contracts* between independent firms. For instance, IBM and Kodak have a 10-year supply contract, where IBM agrees to provide specific computer services to Kodak for a given price. The contract contains many provisions specifying the nature of the service and the duties and obligations of each of the contracting parties. Second, there are *joint ventures*. In the typical joint venture, a new firm is formed that is jointly owned by two or more independent firms. The new firm might be responsible for conducting research, supplying inputs for a subset of the firms or for downstream activities such as marketing or distributing a product. Drug companies form research joint ventures to conduct basic research on new drugs. The output of this research is shared by the partners in the venture. Similarly, an American company and a European company might form a joint venture to market the American company's products in Europe. Third are *lease contracts*, where a firm acquires an asset such as a machine or building through a lease agreement with another firm. Fourth are *franchise agreements*, which grant an independent businessperson the rights to use the parent's proven name, reputation, and business format in a given market area. Fifth are *strategic alliances*. This term is used to describe a variety of agreements between independent firms to cooperate in the development and/or marketing of products. For instance, an airline company and a car rental company might agree to promote each other's products and to participate in joint promotional activities.

Figure 18.2   Outsourcing: Choosing along a Continuum

It often is useful to think of the outsourcing decision as a choice along a continuum of possibilities. At one extreme, a product or service can be purchased from any one of a large number of potential suppliers in the spot market. At the other extreme, the company can produce the product or service internally within a division of the vertically integrated firm. Between these extremes are various long-term contracts. Contracts take a variety of forms, including standard supply and distribution contracts, joint ventures, lease contracts, franchise agreements, and strategic alliances.

Spot markets   Long-term contracts   Vertical integration

---

organization that begins to market its own goods or to conduct additional finishing work is engaging in *forward,* or *downstream,* integration. Lincoln Electric integrated backward when it began manufacturing certain inputs for its welding machines that previously were supplied by outside companies. PepsiCo, on the other hand, integrated forward when it acquired Kentucky Fried Chicken, Pizza Hut, and Taco Bell, which sell PepsiCo's soft drinks. (Note that in 1997, PepsiCo spun off these fast-food restaurants.)

The term *outsourcing* frequently is used to describe a movement away from vertical integration—moving an activity outside the firm that formerly was done within the firm. An example of this usage is "Kodak outsourced its computer operations to IBM." The term *outsourcing* also is used to describe an ongoing arrangement whereby a firm obtains a part or service from an external firm. An example of this usage is "Reebok always has outsourced most of its footwear production to foreign companies."

Often it is useful to think of the outsourcing decision as a choice along a continuum of possibilities. As pictured in Figure 18.2, at one extreme, the part or service is purchased from any one of a large number of potential suppliers in the *spot market* (where the exchange is made immediately at the current market price with no long-term commitment between the buyer and the seller). At the other extreme, a company vertically

---

Vertical Outsourcing by Taiwan Semiconductor

Taiwan Semiconductor Manufacturing Co. had 1998 sales of $1.5 billion. Most of TSMC's revenues were from chip manufacturing. For years companies like Motorola produced most of their chips to control quality and design. By the year 2002, Motorola plans to have 50 percent of its chips outsourced, up from 16 percent in 1999. TSMC is going beyond manufacturing chips to offer semiconductor design services. TSMC will design ordinary chips and help customers design complex semiconductors. TSMC has a library of chip designs that can be "glued together" quickly to build combo chips. New semiconductors can be designed and manufactured faster and cheaper this way. Notice that TSMC plans to vertically integrate design and manufacturing within TSMC to get customers to outsource both of these functions.

Source: J. Moore (1999), "TSMC's Chip Business Booms as More
Companies Outsource," *Business Week* (June 21), 128.

Outsourcing Logistics

Deere & Co., the farm-equipment giant, uses Ryder System, the truck rental company, not only to move parts for its plants, but also to label and package tractor repair kits sent to farmers. A Deere manager says, "We don't think the farmer really cares who stores the parts, but he does want John Deere to build his tractor. You need to decide what you're really good at and focus on that." Trucking companies and shipping lines have been expanding into the often-hidden but enormous business of logistics—the planning, packaging, storing, and shipping of inventory. Logistics seeks to cut costs by slashing inventories and speeding up transportation. Today, 75 percent of big American manufacturers rely on these megashippers. One commentator remarks, "It's one-stop shopping for outsourcing." Nike outsources the running of its huge high-tech warehouse in Atlanta to another firm, Menlo. Menlo employees put air into basketballs, soccer balls, and footballs, which come only half-inflated to save space. They also place the balls in colorful packages and even attach price tags for some retailers.

Source: A Mathews (1998), "Logistics Firms Flourish Amid Trend in Outsourcing," *The Wall Street Journal* (June 2), B4.

integrates and produces the part or service internally.[3] In the middle are long-term contracts between independent or quasi-independent firms. Long-term contracts take many forms, including long-term supply and distribution contracts, franchise agreements, leasing contracts, joint ventures, and strategic alliances. Many of the recent outsourcing decisions move the firm from vertical integration to long-term contracting (Kodak and IBM for computer services, Kodak and Marriott for food service, Du Pont and Lanier for copying services). We begin our analysis of outsourcing by considering some of the advantages of acquiring parts and services in spot markets. We use the term *market transactions* to refer to sales and purchases in the spot market; we use the term *nonmarket transactions* to refer either to vertical integration or to long-term contracts.

Benefits of Buying in Competitive Markets

Figure 18.3 presents the standard diagram of a competitive equilibrium (as discussed in Chapter 6). The figure illustrates that competitive markets result in efficient production: Production occurs at the lowest possible average cost per unit. Price equals average cost, implying that buyers acquire the product at cost (which of course includes a normal rate of return on investment).[4] Over time, suppliers adopt technological advances that lower the costs of production and/or enhance the quality of the product. Lower costs are passed to buyers in the form of lower prices. This analysis suggests that when competitive outside markets are available to purchase goods and services, firms should use them. In most cases, a firm cannot acquire the product more cheaply through a nonmarket transaction; in many cases, it would cost more.

One common concern with internal production is generating high-enough volume to take advantage of scale economies in production. In Figure 18.3, the minimum point on the average cost curve is at a volume of Q^* units. Individual firms in the marketplace produce this volume. If a firm requires less than Q^* units and produces only that

[3]See Chapter 17 for a discussion of how firms organize internal production into divisions. That chapter also examines the corresponding transfer-pricing issues.

[4]Recall that if price is above long-run average cost, firms are making economic profits and new firms enter the industry. The increase in supply drives down the price. Alternatively, if price is below long-run average cost, firms are losing money and exit occurs.

Figure 18.3 Competitive Equilibrium

This figure illustrates that competitive markets result in efficient production. The right panel displays the supply and demand curves for the industry. Their intersection determines the market price. The left panel pictures the output decision of the marginal firm in the industry. Production occurs at the lowest-possible long-run average cost (LRAC). Buyers acquire the product at cost ($P^* = $ LRAC $= $ LRMC, where LRMC $= $ long-run marginal cost). The analysis suggests that when competitive outside markets for inputs are available, firms should use them. In most cases, the firm cannot produce more cheaply itself, and in many cases it will cost more.

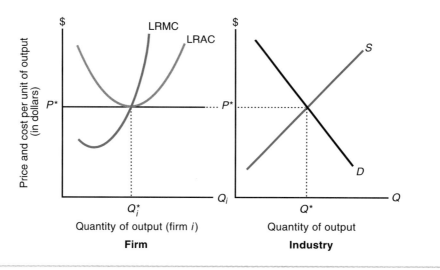

---

amount internally, it will incur higher average costs. The firm could produce Q^* and sell the surplus in the open market. However, this choice requires the firm to enter a new market—one that is not its primary line of business. As we discussed in Chapter 8, diversifying into unrelated fields can reduce value. Empirical studies suggest that diversified firms frequently perform poorly relative to firms that are more focused.[5]

Another concern with nonmarket procurement is the cost of motivating efficient production. Divisions within large firms can be inefficient, yet continue to survive, so long as they are subsidized by more profitable units within the firm. Firms must adopt costly incentive and control systems to motivate internal managers to engage in efficient production. Similarly, parties to a long-term supply contract must be motivated to carry out their parts of the agreement. Independent firms, on the other hand, face more direct market pressures. If they are inefficient in their main line of business, they lose money and eventually are forced to liquidate.

Due to such concerns, most firms use markets to acquire many, if not most, of their inputs. Few companies produce their own automobiles, trucks, fuel, copy machines, pencils, staples, telephones, office furniture, or bathroom fixtures. Most of these products are acquired through market transactions. Also, firms generally rely on external markets for many of their downstream activities, such as product distribution. For

[5]P. Berger and E. Ofek (1995), "Diversification's Effect on Firm Value," *Journal of Financial Economics* 37, 39–65; R. Comment (1995), "Corporate Focus and Stock Returns," *Journal of Financial Economics* 37, 67–87; and K. John and E. Ofek (1995), "Asset Sales and Increase in Focus," *Journal of Financial Economics* 37, 105–126.

Merck and Astra—Joint Venture

United States based Merck and Sweden's Astra formed a 50-50 American joint venture years ago called Astra Merck. Astra gave Astra Merck all of its US business, and Merck helped Astra market and win regulatory approval in the United States. This joint venture has been a huge windfall for Merck and a sore point for Astra. One of Astra's drugs, Prilosec, is the best-selling prescription drug in both the United States and the world. A treatment for ulcers, Prilosec has US sales of $2.4 billion and worldwide sales of $4.2 billion.

   In a restructing of this joint venture, Merck will cede management control and voting rights for royalty payments. Analysts expect the restructuring to generate payments to Merck valued at between $7 and $10 billion while allowing Astra to find a merger partner.

Source: S. Lipin and R. Langreth (1998), "Merck, Astra Reach Restructuring Pact," *The Wall Street Journal* (June 19), B6.

instance, Procter & Gamble sells many of its products, such as soap and toothpaste, through independent grocery stores and drugstores. The key point is that well-functioning markets provide powerful incentives for efficient production and low prices. It is value-maximizing to acquire many goods and services through market transactions.

Reasons for Nonmarket Transactions

Our analysis appears to argue against nonmarket transactions: Firms should concentrate on a particular stage of the production/distribution process and acquire other inputs and services using market transactions with outside suppliers and distributors. There are, however, at least three principal reasons why firms often use nonmarket transactions to acquire inputs and downstream services: contracting costs, market power, and taxes/regulation.

Contracting Costs

In Chapter 3, we discussed the architecture of markets. We argued that markets effectively link specific knowledge and decision rights; moreover, they provide incentives for decision makers to use this information effectively. We posed the question: *Why aren't all economic transactions conducted through markets?* Ronald Coase provided the basic answer to this question by arguing that market transactions are not costless.[6] For instance, they involve the costs of searching for trading partners and negotiating relevant prices. Parties to a transaction have incentives to use other mechanisms, such as internal production, when the transaction can be accomplished at a lower cost. At least four factors can make the costs of nonmarket transactions lower than the costs of market exchanges. These factors include *firm-specific assets, costs of measuring quality, externalities,* and *coordination problems.*

Firm-Specific Assets[7]   Production typically requires investment in assets. As examples, IBM requires mainframe computers to provide computer services to Kodak and suppliers

---

[6]For a collection of Coase's work on this topic, see R. Coase (1988), *The Firm, the Market, and the Law* (University of Chicago Press: Chicago).

[7]This section draws on B. Klein, R. Crawford, and A. Alchian (1978), "Vertical Integration, Appropriable Rents, and the Competitive Contracting Process," *Journal of Law & Economics* 24, 297–326.

Made in the USA

Companies sometimes label their products "Made in the USA." This statement apparently appeals to the sentiment among some consumers that Americans should purchase only American-made products to protect domestic jobs. The claim also helps companies gain contracts from the US government. The common practice of acquiring many inputs from outside suppliers, however, makes it difficult to define what really is made in the USA. In early September 1994, the FTC charged two athletic shoe companies, New Balance and Hyde Athletic Industries Inc., with deceptive advertising for saying that their products were "Made in the USA." Although the companies sew and glue the bulk of their shoes in the United States, they import many of the component parts, such as soles and uppers, from Asia. Hyde Athletic agreed to change its label to "Made in the USA from domestic and imported components." New Balance disputed the claim. This issue could affect many companies, ranging from Dell Computers to General Motors, who emphasize domestic production but rely on foreign companies for various inputs and services.

Source: M. Oneal (1994), "Does New Balance Have an American Soul?"
Business Week (December 12), 86–90.

---

require machines to make parts. Sometimes these assets can be transferred easily among alternative uses. Mainframe computers are general-purpose machines that can be used to serve a variety of other companies in addition to Kodak. Other assets are significantly more valuable in their current use than in their next best alternative. For example, the Alaska Pipeline is materially more valuable for transporting oil than for any other conceivable use. If IBM writes a specialized computer program to run Kodak's payroll, the program is more valuable for Kodak's payroll than for some other firm's payroll (which might offer different fringe benefits, for instance). Although the program could be adapted for use by other firms, changing the program is costly. Assets that are substantially more valuable in their current use than in their next best alternative use are referred to as *firm-specific assets*. Asset specificity is most likely to occur in four particular instances.[8]

- **Site Specificity.** The asset is located in a particular area that makes it useful only to a small number of buyers or suppliers, and it cannot be moved easily. An example is the Alaska Pipeline, which can be used only by oil producers in Alaska.

- **Physical-Asset Specificity.** Product design makes the asset especially useful only to a small number of buyers. An example is a specialized machine tool that is used to make parts for one particular model of automobile.

- **Human-Asset Specificity.** The transaction requires specialized knowledge on the part of the parties to the transaction. An example is the knowledge that IBM employees must acquire about Kodak's unique processes in order to provide computer services to the company.

- **Dedicated Assets.** The expansion in facilities is necessitated only by the requirements of a few buyers. An example is a chip producer who adds extra capacity to serve one particular computer company.

If a supplier invests in a specific asset to serve a particular customer, that supplier places itself in a tenuous position for future negotiations. For example, consider a supplier who invests $50,000 for a machine tool (such as a metal punch-press die) to produce a particular part. The part is used only by one manufacturer, and the die has no

---

[8]O. Williamson (1985), *The Economic Institutions of Capitalism* (Free Press: New York).

Kodak-IBM Outsourcing Renewal

The original outsourcing agreement between Kodak and IBM was formalized in a 10-year contract. Begun in 1989, it expired in 1999. Over this 10-year span, IBM expanded this aspect of their business substantially through its IBM Global Services unit due to its profitability. IBM routinely announces the renewal of contracts—yet, months after the original contract expired, no announcement of a Kodak renewal had been posted.

Presumably, Kodak is arguing that as technology has changed, IBM's costs have fallen by more than was expected in the original contract and thus they should receive more favorable terms. But IBM would be reluctant to cut prices, especially if Kodak is unlikely to be able to move to another vendor without incurring substantial costs. Because each company has made sunk investments in the relationship, a divorce would be an unattractive alternative. But these sunk costs are precisely the kind of relationship-specific investments that lead to holdup problems as well as contentious negotiations when such a contract must be renewed.

Sources: *www.ibm.com* and A. C. Doyle (1893), "Silver Blaze," *Strand Magazine* (December).

other uses or salvage value—it is extremely firm-specific. The variable cost of production is $1 per unit and the useful life of the die is 50,000 units. The supplier must be able to sell the parts for at least $2 per unit to break even. The buyer, however, is in a strong position to argue for a price concession after the investment is made. At this point, the investment is a *sunk cost,* and the supplier will continue to operate as long as it can cover its variable costs of $1 per unit. Thus, the buyer potentially can force the supplier to accept a price as low as $1, even though the supplier loses its initial investment. Anticipating this *holdup problem,* the supplier will not invest in the machine tool in the first place unless it receives some effective guarantee that the buyer will continue to pay $2 per unit and will buy at least 50,000 units.

Buyers face potential holdup problems as well if they purchase key inputs from a single supplier that has invested in the relevant firm-specific assets. For instance, a specialized chip supplier might demand a large price increase when it knows that a computer company has a large backlog of orders and that it has no alternative sources of supply.

These potential holdup problems can be controlled by vertical integration. If the buying firm invests in the machine and produces the part internally, it does not have to worry about subsequently arguing with its supplier over prices. An alternative to integration would be for the buyer and supplier to enter into a long-term supply contract. The buyer might agree to purchase 50,000 units from the supplier over the next 5 years at a cost of $2 per unit. Contracts are not costless to write or to enforce, and so the preferred alternative depends on the relative costs of vertical integration versus contracting. This trade-off is considered in greater detail below.

Measuring Quality   It is difficult to monitor the quality of some inputs and services. The buyer might not learn that a part is defective until long after purchase. In this case, the seller can have the incentive to cheat the buying firm: Once a price is set, the supplier can increase its profits by supplying a lower-quality, lower-cost product. Buyers sometimes can avoid these problems by transacting with companies that have established reputations for quality and/or can offer credible warranties for their products. Otherwise, buyers either should negotiate a long-term supply contract that provides appropriate incentives for quality production or should produce such products in-house. Internal production and long-term contracts are especially useful when maintaining the quality of the part is critical for the overall success of the product. (Recall from Chapter 17 Kodak's decision to own Eastman Gelatine so that it could better control the quality of the gel used in its photo emulsion.) These nonmarket forms of organization do not necessarily change the distribution of information among the parties. However, they allow the company to develop contractual incentives that motivate quality production. (We discuss this issue further in Chapter 21.)

Reducing Externalities   Firms often invest in developing reputations and customer loyalty. This investment can increase the demand for a company's products. However, firms can have problems motivating independently owned distributors to invest sufficient resources to maintain a brand name—there is a free-rider problem. Independent retailers in a distribution system have incentives to shirk on advertising and depend on the efforts of other units in the system to attract customers. These retailers also might want to cut costs by hiring less skilled, lower-priced labor. A given owner of a retail unit receives all the benefits from reducing the unit's labor costs but bears only part of the costs from providing poor service to customers: Any decline in future sales is likely to be shared with other units. The incentives to free-ride are particularly large when the retailer deals with customers who are not likely to make repeat purchases at the particular unit.

This free-rider problem can be reduced through vertical integration, where managers of stores are compensated in ways that discourage free-riding, or through long-term contracts with terms that motivate increased sales efforts. We provide a more detailed discussion of such distribution contracts later in this chapter.

Extensive Coordination   Some activities require extensive coordination. For example, railroads rely on extensive feeder traffic for their routes. In principle, it would be possible to use the price system for each link within this network. Rail companies could pay one another to use their lines, with prices adjusting to changes in supply and demand. Such a system would be complicated and expensive to operate. An alternative is for the railroad companies in the network to merge and to address the various coordination problems internally. Railroad companies were among the first large firms in the United States. These large firms were motivated, at least in part, by the benefits of using internal managers, rather than market transactions, to coordinate rail activity.[9]

A related reason for vertical integration is to coordinate pricing and service decisions among retail units. The pricing decisions of individual retailers can have effects on other units in the system—they produce a kind of externality. For instance, it might be optimal from a companywide standpoint to set prices where some units sustain losses. (When McDonald's stays open, customers are less likely to try Burger King.) Independent retailers cannot be expected to set optimal systemwide prices since they care only about the profits from their own units. In principle, the central company could set the retail prices; but antitrust law limits this solution. The company can coordinate prices if it owns its own retail outlets.

Market Power

A firm with market power might use vertical integration to increase profits in several different ways. The following example illustrates one of these methods—using

[9]A. Chandler (1977), *The Visible Hand—The Managerial Revolution in American Business* (Belknap Press: Cambridge, MA). Also, D. Carlton and M. Klamer (1983), "The Need for Coordination among Firms with Special Reference to Network Industries," *University of Chicago Law Review* 50, 446–465.

vertical integration to price-discriminate.[10] Consider a firm, DrugCo, that has a patent on a particular chemical compound used as an input in the production of two different pharmaceutical products. One of the products is a pain reliever that competes with many other pain relievers. The other helps cure a particular type of cancer, and faces no close substitutes. The industry demand for the two retail products (pain reliever and cancer drug) is given by

$$\text{Pain relief:} \qquad P = 100 - 5Q \qquad (18.1)$$

$$\text{Cancer drug:} \qquad P = 200 - 10Q \qquad (18.2)$$

The marginal cost to DrugCo for producing the chemical compound is $10 per gram. For simplicity, suppose that a drug manufacturer can take the chemical compound and transform it into 1 gram of either retail product (pain reliever or cancer drug) at zero marginal cost incurring no additional distribution or marketing costs. Many manufacturers can produce and distribute the retail drugs. Competition among these retail manufacturers will drive the retail prices of the pain reliever and cancer drug down to the retail manufacturers' marginal costs, which in this example is the wholesale price (see Chapter 7) of DrugCo's chemical compound. Thus, the demand curves facing DrugCo at the wholesale level are the same as the retail demand curves given in Equations (18.1) and (18.2).

To maximize total profits, DrugCo would like to set marginal revenue equal to marginal cost in each market. As shown in Figure 18.4, the optimal price to charge retail drug manufacturers who produce the pain reliever is $55. The optimal price for those who produce the cancer drug is $105.[11] Since both retail markets are competitive and there are no other costs, the price to consumers in the two markets would be $55 and $105. However, if DrugCo tries to sell to some manufacturers at $55 and other manufacturers at $105, potential *arbitrage* is available: Manufacturers who buy at $55 can resell the chemical compound to other manufacturers at less than $105 and make a profit. They will undercut any attempt by DrugCo to sell to manufacturers at $105.

One way that DrugCo can prevent such arbitrage is to integrate forward and manufacture the pain reliever. The company would price the pain reliever at $55 in the retail market and sell the base drug at $105 in the wholesale market. Arbitrage is no longer possible (assuming that the pain reliever cannot be transformed back into the chemical compound at low cost). Integrating forward into the retail market for the cancer drug will not solve the problem. If DrugCo tries to price the cancer drug at $105 and sell the chemical compound at a wholesale price of $55, other retail manufacturers would begin to produce and market the cancer drug (after buying the chemical compound at $55). DrugCo would not be able to maintain a price of $105. It must integrate forward into the lower-priced (more *elastic*) pain-reliever market.

Taxes and Regulation

Taxes and regulation also can motivate vertical integration. If one stage of production is heavily taxed and another is not, total taxes might be reduced by shifting profits to the low-tax activity. A firm potentially can capture these gains by integrating vertically and having the low-tax unit charge higher transfer prices to the high-tax unit. Yet as we

---

[10]For additional methods, see Carlton and Perloff (1990), Chapter 16.

[11]Recall from Chapter 7 that these prices are easily found by setting the marginal revenue in each market (implied by the two demand curves) equal to the marginal cost of $10.

Figure 18.4 Using Vertical Integration to Price-Discriminate

DrugCo has a patent on a chemical compound used as an input in the production of two different pharmaceutical products: a pain reliever that competes with many other products and a cancer drug. The marginal cost to DrugCo for producing the chemical compound is $10 per gram. The industry-level demand curves for the two products are the same demand curves facing DrugCo for the chemical compound. The optimal price to charge manufacturers who produce the pain reliever is $55. The optimal price for those who produce the cancer drug is $105. However, if DrugCo tries to sell to some companies at $55 and others at $105, potential arbitrage is available. One way to price-discriminate effectively is for DrugCo to integrate forward into the retail market for pain relievers. It would sell the pain reliever to consumers at $55 and the chemical compound to the manufacturers of the cancer drug at $105.

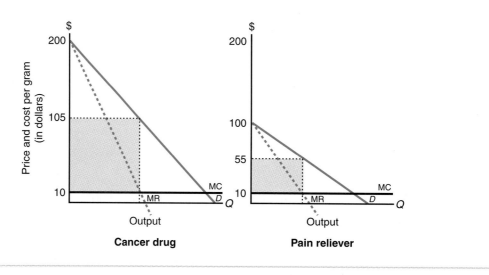

discussed in Chapter 17, tax authorities are aware of this incentive and limit this type of activity.[12]

Similarly, a regulated company might want to integrate vertically to shift profits from a regulated segment of the business, where profits are restricted, to an unregulated segment of the business. In 1984, AT&T settled an antitrust suit with the Department of Justice by splitting into several firms. One of the concerns of the Justice Department was that it was difficult to monitor cost-shifting among AT&T's regulated businesses (for example, telephone service) and other less regulated businesses (for instance, telephone equipment). The breakup of AT&T reduced these concerns.[13]

Other Reasons

Another potential motive for nonmarket procurement is to ensure the supply of an important input. In contrast to the standard economic model, shortages sometimes occur in actual markets. For example, theaters do not always raise ticket prices for popular movies. Rather, tickets are allocated on a first-come, first-served basis when demand

[12]M. Scholes and M. Wolfson (1992), *Taxes and Business Strategy: A Planning Approach* (Prentice Hall: Englewood Cliffs, NJ), Chapter 2.

[13]D. Carlton and J. Perloff (1990), *Modern Industrial Organization* (HarperCollins: New York).

Price Discrimination and Antitrust Law

Firms that integrate vertically to engage in price discrimination can sometimes be held accountable under antitrust law. Alcoa had market power in the production of virgin aluminum ingots, an intermediate good. It integrated into the lower-priced markets (for example, rolled sheet) and "squeezed" competitors in these markets. The judge who wrote the opinion in the antitrust case proposed a "transfer-price test" to assess whether a firm is engaged in a price squeeze. The test considers whether the integrated firm could sell the final output profitably at prevailing prices, assuming it had to pay the same price for the input as it charges downstream competitors. The court determined Alcoa could not. (Note that in our example from the previous section, DrugCo would operate at a loss if it paid $105 for the input and sold the pain reliever to consumers at $55.)

Source: *United States v. Aluminum Company of America* (1945), 148 F. 2d, 416.

exceeds theater capacity for a performance. Similarly, companies sometimes face rationing or short supply of particular inputs. Companies might integrate vertically or enter long-term contracts to increase the reliability of receiving an input.

Firms also use nonmarket procurement to avoid sharing proprietary information with other firms. For instance, a firm might be reluctant to provide an independent supplier with detailed information about its production processes because it fears that the supplier might share the information with other firms. Normally, it is easier to control the leakage of sensitive information when dealing with internal employees or long-term suppliers.

Another common explanation for nonmarket transactions relies on technological factors. For example, some people explain the common ownership of steel milling and steel production by the close technological links of the two processes. But this argument is flawed. Although it is true that there are benefits from having these operations at one location, technology does not dictate ownership. Steel mills could buy hot steel ingots from other companies located in the same building. The reasons they do not are due not to technological factors, but rather result from contracting problems: Independent companies do not want to expose themselves to the holdup problems that arise from such firm-specific investments.

Vertical Integration versus Long-Term Contracts[14]

We have discussed reasons why a firm might acquire a good or service through a nonmarket transaction. We now consider the trade-offs between the two general types of nonmarket transactions, vertical integration and long-term contracts. We examine these trade-offs using the example of AutoCorp, a producer of new automobiles. AutoCorp is considering whether to produce its own auto bodies or to obtain them from an independent supplier through a long-term contract. In either case, a new auto body plant must be constructed. There will be ongoing production, maintenance, and capital-replacement costs. AutoCorp wants to choose the organizational arrangement that maximizes value.

[14]This section draws on Williamson (1985). Important references on this topic include Klein, Crawford, and Alchian (1978); S. Grossman and O. Hart (1986), "The Costs and Benefits of Ownership: A Theory of Vertical and Lateral Integration," *Journal of Political Economy* 94, 691–719; and O. Hart (1995), *Firms, Contracts, and Financial Structure* (Oxford Press: Oxford, UK).

Incomplete Contracting

If contracts were costless to plan, negotiate, write, and enforce, it would not matter if AutoCorp made its own auto bodies or bought them from an outside supplier. In either case, a *complete contract* would be negotiated, one that specified exactly what was expected of each party under all possible future contingencies. Severe penalties would ensure compliance. The actions of each party would be chosen to maximize value (the level of investment, ongoing expenditures, production quantities, designs, and so on). With vertical integration, the contracts would be between the firm and employees, whereas a long-term supply contract would be between two independent firms.

Contracting, however, can be expensive. First, it is difficult to foresee and plan for all possible contingencies. AutoCorp surely will want to make future changes in the design of its auto bodies if customer tastes change or if a competitor develops a superior body design. However, AutoCorp's managers are unlikely to know the appropriate response until the new situation actually confronts them. Second, it is expensive to negotiate contracts. Self-interested parties often find it difficult to agree on contracts—consider the record of strikes by professional athletes. Third, it is costly to enforce contracts. Contracting costs necessitate *incomplete contracts:* Many contingencies will be omitted and thus left open for future negotiation. For example, the Kodak-IBM outsourcing contract stated that IBM must maintain a state-of-the-art data center. The exact technology, software, and communications system are not specified.[15] When contractual disputes arise, the contracting parties are likely to incur legal expenses and spend valuable time either preparing for court or renegotiating contracts.

The prospect of future negotiations can motivate suboptimal investment. Parties to the contract realize that part of the gains from their investments (in capital or effort) are likely to go to other parties: They are not protected by a complete contract. For example, as we discuss below, a supplier will be reluctant to invest effort or capital to reduce production costs if the buyer is likely to capture most of the gains by renegotiating a lower purchase price for the input.

Ownership and Investment Incentives

The owner has the right to determine the *residual use* of an asset—any use that does not conflict with prior contract, custom, or law. Residual rights give an individual increased ability to capture the gains from an investment and can affect investment incentives. For instance, house owners have the residual rights for their properties. As long as their actions are consistent with the law and existing contracts (for example, zoning requirements and restrictive covenants in the deed), they are free to sell or rent their houses. The ability of owners to capture the gains from investing in house repairs through higher selling prices makes it more likely that owners will take better care of houses than renters. Renters are reluctant to invest in repairs if much of the gains goes to owners.[16]

Vertical integration and long-term contracts differ in their assignment of ownership rights. Vertical integration keeps the ownership rights for the relevant assets within one firm, whereas long-term contracting apportions them between firms. As we discuss below, the optimal choice between vertical integration and long-term contracts depends, at least in part, on which ownership structure motivates the most productive investment decisions.

[15]Richmond, Seidmann, and Whinston (1992), 463.

[16]C. Smith and L. Wakeman (1985), "Determinants of Corporate Leasing Policy," *Journal of Finance* 40, 896–908.

Contracting Problems and Investment Incentives: Evidence from China

The early 1990s witnessed a substantial growth in American investment in China. American financial institutions loaned substantial amounts of money to Chinese businesses, and other American companies invested in a variety of Chinese business ventures. By 1995, many of these American companies experienced problems in collecting debts from Chinese businesses. One problem in enforcing contracts with Chinese businesses is that the legal system in China is "primitive." In addition, "China's corporate managers are accustomed to the old socialist system, where they could simply ignore their debts"—there is little market-based enforcement of contracts.

Leasing companies that have financed specific assets have been "particularly vulnerable because the collateral—usually heavy equipment or production lines—is difficult to seize once installed. And even if it can be repossessed, China lacks a good secondary market for equipment." The inability to write enforceable contracts has made American companies question whether it is a good idea to make specific investments in China.

Source: P. Engardio (1994), "Why Sweet Deals Are Going Sour in China," *Business Week* (December 19), 50–51.

Specific Assets and Vertical Integration

Specific assets can cause substantial investment distortions among independent contractors. Consider the investment incentives of BodyWorks, a potential supplier to AutoCorp. BodyWorks would have to construct a plant next to one of AutoCorp's major production facilities. Transportation costs and special designs make this plant quite specific: It is of much less value to other car companies that are farther away and use different body designs. Asset specificity places BodyWorks in a tenuous position. Without the guarantee of a complete contract, BodyWorks will be concerned that AutoCorp will try to lower the price for auto bodies once the investment is made (recall from Chapter 5 that BodyWorks has incentives to operate as long as price is greater than *average variable cost*). AutoCorp might claim that BodyWorks is supplying low-quality products and demand a price concession. Given litigation costs, BodyWorks might be forced to accept the lower price. This concern reduces BodyWorks' incentives to invest in the plant. Similarly, AutoCorp might be reluctant to tailor-make their cars to fit BodyWorks products because it fears that BodyWorks will be opportunistic and increase the price for its auto bodies. In this example, investment incentives can be improved through vertical integration. If AutoCorp constructs its own auto body plant (or buys BodyWorks), it is in a position to capture the gains from its investment. It does not have to worry that some outside firm will try to extract part of the returns by demanding a different price for auto

Renting and Asset Abuse

Renters do not bear the total costs from abusing an asset, since it is owned by the rental company; thus, rental assets frequently are abused. "In one case, a fellow rented a sports car with 12 miles on it. He took out the high-powered engine and installed it in a 'stock car,' to run a high-speed 500-mile race. After crossing the finish line, he reinstalled the engine in the rental car and returned it. The rental company could not successfully prosecute because it failed to establish the number of miles that had been put on the engine. The rental car still showed low mileage, and the rental fee to the customer/car racer was only $24."

Source: D. McIntyre (1988), "Rent a Reck," *Financial World* (September 20), 72.

Owning versus Leasing Networks

Electric Lightwave sells services including local telephone, long-distance, Internet access, and network access to businesses. It decided to build and own a 1,300-mile fiber-optic network from Los Angeles to Portland, Oregon and a 1,600-mile route connecting clusters of cities in the western United States. By making this firm-specific investment and owning these lines, Electric Lightwave can offer higher-quality, lower-cost services and still have higher profit margins. In addition, Electric Lightwave leases lines from other telecommunications companies to fill in gaps in its network until it can build its own lines.

Source: P. Stepankowsky (1998), "Electric Lightwave Sees Advantages in
Owning Network," *The Wall Street Journal* (September 14), B11.

bodies.[17] Other contracting costs might decline as well, since the companies do not have to negotiate a complicated legal contract.

These arguments help explain why vertical integration can be preferred to long-term contracting. Why is this not always the case? What limits the entire economy from being served by one gigantic firm that produces all products? The answer lies again in investment incentives. Consider AutoCorp's purchase of lightbulbs from LightCo. Since lightbulbs are not a specialized product, the purchasing arrangement harms neither LightCo's nor AutoCorp's investment incentives. LightCo is willing to make investments that reduce the costs of making lightbulbs because it benefits from these investments. If AutoCorp tries to capture some of the benefits from LightCo's investment by offering a lower price for lightbulbs, LightCo simply will sell the bulbs to another customer. If LightCo tries to raise the price of its bulbs to extract profits from AutoCorp, it simply will buy bulbs from one of LightCo's rivals, such as Philips Electronics or General Electric. In contrast, if AutoCorp purchases LightCo and operates it as an internal division, investment incentives might be distorted. As divisional managers, LightCo's management might face reduced incentives to invest in innovative activities, since part of the credit for value-enhancing ideas will go to AutoCorp's senior management. In addition, LightCo's management might invest in unproductive activities, such as trying to *influence* senior management's decisions (salaries, allocating capital to the divisions, and so on).[18]

These arguments suggest that *the likelihood of vertical integration increases with the specificity of the asset.* With less specialized assets, market transactions or long-term contracts are more likely to produce efficient investment incentives. This proposition is one of the most important ideas in the economic literature on organizations. Empirical tests support its validity. As an example, J. Stuckey examined aluminum refineries that are located near bauxite mines.[19] Not only are the refineries specific to particular mines owing

---

[17]With costless contracting and risk-neutral individuals, the holdup problem could be solved in the following way: The contract could specify optimal investments by BodyWorks and AutoCorp, and anticipated holdups could be compensated for in advance by appropriate side payments between BodyWorks and AutoCorp.

[18]P. Milgrom and J. Roberts (1994), "Bargaining Costs, Influence Costs, and the Organization of Economic Activity," in J. Alt and K. Shepsle (Eds), *Perspectives on Positive Political Economy* (Cambridge University Press: Cambridge), 57–89.

[19]J. Stuckey (1983), *Vertical Integration and Joint Ventures in the Aluminum Industry* (Harvard University Press: Cambridge, MA). See also E. Anderson (1985), "The Salesperson as Outside Agent or Employee: A Transaction Cost Analysis," *Marketing Science* 4, 234–254; E. Anderson and D. Schmittlein (1984), "Integration of the Sales Force: An Empirical Examination," *Rand Journal of Economics* 15, 385–395; and W. Kim, D. Mayers, and C. Smith (1996), "On the Choice of Insurance Distribution Systems," *Journal of Risk and Insurance* 63, 207–227.

Figure 18.5 Asset Specificity, Uncertainty, and the Procurement Decision

When asset specificity is low, it generally is optimal to use simple market transactions for procurement. As the degree of asset specificity increases, nonmarket transactions (contracts and vertical integration) become more desirable. When uncertainty is low, relatively complete contracts can be written. Thus, contracts can be used to resolve incentive conflicts motivated by firm-specific assets. As uncertainty increases, contracting becomes more expensive. Vertical integration of firm-specific assets becomes more likely as uncertainty increases.

Asset Specificity \ Uncertainty	Low	Medium	High
Low	Market transaction	Market transaction	Market transaction
Medium	Contract	Contract or vertical integration	Contract or vertical integration
High	Contract	Contract or vertical integration	Vertical integration

to transportation costs, the refineries also invest in specialized equipment. Stuckey found that in virtually all cases, there is vertical integration.

Research indicates that specific assets are especially likely to motivate integration in *uncertain environments*. In uncertain environments, the contracting problems with specific assets are particularly severe: It is nearly impossible to specify what actions each party should perform under all future contingencies. In more stable environments, the range of possible circumstances to cover is more limited and relatively complete contracts that mitigate holdup problems can be negotiated at low cost.

The arguments in this section are summarized in Figure 18.5. When asset specificity is low, it is generally best to rely on market exchange, regardless of the level of uncertainty. As the degree of asset specificity increases, the desirability of nonmarket transactions increases. Uncertainty increases the desirability of vertically integrating firm-specific assets;

Lease versus Buy

Firms frequently must decide between leasing and buying an asset. Economic theory suggests that firms are most likely to own assets that are highly firm-specific. For example, Le Roy Industries leases some of its forklifts and other vehicles but buys outright the very specialized machinery it needs to make suspension parts for Ford, General Motors, and Chrysler cars. To quote Charles Teets, vice president and chief financial officer of the company,

> It takes about a year to make the machinery we need. It would be very hard to find a lessor interested in our type of equipment because of the long lead-time. After the lease expired, no lessor would want the equipment back.

Source: B. Gatty and M. Finney (1987), "The New Attraction in Leasing," *Nation's Business* (March), 50–54.

Vertical Integration in the Aerospace Industry

Scott Masten studied the make-versus-buy policies of a major aerospace contractor. The firm made many products for the United States government. The company had to choose between making each product or subcontracting it to another firm for production. Economic theory suggests that internal production is more likely when the assets are specific and the uncertainties in contracting are large.

Masten used two measures of asset specificity for each product. The first measured design (physical-asset) specificity, whereas the second measured site specificity. He also measured the complexity of the product design, which was intended to proxy for uncertainties in contracting. Consistent with the theory, he found that products which were more design specific and quite complex were more likely to be produced internally. When the product was both design specific and complex, there was a 92 percent probability of internal production. If the product was design specific but not complex, the probability of internal production was 31 percent. The probability of internal production was only 2 percent when the product was neither design specific nor complex. For this particular company, site specificity was unimportant.

Source: S. Masten (1984), "The Organization of Production: Evidence from the Aerospace Industry," *Journal of Law & Economics* 27, 403–417.

---

when asset specificity and uncertainty are both high, vertical integration is likely to be the preferred alternative.

This analysis of firm-specific assets helps explain why catering, trucking, copying, and mainframe computing are among the most frequently outsourced services. These activities are sufficiently specialized that spot-market transactions are not viable. Nonetheless, these activities involve assets that are not highly firm-specific. Food-service equipment, trucks, copy machines, and computers can be used by many different companies; therefore, the potential for holdup actions is relatively low. Furthermore, for activities like copying, it is easy to write a relatively complete contract (uncertainty is reasonably low). There also are potential benefits from using independent firms that specialize in large-volume production. Moreover, the transactions are quite *repetitive;* thus, it makes sense to contract with a single supplier on a long-term basis. (The supplier makes customer-specific investments in learning how to serve the customer; hence, it is expensive to change suppliers.) These factors imply that it often is optimal to contract for these services.

One advantage of having IBM provide computer services to Kodak is that IBM provides similar services to other companies. This higher volume can lower the cost for Kodak. The costs of training technical specialists can be spread across more users; software can be written that is used by more than one company. Also, IBM is able to attract higher-quality computer specialists than can Kodak, since IBM's scale of operation provides a much richer set of future career opportunities. Conceptually, Kodak could capture some of these gains by purchasing IBM and operating the two companies as one large enterprise. However, the costs of managing such a large, diverse enterprise likely would outweigh the benefits.

Asset Ownership[20]

We have concentrated on potential holdup problems that occur after the initial investment. Our major point is that these problems can be reduced through vertical integration. However, common ownership can be achieved in our example either if AutoCorp owns BodyWorks or if BodyWorks owns AutoCorp. Which alternative, if either, is best?

---

[20]This section draws on Grossman and Hart (1986).

Considering ongoing specific investment provides a partial answer to this question. In their ongoing interaction, companies like AutoCorp and BodyWorks generally benefit from specific investments, which are difficult to observe or use as the basis for contracts. For example, the management of BodyWorks might invest in learning about AutoCorp's future design plans so that it can plan more effectively for potential changes. This planning might increase the speed at which new models could be developed and thus improve overall corporate performance. Similarly, AutoCorp might invest in learning more about BodyWorks' production processes to develop lower-cost body designs. Investments of this type are hard to observe and depend on the managers' incentives to make them. These incentives, in turn, can depend on ownership structure.

If AutoCorp buys BodyWorks it will structure BodyWorks as a division of the firm. As discussed in Chapter 17, the management of BodyWorks will be evaluated primarily on divisional performance, and will have relatively low incentives to invest in activities that primarily benefit other divisions (although they may have limited incentives to do so through stock ownership and profit-sharing plans). Thus they will invest little in learning about AutoCorp's design plans if the benefits go primarily to AutoCorp. Yet AutoCorp's management, being at the top of the corporation, will be evaluated on overall corporate performance. They will have incentives to invest in all activities that benefit the overall corporation. Thus they will work to invest in lowering BodyWorks' costs if it increases the overall value of the firm. In contrast, if BodyWorks owns AutoCorp the reverse situation holds. BodyWorks' management has incentives to invest in activities that increase total firm value, whereas AutoCorp's management will focus primarily on divisional performance. Which ownership structure is best depends on whose investments are most important. Typically it is better for the party whose investments have the bigger impact on the value of the firm to be the owner. If both parties' investments are important, it can be best to maintain separate ownership and use contracts. This idea is explored in more detail in the appendix.

Other Reasons

Unions are another factor that can affect the choice between vertical integration and contracting. For instance, some of the major airlines have threatened labor unions that they will outsource their kitchen operations to other companies to avoid paying union wages. The major automobile companies have made similar statements with respect to the manufacturing of component parts. Some firms are reluctant to integrate into a unionized activity because they fear that the move might motivate their employees to organize.

Controlling sensitive, proprietary information can affect decisions of outsourcing versus vertical integration. For example, in the specific case of Kodak's outsourcing computing services to IBM, there is a potential problem with Kodak-specific knowledge about electronic imaging. Kodak invests heavily in electronic-imaging R&D. To exploit this investment fully, Kodak must guard this information carefully. Since IBM is an obvious competitor in the electronic-imaging market, outsourcing Kodak's computing services presents a potential problem, one that demands the design of careful controls to keep IBM personnel from accessing Kodak's proprietary information. Note that the costs of designing and administering these controls affects the optimal policy choice. If they are high, Kodak might reject IBM as an outsourcing partner in favor of another vendor with less overlap in the electronic-imaging market (perhaps Electronic Data Systems), or Kodak might reject outsourcing altogether. Along these lines, Prahalad and Hamel argue that it often is unwise for a company to outsource its "core competencies" (those capabilities which are fundamental to a firm's performance and strategy). Rather, according to this argument, firms should keep core competencies within the firm to enhance their development and to prevent other firms from developing similar capabilities (see Chapter 8).[21]

The financial press often argues that obtaining inputs through contracts with other firms "frees companies to use scarce capital for other purposes." This claim is questionable given access to well-developed capital markets. Having another firm produce a product does not reduce investment, it simply shifts the capital expenditures to another firm. Buyers still pay for this investment through the price of the product. The important question is whether more value is created by producing the product internally or externally. If internal production is more valuable, the firm can raise money in the capital market for financing the relevant assets: Capital is not "scarce" for good projects. If external production is more valuable, funds must be raised by the supplier.

Continuum of Choice

Although we have discussed long-term contracting versus vertical integration as a choice between two policies, it is important to keep in mind that the outsourcing decision falls on a continuum. For example, sometimes it is desirable for a firm to maintain ownership of a firm-specific asset and contract with another firm to operate it. This ownership pattern reduces potential holdup problems because if there is a contract dispute, the owner can take the asset and simply contract with an alternative firm to provide the service (neither side faces large losses). This ownership pattern is most viable if the asset can be moved at low cost and the value of the asset is insensitive to asset maintenance or abuse. Alternatively, the owner must be able to provide the service operator with sufficient incentives to maintain and not to abuse the asset.

A related example is Kodak's decision to contract with IBM for providing operating software and hardware but to maintain responsibility for applications software. Development of applications software is likely to be more specific to Kodak than developing of operating software that can be used for many different applications and firms. IBM, therefore, has greater incentives to focus on developing operating software, whereas Kodak has greater incentives to focus on the applications software. The location of specific knowledge reinforces these incentives: Kodak knows more about its specific applications, and IBM knows more about general computing. The observed organizational arrangement reflects these incentive and information effects.

Contract Length

A major advantage of long-term contracts over short-term contracts is that they increase the incentives of the contracting parties to make firm-specific investments. For example, IBM would have limited incentives to invest in learning Kodak's special computing demands if it anticipated only a short-term relationship between the two companies.[22] On

---

[21]C. Prahalad and G. Hamel (1990), "The Core Competence of the Corporation," *Harvard Business Review* (May–June), 79–91.

[22]Long-term contracts provide the greatest incentives when they have uncertain expiration dates (the parties expect the contracts might be renewed). There are strong incentives to cheat in the last period when a contract has a known ending date, since maintaining the reputation as a good partner has no benefit (ignoring third-party effects). The parties, knowing that they will not cooperate in the last period, have incentives to cheat in the next to-last period. (There are no reputational concerns since they know that the other party will not cooperate in the last period.) The incentives to cheat in the next-to-last period affect the incentives in the previous period, and so on. In this case, the contract can unravel, so that the parties have the incentive to cheat in the first period. L. Telser (1980), "A Theory of Self-Enforcing Agreements," *Journal of Business* 53, 27–44.

Short-Term Leases

Car rental companies know something most of us don't. People who rent cars can't drive. They fiddle with the dashboard, eyeball billowing city maps, confuse the horn with the cruise control, and they crash. A lot. Forty percent of Hertz's fleet is damaged some way each year. One rental customer said, "I'm hell on wheels. I'm a good reason not to buy a used car from a rental company." One rental agent says, "They don't even know how to put a car in gear. I have to tell them, 'P is for park, R is for reverse.' Jeez, P should be for 'pray.'" One driver in Florida ran over an alligator, demolishing the car's underside. The man claimed, "The alligator was in my way." Rental companies have started conducting background checks of customers' driving records to turn away high risks. Short-term contracts such as car rental agreements attract customers who are more accident-prone and fail to encourage customers to make investments in safety.

Source: C. Quintanilla (1995), "Hertz Is a Little Wary about Putting You in the Driver's Seat," *The Wall Street Journal* (July 28), A1.

the other hand, it is costly to write and litigate long-term contracts in uncertain environments, where it is difficult to plan for potential changes in technology, input prices, product demands, and the like. Thus, firms might be expected to enter long-term contracts when the desired investment is relatively firm-specific and where the environment is relatively stable. Alternatively, if the firm faces a highly uncertain environment and large investments in firm-specific assets, vertical integration is more likely to be the preferred alternative. Finally, if the investment in firm-specific assets is relatively low or if the lives of the assets are relatively short, the firm can more easily enter into short-term contracts with suppliers or rely on spot market transactions.

Contracting with Distributors

Although our examples have focused on supply contracts, the same analysis applies to distribution contracts. As assets become more specific, vertical integration becomes more desirable. Yet a number of other interesting issues arise in distribution contracts. We now examine these issues.

Free-Rider Problems

Earlier in this chapter, we noted the incentives of independent distributors to free-ride on the reputation of a brand name and how these incentives can motivate suboptimal

Divorce between Outsourcing Partners

Not all outsourcing ventures work—some end in divorce. Hibernia National Bank and Capital Bank used to outsource their computer operations to IBM. To cut its costs, IBM pooled the software support staff for the two banks. Both banks used software from Hogan Systems, a business partner with IBM from 1987. In 1993, Hibernia estimated it could save $40 million over 8 years by switching to a new outsourcing partner, Systematics Financial Services Inc. Capital followed Hibernia and also shifted to Systematics. Subsequently, Hogan and IBM parted ways. This example and others like it suggest that prospective outsourcing partners should anticipate the possibility that the venture will not work out and plan accordingly (for example, by negotiating the equivalent of a prenuptial agreement—what to do with assets, severance payments, and so on).

Source: "ISSC: A Tale of Marriage and Divorce" (1994), *Information Week* (July 18), 13.

Conflicts over Advertising Provisions

Meineke Discount Muffler Shops was ordered to pay $347 million to its franchisees by a federal district court in North Carolina. Franchisees started noticing that the franchiser had been cutting back on advertising. Newspaper ads were waning, and TV spots were appearing after midnight. Eventually, they discovered that instead of the contractually specified 2 percent, Meineke was pocketing $17 million, or 15 percent of the communal ad funds. The judge said the franchiser had a fiduciary duty to ensure that the franchisees' funds were properly managed.

Source: N. Harris and M. France (1997), "Franchisees Get Feisty," *Business Week* (February 24), 65–66.

---

sales efforts—for example, insufficient expenditures on advertising and other inputs. One method of reducing this problem is vertical integration.[23] The other method is to use contracts with specific provisions to control free-rider problems. Two contract terms that specifically address this concern are advertising provisions and exclusive territories.

Advertising Provisions   Firms use several related methods to increase advertising at the local level. First, a company can charge its retail units an advertising fee and have the central company retain the responsibility for advertising. For instance, most franchise contracts require that, in addition to the base royalty payment, individual units pay a percentage of sales to the central company to provide advertising. One potential problem with this approach is that the local unit, not the central company, might have the specific knowledge relevant for effective local advertising. A second alternative that addresses this concern is for the central company to share in the local advertising costs; for example, it might pay half of any advertising expenditures. The decisions on local advertising are made by the local managers, but by reducing the effective cost of advertising, they encourage the local unit managers to advertise more extensively. A third alternative is to require distributors to contribute to regional advertising funds. The distributors have the primary decision rights to decide how to spend the monies in the funds.

Exclusive Territories   One of the most common methods of reducing free-riding is to grant individual distributors exclusive rights to operate in a given market area. For example, an AutoCorp dealership might have a contract that prevents the company from opening another dealership within 30 miles. By giving distributors monopoly rights for specific market areas, there are fewer incentives to free-ride, since the distributors internalize more of the benefits from their sales efforts, fewer benefits go to other units not owned by the given distributor. Exclusive territories also can create extra profits for local distributors. These profits can provide additional incentives not to free-ride: If the manufacturer catches the distributor free-riding and terminates the contract, future profits are lost.[24]

Double Markups

Granting distributors market power within specific areas reduces free-rider problems, but it can create another problem—*double markups*. Since both the manufacturer and

---

[23]H. Marvel (1982), "Exclusive Dealing," *Journal of Law & Economics* 25, 1–25.

[24]B. Klein and K. Murphy (1988), "Vertical Restraints as Contract Enforcement Mechanisms," *Journal of Law & Economics* 31, 265–97 and J. Brickley (1999), "Incentive Conflicts and Contractual Restraints: Evidence from Franchising," *Journal of Law and Economics* 42, 745–774.

Conflicts over Exclusive Territories

Granting distributors exclusive territories reduces free-riding among distributors but can induce dysfunctional behavior within the company. For example, McDonald's generated growth by building thousands of new restaurants in the late 1980s and early 1990s—restaurants which proceeded to divert customers and profits from existing franchises. McDonald's has lots of small franchisees—4,500 worldwide. It got so bad in the mid-nineties that US franchisees told McDonald's management, "It's like you're flying the plane, and we operators are stuck in the back of a smoke-filled cabin with no idea what's going on." To solve this problem, McDonald's began consolidating some of its franchisees. The CEO, Jack Greenberg, said, "From here on out, we're going to grow with our existing licensees rather than add hundreds of new ones each year. I want the stores in the hands of the best operators."

Source: P. Sellers (1998), "McDonald's Starts Over," *Fortune* (June 22) 34–36.

the distributor face downward-sloping demand curves, each has the incentive to mark up the product's price above marginal cost. Unchecked, this results in the customer's facing two markups rather than one. Hence, both the quantity of the product demanded and the combined profits for the manufacturer and distributor are less than they would be if this incentive were controlled. The following is a numerical example illustrating this problem, as well as the contract terms that might be used to control it.

Example   Suppose that AutoCorp faces the following demand for its Rhino automobiles in the Medford, Oregon, market area:

$$P = 55,000 - 100Q \tag{18.3}$$

AutoCorp can produce Rhinos at a constant marginal cost of $5,000. To simplify the computations, assume that there are no fixed costs in producing or selling cars. To maximize profits, AutoCorp must select the quantity and price where marginal revenue equals marginal cost. As pictured in Figure 18.6, the optimal quantity and price are $Q^* = 250$ and $P^* = \$30,000$. The firm's profits are $6.25 million.

Now suppose that AutoCorp sells its vehicles through SUVmart, an independent distributor that has the exclusive right to sell Rhinos in the Medford market area. Under the contract, AutoCorp sets the wholesale price, while SUVmart selects the quantity to purchase and the retail price. For simplicity, suppose that the only marginal cost facing SUVmart for Rhinos is the price charged by AutoCorp. (There are no variable distribution costs.) The owners of SUVmart care only about their own profits, and the managers of AutoCorp care only about AutoCorp's profits. The problem facing AutoCorp is to choose the wholesale price, P_w, that maximizes its profits.

To solve this problem, AutoCorp's management would like to know the quantity that SUVmart would purchase at each possible wholesale price. AutoCorp can infer this demand curve by analyzing the problem from the perspective of SUVmart. SUVmart faces the retail demand curve for autos given in Equation (18.3). SUVmart maximizes its profits by setting its marginal revenue, implied by this retail demand curve, equal to P_w, its marginal cost. Thus, SUVmart's marginal revenue curve is the effective demand curve AutoCorp faces. (At any wholesale price, SUVmart buys the quantity indicated by its marginal revenue curve.) As pictured in Figure 18.6, this curve is

$$P_w = 55,000 - 200Q \tag{18.4}$$

Figure 18.6 Optimal Output in an Example of the Double Markup Problem

AutoCorp can produce automobiles at a constant marginal cost of $5,000. To maximize profits, AutoCorp must select the quantity and price where marginal revenue equals marginal cost. The optimal quantity and price are $Q^* = 250$ and $P_W^* = \$30,000$. Firm profits are $6.25 million (assuming no fixed costs).

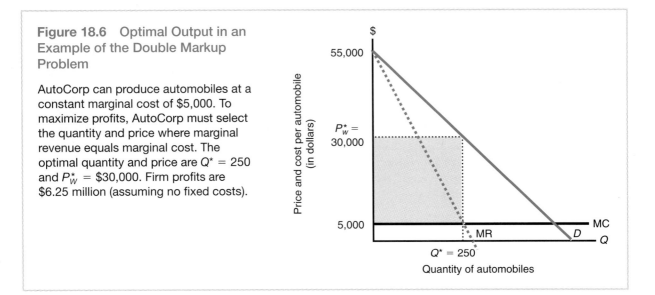

Given SUVmart's demand for Rhinos, what wholesale price will AutoCorp choose? AutoCorp maximizes its profits by setting its marginal revenue equal to its marginal cost of $5,000. Since AutoCorp faces a demand curve of $P_w = 55,000 - 200Q$, its marginal revenue is $\text{MR} = 55,000 - 400Q$. AutoCorp's profits are maximized by selecting a wholesale price of $P_w^* = \$30,000$. At this price, SUVmart will buy 125 Rhinos and set a retail price of $42,500. AutoCorp will have profits of $3.125 million, and SUVmart will have profits of $1.563 million, for combined profits of $4.688 million.

This outcome, which is pictured in Figure 18.7, is inefficient. AutoCorp and SUVmart fail to maximize their joint profits. Both parties could be made better off by coordinating their prices and volume choices—we already have shown that they could

---

Company Ownership versus Franchising

We have discussed how a central company can reduce the incentives of an independent distributor to free-ride on the brand name through contracts with terms that motivate increased sales efforts. When the free-rider problem is severe, it can be less expensive simply to own the distribution units centrally. Managers of a company-owned unit have fewer incentives than an independent distributor to free-ride on the reputation, since they do not get to keep the profits from the unit—the reduction in costs (for example, from decreased advertising) flow through to the central company, not the managers.

Most franchise companies do not franchise all their retail outlets. The typical company franchises about 80 percent of the units and owns the other 20 percent. Our argument suggests that central companies are most likely to own the units that receive a significant amount of business from customers who are unlikely to make repeat purchases at the particular units (the incentives to free-ride in this case are large). On average, fast-food restaurants are more likely to serve transient customers than auto-service companies. (Customers tend to use the same unit repeatedly for oil changes and tune-ups.) Consistent with the theory, the typical restaurant franchise company owns about 30 percent of its units, and the typical auto service franchise company owns about 13 percent of its units.

Source: J. Brickley and F. Dark (1987), "The Choice of Organizational Form: The Case of Franchising," *Journal of Financial Economics* 18, 401.

Figure 18.7 Example of Double Markups

AutoCorp sets the wholesale price for its automobiles, while SUVmart selects the quantity to purchase and the retail price. SUVmart maximizes profits by setting the wholesale price equal to its marginal revenue. Thus, SUVmart's marginal revenue curve is AutoCorp's demand curve. AutoCorp maximizes profit by setting its marginal cost of $5,000 equal to its marginal revenue. AutoCorp selects a wholesale price P_w^* of $30,000, a $25,000 markup above its marginal cost, whereas SUVmart selects a retail price P_r^* of $42,500, a $12,500 markup above its marginal cost. SUVmart sells 125 cars at this price. The combined profits are $4.688 million. The two companies could earn combined profits of $6.25 million if they cooperate and sell 250 automobiles to consumers at a price of $30,000.

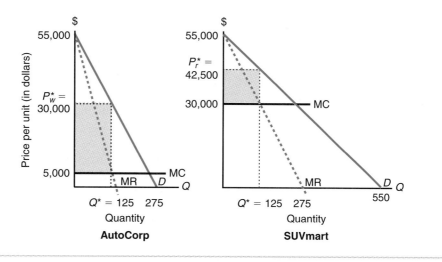

earn up to $6.25 million—versus $4.688 million. In addition, with the double markups, consumers pay $42,500 for 125 Rhinos rather than $30,000 for 250.

This problem does not automatically disappear if AutoCorp merges with SUVmart. We saw in Chapter 17 that exactly the same problem can arise within firms, when products are sold between two profit centers using internal transfer prices. As we discussed, the transfer-pricing problem can be reduced by appropriate organizational design. Our current focus is to look at how this problem might be reduced between two independent firms through specific contractual terms.

Two-Part Pricing SUVmart will purchase 250 Rhinos if AutoCorp sets a wholesale price of $5,000. This quantity maximizes the joint profits of the two firms and results in a retail price of $30,000. The entire profits, however, go to SUVmart, since AutoCorp is selling the automobiles at cost. One solution is for AutoCorp to charge SUVmart an up-front franchise fee—thereby extracting its share of the profits through this fee—and then to sell automobiles to SUVmart at $5,000 each. Since SUVmart's purchasing decision is based on marginal cost, not total cost, it still will purchase 250 automobiles and set a retail price of $30,000. If AutoCorp charges SUVmart an up-front fee of $3.125 million for the exclusive rights to the Medford market area, the combined profits of $6.25 million are split evenly between the two companies. Once the fee is collected, AutoCorp might try to increase the wholesale price of the automobiles to increase its profits. Thus, for such a solution to work, AutoCorp must be able to commit credibly to sell automobiles to SUVmart at marginal cost.

Quotas   An alternative method for maximizing the combined profits is for the two companies to agree on a minimum purchase requirement. SUVmart could agree to purchase at least 250 automobiles at a prespecified wholesale price (above $5,000). Given the details in this example, SUVmart will purchase exactly 250 automobiles and sell them at $30,000 to retail customers. The level of the prespecified wholesale price determines the split of the profits between the two companies. A wholesale price of $17,500 splits the profits evenly (each company nets $12,500). AutoCorp must be able to commit credibly to the wholesale price, and SUVmart must purchase the agreed-upon quota.

Regulatory Issues

Some regulators and scholars are suspicious of contract terms such as exclusive territories that potentially limit competition. Nonetheless, most nonprice contract terms are not *per se* illegal (always illegal) under federal antitrust law. They are judged on a *rule of reason,* where the court attempts to consider the benefits of the terms (such as increased sales efforts) against potential anticompetitive effects. In some states, automobile dealers and franchisees have successfully lobbied their legislators to limit the control that central companies impose—for example, in setting quotas and terminating contracts. In addition, federal law restricts central companies from directly controlling the pricing by distributors at the retail level. A detailed treatment of these regulatory issues is beyond the scope of this book.[25] Suffice it to say that it usually is important for firms to engage expert legal counsel to advise in designing supply and distribution contracts.

Recent Trends in Outsourcing

The 1990s have witnessed a huge expansion in outsourcing by major companies. At least four factors have contributed to this trend. First, new flexible production technologies allow suppliers to adapt more easily to customer demands. Thus, in some cases, assets are becoming less firm-specific—a technological innovation that favors contracting over vertical integration. Second, improvements in information and communications technology make it easier to identify potential partners and to communicate with them after an agreement is reached. Electronic data interchange allows firms to connect their computers to each other. These computers can automatically order inventory directly from a supplier with little human intervention. Third, there has been a dramatic increase in worldwide competition. This competition has placed greater pressure on firms to reduce costs and increase efficiency. Some scholars argue that many American firms were "flush with cash" in the 1960s and 1970s and were more likely to waste this cash through such actions as engaging in too much integration.[26] Some recent outsourcing decisions thus might be corrections for poor investment decisions of the past. Fourth, during the early 1990s, there was a worldwide recession, which caused excess capacity in many industries. In this environment, firms often could obtain large discounts from external vendors. (This effect should be more cyclical than permanent.)

Many recent outsourcing decisions do not move firms from internal production to the other end of the spectrum (spot market transactions). Rather, the movement has

---

[25]For a more detailed treatment of these issues, see R. Posner (1976), *Antitrust Law* (University of Chicago Press: Chicago); and D. Carlton and J. Perloff (1990).

[26]M. Jensen (1986), "Agency Costs of Free Cash Flow, Corporate Finance and Takeovers," *American Economic Review* 76, 323–329.

been to an intermediate arrangement—long-term contracting. Many firms also have moved away from acquiring inputs in the spot market. To improve quality and lower unit costs, firms such as General Motors and Xerox have cut their number of suppliers dramatically and correspondingly have increased the number of long-term partnerships with independent firms. Thus, those trends can be viewed as movements from each end of the spectrum toward the middle.

Technological changes, such as just-in-time production methods, electronic data interchanges, and total quality manufacturing, require close links between manufacturers, suppliers, and distributors. Rather than inspecting parts and materials from numerous suppliers on delivery, a few suppliers are selected and their production processes are certified as meeting high-quality standards. Thus, although the various activities in the manufacturing/distribution process are conducted by different firms, it is important that these firms remain closely linked. In such cases, these factors make spot market transactions undesirable.

CASE STUDY: *AutoCorp*

AutoCorp produces automobiles. It has asked the Amalgamated Fabric Company to consider a proposal to become a supplier of automobile seats. Under the proposal, Amalgamated Fabric would construct a $20 million plant near one of AutoCorp's production facilities. AutoCorp would purchase 100,000 car seats per year at a price of $280 per seat for 15 years—the useful life of the plant. (The actual proposal contains an adjustment for inflation. Ignore this complication in the analysis.)

Amalgamated Fabric's financial analysts have examined the proposal. It appears to be a profitable opportunity. The amortized cost of the plant is $2.6 million per year (at a discount rate of 10 percent). The annual costs are $25.4 million per year. Therefore, the average total cost is $280 per seat—ATC = ($25.4 million + $2.6 million)/100,000 = $280. The financial analysts have examined AutoCorp's financial outlook. Although it has not been highly profitable in all years, there is essentially no probability of bankruptcy over the next 15 years. Since the proposed price covers the cost, the financial analysts think that the proposal should be accepted. (It breaks even with a fair rate of return on invested capital of 10 percent.)

You have been asked to analyze the contract proposal. You have seen the financial analysis and think the cost estimates are reasonable. You are aware that,

due to its location, the proposed plant has no alternative use other than supplying seats to AutoCorp. The salvage value of the plant, in the event of liquidation, is $2 million.

Discussion Questions

1. One concern you have is that AutoCorp might try to lower the effective purchase price of the seats after the plant is built (by reneging on the contract or demanding higher-quality seats for the same price). Once the plant is built, how much can the purchase price fall before Amalgamated Fabric liquidates the plant?

2. What factors would you consider to decide whether opportunistic behavior by AutoCorp is a likely possibility?

3. Does AutoCorp have to worry about any opportunistic actions by Amalgamated Fabric?

4. What factors might make it difficult to write a contract that would limit opportunistic behavior by both companies?

5. What are the costs and benefits of AutoCorp vertically integrating and supplying its own automobile seats?

6. What are the costs and benefits of having AutoCorp construct the plant and letting Amalgamated Fabric operate it on a contractual basis?

Summary

When a firm participates in more than one successive stage of the production or distribution of a product or service, it is said to be *vertically integrated*. Firms change their degree of integration over time. An organization that begins to produce its own inputs is engaging in *backward* or *upstream* integration, whereas an organization that begins to market its own goods or to conduct additional finishing work is engaging in *forward* or *downstream* integration. The term *outsourcing* frequently is used to describe a movement away from vertical integration—moving an activity outside the firm that formerly was done within the firm. The term *outsourcing* also is used to describe an ongoing arrangement where a firm obtains a part or service from an external firm. It is useful to think of the outsourcing decision as a choice along a continuum of possibilities, ranging from spot market transactions to vertical integration with an array of long-term contracts in between.

Well-functioning markets provide powerful incentives for efficient production and low prices; thus, firms acquire many goods and services through market transactions. Economists have identified at least three primary reasons why a firm might want to engage in nonmarket procurement: *contracting costs, market power,* and *taxes/regulation*. Four factors can make the contracting costs of nonmarket procurement lower than the costs of market exchange. These factors include firm-specific assets, costs of measuring quality, externalities, and coordination problems.

Firm-specific assets are assets that are substantially more valuable in their current use than in their next best alternative use. Investment in firm-specific assets can cause enormous problems between suppliers and buyers and is a primary reason for nonmarket transactions. Once the investment in firm-specific assets is made, there is a *sunk cost*—the supplier has incentives to continue the relationship as long as the variable costs are covered—even if total costs are not. This incentive subjects the supplier to a potential *holdup problem*. The buyer also can be held up by the supplier. One way of reducing these problems is to integrate vertically. The other method is to negotiate a detailed contract that spells out the rights and responsibilities of each party.

Due to contracting costs, most contracts are *incomplete:* Many contingencies are unspecified and subject to future negotiation. The prospect of future negotiations can motivate suboptimal investment in both capital and effort. Parties to the contract realize that part of the gains from their investments are likely to go to other parties: They are not protected by a complete contract.

The owner has the right to determine the *residual use* of an asset—any use that does not conflict with prior contract, custom, or law. Residual rights give an individual increased ability to capture the gains from an investment and thus can provide investment incentives. Vertical integration and long-term contracts differ in their assignment of ownership rights. Vertical integration keeps the ownership rights for the relevant assets within one firm, whereas long-term contracting apportions them between firms. The choice between vertical integration and long-term contracts depends, at least in part, on which ownership structure creates more productive investment decisions.

A primary prediction of the economics literature is that as an asset becomes more firm-specific, the firm is more likely to choose vertical integration over long-term contracting. The analysis suggests that firms will enter long-term contracts when the desired investment is relatively firm-specific and where the environment is relatively stable and predictable (in stable environments, the range of possible circumstances to cover is more limited and negotiating more complete contracts is less costly). Conversely, if the firm faces a more uncertain environment and large investments in firm-specific assets, vertical integration is more likely to be the preferred alternative. Finally, if the investment in firm-specific assets is relatively low (the assets are unspecialized) or the lives of the assets relatively short, the firm can either enter into short-term contracts with suppliers or rely on spot market transactions.

Independent distributors can have incentives to *free-ride* on a brand name. One method to reduce this problem is vertical integration. Another method is to use contracts with specific provisions that control free-rider problems. Two types of contract terms that specifically address this concern are *advertising provisions* and *exclusive territories*. Exclusive territories help internalize free-rider problems, but they create another problem—*double markups*. This problem (which is analogous to the transfer-pricing problem examined in Chapter 17) can be reduced through *two-part pricing* or *quotas*.

At least four factors have contributed to the recent trend in outsourcing—increased worldwide competition, the development of less firm-specific production technologies, improvements in information and communication technologies, and excess capacity from a worldwide recession. The recent trend, however, is not from vertical integration to spot market transactions. It is a movement from both ends of the spectrum toward an intermediate solution of some form of long-term contracting. Technological changes, such as just-in-time production methods, electronic data interchanges, and total quality management, require closer links between manufacturers, suppliers, and distributors. These changes reduce the desirability of spot market transactions in many cases.

Appendix

Ownership Rights and Investment Incentives[27]

This appendix provides a more detailed example of how ownership rights can affect investment incentives (in this case, investments in effort). Through this example, some of the important trade-offs between vertical integration and long-term contracts become more evident.

Basic Problem   The AGT Company manufactures computer modems. The company is owned by Valentina Vezzali. The Custom Circuit Company makes circuit boards for AGT. AGT is Custom's only customer, and Custom is AGT's sole supplier of circuit boards. The boards are tailor-made for AGT and cannot be used by other manufacturers (the boards are firm-specific). Custom Circuit is owned by Phillipe Daurelle.

AGT might want to make future design changes in its circuit boards. For simplicity, suppose that the future benefit of a design change to AGT can take only two values, 20 or 40, whereas the costs to Custom of making the change can either be 10 or 30. The likelihood of a high benefit and a low cost is influenced by both Tina's and Phil's efforts. Let x equal the probability that the benefit is 40. Tina can affect this probability through her efforts—in fact, we assume that Tina's efforts completely determine x. For instance, by working with customers, she can determine the best design change to make. She also can spend time marketing the revised product. These types of activities increase the probability that the benefits from the design change will be large. However, the personal cost to Tina of exerting effort is $10x^2$. As an example, if Tina exerts enough effort so that x is 0.5, she incurs a personal cost of $10(0.5)^2 = 2.5$. Similarly, Phil's actions completely determine y, the probability that the cost equals 10, at a personal cost of $10y^2$. For instance, Phil can exert effort on developing more cost-effective ways to manufacture the new circuit boards.

Neither Tina's nor Phil's effort choices are observable by the other party. Tina does not know y and Phil does not know x. Although both Tina and Phil ultimately can

---

[27]This appendix uses elementary probability theory and calculus. This section draws on B. Holmstrom and J. Tirole (1989), "Theory of the Firm," in R. Schmalensee (Ed.), *Handbook of Industrial Organization,* Volume 1 (North Holland: Amsterdam), 69–72.

observe the realized costs and benefits of the design change, they cannot be verified by a third party. Thus, neither effort, costs, nor benefits are contractible; it is not possible to provide either party with incentives through a contract tied to realized costs or benefits of the design change.

Ideal Effort Choices   Value is created by a design change whenever the benefits of the change exceed the costs. The only time that the design change does not create value is when the benefits are 20 and the costs are 30. Both Tina and Phil are risk-neutral. It is in their joint interests to choose effort levels that maximize expected surplus. By maximizing the size of the pie, there is more value to share and both parties can be made better off. Ideally, the joint expected surplus S_J for the two companies is

$$S_J = (40 - 10)xy + (40 - 30)x(1 - y) + (20 - 10)(1 - x)y - 10x^2 - 10y^2$$
$$= 30xy + 10x(1 - y) + 10(1 - x)y - 10x^2 - 10y^2 \qquad (18.5)$$
$$= 10xy + 10x + 10y - 10x^2 - 10y^2$$

This equation is maximized by choosing effort levels of $y = x = 1$.[28] The joint expected surplus net of effort costs is 10.

Actual Effort Choices under the Contract   The specific contract between AGT and Custom requires that a design change be approved by both companies. Since Tina and Phil have equal bargaining power, they anticipate splitting the surplus that is available from any future design change. For instance, if the benefits are 40 and the costs are 10, the total surplus is 30. A price for the circuit boards of 25 splits the gains: Tina gains $40 - 25 = 15$ and Phil gains $25 - 10 = 15$.

Tina and Phil *choose their effort levels privately* (the effort choices cannot be observed by the other person). Each person chooses an effort level that maximizes his or her own surplus, given the anticipated effort choice of the other party. As we shall see, both parties choose effort levels below the values that maximize the joint surplus. The low effort choices result from the standard free-rider problem. Tina and Phil bear the total costs of their personal efforts but receive only half the benefits.

Consider Tina's problem. Her expected surplus S_T is

$$S_T = .5(40 - 10)x\bar{y} + .5(40 - 30)x(1 - \bar{y}) + .5(20 - 10)(1 - x)\bar{y} - 10x^2$$
$$= 15x\bar{y} + 5x(1 - \bar{y}) + 5(1 - x)\bar{y} - 10x^2 \qquad (18.6)$$
$$= 5x\bar{y} + 5x + 5 - 10x^2$$

where $\bar{y}$ is the effort level that she expects Phil to exert.[29] Taking the partial derivative with respect to x and setting it equal to zero,

$$\partial S_T / \partial x = 5\bar{y} + 5 - 20x = 0 \qquad (18.7)$$

Phil's first-order condition is, similarly,

$$\partial S_P / \partial y = 5\bar{x} + 5 - 20y = 0 \qquad (18.8)$$

In a Nash equilibrium, both Phil's and Tina's first-order condition will be met and the effort choices will be $x = 1/3$ and $y = 1/3$ (at these values, neither party has the incentive

---

[28]Technical note: The first three terms in Equation (18.5) are the three possible outcomes of positive surplus multiplied by the probability of the outcome. The last two terms are the effort costs. Note: If the benefits are 20 and the costs are 30, the design change is not implemented; the term $(0)(1 - x)(1 - y)$ drops out of Equation (18.5). The first-order conditions are $10 + 10y - 20x = 0$ and $10 + 10x - 20y = 0$. The solution is $x = y = 1$.

[29]She bears the full cost of her effort, $10x^2$, but receives only half the benefits.

to alter his or her choice). The total surplus, net of effort costs, is 5.6 [substitute $y = x = 1/3$ into Equation (18.5)].

Vertical Integration   One way to change effort incentives is for the two firms to integrate vertically, either by having AGT buy Custom or by having Custom buy AGT. Consider the case where Tina purchases Custom from Phil and hires him as an employee to manage AGT's "Custom Circuit Division." Ownership gives Tina the decision rights to implement the design change without Phil's approval (she has the *residual use rights*). Since Phil has no bargaining power, all the surplus goes to Tina. Phil has no incentives to exert effort on increasing the likelihood of a low production cost: He bears all the costs for his personal effort and reaps none of the benefits. (Recall that we have ruled out incentive contracts tied to realized costs or benefits of design changes.) Given $y = 0$, the cost of implementing the design change is 30 for certain. Tina's benefits from investing are

$$(40 - 30)x - 10x^2 \tag{18.9}$$

Tina will choose $x = 1/2$. The total surplus, net of investment costs, is 2.5.[30] The case where Custom buys AGT is symmetrical, Phil invests $y = 1/2$, and total net surplus is 2.5.[31] Clearly, vertical integration is not superior to a long-term contract.

Optimal Organizational Choice   When Tina and Phil negotiate the sale of either company, they can share the expected surplus in any manner by negotiating the appropriate purchase price. They have incentives to choose the ownership structure that maximizes the expected net surplus. Given the numbers in this example, they will choose not to combine the two companies. Separate ownership creates more value than integration.

This example illustrates that ownership structure can matter because it affects investment incentives. (In this case, investments in effort.) Ownership gives individuals increased power to capture the fruits of their efforts (see Chapter 10) and thus can provide important incentives. In this example, separate ownership is better than integration because both parties' investments are important. It is better to provide moderate incentives to both Phil and Tina than strong incentives to only one party. It is easy to envision cases where integration will be the preferred alternative. For instance, suppose that Tina can exert effort to affect the benefits of the design change, but Phil has little control over the costs. Here, it would make sense for AGT to own Custom. This ownership structure provides strong incentives for Tina to exert effort and weak incentives for Phil. These incentives are optimal, since only Tina's effort matters. Conversely, it makes sense for Custom to own AGT when Phil's effort is substantially more important than Tina's.

In this example, we have ruled out the possibility that effort can be motivated by incentive compensation (making payments based on the realized costs and benefits). We made this extreme assumption specifically to isolate the important incentive effects of ownership. More generally, owners can motivate internal employees through incentive compensation. For instance, if AGT purchased Custom, Tina might be able to pay Phil in a manner that would encourage him to exert some effort to reduce costs. Similarly, in the separate ownership case, AGT and Custom might be able to include incentive clauses in the contract that would encourage investment (for instance, Custom might receive extra revenue from AGT if it can produce the new design at low cost). As we

---

[30]Tina's first-order condition is $10 - 20x = 0$. The solution is $x = 1/2$. The total surplus is found by substituting $x = 1/2$ and $y = 0$ into Equation (18.6).

[31]This symmetry is a result of the cost and benefit functions in our example. More generally, it can matter who buys whom.

discussed in Chapters 15 through 17, incentive schemes and performance evaluation are not costless activities. In a more detailed analysis, AGT and Custom would have to compare the value that could be created using an optimal supply contract without integration to the value that could be created using optimal incentive compensation contracts under integration. The basic point of our analysis continues to hold—*ownership structure matters because it can affect investment incentives.*

Appendix Problems

1. Insurance companies contract with independent agents to sell policies and provide ongoing services to customers. Ongoing client services tend to be more important in auto insurance companies than life insurance companies. In some insurance companies, the agents "own" the client list. If they stop representing the firm, they can take the clients with them to a new company. In other cases, the insurance company owns the list. The agent is not allowed to take clients to another company. (There is a formal contract with this provision.) Do you think life insurance companies or auto insurance companies are more likely to employ independent agents who own their client lists? Explain.

2. In explaining a decision to purchase an independent R&D laboratory, an executive of the acquiring company said,

   We felt we had to purchase the company to give us patent rights on any important discoveries. Without these rights, we would have few incentives to invest in the marketing and distribution systems that are necessary to support the discoveries.

   Evaluate this logic.

Suggested Readings

D. Carlton and J. Perloff (1999), *Modern Industrial Organization,* 3rd edition (HarperCollins: New York), Chapter 16.

O. Hart (1995), *Firms, Contracts, and Financial Structure* (Oxford Press: Oxford, UK).

B. Klein, R. Crawford, and A. Alchian (1978), "Vertical Integration, Appropriable Rents, and the Competitive Contracting Process," *Journal of Law & Economics* 24, 297–326.

P. Rubin (1990), *Managing Business Transactions* (Free Press: New York).

O. Williamson (1985), *The Economic Institutions of Capitalism* (Free Press: New York).

Review Questions

18–1. Discuss the pros and cons of the policy described in the following quote from *Fortune*[32]:

   According to the new thinking, any kind of work to which a company can't bring a special set of skills should be spun off, outsourced or eliminated. Thus AT&T, GE, IBM, and Shell Oil are in the process of spinning off legal, public relations, billing, payroll, and other services. What's left, whether it's a $100 million corporation or a $100 billion corporation, is the ideal size. . . . For example, if marketing is a competitive advantage in an industry, then it should build up its marketing muscle and employ outside suppliers and service firms to do everything else.

18–2. The Black Diamond Company mines coal. It would like to build a processing plant right next to its major mine. The location of this mine is relatively remote and is not near other coal mines. Tax considerations, as well as government regulations, dictate that the processing plant be owned and operated by some independent company (other than Black Diamond). Your company, the Greg Norman Coal Company, is considering building and operating the plant

[32]B. Dumaine and J. Labate (1992), "Is Big Still Good?" *Fortune* (April 20), 50.

for Black Diamond on a contract basis. Your job is to negotiate the contract with Black Diamond. Discuss the terms that you will try to get Black Diamond to agree to in the contract. Explain why these terms are important to you.

18–3. Evaluate the following quote:

The major advantage to outsourcing is that it reduces a company's capital costs, freeing the company to use scarce capital for other purposes.

18–4. Assume that Ford Motor Company can produce an automobile at a constant marginal cost of $4,000. The demand for the car in the Rochester area is $P = 60,000 - 100Q$.
  a. What is the profit-maximizing price and quantity? What are the profits from this activity?
  b. Now suppose that Ford sells its cars through an independent distributor, Rochester Autos, which has the exclusive right to sell new Fords in the Rochester area. Under the contract, Ford sets the wholesale price, and Rochester Motors selects the quantity to purchase and the retail price. The only cost facing Rochester Motors is the wholesale price of the car. Ford and Rochester Autos both strive to maximize their own profits. What are (1) the wholesale price, (2) the retail price, (3) the quantity sold, and (4) the combined profits of Ford and Rochester Autos?
  c. Describe how Ford might use a two-part pricing scheme to eliminate this successive monopoly problem with Rochester Motors. (No calculations are necessary.)

18–5. BioChem has a patent on a chemical product that is used as a key input in producing farm and home agricultural fertilizer. Currently, BioChem produces the product and sells it to companies who manufacture the final products for the farm and home users. BioChem faces the following demand curves from the farm and home market segments:

$$\text{Farm:} \qquad P = 300 - 10Q$$

$$\text{Home:} \qquad P = 100 - 5Q$$

BioChem can produce the product at a constant marginal cost of $1. Calculate the optimal prices that BioChem would like to charge in each market segment to maximize profits. Discuss how vertical integration might be used to accomplish this pricing policy. Be sure to indicate the market into which BioChem should vertically integrate (assume they can integrate only into one). Explain why you chose this market.

18–6. In explaining the recent acquisition of a supplier, an executive made the following argument: "We purchased the supplier so that we could keep the profit rather than pay it to some other firm." Evaluate this argument.

18–7. Cable television companies lay cables to individual households in the communities they serve to carry the television signal. How specific is this investment? What kind of arrangements would you expect the cable companies to make with local communities about the pricing and taxation of cable services? Explain.

18–8. The Hidden Dog Fence Company sells invisible electric fences to contain dogs within yards. For a half-acre lot, the cost is $2,000 for the system and installation. The market for invisible dog fencing is competitive: Several companies sell similar products at about the same price. In each case, the dog wears a battery-powered collar. The collar give the dog a shock if it gets near the boundary of the property. Hidden Fence uses a specially designed collar that uses batteries made specifically for Hidden Fence by the Battery-O-Vac Company. The batteries last for 3 months and cost $25 apiece. Hidden Fence has a patent on these batteries, and there are no alternative sources of supply. Other fence companies produce products that use generic batteries. Currently, the battery costs of these other systems are the same as for Hidden Fence.
  a. Suppose that you purchase the system from Hidden Fence. After you purchase the system, how much will Hidden Fence be able to raise the price of its batteries before you discontinue use of the system and buy a different system from another company? (Suppose that you do want to maintain an invisible fence.) For this question, assume a 10 percent annual discount rate, no inflation, and an infinite life for the invisible fence, yourself, and the patent for the batteries.

b. As the manager of Hidden Fence Company, what might you do to convince a worried prospective customer that opportunistic behavior with respect to battery prices is not a likely occurrence?

18–9. Major oil companies use a dual distribution system for gasoline. Some stations are *direct-serve,* where the oil company delivers gasoline to the station. Other stations are served by distributors. Distributors are independent businesspeople who buy gas from the oil company and sell it to stations. Distributors also own their own stations. The land, tanks, and equipment at the direct-serve stations are owned by the oil company and leased to the dealer (franchisee). The dealer buys gas from the oil company and pays rent for the land. The dealer keeps the profits from the station over the life of the lease. (Some direct-serve stations are centrally owned by the oil company. At these locations, the oil company hires a manager to operate the station.) At direct-serve stations, the oil company is responsible for environmental cleanup, local advertising, monitoring of the station (to protect the brand name), and so on. The distributors are responsible for these activities at the stations they serve. Typically the oil company sells gas to distributors at about 7 cents less per gallon than it sells gas to dealers at its direct-serve stations.

a. Oil companies do not allow dealers (franchisees) to buy gas from distributors. Dealers must buy gas from the central oil company. Dealers often complain that this is unfair. The practice has been the subject of antitrust lawsuits. Oil company executives argue that this policy is important because it limits *free-riding* on the part of the distributors. Explain the executives' arguments in more detail.

b. Suppose the courts ruled that the oil companies must allow the dealers to buy gas from distributors. What effects do you think such a ruling would have on the operational policies of the oil companies?

c. Some direct-serve gasoline stations provide repair services, and others concentrate almost exclusively on self-service gasoline sales. Which type of station is more likely owned by the central oil company and which type is more likely to be franchised? Explain.

d. Typically the stations served (and owned) by distributors are located in rural areas, whereas the direct-serve stations are located in urban areas. Give two economic reasons to explain why you might expect such a pattern.

18–10. Advanced Interconnect Manufacturing Inc. (AIM) is an independent company. It is located in the Elmgrove plant at Kodak. It was formerly owned by Kodak, but was purchased by five managers (with the help of outside investors). AIM assembles wire harnesses for use in machines such as copiers and x-ray machines. The vice president of the company claims that the company is more efficient because "as an independent company, AIM doesn't have to share any of Kodak's corporate overhead." As he notes, "Kodak's CEO doesn't get paid by us."

a. Evaluate the vice president's explanation for the increased efficiency of AIM since the ownership was changed.

b. Give an alternative explanation for the increased efficiency.

18–11. Jimmy's Stereo Company manufactures stereo equipment. Its business strategy is to provide retail customers with high-quality equipment, along with good service and warranty protection. It currently distributes its products through licensed dealers who have exclusive territories. Discuss (1) why Jimmy's might offer its distributors exclusive territories, (2) the potential problems that this policy might create in terms of retail pricing, and (3) potential policies that Jimmy's might use to address this pricing problem.

18–12. BQT Manufacturing produces electric lamps. To produce these lamps, BQT must either make or acquire bases for the lamps. Currently, the company outsources the production of the bases for their lamps to the ACE Lamp Company. BQT maintains ownership of the machinery that is used to produce the bases. ACE uses BQT's machines at plants owned by ACE.

a. Why do you think BQT is subcontracting the production of the bases?

b. Why do you think BQT maintains ownership of the production equipment?

c. What problems might be caused by BQT's maintaining ownership of the production equipment?

d. What might BQT do to reduce the magnitude of these problems?

18–13. Most of the McDonald's restaurants in the Rochester area are owned by one individual. Discuss why this ownership pattern makes economic sense.

18–14. You are at a cocktail party, where you meet the CEO of a pharmaceutical company who has been thinking recently about her overseas distributors who have exclusive sales territories. She can't quite figure out what is troubling her, but she is dissatisfied with these distributors. You describe the "double markup" problem. The CEO's eyes light up. "You are exactly right," she says. "The distributors are setting prices for our product that are too high." A year passes. You meet the CEO at another party. She heads straight for you and says,

> *You were wrong. There was no double markup problem. After our talk a year ago, I terminated the contracts with all our overseas distributors. I sent our own people overseas to set up in-house distributors. To motivate the region managers I tied a big part of their compensation to the profitability of their regions. I was sure I would see a big change, but overseas prices are just about the same as they were when we used exclusive distributors. I guess prices weren't that bad with the distributors.*

Do you think the CEO's conclusions are correct? Why or why not?

18–15. The Boswell Medical Center is the only hospital in a rural community. It requires significant janitorial services to clean its buildings and equipment. It also requires a relatively large lab for conducting tests of various types (for example, MRIs, blood tests, and ultrasound tests). Do you think that Boswell is more likely to outsource its janitorial services or lab work? Explain.

18–16. The Hanson Clinic is a well-regarded medical center located in a semirural area in the Midwest. One of its specialty areas is treating rare forms of cancer. To support this activity Hanson wants to construct a new lab. The lab will require very specialized equipment, a specially designed building, and a skilled staff. The estimated cost of the equipment and building is $50 million.

The clinic is considering three possible organizational arrangements. The first is vertical integration. The second is outsourcing (where another company constructs the building, purchases the equipment, and provides contractual services to the clinic). The third is for the clinic to purchase the equipment and building, and lease them to an independent operator (who would provide contractual services to the clinic).

Discuss the pluses and minuses of each of the three alternative structures. What factors do you think are most important in making this choice?

18–17. Koji Incorporated produces high-end cameras. Its typical camera comes with an array of options. The company has a good brand name.
   a. Koji distributes its cameras through independent dealers who are given exclusive distribution rights for their respective market areas. Discuss why it might make economic sense for Koji to grant its distributors exclusive territories.
   b. Since Koji adopted this distribution system, it has experienced a double markup problem. What is a double markup problem?
   c. Discuss how Koji might use a two-part pricing scheme to reduce the double markup problem. (Be sure to specify what the two-part pricing scheme would entail.)
   d. Describe one other method that Koji might use to address the double markup problem.

Chapter 19
Leadership: Motivating Change within Organizations

In 1982, David Kearns was appointed CEO of Xerox Corporation, the leading producer of copy machines in the world.[1] At that time, the company faced serious problems. Between 1976 and 1982, Xerox's share of installations of new copiers in the United States dropped from about 80 percent to 13 percent. Japanese

[1] Details of this example are from D. Kearns and D. Nadler (1992), *Prophets in the Dark* (Harper Business Press: New York).

companies—Canon, Minolta, Ricoh, and Sharp—had become major players in this market. These companies were selling copiers at prices that at times were lower than Xerox's costs for producing competing machines.

A major reason for Xerox's decline in market share was poor product quality. As Kearns put it,

> *Our customer cancellations were rapidly on the rise, our response to the problem was to try to outrun them by pushing hard to get enough new orders to offset the customers we had lost. Customers were fed up with our copiers breaking down and our service response.*

Kearns reasoned that if something was not done, "Xerox was destined to have a fire sale and close down by 1990. [The] only hope for survival was to urgently commit the company to vastly improving the quality of its products and services."

According to Kearns, most Xerox employees understood neither the extraordinary gravity of the problem nor the fundamental importance of improving product quality. He realized that even as CEO, he could not implement his vision of increasing product quality simply by ordering thousands of employees to focus more on quality. First, employees did not necessarily possess all the skills required to produce quality products. Second, unless employees were convinced that it was in their individual interests to focus more on quality, it would be difficult to motivate them to alter their behavior. Certainly, Kearns did not have the time to monitor each employee to see if his vision was being implemented. Third, Kearns faced a difficult balancing act; he feared that painting too dismal a picture would induce some key people to leave the company.

In response to these concerns, Kearns initiated a strategy to shift corporate direction. He realized that many Xerox employees would oppose the kind of dramatic change he envisioned. They might fear for their jobs, worry about changes in job assignments, or be concerned about having to relocate. Kearns began by convincing a select group of key executives that additional focus on quality was essential. These individuals helped refine this quality vision and convince other employees of the potential benefits of this change in focus. Employees throughout the company received substantial training in quality techniques. The importance of quality was emphasized at every opportunity—media releases, management speeches, signs on bulletin boards, and so forth. In addition, they stressed the potential crisis posed by the Japanese successes.

Yet after much training and promotion, the desired change in culture simply was not occurring. It was then that Kearns realized that to affect employee behavior, senior management had to do more than just exhort, cajole, and plead—the performance-evaluation and incentive systems also had to change. As Kearns says,

> *Unless people get rewarded and punished for how they behave, no one will really believe that this is anything more than lip service. A widespread problem [with implementing change] that was singled out was that people said we were still promoting and rewarding employees who weren't true believers and users of the quality process. This was creating noise in the system and sending mixed signals. It had to stop.*

Kearns thereafter initiated changes in the criteria for promotions and compensation decisions, placing major emphasis on customer satisfaction and quality. Eventually, the culture at Xerox did change. In 1989, Xerox won the Malcolm Baldrige National Quality Award.

This example suggests that effective leadership involves a great deal more than just developing an appropriate vision for the company. It is critical to motivate people to implement that vision. Changes in a firm's organizational architecture—the assignment of decision rights, reward system, and performance-evaluation system—can play an important role in motivating material organizational change. Marketing the concept to other employees also is important.

In this chapter, we use the framework developed in this book to provide insights for more effective leadership. The analysis presents an important example of how this framework can be used to provide a structured discussion of this popular (though ill-understood) topic. The insights in this chapter are useful not only for people at the top of the organization but also for employees who have the opportunity to assume various leadership roles throughout the firm. Indeed, the analysis is helpful for all individuals who want to have their ideas implemented within any organization.

We begin by discussing the concept of leadership in more detail. Next, we discuss decision making within firms and present a framework for understanding attitudes toward change within organizations. We use this framework to analyze various strategies for motivating employees to endorse proposals for change. These strategies include changing the organizational architecture, analyzing the strategic design of the proposal, and marketing the proposal. In the final sections of the chapter, we provide an analysis of the sources of individual power within an organization and a brief discussion of the use of symbols—role modeling, formal creeds, stories, and legends—in leadership. In the appendix, we present a simple example of the strategic value of commitment and crisis.

Leadership

Webster's defines *leadership* as "leading others along a way, guiding." This definition suggests that there are at least two important characteristics of good leadership. First, the leader must help the organization choose the right path—vision, goal, or plan. Second, the leader must help motivate people to follow it. Much of the popular literature on leadership stresses these two characteristics. To quote John Gardner, "The two tasks at the heart of the popular notion of leadership are goal setting and motivating."[2] Since these tasks are performed by people throughout the organization, leadership is in no sense the exclusive domain of senior executives. Throughout the firm, many employees assume important leadership roles.

Vision Setting

By vision, we simply mean a course of action for the firm.[3] Sometimes leaders devise a corporate vision by themselves. According to Kearns, he was among the first people to envision Xerox as a quality-based organization. But senior executives normally do not have all the relevant specific knowledge and cannot be expected to conceive important visions entirely by themselves. In many cases, a vision emanates from a lower-level employee or even from a person outside the firm—for example, a consultant. Often, the information for formulating a vision has to be assembled by combining the knowledge of numerous individuals. Firms typically involve many employees in developing mission statements. One aspect of effective leadership involves structuring organizational architecture in a manner that motivates employees with the relevant specific knowledge to initiate value-enhancing proposals—to take part in vision setting. It is this view that has

---

[2]J. Gardner (1990), *On Leadership* (Free Press: New York), 11.

[3]The management literature differentiates among the terms *vision, strategies,* and *plans.* Visions represent goals and objectives, whereas strategies and plans relate to how to achieve them. For our purpose, this differentiation is unimportant. We are interested in any type of proposal that implies change for the organization. We use the term *vision* as a catchall for these proposals.

Vision Setting: Lessons from the Enterprise

In my experience, the best-run companies have a basic philosophy that the people in the company know and understand. Sometimes this philosophy is formalized in a mission statement. Here is the best mission statement I have ever heard:

> These are the voyages of the Starship Enterprise. Her 5-year mission: To explore strange new worlds, to seek out new life and new civilizations, to boldly go where no man has gone before.

Crew members of the Starship *Enterprise* know exactly what they are supposed to do. Suppose you are the dumbest person on the ship. And suppose you encountered a strange new world. What should you do? Explore it, perhaps. There is even an emotion telling you how you should go about exploring it. Boldly.

What if your company encounters a strange new opportunity? Without a basic philosophy, even a business's smartest employees have to improvise when they meet a new or challenging situation. We could do worse than rewriting the Star Trek mission statement for whatever venture we are on. Make the language exact, the goal specific, and even your worst employee will make you proud.

Source: D. Marinaccio (1994), *All I Really Need to Know I Learned from Watching Star Trek* (Crown Publishers: New York).

prompted much of the current literature on the role of managers in empowering employees to "unleash their untapped creativity."

Motivation

Although an appropriate vision is important, it cannot increase a firm's value unless it is implemented. Thus, the task of motivation is at least as important as the task of goal setting. It is often better to implement a pretty good plan than to identify yet fail to implement the perfect plan. Literature on leadership often emphasizes motivation skills[4]:

- *Leadership is the* process of persuasion *or example by which an individual induces a group to pursue objectives held by the leader or his or her followers.*

- *I define leadership as leaders* inducing *followers to act for certain goals that represent the values and the motivations—the wants and needs, the aspirations and expectations—of both leaders and followers.*

- *The one who knows the right thing but cannot achieve it fails because he is ineffectual. The great leader* needs . . . the capacity to achieve.

Some people argue that leaders motivate people to follow visions through personal charisma, style, and inspiration. Under this view, the bonds between leader and follower are more emotional than rational. Certainly, strong emotional ties sometimes motivate individuals to follow a leader's call to action. Leaders often cited as charismatic include Mahatma Gandhi, John F. Kennedy, and Martin Luther King, Jr. Charisma undoubtedly explains much of the behavior of individuals in particular settings (for example, in certain religious cults). Business managers might glean some valuable lessons from studying the styles of inspirational leaders, but for most people, charisma is difficult to learn.

Yet the economic framework suggests that other attributes of effective leadership can be learned. Economics stresses that people make choices that are in their own

---

[4]Emphases in the following quotes are ours. The quotes are taken, respectively, from Gardner (1990), 1; J. Burns (1978), *Leadership* (Harper & Row: New York), 19; and R. Nixon (1982), *Leaders* (Warner Books: New York), 5.

self-interest. They are more concerned about their own welfare (which can include concerns about family, community, and so on) than they are about the welfare of the owners of the company. Under this view, the problem of motivating employees to follow a proposed direction or course of action is just the standard incentive problem. Below, we discuss techniques that managers can use to address this problem.

Decision Making within Firms

Incentive Problems and Organizational Politics

Academic discussions often treat decision making as a purely intellectual exercise: Relevant alternatives are identified, analysis is conducted, and the best alternative is chosen. (Consider the standard treatment of capital budgeting in finance courses.) Implementation problems often are ignored. In this context, good leadership is equivalent to *initiating* good proposals and conducting careful analysis. Within most firms, the decision process is much more complicated than this simple characterization reflects. Although developing good proposals and conducting careful analysis are important, they are far from sufficient for effective leadership. Just because a proposal would enhance the value of the firm is no guarantee that it will be either *ratified* or *implemented*.[5] Due to incentive problems, decision making within firms often resembles decision making in *political settings* such as government. There are self-interested people involved in group decision making.[6] To quote Jeffrey Pfeffer,

> Organizations, particularly large ones, are like governments in that they are fundamentally political entities. To understand them, one needs to understand organizational politics, just as to understand governments, one needs to understand government politics.[7]

Understanding Attitudes toward Change

To provide deeper insights into the decision-making process within firms, consider the problem facing Christian Seidler, a general manager at the BCT Corporation. Like David Kearns at Xerox, Chris is convinced that his division must adopt a quality-improvement program to remain competitive. He needs support from Claudia Kobatzki, the CEO, for ratification of the program and support from employees in his division for implementation. Chris does not think that the quality program will be a success unless he has the full support of his department managers. He also depends on these managers for advice, because they have important specific knowledge about whether his proposal is a

---

[5]Recall that four important steps in the decision-making process are initiation, ratification, implementation, and monitoring (see Chapter 12).

[6]As we have discussed in previous chapters, if there were no transaction costs, individuals in the group would agree unanimously on a course of action to maximize value. By maximizing the size of the pie, all of the individuals are made better off: Every individual's piece of the pie can be enlarged by the appropriate side payments. Transaction costs limit the likelihood of this outcome in large organizations. For example, suppose that laying off a group of workers will create value and that the labor union has the power to veto the layoff. With no transaction costs, the owners and labor will agree on the layoff. The owners share the increase in value by making appropriate severance payments to the workers. Both parties are better off. Bargaining costs often prevent this result from occurring (asymmetric information is a particular problem). In this case, the parties do not have a shared common interest in maximizing value. Similar to other political settings, conflicts arise as all parties try to increase their own share of the pie.

[7]J. Pfeffer (1992), *Managing with Power* (Harvard Business School: Boston), 8.

Figure 19.1 Framework for Understanding Attitudes toward Change

In this example, Lynn Vestergaard is a department manager at the BCT Corporation. Lynn is risk-averse. Her utility increases with her expected payoffs from the company and falls with the standard deviation of these payoffs. This figure displays her indifference curve associated with the *status quo* (assuming the company does not change its direction). Lynn will support proposals for change in the *favor proposal region* of the figure and be against proposals in the *oppose proposal* region.

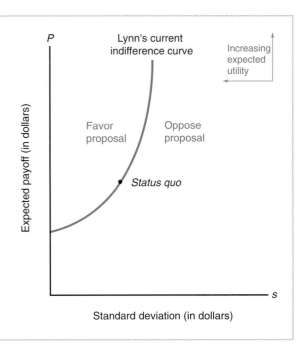

good idea. If the managers were to oppose his proposal strongly, Chris would consider withdrawing it. We focus on Lynn Vestergaard, a department manager who reports to Chris.

Consider the proposal from Lynn's perspective. She is risk-averse and interested in maximizing her own utility, which increases with the expected payoffs that she receives from BCT, P_L, and falls with the standard deviation of these payoffs, s_L (see Chapter 2):

$$U_L = f(\overset{+}{P}_L, \bar{s}_L) \qquad (19.1)$$

Expected payoffs include both monetary and nonmonetary compensation from the company. For instance, Lynn gains utility from her salary, supervising a large number of employees, administering a large budget, and working in California. She will not support Chris's proposal simply because it increases the firm's value. It must increase her personal utility.

Figure 19.1 displays Lynn's expected payoff and standard deviation under the *status quo* (assuming the company does not adopt the proposed program). Also displayed is the indifference curve, which contains all combinations of expected payoffs and

Henry Kissinger on Decision Making

Former Secretary of State Henry Kissinger offers the following observation about decision making:

> Before I served as a consultant to Kennedy, I had believed, like most academics, that the process of decision-making was largely intellectual and [that] all one had to do was to walk into the President's office and convince him of the correctness of one's view. This perspective I soon realized is as dangerously immature as it is widely held.

Source: H. Kissinger (1979), *The White House Years* (Little, Brown: Boston), 39.

Mismanaging Organizational Politics at Xerox

Good analysis is not enough to motivate the implementation of new ideas in an organization. Often, a concerted effort to gain the support of other employees is necessary. Xerox's Palo Alto Research Center (PARC) invented the first personal computer, the first graphics-oriented monitor, one of the first handheld computer mouses, the first word processing program for nonexpert users, the first local area communications network, the first object-oriented programming language, and the first laser printer. Xerox failed to capitalize commercially on this inventive technology. One reason was that PARC was physically removed from the rest of Xerox and apparently did not understand the importance of motivating other units in the firm (such as marketing) to support its technological visions. Employees at PARC were characterized as being arrogant and suffering from a "we/they attitude toward the rest of Xerox." In the words of Jeffrey Pfeffer,

> By not appreciating the interdependence involved in a new product launch and the skills required to manage that interdependence, PARC researchers lost out on their ambition to change the world of computing, and Xerox missed some important economic opportunities.

Source: J. Pfeffer (1992), *Managing with Power* (Harvard Business School: Boston), 38–39.

standard deviations that provide Lynn with the same utility as the *status quo*. (Recall that northwest movements in the graph are utility-increasing.) For Lynn to favor Chris's proposal over the *status quo,* she must view the proposal as placing her in the region of the graph labeled "favor proposal."

Lynn will oppose the proposal if it reduces her utility. For instance, if she thinks that the proposal will increase the likelihood that she will be laid off, she is likely to be against the change. Now Lynn is unlikely to come right out and say that because she fears for her job; she does not like the proposal. She is more likely to question his underlying analysis—even if she thinks it is right. She might waste time developing spurious evidence to convince people that the proposed program is unworkable. She might try to block the program by failing to do her part during implementation. If many employees in the firm undertake similar actions, the proposal will fail.

Chris cannot observe Lynn's personal preferences. But he can analyze how the proposal is likely to affect her and make an educated guess of how she will react. One important factor to consider is the existing organizational architecture. What decision rights does she have currently and how will she be affected by the proposal? How is she rewarded? If Lynn is paid a bonus based on divisional sales and the proposal is likely to reduce those sales, it is reasonable for Chris to assume that Lynn will oppose the proposal.

Suppose that Chris forecasts that Lynn will oppose the proposal. He might gain her support by employing one of three general tactics. First, he could change organizational architecture so that it is in Lynn's interest to support the proposal. Second, he could change the proposal so that she is more likely to support it. Third, he might be able to market the proposal to Lynn by convincing her that actually it is in her self-interest to support the proposal. We discuss each of these general tactics below.

Changing Organizational Architecture

Chris can make two general changes in his division's architecture that would help him gain support for his proposal. First, he can identify individuals who are likely to support the proposal and give them increased decision rights, and he correspondingly can reduce the decision rights of individuals who are likely to oppose the proposal. Second, he can change the performance-evaluation and reward systems so that it is in the self-interest of

Figure 19.2   Changing the Architecture to Gain Support for a Proposal

In this example, Lynn Vestergaard will not support Chris Seidler's proposal, given her current compensation plan. The *status quo* provides her with higher utility. Chris changes the architecture so that the *status quo* is worse—if Lynn does not improve quality, she is likely to be fired. Now, when Chris introduces the proposal, Lynn will support it and will do her part during the implementation phase.

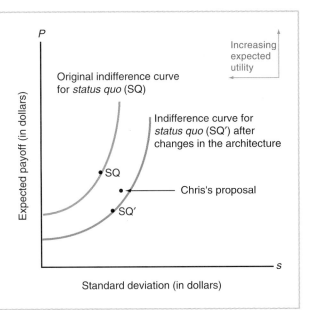

more employees to support the new program. Kearns implemented both types of changes in architecture at Xerox.

To illustrate the effect of changes in the performance-evaluation and reward systems, suppose that Lynn currently is paid a salary plus an additional bonus, based on sales by her department. Denote Lynn's expected payoff and standard deviation, given this compensation plan *without implementing* Chris's proposal, as the *status quo* (SQ). The indifference curve associated with SQ is depicted in Figure 19.2 (labeled "original indifference curve"). His proposal makes Lynn worse off relative to the *status quo*: The expected payoff is lower and the standard deviation is higher. Lynn will try to convince Chris that his proposal is a bad idea and is unlikely to exert great effort in implementing it, should it be adopted. Now suppose that before suggesting the proposal, Chris changes the performance-evaluation and reward systems. Lynn now will be evaluated on product quality. If the quality in her department is poor, she has an increased likelihood of job loss. This change in the reward system produces a new *status quo* (SQ'). Without adopting a quality program, chances are that Lynn's quality would suffer and she might be fired. This change in architecture places her on a lower indifference curve (labeled "after changes in architecture"). Now when Chris proposes his quality program, he receives Lynn's support. She will want to attend quality workshops, provide instruction to her employees in quality techniques, and participate in the program in other ways.[8] She wants to take actions to improve quality in her department because now, participation makes her better off.

Obtaining the approval of the CEO for the program and the support of department managers will not ensure that Chris's proposal will be implemented successfully. There are potential incentive problems with other employees within the division (for example, production workers). He can anticipate some of these problems by carefully analyzing these employees' incentives. For instance, will these employees fear for their jobs, face fewer promotion opportunities, or have less challenging task assignments? Through this analysis, he can identify the employees who are most likely to resist implementation.

[8]In this illustration, the change in the reward system affects Lynn's assessment of the *status quo*. Chris's changes in the reward system also might affect Lynn's expected payoffs and risk under the proposed change. The basic point continues to hold: Chris can influence Lynn's attitude about the proposal by making changes in the architecture.

Chris can make changes in the architecture to reduce the anticipated problems. He can make sure that certain groups of employees are monitored closely in the implementation phase (recall from Chapter 12 that monitoring is the fourth step in the decision-making process). He also might make additional changes in the performance-evaluation and reward systems. For example, he can reward employees—perhaps, through promotions—for successfully implementing the quality concept. Or he can promise employees that they will not lose their jobs due to quality improvements. This promise increases support for these programs (see Chapter 22).

David Kearns wanted to make dramatic changes in the culture at Xerox. To motivate employees to support these changes, he altered the firm's performance-evaluation and reward systems. But most employees *must exercise leadership within the existing architecture:* They do not have the authority to make changes in either the performance-evaluation or reward systems. Even CEOs often choose to work within the existing organizational architecture, since changing the architecture can be expensive. (Remember, frequent changes in the evaluation and reward systems can discourage employees from making long-run investments and developing relationships with teammates—see Chapter 11.) The following discussion suggests methods that managers can use to get their proposals implemented within the existing organizational architecture. These techniques also can be used in conjunction with changes in the architecture.

Proposal Design

Managers can analyze the incentives of key decision makers and design proposals that are likely to be supported. We discuss three issues relating to proposal design: flexibility, commitment, and distributional consequences.

Maintaining Flexibility

Holding the expected payoffs of a proposal constant, employees are more likely to support new proposals if they entail lower risk. One way to convince people that the risk of a proposal is low is to design the proposal so that it can be modified easily once it is under way. A manager might suggest starting with a limited pilot program, involving only one region or a single product. If this pilot is successful, the program can be expanded. If not, it can be discontinued at low cost. A small-scale test does not commit the firm to adopt the program throughout the company: It provides an option to do so. Experiments of this type commit only limited resources while providing more precise estimates of the costs and benefits of proposed actions. And this information is available both to senior executives who must approve an expanded program as well as to the employees in other areas of the firm where the program might be implemented subsequently.

Commitment

Maintaining flexibility has benefits, but it also can impose costs. If employees think that senior management is not committed to the change, they have less reason to take the change seriously. In addition, employees who are against the change have increased incentives to take actions to convince senior management that the change is a poor idea. David Kearns made it quite clear that he was committed to the quality program at Xerox and that employees should take the change seriously. The appendix presents a more detailed example of the strategic value of commitment.

Figure 19.3 Analyzing the Distributional Consequences of a Proposal

In this example, Chris Seidler's initial design of a proposal would be highly favored by Rob Lewis and slightly opposed by Lynn Vestergaard (both have the same initial indifference curve under the *status quo*). Chris can obtain both managers' support by redesigning the proposal. For instance, Chris might reassign some employees that would have reported to Rob under the original proposal to Lynn. Assuming that both Rob and Lynn gain utility from supervising larger departments, Lynn gains and Rob loses utility. Chris's objective is to make changes until both Lynn and Rob view the proposal as being better than the *status quo*.

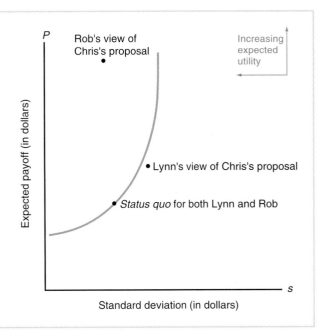

Distributional Consequences

Most proposals for change have distributional consequences—some employees gain and others lose. For instance, a plan to reduce the power of middle managers will harm middle mangers but benefit certain line employees. Managers can design proposals so that the distributional effects promote support among key decision makers. Returning to our example, Figure 19.3 considers the case of Lynn and another department manager, Robert Lewis. Both Rob and Lynn have the same utility function. They also view the *status quo* exactly the same (so they are on the same initial indifference curve). Chris's proposal greatly benefits Rob but harms Lynn slightly. Chris can obtain support from both Rob and Lynn by modifying the proposal so that Rob is less well off and Lynn is

---

Leverage and Commitment

Firms obtain financing through combinations of equity and debt. Common stock is the most frequently used source of equity capital for large firms. Dividend payments to holders of common stock are discretionary. The board of directors can reduce dividend payments without placing the firm in bankruptcy. Payments to debt holders must be made in a timely fashion to avoid bankruptcy. During the 1980s, many firms increased their amount of debt substantially through activities such as selling bonds and repurchasing common stock.

High leverage can serve as a commitment that management intends to make changes in the firm to increase cash flows to meet the higher debt payments (for example, through cutting costs), since failure to increase cash flows can result in bankruptcy. Managers have their "feet to the fire," since they do not want to lose their jobs. Managers in firms financed primarily by equity can be under less pressure to make changes to increase cash flows, since they have more flexibility to decrease cash payouts to security holders. There are many determinants of the optimal amount of debt in a firm's capital structure. This discussion suggests that one determinant can be the desire of senior managers to commit to employees and outside stakeholders that they will take actions to increase or maintain high cash flows.

Source: M. Jensen (1986), "Agency Costs of Free Cash Flow, Corporate Finance, and Takeovers," *American Economic Review* 76, 323–329.

slightly better off. For instance, some of the employees that would have reported to Rob under the initial proposal might be reassigned to report to Lynn. If Lynn values supervising a larger number of employees, she is more likely to support the proposal.

Marketing a Proposal

Employees' attitudes toward a proposed change depend on their assessment of the expected payoffs and risk under the new proposal, relative to the *status quo*. The sponsor of the proposal often will have information that can affect this assessment. The sponsor might be able to convince the employee to support the proposal by conveying this information credibly to the employee.

Careful Analysis and Groundwork

Chris can anticipate initial opposition to his quality proposal because people are risk-averse. Individuals who are confronted with a new idea are likely to be unsure of the personal consequences of the action relative to the *status quo*—thus, they are likely to oppose it. Chris correspondingly should take time to explain his analysis to key employees and to convince them that his analysis is correct. He might meet with these employees to discuss the proposal and answer questions. He might give speeches on the topic, write an article for the company paper, and so on. By carefully communicating the reasons he supports the plan, uncertainty is reduced. Correspondingly, there is increased support for the proposal: More people view the proposal as being in the "favor proposal" region of Figure 19.1.

As a general rule, it is unwise to introduce important proposals at meetings and then request on-the-spot decisions. Without laying the appropriate groundwork, such proposals are likely to be tabled for further study or simply rejected. Since people are risk-averse, they tend to favor the *status quo* until they are convinced otherwise.

Relying on Reputation

People have reasons to listen to a person with an established reputation for offering sound proposals. First, past success is an indicator of analytical and organizational skills

---

Reputation and Influence

Decision makers often rely on the advice of people with established reputations. This tendency is emphasized by H. Mintzberg:

> I found that chief executives faced complex choices. They had to consider the impact of each decision on other decisions and on the organization's strategy. They had to ensure that the decision would be acceptable to those who influence the organization as well as ensuring that resources would not be overextended. They had to understand the various costs and benefits as well as the feasibility of the proposal. They also had to consider questions of timing. All this was necessary for the simple approval of someone else's proposal. At the same time, however, delay could cost time, while quick approval could be ill considered and quick rejection might discourage the subordinate who had spent months developing a pet project. One common solution to approving projects is to pick the man instead of the proposal. That is, the manager authorizes those projects presented to him by people whose judgment he trusts.

Source: H. Mintzberg (1975), "The Manager's Job: Folklore and Fact,"
Harvard Business Review (July–August), 49–61.

as well as the likelihood of future success. Second, a successful person has strong incentives to conduct a careful analysis to avoid damaging that established reputation. If other employees are confident that a manager usually makes good decisions, they will attach less risk to that manager's proposals and hence are more likely to support them. A manager with an established reputation can garner support for a proposal by asserting forcefully that it is beneficial. It is important for managers not to misuse their reputations by arguing passionately for marginal proposals. A manager's reputation is diminished whenever proposals turn out to be unsuccessful.

A sponsor also can increase support for a proposal by obtaining the endorsement of other managers with good reputations. Therefore, it is often useful to conduct detailed discussions with these managers. If they agree with the analysis, it is more likely that it is correct. Moreover, their endorsements will garner additional support and forestall opposition throughout the organization.

Emphasizing a Crisis

A complementary strategy to overcome the normal preference for the *status quo* is to argue that the current situation is worse than people think. The popular literature frequently argues that employees are most likely to favor change when an organization faces a *crisis*: If change doesn't occur, the organization is going to fail. Managers can promote a willingness to change if they can convince employees that the firm does face a crisis. Kearns gained support for his program at Xerox by repeatedly highlighting the threat from Japanese competition. Of course, this strategy works best if in fact the firm faces an actual crisis. Individuals understand the incentives that proponents of proposals have to state that the organization faces a crisis and correspondingly are unlikely to accept this argument unless it is credible. In the case of Xerox, it was easy to document the lost business. Also, it was easy to point to other industries, such as steel and automobiles, which were having similar experiences. The effect of this action is to reduce employee assessments of the utility associated with the *status quo*. This shift enlarges the support region, similar to the analysis in Figure 19.2. Thus, Chris can gain Lynn's support if he provides her with new information that causes her to be less optimistic about the *status quo*. The appendix illustrates how an employee's attitude toward change can depend on whether the firm faces a crisis.

Organizational Power

Economics suggests that an employee's attitude toward change will depend on the personal effects of the proposal. These effects are likely to depend on the identity of the sponsor. Some proposal sponsors have more personal *power* than others to affect the payoffs received by other employees. To be effective, it is important for managers to understand the sources of this power and how to acquire it.

Sources of Power[9]

What is the source of power within organizations? There are no laws that require people to obey or support the wishes of others within the firm. Corporate power does not come from the ability to force others to follow commands. Ultimately, it comes from other people who *voluntarily agree* to comply with a leader's wishes or proposals. For this

---

[9]This section draws on Pfeffer (1992).

Ford Motor Company and the $5 Day

In 1914, Ford Motor Company paid a wage rate of $2.20 per day to factory workers. This rate was very close to the prevailing market rate in the Detroit area. Annual turnover at Ford was over 300 percent, as employees would take jobs at different companies for slightly higher wages. Management had little power over its employees. If a supervisor was too demanding or difficult, employees would simply quit and go to work for a different firm. To combat this problem, Henry Ford increased the daily wage to $5 per day. This wage rate gave Ford tremendous power over his employees since they did not want to lose their jobs and work for someone else at $2.20 per day. To quote Henry Ford,

> I have a thousand men who if I say "Be at the northeast corner of the building at 4 AM" will be there at 4 AM. That is what we want: Obedience.

Sources: D. Halberstam (1986), *The Reckoning* (Avon Books: New York); and
S. Meyer (1981), *The Five Dollar Day: Labor, Management, and Social Control in the Ford Motor Company, 1908–1921* (State University of New York Press: Albany, NY).

voluntary action to occur, it must be in the interests of these people to cooperate with the leader. This section discusses potential sources of power and influence.

Formal Authority Some power comes from the formal position within the organization. If a manager has the right to fire, promote, and compensate an employee, the employee obviously has an economic incentive to comply with the manager's wishes.[10] In our example, Chris can count on some support from his employees even if the employees think that the proposal will harm them because not supporting it might harm them even more—Chris might fire them. For instance, these employees are likely to speak in favor of the proposal at public meetings. In addition, his formal authority gives Chris the right to make certain decisions without consulting others. But power attached to a formal position is not without limits. There is the usual incentive problem that employees might ignore their manager's wishes. Also, employees can take actions to get the manager replaced (a "palace revolt"). Disgruntled employees might form a coalition to complain to the CEO that Chris is incompetent. Finally, some companies conduct 360-degree performance reviews where employees provide formal input into the performance evaluations of the managers.

Control of Budgets and Resources People are granted rights to control resources within organizations. Some individuals have budget authority, and others decide on the allocation of office space or the priority for using copy machines. Control over these resources is a source of power. Individuals are reluctant to challenge a person who controls an important resource because they fear that it will affect their access to the resource. For example, department managers might support Chris because he controls the budget from which they receive funds.

This discussion suggests that individuals can increase their organizational power by gaining control over key resources. This concept can be important in deciding whether to apply for a particular job or task within the firm: Jobs and tasks are more attractive if they contain decision rights over resources others value. Also, a person sometimes can create power by developing a service or product that becomes important to other people within the organization. For example, the data processing manager in a company might

---

[10]Assuming the employee cannot shift to a comparable position costlessly at another firm.

Power and Resource Control—Voting on Antitakeover Amendments

Economic theory suggests that the control of important resources provides a person with power. Other people are afraid not to support the person's proposals because they fear that they will lose access to the important resource.

An illustration of the importance of this argument is provided by studies of corporate voting on antitakeover amendments. These amendments make it more difficult for outsiders to take control of a company through a corporate takeover. The existing evidence suggests that some of these amendments reduce the wealth of shareholders but benefit incumbent managers who become more secure in their jobs. The decision on whether to adopt these management-sponsored amendments is held by the shareholders, who would appear to have the incentives to vote against the amendments. Management, however, has power over certain institutional investors, such as banks and insurance companies, because they derive business from the firm that is under management control: If they don't vote in favor of management-sponsored amendments, they risk losing important business. Empirical evidence indicates that these types of institutional investors are more likely to support management-sponsored antitakeover amendments than other, more independent, investors. The evidence also suggests that management groups who do not have enough power to get amendments passed tend not to propose amendments because they do not want to bear the reputation costs of proposing an amendment that fails.

Source: J. Brickley, R. Lease, and C. Smith (1994), "Corporate Voting: Evidence from Charter Amendment Proposals," *Journal of Corporate Finance* 1, 5–31.

increase personal influence and power by offering a repair service for computers within the organization. This action will create greater power if the firm prohibits the use of external vendors, requiring employees to use this internal service for computer repair.

Throughout this book, we have argued that it is important to link decision rights and specific knowledge. Our current discussion suggests a secondary factor that executives might consider in assigning decision rights over key resources: It can be important to grant power to managers who have the most potential to increase firm value.[11] For example, suppose that an executive can assign decision rights over corporate computing to one of two divisional managers, Sanjai Kumar or Maria Lopez. Both managers have the specific knowledge to manage the computer resources effectively. Sanjai, however, has a greater potential to affect the firm's value through his proposals than Maria (Sanjai manages a division with greater opportunities to create value). Further, Sanjai's proposals require the support and cooperation of employees in other divisions of the firm. In this case, the executive will want to assign the decision rights over computing to Sanjai, since they will give him control over additional resources that he can use to persuade other employees to support his proposals.

Control of Information   A particularly important resource in most organizations is information. The information held by any particular employee depends on things like the employee's position, office location, social network, and special skills. Not all employees have equal access to information. Since most employees require various types of information to be effective in their jobs, people with information have power—they can trade information for support. Some employees at BCT might support Chris because they depend on him to keep them informed about what is going on in the company. Individuals can attempt to increase their access to information (and power) by lobbying for centrally located office space (for example, at the corporate headquarters), developing

---

[11]This point relates to Hart's argument that the allocation of power and control of resources can affect investment decisions and thus value. O. Hart (1995), *Firms, Contracts, and Financial Structure* (Oxford Press: Oxford, UK).

The Power of Information: Evidence from a French Tobacco Factory

An interesting example of the power of information comes from a French cigarette plant in the 1960s. The equipment in this plant was highly automated and subject to mechanical failures. The manuals that explained how to repair this equipment had been destroyed in a fire, and the only people with the knowledge to fix the machines were the maintenance engineers at the factory. This monopolistic access to important information gave the engineers enormous power. Without them, the plant could not run, and it was impossible to replace them. Indeed, the engineers had sufficient power to have a managing director of the company removed from his job. When new engineers were trained in the plant, they were instructed verbally and asked to destroy any notes once they mastered the material. These actions helped the engineers to maintain their power over time.

Source: M. Crozier (1964), *The Bureaucratic Phenomenon* (University of Chicago Press: Chicago).

a social network within the organization, applying for jobs that are "in the information loop," or volunteering for key committee assignments.

Viewing the firm as the focal point for a set of contracts (see Chapter 10) provides a useful way to think about the control of information in a firm. Under this view, the firm is characterized as a network of contracts between the firm and other parties such as suppliers, customers, and employees. Many of these contracts are informal, and important information is held by people at the various contracting nodes. Controlling access to this information can vest a person with substantial power. It would be quite difficult for a firm to fire an employee who has been the primary contact with a key customer for 20 years. The employee possesses specific information on issues from company promises to customer requirements, and turnover in this position would be costly for the firm.[12]

Friends and Allies   Having close personal ties with decision makers increases the likelihood that they will act on your behalf. Managers sometimes hire or promote their friends into key positions over more qualified candidates. One reason for such actions is that the managers expect that their friends will provide support. Some employees make a point of doing favors for other individuals within the firm (for example, providing assistance on difficult projects or filling in for other people when they are on vacation) to increase the likelihood that these individuals will support them in the future. Chris is more likely to obtain support for his proposal if he has developed allies within the company.[13]

Tying the Proposal to Another Initiative

Sometimes it is possible to free-ride on the power of other people in the firm to gain support for a proposal. Perhaps, in our example, BCT's CEO has stressed the importance of product quality to the media and to customers through a program entitled "Quality 2000." Chris might claim that his proposal is an integral part of the CEO's vision for the company and fits nicely within the Quality 2000 program. Casting up the proposal in

[12]Andre Shleifer and Robert Vishny argue that managers sometimes choose investment projects that give them an informational advantage and thus make it more costly for shareholders to replace them. A. Shleifer and R. Vishny (1989), "Management Entrenchment: The Case of Manager-Specific Investment," *Journal of Financial Economics* 25, 123–139.

[13]For an economic analysis of gift giving and exchange, see G. Akerlof (1982), "Labor Contracts as Partial Gift Exchange," *Quarterly Journal of Economics* 97, 543–569; and J. Rotemberg (1994), "Human Relations in the Workplace," *Journal of Political Economy* 102, 684–718.

Logrolling in Government and Business

Many of the classic examples of logrolling come from government. For example, one stylized example involves big business, unions, and farmers, where a winning coalition consists of any of the two groups. Farmers have an advantage in this setting because their demands are more likely to be consistent with the demands of unions and big business than are the demands of big business and unions likely to be consistent with each other. Indeed, farmers often want things that are relatively unimportant to the other two groups. Farmers, in turn, often don't care much about the demands of the other groups. This mutual indifference makes farmers good partners in a coalition. In contrast, big business and labor unions are likely to make a poor coalition. This helps explain why farmers have been unusually successful in getting favorable regulation established by the government.

Although many of the examples of logrolling come from government, it is also prevalent in most types of organizations. For example, a marketing executive and a manufacturing manager might form a logroll to provide mutual support for each other's funding requests. In contrast, two manufacturing executives who are interested in mutually exclusive projects would not enter into a coalition. To quote Professor James March,

> Logrolls are found not only in the United States Congress, but also in business firms, military organizations, and universities.

Source: J. March (1994), *A Primer on Decision Making* (Free Press: New York), 157–159.

this manner makes it less likely that other employees will raise objections because they will hesitate to argue against an important initiative sponsored by the CEO.

Coalitions and Logrolling[14]

A manager sometimes can increase power through *logrolling*. A logroll consists of a coalition of individuals who are largely indifferent to one another's proposals but agree to support the various requests so that each can get what he or she wants. A classic example is the coalition that forms each year in the United States Congress to pass the Rivers and Harbors Act. This act contains many local projects that individually would receive support from only a few legislators. Yet this act regularly passes by a comfortable majority because certain legislators band together to provide mutual support for one another's proposals. In our example, Chris might form a logroll with other general managers in the company to support his proposal. He can agree to support proposals by these managers to expand their divisions if they back his quality proposal. In business firms (as in many other settings), these types of agreements virtually always take the form of implicit promises or understandings rather than formal contracts.

Coalition Obstacles   In trying to form a logroll, Chris should anticipate at least two potential problems. First is the issue of credible promises. Major decisions in firms do not occur simultaneously. He might need immediate support from other managers, whereas proposals from these managers might not be considered until later. Other managers might be reluctant to support Chris because they fear that he will not follow through on his part of the bargain. Second, identifying potential candidates for the logroll is not always easy. There is likely to be asymmetric information about how the proposal affects other people's welfare. Chris does not know for certain who is indifferent to his proposal. Individuals who are truly indifferent might claim that they would be

[14]This section draws on W. Riker (1962), *The Theory of Political Coalitions* (Yale University Press: New Haven, CT).

Logrolling at General Motors

J. L. Pratt, who was chairman of General Motors' Appropriations Committee, noted that there was no corporate headquarters coordinating the company's various divisions before Alfred Sloan became CEO. The Executive Committee was composed of division managers. "When one of them had a project, why he would get the vote of his fellow members; if they would vote for his project, he would vote for theirs. It was a sort of horse trading."

Source: A. Chandler (1962), *Strategy and Structure* (MIT Press: Cambridge, MA), 127.

---

harmed by the proposal and are unwilling to support him unless he makes many concessions to their wishes. As discussed in Chapter 10, this type of strategic misrepresentation can result in bargaining failures—in this case, the logroll might fail to materialize. Despite these problems, however, effective coalitions often are formed. Indeed, this type of deal making, or "horse trading," is common within organizations.

Proposal Detail and Logrolling   As we discussed, Chris is concerned not only about getting his proposal adopted, he also is concerned about incentive problems that could occur after the program is under way. He can reduce these incentive problems by being quite specific about what is expected of each key employee (so he leaves little discretionary decision authority). This strategy, however, entails two potentially significant costs: First, it limits the ability of employees to act on their specific knowledge in the implementation phase. In this sense, Chris faces a basic trade-off in project design that we have emphasized throughout this book—the trade-off between the effective use of specific information and incentive problems. Second, being overly specific in the ratification phase can make it more difficult for Chris to assemble an effective coalition. Logrolling often requires that terms of the proposal be somewhat vague to limit potential conflicts. Specific proposals provide employees with greater opportunities to argue about details.[15]

Is Organizational Power Bad?

We have argued that leaders often use personal power and political skills to motivate change within organizations. Yet words like *power* and *politics* frequently connote negative images to many people. It is easy to conjure up visions of Machiavelli offering insidious advice to the prince on how to increase his power. Similarly, one easily can envision managers becoming completely absorbed in office politics.

Obviously, attempts to gain power involve costs. For instance, having key employees spend time on logrolling can be expensive. In Chapter 12, we discussed how these influence costs can affect the appropriate architecture of the organization. Firms that survive in the marketplace are likely to be those which effectively limit unproductive uses of employee time. It also is important to recognize that power and political skills can provide important benefits. Organizations involve people working together. Without political skills and power, leaders might fail to implement value-increasing plans and the organization would suffer immensely.

In summary, power and political skills are, in and of themselves, neither good nor bad. They are important attributes that can be used either for productive or unproduc-

---

[15]J. March (1994), *A Primer on Decision Making* (Free Press: New York), 170–171.

Political Skills and Organizational Productivity

The development and exercise of power in organizations is about getting things accomplished. The very nature of organizations—interdependent, complex systems with many actors and many points of view—means that taking action is often problematic. Failures in implementations are almost invariably failures to build successful coalitions. Although networks of allies can obviously be misused, they are nevertheless essential in order to get things done.

Source: J. Pfeffer (1992), *Managing with Power* (Harvard Business School: Boston), 108.

---

tive purposes. Managers would be naive to think that they could be effective without such attributes.

The Use of Symbols

Our analysis thus far in this chapter has focused on the formal organizational architecture and strategies for garnering support for proposals. The popular literature often stresses that effective leadership requires the clever use of symbols such as role modeling, formal creeds, stories, and legends. For example, an executive interested in increasing customer service might take the time to talk to customers directly—ensuring that these actions are visible to other employees through media releases and videotapes. The executive might retell stories about employees who have gone out of their way to serve customers. The company also might adopt formal creeds and statements to emphasize the manager's basic vision for the company.

We view such symbols as an aspect of corporate culture that performs a potentially important communication function; the symbols inform employees about what is valued in the company (see Chapters 11 and 21). But again, symbols are unlikely to be effective in motivating employees to take particular actions unless reinforced by the firm's performance-evaluation and reward systems. David Kearns came to realize this and ultimately had to change the reward system at Xerox before he could implement his quality program successfully.

The Use of Symbols at Nordstrom's

Nordstrom's is a department store chain that is famous for stressing customer service and satisfaction. The vision of the Nordstrom family (who manage the firm) is to offer the customer the best in service, selection, quality, and value.

The importance of customer service is stressed to employees by the frequent telling of stories about sales clerks who performed such heroics as changing a customer's flat tire in a store parking lot, paying a customer's parking ticket, and lending money to a customer who was short on cash to make a purchase. One particularly interesting story is the one about the sales clerk who refunded money to a customer irate about some newly purchased tires. The clerk cheerfully refunded the money even though the customer did not have a receipt. The fascinating part of the story is that Nordstrom's does not sell tires!

Nordstrom's does not rely on these types of stories alone to motivate employees to provide customer service. It has an extensive incentive system that stresses sales and customer service.

Source: H. Weston (1991), *Nordstrom: Dissension in the Ranks,* Harvard Business School Case, N9-191-002.

CASE STUDY: *Global Insurance*

Global Insurance is a disability insurance company. Traditionally, it has organized its corporate headquarters around functional specialties. After an application for an insurance policy arrives at headquarters from a field agent, it is processed through a series of functional departments. One department checks to see if the application is filled out correctly, another department checks the medical history of the applicant, and so on. Among the final steps is the underwriting decision, where the company agrees to accept the policy. This task is handled by trained underwriters.

One of the more important departments at Global is human resources. The human resources department administers the personnel system (for instance, screening job applicants, reviewing promotion decisions, having key decision rights on salary levels and job classifications, and providing training throughout the organization). Currently, the system includes nearly 2,000 discrete job titles. The director of human resources is viewed by most employees as a key person in the organization.

A major problem at Global is that it takes nearly a month to process an insurance application. Applications can sit for days in in-boxes, as they move from department to department. Global's CEO has decided that the company must reorganize to remain competitive. He has a vision to do away with most of the functional departments. Insurance applications would be handled by *caseworkers* responsible for all the steps from initial inspection of the application through underwriting. These caseworkers would be supported by a computer system that would allow access to medical record databases and other information necessary for processing an application. The management information system manager would be charged with developing the information system. Caseworkers would receive training in underwriting from the existing underwriters in the firm. Entry-level caseworkers would be required to have at least a 2-year degree from a community college. The number of job titles would be reduced significantly. Most of the people would have titles like *associate* or *partner*. Training, promotion, and hiring rights, currently held by human resources, would be decentralized to senior case managers (partners). The human resources department would play an important role in transitioning to the new system (dismantling existing training programs and turning them over to case managers, reducing the size of its staff, and so on). Through similar programs, other insurance companies have been able to reduce their application processing times dramatically. They also have reduced their workforces significantly.

Discussion Questions

1. Which employees in the organization do you think will oppose the new proposal? Who will support it?
2. What problems can the opponents cause in implementing the plan?
3. What actions should the CEO take to increase the likelihood that his plan will be implemented successfully?

Summary

This chapter uses the framework developed in Part 3 of this book to provide insights into more effective *leadership*. The analysis presents an important example of how this framework can be used to provide a structured discussion of this popular, but not necessarily well-understood, topic.

The leadership literature stresses two important tasks that all leaders must perform—setting goals and motivating employees. To accomplish these tasks, management must design decision-right, performance-evaluation, and reward systems that effectively link relevant specific knowledge with decision-making authority and provide appropriate incentives for decision makers to act on their information. In this sense, much of this book has focused on key components of leadership.

Academic discussions often treat the process of decision ratification as a purely intellectual exercise. In most firms, however, the decision process involves significant incentive problems. As a result, decision making in firms often resembles decision making within political settings.

Effective leadership is facilitated by careful consideration of other employees' perspectives on proposals for change. It is important to recognize that people typically are risk-averse and interested in their own well-being. An important factor to consider is the existing organizational architecture. How will a proposed change affect specific employees in terms of their decision rights and rewards from the organization?

Managers can make two general types of changes in architecture that can assist in gaining support for their proposals. First, they can identify individuals who are potential supporters of their proposals and give them increased decision rights. Second, they can change the performance-evaluation and reward systems so that it is in the self-interest of more employees to support their suggestions.

Developing proposals that can be discontinued at low cost can increase support. Flexibility, however, has costs as well as benefits. Sometimes it is better for managers to demonstrate a greater commitment to a change so that employees take the change more seriously. Managers can analyze the incentives of key decision makers and design proposals that are more likely to be supported.

The sponsor often will have information that can affect other employees' assessments of a proposal. The sponsor might be able to convince other employees of the merits of the proposal through careful analysis and groundwork, relying on a reputation for good decision making, and/or emphasizing a crisis.

Some managers have more personal *power* than others to affect the payoffs to other employees. Power within organizations generally does not come from the ability to force others to follow commands. Rather, power comes from other people who *voluntarily agree* to comply with a leader's proposals. For this voluntary action to occur, it must be in the interests of these other people to cooperate with the leader. Sources of power include formal authority derived from the position in their firm, control over important physical or budgetary resources, control over information, and friends/allies. Sometimes it is possible to use the power of another employee by tying the proposal to a program backed by the powerful employee.

Employees can gain support for proposals by *logrolling*. A logroll consists of a coalition of individuals who are largely indifferent to one another's proposals but agree to support the various requests so that each can get what he or she wants.

Words like *power* and *politics* often conjure up negative images. Our view is that power and political skills are neither universally good nor bad. Rather, they are important attributes that can be used for either productive or unproductive purposes. Managers are naive if they think that they can be effective without such attributes.

Symbols such as role modeling, formal creeds, stories, and legends can play an important role in communicating a manager's vision to employees. However, they are unlikely to be effective in motivating employees to take particular actions unless they are reinforced by the firm's performance-evaluation and reward systems.

Appendix

Strategic Value of Commitment and Crisis

In this chapter we discussed how a crisis and a leader's demonstrated commitment to change sometimes helps motivate change within an organization. In this appendix we use a simple game-theoretic example to illustrate these ideas.

Tomoka Hayashi is chief financial officer of the GSA Company. Simon Lewellen is the general manager of the company's largest division. The board of directors is

Figure 19.4   Strategic Value of Commitment

Tomoka Hayashi is CFO of the GSA Company, and Simon Lewellen is the general manager of the company's largest division. At the next board meeting Tomoka will recommend the degree of leverage; Simon will recommend whether his division should invest in a new technology. If they both wait until the board meeting to announce their policy choices, the Nash equilibrium is low leverage and no investment. Tomoka may be able to achieve a preferred outcome— high leverage and investment—by effectively *committing* to recommend high leverage prior to the meeting.

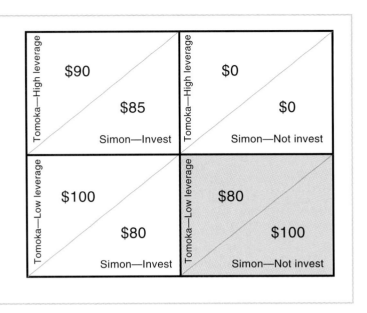

scheduled to meet next week. Tomoka will recommend the firm's leverage ratio for the next year. She will recommend either high leverage, where the firm will borrow money to repurchase common stock, or low leverage, where the company maintains its current low debt-to-equity ratio. Simon will recommend whether his division should invest in a major new technology. The board is expected to accept Tomoka's and Simon's recommendations.

Figure 19.4 displays the personal payoffs to Tomoka and Simon for the four possible combinations of leverage and investment. Tomoka prefers low leverage and investment in the new technology, whereas Simon prefers low leverage and not investing in the new technology.[16] Tomoka, however, prefers high leverage and investing to low leverage and not investing. Currently both are scheduled to make their first public disclosures of their recommendations at the board meeting. This schedule effectively requires them to make simultaneous announcements. Each must prepare extensive presentations supporting their recommendations. It is unlikely that either person will want to change his or her recommendation in the middle of the board meeting: Board members would view such a change as troublesome evidence with respect to that person's abilities. The Nash equilibrium is for Tomoka to propose low leverage and for Simon to propose no new investment.[17]

Tomoka potentially can affect Simon's choice by *committing* to propose high leverage. Simon views high leverage as placing the firm in a financial *crisis*. If the company does

---

[16]Tomoka anticipates that the new technology will increase the firm's value. As CFO she is evaluated based on the stock-price performance of the company. She favors low leverage because of its lower likelihood of bankruptcy. Simon, on the other hand, views the investment as more work for him, with little direct personal benefit. Also, the new investment will reduce his division's reported profits for a few years (there are initial startup expenses, and it will take some time to build sales) and thus the size of his annual bonus. He expects to retire in 3 years and will not be with the firm when the division begins reporting higher profits.

[17]Simon knows that Tomoka will recommend low leverage regardless of what she expects him to do. (Holding Simon's recommendation fixed, she always receives a higher payoff by recommending low leverage.) Thus, Simon's optimal strategy is to recommend not to invest in the new technology.

not invest in the new technology, the firm will not generate sufficient cash flow to service the debt, the firm will go bankrupt, and both will lose their jobs. The new technology, on the other hand, is likely to generate enough cash flow to avoid this outcome. If Simon were convinced that Tomoka would recommend high leverage, he would propose investing in the new technology. She might effectively commit to high leverage by announcing to the financial press that she intends to make this recommendation. Simon will realize that Tomoka has "backed herself into a corner"; surely she would not alter her recommendation—it would ruin her reputation as a decisive CFO. To affect his choice, it is important that Tomoka's commitment is binding. If he is not convinced, he is more likely to recommend not to invest, expecting that she will recommend low leverage to the board. Simon also might be able to influence the outcome in his favor by being the first to commit to a specific recommendation—in this case, to reject the new technology.

Appendix Question   The analysis in this appendix suggests that a leader can sometimes motivate desired change by making a strong commitment to a particular action. Do you think it is always in the leader's interest to make this type of commitment? Explain.

Suggested Readings

J. Gardner (1990), *On Leadership* (Free Press: New York).

D. Kearns and D. Nadler (1992), *Prophets in the Dark* (Harper Business Press: New York).

D. Kreps (1990), "Corporate Culture and Economic Theory," in J. Alt and K. Shepsle (Eds.), *Perspectives on Positive Political Economy* (Cambridge University Press: Cambridge).

J. March (1994), *A Primer on Decision Making* (Free Press: New York).

J. Pfeffer (1992), *Managing with Power* (Harvard Business School: Boston).

Review Questions

19–1. What is leadership?

19–2. It is frequently claimed that meaningful change is difficult to achieve in large companies. Why do you think this might be the case?

19–3. What does leadership have to do with organizational architecture?

19–4. What is organizational power, and where does it come from?

19–5. The PPP Company recently purchased a large chain of supermarkets (over 1,000 stores). Following this acquisition, PPP's management announced its plan to cut labor costs dramatically so that the stores could remain competitive. Labor unions responded by saying that they would not agree to large wage cuts. After negotiating with a labor union for a short time, PPP announced that it was closing several of its most profitable stores because labor would not agree to wage cuts. On the surface, this seemed like a silly move, given that the stores were profitable. Why do you think PPP made this move?

19–6. The TRF Company has not fared well with recent increases in foreign competition. Management indicates that it must substantially cut costs to survive. Cost cutting entails dramatic change for the company. TRF had been an all-equity firm. Recently, the company borrowed nearly 90 percent of its value and used the money to repurchase shares. The required annual debt payments exceed the company's realized earnings over the past few years. What might have motivated management to make this dramatic increase in leverage, given that it placed the firm in a near "financial crisis?"

19–7. Alex Cohen is the general manager of the textile division in a large diversified company. Recently, Alex argued strongly to the CEO that an expansion request by the drug division be approved. On the surface, Alex's actions seem strange, given that Alex is not affected by this decision (it does not affect his budget or his compensation). Further, Alex spent substantial time developing his presentation for the CEO.

a.   Why do you think Alex took such an active role in supporting the drug division's request?

b.   Since Alex is not affected by the decision, should the CEO consider Alex as an unbiased observer who is focused on trying to maximize company value? Explain.

19–8.   Poorly performing employees in Japanese firms are sometimes punished by being sent to remote locations or placed at desks away from their colleagues. Discuss the effects that such a penalty will have on the leadership effectiveness of the punished employees.

Chapter 20
Understanding the Business Environment: The Economics of Regulation

I n May 1998, the US Justice Department charged Microsoft Corp. with crushing competition and stifling innovation in the software industry.[1] Even though the lawsuit had been rumored widely, Microsoft shares still fell 3.8 percent upon filing the legal action. Nineteen states ranging from California to New York joined the suit. This litigation alleged that Microsoft's long-standing practice of adding features to its Windows operating system without a separate charge amounts to predatory pricing: It drives out existing competitors and dissuades other firms from entering the software

[1]J. Wilke (1998), "U.S. Sues Microsoft on Antitrust Grounds," *The Wall Street Journal* (May 19), A3; "Microsoft Says It Was 'Set Up,'" *Democrat and Chronicle* (October 27, 1998), D12; D. Bank (1998), "Is Microsoft a New Public Utility?" *The Wall Street Journal* (May 19), B1; and M. France, P. Burrows, L. Himelstein, and M. Moeller (1999), "The Microsoft Ruling," *Business Week* (November 22), 38–41.

market. In particular, Microsoft was accused of damaging rivals Netscape and Sun Microsystems.

The federal government contended that Microsoft has used its Windows, which was installed on 90 percent of new machines, to pressure personal computer makers to favor Microsoft's browser over Netscape's. Offered as evidence were records of a meeting between Microsoft and Netscape executives in June 1995 where Microsoft allegedly proposed dividing the browser market between the two companies. At the trial in October 1998, Microsoft argued that it was "set up" by Netscape. According to Microsoft, Netscape used the June 1995 meeting to create a record that could be passed to the Justice Department to further its case against Microsoft.

The government's case was based on the assumption that the PC operating system is an "essential facility." So many people rely on their Windows-based computers that software "competitors now need the hand of government to give them a place on the PC screen." Microsoft had acquired a virtual monopoly in the market for PC operating systems—but by itself, that was not illegal. The government also had to show that the company used predatory practices to restrain trade. For example, the government made much of a quote from a Microsoft vice president who stated that it was "necessary to fundamentally blunt [Sun Microsystems'] Java to protect our core Windows assets." But Microsoft Chairman Bill Gates scoffed at the idea that such statements indicate illegal actions. "It's no surprise to me that there are quotes from inside Microsoft that say, 'Let's compete, let's do a better product.'" Microsoft defended its actions by arguing that consumers have not been harmed and that "this suit is about Microsoft's right to innovate."

One remedy the government might pursue would be to prohibit Microsoft from dictating what Internet content appears on the Windows desktop. For example, users seeking travel reservations on the web were routed to Microsoft's Expedia site. Such routing was unfair, claimed Terrell Jones, president of Sabre Interactive, which operated the competing travel-arrangement site, Travelocity. Jones claimed that Microsoft denied him a favored position on desktops.

On November 5, 1999, US District Judge Thomas P. Jackson released his finding of facts declaring that Microsoft routinely used its monopoly power to crush competitors. Judge Jackson's fact findings were so critical of Microsoft that the breakup of Microsoft became a real possibility. Even if it is not broken up, Microsoft faces other court-imposed remedies. And now that it has been officially labeled a monopoly, it becomes the target of civil suits involving billions in damages suffered by competitors.

Importance of Regulation to Managers

Recall Figure 11.1, which provides a flowchart of the framework underlying this book. In that figure the external business environment—technology, markets, and regulation—drives the firm's choice of business strategy and in turn the firm's organizational architecture. Numerous examples have been provided throughout the book regarding how the three legs of the organizational architecture stool can become unbalanced when the firm's business environment and its strategy change. In Chapter 8 we discussed how a firm might develop a business strategy that both creates consumer value and allows the firm to capture that value.

In the federal and state lawsuit against Microsoft, government regulators argued that they were trying to protect consumers by fostering competition. Yet government regulation often limits entry into industries. For instance, electric utilities explicitly were granted effective monopolies to supply electricity to customers within specific geographic regions. New entrants were prohibited from building generating plants or selling electricity at lower prices. As states now deregulate power production, new companies are competing for customers. This has lowered prices and created new businesses ranging from consulting firms who advise large power customers about ways of exploiting the new competitive environment to power brokers who buy electric power from new power plant operators and resell it to large consumers of electricity. Thus, these regulatory changes have altered firms' strategies as well as their organizational architectures.

Government regulation takes a variety of forms: The Microsoft lawsuit is but one example of the government regulating business conduct. The following is but a partial list of the many ways regulation affects business:

- The US government has enacted an array of antitrust legislation that makes illegal such practices as collusive pricing that restrict trade.

- The Environmental Protection Agency (EPA) was established in 1970 to limit pollution of air and water by controlling the disposal of solid waste, pesticides, radiation, and toxic substances.

- All companies with publicly traded stock must follow the Securities and Exchange Commission regulations; for instance, financial disclosure regulation requires that these companies file audited financial statements prepared in accordance with Generally Accepted Accounting Principles with the SEC.

- Intellectual property laws, price and entry restrictions, labor laws, occupational safety regulations, import and export laws, and immigration acts both protect and constrain commercial activities.

- Some regulations focus on specific industries; for example, financial services (banks, savings and loans, credit unions, mutual funds, investment banks, and insurance companies), energy (electric utilities, gas pipelines, coal, and oil), and transportation (airlines, railroad, and trucking).

- Federal corporate tax rates of roughly 33 percent imply that all firms in effect have a partner who is entitled to about one-third of the firm's profits.

This chapter discusses various roles of government including its role in regulating business, how the market for regulation works, and how successful managers manage the regulatory process.

Europe Relaxes Its Labor Laws

Europe has rather strict worker protection laws that regulate the days people work, their vacations, layoffs, and other aspects of the employment relationship. One manager said, "We can divorce from our husbands and wives, but we can't divorce from our employees." These laws have made it quite expensive to dismiss employees when business slowed. This has caused companies to be extremely cautious in expanding within Europe during upturns, preferring to expand production in less regulated countries, often in Asia. The result has been slow job growth in Europe. But since the mid-1990s, with the support of politicians, companies are increasingly getting around these restrictive labor laws by hiring temporary employees—many of the most restrictive laws apply only to permanent employees.

Most European countries now have adopted laws legalizing temporary employee agencies, such as Manpower. These temp companies provide employers great flexibility to dismiss "long-term temporary help." And the countries that have relaxed their labor laws the most have enjoyed the greatest job growth.

Source: H. Cooper and T. Kamm (1998), "Much of Europe Eases Its Rigid Labor Laws, and Temps Proliferate," *The Wall Street Journal* (June 4), A1.

Economic Reasons for Government Intervention

Governments perform various functions; they provide a system of laws and legal institutions that define and enforce property rights, and they address market failures. Markets are said to fail whenever a competitive, unfettered market does not generate an efficient resource allocation for the people in the economy. Later we describe a number of reasons for such market failures: externalities, public goods, monopolies, and information asymmetries. To finance these potentially beneficial government functions of enforcing property rights and resolving market failures, revenues must be raised—usually through taxes. However, governments also use taxes as well as other means to redistribute resources in ways that impose costs on society. We now discuss each of these aspects of government intervention.

Defining and Enforcing Property Rights

When engaging in trade, each party to the transaction generally expects that its rights in the contract will be enforced. If Mark Danchak promises to deliver 200 spring suits to Melanie Caoile's store next February in return for $20,000 today and $80,000 in April, Mel expects that Mark will deliver the clothing that she ordered and Mark expects that he will receive the $80,000. If the suits do not arrive and she has no legal recourse, her future willingness to buy clothing from his factory is reduced. Similarly, if Mel does not pay the $80,000 she promised and Mark has no legal recourse, his willingness to sell Mel clothing in the future is reduced.

The government creates legal institutions, such as courts, that enforce property rights. To enforce its rulings, the court has access to police powers of the state. If Mark abrogates a contract that states he will deliver 200 suits, the court can force him to make restitution. If Mel does not pay, the court has the power to force compliance.

By enforcing contracts between private parties and adjudicating disputes, the government reduces transaction costs. With lower transaction costs, there are greater gains from trade, more transactions, more consumer and producer surplus,[2] and greater wealth. If Mel could obtain comparable suits from an extremely reputable supplier (one with no risk of default) for $102,000 and she expects to incur more than $2,000 in costs of litigating the transaction with Mark, she will not buy his suits. But if she believes the government will enforce the contract at a cost to her of less than $10 per suit, then she will buy the 200 suits and will have consumer surplus of as much as $2,000. If the government can enforce this contract for less than $2,000, then it's efficient for the government to perform this role (even ignoring any producer surplus).

Chapter 3 discussed the importance of property rights and gains from trade. A system of well-enforced, stable property rights increases incentives for people to make investments. Knowing that Mark can sell his output incurring low transaction costs supports his incentives to build a suit factory. Not only will more customers be willing to buy Mark's products because their transaction costs will be lower, his transaction costs also will be lower. The government enforces property rights in other ways as well; for instance, Mark expects that the state will provide protection against someone stealing his goods prior to their delivery.

---

[2]Chapter 7 defined consumer surplus as the difference between what the consumer is willing to pay and what is actually paid for a product. Analogously defined, producer surplus is the difference between the price the producer receives for the product and the cost of producing it.

War and Hunger

Wars, such as those in Africa, Kosovo, and Chechnya, regularly produce widespread hunger among the population. During wars, the power of the central government to enforce property rights and contracts is reduced dramatically. Without protection from the government supporting their ability to reap the rewards of a harvest, farmers are reluctant to plant crops. Especially near contested areas, farmers fear that their land might turn into a battlefield and any crops they grow might be seized by one of the combatants. Agricultural output is slashed due to the reduced incentives to plant because the farmers' ability to capture the fruits of their investments is diminished. Besides the obvious reason that wars create hunger by consuming real resources (labor and property), wars also create hunger by reducing incentives to invest in agriculture.

Most governments enforce patents, copyrights, and trademarks. By granting inventors patents (which protect the inventor from others copying their inventions for a stipulated time period), inventors and investors devote more resources to inventive activities. Developing countries without strong patent and trademark protection often have difficulty attracting investment because people fear that their investments will be expropriated.

The transaction costs of writing and enforcing contracts are higher in countries with poorly enforced property rights. For instance in the former Soviet Union, large firms employ their own security forces for protection. Workers are frequently paid in cash because the banking system is unreliable. Delivering the payroll to remote sites requires expensive security measures. All these transaction costs reduce gains from trade, lower the volume of transactions, limit investment incentives, and reduce wealth.[3]

In developed countries, relatively few commercial transactions are litigated. The threat of litigation as well as concerns about one's reputation—especially in repeated business dealings—cause most businesspeople to honor contracts voluntarily.[4] Nonetheless, commercial litigation is a growing problem in the United States. Between 1971 and 1991 more than 4 million federal lawsuits were filed, with almost 2.5 million involving at least one business entity. Moreover, this litigation is quite expensive. Combined wealth losses by firms have been estimated to be 1 percent of their equity value or about $21 million per lawsuit.[5] Lawsuits also increase operating costs. For instance, experts argue that one reason health care costs are so high is that doctors practice defensive medicine—for example, by ordering extra tests to bolster their legal defense in the event that they are sued. Similarly, to limit their liability, few public swimming pools have diving boards. Excessive litigation limits consumers' choices and thus their welfare.

On the one hand, the legal system can promote efficiency by lowering transaction costs by making property rights more secure; on the other, the legal system can raise costs by creating incentives to litigate frivolous suits. A jury ordered McDonald's to pay $2.7 million to Stella Liebeck, a drive-through customer who burned herself with hot coffee after placing the cup between her legs to remove the top and add cream: She claimed the coffee was just too hot. The US Securities Acts potentially lower transaction

[3]A. Grief and E. Kandel (1995), "Contract Enforcement Institutions: Historical Perspective and Current Status in Russia," in E. Lazear (Ed.), *Economic Transition in Eastern Europe and Russia: Realities of Reform* (Hoover Press: Stanford, CA).

[4]In Chapter 21, we discuss these issues in greater detail.

[5]S. Bhagat, J. Brickley, and J. Coles (1994), "The Costs of Inefficient Bargaining and Financial Distress," *Journal of Financial Economics* 35 (April), 221–247.

Pirated CD-ROMs

In Beijing, a peddler hawks one of China's hottest consumer products: pirated CD-ROMs. Just across the street from the US Embassy, he and other street merchants sell ripped-off versions of everything from Microsoft's Windows to music CDs. Most of these CDs come from underground factories in Hong Kong and Macao that satisfy soaring demand in China. Price—less than $5. Conservative estimates put the counterfeit disk market in China at $1 billion. CD piracy is now the No.1 problem between the US and Hong Kong.

Under US pressure, Beijing began to crack down. In 1997 Hong Kong's Customs & Excise Department had 188 agents conducting approximately 30 raids a week. Although that contributed to an eightfold rise in seizures of counterfeit goods over the previous two years, the agency said that it still could not keep up. Beijing is drafting a new copyright law, which the National People's Congress might pass. Experts hope it will help close loopholes in existing legislation.

All three governments have incentives to protect the intellectual property of software and music. The US government is trying to enforce the property rights of American firms. Hong Kong and Beijing are trying to avoid commercial sanctions that could be imposed on them if they appear lax in preventing counterfeiting.

Source: B. Einhorn (1997), "China's CD Pirates Find a New Hangout," *Business Week* (December 8), 33.

costs in security markets by regulating brokers and requiring publicly traded firms to make timely operating information disclosures. However, these acts also allow investor lawsuits if the firm makes what turn out to be false disclosures. The out-of-pocket cost to plaintiffs of filing such a lawsuit is under $200, whereas the average settlement is $7 million. Such a disparity encourages frivolous suits. (In some other countries, the incentive to file frivolous suits is reduced by making the losing party responsible for part of their opponent's legal expenses.)

Redressing Market Failures

Chapter 3 describes how a well-functioning market provides an efficient allocation of resources without shortages or surpluses. But unregulated markets do not always function well. Externalities, public goods, monopolies, and informational failures can produce "market failures" that limit the efficient allocation of resources. In these cases, some economists argue that an appropriate role of government is to enter and regulate the market to redress the failure. Yet, even after accepting the fact that such market failures exist, two questions still must be addressed before one should conclude that government regulation will help. First, can government resolve the problem at a cost lower than that of the inefficiency caused by the market failure? Government intervention is not free. Regulators must be hired and their regulations enforced. These actions consume real resources. Are these total resources lower than the cost of the market failures eliminated?

Alternative Dispute Resolution

To reduce the high cost of commercial litigation, many companies are turning to alternative dispute resolution (ADR) mechanisms: arbitration and mediation. Many commercial contracts now contain provisions binding the parties to use ADR instead of litigation. Professional ADR firms providing such services streamline the dispute process by avoiding lengthy court delays and more costly legal procedures.

Frivolous Lawsuits

In June 1994 Orange County, a California municipality, which defaulted on its debt payment because of losses from trading interest-rate derivatives, received $400 million from Merrill Lynch in an out-of-court settlement. Merrill Lynch was the investment bank that sold the derivatives to Orange County. The dispute revolved around whether Merrill should have known that the county officials were trading inappropriately and, if so, whether it should have refused to do business with the county. Merrill argued that county officials were sophisticated, acting in full public view.

> Because cases such as these tend to be settled out of court, precisely what duty a seller of financial products owes to its clients remains horribly vague. As a result, there is nothing to stop a loss-making client's imagination from running wild over the settlement that threats might achieve. Until legal uncertainties are resolved, bankers had better remember that they cannot know their clients too well.

Orange County is an extreme example of the hindsight often employed by courts. As long as Orange County was not losing money on its derivatives, there was no lawsuit. Courts enter and undo deals that go sour. Thus lawsuits are like embedded options. If the product or service works, there's no legal action. If the product or service fails, a lawsuit results. This is all right as long as the seller of the product or service can price the option at the time of sale and the buyer is willing to pay for this option. The market for the product or service collapses if the seller and buyer cannot agree on a price for the product/service including the embedded option.

Source: "Orange County Seller Beware," *The Economist* (June 6, 1998), 75.

Second, will the regulators act in the public interest to resolve the market failure and not in their self-interest? Later in this chapter we examine this second question.

Externalities   Government regulation can reduce market failures caused by externalities. Chapter 3 describes externalities as the costs or benefits created by the actions of one party imposed on involuntary participants where the consequences of these actions are not regulated by the system of prices. Air pollution is an example of an externality. When you buy and consume gasoline, the purchase price compensates everyone in the supply chain from landowners to oil explorers, drillers, refiners, and gas station owners for providing that gallon. But the people who breathe the carbon monoxide produced when you use that gasoline are not compensated. The Coase Theorem (Chapter 3) states that resource allocations remain efficient, even in the presence of externalities, as long as property rights are clearly assigned and the transaction costs of enforcing and exchanging them are sufficiently low. Hence, government can reduce market failures caused by externalities by defining property rights or by reducing the transaction costs of enforcing property rights.[6]

Consider the example of the federal government's creating a market in pollution rights. In 1995, it set a cap on the number of tons of sulfur dioxide allowed into the air.[7] Each year thereafter, the cap declines. The government issued to the 110 dirtiest power plants tradable certificates that matched their share of the cap. If companies cut their emissions below their caps, they could sell the excess to other companies that hadn't

---

[6]Note that some regulations establish and enforce property rights, but effectively make them nonmarketable (inalienable). For example, the Occupational Safety and Health Administration is charged with enforcing workplace safety regulations that specify an employee's right to work in an environment that satisfies certain conditions. Employees cannot waive these rights. Thus, even though an employee might be willing to bear a risk for additional compensation that was lower than the cost of reducing the risk, such an employment agreement is not allowed, and potential gains from trade are unexploited.

[7]J. Fialka (1997), "Breathing Easy," *The Wall Street Journal* (October 3), A1; J. Fialka (1998), "EPA Plans Emission-Trading Program to Reduce Nitrogen-Oxide Pollution," *The Wall Street Journal* (April 30), B11.

Direct and Indirect Costs of the Food and Drug Administration

"The FDA ensures that the food we eat is safe and wholesome, that the cosmetics we use won't harm us, and that medicines, medical devices . . . are safe and effective." To accomplish its mandate, the FDA has 9,000 employees and a 1999 budget of over $1 billion. Yet, the cost of protecting consumers from unsafe drugs includes more than just the FDA's $1 billion budget. Following FDA-mandated procedures, it can take 15 years to approve a new drug; in the meantime, people who could have been helped are not. And despite all its efforts, the FDA process is not foolproof. Many new drugs are pulled off the market because of some unforeseen problem. Duract was yanked after 4 patients died and 8 needed liver transplants. Pretrial tests cannot include all the possible drug interactions from other medications. And doctors often prescribe drugs for conditions other than those for which the drugs were approved.

This example illustrates that regulation generates both direct costs and indirect costs. The indirect costs are opportunity costs—drug therapies denied to potential patients because of delays in the approval process.

Sources: *www.fda.gov/opacom/faqs/genfaqs.html;* and A. Barrett (1998), "The Big Hole in the Drug Safety Net," *Business Week* (July 6), 37.

---

made the necessary cuts. Companies can save certificates from year to year, but federal clean-air standards still limit pollution. Sulfur dioxide certificate trading reached $650 million in 1997. One company had to reduce emissions by 30,000 tons. It removed 20,000 tons cheaply by switching to low-sulfur coal. The remaining 10,000 tons could be removed only by spending $130 million on scrubbing equipment. Instead, it bought certificates for the remaining 10,000 tons, saving the company $100 million. This program, which reduced emissions 30 percent nationwide, is an example of the government's reducing an externality using market-based mechanisms by defining and enforcing tradable property rights in pollutants.

The market for pollution rights works because firms whose costs to reduce pollution are lower than the market price of the rights can sell their rights to firms that face higher costs of pollution abatement. Thus, society gets the greatest reduction in pollution for the least aggregate cost.

Public Goods   Public goods are those commodities whose consumption by one person does not diminish the amount available to others. Moreover, purchasers of a public good cannot exclude nonpurchasers. A classic example of a public good is national defense; defending you against foreign attack does not necessarily reduce the amount of protection available to others. Moreover, it is difficult to exclude your neighbors from national defense if they don't pay their share. A lighthouse guiding ships at sea is a public good; one ship's use of the lighthouse does not diminish another's use of the lighthouse, and it is difficult to exclude nonpurchasers. An apple is a private good: Your consumption of an apple precludes others' consumption of that apple. It often is difficult for a market to determine the appropriate quantity and price of a public good because free-riders are not excluded easily.

Total welfare would be maximized if quantity produced were set where the public good's marginal cost equaled the sum of each consumer's marginal value. For example, suppose a firm is considering launching a new satellite that will broadcast 500 channels. Aggregate welfare increases so long as the satellite's cost is less than the sum of what each user would be willing to pay. Suppose there are 1 million potential users—half willing to pay $100 each ($50 million) and the other half willing to pay only $10 each ($5 million). If the cost of the satellite is less than $55 million, it is efficient to launch. But a competitive market might not reach this outcome if satellite transmissions are a public good. If the company tries to charge consumers for receiving the signals, all users might claim they only value the signal at $10, so the firm would collect only $10 million. Each user might try to *free-ride*. (Recall the incentive conflicts from free-riders involving joint ownership of assets described in Chapter 10.) Aware of this free-rider problem, the satellite firm will launch the satellite only if its cost is lower than $10 million. The problem is how to identify and charge the users who value the service at $100—a price above $10.

One solution to this free-rider problem is for the government to launch the satellite and pay for it with a tax. This is the basic rationale for using general taxes as the mechanism to finance such government-supplied public goods as defense, police, and fire services. Note that this rationale presumes that the government somehow can estimate the consumers' level of demand accurately. Yet, the government is not immune to particular groups of consumers' overstating their valuation in order to ensure that their desired project is completed. Moreover, the government will be lobbied by satellite makers and others who will profit from this endeavor should the project be undertaken.

Besides having the government provide the public good, another possibility exists: Convert the public good into a private good and exclude those potential customers with low valuations. For example, the company might scramble the satellite signals; those wishing to purchase the signal would have to rent a decoding box for something less than $100. Now, if the satellite costs plus the cost of the scrambling and decoding equipment is less than $50 million, a private firm will provide the service.

Monopoly   Chapter 6 describes how monopolies create resource misallocations. A monopolist sets prices above the competitive price (long-run marginal production cost) and output below the competitive output level. Some customers are willing to pay more than marginal cost, yet do not receive the product. Thus, not all gains from trade are exhausted. One potentially beneficial role of government is to limit the amount by which the monopolist's price exceeds marginal cost, and thus realizing more of the potential gains from trade. For example, state and federal regulators retain the authority to set or approve public utilities' prices. However, performing this role well requires the regulator to know the utility's true cost function.

In the United States, antitrust laws dating back to the 1890 Sherman Act give the federal government the power to limit the ability of these monopolies to set prices above competitive levels. The US Justice Department and the Federal Trade Commission have broad powers to ensure the effectiveness of the market and protect competition by overseeing pricing practices, approving mergers, scrutinizing advertising, and regulating other business practices.

In determining whether a monopoly exists, the government must show that the alleged defendant has substantial market power to set prices above the competitive level. In most antitrust cases, the definition of the relevant market becomes a central focus of the lawsuit. In the Microsoft case the government argued that the relevant market that Microsoft controlled involves operating systems, and Microsoft has 90 percent of that market. Microsoft contends that the relevant market is for browsers and that in that market Microsoft's Explorer does not have a dominant position.

Moreover, for this regulation to improve the overall resource allocation, regulators must operate in the public's interest and not be "captured" by the utility or some other party. For example, some politicians think that Internet users should pay a tax to subsidize low-income individuals' access to the Internet. These politicians argue that the poor deserve the same Internet access as the wealthy and that an Internet tax is a good way to achieve such an important social end. While this goal might be laudatory, such taxes are

Interstate Commerce Commission

During the 1880s, midwestern farmers complained bitterly that rail rates were unfair; the sum of the costs to ship goods from Chicago to Cleveland, Cleveland to Buffalo, and Buffalo to New York City was substantially greater than the cost of shipping from Chicago to New York—the sum of the short-haul rates exceeded the long-haul rates. At this time, railroads competed on long hauls but not on short hauls because there was usually just one railroad serving adjacent cities such as Chicago and Cleveland, but several railroads serving more distant cities such as Chicago and New York. The federal government created the ICC to regulate railroad freight rates. To ensure that the commissioners understood the industry they were to oversee, railroad executives were appointed to the commission. The ICC "fixed" the rate disparities by raising the long-haul rates and prohibiting price competition. When the trucking industry began competing with railroads for short hauls (competition that would have eliminated the initial problem if the industry had been left unregulated), the ICC expanded its scope to regulate the interstate trucking industry as well. Regulation raised interstate trucking rates where trucks had been taking short-haul business from the railroads. The ICC provides an example of how regulators can be "captured" by the industry they are regulating and end up protecting producers and not consumers.

inefficient: They discourage Internet use whenever the tax exceeds the user's marginal benefits. Moreover, some low-income individuals value receiving other goods and services more than they value being connected to the Internet.

It is somewhat ironic, given this array of efficiency issues raised by firms with market power, that many of the monopolized industries were created by various government acts. For example, public utilities (such as electric companies, cable TV, or telephone companies) often are granted exclusive operating franchises to provide services within a specific geographic region.

Finally, some advocates of additional regulation presume that the government can act with almost surgical precision, identifying and stopping inappropriate activities while leaving appropriate activities unaffected. Yet it is difficult to implement regulation perfectly. Even well-meaning regulators make mistakes. Recognizing that regulatory sanctions still might be imposed on managers who are not behaving illegally (or inappropriately), these managers still might modify their actions quite rationally to reduce the likelihood that sanctions will be imposed. And such modified actions reduce the firm's value to the extent that they are costly—perhaps because managers are diverted from actions that would have increased value.

Informational Failures   Chapter 10 describes how adverse selection can lead to market failures. Adverse selection refers to the situation in which an individual with private information that affects a potential trading partner's benefits makes an offer that is detrimental to the trading partner. The classic example is the "lemons" problem—sellers of used cars generally know more about their mechanical condition than buyers.[8] Thus, at any given price, sellers are more likely to offer "lemons" than high-quality cars. Suppose the average resale price of 1-year-old Ford Broncos is $20,000. Used-car buyers do not expect vehicles offered will be in perfect mechanical condition. The $20,000 price thus reflects buyers' forecasts of mechanical problems for 1-year-old Broncos offered in the used-car market. For instance, Lena Cardone is the owner of a 1-year-old Bronco with no mechanical problems. But if she cannot credibly convince a potential buyer that her

---

[8]G. Akerlof (1970), "The Market for 'Lemons': Quality Uncertainty and the Market Mechanism," *Quarterly Journal of Economics* 84, 488–500.

Bronco has no problems and that she has another reason for selling, she must sell her Bronco for $20,000. Knowing that it is worth more than $20,000, Lena might prefer to keep it—some economists argue that a market failure results.[9] Some state governments have tried to limit this market failure by passing a "lemon law," which requires used-car dealers to fix mechanical defects in used cars up to 30 days after the sale. (Note that although this law might raise retail prices of used cars by increasing the demand by buyers, it will not raise the wholesale price to sellers.)

The US securities laws attempted to overcome alleged market failures that were blamed for the 1929 market crash. Here the information asymmetry involved investors and corporate executives. Advocates for the securities acts claimed that investors were fooled into buying overvalued securities because unscrupulous executives did not disclose information about companies honestly. Of course investors have incentives to anticipate such behavior and only offer prices that reflect expected quality.[10] The US securities acts require such disclosures to reduce the asymmetry, thereby increasing the demand for securities.

Again, these laws are not costless. Regulators must be hired, and firms must expend real resources publishing financial results. Some of the mandated disclosures might involve proprietary information that is more valuable to competitors in crafting effective corporate strategies than to potential investors. And knowing that the information cannot be kept confidential, managers might be less likely to invest in its production. Moreover, external auditors must be hired to attest to the accuracy of the disclosures. Note that private solutions might be less costly than government regulation. Investors discount the price of securities unless the company makes credible disclosures. Thus, firms face private incentives to provide information for investors. Similarly, used-car buyers can hire auto inspectors or used-car sellers can certify that their preowned cars do not

Cost of Regulation: Proprietary Information

IRS officials now release portions of the "advance pricing" agreements they make with businesses. Through these APAs, companies agree in advance with the IRS on how to set transfer prices for internal transactions among units. Although the IRS says it removes sensitive details (taxpayer's identity, trade secrets, and other confidential information), some tax specialists worry. "Companies really bare their souls in filing for APAs," says Timothy McCormally of Tax Executives Institute. He says companies may skip the program rather than risk disclosure.

This is an example of the opportunity costs imposed by regulation. A firm can reduce expected legal costs by negotiating an APA with the IRS. However, filing an APA can expose the firm to considerable risk by having some of its most sensitive cost information outside its control in the hands of a government regulatory agency.

Source: "Tax Report," *The Wall Street Journal* (February 3, 1999), A1.

[9]We believe that this argument requires care. It is true that if information were costless, unexploited gains from trade would exist. But information is a good, one that is expensive to produce and transfer. Given the distribution of information and technology for producing and transferring information, the allocation of resources is efficient. We see little difference in arguing that "compared to a world where information costs are lower, the current allocation of resources is inefficient" and that "compared to a world where the cost of steel is lower, resources are misallocated." Ultimately, efficiency must be judged given the costs implied by available technology—not against a benchmark of zero costs. This is another example of the Nirvana fallacy discussed in Chapter 17.

[10]Moreover, for the price to be too high, it is not enough that some investors are misled (or even that the average investor is unsophisticated and is misled); the marginal investor must be misled to affect prices. The marginal investor—that investor who is just on the fence between buying and not buying, so that small differences in price or information may change the decision to buy—is likely to be knowledgeable.

have mechanical defects. Car buyers will pay more for used cars with warranties. In these cases, the contracting parties have incentives to overcome potential information asymmetries.

Redistributing Wealth

So far we have discussed two potentially beneficial roles of government: enforcing contracts to facilitate trade and eliminating market failures. In both roles the invisible hand of the free market can be improved (at least in principle) by government intervention. However, details of the implementation of policies to address these problems create opportunities for self-interested individuals to use this intervention as an opportunity to enrich themselves. For example, national defense clearly is a valuable service provided by the government—one that addresses a potential market failure. But if an influential legislator can ensure that a defense contract is granted to a favored firm on lucrative terms, a large transfer of wealth results. Moreover, government must finance this intervention. It generally does so by levying taxes, but governments also raise revenue through user fees for toll roads, tariffs on imports, and licensing and registration fees. In financing government intervention, there are additional opportunities to engineer wealth transfers. Throughout this book (see especially Chapters 2 and 10) we adopt the standard assumption that individuals operate in their own self-interest. This assumption also is useful in explaining how individuals behave when working for the government or interacting within the political process. For example, auditors have an incentive to lobby for securities laws that increase the total demand for audited financial statements, especially if they can restrict entry into the auditing profession.

As an example of government effecting wealth transfers, consider taxi licensing that restricts the number of cabs. Figure 20.1 depicts the supply and demand curves for taxi rides in a perfectly competetive, unregulated market. Each cab owner charges price P^* equal to average (and marginal) cost and hence (assuming identical suppliers) makes no economic profit. Absent government intervention, the price of a cab ride is P^* and the number of cab rides is Q^*. Suppose the government—in the name of protecting the public from low-quality cabs—restricts the number of taxis and thus the number of cab rides to Q'. To operate a cab, the driver must display a taxi medallion, which are limited in number. The price of a taxi ride rises to P', and the marginal cost per ride is P^*. Consumer surplus falls by the shaded area. Profit per ride is $P' - P^*$, and total industry profit is the rectangular area π. There are fewer taxi owners, but those expecting to be in business are willing to spend up to π, lobbying the government to restrict the number of cabs. In the extreme case, this entire profit stream will be expended on lobbyists and political campaign contributions.[11]

Consumers should be willing to spend their forgone consumer surplus (the shaded area) lobbying to prevent restricting the number of cabs. Yet because of free-rider problems, it is difficult to raise this amount for an effective lobbying campaign. So long as the cab owners are easier to organize—there are fewer of them and their wealth implications are more concentrated—taxi regulation can be passed despite the fact that the forgone consumer surplus for the riders exceeds the surplus gained by the owners. The lobbying expenditures by the surviving cab owners and consumers yield no productive benefits to society. If the number of taxis is limited to, say, Q', there is a wealth transfer from cab riders to taxi owners, lobbyists, politicians, and regulators. This example illustrates how

---

[11]Note that profit π is a flow. Thus, the taxi owners should be willing to spend up to the present value of the incremental profit stream on lobbying activities.

Figure 20.1 Wealth Transfers via Government Quotas on the Number of Taxis

S and *D* are the supply and demand curves for taxicab rides. Absent government intervention, the price is *P** and *Q** is the equilibrium number of cab rides. If the government restricts the number of cabs and thus cab rides to *Q′*, the price of a ride increases to *P′*. Consumer surplus falls by the shaded area. Industry profit is the area π. Those cab owners expecting to survive should be willing to spend up to π, lobbying government to restrict the number of taxis.

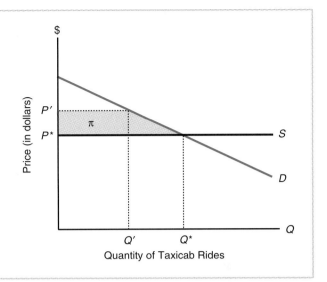

government regulation can transfer wealth among various parties. The example also indicates that both consumers and producers have incentives to lobby.

Other examples of wealth transfers exist. Taxes are among the most obvious. Import quotas and tariffs transfer wealth from domestic consumers to domestic producers. Import quotas also help foreign producers act as a cartel. Licensing of doctors, dentists, and lawyers restricts entry into these professions and transfers wealth from the consumers of these services to the incumbent members of the professions. Although zoning restrictions can address externalities, thereby raising land values, they also transfer wealth. These wealth transfers generally are from the initial landowners whose property is restricted to those landowners whose land has no restrictions. Subsequent owners of the restricted-use land buy the land at lower prices that reflect the value of the restrictions. Government farm supports, which pay farmers not to grow certain crops, transfer wealth from consumers to the producers when the subsidy is created. (Again, subsequent

Regulated Limos in Las Vegas

The Nevada State Transportation Services Authority (TSA) requires all limousine operators to have a certificate of public convenience and necessity. One would-be limo owner describes the system like this: "The TSA regulatory system is designed to protect large companies and to prevent entrepreneurs like me from competing." To get a limo certificate, applicants must show that "the granting of the certificate will not unreasonably and adversely affect other carriers operating in the territory." Existing certified limo companies can pose questions and raise objections that the applicant must answer. One applicant filed 1,000 pages of information ranging from maintenance records to customer lists and spent over $15,000 on the process. His application was denied. In 20 years, only 3 new certificates have been granted. The area's two largest firms (with 170 limos between them) have lodged objections to all new applicants.

Clearly, the two largest limo firms successfully used the TSA system to help limit entry, reduce competition, and maintain high prices for limo services.

Source: R. Fitzgerald (1999), "Mugged by the Law," *Readers Digest* (January), 98–103.

purchasers of the farm land pay a higher price for the land as long as the subsidy is linked to the land.) Student financial aid, government support of university research, welfare, and Small Business Administration loans with below-market interest rates all involve wealth transfers.

Managers interested in understanding how government regulation affects the value of their firms must understand the inherent "market" for government regulation. There is both a demand for and a supply of government regulation. If they ignore this market, managers place themselves and their firms at risk. Most organizations find themselves at times lobbying for or against various proposed regulations at the local, state, federal, and even international levels. For example, General Motors argues for lower property assessments and local property taxes, fewer state environmental regulations, increased federal defense department procurement of its products, and more aggressive intervention by international trade organizations to help it gain better access to foreign consumer markets. The next section presents an economic theory of this market for government regulation.

Economic Theory of Regulation

Before presenting the theory of how the market for regulation works, we begin by first describing the underlying principles (demand, supply, self-interested politicians, and coalition formation).

Demand for Regulation: Special Interests

Special interest groups are composed of self-interested individuals who, because of their current circumstances stand to benefit from a proposed government legislation. The special interest group might be bicycle riders seeking a bike lane; they might be landowners, construction companies, and labor unions seeking a new federal highway project in their area; they might be milk farmers, organized labor, or the Sierra Club sponsoring legislation that furthers their causes. In most cases the demanded legislation comes at the expense of some other group who either will pay for the legislation or will have their rights restricted by the legislation. The special interest group backing legislation to raise the sales tax collections to pay for a new sports stadium might consist of football fans, construction companies, skilled trades people, hotel and bar owners in the area, and sports reporters working for the local media. A new stadium would make each of these individuals better off. People who are not sports fans are made worse off by the

---

Special Interests and the Microsoft Antitrust Suit

Only 19 of the 50 states joined the federal government suit alleging Microsoft violated the antitrust laws. It is interesting to look at which states participated in the suit and the special interests located in the state. Microsoft's major competitors, Sun Microsystems and Netscape, are California-based companies; Novell is located within Utah. Both California and Utah joined the suit. Washington, home of Microsoft, is not participating, nor is Texas. Texas computer makers Dell, Compaq, and Tandy—who bundle Microsoft Windows into their machines—oppose the suit. It appears as though politicians and regulators in the various states represent the interests of the computer firms in their states when it comes to joining the federal government suit against Microsoft.

Source: C. Georges (1998), "Politics Play a Role in States' Status in Microsoft Suit," *The Wall Street Journal* (May 28), A24.

Political Support

U.S. Senator Trent Lott collected $850,000 from 144 individuals for his and other Republican representatives' campaigns. *The Wall Street Journal* contacted these individuals and reported that "four out of five donors to the Lott [Political Action Committee] had identifiable stakes in specific programs and policies pending before government. One shipping executive said, 'I gave because I have an interest in how he votes on maritime issues. It's self-interest.'"

Source: G. Hitt and P. Kuntz (1998), "The Money Trail," *The Wall Street Journal* (May 28), A1.

higher sales taxes. For most proposed government action, two special interest groups can be identified—those made better off and those made worse off.

Supply of Regulation: Politicians

Politicians, including members of the legislative and executive branches of government, are the primary market participants who supply the regulations. They act as brokers among special interest groups favoring and opposing regulations. But more than just brokering these transactions, they often are active entrepreneurs in proposing regulations and then helping mobilize special interest groups. Politicians must get elected and reelected. They do this by promising to pass (or defeat) legislation that helps (or harms) their constituents. This frequently involves proposing new legislation.

Economists assume that consumers, business owners, and managers are self-interested (Chapters 2 and 10); politicians are similarly motivated. Just because politicians claim that they are public-spirited does not make it so. As in private organizations, agency problems exist within the government. Politicians' activities are difficult to monitor. Simply promising to help deliver a particular regulation does not mean a politician will exert maximum effort to do so. It is difficult for voters to observe the level of effort exerted: Although politicians' voting records are observable, their behind-the-scenes actions generally are not.

This view of public officials as self-interested individuals seeking to enrich themselves by supplying legislation that benefits some group is based on numerous, carefully executed studies of public choice.[12] Our purpose here is to summarize the major managerially relevant insights from that research.

Incentives to Free-Ride and Form Coalitions   The market for government regulation is a competition among those special interest groups supporting and opposing the regulation. The political power of a coalition depends both on its size and how well it is organized to deliver votes and political contributions relative to its opposition. For instance, opinion polls typically show that the majority of Americans favor stricter gun control. Yet the relatively small, but quite well-organized and well-financed National Rifle Association regularly defeats most proposed firearm regulation. Although most Americans favor additional firearm regulation, they do not feel strongly enough to take the time and expend the resources to organize an effective coalition. They rationally choose to stay on the sidelines. This example illustrates several important points. Forming a politically

---

[12]For a review of the material, see R. McCormick (1993), *Managerial Economics* (Prentice Hall: Englewood Cliffs, NJ), Chapter 15.

effective special interest group is costly. Its members must be kept informed of pending legislation. They must be willing to write letters to politicians, to make campaign contributions, and ultimately to vote for those who support their position. Whether for emotional or financial reasons, people must feel strongly enough about the cause to overcome their incentives to free-ride on the actions of others. Organizing an effective coalition involves many of the same organizational architecture issues described throughout this book—namely, creating incentives and monitoring devices to generate participation in the process.

For a coalition to be effective, the benefits of the government regulation each party in the coalition expects to receive must exceed the costs they bear in forming the coalition and lobbying. Consider a government import quota on foreign cars that raises the price of domestic cars $100. If consumers keep their cars an average of 5 years, they could save about $20 per year by opposing such quotas effectively. Yet these diffuse costs are generally too small to justify incurring the costs of forming a broad coalition, becoming informed of pending legislation, and acting on this information. Thus, most consumers rationally choose to remain uninformed. However, a $100 price hike on each car amounts to hundreds of millions of dollars for each domestic car company. These concentrated benefits are more than sufficient to justify the costs of forming and maintaining their coalition.

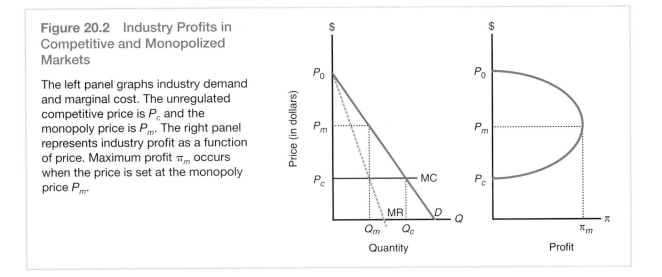

Figure 20.2 Industry Profits in Competitive and Monopolized Markets

The left panel graphs industry demand and marginal cost. The unregulated competitive price is P_c and the monopoly price is P_m. The right panel represents industry profit as a function of price. Maximum profit π_m occurs when the price is set at the monopoly price P_m.

Market for Regulation[13]

To illustrate the market for regulation, consider an industry represented by the demand curve in the left panel of Figure 20.2. Marginal cost is constant at MC. If the industry is competitive and unregulated, the market price is $P_c =$ MC. But if all the firms in the industry could collude and behave as a single monopolist, the price would be P_m—the monopoly price would be set where marginal cost and marginal revenue are equal. The right-hand panel of Figure 20.2 represents industry profit as a function of price.[14] Maximum profit π_m occurs when the price is set at the monopoly price P_m (assuming no price discrimination among customers). If the price is P_0, nothing is sold and hence (with no fixed costs) profit is zero. Profit also is zero when the price is at the competitive level, P_c.

In Figure 20.3 suppose an industry regulator, Ann Melville, is interested in maximizing political support from her constituents—owners of the firms in the industry and the consumers of the industry's output. Regulation gives her the right to set the price in this industry and thus to determine industry profits. Owners want high profits; consumers want low prices.

Figure 20.3 displays two curves that represent those combinations of prices and profits that yield equal political support in terms of campaign contributions and votes.[15] For example, Ann is indifferent between setting price at P_x and profit at π_x and setting price at P_y and profit at π_y. Both combinations yield equivalent political support. At P_x and π_x she gets more support from consumers but less from producers. At P_y and π_y she gets less consumer support but more producer support. Ann prefers to be on political support curves that are lower and to the right—for instance, she prefers PS_2 to PS_1. On PS_2, consumers have lower prices (and hence Ann gets more consumer support) for a given level of profit. For example, hold industry profits constant at π_x; if Ann is on PS_2, consumers face a lower price P_x than if Ann is on PS_1 and consumers face a higher price P_z—Ann

---

[13]This section draws on G. Stigler (1987), *Theory of Price,* fourth edition (Macmillan Publishing Company: New York), Chapter 20.

[14]Although we usually think of profit as a function of price, we plot price as the vertical axis to make comparisons across the graphs easier.

[15]Note that these curves are similar in concept to indifference curves in Chapter 2 and isoquants in Chapter 5.

Figure 20.3   Political Support Functions

A PS curve graphs combinations of profit and price levels that produce equivalent political support from industry and consumers. Thus, the regulator is indifferent between setting price at P_x and profit at π_x and setting price at P_y and profit at π_y—both combinations yield equivalent levels of political support. However, the regulator prefers to be on PS$_2$ than on PS$_1$.

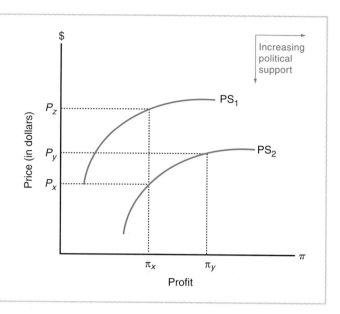

thus receives less consumer support. These political-support functions have positive slope. Higher prices reduce consumer support that can be offset only with higher support from industry via higher profits. These curves are concave because at low prices, small price changes are little noticed by consumers. But at higher prices, they garner greater notice, thereby requiring larger industry profits to offset them. For example, when gasoline prices increased dramatically in 2000 following OPEC's production cuts, politicians appeared on television supporting consumers and promising to investigate the high prices.

Although Ann prefers to be on a political support function as far to the right as possible, the actual political support function she can achieve depends on the trade-off between profits and prices as determined by specific conditions in the industry. Figure 20.4 combines the analysis in the earlier two figures. Given the profit-price profile in Figure 20.2, Ann is able to achieve political support PS$_2$. Here she will set the regulated price at P_r^*. Industry profits are π_r^*, which is less than maximum profits of π_m. Ann favors a price between the monopoly and competitive prices. If she sets a higher price to generate more support from the industry, she loses support from consumers and finds herself on a lower political support curve. If she sets a lower price to garner more consumer support, she loses so much industry support that again she finds herself with lower overall political support.

Cost of Protection: Automobile Import Restrictions

In the 1980s, the US and Japanese governments agreed on a "voluntary restriction" on Japanese cars imported into the United States to protect American auto jobs. By limiting the number of cars imported, the price of Japanese cars rose about $1,000, the price of European cars rose about $2,000, and the price of US cars rose about $500. By one estimate, the cost of saving one US automotive job via this voluntary import restriction approached $200,000. Thus, US consumers paid about $200,000 per American auto job saved.

Source: E. Dinopoulos and M. Kreinin (1988), "Effects of the U.S.–Japan Auto VER on European Prices and on U.S. Welfare," *Review of Economics and Statistics* 70, 484–491.

Figure 20.4   Equilibrium Regulated Price

The regulator sets the regulated price P_r^* to be less than the monopoly price P_m, but more than the zero-profit competitive price P_c. At higher prices, the regulator loses more support from consumers than is gained from industry. At lower prices, the regulator loses more industry support than is gained from consumers.

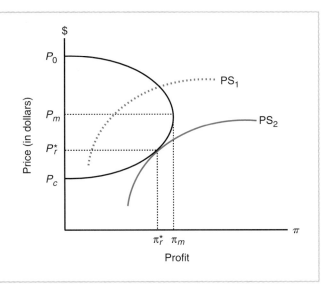

Several important insights arise from this analysis:

- Regulators do not always behave in obviously consistent ways. They might reduce monopoly prices but seek to form cartels in competitive industries where they can raise prices. Although appearing inconsistent, both types of regulation move price away from favoring entirely either consumers or producers.

- If consumers are unorganized, they offer regulators little political support relative to an organized industry group. In the case of completely unorganized and ill-informed consumers, the political support function in Figure 20.4 becomes vertical (at least over the relevant range) and the regulator maximizes support by setting the monopoly price. Conversely, if consumers are well organized but industry owners are disorganized and offer no political support, the regulator faces a horizontal support function and will set the price at the competitive, zero-profit level.

- The outcome of the political process depends on the relative political support a special interest group can achieve. The more organized and the larger the special interest group, the more political support it can offer. Executives attempt to make the political support function steeper by increasing political contributions, organizing their employees to vote for the candidate, and reducing consumer opposition through a public relations campaign.

Brazil Deregulates Airfares

"For decades, Brazil's airlines competed only in the corridors of [the capital] Brasília, where politicians dispensed favors in return for free airline tickets and other goodies." Airfares between Rio de Janeiro and São Paulo averaged $500 (round trip). Deregulation has sparked intense competition. Fares on this route have fallen to about $200, and Brazil's largest airlines are currently complaining that they are losing money. This is an example of how regulators can choose between prices and industry profits.

Source: P. Fritsch (1998), "Brazilian Carriers Plunge into First Fare War as Deregulation Ignites Ferocious Competition," *The Wall Street Journal* (May 12), A15.

Conservative Choices of Accounting Methods

Large, highly visible firms like IBM, General Motors, and Microsoft tend to use more conservative accounting procedures than smaller, less visible firms. For example, large firms are more likely to use depreciation methods that write assets off faster, thereby lowering reported earnings. This evidence is consistent with these firms' seeking to reduce their political exposure by reporting lower accounting earnings. Since large accounting profits are often viewed as measures of monopoly profits and hence attract more media attention, managers of firms subjected to these charges attempt to blunt them by choosing income-decreasing accounting methods. This can reduce the amount of political opposition these firms face.

Source: R. Watts and J. Zimmerman (1986), *Positive Accounting Theory*
(Prentice Hall: Upper Saddle River, NJ).

- Government programs tend to benefit small groups (aerospace contractors) at the expense of large groups (taxpayers). Holding constant the total amount of wealth transferred, the larger the losing group, the smaller the average loss per loser. Similarly, the smaller the winning group, the larger the benefits per winner.

Deadweight Losses, Transaction Costs, and Wealth Transfers

Because special interest groups can enrich themselves at the expense of others, each group is willing to spend up to the amount they are expected to win or lose providing political support. Recall from Figure 20.1—where government restricts the supply of taxis, thereby driving up the cost of cab rides—that the lost consumer surplus (the shaded area) is a deadweight loss to society. The surviving cab owners are making a profit because now price is above their cost. But to limit the number of cabs, a government taxi licensing office must be created to issue permits. Police and courts must incur costs as they attempt to catch and punish unauthorized cab drivers. In addition to these costs, each side will incur costs of organizing, lobbying, and providing political support for the politician. Minimizing these costs and deadweight losses is in both the winners' and losers' interests. Thus, government policies that generate smaller reductions in economic efficiency are more likely to be adopted because the losers are harmed less and will oppose the regulations with less zeal, and winners will lobby harder since they have more to share.

Managerial Implications

Having laid out the essential features of the market for regulation, in this section we describe the important managerial implications such as entry restrictions, forming coalitions, and business participation in the political process.

Restricting Entry and Limiting Substitutes

In Chapter 8 we describe how firms develop strategies that both create value and capture value. Recall that it is not enough to build a better mousetrap; you must prevent others from copying your ideas and entering the market. We discussed patents, copyrights, and trademarks as means to protect intellectual property. Now we examine how government regulations might be used to create additional barriers to entry.

Restricting Entry into European Retailing

"The fight against outlet malls will continue. If we allow one, the dam will break, and we'll be swamped," stated the director of the German Retailers' Association. US and UK retailers are trying to enter European markets. To keep them out, shops cannot stay open evenings and Sundays. Mall developers must contend with high wage rates, restrictive zoning laws, and high property taxes. Public officials battle developers over signage and government permits. In Austria, the chamber of commerce is lobbying hard to keep out foreign competitors. One retailer says, "Low prices will be our downfall." Thus, to limit the competition they face (especially from foreign firms), European retailers use a wide variety of government regulations to restrict entry.

Source: E. Beck (1997), "Outlet Malls Make Headway in Europe Despite Opposition by Local Retailers," *The Wall Street Journal* (September 17), A17.

The most direct way to restrict competition is a government regulation limiting entry. For example, labor union laws that prevent unionized firms from hiring nonunion employees raise wages in these firms. Immigration laws limit the numbers of foreign workers allowed into the country to protect the domestic labor force. It is illegal for private delivery services to deliver mail to a customer's mailbox. Professions like law, medicine, accounting, and dentistry limit competition by setting professional licensing standards such as passing exams and requiring work-related experience. Public utilities such as telephone, gas, electric, and cable television companies have been granted exclusive franchises within specific geographic areas.

A less direct method of limiting competition is a government regulation that imposes a cost on certain competitors and potential entrants. For example, consider health codes that require restaurants to meet various regulations concerning the preparation and storage of food. Although such health codes increase all restaurants' costs, they increase street vendors' costs proportionately more than those of full-service restaurants. Thus, health codes restrict the number and types of street vendors and hence potential competition from new entrants. Or, recall Netscape's involvement in the federal government's antitrust suit against Microsoft. Microsoft argues that it was "set up" by Netscape in a June 1995 meeting where Netscape allegedly created a record that Microsoft proposed splitting the browser market with Netscape. Documents referring to this meeting are a key argument in the government's case. If Microsoft loses this case, possible remedies include breaking up Microsoft or preventing it from bundling its browser with its Windows desktop software. Both remedies impose costs on Microsoft and make Netscape more competitive.

To illustrate how government regulation can change the relative competitiveness of firms, consider the market for rugs.[16] Suppose there are two ways to produce the same rug. Labor-intensive firms employ 10 workers an hour at $15 per hour and use 30 pounds of wool at $5 per pound. It takes 1 hour to produce a rug at a total cost of $300 ($10 \times \$15 + 30 \times \$5$). Material-intensive firms also produce 1 rug per hour, also at a cost of $300, but they use 5 workers at $15 per hour and 45 pounds of wool at $5 per pound. Material-intensive firms cannot switch to become labor-intensive firms, and vice versa; moreover, firm sizes are fixed. The rug market is competitive and each rug sells for $300. There are only 200 labor-intensive firms and only 200 material-intensive firms. Total quantity produced and sold is 400 rugs per hour. In Figure 20.5 the market

---

[16]This example is based on R. McCormick (1993), Chapter 15.

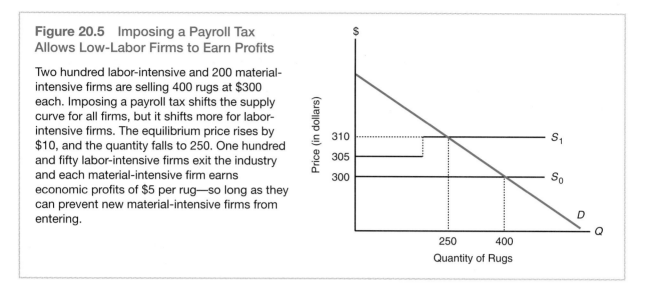

Figure 20.5 Imposing a Payroll Tax Allows Low-Labor Firms to Earn Profits

Two hundred labor-intensive and 200 material-intensive firms are selling 400 rugs at $300 each. Imposing a payroll tax shifts the supply curve for all firms, but it shifts more for labor-intensive firms. The equilibrium price rises by $10, and the quantity falls to 250. One hundred and fifty labor-intensive firms exit the industry and each material-intensive firm earns economic profits of $5 per rug—so long as they can prevent new material-intensive firms from entering.

demand curve and the original supply curve intersect at a quantity of 400 rugs and a price of $300. Neither type of firm makes abnormal profits.

Now the material-intensive firms are able to get a $1 per employee per hour payroll tax implemented by the government. All firms are required to pay this tax. The total cost of a labor-intensive firm rises to $310 ($10 \times \$16 + 30 \times \$5$). The total cost of a material-intensive firm rises to $305 ($5 \times \$16 + 45 \times \$5$). The price of rugs rises to $310 because the demand curve intersects the new supply curve at a price of $310. The material-intensive firms are making abnormal profits of $5 per rug. The remaining labor-intensive firms are breaking even. But only 250 rugs per hour are produced. The result is that 150 labor-intensive firms go out of business. The 200 material-intensive firms continue to make abnormal profits of $5 per rug so long as they can prevent new material-intensive firms from entering.

This example illustrates an important managerial implication. A firm might rationally support government regulations that impose costs on itself, as long as competing firms incur higher costs. This drives the high-cost firms from the industry, and allows remaining firms to earn economic profits because the marginal firm (or the next firm to enter) is a high-cost firm. Managers often support these regulations by arguing that they are in the public interest. For example, managers might argue the payroll tax is used to support social programs such as employee health benefits.

Other examples illustrate the pervasiveness of cost-increasing regulations that restrict entry. General Motors lobbied for stringent miles-per-gallon standards in the early 1980s. Burlington Industries supported Occupational Safety and Health Administration cotton dust standards for textile manufacturers. These standards imposed relatively higher costs on smaller plants, thereby allowing the larger plants to generate economic rents. Truckers support train safety regulation. Local merchants want tougher building codes. In the 1800s, English steam-powered mill owners argued for rules limiting child labor in factories. (This example is analogous to Figure 20.5 where a payroll tax is imposed; it favors capital-intensive firms—steam-powered mills—at the expense of other labor-intensive firms.) Finally, large accounting firms supported regulations that required all CPAs to have extensive periodic peer review evaluations. These requirements impose relatively higher costs on smaller CPA firms, forcing them out of markets (such as those for publicly traded client firms) where large CPA firms dominate.

Skyway Robbery

In June 1997, Southwest Airlines ran ads urging travelers to lobby their elected representatives to oppose a change in the federal tax on airline tickets. The largest seven airlines proposed a fixed head tax on each ticket instead of a tax based on the ticket's cost. For a given route, this change would raise the ticket price of low-fare airlines such as Southwest more than that of the seven big airlines. This is an example of how the largest airlines tried to use details of the structure of federal taxation of airline tickets to reduce competition from low-fare carriers.

Source: *The Wall Street Journal* (June 15, 1997), A5.

Forming Coalitions

The economic theory of regulation emphasizes the critical importance of coalition formation. Winning coalitions supply more political support to politicians (votes and campaign contributions) than losing coalitions. One way to increase political support is to expand the number of people supporting the regulation. This process sometimes produces unusual alliances. For instance, in the South during the early 1900s, illegal liquor producers (bootleggers) wanted to reduce competition from legal distillers. Bootleggers supported a coalition of church members who wanted to ban the sale of all alcohol. Responding to this lobbying, a number of counties in southern states became "dry" by passing legislation prohibiting the sale of alcoholic beverages. Since the bootleggers had been operating illegally for years and avoiding prosecution from federal alcohol tax collectors, continuing to operate their underground businesses posed relatively few problems. This is a classic case of "politics make strange bedfellows" and has been called the "Bootleggers and Baptists Phenomenon."[17]

We often observe a special interest group that lobbies to restrict entry because it furthers its economic interest (bootleggers) joining forces with a special interest group that lobbies to correct a social ailment (Southern Baptists). Another example is western coal producers supporting environmental groups who lobby for tighter air-quality emission standards that make burning high-sulfur eastern coal more expensive than their low-sulfur coal. Winning coalitions frequently contain industry groups, "public interest" groups, and regulators to produce a strong political force pitted against consumers and rival companies. For example, aerospace contractors to the space program form coalitions with science "buffs" to lobby Congress for more space funding.

Recall the discussion in Chapter 19 regarding leadership. Forming political coalitions is similar to forming coalitions within the firm to advocate new proposals. Members of a political coalition are usually risk-averse, and so new government regulations that are uncertain will likely be opposed. Ways of increasing the coalition's support of a proposed regulation is to reduce the uncertainty in the regulation, emphasize a crisis, and organize a logroll.

On Business Participation in the Political Process

Some will question whether a firm should be an active participant in the political process. Certainly our analysis suggests that collectively, we would be better off if we could limit the government's ability to pass regulation that restricts competition. In such

---

[17]McCormick (1993), 649.

Effect of the Microsoft Case on Other Computer Firms

One might expect that the government's antitrust actions against Microsoft would have affected the values of other computer firms. In particular, direct competitors such as Netscape and Sun should be made better off, whereas firms selling complementary products such as Dell and Compaq are made worse off. A study of the stock price movements of 159 computer-related firms surrounding major news announcements of antitrust actions against Microsoft from March 1991 to December 1997 yields some interesting findings. These 159 computer firms (excluding Microsoft) had a total stock market value of $754 billion in December 1997. This group experienced an aggregate drop in stock value of $35 billion on the 3 days surrounding the 29 news announcements that increased the antitrust enforcement against Microsoft. Conversely, when antitrust news favorable to Microsoft was announced, these firms' value increased $70 billion. Negative (positive) movements of Microsoft stock at the time of antitrust enforcement actions coincide with negative (positive) returns for the industry. Notice that the 159 computer firms include those firms supposedly wanting the government antitrust suit to succeed. Surprisingly, there is no evidence that individual firms such as Netscape, Sun, Novell, or Apple realized higher stock returns when antitrust actions were taken against Microsoft. Repeated antitrust actions against Microsoft have not increased the expected earnings of other computer firms. "Surprisingly, government action against Microsoft appears to inflict capital losses on the computer sector as a whole. . . . Withdrawals from policy enforcement have been accompanied by positive shareholder returns throughout the computer sector."

Source: G. Bittlingmayer and T. Hazlett (2000), "DOS *Kapital*: Has
Antitrust Action against Microsoft Created Value in the Computer Industry?"
Journal of Financial Economics 55, 329–359.

a case, consumer prices would be lower and we would save the deadweight costs and transaction costs associated both with lobbying for government regulations and enforcing the regulations.

Yet in evaluating company participation, we believe several points are important to consider. First, managers have a fiduciary responsibility to maximize the value of their firm, not to maximize social welfare. Regulation can have a material impact on a firm's value. Second, companies did not create this system that allows these welfare-reducing regulations to be adopted—politicians did. Unfortunately, eliminating this wasteful activity seems unlikely. Far too much wealth is at stake. Too many vested interest groups (including politicians, regulators, lobbyists, and lawyers) exist to expect that these very same people will pass new laws reducing the demand for their services. Third, even if a firm decides not to pursue political activities designed to produce wealth transfers, it almost certainly will be confronted with trying to prevent regulation aimed at reducing its value. Remaining passive does not mean that everyone else will leave it alone. Managers who avoid participation in the political process that would benefit their firms reduce shareholder wealth. This places their company's continued existence at risk and calls into question their fiduciary responsibility to shareholders.

Finally, it is important to evaluate carefully the strategic aspects of participation in the political process. As described in Chapter 9, managers must consider carefully how government regulators and other affected parties will react to the manager's lobbying activities. For example, managers must decide whether it is better to be a "first mover" or "second mover" in lobbying. Managers must ensure that their lobbying is "credible" in the sense that rivals change their beliefs because the manager has sufficient commitment to the strategy. And, managers must consider how their lobbying on the current government regulation will affect repeated interactions in the future. Government regulation is another example of where game theory (Chapter 9) can help managers better understand and plan their actions.

CASE STUDY: *World Motors*

World Motors (WM) is a large US automobile manufacturing company. Eighty percent of its plants and sales are in the United States. WM is considering whether it should hire lobbyists to try to influence a variety of pending legislation. There are bills in Congress proposing to tighten automobile emission standards as part of the clean air laws, laws restricting union activity, increasing worker safety rules, reducing the miles-per-gallon standards on automobiles, and imposing import quotas. WM supports legislation that increases its firm's value. Each piece of pending legislation is evaluated using this criteria. The following briefly describes each piece of pending legislation.

Emission Standards   Tighter emission standards increase the cost of cars because they require more expensive emission-control devices such as more precise fuel injection systems and catalytic converters. One of WM's major competitors has a patent on a proprietary fuel emission system that allows cars equipped with its technology to meet the tighter emission standards. WM's competitor can install this proprietary technology on its cars cheaper than WM can install its device required to meet the higher emission standards.

Labor Union Laws   Labor laws increase the bargaining power of unions and thus their ability to extract higher pay or benefit concessions or provide lower amounts of work. The pending legislation proposes rules that make it harder for a local union to call a labor strike.

Worker Safety Rules   The Occupational Safety and Health Administration (OSHA) is proposing that plants making metal castings (such as automobile engine blocks) be equipped with air ventilation systems that replace the air in the plant more frequently than the current air-quality standard requires. Most of WM's engines are cast off shore, whereas most of its competitors cast their engine blocks in the United States.

Miles-per-Gallon Standards   To conserve gasoline, the federal government has mandated that automobiles produced by each company must comply with a minimum miles-per-gallon standard. These standards are met by producing lighter cars with more efficient fuel systems. New rules requiring tighter, more fuel-efficient vehicles are being proposed. The mix of WM's produced vehicles is very similar to those of its major competitors in terms of car sizes and their fuel efficiency. No auto company has any proprietary technology to improve fuel system efficiency.

Import Quotas   Citing the unfavorable trade deficit, the US government is considering regulations limiting the number of foreign cars imported into the United States.

Discussion Questions

1.   For each piece of proposed legislation, should WM support or oppose it?
2.   Which pieces of legislation do you expect WM's local labor unions to oppose or support?

Summary

This chapter presented a framework for understanding how government regulation affects a firm's strategy and hence the value of a firm. Chapter 8 and Figure 11.1 emphasize that government regulation is a key environmental factor affecting a firm's value. From changing the extent and nature of the competitiveness of markets, to regulating labor and capital markets, to taxation, governments touch virtually all aspects of organizations. In this chapter we discuss the managerial importance of government regulation and the benefits and costs of this regulation, and present an economic theory of regulation. This theory helps managers to understand better how various regulations come about and how to better participate in the markets for regulation more effectively.

Governments provide a system of laws and legal institutions that facilitate production and exchange; they also address various market failures. Legal institutions which define and enforce property rights lower transaction costs, thereby increasing both producer and consumer surplus. For example, the patent process increases the amount invested in research and development and ultimately the value of goods and services flowing from this R&D. Governments also seek to redress market failures such as externalities (air pollution), public goods (national defense), monopolies (antitrust laws), and informational failures (lemon laws).

It is important to realize that it is costly to enforce property rights and to resolve these market failures. To finance these beneficial functions, governments must raise revenues, usually through taxes. In the process of performing these functions and raising the revenues to finance them, governments also can redistribute wealth, which imposes costs on society. Government agencies, courts, and legislative processes must be financed out of taxes and fees. And besides the direct costs of operating governments, there are indirect costs imposed on society because of the wealth transfers that undoubtedly arise from most government actions. These wealth transfers are not merely zero sum games, in the sense that what one group receives another loses. Rather, there are transaction costs and deadweight losses (reduced consumer and producer surplus). In the process of transferring some of the pie from Peter to Paula, the pie is smaller because knowing that he might lose some of the pie to Paula, Peter has *less* incentive to make the pie as big as possible. Income taxes are another example. Paying, say, 30 percent of my income to the government in the form of income taxes causes me to engage in less work[18] and consume more leisure.

The economic theory of regulation is based on those who demand regulation (special interests) and those who supply it (politicians). Special interest groups who are made better off by the regulation will lobby in its favor, whereas those harmed will lobby against it. Politicians are made better off by brokering these transactions. They generate political support in the form of campaign contributions and votes from the various coalitions formed to support or oppose the regulation. The size and political power of a coalition depend both on how well it is organized to deliver votes and political contributions as well as how poorly organized is its opposition. People must feel strongly enough about the cause for either emotional or financial reasons to overcome their incentives to free-ride on the actions of others. If consumers are unorganized, they offer regulators little political support relative to an organized industry group. The outcome of the political process depends on the relative political support a special interest group can achieve. The more organized and the larger the special interest group, the more political support it can offer the regulator.

This theory of regulation has several important managerial implications. To develop strategies that both create value and capture value—it is not enough to build a better mousetrap—you must limit entry by competitors. The most direct way to limit competition is a government regulation limiting entry (for instance, zoning laws or taxi medallions). A less direct method for limiting competition is a government regulation that imposes a cost on certain competitors and potential entrants (for instance, health codes, worker safety standards, and pollution emission laws).

Another implication of the economic theory of regulation emphasizes the importance of coalition formation. Effective coalitions supply political support to politicians

---

[18]Suppose I am paid $20 per hour, H, and my utility function for work is $\$20H(1 - t) - 0.5H^2$. I have disutility of work that is quadratic. The tax rate on income is t. Taking the first derivative with respect to H and setting it equal to zero yields $H^* = 20 - 20t$. If $t = 0$, I work 20 hours. If $t = 50$ percent, I work only 10 hours.

(votes and campaign contributions). One way to increase political support is to expand the number of people supporting the regulation. Coalitions are like other types of organizations—they have organizational architectures. To make coalitions more effective within the political process, the coalition should be structured using the concepts of organizational architecture presented throughout this book. In particular, incentives to participate and performance measures can be used to reduce free-rider problems within the coalition.

Finally, regulation can have a material impact on a firm's value. Managers must decide whether or how to participate in the market for regulation. Remaining neutral does not guarantee that your firm's value is unaffected. Managers who avoid participating place their company's continued existence at risk and call into question their fiduciary responsibility to shareholders.

Review Questions

20–1. "When I bought this land, it was zoned only for farming. But the longer I live here, the more I resent the wealth transfer I'm paying to other landowners without such restrictions." Comment.

20–2. Adam Smith often is quoted as saying, "People of the same trade seldom meet together, even for merriment and diversion, but the conversation ends in a conspiracy against the public or in some contrivance to raise prices." If Smith is right, does this justify a role for government?

20–3. At a city council meeting, the Taxi Cab Owners Association argued for a fare increase. They note that the market price to buy or rent taxi medallions has been rising, and with these higher costs, profitability is reduced. Evaluate this argument.

20–4. In 1997 Canadian 2 × 4 lumber studs with two holes drilled in them (so that electricians could run wires) were categorized by customs agents as Category #4418 and free of any tariffs. If they had been categorized as #4407, they would have fallen under a quota system whereby only the first 14.7 billion board-feet of lumber Canada imports to the United States are duty free. The next 650 million are subject to a $50 export fee per 1,000 board-feet, and beyond that, a $100 fee. Roughly 15 billion board-feet of lumber is imported to the United States each year from Canada. If the Canadian 2 × 4 studs with holes are classified as #4407, this adds about $3,000 to the cost of a new home. Discuss the expected lobbying behavior of lawmakers from timber producing states (Montana and Alabama), the National Association of Homebuilders, and US lumber companies (for instance, Georgia Pacific).

20–5. What would be the impact of raising the federal minimum wage?

20–6. What are the benefits and costs of government regulation of air quality within cotton mills—for instance, specifying maximum levels of cotton dust (prolonged exposure leads to "white lung" disease)?

20–7. What are the benefits of government regulation of air pollution from automobiles? What are the costs of this regulation?

20–8. Sun, Netscape, and Apple have encouraged the government to pursue its antitrust suit against Microsoft; California, where these firms are headquartered, has joined the suit; yet Bittlingmayer and Hazlett (2000) find no evidence that these firms realize higher stock returns when antitrust actions are taken against Microsoft. How might you explain these facts?

20–9. Various politicians have proposed an Internet tax. One proposal would be to tax both outgoing e-mail and every web page downloaded. What groups are likely to support such a tax and what groups would oppose it?

20–10. Dubliners often complain that there are too few pubs in their city. At night pubs can be quite crowded and prospective customers often are turned away. Some Dubliners blame this pub "shortage" on the English who originally enacted laws restricting pubs centuries ago when they ruled Ireland. Is it appropriate to blame the English? Explain.

20–11. Proposed legislation would required 48-hour notification to all neighbors (within 150 feet of your property) for all pesticide applications that may be made to your property by trained, professional applicators. This legislation is labeled "environmentally friendly." Analyze the impact to the environment. (Note that pesticides come in varying strengths with more toxic products having a longer residual impact and thus requiring less frequent application.)

20–12. California (and other states) has passed laws that restrict the exercise of termination provisions in franchise agreements. Your boss says that he thinks this is a good idea—firms have an incentive to terminate profitable franchises and replace them with company-owned outlets. He asks what you think.

Chapter 21
Ethics and Organizational Architecture*

In December 1990, the head of Salomon Brothers' government-bond trading desk, Paul W. Mozer, submitted bids for 35 percent of a 4-year Treasury note auction. He also submitted another $1 billion bid under the name of Warburg Asset Management—a Salomon Brothers customer—but without the customer's knowledge or permission. The two bids, which represented 46 percent of the issue, violated the Treasury's auction rules limiting the amount sold to any single bidder to 35 percent of the issue.[1] Mozer repeated this tactic at Treasury note auctions in February and April.

---

*Portions of this chapter were published in C. Smith (1992), "Economics and Ethics: The Case of Salomon Brothers," *Journal of Applied Corporate Finance* 5:2, 23–28; and J. Brickley, C. Smith, and J. Zimmerman (1994), "Ethics, Incentives, and Organizational Design," *Journal of Applied Corporate Finance* 7:2, 20–30.

[1]In auctioning Treasury bonds, the US Treasury awarded bonds first to the highest bidder at their quoted prices, then they moved to the next-highest bidder. This process continued until the issue was exhausted. If the Treasury received multiple bids at the price that exhausted the issue, it allocated bonds in proportion to the bid size. But Treasury auction rules limited the amount of an issue sold to a single bidder to no more than 35 percent of the issue.

In April, Mozer became concerned that the Treasury was about to uncover his illicit bidding tactics. He admitted his unauthorized bidding in the February auction at a meeting with Salomon Chairman John Gutfreund, President Thomas Strauss, Vice Chairman John Meriwether, and General Counsel Donald Feuerstein. They apparently accepted his confession to a one-time, not-to-be-repeated mistake and no immediate action was taken.

In May, he again employed this bidding tactic in another Treasury note auction. In June, the Securities and Exchange Commission and the Justice Department issued subpoenas to Salomon and some of its clients for records involving bond auctions. Salomon then initiated a review of its government-bond operations and in August disclosed its unauthorized bids over the period between December and May.

By May 1992, the government had imposed a number of penalties on Salomon Brothers. The Treasury barred Salomon from bidding in government securities auctions for customer accounts. While allowing Salomon to retain its designation as a primary dealer, the Federal Reserve Bank of New York suspended its authority to trade with the bank for 2 months. The firm agreed to pay $122 million to the Treasury for violating securities laws and $68 million for claims made by the Justice Department. It established a $100 million restitution fund for payments of private damage claims that might result from approximately 50 civil lawsuits that the firm still faced stemming from the scandal. Monies in this fund not paid to the plaintiffs reverted to the Treasury, not Salomon.

Although these legal and regulatory penalties were substantial, they represent but a fraction of the total costs borne by the firm. In the week that the information about the unauthorized bids was released, Salomon Brothers' stock price dropped by one-third. This $1.5 billion fall in market value suggests that the market expected Salomon to bear significant costs as a result of these actions. Further, the drop seems too large to reflect simply fines and other expected legal and regulatory sanctions. In addition to the penalties and decline in the market value of Salomon's stock, all of the senior officers who knew of the illicit bids, but failed to act swiftly, were forced to leave the firm—and none of these individuals has since worked in a major securities firm. The case of Salomon Brothers illustrates that market forces can impose material sanctions on parties engaged in unethical behavior.[2]

Over the past decade, much public attention has been devoted to the issues of business ethics and corporate social responsibility. Politicians and social critics have deplored the materialism of the eighties and nineties; the media have treated the public to sensational accounts of corporate scandal; and business schools across the country offer courses in ethics.

In recent years, many United States corporations have responded by issuing formal codes of conduct, appointing ethics officers, and offering employee training programs in ethics. Such codes and programs cover a wide range of behavior, but most emphasize the following:

- Compliance with laws and statutory regulations
- Honesty and integrity in dealings with customers and other employees
- The avoidance of conflicts of interest with the company

Although few would quarrel with such aims, equally few proponents of such corporate initiatives have bothered to ask questions like the following: Are such codes and programs likely to be effective in deterring unethical behavior by corporate managers

---

[2]For a more complete discussion of the Salomon Brothers case, see C. Smith (1992), "Economics and Ethics: The Case of Salomon Brothers," *Journal of Applied Corporate Finance* 5:2, 23–28.

and employees? And, more pointedly, is the behavior enjoined by such codes consistent with the normal incentives of employees or managers, *given the current organizational architecture* of the firm?

Although it is recognized rarely in most public discussions of the subject, corporate ethics and organizational architecture are closely related. To increase the likelihood that businesspeople will behave ethically in their roles as managers and employees, corporate performance-evaluation systems, reward systems, and assignments of decision rights can be designed to encourage such behavior.

In this chapter, we present five basic arguments:

First, the term *ethics* is elusive. It has many different meanings, and these meanings vary across cultures and over time. The term *business ethics* can mean everything from corporate social responsibility to maximizing shareholder value.

Second, if the corporation is to survive in a competitive environment, it must maximize its value to its owners (primarily the stockholders). Taking care of other corporate stakeholders such as employees and local communities is important, but such care can be taken too far. If the firm reduces the owners' value, this care can imperil corporate survival.

Third, a company's reputation for ethical behavior, including its integrity in dealing with noninvestor stakeholders, is part of its brand-name capital; as such, this component of the firm's value is reflected in the value of its securities. By the same token, individuals' human capital—that which determines their future earnings prospects—is based in large part on their reputation for ethical behavior. In this sense, private markets provide important incentives for ethical behavior by imposing substantial costs on institutions and individuals that depart from accepted ethical standards. The Salomon Brothers trading scandal illustrates that the magnitude of these costs can be enormous.

Fourth, considerable emphasis in corporate ethics programs is put on what we would argue are misplaced efforts to change employees' preferences by attempting to persuade them to put the interests of the organization or its customers ahead of their own. Our approach, instead, accepts people's preferences as given and assumes they will follow their perceived self-interest. We focus on structuring the organization in ways that better align incentives of managers and employees with the corporate aim of maximizing value.

Fifth, even if ethical guidelines and training programs are unlikely to alter fundamental preferences, they have the potential to add value by more explicitly communicating the firm's expectations to its employees. To be most effective, however, such guidelines must be reinforced by formal aspects of the firm's organizational architecture.

Ethics and Choices

People make choices. A cornerstone of this book is that individuals make choices to maximize their utility. Individuals have preferences over just about everything and choose how much to spend on food, transportation, housing, charitable contributions, and other purchases. People choose how to allot their time between work, leisure, and charitable activities as well as how to allocate their time among alternative leisure activities—for example, watching television, playing golf, or attending a symphony concert. Economics is the study of how people make choices; it is basically a descriptive study seeking to explain people's observed decisions. In this book, our analysis has been descriptive, not normative. We have avoided suggesting what decisions people should make; we have not suggested that people should spend more time fund-raising for their local charities and less time watching television. We have argued that given people's preferences, they will tend to select those activities which maximize their perceived well-being (see Chapter 2).

This chapter is also about choices—in particular, choices among actions that are perceived to have ethical implications. Much of the study of ethics specifically focuses on how people should make choices: It is the study of those behaviors people should pursue. In large part, ethics is normative, not descriptive. When philosophers speak of ethics, they are dealing with the 25-century-old discipline that seeks to identify those behaviors which are right or wrong, good or bad, virtue or vice. Moral philosophers have been debating ethics since ancient times, and all religions involve statements of which behaviors are ethical and which are unethical. All major religions—Buddhism, Christianity, Confucianism, Hinduism, Islam, and Judaism—espouse the Golden Rule: "Do unto others as you would have them do unto you."[3] Western religions are based on the Ten Commandments, a code of ethical behavior.

Behaviors such as lying, cheating, stealing, and killing are almost universally viewed as wrong—except under mitigating circumstances (murder in self-defense is usually justifiable, for instance). However, certain behaviors viewed as wrong by some are viewed by others as right. For example, some people view abortion as wrong, whereas others view denying women the right to choose as wrong. Similar conflicts exist regarding birth control and a person's right to die. In these cases, there simply is no universally accepted code of ethics on which one can rely to assess right and wrong.

Business ethics seeks to proscribe those behaviors in which businesses should not engage. Such actions range from the giving or taking of gifts, bribing government officials, misrepresenting data, discriminatory hiring practices, and boycotting third parties. For example, some deemed it unethical for a company to do business in South Africa while that country practiced apartheid.

Business ethics and organizational architecture are interdependent. Organizational architecture, we have argued throughout this book, establishes incentives and thus affects the decisions managers and employees undertake. If it is important for businesspeople to behave ethically in their roles as managers and employees, it is important that the organization be structured to foster ethical behavior. In examining these issues, we first focus on external ethics policies controlling interaction between the firm and parties like customers, investors, and the local community. We then turn to internal ethics policies that deal with employees and managers.

Corporate Mission: Ethics and Policy Setting

What is the mission of the corporation, and does it involve ethics? Most people have a pretty good idea about what they mean when they describe an individual as "ethical." Most of us feel an emotional allegiance to the Golden Rule that urges us to treat others as we would have them treat us, and we value qualities such as honesty, integrity, fairness, and commitment to the task at hand. But what does it mean for a corporation to behave ethically? First, we have to understand what the term *ethical* means and then how it relates to the firm's mission.

Ethics

Ethics is a branch of philosophy. Western ethical philosophy can be traced back at least 2,500 years to Socrates, Plato, and Aristotle. These ancient Greeks searched for a

---

[3]W. Shaw (1991), *Business Ethics* (Wadsworth Publishing: Belmont, CA), 12.

generally understood set of principles of human conduct. Their treatises revolve around the terms *happiness* and *virtue*. Writing in the thirteenth century, St. Thomas Aquinas "argues that the first principle of thought about conduct is that good is to be done and pursued and evil avoided."[4]

There are numerous ethical theories, ranging from egoism (an act is correct if and only if it promotes the individual's long-term interests)[5] to utilitarianism (behaviors should "produce the greatest possible balance of good over bad for everyone affected by our action")[6]. Kantian ethics judges the nature of the act, not the outcome; Kant argued that only good deeds matter.[7] Adam Smith argued that through the invisible hand of market competition driven by self-interested traders, resources are directed to their most productive use and societal wealth is maximized. Ethical relativism holds "that moral principles cannot be valid for everybody; and . . . that people ought to follow the conventions of their own group."[8]

Even a cursory review of the major ethical philosophies yields two immediate observations. First, ethics is an enormous subject area that has engaged some of history's best minds. Second, despite considerable effort, there is no universally accepted philosophical consensus across time and societies as to which behaviors are ethical and which are not.

Furthermore, when it comes to defining the ethics of organizations like public corporations that encompass large groups of people, there is bound to be confusion. A corporation, after all, is simply a collection of individuals—or, more precisely, a set of contracts that bind together individuals with different, often conflicting, interests (see Chapter 10). In this sense, organizations themselves do not behave ethically or unethically—only individuals do. And if managers and employees are not pursuing their own interests, then whose interests are they serving? Their bosses'? The shareholders'? The board's? And what if there are major conflicts among these various interests?

Value Maximization

Economic Darwinism   Maximizing the firm's value is the mission most economists ascribe to managers. By maximizing the size of the pie, each party contracting with the firm can receive a larger slice—including shareholders, bondholders, managers, employees, customers, suppliers, charities, and local cultural institutions. If the firm faces competition for both inputs and outputs, the prices the firm pays for its inputs and receives for its outputs will be driven to competitive levels (Chapter 6), and the firm will not receive any abnormal profits. Economic Darwinism and survival were discussed in Chapter 1. Long-run survival in a competitive environment dictates that firms seek to produce products at the lowest possible cost. In the absence of barriers to entry, firms that survive in the long run are those that deliver products consumers want at the lowest cost. This means that managers must adopt policies that maximize the value of the firm—or, what amounts to the same thing, the net present value of future cash flows distributable to the firm's investors. If managers follow other policies that raise their

---

[4]J. Haldane (1991), "Medieval and Renaissance Ethics," in P. Singer (Ed.), *A Companion to Ethics* (Basil Blackwell: Oxford), 135.

[5]K. Bair (1991), "Egoism," in *A Companion to Ethics,* 197.

[6]W. Shaw (1991), *Business Ethics,* 49.

[7]Shaw (1991), 74.

[8]R. Brandt (1970), "Ethical Relativism," in T. Donaldson and P. Werhane (Eds.), *Ethical Issues in Business: A Philosophical Approach* (Prentice Hall: Englewood Cliffs, NJ), 78.

Corporate Philanthropy Comes under Fire

Pioneer Hi-bred International, the world's largest seed company, provided financial support for Planned Parenthood of Greater Iowa. But when right-to-life groups voiced strong objections and organized boycotts in the farming communities where the firm does business, the company was forced to withdraw its sponsorship. As *The Wall Street Journal* reported,

> "We were blackmailed," declares Pioneer chairman and president Thomas Urban. "But," he says, . . . "you can't put the core business at risk," even though the company concedes that canceling funding probably upset as many farmers as it appeased and the boycott didn't end.

Source: R. Gibson (1992), "Boycott Drive Against Pioneer Hi-Bred Shows
Perils of Corporate Philanthropy," *The Wall Street Journal* (June 10), B1.

---

costs, value-maximizing competitors enter, supply products at lower costs, and sell them at lower prices. Eventually, firms that deviate materially from value maximization will fail.

Role for Regulation   There are two important cases where value maximization leads to predictable resource misallocation. First, if the firm has monopoly power, it will reduce output and set price above long-run marginal cost (see Chapter 6). Second, if there are externalities—if firms' actions impose costs or benefits on uninvolved third parties—the firm has incentives to produce too much or too little of an item (see Chapters 3 and 20). For example, because no one has readily enforceable property rights to clean air, factories may produce too much air pollution. In both cases, one potential limiting factor in these problems is government regulation. Thus, if appropriate regulation constrains any resource misallocation from monopolies or externalities, firms can focus on value maximization within the bounds of the regulation.[9]

Compensating Differentials   Maximizing a firm's value requires managers to assess all costs and benefits of proposed actions accurately. Suppose George Wilson, manager of DisposeCo, is considering entering the business of the disposal of hazardous wastes. Employees exposed to such hazards usually demand a compensating wage differential to offset the higher risks of illness from such work (see Chapter 14). Therefore, when evaluating whether to enter this business, George must include these compensating differentials in his estimated costs.

Suppose Etsuko Kitagawa is CEO of PharmInc, which is considering the production of birth control products, a business with potential ethical dimensions. Some employees of the firm may have personal beliefs that conflict with this new business. Some of these employees might leave the firm; some might seek transfers to other divisions; others may require compensating differentials to stay; and employees with strong moral beliefs opposed to the company's position might even sabotage the project or misreport data to dissuade Etsuko from undertaking the project. In such cases, the costs of business decisions that some view as unethical are higher because of these higher compensating differentials, additional labor turnover, more pronounced incentive problems, and potential adverse publicity associated with such decisions.

---

[9]There are a number of issues implied by this brief discussion. In general, within the government, individuals are not always acting to maximize social welfare. Thus, even if appropriate regulation could reduce these problems in principle, there is no assurance that regulations are adopted to do so. See Chapter 20 and G. Stigler (1971), "The Theory of Economic Regulation," *Bell Journal of Economics* 2, 3–21.

Coca-Cola's View of Corporate Responsibility

In the 1996 Coca-Cola annual report, CEO Roberto Goizueta wrote, "Governments are created to help meet civic needs. Philanthropies are created to meet social needs. And companies are created to meet economic needs." In 1997 four Atlanta-based philanthropies donated $220 million to local causes. These four foundations held Coke stock valued at $7.6 billion.

Source: A. Ehrbar (1998), *EVA The Real Key to Creating Wealth* (John Wiley & Sons, Inc.: New York), 18–19.

Corporate Social Responsibility

One source of confusion about the corporate mission is the concept of "corporate social responsibility," which often is used interchangeably with corporate ethics. In 1969, Ralph Nader along with several other lawyers launched their Project on Corporate Responsibility with the following statement[10]:

> Today we announce an effort to develop a new kind of citizenship around an old kind of private government—the large corporation. It is an effort which rises from the shared concern of many citizens over the role of the corporation in American society and the uses of its complex powers. It is an effort which is dedicated toward developing a new constituency for the corporation that will harness these powers for the fulfillment of a broader spectrum of democratic values.

As Nader's statement suggests, the goal of some advocates of corporate social responsibility is nothing less than to change the objective function of the corporation. In Nader's view, the corporation is to be transformed from a means of maximizing investor wealth into a vehicle for using private wealth to redress social ills. The corporate social responsibility movement seeks to make management responsible for upholding "a broader spectrum of democratic values." Corporate support for such values could take the form of philanthropic activities, the provision of subsidized goods and services to certain segments of the community, or the use of corporate resources on public projects such as education, environmental improvement, and crime prevention. If all firms in the marketplace face the same social requirements, then the survival of any given firm is less of an issue. However, if some firms are exempted from redressing social ills, others' survival in a competitive environment is more in doubt.[11]

Economists' View of Social Responsibility

The conflict between Nader's and economists' views of the corporation is perhaps not as pronounced as it might appear. Corporations intent on maximizing firm value generally find it in their interest to devote resources to noninvestor stakeholders such as employees, customers, suppliers, and local communities. For example, a company with a large plant in an inner city might decide that investing corporate resources and personnel to improve area schools leads to better-trained job applicants, more productive employees, and lower-cost products. Giving money to the local university might benefit the firm by

[10]J. Collins (1979), "Case Study—Campaign to Make General Motors Responsible," reprinted in *Ethical Issues in Business,* 90.

[11]M. Jensen and W. Meckling (1978), "Can the Corporation Survive?" *Financial Analysts Journal* 34, 31–37.

Phone Companies Charged with Electronic "Redlining"

A coalition of public-interest groups recently charged that four leading telephone companies engage in "electronic redlining" by bypassing low-income and minority communities as they begin to build advanced communication networks. These groups asked the Federal Communications Commission to clarify its rules and issue a policy statement opposing discrimination in the building of such networks. By raising charges of redlining, these groups seek to persuade the firms to provide early, subsidized service to less profitable markets. A spokesperson for one firm pointed out that to achieve its plan of "wiring" half the state of California by 2000 "without raising rates," the company "must [first] bring the network to areas where it will generate some new business and revenues, so ultimately we can bring it to everyone in the state."

Source: M. Carnevale (1994), "Coalition Charges Phone Firms with
'Redlining' in Adding Networks," *The Wall Street Journal* (May 24), B6.

improving its R&D, increasing its access to top graduates, or enhancing cultural and educational opportunities for its employees. Improving the environment lowers the company's legal exposure to damage claims and also might reduce its wage bill to the extent that a cleaner local environment lowers the cost of attracting and retaining employees.

Maximizing firm value requires expending the firm's resources on members of each important corporate constituency to improve the terms on which they contract with the company, to maintain the firm's reputation, and to reduce the threat of restrictive regulation. More precisely, it means allocating corporate resources to all groups or interests that affect the value of the firm—but only to the point where the incremental benefits from such expenditures at least equal their additional costs.

Many managers are inclined to endorse Nobel Laureate Milton Friedman's prescription that the social mission of the corporation is "to make as much money for its owners as possible while conforming to the basic rules of society." As we have noted, some companies will find it in their shareholders' interest to "invest" in social causes of various kinds, but corporate investments that systematically fail to provide adequate long-term returns to private investors are wealth transfers that end up reducing social as well as private wealth.

Absent tax benefits, it usually is more efficient for the corporation to focus on creating wealth and to let its shareholders, employees, and customers choose the beneficiaries of their charitable contributions. By maximizing their shareholders' (or owners') wealth, corporations effectively enlarge the pool of individual (noncorporate) resources available for charity.[12]

People who advocate ever-larger corporate contributions to charities and social causes such as retraining displaced workers and environmental cleanup (without consideration of their own long-run profitability) are effectively calling for higher implicit taxes on corporations. If all companies are so taxed, the taxes are borne ultimately by shareholders in the form of lower returns to capital, by employees in the form of lower wages, and by customers in the form of higher prices. Thus, ironically, the potential social consequences of such an increase in corporate social responsibility are lower rates of economic growth, lower corporate values, lower employment, and even overall reductions in charitable donations (if reductions in donations by individuals more than offset the increases in corporate giving).

[12]J. Brickley (1988), "Managerial Goals and the Court System: Some Economic Insights," *Canada–United States Law Journal* 13, 79.

Milton Friedman's View of Corporate Social Responsibility

What does it mean to say that the corporate executive has a "social responsibility" in his capacity as businessman? If this statement is not pure rhetoric, it must mean that he is to act in some way that is not in the interest of his employers. For example . . . that he is to make expenditures on reducing pollution beyond the amount that is in the best interests of the corporation or that is required by law in order to contribute to the social objective of improving the environment . . .

[The problem in this case is that] the corporate executive would be spending someone else's money for a general social interest . . . [when] the stockholders or the customers or the employees could separately spend their own money on the particular action if they wished to do so.

Source: M. Friedman (1970), "The Social Responsibility of Business Is to Increase Its Profits," *New York Times Magazine* (September 13).

Corporate Policy Setting

Once a corporation has determined its mission, implementing the mission requires a set of operating policies. Again, ethical issues arise. It is futile to think that one can reduce excruciatingly difficult corporate policy issues to simple, universally applauded policy decisions. Consider questions like

- Should we use laboratory animals for product testing?
- Should we market infant formula in Central Africa?

Taxes and Corporate Philanthropy

One potential benefit to the owners of a firm from having the corporation donate to charities is a reduction in taxes paid to the government. Assume that both the corporate and personal tax rate is 50 percent. Suppose a corporation has profits of $5,000 before taxes and distributes all its after-tax profits to the shareholders as dividends. The firm has four equal shareholders who collectively wish to contribute $1,000 to a particular charity. If the firm makes the contribution, it is deductible from corporate income before taxes. Thus, the corporation has $4,000 of taxable income ($5,000 − $1,000), of which $2,000 is paid in taxes and $2,000 is paid to the owners who pay personal taxes on the dividends they receive. After personal taxes, each shareholder has $250 ($2,000 ÷ 4 × 50%).

Now suppose the shareholders donate $250 each to the charity and the corporation makes no contribution. The firm has pretax profits of $5,000, pays taxes of $2,500 (50% of $5,000), and distributes $2,500 to shareholders. Each shareholder receives $625 ($2,500 ÷ 4) before personal taxes, makes the contribution ($250), and has taxable income of $375 ($625 − $250). Each pays taxes of $187.50 and has after taxes $187.50 ($625 − $250 − $187.50). By having the firm make the charitable contribution, each shareholder has $62.50 ($250 − $187.50) more than when the shareholder makes the charitable contribution. When the firm makes the contribution, the gift shields $1,000 from corporate taxation.

These tax reduction gains for corporate philanthropy are most compelling when all the shareholders agree on the amount and nature of the donations. Gifts to charities not valued by some shareholders reduce these shareholders' welfare. Unfortunately, corporate stakeholders are unlikely to agree about which charities should receive corporate donations and how much each should receive. Customers, employees, or independent sales agents objecting to the firm's choice of charities may take their business or services elsewhere. Moreover, corporate managers do not have an obvious comparative advantage in choosing which charities to support. If it is time-consuming for managers to sort through charitable requests and make the selections, this is time that could have been spent on other activities that more predictably increase the firm's value. Thus, even with the tax advantage of corporate philanthropy, shareholders are not necessarily better off by having the firm make charitable donations instead of doing it themselves.

- Should we do business with a company that employs child labor in its Asian textile factory?
- Should we adopt different procedures for handling and disposing of hazardous wastes in Latin American plants than we use in the United States?
- Should we pay "fees" to expedite paperwork for export permits to an African market?
- Should we tow our obsolete North Sea oil rig to deep water and sink it?

Because there is no widely embraced definition of ethical behavior, these problems require careful analysis in establishing appropriate corporate policy. In particular, managers should be careful to collect data for estimating the total cost and benefits of alternative actions, including costs of adverse publicity, tarnished reputation, and lost customers. Although we cannot solve the above problems, we can suggest steps to help craft an appropriate policy.

Diversity of Input In questions with potentially contentious ethical implications, it is particularly important to obtain input from a broad cross section of potentially affected stakeholders in the firm. Here, diversity in perspective can be especially valuable in identifying potentially sensitive areas that require additional analysis prior to setting policy. Diversity in backgrounds can help the management team better assess the potential total costs of alternative policies.

Legal Standards It is important to understand the legal consequences of potential policy choices. The first, most obvious, question is—*Is it legal?* Yet this knowledge alone is generally far from sufficient to frame policy. For example, after the United States bombed Libya in 1986, some US banks faced a dilemma: The US Federal Reserve and the State Department required that Libyan funds in US banks be frozen. But the Central Bank of Greece simultaneously announced that under Greek law, any Libyan funds on deposit in Greece must be available on demand. If Libya had funds on deposit in Citibank's Athens branch and requested the funds, the bank would have to choose between violating US law or Greek law. Or, consider potential consequences of hiring child labor in a textile mill in Pakistan, even if it is legal there; some customers might object because the practice would be illegal in the United States or Europe.

Moreover, illegality may not be the determining factor. For example, it is doubtful that Federal Express would adopt a policy of firing a driver who violates the law by receiving a parking ticket. Hence, it is important to understand what sanctions might be imposed if a law is violated.

Finally, laws are not constant over time. For instance, although the 1995 Congress rolled back certain environmental regulations, some firms appear reluctant to take advantage of the entire range of newly allowed activities. They appear to be concerned that if the political pendulum swings back, they might face some future liability.

Business Norms In the business community, there are expectations in transactions that do not have the force of law but nonetheless represent expected behavior. These norms are rarely written down; knowledge of them accumulates primarily with experience. These issues can be especially important when entering a new market. For instance, when Lincoln Electric decided to expand into Japan, it encountered unexpected difficulties in selling its products. Lincoln's managers had not appreciated the strong preference accorded long-standing business partners by Japanese companies.

Adam Smith on Merchant Reputation

Of all the nations in Europe, the Dutch, the most commercial, are the most faithful to their word. The English are more so than the Scotch, but much inferior to the Dutch, and in the remote parts of this country they [are] far less so than in the commercial parts of it. This is not at all to be imputed to national character, as some pretend; there is no natural reason why an Englishman or a Scotchman should not be as punctual in performing agreements as a Dutchman. It is far more reducible to self-interest, that general principle which regulates the actions of every man, and which leads men to act in a certain manner from view of advantage, and is as deeply implanted in an Englishman as a Dutchman. A dealer is afraid of losing his character, and is scrupulous in observing every engagement. When a person makes perhaps 20 contracts a day, he cannot gain so much by endeavoring to impose on his neighbors, as the very appearance of a cheat would make him lose. When people seldom deal with one another, we find that they are somewhat disposed to cheat, because they can gain more by a smart trick than they can lose by the injury which it does to the character.

Source: A. Smith (1964), *Lectures on Justice, Police, Revenue, and Arms*, E. Cannan (Ed.) (Augustus M. Kelley: New York).

In special cases, these norms are codified. Adopting procedures developed by an external group to handle sensitive issues can be quite useful. For example, standards for using laboratory animals in product testing are established by the US Department of Agriculture, the National Institutes of Health, and the Public Health Service. Most organizations that undertake animal research adhere to these standards. Nongovernmental groups also participate in this process. For instance, firms in the motion picture industry frequently voluntarily adopt standards developed by the American Society for the Prevention of Cruelty to Animals. By simply stating that you adhere to the ASPCA code, a film company may be able to deflect much criticism.

Press Standard   Another useful device managers use in determining the ethical issues in setting corporate policies involves assessing the public's likely reaction. The example of Pioneer Hi-bred International's withdrawal of support for Planned Parenthood illustrates the often important interaction among ethics, public relations, and the media. Ethics consultants regularly counsel corporate managers to apply the press standard to help determine which behaviors are ethical. This criteria suggests that to judge whether an action is ethical, you should ask yourself whether you would be comfortable reading about your decision on the front page of the newspaper or seeing it reported on television.[13] Suggesting that a decision is a good idea only if it is kept confidential is quite likely to be a mistake. Remember, the business press is quite sophisticated. Counting on a questionable decision being overlooked or ignored might be characterized better as wishful thinking than thoughtful analysis.

Using publication of your behavior as an ethical benchmark for judging a decision highlights the linkage between ethical behavior and reputation. Below, we discuss market forces that create incentives for people and firms to behave ethically. The argument is that unethical behavior adversely affects reputation, and one way to assess a decision's

---

[13]Thomas Jefferson offered similar advice in a letter to Peter Carr: "Whenever you are to do a thing, though it can never be known but to yourself, ask yourself how you would act were all the world looking at you, and act accordingly." T. Jefferson (1785), in N. Beilson (Ed.), *Thomas Jefferson: His Life and Words* (1986) (Peter Pauper Press: White Plains, NY), 47.

reputational effects is to ask how it would read in *The Wall Street Journal* or the *Financial Times*.

Mechanisms for Encouraging Ethical Behavior

Ethical lapses generally are manifestations of conflicts of interest—incentive problems. As stated earlier, in most market exchanges, parties to the contracts have incentives to devise mechanisms to reduce contracting costs, thereby raising the prices they receive for their products or services. For example, when taking their firms public for the first time, founders of companies frequently retain large positions in the stock and voluntarily impose restrictions on their own future sales to help ensure that their interests are consistent with those of their new investors. Such arrangements effectively raise the price investors are willing to pay.

Likewise, external public auditors voluntarily prohibit themselves from owning stock in the companies they audit. By not owning any stock, auditors do not gain by withholding unfavorable financial information. This increases their independence from their clients, raises the value of the audit, and hence increases the price firms are willing to pay for it.

As we noted earlier, because reputational capital is an important determinant of future earnings, market forces provide incentives for firms and individuals to behave ethically. But the effectiveness of market forces in controlling conflicts of interest and enforcing contracts varies among different kinds of transactions. Among the most important characteristics of such transactions are the difficulty of ascertaining product quality prior to purchase and the likelihood that the transaction will be repeated.

Take the case of a buyer purchasing a product. For products whose quality can be determined at low cost prior to purchase, markets readily solve this problem. If buyers can cheaply monitor quality, they will do so. For example, a buyer negotiating a purchase of silver for Kodak can confidently and cheaply ascertain its quality by assay.

For some products, quality is virtually impossible to determine prior to purchase. For example, you can know the quality of an airplane ticket only after the plane has landed, it is parked at the gate, and you have deplaned and retrieved your luggage. Although

---

Signaling Quality by External Monitoring: Rice Aircraft

In 1991, Rice Aircraft Company became the first company in its industry to earn ISO 9002 accreditation, an international standard for quality management. This was a significant, highly visible signal of change within the firm. For in August 1989, Bruce J. Rice, CEO of Rice Aircraft, had pled guilty to fraud and was sentenced to 4 years in prison. The Defense Department forbade its contractors to do business with the company for 5 years, and annual sales fell from $15 million to $5 million. At this point, Paula DeLong Rice, Rice's wife, took over and set out to save the company by visibly and radically transforming it. She implemented a total quality initiative and provided classes in statistical process control, time management, and communications for all the company's employees.

Paula DeLong Rice's strategy appears to have been quite effective. Profit margins increased from 12 percent in 1992 to 27 percent in 1993 without benefit of price increases; order cycle time was reduced by 50 percent; and on-time deliveries increased 98 percent. Paula DeLong Rice, moreover, is now in great demand as a speaker on managing for quality.

Source: T. Pare (1994), "Rebuilding a Lost Reputation," *Fortune* (May 20), 176.

Evidence on the Penalty from Fraud

Researchers have examined the stock market's reaction to announcements of fraud charges against corporations. They specifically focus on cases where the damaged party does business with the accused firm—thus, they focus on frauds alleged against customers, suppliers, employees, and investors (but not damages to third parties such as in pollution dumping). The evidence suggests that in the days around the first announcement in *The Wall Street Journal,* the average fall in the firm's stock price is 1.58 percent. Thus, press reports of alleged fraud are associated with statistically significant and economically material losses in value. Moreover, these losses were much too large to be explained by legal costs and fines.

Source: J. Karpoff and J. Lott (1993), "The Reputational Penalty Firms Bear from Committing Criminal Fraud," *Journal of Law & Economics* XXXVI, 757–802.

sellers have incentives to cheat on quality when quality is expensive to measure, rational sellers will provide products of lower-than-promised quality only if the expected gains exceed the expected costs.

Repeat Sales   One important constraint on such cheating is the potential for future sales.[14] Moreover, corporations with established market positions and valuable brand names face higher costs of cheating and hence are less likely to cheat than startup firms. The costs of cheating on quality also are higher if the information about such activities is more rapidly and widely distributed to potential future customers. For example, in markets like the diamond trade in New York, which is dominated by a close-knit community of Hasidic Jews, cheating on quality is extremely rare.[15]

Warranties   Seller-provided product warranties are another mechanism to reduce the likelihood of cheating. Since sellers bear higher warranty costs if they cheat on quality, they have less incentive to cheat. Seller warranties will be most prevalent when product failures result from factors that are under the firm's control (such as manufacturing tolerances). In this case, warranties directly impose the cost of failure on the parties who have the most control over product quality or failure. However, when failures are due primarily to factors that are under the customers' control (such as the way the product is used or maintained), the moral-hazard problem will be greater and warranties are less useful as a quality-assurance mechanism.

Third-Party Monitors   In some markets, specialized information services monitor the market, certify quality, and help ensure contract performance. For example, *Consumer Reports* evaluates products from toasters to automobiles, the *Investment Dealer Digest* details activities of investment bankers, and A.M. Best Company rates financial conditions of insurance companies. These third-party information sources lower the costs for potential customers to determine quality and so increase the expected costs of cheating.

In credit markets, specialized credit information services like Moody's and Dun & Bradstreet perform both a monitoring and an information dissemination function. The

---

[14]L. Telser (1980), "A Theory of Self-Enforcing Agreements," *Journal of Business* 53, 27–44.

[15]Other examples of ethnic communities, like the Chinese in Singapore, support the view that choosing trading partners from within one's own ethnic community economizes on the costs of contracting. J. Landa (1981), "A Theory of the Ethnically Homogeneous Middlemen Group: An Institutional Alternative to Contract Law," *Journal of Legal Studies* 10, 349–62.

existence of such intermediaries provides an opportunity for the firm to guarantee quality. For this reason, corporate issuers pay Moody's to have their debt rated over the life of the bond issue. By issuing rated public debt, a firm lowers the cost to other potential corporate claimholders (including potential customers) of ascertaining the firm's financial condition.[16]

Disclosure   The required level of disclosure in markets can also be important in determining quality. For example, a study of two wholesale used-car markets with different levels of required disclosure found higher prices in the market with more required disclosure.[17] The ability to "precommit" to disclose information reduces the potential information disparity between buyer and seller and so reduces the discount buyers apply to their demand prices. Also, eBay.com, the online auction web site, encourages participants to write messages about their experiences with their partner in the transaction. This provides future participants with more information about the performance of a potential trader and thus enables them to have more confidence in their transactions. Moreover, by creating this feedback mechanism, eBay provides sellers with a means of developing a reputation. This improves the performance of auction participants.

Ownership Structure   Incentives to provide high-quality products vary across ownership structures. Take the case of franchise companies such as fast-food and lawn-care firms. Such companies typically franchise some units rather than own all their stores in order to take advantage of the incentive benefits of decentralized ownership while retaining scale economies in advertising and brand-name promotion.

Yet outlets that have little repeat business create a special problem. The franchise owners of these stores have an incentive to cheat on quality because they can benefit from a steady stream of one-time sales while reducing the reputation of the entire organization; this is another example of the standard free-rider problem. At these locations, the central company is more likely to own the unit than to franchise it, in part because a salaried manager has fewer incentives to cheat on quality.[18]

Companies with large amounts of debt in their capital structure can face a significant probability of financial distress. Such firms are more likely to cheat on quality than financially healthy firms because repeat sales are less likely. Therefore, some firms "bond" product quality by adopting conservative financial policies. Since financial distress is more costly for firms that market products where quality is difficult to ascertain, such firms have incentives to adopt financing policies that lead to a lower probability of financial distress—policies such as lower leverage, fewer leases, and more hedging.

Contracting Costs: Ethics and Policy Implementation

In our examples of Barings Bank (Chapter 1), Sears Auto Centers (Chapter 2), and Salomon Brothers (Chapter 21), none of these firms had formal corporate strategies of engaging in unethical behavior. Rather, their ethical problems arose from controlling the

---

[16]L. Wakeman (1983), "The Real Function of Bond Rating Agencies," *Chase Financial Quarterly* 1, 18–26.

[17]H. Grieve (1984), "Quality Certification in a 'Lemons' Market: An Empirical Test of Certification in Wholesale Used-Car Auctions," working paper, University of Rochester.

[18]One study finds that franchise companies in lines of business with more repeat sales at individual units (e.g., lawn-care and beauty shops) are likely to franchise a higher percentage of total units than franchise lines with less repeat business (such as motels, car rental agencies, and restaurants). J. Brickley and F. Dark (1987), "The Choice of Organizational Form: The Case of Franchising," *Journal of Financial Economics* 18, 401–20.

behavior of individuals granted particular decision rights within the firm. They are examples of incentive problems within firms. Chapter 10 described the general incentive problem as the difficulty in making corporate managers and employees perform in ways consistent with the aims of the firm's owners. In addressing these internal ethical issues, this section makes two key points: First, the incentive problem of shirking or of opportunistic actions by an employee often is labeled an ethical lapse; and second, if all employees reduced their opportunistic actions (behaved more ethically), contracting costs would be lower.

To review the incentive problems that can arise with performance evaluation and monitoring, take the simple case of Alice Brown's hiring Olaf Kolzig to paint her house. Especially in performing tasks that are hard to monitor by inspection after the job is completed, such as surface preparation (sanding, scraping, and priming), Olaf has incentives to shirk—or, at least, to do a job that may not be as thorough as Alice might like. Of course, Olaf also will be prompted by other considerations to do a good job. It may be a matter of private conscience; that is, Olaf's sense of self-worth might be tied up with the quality of the workmanship, and violating such a self-imposed standard would impose major "costs" in the form of a tarnished self-image. Or Olaf might be constrained by the desire to maintain his commercial reputation (and, though it might take some time for a poor job of surface preparation to show its effects, quality eventually will reveal itself). As we noted earlier in this chapter and discussed in Chapter 10, reputation is an important contributor to the capitalized value of one's expected future earnings.

But because the prompting of conscience and the desire to maintain a reputation are neither universal nor constant, it's impossible for Alice to know the extent to which Olaf is bound by such considerations. Alice faces an information problem: When hiring Olaf, she does not know the kind of surface preparation she will get, nor will she be capable of ascertaining that until well after the job is done and the bill is paid.

To reduce her vulnerability in such circumstances of informational asymmetry, Alice likely will ask for a list of references (if Olaf has not already provided one). Such references should give Alice a better basis for assessing Olaf's time horizon and the importance he attaches to reputation. Olaf also might offer, or Alice might insist on, a one-or-more-year warranty on the job. (As discussed above, such common practices as the use of warranties, third-party references, and credit checks play an important role in reducing contracting costs in the business world.)

But despite such assurances, some uncertainties about Olaf's level of performance remain. For example, will he be around to make good on the warranty if the paint peels in a year? Perhaps Olaf has heavy debts and is about to declare personal bankruptcy. Or perhaps the job he does for Alice will be Olaf's last before he embarks on a new career painting still lifes and family portraits.

As a consequence of the possibility of shirking and her own remaining uncertainty, Alice effectively reduces the price she is willing to pay. Or, to state the converse of this proposition, if there were some means for Olaf to provide Alice with complete assurance about his level of commitment, Alice would be willing to pay a higher price for the job.

Three points emerge from this simple example. First, let's assume Alice was able to design a perfect contract; for the sake of argument, let's say that Alice had a camera which enabled her to observe Olaf's activity at random intervals (and Olaf knew she had it) and that Alice was able to structure a pay schedule based on the observed effort. Even if she were able to devise such a monitoring and reward system, it would clearly not pay her to do so. The cost to Alice of writing, of administering, and, most important, of

---

A CEO's View of Verbal Contracts

Most of our products were custom-made. Customers called in their orders over the phone. The orders, ranging in value from a few hundred dollars to tens of thousands of dollars, generally required delivery of goods within one or two days. It meant we would usually begin production before receiving a confirming purchase order. (This was before faxes.) The customer's word alone was enough. In my 20-year stint as CEO, not once did a customer go back on it. Unusual? Not at all. Without such trust, business couldn't be conducted. Similar transactions happen every day. . . . [W]e learned there are two ways to go: An eye for an eye, or do unto others what you would have them do unto you. In business, the latter philosophy is far more common, simply because it makes things work better.

Source: H. Aaron (1994), "The Myth of the Heartless Businessman," *The Wall Street Journal* (February 7), A14.

---

monitoring compliance with such a contract would be substantial—perhaps even greater than the value of the painting job itself. Thus, as this simple illustration is meant to point out, in most cases it does not pay to attempt to eliminate all possible shirking; because of the costs of writing and monitoring compliance with contracts, it is efficient to leave some slack in the system. As explained in Chapter 10, the *optimal* amount of shirking or opportunistic behavior by an agent is not zero.

Second, the *expected* level of opportunism or shirking—which, again, is greater than zero—is priced in the contract. Thus, the principals do not bear the full costs of opportunistic actions by their agents. Typically, at least some of these costs are shifted back to agents in the form of lower prices for their services or products.

Third, higher ethical standards among agents, whether corporate employees or participants in market exchanges, would lead (over time) to a reduction in the level of *expected* opportunistic behavior and hence a reduction in contracting costs. As a result, there would be more transactions (including more jobs created) and higher prices paid to agents by principals (including higher corporate wages). This would occur not only because of a reduction in the amount of shirking but also because the costs of writing and monitoring contracts would fall. Both principals and agents would be better off. Economist Jack Hirshleifer makes this last point: "Altruism economizes on the costs of policing and enforcing contracts."[19] In discussing economic development, one writer lists low business ethics as an important factor impeding growth. During the late nineteenth century, such practices as confidence men selling shares, bankruptcy with concealed assets, and squandering capital increased the difficulty of raising capital to finance new ventures such as the construction of the railroads.[20]

The retired CEO's story in the accompanying box illustrates an important point about the economic consequences of ethics: Ethical standards within an organization—or within an economy—affect the resources devoted to ensuring contract compliance and hence, help determine overall productivity. If everyone voluntarily were to reduce opportunistic behavior (such as withholding important information about product quality), then resources devoted to monitoring and enforcing exchanges could be used in other, more productive pursuits.[21]

---

[19]J. Hirshleifer (1977), "Economics from a Biological Viewpoint," *Journal of Law and Economics* 20, 28.

[20]T. Cochran (1964), *The Inner Revolution* (Harper & Row: New York).

[21]E. Noreen (1988), "The Economics of Ethics: A New Perspective on Agency Theory," *Accounting, Organizations and Society* 13, 359–369.

Codes of Ethics

We view important aspects of the corporate ethics problem primarily as problems of controlling incentive problems. And generalizing from the above discussion, there are several potential ways to control them. One way to control incentive problems would be to get corporate managers and employees to voluntarily adopt higher, more stringent ethical standards. A second is to use contracts that better align the interests of managers and employees with those of shareholders. Examples of such contracts in corporations are executive or employee stock options, bonus plans, and profit-sharing arrangements (see Chapter 15). (Such contracts also will act to reinforce voluntary codes.) Both more cost-effective incentive contracts and higher ethical standards can be expected to lead to lower contracting costs, greater corporate efficiency, higher corporate values, and greater social welfare.

As mentioned earlier, many companies and most professions have written codes of conduct, and some companies also have educational programs dealing with ethics for their employees. Such codes and programs regularly emphasize the following[22]:

- Employees must obey the laws and observe statutory regulations.
- Customer relations in terms of the reputation and integrity of the company are of great importance.
- Employees must support the company's policies to customers.
- Conflicts of interest between the company and the employee must be avoided.
- Confidential information gained in the course of business must not be used improperly.
- It is improper to conceal dishonesty and protect others in their dishonesty.
- Advice to customers should be restricted to facts about which the employee is confident.

Why have corporations adopted such codes? The most cynical view is that a corporate code of ethics is nothing more than a document that helps the firm defend itself against charges of illegal behavior. Sentencing guidelines issued by the U.S. Sentencing Commission in November 1991 strongly encourage corporations to establish and communicate compliance standards and procedures for employees and other agents through training programs and publications. For example, when an individual is found guilty of wrongdoing, the organization also might be vulnerable to federal sanctions such as fines. These penalties can be reduced by more than 50 percent simply by demonstrating that the organization has a compliance program that meets the Sentencing Commission's standards.[23] A compliance program consists at least of a code of ethics and a training program. These federal sentencing guidelines thus have blurred the line between legal and ethical issues.

But corporate ethical codes, as we just have argued, also have the potential to perform the economically valuable function of reducing the costs of monitoring and enforcing contracts. To the extent that they reduce managerial and employee opportunism, better ethical standards enhance the organization's reputation and hence increase shareholders' wealth.

---

[22]These codes are not unique to the United States. For example, similar codes are observed in Australian firms. B. Kaye (1992), "Codes of Ethics in Australian Business," *Journal of Business Ethics* 11, 857.

[23]N. Gilbert (1994), "1-800-ETHICS," *Financial World* (August 16), 20–25.

The critical questions, however, are these: *Are ethical codes effective in deterring unethical behavior? And if they are, how and why are they effective?*

Altering Preferences

There are two basic ways to view the function of corporate codes of conduct in reducing opportunistic behavior. One way is by appealing directly to employees' consciences, attempting to instill in them loyalty to the organization and its goals. An economist might describe this as an attempt to alter people's "preferences."

Now, there is undoubtedly some value to this approach. As we noted earlier, personal codes of conduct and the guilt one suffers in violating such codes are undeniably constraints on many people's behavior. As described in Chapter 2, individuals' utility functions contain many nonpecuniary factors, including conscience and guilt. As the following statement by Nobel Laureate Kenneth Arrow suggests, subjective concepts like ethics and morality surely are consistent with the economist's notion of rational self-interest:

> *Certainly one way of looking at ethics and morality . . . is that these principles are agreements, conscious or, in many cases, unconscious, to supply mutual benefits. . . . Societies in their evolution have developed implicit agreements to certain kinds of regard for others, agreements which are essential to the survival of the society or at least contribute greatly to the efficiency of its working. . . . The fact [that] we cannot mediate all our responsibilities to others through prices . . . makes it essential in the running of society that we have what might be called "conscience," a feeling of responsibility for the effects of one's actions on others.[24]*

The problem in applying this logic to corporate management, however, is that such "agreements to supply mutual benefits to others" are likely to be too amorphous to serve as a practical guide to individual behavior in large public companies with diffuse stock ownership. If employees are understandably unmoved by serving an anonymous group of "wealthy" shareholders, then who precisely are "the others" whose interests their morality is intended to serve? And what should employees do in those cases, noted earlier, where there appear to be (at least short-run) conflicts between the interests of the corporation and those of its noninvestor constituencies? After all, as we have seen earlier, the effective management of scarce resources often means saying no to the requests or desires of some employees, customers, and local communities. Moreover, the entire situation is complicated by the fact that the fundamental goal of the corporation—making money for its owners—is viewed as immoral or unethical by many advocates of corporate ethics.

Given this confusion about, and even conflict between, some professed ethical objectives and the goal of the corporation, we are skeptical about organizational attempts to instill conscience or a sense of guilt in their employees—that is, to alter employees' preferences. To the extent that these corporate ethics programs are aimed at trying to bring about material changes in employees' preferences, we are skeptical that they will succeed.

Consider the transfer-pricing problem faced by corporations with multiple divisions that buy and sell to one another. In Chapter 17, the firm value–maximizing solution to this problem was described as setting the transfer price to the buyer at the seller's opportunity cost of producing one more unit. But let's assume (as tends to be the case) that managers of the selling division have better information about their costs than the purchasing division's managers.

---

[24]K. Arrow (1974), *Limits of Organization* (W.W. Norton: New York), 26–27.

In such a situation, to the extent that a manager's compensation is based on divisional profits, the selling division's managers have the incentive to set the transfer price substantially above opportunity cost. In such a case, managers' pursuit of their own division's profits will come at the expense of total firmwide profits (because the managers of the buying division will purchase less than the optimal number of units).

Now, if adoption of a code of ethics somehow were to succeed in inducing divisional managers to reveal their private information about costs, units within the firm would be transferred at opportunity cost, and the firm's profits would be increased. But as long as division managers are being *paid* based on the profits of their own divisions, they are unlikely to reveal their actual costs.

Most economists generally assume that individuals' preferences are given and for the most part are difficult to alter. We thus suggest that managers, rather than attempting to alter preferences, should redesign the firm's architecture to change their employees' incentives to take certain actions. For example, in the above case, senior management might attempt to find a means of giving the divisional managers some stake in the profitability of the division to which they "sell" the product. A common, though only partly effective, solution to this problem is to give divisional managers stock options with payoffs tied to the overall value of the company as well as bonuses for divisional performance.

Education

Even if corporate codes of ethics are unlikely to either change preferences or eradicate self-interest, such codes still can play a potentially important role in modifying behavior. Up to this point, we have assumed that corporate managers and employees know the "right thing" to do to promote the interests of the organization. But this assumption does not always hold. In many cases, managers' and employees' uncertainty about ethical standards—or how to live up to them in practice—may well be a greater corporate problem than their failure to work hard or to act in accordance with standards that are well established and clearly defined.

We earlier described the confusion about the corporate mission stemming from the aims and actions of the social responsibility movement. Another potential source of confusion resides in the variability of ethical standards. What might have been acceptable behavior 10 or 20 years ago may not be so today. Social changes such as those brought

---

The Appearance of Impropriety at Citibank, Argentina

A newspaper article reported that H. Richard Handley, the president of Citibank Argentina, had sold portions of Citibank's Argentine assets to some of his friends at "what now look like bargain prices." Citicorp spokesmen dismissed that talk as "Monday morning quarterbacking," pointing out that, at the time of the first sales, there was an equal chance that the value of Argentine investments would rise or fall thereafter.

It is not important whether the terms of this particular set of transactions were appropriate or not; they may well have been deals that furthered important business interests of Citicorp in Argentina. What this case highlights, however, are the costs associated with the *potential* for self-dealing by corporate managers and the importance of stating and enforcing policies for business dealings on less than an arm's-length basis. The structure of this deal has forced Citibank to defend its actions to employees, investors, and regulators.

Source: *Miami Herald* (April 24, 1994).

about by movements as disparate as civil rights and women's rights, on the one hand, and corporate restructuring, on the other, clearly have altered conceptions of socially accepted behavior. Moreover, the progressive globalization of product markets and a more diverse workforce are increasingly forcing corporate employees to recognize and adapt to differences in national or regional cultural expectations.

Given this large and, in some ways, growing uncertainty about what constitutes ethical behavior within large organizations, corporate codes of ethics and training programs potentially play an important educational role by communicating corporate expectations to employees effectively and by demonstrating to them how certain kinds of behavior reduce the value of the firm. For example, misrepresentations of products and services to customers for short-term gain can be shown to reduce the value of the firm by hurting its reputation and thus lowering its brand-name capital. Moreover, in the process of globalizing and thus dealing with customers worldwide, companies might be forced to respond to the increasing cultural differences—or absence of shared expectations—among their managers and employees by providing more explicit communication of standards and expectations.

Besides issuing a clear set of rules governing employee relations with consumers, corporations also are likely to benefit from communicating guidelines for dealings among managers and employees within the firm. For example, many companies develop their executives by rotating them through a series of jobs. The resulting management turnover can undermine informal agreements among managers and employees. Explicit, corporatewide communication of expectations can reduce uncertainty about enforcing unwritten agreements and thereby increase internal efficiency.

Virtually all professions—medicine, law, accounting—have professional ethics codes. Prospective candidates must pass entry exams that test their understanding of these codes. Most professional codes contain detailed descriptions of behaviors that reduce the value of the profession's services. For example, professional accountants are prohibited by their code of ethics from serving on the board of directors of their client firms. Such memberships reduce the appearance of independence of the auditor when rendering an opinion on the client's financial statements. If one accountant is caught not disclosing a known financial fraud, this reduces the value of other accountants' audit opinions. Thus, professions, like firms, have incentives to monitor their members for ethical breaches.

Corporate Culture

More generally, codes of conduct and training programs in ethics have the potential to contribute to the building and maintaining of a value-based corporate culture. Like corporate ethics, *corporate culture* is an ill-defined term, but as discussed in Chapter 11, it generally encompasses such factors as the ways in which work and authority are organized within a company as well as organizational features such as customs, taboos, company slogans, heroes, and social rituals. For example, a slogan like that of Federal Express—"When it absolutely positively has to be there overnight"—helps communicate the message that employees are expected to focus on meeting delivery schedules and that this focus will be recognized and rewarded by the organization. Singling out role models or heroes for special awards is another way of communicating the values of the company. Similarly, social rituals such as training sessions and company parties can help disseminate information by increasing interaction among employees and encouraging discussion of ethical standards. Indeed, the *process* by which a code of ethics is produced and the training programs through which these standards are communicated

CASE STUDY: *The Tylenol Tragedy and J&J's Credo*

Johnson & Johnson sells a diverse array of products, including baby care, first aid and surgical products, prescription drugs, and industrial products. It operates in a decentralized fashion through 190 companies in 175 countries. Each business unit has its own focused mission. Some units employ thousands of people, and others, as few as six. Each business unit is organized around a given market and a given set of customers. In 1943, General Robert Wood Johnson, who led J&J in its metamorphosis from a small family-owned business to a worldwide enterprise, articulated the company's basic philosophy in the J&J *credo*. It has the following basic elements:

- Our first responsibility is to our customers—doctors, nurses, patients, and mothers—to supply high-quality services and products at reasonable prices.

- We are responsible to our employees to respect their dignity and job security in a safe working environment; compensation must be fair and adequate.

- We are responsible to our communities to support education, good works, and charities and bear our fair share of taxes.

- Our final responsibility is to our stockholders. To provide a sound profit, we must make investments in R&D, new products, and facilities. When we operate according to these principles, the stockholders should realize a fair return.

One manager described how the *credo* affects J&J managers:

All of our management is geared to profit on a day-to-day basis. That's part of the business of being in business. But too often, in this and other businesses, people are inclined to think, "We'd better do this because if we don't, it's going to show up on the figures over the short term." The credo allows them to say, "Wait a minute. I don't have to do that. The management has told me that they're really interested in the long term, and they're interested in me operating under this set of principles. So I won't."

In 1982, J&J was stunned when seven people died in the Chicago area after taking Tylenol capsules that had been adulterated with cyanide. Tylenol (capsules and tablets), manufactured by McNeil Consumer Products division, was one of J&J's most profitable businesses and accounted for 8 percent of J&J's sales. Subsequent investigation determined that tampering with the capsules occurred outside of J&J's facilities. McNeil's operating managers took immediate action, withdrawing all Tylenol capsules from the United States and replacing them with tablets (not involved in the tampering.) They stopped producing Tylenol capsules and began redesigning the packaging to make the capsules tamperproof. This redesign process took several months. J&J's profits fell by over $100 million and its stock dropped from over $46 at the time of the announcement of the first death to below $39.

Press coverage of the unfolding tragedy was extensive. In an interview, a McNeil executive was asked whether employees would receive any remuneration during the time it would take to redesign the packaging and reconfigure the production line. Rather than simply state that no decision had been made, he made the commitment that no employees involved in producing Tylenol would be laid off over this period. Similarly, a reporter probing the costs of this packaging redesign asked an executive how much this would increase Tylenol's price. Although the issue had not been discussed, he announced that the product price would not be increased.

Discussion Questions

1. Explain how the *credo* helped guide the managers in the McNeil division.
2. Most discussions of J&J's handling of this tragedy have been laudatory, yet J&J's stock price fell by more than $7. Does this mean that the stock market thinks J&J's managers reacted poorly?
3. Analyze the decision not to raise Tylenol prices.
4. Discuss the advantages and disadvantages of listing shareholders as fourth priority in J&J's *credo*, especially in light of the Tylenol tragedy.
5. Suppose the packaging redesign and retooling required a longer time period, extensive cost, and that all Tylenol products were affected—not just capsules. Might McNeil managers have taken a different set of actions and how might the *credo* have guided these decisions?

are potentially as important as the code itself in developing and maintaining the desired corporate culture.

Nonetheless, to create the value-based or consumer-focused organization that many companies seek to become, these less tangible aspects of corporate culture must be reinforced by more tangible actions. That is, the more formal organizational systems that partition decision rights and evaluate and reward performance, as well as sanctions for unethical behavior, all must be internally consistent and designed to encourage firm value–increasing behavior.

Summary

Business ethics is the study of those behaviors that businesspeople should or should not follow. This book is also about business behaviors, in particular, about how firms are organized to motivate and control the behavior of self-interested employees to maximize a firm's value. The focus of this book has been primarily descriptive. Assuming that people are motivated by self-interest, how are they expected to behave under alternative organizational architectures? Ethics is primarily normative: It is about how people should behave. Managers often endorse the ethical philosophy espoused by Adam Smith. In Smith's view, through private ownership of property, self-interest, and competition, a society's resources are put to the best use and produce the highest quantity and quality of goods and services at the lowest prices—value maximization.

Value maximization requires that all costs and benefits be considered. If a particular business decision conflicts with an employee's or customer's own personal belief, that person is worse off. If enough people are affected, costs are imposed on the firm through compensating wage differentials, higher turnover, and forgone sales.

Moral philosophers and all religions have debated ethics since ancient times and yet we still do not have a universally accepted code of ethics. Witness the current debates over abortion or the use of animals for product testing. There is considerable confusion about the meaning of corporate ethics. It appears unlikely that a universally accepted code of business conduct will emerge. The corporate social responsibility movement has focused less on raising corporate ethical standards than on transferring shareholders' wealth to other parties such as customers, employees, local communities, charities, or cultural institutions. Although other corporate stakeholders are important, if the corporation is to survive, it must maximize its value to its owners—a goal that in turn promotes efficient use of scarce resources.

Many of the issues raised in this chapter are recurring themes in the popular press and are likely to continue to be in the future. You may be called on to resolve a sexual harassment case, an environmental issue, or a product recall dispute. There is no doubt that at least once during your career you will be faced with a key decision that some will label a major ethical dilemma. This chapter seeks to demonstrate that the same basic framework we presented in the earlier chapters can provide guidance for understanding issues involving ethics.

A number of important managerial implications are raised by the discussion in this chapter.

First, behaviors that others classify as unethical impose real costs on the firm by lowering the firm's brand-name capital, especially when they are reported in the media. These costs from reduced reputation include forgone sales or higher costs because parties outside the firm are less willing to contract with the firm. Many ethical problems are similar to other incentive problems discussed throughout the text, and much of the same analysis of incentive problems can be used to analyze ethical problems.

Second, ethics has many different meanings, ranging from making firms socially responsible (transferring wealth from the firm to other parties) to trying to make employees less self-interested. Another use of ethics means informing employees that certain behaviors impose large reputational costs on the firm, and hence the firm will impose sanctions on employees found engaging in such actions.

Third, mechanisms arise to constrain unethical behavior. Like contracting costs, costs of unethical behavior create incentives to minimize these costs. Managers should understand these mechanisms to ascertain under what conditions unethical behavior is most likely. For example, extra care should be exerted when structuring deals with firms in financial distress.

Fourth, decisions that have major ethical dimensions almost invariably involve potential adverse publicity and a decline in the firm's brand-name capital. How the firm responds to the press affects how the public perceives the issue. In dealing with the media, the following application of our framework usually is helpful:

- News reporters are pursuing their own self-interest—not yours. They are trying to maximize their value, which usually means increasing their audience in order to sell more newspapers or TV and radio advertising. Reporters know more about their job than you do.

- Having access to the media is valuable. Developing brand-name capital is quite costly to do through advertising. Use your access to the media to present the firm's position in a credible, honest way. Lying or misrepresenting the facts to the media is likely to backfire because reporters have the incentive and skills to uncover these misrepresentations—again, because such uncovered lies make juicy stories.

Fifth, ethics programs occasionally are used to try to alter people's preferences. Senior managers concerned about the ethical conduct of their employees would do better to spend less time searching, like Diogenes, for "an honest man." Rather, they should pay more attention to the incentives created by the firm's organizational architecture (the three-legged stool). As discussed in Chapter 2, it is unlikely that Sears would have faced widely reported consumer indignation and legal sanctions from unnecessary auto repairs had it anticipated the (quite predictable) incentives its compensation plan would give its employees to overcharge customers. Incentives work. If the compensation plan pays employees for unethical behavior, then unethical behavior is exactly what the company will get. Our approach suggests recognizing the potential incentive problems and then redesigning organizational architecture—not people's preferences. Managers must structure their subordinates' incentives to ensure that they do not reduce the total value of the firm.

Sixth, ethical guidelines can highlight behaviors that increase, as well as behaviors that reduce, a firm's value. Codes of conduct, rather than trying to change employee's preferences, can communicate to employees those value-reducing actions that will not be tolerated and would lead to sanctions imposed on the employee, in addition to those value-increasing actions that are encouraged and would be rewarded.

Suggested Readings

T. Cochran (1964), *The Inner Revolution* (Harper & Row: New York).

T. Donaldson and P. Werhane (Eds.) (1999), *Ethical Issues in Business: A Philosophical Approach,* 6th edition (Prentice Hall: Englewood Cliffs, NJ).

M. Jensen and W. Meckling (1978), "Can the Corporation Survive?" *Financial Analysts Journal* 34, 31–37.

L. Nash (1991), "Ethics without the Sermon," *Harvard Business Review* (November–December).

L. Newton and M. Ford (1998), *Taking Sides: Clashing Views on Controversial Issues in Business Ethics,* 5th edition (Dushkin/McGraw-Hill: Guilford, CT).

E. Noreen (1988), "The Economics of Ethics: A New Perspective on Agency Theory," *Accounting, Organizations and Society* 13, 359–369.

W. Shaw (1999), *Business Ethics,* 3rd edition (Wadsworth Publishing: Belmont, CA).

W. Shaw and V. Barry (2000), *Moral Issues in Business,* 8th edition (Wadsworth Publishing: Belmont, CA).

C. Smith (1992), "Economics and Ethics: The Case of Salomon Brothers," *Journal of Applied Corporate Finance* 5:2, 23–28.

B. Toffler (1986), *Tough Choices: Managers Talk Ethics* (John Wiley & Sons: New York).

Review Questions

21–1. Seventh Generation of Colchester, Vermont, manufactures and markets "environmentally friendly" household products—vegetable-based, chlorine-free laundry products and nontoxic cleaners. Seventh Generation used to sell its products through natural-food outlets and direct mail catalogs. In 1992, the CEO of Seventh Generation, Jeffrey Hollander, concluded that to continue to grow, his company had to appeal to a broader range of customers. The only way to do this was to lower his prices. He concluded, "The research that says people will pay more for socially responsible goods simply isn't true."

Hollander reformulated his products and compromised on environmental purity. Environmentally harmful phosphates and chlorines were still excluded, but cheaper petroleum-based cleaning agents were substituted. These changes allowed a dish detergent's price to be lowered from $3.50 to $2.50. While margins are lower, sales are up 20 percent. Also, the new formulas work better.

Seventh Generation is criticized by some of its old customers for paying less attention to core customers and substituting profits for idealism. Hollander says to his critics, "They not only have greater access to our products, they also can get them cheaper."

   a. Do you agree with Hollander that people aren't willing to pay more for socially responsible goods? Explain why or why not.

   b. Is Seventh Generation behaving ethically by substituting petroleum-based cleaners into its products?

   c. What additional information would you request to help Seventh Generation address its ethical questions?

21–2. Ben and Jerry's Homemade Inc. has received much favorable press for its Rainforest Crunch ice cream. It uses official rain forest nuts and berries and all natural ingredients; it also sends a percentage of profits to charities. However, another flavor, Cherry Garcia, contains sulfur dioxide preservatives, and other flavors use margarine, not butter. What are the problems a firm faces if it is "politically correct" in some products but not others?

21–3. The Body Shop has been widely noted for its ethical stands in its business: natural cosmetics, "Products for People Tested by People," and First World wages for Third World products. Recently, Jon Entine published an analysis of the Body Shop in *Business Ethics,* alleging false advertising and other ethical lapses. Would you expect such charges to have more or less of an impact on a company like the Body Shop that touted its business ethics than if the same charges were leveled against a competitor who made fewer claims?

21–4. The Body Shop started its business by developing an extensive network of franchisees. Recently, franchisees have complained about the company's competing with their franchises through direct catalog sales and over the Internet. How does an expansion of Internet and direct catalog selling affect the Body Shop?

21–5. Eastman Kodak charged that the Fuji Corporation of Japan was illegally dumping film in US markets. It asked the US government to investigate and impose sanctions on Fuji for its unfair practices. But the world film market is dominated by Kodak and Fuji. If the government agrees to sanction Fuji, Kodak will obtain significant market power in the US film market. Is it ethical for Kodak to attempt to use the government to undermine its competitor?

21–6. Wilmorite Corporation owned a large tract of land and proposed erecting a large, modern enclosed shopping mall south of town. The mall was opposed by an environmental group that argued that the land had areas with standing water that waterfowl used in their spring and fall migrations. The challenges resulted in a substantial delay in the development of the land; more extensive environmental impact statements had to be prepared and plans had to be redrawn.

a. Was this development ethical?

b. The largest contributor to the environmental group happened to own Southtown Mall, an older strip mall across the road from the proposed new mall. Was his contribution to the environmental group ethical?

Chapter 22
Organizational Architecture and the Process of Management Innovation

H umana Hospital, a 555-bed institution in Dallas, Texas, fundamentally reorganized the way it was structured for delivering care to its patients. Beginning in 1990, it applied a process called *reengineering* to develop patient-focused care, enhancing the delivery of health care and reducing costs.[1]

Hospital costs in the 1980s and early 1990s had increased faster than inflation, thereby precipitating a health care crisis. The parties that paid for health care services—private individuals, employers, insurance companies, and the government—bore the higher expenses. To stem the rising health care costs, the government began reimbursing hospitals using a fixed fee for each procedure rather than paying for total costs incurred. And large employers, through their insurance companies, began to pressure local health care providers by threatening to require that their employees be treated only at those hospitals and by those physicians that better controlled costs. As a result, hospitals initiated cost containment programs and began competing for patients.

Prior to reengineering, Humana employed the traditional hospital architecture wherein patient care was provided primarily by functionally organized individuals:

[1]Details of this example are from J. Lathrop (1991), "The Patient-Focused Hospital," *Healthcare Forum Journal* (July–August), 17–20.

physicians, nurses, and a score of specialists drawing blood samples and taking x rays and administering EKGs. Most large hospitals are organized around numerous, small, clinically focused nursing units with dedicated staffs and large centrally dispatched services—physical therapists, phlebotomists, and transporters, for instance. They have 60 to 100 department heads and seven to nine layers of management between CEO and bedside caregiver. Patient care units generally are designed with excess capacity; this enables them to handle all but the sickest patient with the most complex needs. Yet 60 to 80 percent of all medical procedures are for routine services (chest x rays, basic lab tests, EKGs). Therefore, infrastructure costs and idle time account for as much as 75 percent of costs for simple procedures. For example, in a typical 650-bed hospital only $.16 of each health care dollar spent reflects direct patient care. Scheduling, documentation, and idle time account for $.63 out of every dollar. The remaining $.21 covers occupancy costs, transportation, management, and supervision.

As a result of increased pressure to attract patients and control costs, some hospitals embraced process reengineering and the patient-focused care movement was born. Nursing roles were reevaluated and tasks reassigned. After the reorganization, patient care was delivered through teams, where two-person caregiver teams of nurses and technicians were responsible for most procedures performed on each patient.

The following characteristics describe a hospital with patient-focused care[2]: At admission, each patient is assigned to a unit and given a standard protocol—sometimes called a *care map*—which details the standard set of tests and procedures to be followed by the caregivers. Instead of documenting every procedure and test performed, the staff documents only exceptions to standard protocols. Exception-based charting reduces documentation by as much as 50 percent.

Each caregiver is trained to provide basic bedside nursing, basic x ray, respiratory care, EKGs, and the like. Routine care is provided by nurses, medical technicians, laboratory technicians, phlebotomists, and other staff working in the two-person teams assigned to patients. The team "owns" the patient: They admit the patient, document the care, serve the meals, change linen, and even clean the room after discharge. During a three-day stay, patients interact with an average of 15 employees instead of 55. Rather than being transported throughout the hospital for routine tests and waiting while they are performed, patients remain in their rooms for most tests.

Traditional hospitals are arranged by level of acuity and broad medical category. For example, cardiac intensive care units and orthopedic intensive care units are two separate acute care units specializing by medical category. Patient-focused care locates patients by the type of tests, therapies, and health care resources required. Wireless technology (pagers and cellular phones) allows more flexibility in how patients are grouped. Instead of a 15- to 20-bed dedicated unit, 50- to 100-bed patient centers provide more effective service lines to be developed.

Large centralized service bureaucracies are dismantled and their resources disbursed under the control of the patient centers. Each patient service center has satellite lab, radiology, and pharmacy units. The caregivers are cross-trained to perform many of the functions that formerly had been centralized. The extent to which decentralized satellites are efficient depends on the costs of the equipment. Basic x rays are decentralized, but CAT scans are not: Small inexpensive, simple-to-operate x-ray machines are available whereas CAT scan equipment is still quite expensive and requires more specialized training to operate.

---

[2]C. Schartner (1994), "Principles of Patient-Focused Care," *Journal of the Healthcare Information and Management Systems Society* 7, 11–15.

Advocates of patient-focused care emphasize that achieving these benefits requires a constellation of organizational changes. Unless the old hierarchy of specialized departments is dismantled and replaced with a new structure with new reporting mechanisms and incentives, many of the benefits of patient-focused care will remain unrealized. That is, the elements of reorganization are complements—not substitutes.

> *The kind of improvement our health care system requires cannot be obtained by isolating a re-design initiative to any one of the patient-focused care principles. We need a more comprehensive effort that understands the complex interrelationships between the principles.*[3]

This example of patient-focused care illustrates how one management innovation, reengineering, was applied within a specific hospital. Many organizations successfully implemented reengineering programs. Others tried it with less success. Besides reengineering, other management innovations have come and gone. This chapter examines the general topic of management innovations—why they are popular, why some succeed while others fail, and how managers implement changes in their organizational architecture.

Management Innovations

The titles currently displayed in the business section of any good bookstore present a seemingly endless array of management prescriptions: total quality management, reengineering, benchmarking, activity-based costing, just-in-time production, quality circles, outsourcing, economic value added, balanced score cards, empowerment, self-directed teams, venturing, incentive compensation, cycle-time reduction, strategic alliances, 360-degree performance reviews, matrix organizations, downsizing, learning organizations, market-based management, core competencies, groupware, and so on. Given this cornucopia of management innovations, one might expect corporate executives' appetite for novelty to show signs of satiation. Yet judging from consulting fees, book sales, and the proliferation of seminars, the corporate thirst for managerial innovations appears to be unquenchable.

Take the cases of reengineering and total quality management, two of the more popular management techniques of the 1990s. One survey of 500 United States managers from large companies reported that 76 percent of the companies represented in the survey at least had tried TQM and that 69 percent had employed some form of reengineering.[4] Such remarkable adoption rates spawned legions of management consultants, many of whom can be counted on to claim that TQM or reengineering is essential for the success of most if not all companies. There is even a highly coveted national prize, the Malcolm Baldrige National Quality Award, which is presented each year to the most successful application of the principles of total quality management.

But for all the hype, a significant number of TQM and reengineering programs have failed to live up to expectations. Press stories have expressed growing dissatisfaction with reengineering programs, to the point where the founders of the movement, James Champy and Michael Hammer, have shifted the focus of their consulting efforts away from downsizing initiatives and toward the pursuit of growth opportunities. And reports of discontent with TQM began to appear in the early 1990s. For example, a Gallup poll of over 1,200 corporate employees in 1990 reported that although over half

---

[3]Schartner (1994), 15; and P. Milgrom and J. Roberts (1995), "Complementarities and Fit: Strategy, Structure, and Organizational Change in Manufacturing," *Journal of Accounting and Economics* 19, 179–208.

[4]"Missions Possible," *The Globe and Mail* (September 13, 1994), B22.

said that quality was *top priority,* only one-third considered their companies' programs to be *effective.*[5] A survey of 300 large companies conducted by *The Wall Street Journal* in 1991 found that executive satisfaction levels with TQM were only 40 percent.[6] Some companies, such as McDonnell-Douglas Aircraft and Florida Power & Light, abandoned their TQM programs. After winning the Baldridge Award in 1990, Wallace Company filed for bankruptcy in 1992.[7] Finally, a study of 584 United States, Canadian, German, and Japanese firms in 1991 concluded, "Many businesses may waste millions of dollars a year on quality-improvement strategies that don't improve their performance and may even hamper it."[8]

Such mixed reviews are not confined to TQM and reengineering. Evidence of the rise and fall of a larger sample of recent management innovations is presented in Figure 22.1, which displays the percentage of published business articles that mention a particular management technique in a given year. For example, as displayed in the first graph in Figure 22.1, almost 1.5 percent of all business articles published in 1993 contained the words *total quality management* or *TQM.* The graph also shows that, after reaching a peak in 1993, citations of TQM have fallen sharply. A similar pattern can be observed for *reengineering,* which achieved peak prominence in 1995. And two much-noted management preoccupations of the 1980s, *just-in-time production* and *quality circles,* have lost virtually all press coverage. The last four graphs—*benchmarking, activity-based costing, outsourcing,* and *economic value added*—represent still more recent innovations. Benchmarking and ABC are starting to fade; EVA and outsourcing continue to rise.[9]

If history offers any guide to the future, management techniques will continue to wax and wane. And new techniques—many of them reviving elements of older innovations—will doubtless appear.[10] The rise and fall of such management techniques raise a number of important questions:

- What explains the popularity of these management innovations?
- Why do they often fail to produce their touted benefits?
- How can managers tell if a particular technique is appropriate given their firm's circumstances?
- What can managers do to increase the likelihood that an adopted technique will be successful?

We use our organizational architecture framework to address these questions. Thinking in terms of organizational architecture can help managers evaluate expected benefits and costs of management innovations for their own companies. As we argue below, virtually all management techniques focus on a specific problem confronting the organization, while

---

[5] *The Wall Street Journal* (October 4, 1990), B1.

[6] F. Bleakley (1993), "Best Laid Plans: Many Companies Try Management Fads," *The Wall Street Journal* (July 6), A1.

[7] J. Mathews (1992), "The Cost of Quality," *Newsweek* (September 7), 48–49.

[8] G. Fuchsberg (1992), " 'Total Quality' is Termed Only Partial Success," *The Wall Street Journal* (October 1), B7.

[9] "FirstSearch," an online referencing software, was used to gain access to ABI/Inform, a database containing over 800,000 articles in 1,000 US and international publications on business and management topics. To calculate the percentage of articles published, the total number of business articles in a year was determined by searching for the following: *business, management, firm,* or *managers.*

[10] The reader is cautioned against reading too much into Figure 22.1. Some of these management techniques still may be used actively, but under another term. The press publishes articles about "new" topics. "Old" topics are more difficult to attract the attention of journalists. However, the articles counted in Figure 22.1 are not just articles that describe the particular technique, but rather are articles that simply mention the technique.

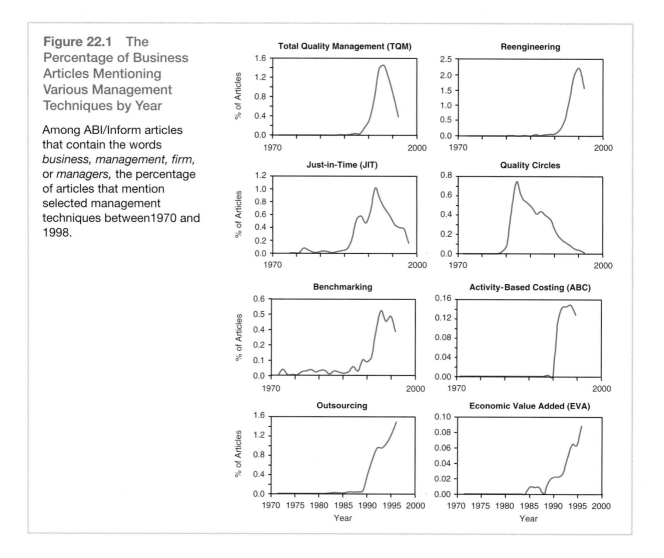

Figure 22.1 The Percentage of Business Articles Mentioning Various Management Techniques by Year

Among ABI/Inform articles that contain the words *business, management, firm,* or *managers,* the percentage of articles that mention selected management techniques between 1970 and 1998.

ignoring possible effects of their proposed solution on other aspects of the firm. In our terms, such programs typically affect one or two legs of the organizational architecture stool without careful consideration of their effect on the others. As one obvious example, a too rigid insistence on just-in-time principles can lead to big customer service problems; adopters of JIT at least should consider increases in the staffing (and perhaps the incentive pay) of their customer service department to accommodate such change. The organizational architecture framework we develop in this book can help managers considering one potentially valuable set of organizational changes to identify other facets of the organization that also require attention and complementary adjustment.

The Demand for Management Innovations

With dramatic shifts in the business environment created by expanding deregulation, more rapid technological change, and more intense global competition, whole classes of firms face new challenges (recall Figure 11.1). For many companies, what once might have been appropriate architectures began to show signs of obsolescence. As a growing number of large, once-successful companies lose opportunities to smaller, more flexible (and in some cases, overseas) competitors, the opportunity costs of ill-structured organizations are reflected in declining shareholder returns. This in turn increases the demand for management prescriptions that enable companies to respond more effectively to their new environment. Thus, we believe the demand for management innovations (or *fads,* as some refer to them) can be viewed as a rational economic response by executives to changes that cause aspects of their organizational architectures to become obsolete.

The Rise of TQM[11]

Take the case of the broad-based adoption of TQM principles in the 1990s. Before TQM, the standard approach to ensuring product quality was to *inspect it in.* Inspection stations and quality-assurance inspectors were placed along the production line to weed out defective units. Statistical sampling methods were used to draw random samples from each batch and, if an unacceptable number of substandard units was detected, the entire batch would be rejected.[12] Defects were stored waiting to be reworked or scrapped. In some cases, if market demand exceeded production over a period, marginally defective products might be released with problems corrected by the field service organization under warranty arrangements.

By the mid-1980s, two factors worked together to change this traditional approach to quality within many industries. First was a change in technology: The cost of detecting problems and monitoring production using new computerized instrumentation fell sharply relative to the cost of maintaining quality via manual inspection or warranty repairs. Increases in the cost of labor (including fringe benefits) made the manual identification of errors and field service repairs considerably more expensive than doing it electronically. Instead of manually detecting and remedying defects after production, improved instrumentation allowed identification and correction of problems during the manufacturing process.

A second key factor in the rise of TQM was the expansion of worldwide competition. Besides price wars, competition also took the form of a push for higher-quality products. Customers shifted to more reliable products, many of whose producers were based overseas. Perhaps the most dramatic case of such quality-driven competition was the auto industry in the early 1980s. Once Japanese companies gained price competitiveness against American automakers, they focused their attention on achieving quality advantages.

Thus, the total quality movement was spurred both by lower costs of identifying defects and increased global competition. To reduce defects, companies redesigned their products to require fewer different parts, making it easier to maintain tighter controls on the quality of their suppliers. Product designers redesigned parts that failed. Production

---

[11]This section draws on J. Zimmerman (2000), *Accounting for Decision Making and Control,* third edition, (Irwin/McGraw-Hill: Burr Ridge, IL), Chapter 14.

[12]Statistical quality control (SQC) consists of a set of statistical methods used to determine if a particular repetitive manufacturing process is in or out of control. By employing common statistical procedures (means and standard deviations), normal variation of the process is established. If products exceed the normal bounds, the process is deemed "out of control" and subject to management investigation.

processes were changed to reduce defects. Robots and additional instrumentation in the manufacturing process ensured more uniform production.[13]

Other Innovations

Although many TQM programs initially were started to improve the tangible aspects of product and service quality for external customers, TQM programs expanded to include efforts to improve both the quality and the efficiency of processes and services for internal as well as external customers. In this sense, the boundaries between TQM and another popular innovation, reengineering, have become somewhat blurred.

Reengineering   One way of distinguishing between the two movements is to view reengineering as accomplishing a set of major, one-time changes,[14] as opposed to TQM's widely heralded emphasis on continuous improvement. Like TQM, the demand for reengineering stems from both technological changes and heightened competition in the 1980s. As Michael Jensen argued, we have experienced what amounts to a "third industrial revolution" over the past several decades.[15] One major by-product of this wave of technological change has been more rapid product obsolescence and, as a consequence, overcapacity in certain global industries. Many of the major restructurings, consolidations, and downsizings associated with reengineering can be seen as value-adding (if not entirely voluntary) managerial responses to excess capacity.

JIT   Technological advances in instrumentation, computers, and telecommunications also have been a key element in the rise of just-in-time production. Such advances have allowed factories to be redesigned along the continuous-flow lines required by JIT. Suppliers' computers are linked electronically to their customers' computers, and electronic order processing is commonplace. But, if JIT has been made possible by technological change, its demand also reflects a major change in market conditions. Large corporate customers increasingly are demanding that their suppliers deliver products in continuous, small-order lot sizes—in part to reduce their own inventories and hence to improve efficiency.

Outsourcing   As part of the process of shedding excess assets and capital to increase operating efficiency and shareholder value, many US companies also pursued a refocusing strategy during the 1980s and 1990s. Along with selling or spinning off unrelated businesses, outsourcing of previously internal functions was a widely practiced method for sharpening corporate focus. As we noted in Chapter 18, outsourcing involves a fundamental change in organizational architecture. It reassigns ownership of certain assets, decision rights, and, in many cases, the employees who exercised them from inside the

---

[13]Other factors contributing to TQM were factory automation and flexible manufacturing that allowed firms to broaden their product lines and to change products more rapidly. Because of these factors, at any time, there are more products and more new products on the factory floor. This means there is likely more specific knowledge on the shop floor now.

[14]As defined by Hammer and Champy, reengineering is "the fundamental rethinking and radical redesign of business processes to achieve dramatic improvements in critical, contemporary measures of performance, such as cost, quality, service, and speed." M. Hammer and J. Champy (1993), *Reengineering the Corporation: A Manifesto for Business Revolution* (Harper Business: New York), 32.

[15]M. Jensen (1993), "The Modern Industrial Revolution, Exit, and the Failure of Internal Control Systems," *Journal of Finance* 48, 831–880.

company to another firm. Recall the Chapter 18 example in which Eastman Kodak sold its mainframe computers to IBM and contracted with IBM to do much of Kodak's data processing. Such partnerships have been prompted in part by changes in the information technology that has made it easier to identify and communicate with partners outside the firm. Also, more flexible production technologies have reduced asset specificity, thus reducing the costs of outsourcing. Besides allowing management to focus more of their attention on those internal activities where they have a comparative advantage, outsourcing also enables companies to acquire goods and services from other firms at lower prices by allowing the latter to specialize and achieve economies of scale.

Why Management Innovations Often Fail

As we noted earlier, many companies adopting new management techniques have been less than enthusiastic with the outcomes. We now explore potential explanations for this dissatisfaction—and more generally, for the tendency for successful innovations to rise sharply and then (often just as abruptly) to fall out of favor, thus prompting skeptics to brand them as *fads*.

Marketing

The demand for management solutions is met predictably by responses from consulting firms, academics, and management gurus (and these groups are not mutually exclusive). Frequently, a consultant working with a client firm identifies a specific set of problems and recommends a package of changes. Especially if implementing the changes appears to improve the operation of the client firm, the consultant quite naturally next seeks to identify other potential clients who are in similar circumstances. Producing a successful management innovation is difficult, but the rewards can be enormous. One challenge potential innovators face is that property rights in management innovations are generally ill-defined. Because of this, labels are quite important. Innovators frequently attempt to brand their innovation with a new term like *reengineering, benchmarking,* or *organizational architecture.*[16]

Setting Inappropriate Expectations   One potential explanation for managerial dissatisfaction is that consultants create inappropriate expectations in marketing management innovations. They frequently claim that their technique will increase productivity and raise profits. But if competing firms in the industry also adopt the technique, any abnormal profits are competed away. As we argued in Chapter 8, a basis for sustainable profits cannot be an asset that competitors can replicate. Thus, although effective and productive, adoption is not followed by higher profits. Here, the appropriate comparison is not future profits against past profits, but future profits with the innovation versus future profits were it not adopted.

A second explanation focuses on the incentives of purveyors of a given management innovation to emphasize expected benefits while understating costs. This is not to suggest that management consultants are less honest or less forthright than the rest of us. Yet as proponents as well as beneficiaries of change, consultants are likely to provide

---

[16]Good acronyms appear helpful (TQM, ABC, MBO). The Holy Grail in this business appears to be having a new acronym registered (EVA®).

detailed information on companies where their techniques appeared to work but less information on those where their techniques failed. And having acquired knowledge and experience in addressing a set of specific corporate issues and problems, consultants are understandably less informed about other aspects and concerns of the organization. As we argue later, it is the potential linkages or interdependencies among these sets of problems that frequently lead to unintended and undesired consequences when making organizational changes.

Of course, managers recognize that consultants have incentives to present an optimistic view of their services. And most managers attempt to adjust for such bias when deciding whether, or to what extent, to implement a consultant's recommendations. But even so, the corporate failure rate in adopting management innovations obviously would be lower if managers had a low-cost, unbiased source of information at their disposal.

Quality Is Not Free   In some instances, management consultants have offered advice that simply defies economic logic. Perhaps the most egregious example is noted quality expert Phillip Crosby's assertion, contained in the title of his 1980 book, that *Quality Is Free*. On page one Crosby writes,

> *If you concentrate on making quality certain, you can probably increase your profit by an amount equal to 5 to 10 percent of your sales. That is a lot of money for free. . . . What costs money are the unquality things—all the actions that involve not doing jobs right the first time.*[17]

Included in Crosby's list of the costs of "not doing things right the first time" are unnecessary or excessive costs associated with prevention of defects (design reviews, supplier evaluations, tool control, preventive maintenance), quality monitoring (prototype tests, receiving inspection and test, packaging inspection), and the costs associated with preventable failures (including the costs of redesign, engineering change orders, rework, scrap, product warranty, and product liability).

But what does Crosby really mean when he says, "Quality is free"? Taken literally, the statement suggests that managers can achieve substantial reductions in product failures, and in the costs associated with preventing them, at no cost to the organization. But this can't be the intended meaning for, as Crosby surely knows, improving product quality clearly requires a major commitment of management time as well as other corporate resources. Defects must be discovered, their causes investigated and corrected, employees must be trained in quality methods, and products redesigned. In fact, improving quality can be quite costly.

Rather than think of quality in Crosby's terms, it makes economic sense to view a TQM initiative as an investment of corporate resources with an uncertain future return in the form of lower costs or higher revenues, or both. Improving product quality usually lowers the cost of reworking defects along with inspection costs, warranty costs, and customer complaints. And, to the extent the firm's brand-name capital is higher when product quality is increased, product demand and hence revenues will increase. But, given the commitment of resources necessary to achieve such increases in quality, the critical question for senior management becomes: *Does the expected rate of return justify the initial and ongoing investment, including the management effort and other costs associated*

---

[17]P. Crosby (1980), *Quality Is Free* (Mentor: New York), 1.

Figure 22.2   The Relation between Quality and Firm Value

Firm value increases as quality increases because consumer demand increases and costs decline. Beyond Q*, the cost of increasing quality is greater than the manufacturing cost savings and the increased consumer demand. Maximizing quality does not maximize firm value. Too much quality lowers value.

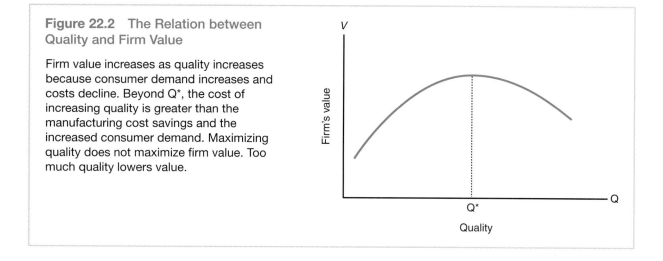

with changing the organization?[18] Crosby asserts that the answer to this question—for all companies and for arbitrarily large commitments, as far as we can tell—is yes. We are unconvinced.

The assertion that quality is free also obscures the reality that it typically requires larger investments of corporate resources to attain higher levels of quality and that, at some point, all companies face diminishing marginal returns from further investments in quality programs. This is turn implies that there is generally an "optimal," or value-maximizing, level of quality.

Figure 22.2 illustrates the relation between quality and the firm's value. At relatively low levels of quality (where the curve is rising), increases in quality lead to increases in firm value in two ways: by reducing production, inspection, and warranty costs and by increasing consumer demand for, and the prices commanded by, the products. But, at some point (represented by Q*), the returns to further investment in quality-increasing measures fall below acceptable levels. Ultimately, it is the company's customers who must pay for the cost of enhanced quality. At some point, the costs of additional improvements in quality exceed the premium customers are willing to pay—along with any further production cost savings. To illustrate, wine lists at many restaurants contain a wide selection encompassing a range of prices; yet even though the quality of the highest-priced wine presumably is commensurate with its price, few diners seem to place enough value on the higher quality of the $275 bottle of 30-year-old imported Chateau Margeaux to order it instead of the $20 bottle of the 3-year-old domestic house wine. Value-maximizing managers will want to undertake only those quality improvements where the incremental benefits exceed the incremental costs of enhanced quality.

Perhaps one way to make sense of Crosby's statement would be to argue that some managers systematically underestimate the total costs of poor quality. For example, some companies might place too much emphasis on short-term financial measures. Or, if managers are about to retire, they might be reluctant to spend money today on quality

---

[18]P. Lederer and S. Rhee (1995), "Economics of Total Quality Management," *Journal of Operations Management* 12, 353–367.

programs that yield benefits after they retire. But this is just the standard horizon problem that confronts all decisions where the expected benefits of present outlays span several periods. In this sense, quality programs are no different from capital investments, R&D, or advertising. Successful firms find ways to control these horizon problems.

An alternative explanation is that some managers underestimate the costs of low quality out of ignorance. Those managers who fail to appreciate the costs of reduced consumer confidence in their products will underestimate the benefits of reducing defects and so underinvest in programs to improve quality. In cases where such myopic behavior is common, companies might benefit from educational programs focused on the importance of quality.

But regardless of whether underinvestment in quality might be attributed to ignorance or distorted incentives, quality still is not free. Decisions to improve quality, like all corporate investment decisions, require accurate estimates of all expected costs and benefits. It is just as dangerous to underestimate the costs of quality programs by arguing that quality is free as it is to underestimate their benefits. As many companies likely have discovered, overinvestment in quality-improvement programs can end up destroying just as much value as underinvestment. Management's job is to find the value-maximizing level of quality—neither too much nor too little—based on the firm's markets and internal capabilities.

Underestimating Costs of Change

Another important reason TQM and other management innovations can prove ineffective is that some managers underestimate the costs of change. As we saw earlier, changes in market conditions, technology, or government regulation can affect optimal architecture. But as we argued in Chapter 11, organizational change is by no means a costless process. In evaluating the merits of an organizational restructuring, it is important to assess these costs in addition to its benefits.

First, there are direct costs. The new architecture has to be designed and communicated. Changes in reporting structures and performance-measurement systems frequently impose costly changes on the firm's accounting and information systems; what might appear to be a minor change in the performance-evaluation system sometimes becomes a quite costly project for the firm's information systems and accounting departments. (Just look at the reported costs of identifying and correcting Y2K problems.)

Second, and at times more important, are indirect costs. Most changes in architecture will affect some employees positively but others negatively (recall our discussion in Chapter 19). Thus, attitudes toward change can be expected to vary among employees, creating incentive problems that are costly to control. And recurrent changes in architecture can have undesirable incentive effects. Increasing the likelihood of change reduces employees' incentives to invest in learning current assignments, devising more efficient production processes, or developing relationships with teammates. Constant restructuring promotes more focus on shorter-run payoffs and less on longer-run investments.

Failure to Consider Other Legs of the Stool

Perhaps the most important reason management innovations often fail, however, is their failure to address all three components of organizational architecture. In Table 22.1 we list a set of popular management techniques along with their primary focus.

	Assignment of Decision Rights	Performance Evaluation	Reward System
Total quality management	X	X	
Reengineering	X		
Outsourcing	X		
Just-in-time production	X		
Quality circles	X	X	
Benchmarking*	X	X	X
Activity-based costing		X	
Economic value added		X	X
Empowerment	X		
Self-directed teams	X	X	
Venturing	X		
Incentive compensation			X
Cycle-time reduction	X		
Strategic alliances	X		
Management by objectives		X	
360° performance reviews		X	
Matrix organizations	X		

*Any corporate policy can be benchmarked; thus benchmarking can be applied to all parts of the organization's architecture. However, in practice, firms often benchmark only one facet of the organization.

Table 22.1 Focus of Management Techniques
For each management technique, we indicate whether it focuses on decision rights, performance evaluation, or the reward system.

For example, let's go back to the case of TQM. As shown in Table 22.1, TQM programs typically change both decision rights and performance measures, but leave the reward system largely unchanged. And this appears to be by design. Echoing quality-guru W. Edwards Deming's well-known disdain for financial incentives, Crosby argues,

> *People really don't work for money. They go to work for it, but once the salary has been established, their concern is appreciation. Recognize their contribution publicly and noisily, but don't demean them by applying a price tag to everything.*[19]

Apparently, this strategy has been adopted widely. For instance, a 1992 study by the American Quality Foundation and Ernst & Young found that quality performance measures were not important variables in determining senior manager's compensation in 80 percent of the firms surveyed.[20]

We would suggest otherwise. In pushing decision rights down to the people with the knowledge about processes and customer preferences, it is important that companies use their reward systems to reinforce their new performance-evaluation systems.[21]

[19]Crosby (1980), 218.

[20]R. Jacob (1993), "TQM: More Than a Dying Fad?" *Fortune* (October 8), 68.

[21]See K. Wruck and M. Jensen (1994), "Science, Specific Knowledge, and Total Quality Management," *Journal of Accounting and Economics* 18, 247–287.

Critics of incentive compensation like Crosby argue that pay for performance does not work because it ends up rewarding people for doing the wrong things. And such criticism is undoubtedly correct in the sense that an ill-designed compensation system indeed can elicit dysfunctional behavior. But Crosby's argument alone is not sufficient reason to conclude that incentive pay should be abandoned. Monetary and nonmonetary incentives are not mutually exclusive—employees clearly value both types of rewards.[22] A recurring theme in this book is that appropriately linking financial incentives to the new performance measures will reinforce the desired changes in behavior.

Reengineering A similar criticism can be directed toward many reengineering programs. As suggested in Table 22.1, reengineering focuses almost exclusively on a single leg of our three-legged stool: the reassignment of decision rights. Most advocates of reengineering pay lip service to the importance of the performance-evaluation and reward systems, but offer little guidance—and in some cases, inappropriate advice—as to how the evaluation and reward systems must change. For example, the best-known advocates of reengineering, Hammer and Champy, are content to provide only the following advice: "Substantial rewards for outstanding performance take the form of bonuses, not pay raises."[23] But as we discussed in Chapters 14 and 15, the compensation decision is far more critical to outcomes than this treatment by Hammer and Champy suggests.

For example, one important part of corporate performance/reward systems is promotions. By creating smaller, flatter organizations, reengineering reduces advancement opportunities. But most reengineering articles are completely silent about how to create new career paths and promotion systems to motivate individuals within a flatter, process-oriented organization. As in the case of TQM, to increase the chances that reengineering efforts will succeed, significant managerial thought and effort also must be focused on reengineering the performance-evaluation and reward systems.

EVA On the other hand, an exclusive concern with performance evaluation and rewards also can cause problems. Take the case of *economic value added,* which attempts to make the economist's concept of residual income the basis for incentive compensation, not only for corporate executives and senior divisional managers, but for rewards that extend "all the way down to the shop floor." Yet such a prescription easily can backfire if it fails to take into account the limited decision rights (and risk-bearing capacity) of lower-level employees. Employees with little control over factors that drive their business unit's EVA may find little motivation—in fact, may be subjected to excessive risk bearing—by such an evaluation and reward system.

ABC As one final example, let's use our organizational architecture framework to explore why the practical achievements of another innovation listed in Table 22.1 have fallen well short of some managers' expectations. In the late 1980s and early 1990s a new accounting system, *activity-based costing,* appeared to great acclaim. An article in *Fortune* magazine declared, "Trim waste! Improve service! Increase productivity! But it does all that—and more."[24]

---

[22]G. Baker, M. Jensen, and K. Murphy (1988), "Compensation and Incentives: Practice vs. Theory," *Journal of Finance* 43, 593–616.

[23]Hammer and Champy (1993), 73.

[24]T. Paré (1993), "A New Tool for Managing Costs," *Fortune* (June 14), 124–129.

How does ABC work? Under traditional accounting systems, overhead costs of common resources such as engineering services are allocated to products or lines of business using very simple formulas, such as percentage of direct labor or percentage of total revenue. For example, suppose both riding and walk-behind lawn mowers are produced in the same plant and both models use common resources. In calculating the accounting costs of the mowers, the plant's overhead costs traditionally are allocated to mowers based on the percentage of direct labor charged to each mower. If direct labor is an unreliable indicator of the level of manufacturing overhead a given operation really generates, this traditional system misrepresents costs. For example, in the case of more complicated products involving little direct labor but a great deal of engineering services, the costs of these products will be understated; managers using such costs to guide pricing decisions might charge too little for them.

Under ABC, different categories of overhead such as purchasing, engineering, and inspection are assigned to products based on underlying cost drivers of that overhead department. For example, purchasing department costs are allocated to different products based on the quantity of purchase orders issued or the number of different parts purchased for each product. By so doing, ABC is said to provide a more accurate estimate of a product's real costs and, hence, a more reliable basis for decision making than the traditional numbers.

But for all its theoretical appeal, the promise of ABC largely has failed to materialize. Although many companies have investigated ABC systems and some have conducted pilot studies, few have abandoned their older, simpler cost-allocation methods. Even though some firms employ ABC-based numbers for special studies, they continue to base performance evaluation on their traditional accounting systems.[25]

One important reason ABC is not replacing traditional accounting systems for purposes of performance evaluation goes back to the standard admonition against giving control of the accounting system to the people being monitored by that system—the separation of decision management and decision control. ABC systems typically must be designed by operating managers because they are the people with the greatest specific knowledge of the overhead cost drivers. Yet these are precisely the people whose performance the ABC measures are intended to evaluate.

But it's not just the opportunity it provides operating managers for self-enrichment that makes most companies reluctant to adopt ABC for performance evaluation. It's the internal turmoil that such changes potentially unleash—influence costs that we discussed in Chapter 12. Altering accounting cost allocations creates both winners and losers in the process. And people can be counted on to struggle mightily to ensure that they are among the winners. The fact that a good deal of subjective judgment goes into determining these ABC measures means that the internal battles are likely to be long, hard-fought, and costly.

As an example of influence costs, one firm implemented and then abandoned activity-based costing after only a year. The controller explained that under the old system, with just a few cost drivers, everyone understood the weaknesses of the system and accepted its faults. With the new system, managers were constantly arguing over the appropriate cost drivers because switching cost drivers changed product costs and thus managers' performance measures. Valuable management and employee time was

---

[25]See A. Sullivan and K. Smith (1993), "What Is Really Happening to Cost Management Systems in U.S. Manufacturing?" *Review of Business Studies* 2, 51–68; R. Cooper, R. Kaplan, L. Maisel, E. Morrissey, and R. Oehm (1992), "From ABC to ABM," *Management Accounting* 74, 54–57; and *Cost Management Update,* newsletter published by the Cost Management Group of the National Association of Accountants, Inc. (January 1991).

ABC and Business Strategy

Although ABC strives to produce more accurate product costs—a laudable goal—obtaining and using more accurate product costs could actually work against the firm's business strategy. For example, suppose a firm is unionized, and reducing labor content is part of its business strategy. Changing the overhead allocation base from direct labor to, say, number of different parts in the product will weaken managers' incentives to reduce labor content by effectively lowering the implicit tax on labor because overheads are no longer allocated on the basis of direct labor content.

Take the case of Hitachi, a large Japanese electronics producer, which manufactures VCRs in one of its plants. Even though this plant is highly automated, and the managers know that direct labor does not reflect the cause-and-effect relation between overhead and the overhead cost drivers, Hitachi continues to allocate overhead using direct labor to reinforce the managers' commitment to further automation. Taxing direct labor through conventional cost accounting is one way to accomplish this aim, thereby lowering production costs.

Source: T. Hiromoto (1988), "Another Hidden Edge—Japanese Management Accounting," *Harvard Business Review* 66, 22.

consumed debating the merits of particular cost drivers. To put an end to the bickering, the controller abandoned ABC.

Because ABC changes product costs and hence product-line profits, successful implementation of ABC throughout the firm requires that new profit targets be established for managers with profit responsibility. To control influence costs, the new profit targets should attempt to eliminate any windfall gains and losses for these managers arising from the change to ABC. This requires detailed changes in compensation plans.

Thus, one of the main reasons ABC has failed to achieve widespread adoption is that it changes only one of the three legs of the firm's organizational architecture stool—the performance-evaluation system. Without complementary changes in decision-right assignments and performance rewards (such as establishing new profit targets in compensation plans), there is little basis for expecting that firm performance will be enhanced.

Managing Changes in Organizational Architecture

Our point in insisting that changes in architecture be coordinated is not to suggest that all facets of the firm's architecture must be changed simultaneously. Rather, we argue the importance of understanding the entire set of policies that must be changed and to develop a plan for implementing that set of changes. An effective plan for implementing a major reorganization often will specify that changes be accomplished sequentially—perhaps in stages—rather than all at once.

Perhaps an analogy will help. Watch a good teaching golf pro giving lessons. The pro knows that there are at least 30 different factors that have to come together to hit a perfect shot—factors such as grip, stance, take-away, position at top, swing plane, release, tempo, and follow-through. After watching a new pupil hit only a few balls, the pro recognizes at least a dozen things that are not quite right. But rather than tell the duffer to think about the dozen things at once, a good teacher will identify the major problem and focus the pupil's attention on fixing that one aspect of the game. In future lessons, the other problems will be addressed in turn. The pro knows that asking someone to think about too many things at once makes it virtually impossible to hit the ball. Thus, to produce better shots, the pro plans a sequence of lessons that, over time, will correct the problems and improve the game.

Fostering major change within an organization frequently takes the same tack. Telling employees that everything is going to be changed creates uncertainty, anxiety, and con-

Sequencing Organization Changes at GM

Choosing the appropriate sequence for implementing organizational changes can be quite important; costly problems can arise if this is not done well. Consider the case of General Motors in its attempts to implement additional outsourcing after adopting just-in-time inventory policies. When GM announced that it was planning to outsource more of its activities, workers at its Dayton brake plant went out on strike. Because of its JIT program, within a week, GM auto production throughout North America was severely curtailed. The walkout by this local's 3,000 members idled over 43,000 GM workers and closed 12 assembly plants.

In effect, the JIT program had increased the local union's bargaining power substantially. Under its old policy, GM would have had an inventory of brakes sufficient to meet production demands for several months, thus giving the company more time to negotiate without affecting overall auto production.

fusion—productivity suffers. Senior management does not have enough resources to oversee changing everything. Identifying the organization's major problem and focusing employees' attention on changing that facet of the organization is difficult enough. After that change is digested, additional complementary changes can be instituted.

This view of the process of organizational change suggests that corporate executives should understand their basic business environment and have a good sense of the kinds of organizational changes that are required to enhance performance. To help form a better sense of the entire set of changes, they might retain a consulting firm for assistance. But again, it is important to recognize that consulting firms naturally specialize in specific problems and techniques. And even though management might benefit from the specific knowledge and experience of such specialists in implementing particular types of organizational change, costly problems may arise from consulting firms' lack of experience in dealing with issues of required complementary changes in other facets of the organization outside their area of expertise.

CASE STUDY: *Software Development, Inc.*

Software Development, Inc. produces and markets software for personal computers, including spreadsheet, word processing, desktop publishing, and database management programs. SDI has annual sales of $800 million.

Producing software is a time-consuming, labor-intensive process. Software quality is an extremely important aspect of success in computer software markets. One aspect of quality is program reliability. Does the software perform as expected? Does it work with other software in terms of data transfers and interfaces? Does it terminate abnormally? In spite of extensive testing of the software, programs always contain some "bugs" (defects). Once the software is released, SDI stands behind the product with phone-in customer service consultants who answer questions

and help the customer work around existing problems in the software. SDI also has a software maintenance group that fixes bugs and sends out revised versions of the programs to customers.

SDI has been tracking the relation between quality costs and quality. The quality measure it uses is the number of documented bugs in a software package. These bugs are counted when a customer calls in with a complaint and the SDI customer service representative determines that this is a new problem. The software maintenance programmers then set about fixing the program to eliminate the bug. To manage quality, SDI tracks quality costs. It has released 38 new or major revisions in existing packages during the last three years. Table 22.2 reports the number of defects documented in the first six months following

(Continued)

	Number of Defects	Product Cost	Training Cost	Prevention Cost	Software Maintenance and Customer Service Cost	Total Cost
1	66	$3,455	$442	$ 770	$2,160	$6,827
2	86	3,959	428	447	2,658	7,492
3	14	3,609	417	1,167	687	5,880
4	73	3,948	211	655	2,334	7,148
5	17	3,104	290	1,013	544	4,951
6	48	3,179	253	547	1,556	5,535
7	80	3,112	392	508	2,633	6,645
8	41	3,529	276	577	1,563	5,945
9	50	3,796	557	634	1,666	6,653
10	67	3,444	365	947	2,140	6,896
11	42	3,922	453	869	1,444	6,688
12	64	3,846	378	1,108	1,942	7,274
13	71	3,014	555	762	2,384	6,715
14	1	3,884	301	773	423	5,381
15	18	3,183	378	1,080	857	5,498
16	85	3,475	528	1,010	2,572	7,585
17	17	3,445	357	666	631	5,099
18	50	3,203	285	427	1,546	5,461
19	22	3,839	239	1,080	891	6,049
20	73	3,060	540	1,054	2,309	6,963
21	52	3,182	329	1,079	1,867	6,457
22	75	3,075	395	832	2,697	6,999
23	35	3,456	447	969	1,518	6,390
24	53	3,987	355	651	2,042	7,035
25	25	3,836	309	1,160	1,036	6,341
26	6	3,886	234	794	252	5,166
27	78	3,846	418	833	2,800	7,897
28	82	3,106	409	1,092	2,871	7,478
29	39	3,506	448	899	1,342	6,195
30	47	3,545	450	442	1,450	5,887
31	30	3,376	456	784	1,260	5,876
32	17	3,740	542	420	607	5,309
33	67	3,479	411	821	2,018	6,729
34	51	3,773	351	1,145	1,873	7,142
35	74	3,034	497	671	2,389	6,591
36	25	3,768	268	887	1,094	6,017
37	14	3,168	356	645	837	5,006
38	77	3,561	492	1,167	2,597	7,817
Average	48	$3,509	$390	$ 826	$1,671	$6,395

Table 22.2 SDI Defects and Costs by Program Release (per 100,000 lines of computer code)

release. Also listed in Table 22.2 is total product cost and quality cost per software package release.

Product cost includes all the costs incurred to produce and market the software, excluding the quality cost in Table 22.2. Quality cost consists of these components: training, prevention, and software maintenance and customer service costs. Training costs are those expenditures for educating the programmers and updating their training. Better-educated programmers produce fewer bugs. Prevention cost includes the expenditures for testing the software before it is released. Maintenance and customer service costs are those of the programmers charged with fixing the bugs and reissuing the revised software and the customer service representatives answering phone questions. The training and prevention costs are measured over the period the software is being developed, and the number of bugs and the maintenance and service costs are measured in the first 6 months following release.

All the numbers in Table 22.2 have been divided by lines of computer code in the particular program release. Programs with more lines of code cost more and also have more bugs. Prior studies find that using lines of code is an acceptable way to control for program complexity. Thus, the numbers in Table 22.2 are stated in terms of defects and cost per 100,000 lines of code.

Figure 22.3 depicts the relation between total quality cost and number of defects. The vice president of quality of SDI likes to use Figure 22.3 to emphasize that costs and quality are inversely related. She is fond of saying, "Quality pays! Our total costs are a declining function of the number of defects. The more we spend on quality, the lower our costs." Based on this analysis, the vice president has recommended a major investment in quality improvement, focusing specifically on prevention and training.

Discussion Questions

Evaluate the vice president's analysis:

1. What criteria should be used in deciding whether to invest more in quality?
2. Do you have sufficient data to evaluate such an investment proposal?

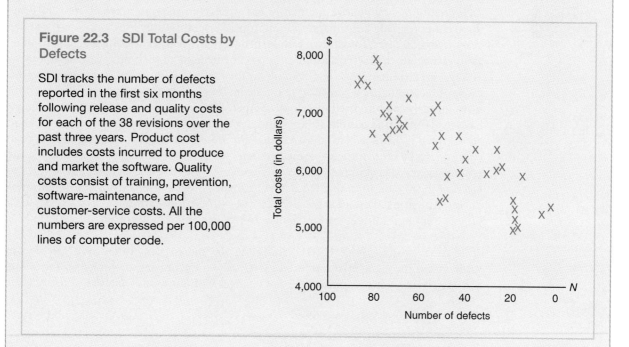

Figure 22.3 SDI Total Costs by Defects

SDI tracks the number of defects reported in the first six months following release and quality costs for each of the 38 revisions over the past three years. Product cost includes costs incurred to produce and market the software. Quality costs consist of training, prevention, software-maintenance, and customer-service costs. All the numbers are expressed per 100,000 lines of computer code.

Summary

In reviewing the business literature over the past thirty years, we find an essentially continuous stream of articles decrying then current management fads. Here are two samples from the 1970s:

> Companies have developed many special devices to meet specific needs in their executive compensation plans. But other companies, wishing to be up to date, have indiscriminately put these devices in their own plans. The results have been—to say the least—embarrassing. The fads include: see-saw options, split-dollar insurance, . . .[26]

> Perhaps the greatest time waste of all is the casting about after fads in Organizational Development, such as constantly jumping on the bandwagons and mindlessly switching from T Group to Team Building, Transactional Analysis, Gestalt Approaches, etc.[27]

Or consider a more recent example:

> If a manager achieves success, the world comes asking for the key to that success. Organization after organization embraces the latest management fads, of which there certainly is no shortage. . . . Total Quality Management (TQM), like so many other elixirs, did not fail for companies because the idea was bad. TQM failed because managers dealt with it superficially.[28]

These articles all argue in one way or another that uncritical adoption of the managerial innovation *du jour* is a prescription for disaster. Yet new management tools are being introduced and adopted continually. We believe it is helpful to understand the market for management innovations in order to make reasoned decisions about whether your organization might benefit from the newest management technique.

Environmental Change Prompts Innovation   Management innovations generally arise as responses to material changes in technology, competition, or regulation. Since such environmental change frequently has similar impacts on a broad array of firms, there is a potentially large market for appropriate organizational responses to those new circumstances. Thus, for all their fadlike behavior, the persistence of management innovations suggests they serve a useful purpose; the benefits of such innovations, at least on average, exceed their costs. For example, if the external environment changes—say, because of technological advances or global competition—a formerly successful, growing firm suddenly can find itself unable to compete effectively; these environmental changes have made the firm's current strategy and organizational architecture obsolete. Changes are required if the firm is to survive and again prosper. And because changing corporate cultures can be quite difficult, some external change agent frequently is useful. The latest management technique often can prove a productive mechanism for suggesting facets of the organization that require adjustment as well as for focusing the organization on implementing these changes. Hence, the current innovation can provide a special opportunity to introduce major changes in strategy and architecture.

If It Ain't Broke, Don't Fix It   Adopting the most recent innovation can destroy value unless the change is warranted by the actual circumstances your firm faces. Unfortunately, some firms appear to adopt changes without careful analysis of the relevant

---

[26]D. Thomsen (1973), "Executive Compensation Gimmicks: Look Out!" *Financial Executive* (August) 58–66.

[27]T. Patten (1977), "Time for Organizational Development," *Personnel* (March–April), 26–33.

[28]G. Shelley (1996), "The Search for the Universal Management Elixir," *Business Quarterly* (Summer), 11–13.

costs and benefits. Figure 11.1 describes the interrelations among a firm's external environment, business strategy, organizational architecture, and value. As discussed in Chapter 8, it is important that managers continually monitor their external business environment as well as internal strengths and weaknesses to identify potentially appropriate strategic changes. Material changes in the external environment require modification of your business strategy, and likely adjustments to your organizational architecture. But if the environment is relatively stable, a successful firm should be extremely cautious about undertaking massive changes in corporate strategy or organizational architecture.

One Size Doesn't Fit All   Not all firms would benefit from outsourcing, improving quality, empowerment, or any other management innovation. Just because a particular management technique appears to have increased value for one firm in no sense implies that adoption would raise your firm's value, as well. Again, only if your firm's current strategy or architecture no longer fit should you consider major changes.

Ensure that the Stool Balances   At any point in time, you face an array of prominent management techniques—each touted as the key to success. Most of these techniques involve fundamental changes in organizational architecture but tend to target one aspect of business strategy or organizational architecture—decision rights, performance evaluation, or rewards—while slighting the rest. For example, advocates of reengineering recommend changing the delegation of decision rights and task assignments. Just as none of these recent management techniques provides coordinated advice for changing all three components of the firm's organizational architecture, we expect that future innovations will fail to do so, as well. Yet changes that leave one leg of the stool out of balance mean that the firm's organizational architecture no longer fits and hence requires coordinated adjustment.

Don't Bite Off More Than You Can Chew   If you do decide to make a change in one aspect of the organization, then you should anticipate the effects of such change on other aspects and plan the implementation of complementary adjustments necessary to accommodate such change. Arguing that it is important to consider all three legs of the stool in designing an appropriate architecture does not imply that all changes must be implemented simultaneously. Changing too many aspects of the firm at one time can be difficult to digest and productivity can suffer. You need to understand your environment, formulate strategy, and devise a plan for implementing the entire array of required changes.

Organizational Change Checklist   When analyzing business problems and challenges, managers often find it useful to ask themselves the following set of questions:

- Does our existing business strategy fit the business environment—technology, market conditions, and regulation—and the capabilities of our firm?
- What are the key features of our current architecture? And does our architecture fit our business environment and strategy?
- Are the three legs of the organizational architecture stool mutually consistent? Given the decision-right system, do the control and reward systems fit and vice versa?

- If the answers to any of the previous questions suggest a problem, what changes in strategy and architecture should the firm consider?
- What problems will our firm face in implementing these changes? What can be done to increase the probability of success?

In Closing   It is critical to recognize that these policy choices represent fundamentally difficult organizational decisions. Across firms, public data on these internal organizational policies are limited, in part because management considers this information proprietary and in part because this information is not easy to summarize and aggregate. Finally, the interrelations among the various dimensions of the problem imply that these policy choices are inherently complex. When making such decisions, information costs are high and errors are potentially substantial. Thus, it is useful to recall Yogi Berra's observation: "You got to be careful if you don't know where you're going, because you might not get there." We believe that the organizational architecture framework we develop in this book can help by giving you a more detailed understanding of "where you're going"—it better focuses your attention and thus helps you frame better questions. Nonetheless, answers still are quite difficult. Yet by asking better, more focused questions and structuring more complete, coherent analysis, this framework helps ensure that you will in fact "get there."

Suggested Readings	

P. Crosby (1980), *Quality Is Free* (Mentor: New York).

M. Hammer and J. Champy (1993), *Reengineering the Corporation: A Manifesto for Business Revolution* (Harper Business: New York).

J. Juran (1989), *Juran on Leadership for Quality* (Free Press: New York).

J. Juran and Gryna, Jr. (1993), *Quality Planning and Analysis* (McGraw-Hill: New York).

S. Keating and K. Wruck (1994), "Sterling Chemicals Inc.: Quality and Process Improvement Program," Harvard Business School Case 9-493-026.

K. Wruck and M. Jensen (1994), "Science, Specific Knowledge and Total Quality Management," *Journal of Accounting and Economics* 18, 247–287.

Review Questions	

22–1. "Hewlett-Packard now treats TQM like any other investment: If a particular total-quality initiative doesn't show a quick return in terms of higher sales, lower costs, or happier customers, it is redesigned or scrapped."[29] Critically evaluate Hewlett-Packard's policy.

22–2. Guest Watches is a division of Guest Fashions, a large, international fashion designer. Guest Watches manufactures highly stylish watches for young adults (ages 18 to 30) who are fashion-conscious. It is a profit center and its senior management's compensation is tied closely to the watch division's reported profits. Guest Watches has succeeded in capturing the fashion market, but a lack of product dependability is eroding these gains. A number of retailers have dropped or are threatening to drop the Guest watch line because of customer returns. Guest Watches carry a 1-year warranty, and 12 percent are returned, compared to an industry average of 4 percent. Besides high warranty costs and lost sales due to reputation, Guest has higher-than-industry average manufacturing scrap and rework costs.

Senior management, worried about these trends and the possible erosion of its market dominance, hired a consulting firm to study the problem and make recommendations for reversing the situation. After a thorough analysis of Guest's customers, suppliers, and manufacturing facilities, the consultants recommended five possible actions, ranging from the *status quo* to a complete total quality management, zero defects program (level IV). The table below outlines

[29]"The Straining of Quality," *The Economist* (January 14, 1995), 55.

the various alternatives (in thousands of dollars):

	Additional Training Cost*	Additional Prevention/Compliance†
Status quo	$ 0	$ 0
Level I	80	180
Level II	200	240
Level III	350	340
Level IV	550	490

*Includes the annual costs of training employees in TQM methods.
†All annual costs, including certifying suppliers, redesigning the product, and inspection costs to reduce defects.

The consultant emphasized that although first-year startup costs are slightly higher than subsequent years, management must really view the cost estimates in the table as annual, ongoing costs. Given employee turnover and the assumption that supplier changes, training, prevention, and compliance costs are not likely to decline over time, the costs in the preceding table will be annual operating expenses.

The consulting firm and the newly appointed vice president for quality programs estimated that under level IV, rework and scrap would be $25,000 and warranty costs zero. Level IV was needed to get the firm to zero defects. A task force was convened, and after several meetings, it generated the following estimates of rework/scrap and warranty costs for the various levels of firm commitment:

	Total Rework/Scrap Cost*	Total Warranty Costs†
Status quo	$500	$350
Level I	300	280
Level II	150	140
Level III	75	80
Level IV	25	0

*The costs of manufacturing scrap and rework.
†The costs of repairing and replacing products that fail in the hands of customers.

There was considerable discussion and debate about the quantitative impact of increased quality on additional sales. Although no hard-and-fast numbers could be derived, the consensus view was that the total net cash flows (contribution margin) from additional sales as retailers and customers learn of the reduced defect rate would be as follows:

	Contribution Margin on Additional Sales
Status quo	$ 0
Level I	600
Level II	1,000
Level III	1,200
Level IV	1,300

a. Assuming that the data as presented are reasonably accurate, what should Guest Watches do about its deteriorating quality situation? Should it maintain the *status quo* or should it adopt the consultant's recommendation and implement level I, II, III, or IV?

b. Critically evaluate the analysis underlying your policy recommendation in part (a). Will the senior management of the watch division make the same decision as the senior management of Guest Fashions?

22–3. According to a *New York Times* article,[30] LDS Hospital in Salt Lake City installed a computer in every hospital room in the mid-1980s. These computers replaced paper charts so everything the doctor or nurses did was entered into a database as it happened. A small number of patients get infections following surgery, which adds to the length of their hospital stay and ultimately to the cost of treating the patient. After several years, hospital personnel began using the computerized data to determine the best time to begin antibiotics for patients undergoing surgery. They found that by starting antibiotics a few hours before surgery, the rate of infections fell from 1.8 percent to 0.4 percent, saving the hospital about $9,000 per case. By using the computer system, the head of LDS's quality control program can improve quality and cut hospital costs.

Analyze the LDS quality control program in terms of basic TQM principles.

22–4. LDS Hospital in Salt Lake City has a computer system that records all procedures performed on patients and all drugs administered.[31] The computer system can track which surgeons are the best and which ones are the worst in terms of length of patient stays, complications, and death rates. They found that once a new quality-improvement program was imposed after an extensive study of past practices, nearly all the doctors improved. But some did not.

The doctor in charge of the quality-improvement program said, "I have a few bad apples. And I know who they are. But for quality improvement to work, you have to construct a 'safe' environment where doctors trust you. Any time you start taking names, you're going to start a cycle of fear, and quality improvement will not occur."

When he learned of LDS tracking system, the head of the Utah medical board said, "That's a terrible indictment of them and of the practice of medicine that they are willing to sacrifice patients to unnecessary mortality, morbidity, injury, and pain by these doctors. It's unconscionable!"

Discuss the dilemma LDS faces in terms of using its computer system to improve quality.

22–5. A company chairman was given a ticket for a performance of Schubert's *Unfinished Symphony*. Since he was unable to go, he passed the invitation to the company's quality-assurance manager. The next morning the chairman asked him how he enjoyed it and, instead of a few plausible observations, he was handed a memorandum which read as follows:

- For a considerable period, the oboe players had nothing to do. Their number should be reduced, and their work spread over the whole orchestra, thus avoiding peaks of inactivity.

- All 12 violins were playing identical notes. This seems unnecessary duplication, and the staff of this section should be drastically cut. If a large volume of sound is really required, this could be obtained through the use of an amplifier.

- Much effort was involved in playing the demi-semiquavers. This seems an excessive refinement, and it is recommended that all notes should be rounded up to the nearest semiquaver. If this were done, it would be possible to use trainees instead of artisans.

- No useful purpose is served by repeating with horns the passage that has already been handled by the strings. If all such redundant passages were eliminated, the concert could be reduced from two hours to twenty minutes.

In light of the above, one can only conclude that had Schubert given attention to these matters, he probably would have had the time to finish his symphony.

Although the memo obviously was written in jest,[32] how would you respond?

---

[30]J. Brinkley (1994), "At Utah Hospital, Innovative Way to Track Medical Quality," *The New York Times* (March 31), B8.

[31]J. Brinkley (March 31, 1994).

[32]Doug Rathbun, Internet.

Glossary*

Absolute performance evaluation is based on a predetermined standard of performance; the employee is not evaluated on performance relative to peers.

activity-based costing (ABC) assigns different categories of overhead (purchasing, engineering, inspection) costs to products by first estimating the underlying cost drivers of the activities performed within the overhead department and then assigning these activity costs to the products that benefit from or consume these resources.

adverse selection refers to the tendency of individuals with private information about factors that affect a potential trading partner's benefits to make offers that are detrimental to the trading partner—see *precontractual information problems*.

agency relationship is an agreement under which one party, the principal, engages another party, the agent, to perform some service on the principal's behalf.

alienable property rights are private property rights that can be transferred (sold or given) to other individuals.

arbitrage is a simultaneous set of transactions designed to make profits without risk (for example, if equivalent assets are traded in two markets, buying at the lower price and selling at the higher price).

arc elasticities are estimated between two points (elasticities also can be calculated at a point); they relate the percentage change in one variable, such as quantity, to a percentage change in another variable, such as price.

asset specificity occurs when a given asset is especially useful to one or to a small number of buyers—for physical assets, this results from product design or *site specificity;* for *human capital,* it results from investments in specialized knowledge or skills.

asymmetric information occurs when one party to a transaction has information different from that of another party.

average cost (AC) is the *total cost* divided by total output; average cost can be defined for either the *long run* or the *short run.*

average product (AP) of an input is the *total product* divided by the quantity of the input employed.

average revenue (AR) is the *total revenue* divided by total output.

Backward integration occurs when an organization produces its own inputs—also called upstream integration.

bargaining failures occur due to *asymmetric information;* parties fail to reach an agreement, even when in principle a contract could be constructed that would be mutually advantageous—see *precontractual information problems.*

barriers to entry are factors that limit the entry of new *firms* to a *market,* even though the existing firms are making *economic profits.*

benchmarking is identifying the best practices of *firms* operating within similar environments, so that the benchmarking firm can learn from the experience of the others.

Bertrand model examines producer interaction, assuming each firm treats the product price chosen by its competitors as fixed and then decides how to set its price—see *oligopolistic market.*

block pricing sets a high price for the first unit or block of units purchased and lower prices for subsequent units or blocks.

boundary setting occurs when managers empower employees to make decisions within prespecified limits.

brand-name capital refers to a firm's intangible reputational capital; by establishing a reputation for quality products or living up to its end of a contract, the firm can receive more favorable terms from contracting parties because it is a more desirable partner.

broad task assignment has individual employees performing a relatively large set of tasks.

bundling occurs when a company packages two or more products together and offers the package for sale as a unit.

business environment includes the technology, *markets* (product and input), and regulations facing the *firm.*

business ethics is the study of behaviors that businesspeople should and should not follow (however, this term also is used in a variety of ways that range from making *firms* socially responsible to attempting to induce employees to ignore their self-interest).

*Italicized terms are defined elsewhere in the glossary.

595

business norms are expectations in *market* transactions that do not have the force of law, yet nonetheless represent expected behavior.

business strategy focuses on *strategy* at the business-unit level; the primary consideration is whether to focus on being the low-cost producer in an industry or to develop differentiated products for which customers are willing to pay a price premium.

Cafeteria-style benefit plans are plans in which individual employees allocate a fixed-dollar *fringe-benefit* allowance among a variety of choices—also called menu plans.

career earnings are the total wages that employees expect to earn over their entire careers.

cartels consist of formal agreements among a set of *firms* to cooperate in setting prices and output levels.

centralized decision system is one that assigns the most important decisions to senior executives within the organization.

certainty equivalent is the certain income that an individual considers equivalent to an activity with risky payoffs.

changes in demand are movements of the *demand curve* motivated by factors other than changes in the good's own price (such as changes in income or changes in the prices of related goods).

changes in the quantity demanded are movements along a *demand curve* that are motivated by changes in the good's own price, holding all other factors constant.

Coase theorem states that the ultimate resource allocation will be efficient, regardless of the initial assignment of property rights, as long as *contracting costs* are sufficiently low, *property rights* are assigned clearly, and these rights can be exchanged readily.

comparative advantage occurs when one party can produce a good relatively more efficiently than other parties (relative efficiency means that alternative products which could have been produced from the same inputs are less valuable). It is conceptually possible for a party to have an absolute advantage in producing all goods (meaning that it can produce all goods with fewer inputs); however, it cannot have a comparative advantage in all goods. Aggregate output is higher if parties specialize in producing products in which they have a comparative advantage.

compensating wage differential is the extra wage that is paid to attract an individual to a less desirable *job*.

competitive market is a *market structure* in which no buyer or seller has *market power* (all trades are made at the going *market price*); it is characterized by a large number of potential buyers and sellers, low costs of entry and exit, product homogeneity, and rapid dissemination of accurate information at low cost.

complementarities exist when doing more of one activity either increases the benefits or reduces the costs of doing another activity.

complements are products that tend to be consumed together; a price reduction of one good tends to increase the quantity demanded of the other good.

complete contracts are contracts that specify exactly what is expected of each party under all possible future contingencies.

constant returns to scale for a production function occur when a 1 percent change in all inputs results in 1 percent change in output.

consumer surplus is the difference between the maximum amount a consumer would be willing to pay for a product and what the consumer actually pays when buying it.

contracting costs are the out-of-pocket and *opportunity costs* of negotiating, drafting, and enforcing contracts; they include search and information costs, bargaining and decision costs, and policing and enforcement costs, and the efficiency losses that result because incentive conflicts are not completely resolved.

contracting problems occur within contracts because individuals have incentives to take actions that increase their well-being at their contracting partner's expense; they occur within both *explicit* and *implicit contracts.*

control system encompasses the reward and *performance evaluation* systems within the *firm.*

corporate culture is the set of explicit and implicit expectations of behavior within the *firm;* it usually encompasses the ways work and authority are organized, the ways people are rewarded and controlled, as well as organizational features such as customs, taboos, company slogans, heroes, and social rituals.

corporate strategy focuses on *strategy* at the *firm* level; the primary consideration is the degree of corporate diversification chosen by the firm (the array of different products that the firm sells).

cost centers are business units whose performance is evaluated based on their efficiency of production.

cost-plus pricing is where *firms* set prices by marking up average total cost by an amount designed to yield a target rate of return.

Cournot model examines producer interaction, assuming each *firm* treats the output level of its competitors as fixed and then decides how much to produce—see *oligopolistic market.*

cross elasticity relates the percentage change in the quantity of a good purchased to a percentage change in the price of some other good.

cross-training occurs when employees are taught to complete more than one task or *function.*

cumulative production is the total output produced by the *firm* across all previous production periods.

Deadweight loss involves the forgone gains from trade (for instance, the forgone producer and *consumer surplus* when a *firm* with *market power* sets price above *marginal cost*).

decentralized system is one which assigns many important *decision rights* to lower-level employees.

decision control encompasses the *ratification* and *monitoring* of decisions.

decision management encompasses the *initiation* and *implementation* of decisions.

decision rights represent the authority to decide how resources will be used within the organization.

decreasing returns to scale for a production function occur when a 1 percent change in all inputs results in a less than 1 percent change in output.

dedicated assets are those whose purchase is necessitated by the requirements of one or only a few buyers.

demand curve displays the relation between the quantity of a product that will be purchased at each price over a stated period of time, holding all other factors fixed; demand curves slope downward because customers are more likely to purchase if the price is lower—see *law of demand.*

demand function is the relation between the quantity demanded for a product and all factors that influence its demand.

dominant strategies exist when it is optimal for a *firm* to choose a particular *strategy* no matter the choices of its rivals—especially used in *game theory.*

double markups are the increments in the product's price above *marginal cost* first by the manufacturer and then by the distributor; this problem occurs with decentralized pricing decisions when the producer has *market power.*

downstream integration—see *forward integration.*

duopoly is a market setting in which two *firms* compete in a *market*—see *oligopolistic market.*

Economic Darwinism is the economic counterpart of the biological theory of natural selection; an organization selects features that increase its ability to survive within its environment; the basic idea is that a competitive marketplace creates pressures that favor organizations that are relatively most efficient.

economic profit is an above-competitive (or extra-normal) rate of return on assets; *economic profits* are eroded in *competitive markets.*

economic value added (EVA—registered trademark of Stern Stewart) is a measure of *residual income;* it is the after-tax operating profit of the division minus the total annual cost of capital invested in the division.

economies of scale occur in industries in which *average cost* declines over a broad range of output levels.

economies of scope occur when the cost of producing a set of products jointly within one *firm* is lower than the cost of producing the products separately across independent firms.

efficiency wages are wage premiums paid to reduce shirking because employees are afraid that if they are caught, they will be fired and lose this premium; efficiency wages also discourage employee turnover.

elastic demand occurs when the *price elasticity* is greater than one; in this case, a small increase in price decreases *total revenue.*

elasticity of demand relates the percentage *change in the quantity demanded* to a given percentage change in its price. Higher price elasticities mean greater price sensitivity. Although the *law of demand* implies that this ratio will be negative, convention dictates that this elasticity is stated as a positive number—also called price elasticity of demand.

equilibrium refers to a stable situation where no party has a reason to change its *strategy* (for example, in a *competitive market,* this occurs when the quantity supplied of a product equals the quantity demanded).

ethics is the study of behaviors that people should and should not follow.

exclusive territories grant individual distributors the exclusive rights to operate within a specified *market* area.

expense centers are business units that are given fixed budgets and asked to maximize some hard-to-measure service or output; it is essentially a *cost center* that does not produce an easily measurable output.

experience goods are those which must be tried by the customer to ascertain *quality.*

explicit contracts are formal written agreements with a party related to the *firm* (for example, employees, customers, suppliers, and capital providers).

externalities are costs of or benefits from the actions of one party that affect the *utility* or production possibilities of another party.

Factor-balance equation states that at the cost-minimizing level of output, the ratios of *marginal product* to price for each factor are equal.

factor demand curves display the relation between the quantity of an input the *firm* demands and its price, holding other factors constant.

firm is a basic organizational unit of production; for purposes of this book, it is a focal point for a set of contracts.

firm-specific assets are assets that are significantly more valuable in their current use within the *firm* than in their next best alternative use outside the firm.

first-degree price discrimination—see *personalized pricing.*

first-mover advantages are the expected benefits derived by the first *firm* to introduce a product.

fixed costs are those costs which do not vary with output over the time horizon of the analysis.

formal authority is the power that comes from explicitly assigned decision rights within the organization.

forward integration occurs when the *firm* begins to conduct additional finishing work or to market its own goods—also called downstream integration.

franchise agreements are contracts between the franchisor (parent) and the franchisee that grant to the franchisee the rights to use the parent's name, reputation, and business format at a particular location or within a stipulated *market* area.

free cash flow problems are incentive conflicts between owners and managers over retaining cash within the *firm* beyond that necessary to fund value-increasing investment projects; managers prefer to take projects which expand firm size beyond that which maximizes the firm's value, rather than to distribute the cash to owners.

free-rider problems occur in team efforts; each member of the team has an incentive to shirk because each receives the full benefit from shirking, but bears only a part of the costs.

fringe benefits are components of the compensation package other than salary and incentive compensation; they are either in-kind or *deferred* (such as medical insurance and pensions).

full-cost transfer prices use full cost to value goods exchanged between business units; full cost is the sum of *fixed* and *variable cost.*

function refers to a primary activity within the process that a *firm* employs to provide a product to customers; major functions include research, manufacturing, finance, marketing, sales, and service.

functional myopia occurs when employees focus on their individual *function* at the expense of the larger array of activities that must be accomplished to capture as much value as possible given the firm's business opportunities.

functional subunits group all *jobs* performing the same *function* into the same department.

Gain from trade is the difference between the minimum value that an owner or a supplier is willing to accept for an item and the maximum price that a prospective buyer is willing to pay.

game theory is concerned with the general analysis of strategic interaction; it focuses on optimal decision making when all decision makers are presumed to be rational, with each attempting to anticipate the likely actions and reactions of its rivals.

general human capital consists of training and education that is useful across a wide variety of different *firms.*

general knowledge is that which is relatively inexpensive to transfer.

Generally Accepted Accounting Principles (GAAP) are that set of accounting methods commonly used or proscribed by the Securities and Exchange Commission (SEC) and the Financial Accounting Standards Board (FASB) for financial reporting.

goal-based system provides each employee a set of goals for the year and then evaluates employees based on the extent to which the goals are achieved.

group incentive pay bases employee compensation on group performance.

group pricing occurs when a *firm* separates its customers into classes and sets different prices for each class—also called third-degree price discrimination.

Historical costs reflect the original purchase price of resources and not necessarily their current *opportunity cost;* historical costs generally are not relevant for decision making (except for their tax effects).

holdup problems can occur when parties invest in *specific assets;* for example, after the investment is made, the buyer might be able to force a price concession, since it will be in the interests of the seller to continue to operate as long as *variable costs* are covered.

horizon problems are the incentive conflicts that can arise between owners and employees due to differential horizons with the *firm;* employees' claims on the firm generally are tied to their tenure with the firm, but owners are interested in the present value of the entire stream of future cash flows.

human asset specificity—see *specific human capital* and *asset specificity.*

human capital is a term that characterizes individuals as having a set of skills that can be "rented" to employers.

Identification is a statistical problem that arises in separating the effects of simultaneous equations; for example, separating supply versus demand shifts in explaining the observed changes in market prices and quantities.

implementation rights involve the execution of ratified business decisions.

implicit contracts consist of promises and shared understandings that are not expressed by formal legal documents.

incentive coefficients are weights that the compensation plan places on the various tasks assigned to an employee.

income elasticity relates the percentage change in the quantity purchased for a good to a given percentage change in income.

incomplete contracts do not specify actions under all possible contingencies.

increasing returns to scale for a production function occur when a 1 percent change in all inputs results in a greater than 1 percent change in output.

indifference curves display all the combinations of goods that yield the same *utility.*

industry demand curve relates total quantity demanded across all *firms* in an industry to price of the product.

inelastic demand occurs when the *price elasticity* is less than one; in this case, a small increase in price raises *total revenue.*

inferior goods are goods for which the quantity purchased declines with income.

influence costs include those nonproductive activities in which employees engage to influence decisions.

information failures refers to the case where information asymmetries and *adverse selection* can lead to a breakdown of markets and the failure to consummate potentially beneficial exchanges.

informativeness principle states that it is typically desirable to include in the compensation plan all performance indicators that provide incremental information about the employee's effort, assuming the measures are available at low cost.

initiation rights are the *decision rights* to generate proposals for particular business decisions such as resource utilization or contract structure.

internal labor markets fill *jobs* from within the *firm.* In firms that rely primarily on internal labor markets, they are used to fill most non-entry-level jobs; employees typically spend a significant fraction of their careers with the firm.

investment centers are business units that have all the *decision rights* of *cost centers* and *profit centers* as well as the *decision rights* over the amount of capital to be invested.

isocost lines display all combinations of the factors of production with the same cost.

isoquants display all possible ways to produce the same quantity (*iso* meaning "the same," *quant* from "quantity").

Jobs define the basic roles and responsibilities of employees; jobs have at least two important dimensions: the variety of tasks that the employee is asked to complete and the decision authority that is granted to the individual to complete the tasks.

joint ventures establish new *firms* that are owned jointly by two or more independent firms.

just-in-time production (JIT) is a production system whereby each component is produced immediately as needed by the next step in the production process.

Keiretsu is a form of *network organization* employed in Japan; it consists of an affiliation of quasi-independent *firms* with ongoing, fluid relationships; typically, the firms have cross-holdings in each other's common stock.

Law of demand states that normal *demand curves* slope downward to the right—quantity demanded varies inversely with price.

law of diminishing returns states that the *marginal product* of a variable factor will eventually decline as the use of the factor is increased—also called the law of diminishing marginal product.

leadership is the process of persuasion or example by which an individual induces a group to pursue objectives held by the leader; it has at least two important components: establishing goals and motivating others.

learning curves display the relation between *average cost* and *cumulative production;* learning-curve effects refer to average cost falling as production experience accumulates.

logroll consists of a coalition of individuals who are largely indifferent to one another's demands, but agree to support a variety of requests so that each can get what he wants.

long run is the period of time over which the *firm* has complete flexibility; no inputs are fixed.

long-run cost curves—see *planning curves.*

M-form organization—see *multidivisional form.*

Malcolm Baldrige National Quality Award was instituted in 1987 by the U.S. government to recognize *quality* achievement by American companies.

marginal analysis considers only the incremental costs and benefits in making a decision; costs and benefits that do not vary with the decision are sunk and hence are irrelevant.

marginal benefits are the incremental benefits associated with making a decision.

marginal cost (MC) is the change in total costs associated with a one-unit change in output—*marginal costs* can be defined for either the *long run* or the *short run.*

marginal-cost transfer prices use marginal production cost to value goods exchanged between business units.

marginal product (MP) of an input is the change in total output associated with a one-unit change in the input, holding other inputs fixed.

marginal revenue (MR) is the change in *total revenue* given a one-unit change in quantity.

marginal revenue product (MRP) is the incremental revenue that the *firm* obtains from employing one more unit of the input (the incremental output times the incremental revenue)—also called the value of the marginal product.

market consists of all *firms* and individuals who are willing and able to buy or sell a particular product.

market-based transfer prices use external market prices to value goods exchanged between business units.

market-clearing price is the price at which the quantity supplied of a product is equal to the quantity demanded.

market failures occur because of *externalities, public goods, monopolies,* and *information failures;* they keep *markets* from then providing an efficient allocation of resources.

market power occurs when a *firm* faces a downward-sloping *demand curve;* it can raise prices without losing all sales.

market structure refers to the basic characteristics of the *market* environment, including (1) the number and size of buyers, sellers, and *potential entrants,* (2) the degree of product differentiation, (3) the amount and cost of information about product price and *quality,* and (4) the conditions for entry and exit.

markup pricing sets price by estimating its price elasticity and marking up *marginal costs;* the *firm* substitutes these estimates into $MC^*/[1 - 1/\eta^*]$.

matrix organizations are those which are characterized by intersecting lines of authority; they have functional departments (such as finance, manufacturing, and development), but employees from these functional departments also are assigned to subunits organized around product, geography, or some special project—individuals report to both a functional manager and a product manager. See *function* and *functional subunits.*

meeting-the-competition clause is a contractual provision that guarantees that the seller will match the price offered by a competitor.

menu plans—see *cafeteria-style benefit plans.*

menu pricing involves offering all potential customers the same menu of purchase options. Customers self-select among the alternatives, thus revealing information about their *demand elasticities*—also called second-degree price discrimination.

minimum efficient scale is the plant size at which *long-run average cost* first reaches its minimum.

monitoring rights represent the opportunity to oversee whether the obligations of another party have been met.

monopolistic competition is a *market structure* that is a hybrid between *competitive markets* and *monopoly; firms* have downward-sloping *demand curves* for their differentiated products, but *economic profits* are limited by entry and competition (examples include the *markets* for toothpaste and golf balls).

monopoly is a *market structure* where there is only one *firm* in the industry; here, industry and firm *demand curves* are the same.

moral-hazard problems—see *postcontractual information problems.*

most-favored-nation clause is a contractual provision which guarantees that the seller will not sell to another buyer at a lower price.

motion studies are the systematic analysis of work methods considering the use of raw materials, the design of the product or process, the order of work, the tools, and the activities at each step.

multicollinearity is a statistical problem which arises when the factors that affect a dependent variable in a regression are highly correlated (tend to move together); it can make it difficult to estimate the individual effects of the explanatory variables with much precision.

multidivisional form of *firm* organization groups *jobs* into a collection of business units based on factors such as product or geographic area; operating decisions such as product offerings and pricing are decentralized to the business unit and each business unit has its own *functional* subunits—also called M-form organization.

multitask principal-agent model examines the incentive problems that arise when an employee is assigned multiple tasks.

Nash equilibrium occurs when each *firm* is doing the best it can, given the actions of its rivals.

negotiated transfer prices use prices set by negotiation between the two business units to value goods exchanged between them.

network effects occur where the demand for a product increases with the number of users (for example, fax machines are more useful the more people that use them).

network organizations are those which are organized into work groups based on *function,* geography, or some other dimension; the relationships among these work groups are determined by the demands of specific projects and work activities, rather than by formal lines of authority; these relationships are fluid and frequently change with changes in the *business environment.*

normal goods are those for which the quantity purchased increases with income.

Objective performance measure is a measure that is easily observable and quantifiable.

oligopolistic market is a *market structure* that has only a few *firms* which account for most of the production in the *market;* products may or may not be differentiated; firms can earn *economic profits.*

omitted variables problem is a statistical problem that arises from estimating equations without all the relevant explanatory variables.

operating cost curves are used in making near-term production and pricing decisions—also called short-run cost curves.

opportunity cost is the value of the resource in its next best alternative use.

organizational architecture comprises the three critical aspects of corporate organization: (1) the assignment of *decision rights* within the company, (2) the methods of rewarding individuals, and (3) the structure of systems to evaluate the performance of both individuals and business units.

outsourcing is moving an activity outside the *firm* that formerly was done within the firm; it can also refer to an outgoing arrangement for using external firms either to supply inputs or distribute products.

Pareto efficiency occurs when there is no feasible alternative that keeps all individuals at least as well off but makes at least one person better off.

performance evaluation is the process of appraising the correspondence between employee productivity and employer expectations.

personalized pricing occurs when the producer extracts all potential *consumer surplus* from each potential consumer—also called first-degree price discrimination.

physical asset specificity—see *asset specificity.*

planning curves play a key role in longer-run planning decisions relating to plant size and equipment acquisition—also called long-run cost curves.

postcontractual information problems are *agency problems* that occur because of *asymmetric information* after the contract is negotiated; individuals have incentives to deviate from the contract and take self-interested actions because the other party has insufficient information to know whether the contract was honored—also called moral-hazard problems.

potential entrants are all *firms* that pose a sufficiently credible threat of *market* entry to affect the pricing and output decisions of incumbent firms.

precontractual information problems are contracting problems that occur because of *asymmetric information* at the time the contract is being negotiated; these problems include *adverse selection* and *bargaining failures.*

price discrimination occurs whenever a *firm's* prices in different *markets* are not related to differentials in production and distribution costs; it involves charging different consumers different prices based on their *elasticities of demand.*

price elasticity of demand—see *elasticity of demand.*

principal-agent model examines incentive problems among contracting parties, especially within organizations.

prisoners' dilemma is a *game-theory* model which examines the tension between group interest and individual self-interest; the *equilibrium* is for the two prisoners to confess, even though it is in their joint interest not to confess.

product attributes are the various characteristics of a product that buyers value.

product life cycle is the pattern in the demand for products over their life cycles; it is divided into four stages: introduction, growth, maturity, and decline. Typically, the demand for a successful product increases rapidly through the growth phase; the demand tends to level off during the maturity phase; it eventually drops when the product enters the decline phase.

production function specifies the maximum feasible output that can be produced for given quantities of inputs.

profit centers are business units whose managers are given *decision rights* for input mix, product mix, and selling prices (or output quantities) and are asked to maximize profits given a fixed capital budget.

profit-maximizing level of production occurs when *marginal revenue* equals *marginal cost.*

property right is an enforceable right to select the uses of a good.

public goods are those commodities whose consumption by one person does not diminish the amount available to others.

Quality can refer to high mean, low variance, more options, or meeting customer expectations.

quality circles are voluntary work groups who meet regularly to discuss how to improve the *quality* of products and work processes.

Ratchet effect refers to basing next year's performance standard on this year's actual performance; such standard setting can induce employees to restrict production in the current period in order to limit the increase in their future performance benchmarks.

ratification rights are those which involve the choice of the business-decision initiatives to be implemented.

reaction curve displays one *firm's* optimal choice (of output, for instance), given the choice of another firm.

reengineering is a management technique defined as the fundamental rethinking and radical redesign of business processes to achieve improvements in measures of performance, such as cost, *quality,* service, and speed.

relative-performance evaluation measures employees' performance relative to peers.

relative price is the price of one good as compared to another.

repeated relationship occurs when two parties expect to interact with each other over time; sometimes it is possible for the parties to cooperate in a repeated relationship, even though they would not cooperate in a one-time interaction due to incentive conflicts.

reservation price is the maximum price that the buyer is willing to pay, or the minimum that the seller is willing to accept.

reservation utility is the *utility* that the employee can obtain in the next best alternative; the employee must be paid her reservation utility or she will not work for the *firm.*

residual claimants have the legal rights to the profits of the enterprise once the fixed claimants of the *firm* (for example, bondholders and employees) are paid.

residual income measures business-unit performance by subtracting a stated return on investment from division profits.

residual loss is the dollar equivalent of the remaining loss in value that results because incentive problems have not been completely resolved by out-of-pocket expenditures on monitoring and bonding.

residual use rights for an asset are the rights to select any use that does not conflict with prior contract, custom, or law.

return on assets (ROA) is the ratio of accounting net income generated divided by total assets; ROA is a commonly used investment-center performance measure.

returns to a factor define the relation between output and the variation in only one input, holding other inputs fixed.

returns to scale is the relation between output and a proportional variation of all inputs taken together.

revenue centers are business units that evaluate performance based on revenue generation.

risk-averse individuals prefer a lower level of risk, holding the expected payoff fixed.

risk-neutral individuals care only about expected value and are indifferent to the level of risk.

risk premium is the difference between the expected value of a risky income stream and its *certainty equivalent.*

Second-degree price discrimination—see *menu pricing.*

self-selection occurs when people with differential private information identify themselves to outsiders by choosing contracts that best fit with their private information.

short run is the operating period during which at least one input (frequently capital) is fixed in supply.

short-run cost curves—see *operating cost curves.*

short-run profit maximization occurs when *marginal revenue* equals *short-run marginal cost.*

shortage occurs when the price in the *market* is lower than the *market-clearing price* and quantity demanded is greater than quantity supplied; as inventories are depleted, suppliers have incentives to raise prices.

shut-down condition in the *short run* occurs when price is lower than *average variable cost;* in the *long run* it occurs when price is lower than *long-run average cost.*

site specificity occurs when an asset is located in a particular place that makes it useful only to a small number of buyers or suppliers and it cannot be moved easily—see also *asset specificity.*

specialized task assignments are those in which individual employees concentrate on a limited set of tasks.

specific assets are those which are worth more in their current use than in alternative uses.

specific human capital is created by learning things that are expected to be useful only within a specific contractual relationship—see *asset specificity.*

specific knowledge is that which is relatively expensive to transfer.

spot market is one in which the exchange is made immediately at the current market price with no long-term commitment between the buyer and the seller.

standard rating scales require the performance evaluator to rank the employee on a number of different performance factors using a scale (for example, far exceeds requirements, exceeds requirements, meets all requirements, partially meets requirements, does not meet requirements).

strategic alliances are any of a variety of agreements between independent *firms* to cooperate in the development and/or marketing of products.

strategy refers to the general policies that managers adopt to generate profits; rather than focus on operation detail, a firm's strategy addresses broad, long-term issues facing the *firm.*

subjective performance evaluation is an evaluation that is based on the personal opinion of the supervisor rather than on some objective measure (such as the quantity of output).

substitutes are goods that compete with each other; if the price of one good is increased, the consumer will tend to shift purchases to the other good.

substitution effect in producing a product occurs when the *firm* shifts among inputs due to changes in their *relative prices.*

sunk costs are those nonrecoverable costs that have already been incurred and the resources have no alternative use.

supply curve displays the quantity producers are willing to sell at each price; the curve typically slopes upward—at higher prices producers are able and willing to produce and sell more units.

surplus occurs when the price in the *market* is higher than the *market-clearing price* and quantity supplied is greater than quantity demanded; as inventories build, suppliers have incentives to reduce prices.

survival of the fittest is a principle implied by the concept of *economic Darwinism;* companies have the greatest chance of survival if they are organized efficiently given their particular environment.

Team production occurs when interdependencies among employees and assets cause the value of the inputs as a team to be greater than their *opportunity costs.*

telecommuting occurs when employees work out of their homes and communicate with the central office via fax, computer, or telephone.

third-degree price discrimination—see *group pricing.*

three legs of the stool is an analogy used to characterize *organizational architecture;* like a balanced stool, a well-designed organization should have an architecture in which the three components (the assignment of *decision rights,* the *reward system,* and the *performance-evaluation system*) are coordinated.

time studies are a wide variety of techniques employed for determining the duration a particular activity requires under certain standard conditions.

total cost curve (TC) displays the relation between total costs (total *fixed costs* plus total *variable costs*) and output.

total product (TP) of an input is the schedule of output obtained as the input increases, holding other inputs fixed.

total quality management (TQM) includes those management processes and organizational changes necessary to meet customer expectations and to achieve continual improvement.

total revenue is the product of price times quantity sold.

transaction costs—see *contracting costs* (note that this term frequently is used to refer only to out-of-pocket contracting costs).

transfer price is the amount one business unit pays another for goods and services that are exchanged between them.

two-part tariff is a *pricing* mechanism in which the customer pays an up-front fee for the right to buy the product and then pays additional fees for each unit of the product consumed; two-part pricing is sometimes used in contracts between manufacturers and distributors.

U-form organization—see *unitary organization.*

unitary elasticity of demand occurs when the *price elasticity* is equal to one; a small increase in price is associated with no change in *total revenue.*

unitary organization groups *jobs* by *function* (engineering, design, sales, finance, and so on); it places each primary function in one major subunit (rather than in multiple subunits)—also called U-form organization.

upstream integration—see *backward integration.*

utility is an index of personal well-being.

utility function is the relation between an individual's well-being (*utility*) and the level of goods consumed.

Value of the marginal product (VMP)—see *marginal revenue product*.

variable costs are costs which change with the level of output.

vertical chain of production is the series of steps in the production process.

vertically integrated *firms* are those which participate in more than one successive stage in the *vertical chain of production*.

vision refers to a course of action for the *firm*—see also *corporate strategy*.

Work sampling is one type of *time study* that involves selecting a large number of observations taken at random intervals and observing how long employees take in performing various components of the *job*.

Index